Canadian Environmental Policy

Canadian Environmental Policy: Context and Cases

Second Edition

Edited by

Debora L. VanNijnatten and Robert Boardman

OXFORD
UNIVERSITY PRESS

OXFORD
UNIVERSITY PRESS

70 Wynford Drive, Don Mills, Ontario M3C 1J9
www.oup.com/ca

Oxford University Press is a department of the University of Oxford.
It furthers the University's objective of excellence in research, scholarship,
and education by publishing worldwide in

Oxford New York

Auckland Bangkok Buenos Aires Cape Town Chennai
Dar es Salaam Delhi Hong Kong Istanbul Karachi Kolkata
Kuala Lumpur Madrid Melbourne Mexico City Mumbai
Nairobi São Paulo Shanghai Taipei Tokyo Toronto

Oxford is a trade mark of Oxford University Press
in the UK and in certain other countries

Published in Canada by Oxford University Press

National Library of Canada Cataloguing in Publication Data

Main entry under title:

Canadian environmental policy: context and cases
2nd ed.
Previously published under title: Canadian environmental policy: ecosystems, politics and process.
Includes bibliographical references and index.
ISBN 0-19-541590-6

Environmental policy—Canada.   2. Environmental protection—Canada.
I. VanNijnatten, Debora, 1967- .   II. Boardman Robert

HC120.E5C355 2001   333.7'0971   C2001-930621-0

Cover Design: Brett J. Miller
Cover Image: Satellite Image of Part of Vancover/RADARSAT International

2 3 4 - 05 04 03

This book is printed on permanent (acid-free) paper ∞.
Printed in Canada

Contents

Part Two: Cases

For my parents, Jack and Eileen

and

For Emma

Introduction

Debora L. VanNijnatten and Robert Boardman

The first edition of this book, *Canadian Environmental Policy: Ecosystems, Politics, and Process* (1992), was compiled almost a decade ago. At that time 'sustainable development' and 'ecosystems' were relatively new concepts in the political vocabularies of Canadians and environmentalism was experiencing its 'second wave'. New information on the extent and complex nature of environmental degradation was being discussed in various political and social fora, and the public appeared to be worried about the environment, at least according to opinion polls. Moreover, the federal government looked as if it just might flex its regulatory muscles, despite provincial and private-sector opposition. The Canadian Environmental Protection Act (CEPA) of 1988 was brand new, the Canadian Environmental Assessment Act (CEAA) was being proposed, and the federal Green Plan of 1990 appeared to provide some strategic direction for environmental policy as well as monies to pursue ecological objectives.

Moreover, these new legislative and policy initiatives were being constructed in a more transparent manner, with the input of environmental groups, industry, and scientists. In a departure from past practice, consultative processes and new legal mechanisms promised non-governmental and non-industry actors a more significant role in decision-making. Round tables on the environment and economy were established at the national level and in the provinces to explore the implications of sustainable development for Canada's future. On other fronts, Canada and the US had just negotiated an Air Quality Agreement under which both countries agreed to reduce emissions causing acid rain. In addition, Canada, along with the other countries of the world, was making plans to endorse formally sustainable development and to sign international conventions on global climate change and biodiversity at the 1992 Rio Earth Summit.

The first edition of *Canadian Environmental Policy* explored these developments both inside and outside Canada's borders. Its main focus was on domestic political behaviour—public opinion and elections, environmental groups, political parties, and the media—within an institutional framework consisting of executive federalism, an increasingly active Environment Canada, the courts, and the legislative system. Other chapters examined trends in Canada-US relations and international environmental politics, as well as comparative policy developments in other countries. The overarching theme of the first edition was how these actors, institutions, and processes would adapt, or be adapted, to the challenges posed by environmentalist critiques and the complexities inherent in addressing the crosscutting problems associated with environmental degradation.

What, then, has transpired over the last decade? Almost 10 years after the appearance of the first edition, and with both feet planted firmly in a new century, Canada's (and indeed global) environmental problems have been shown to be more complex than originally thought, some even intractably so. Canadians still confront an environmental crisis. The environmental challenges from the early 1990s have been joined by other more subtle, but perhaps more insidious, problems. Scientists tell us that, while progress has been made in reducing emissions of acid rain-causing pollutants, further cuts are necessary to save our forests and lakes. Problems continue to be associated with the control and disposal of toxic substances such as organochlorines. The atmospheric buildup of carbon dioxide and other greenhouse gases continues, despite increasing scientific consensus as to its causes (and to a lesser extent its effects), as well as successive rounds of international negotiations designed to decrease emissions (the most recent round in The Hague in November 2000 failed to achieve agreement on how to achieve reductions). In addition, research has shown that continuing air quality problems, such as ground-level ozone and particulate matter, pose threats to human immune, cardiac, and respiratory systems. Water quality and management also are enduring concerns; the 1990s brought us continued warnings about toxic overload in the Great Lakes, debates about bulk water transport, and the Walkerton drinking water disaster.

Natural resource management issues have long occupied a prominent place on Canadian political and environmental agendas. The collapse of the east coast cod fishery was one of several indications in the 1990s that approaches to environmental issues centring on the management and use of natural resources require continuing and critical evaluation. While there has been a doubling of protected lands in Canada over the last decade, this is offset by statistics such as those brought forward by World Wildlife Fund Canada noting that one acre of Canada's forests is logged every 13 seconds and that 174 million acres were staked by the mining industry in 1998 alone. The Canadian endangered species list continues to grow as the habitats occupied by these species—temperate rain forests, grasslands, wetlands, and Carolinian forests—are reduced, in some cases to a fragment of their former expanse.

Some problems we now face were not even on the agenda in the early 1990s. For example, great uncertainty surrounds the health and environmental impacts of genetically modified organisms. In addition, scientists are trying to determine the risks associated with exposure to trace residues of pesticides that appear to disrupt human and animal endocrine cycles. Fertilizer runoff from thousands of farms and yards and emissions from dry-cleaning operations and gas stations are also relatively new issues.

While the concept of sustainable development has increasingly given way in environmental policy discourse to the more prudent 'sustainability' approach, which focuses on the capacity of ecosystems to absorb pollution and waste, this shift has not been reflected in public policy. In fact, public policy and the infrastructure supporting it have experienced considerable difficulty coming to grips with even the milder sustainable development approach. For example, CEPA, revised over 1997–9, has been a disappointment in terms of its ability to deal with the hazardous substances identified in the early 1990s, let alone those that have come to the fore more recently, such as 'estrogen mimics'. And what the federal government does is only part of the picture. The provinces appear to be calling most of the shots with regard to environmental policy these days, with a reluctant (or otherwise engaged) federal government standing on the sidelines. Looking outward, international action, an increasingly important context for Canadian debate and policy during the 1990s, has often foundered on the shoals of greenhouse gas reduction politics, genetically engineered foods, and trade-environment linkages.

This second edition reflects on the Canadian environmental policy experience of the 1990s, the state of play in the diverse areas of environmental policy, and the character of the environmental policy regime as we face a new century. There are signs of both continuity and change in the context of environmental policy. There is continuity, of course, in the basic societal structures underlying environmental policy-making in Canada. Our society continues to favour the individual accumulation of consumer goods and wealth, as opposed to reducing production and changing consumption patterns for environmental gain. This cultural and economic fact has profound implications for our ability and willingness to incorporate concern for the environment into public policy design. Real progress might have been expected in many areas in the early 1990s, such as greenhouse gas reductions, public transit articulation, energy use, the protection of endangered species, Great Lakes water pollution, and toxic substance control, particularly chlorines. While there have been improvements, an observer time-warped from 1990 to 2000 might be forgiven for her disappointment at what has actually happened, as the hard decisions most certainly have not been made. In their own way, each of the chapters in this volume contributes to our understanding of why this is the case.

There is also continuity in the federal government's reluctance to test its regulatory powers, the provincial opposition to accept an expanded, or perhaps any significant, federal role in environmental policy, and the use of intergovernmental accommodation to steer Canadians among these treacherous rocks. The trend towards the 'intergovernmentalization' of environmental policy-making deepened with the advent of the Canada-Wide Accord on Environmental Harmonization in 1998. The Accord was designed to eliminate overlap and duplication in federal and provincial environmental policies and facilitate the creation of a framework for national standard-setting. Negotiations on harmonization, which took place over 1993–8, provoked much critical commentary, however. Was this simply a means by which the federal government could offload its environmental responsibilities onto the provinces? Would harmonization, with its enhanced reporting responsibilities and formalized decision-making processes, truly bring about national action, or would it result in the further fragmentation of the environmental protection regime in Canada? There are as yet no definitive answers to these crucial questions. Certainly, the barbs traded between Ottawa and Ontario at recent federal-provincial meetings do not indicate any great meeting of the minds with regard to national environmental strategies.

There is also evidence of change. Although the public has continued to express moderate levels of concern about environmental degradation, such concerns have ranked well behind other issues such as the deficit (in the mid-1990s), and health care and education (more recently). Canadians' personal habits do not reflect a growing concern for the environment; indeed, they seem to be going in the opposite direction, as our recent love affair with gas-guzzling sport utility vehicles would indicate. Not surprisingly, political parties have paid relatively little attention to the environment in their election platforms and campaigns, and governments have often lacked the political will required to effect sound legislation and programs. In fact, all environmental actors have changed their tactics to reflect the reality that public concern is unlikely to force political change, except in the rare event that a crisis, such as the Walkerton tragedy, arises.

Governments also moved away from formal legislative and regulatory means of achieving environmental goals over the 1990s, to an extent unforeseen in the first edition, towards a reliance on voluntary corporate initiatives. At the start of the decade, general alarm and disbelief would have greeted the suggestion that industry could be relied upon to meet environmental policy objectives voluntarily. It is probably fair to say that command-and-control regulatory measures seemed at that point the best means for bringing about higher levels of environmental protection. However, with the budget-cutting and program review exercises of the federal government beginning in 1994, the deficit-cutting and 'red tape reduction' exercises of the Ontario government beginning in 1995, and various reductions and 'rationalizations' in other provinces, all against a backdrop of minimal public concern about the environment, the regulatory landscape changed. Governments in Canada, propelled by mounting debts and encouraged by New Public Management advocates, have embraced 'alternative' instruments for achieving public policy goals, such as purely voluntary pollution control measures by industry and negotiated performance agreements between governments and industry. Emissions-trading regimes and tax 'shifting' are also under discussion or being employed in various jurisdictions.

Considerable debate has accompanied this development. Some observers have argued that such instruments are more the product of deregulatory, off-loading impulses than of any concern with achieving higher levels of environmental protection. But other critics claim that traditional regulatory measures are in any case outdated and unlikely to bring further environmental benefit, and they run the risk of backfiring by antagonizing the players whose support is essential for the achievement of environmental policy goals. Looking forward, it is likely that the trend towards the use of voluntary initiatives has peaked and that there is now greater interest in combining regulatory and non-regulatory initiatives in innovative ways. Above all, there is growing awareness that government cannot be the sole initiator, implementer, and enforcer of environmental policy, and that performance and compliance methods need to be revamped. As of the year 2000, government policy tool boxes are filled with a number of mechanisms that were not there in 1990.

These contextual shifts have had implications for the routes open to environmental groups, the access they have to governments, and how they go about working towards policy change. The early 1990s represented the apex of multi-stakeholder consultation in environmental policy-making. Over the late 1980s–early 1990s, multi-stakeholder consultations were being employed in conjunction with the formulation of almost all new environmental policies at the federal level: the CEPA, the CEAA, the Green Plan, the Federal Pesticide Registration Review, and the National Pollutant Release Inventory, to name a few. Extensive consultations were also being conducted by the provinces on a range of new environmental initiatives. However, as a result of budget-cutting measures, the increased reliance on non-regulatory environmental measures undertaken by industry actors, and the growth of federal-provincial negotiations to achieve intergovernmental administrative agreements, the role of non-governmental environmental groups in the policy process has changed. They have had to find new ways of operating in a changing political milieu in which the doors of negotiating rooms are not as open to them as they were at the beginning of the 1990s. Some have chosen to direct their energies at the grassroots rather than continue to pursue policy-makers.

Aboriginal peoples, by contrast, increasingly find themselves seated inside. One of the most significant developments over the 1990s has been the evolution in the role that First Nations play in resource management. This has been a gradual, often confrontational development, punctuated by Supreme Court cases such as *Sparrow* (1990), *Sioui* (1990), *Delgamuukw* (1997), and *Marshall* (1999), which have strengthened the legal basis of Aboriginal title and rights. The conflicts over resource use and conservation of the late 1990s, however, speak to continuing uncertainty about the long-term resolution of key issues of environmental governance. Yet innovations on the ground are numerous; co-management mechanisms in the North combining Aboriginal and non-Aboriginal approaches to resource management are one example.

Other portents of change have been continental and global. The processes of economic, social, and political integration now associated with trends towards continentalization and globalization were highlighted from 1994 onward in debates about the North American Free Trade Agreement. Canadian environmental policy has been affected by the multiple phenomena associated with economic globalization, including the rise of international trade agreements, and it also has been increasingly internationalized, as agendas and processes are shaped to a significant extent by developments in international organizations and international law. Canadians have reacted in different ways, taking part in grassroots protests at World Trade Organization and World Bank summits to draw attention to the social and environmental impacts of trade liberalization, and, on the other hand, bargaining hard in international conferences on climate change and biotechnology. In many ways, the Canada-US relationship, environmental and otherwise, is reflective of the problems and promise of a more integrated world.

A final, very important development over the last decade has been a significant expansion of the environmental policy literature in Canada, which uses the tools and perspectives of political science, the policy sciences, public administration, economics, and the environmental sciences (among others). In part, this maturation of the literature reflects the growth and vitality of policy-related environmental studies classes and programs in Canadian universities. Many of the authors in the present volume have been notable contributors to this process. The study of environmental policy now constitutes a 'field' in itself, which thrives on the energies of seasoned scholars as well as new recruits.

Organization of the Book

This book is divided into two parts. The chapters in Part One discuss the context of Canadian environmental policy, while Part Two consists of a set of detailed case studies of specific policy issues.

In Chapter 1, Marcia Valiante examines the legal foundations of Canadian environmental policy and, in the process, highlights many of the above themes. She notes the constraints that federal-provincial accommodation has placed on establishing a strong federal role in environmental law, despite the continuing tendency of the courts to interpret this role rather generously. A detailed analysis of the revised Canadian Environmental Protection Act shows that the Act retains many of the defects of its predecessor, despite innovations in the range of instruments available to policy-makers. Valiante also addresses the new Supreme Court judgements resulting in an expanded role for Aboriginal groups in resource management. As she concludes, the federal government 'seems bent on sharing authority' with provinces, industry, First Nations, and the public through administrative and procedural means, rather than testing the constitutional limits of its authority in legislation.

Similar themes surface in Michael Howlett's chapter on environmental policy instruments and implementation styles in Canada. Chapter 2 traces the evolution of instrument choice (or the choice of policy implementation tools) in Canada, from the development of a public regulatory regime for environmental assessment and pollution abatement over 1960–90 to more recent forays into voluntary and market-based instruments over the 1990s. Howlett argues that the public regulatory regime has been characterized by accommodative relations between government and industry over the enactment of environmental standards and their implementation; recourse to penalties and coercion, by government or via the courts, has existed only as a last resort. Perhaps not surprisingly, this regime has not adequately protected the environment. The more recent forays into market- and tax-based incentives as well as industry self-regulation also have proven disappointing and have not fundamentally changed the environmental policy regime in Canada, which continues to be dominated by government and industry and oriented towards cost-effectiveness.

The next four chapters examine those actors at the heart of these shifts in law, policy, and process: environmental groups, business, Aboriginal peoples, and Environment Canada. In Chapter 3, Jeremy Wilson provides insights into the activities of Canada's environmental movement. While acknowledging the variety and contributions of local and regional environmental groups, Wilson focuses primarily on the strategies of a representative sample of eight of the largest environmental organizations in Canada. He shows how these organizations have adapted to changes in the political context by becoming broader-based organizations able to engage in co-operative, often cross-border, campaigns, reach out to international publics, and employ research and technology to support their activities. Groups have become heavily networked into alliances with other environmental groups and organizations from other sectors. Wilson argues that, although Canada's environmental groups have traditionally put greater emphasis on outside lobbying than on the direct lobbying of government officials, key figures within the movement have invested considerable effort in building relationships with bureaucrats and politicians. Despite its having achieved a level of institutionalization, Wilson argues that the environmental movement has failed to bring about the kinds of changes that ecologists of the 1980s and early 1990s believed were necessary.

Doug Macdonald (Chapter 4) then looks at how regulated industry participates in the policy process and poses two questions: how have industries worked to influence policy intended to influence them, and why have some industries voluntarily improved their environmental performance even when not mandated by law? Through an analysis of three cases—acid rain emissions by Inco, the blue box program, and the chemical industry's Responsible Care initiative—Macdonald shows that business engages in a two-pronged strategy to achieve a certain level of social legitimacy and, at the same time, to delay or divert more stringent regulatory action. While business has improved its environmental performance and has at times used voluntary action to achieve this, it has also engaged in obstructionist lobbying of governments behind the scenes. Business, according to Macdonald, makes behavioural changes only as long as it can achieve its main goal: profit maximization.

Greg Poelzer begins Chapter 5 by noting that 'It is increasingly clear that Aboriginal peoples are central to environmental policy and politics in Canada.' Poelzer argues that the emergence of a more open society in Canada, international pressures, increasingly effective Aboriginal organizations, and court cases have combined to move First Nations from the margins to the centre of environmental decision-making. However, Poelzer argues that First Nations must not be understood merely as societal actors but as diverse 'political communities' consisting of state and societal actors, with both productive and non-productive interests. This diversity is demonstrated in three cases of natural resource management involving First Nations: opposition to the James Bay hydroelectric development; advocacy for sustainable forestry in Clayoquot Sound; and clear-cutting on the Stoney Reserve in Alberta. In each of these cases, First Nations have adopted different roles, sometimes as advocates of preservation, at other times as the resource harvester.

G. Bruce Doern, in Chapter 6, describes the Environment Canada of the 1990s as a more 'networked institution' that has had to respond to a wider array of demands yet decreased resources. Budget and personnel reductions, coupled with the adoption of policy approaches derived from a government-wide focus on innovation, sustainable development, and New Public Management techniques, have produced an impetus for more fluid and flexible or systemic ways of conducting departmental activities. Doern also shows that, while Environment Canada has traditionally faced challenges from 'the lobby from within', i.e., Industry Canada and Natural Resources Canada, the adoption of these policy approaches across government and the increased linkages that accompany them have ameliorated such opposition somewhat. Moreover, Doern notes that Environment Canada's commitment to science-based governance and to conduct science that meets the needs of policy-makers also has encouraged networking.

The next two chapters focus on one institutional reality that permeates almost all aspects of environmental policy in Canada: the federal-provincial division of powers. In Chapter 7, Kathryn Harrison explores the dynamics of federalism and intergovernmental relations over the last two decades, through a period of 'unilateralism' and federal-provincial conflict over 1969–72, to 'collaboration' in the 1970s and 1980s, back to conflict in the late 1980s as a result of renewed federal activism, and, finally, to 'rationalization' over the 1990s culminating in the Canada-Wide Accord. Harrison reviews the theoretical arguments for centralization and decentralization of environmental policy and shows how these arguments have informed various perspectives on federal-provincial developments. While environmentalists have favoured unilateralism and a strong federal role, governments and business favour rationalization as a way of eliminating duplication and conserving scarce public resources. The Canadian Council of Ministers of the Environment (CCME) has played a crucial role in the most recent trend towards rationalization and is now the forum for setting Canada-wide standards on pollutants such as dioxins/furans and ground-level ozone, cases examined by Harrison. Yet, as she notes, it is not clear that intergovernmental co-operation has been beneficial for the environment and there is some cause for concern about the direction that federal and provincial governments have taken with the Canada-Wide Accord.

The inclusion of a chapter specifically on provincial environmental policies is a recognition of the increasingly important role that the provinces have come to play in environmental protection. Debora VanNijnatten's discussion in Chapter 8, comparing provincial environmental policies, highlights the diversity that does exist and the challenges that face the architects of harmonization. The chapter examines provincial policies in a representative range of areas: environmental assessment, air quality, solid waste management, endangered species protection, and parks/protected areas and concludes that, although differences in provincial policies do exist, these differences could not be characterized as stark. More significant is VanNijnatten's finding that there are important differences among the provinces in their levels of commitment to implement policies for environmental protection. These differences are revealed through a comparison of public and private expenditures on environmental protection and natural resource management, numbers of personnel associated with environmental protection tasks, and enforcement activities. The overall trend is one of certain western provinces showing relatively high commitment levels, with Ontario and Quebec showing minimal commitment, and a mixed pattern in the Maritime provinces. This has obvious implications for the actual attainment of Canada-wide standards set collaboratively by the CCME but implemented by individual provinces.

While many of the chapters in Part One touch on the processes of continentalization and globalization and their implications (for example, Jeremy Wilson's observation that environmental groups have become more internationalist in their orientation), the final three chapters in Part One deal specifically with these trends.

In Chapter 9, George Hoberg provides something of a primer for Canadians who want to know how the US influences Canadian environmental policies and processes and what domestic conditions underlie these influences from south of the border. Hoberg first examines the mechanisms for US influence, such as policy emulation, bilateral diplomacy, and trade agreements. He then compares the policy regimes in the two countries, focusing on the greater role played by Congress, the courts, and interest groups in the more open (and complex) American policy process. He also points to the dominant role of the federal government in environmental protection in the US and the tendency of that government to use regulatory measures. Of particular note is that US influence on Canadian environmental policy is in many cases positive, which indicates that continentalization, at least in this area, may offer certain benefits. Hoberg also speculates on the implications for Canadian-American environmental relations of a new Republican administration in Washington.

Robert Boardman's account in Chapter 10 looks at the internationalization of Canadian environmental policy. While international influences made their mark in the 1980s, for example, through the responses of Canadian governments to the 1987 report of the Brundtland Commission, these have intensified over the last decade. The negotiation and implementation of international agreements such as those on the ozone layer, climate change, biodiversity, and transboundary pollution have had far-reaching implications for several key sectors of Canadian industry. At the same time, continental and global trade agreements, such as NAFTA and the regime of the World Trade Organization (WTO), have generated sustained criticism from many environmentalists for the restrictions they place on the capacities of governments to effect environmental policy measures. A major theme of the chapter centres on how the federal government's pursuit of international environmental agreements fits into broader conceptions of Canadian foreign policy, particularly the continuing importance of multilateralism in Canadian diplomacy.

Steven Bernstein and Ben Cashore, in Chapter 11, consider non-domestic factors that shape Canadian environmental policies, focusing specifically on interactions between the forces of globalization and internationalism. They argue that, in the context of increasingly integrated global markets, an overarching liberal environmentalism norm complex constrains and directs action on global environmental problems, with implications for domestic policies. For example, international negotiations on a Global Forest Convention proved unsuccessful, as proposals were perceived as violating the norms of free trade. On the other hand, negotiations on the Framework Convention on Climate Change and the Biosafety Protocol fared better because the mechanisms to be used under these agreements fit more easily within the legitimating norm complex of liberal environmentalism. Interestingly, Bernstein and Cashore note that, in many cases, the 'downward harmonization' of standards expected by the critics of globalized trade has not occurred; instead, Canada's policies have been pushed to higher levels of stringency than would have been the case in the absence of these non-domestic pressures.

The second section of the book represents a significant departure from the first edition. Here, six in-depth cases of environmental decision-making illustrate the range of contextual factors and trends discussed in Part One. Many of the same themes arise again and again. At the same time, particular environmental policy areas often reveal significant differences and special attributes. Some significant issues that could not be accommodated in this volume as full case studies, such as Arctic/northern environmental challenges and the urban environment, are addressed briefly in bibliographies at the end of the book. It is hoped that these reference lists will spur student interest in these issues and guide their research efforts.

In Chapter 12, Mary Louise McAllister argues that conventional approaches to public policy are ill-suited to the resolution of environmental problems in rural and remote communities, which suffer from the vagaries of resource-based economies, international markets, and external political agencies. Instead, McAllister advocates the use of a 'political ecology' approach, which recognizes the integral role that politics and the distribution of power play in shaping ecosystems. The chapter shows how downsizing in Ontario revealed little recognition on the part of the government of the need to support and maintain the environmental basis of Ontario's wealth, largely situated in rural regions, with the result that a crisis such as that in Walkerton, where seven people died from contaminated groundwater, can occur. McAllister also explores the problems facing mining communities that must deal with the fallout of environmental problems associated with events that occur outside their boundaries. She uses the case of the Adams Mine in Kirkland Lake, Ontario, which was to become a solid waste disposal site for Toronto, to illustrate the nature of these centre-periphery relations. McAllister argues for the use of approaches that can identify and deal directly with the forces that cause environmental degradation in rural regions, as well as recognize the important role that local actors and communities must play to achieve long-term biophysical and socio-economic sustainability.

The focus turns to air quality policy in Chapter 13, as Debora VanNijnatten and W. Henry Lambright explore domestic and continental influences on the formulation of 'smog' policy at the federal and provincial levels in Canada. They argue that the persistence of varying policy regimes at the provincial and federal levels remains a stumbling block for co-ordinated national action on air pollution. Attempts at collaborative intergovernmental policy-making through the CCME, whose agreements are not binding on the provinces, have failed to secure policy actions that would result in serious reductions in emissions of nitrogen oxides and volatile organic compounds, the primary components of smog. However, continental pressures emanating from the national and state levels in the US, as well as critical comment from the trilateral NAFTA Commission on Environmental Co-operation, have had more success in spurring action, especially on the part of Canada's largest smog producer, Ontario. In a manner similar to trends observed in Chapters 9 and 11, this chapter shows that continental pressures have pushed Canadian standards to higher levels of stringency, whereas domestic forces have provided limited impetus for increased stringency.

In Chapter 14, Éric Montpetit argues that domestic Canadian policies on agricultural non-point-source pollution are also weak and this weakness stems mainly from domestic factors. In contrast to Europe and the US, which have adopted regulatory approaches aimed at reducing non-point-source pollution, Canada has preferred to rely on science-based 'moral suasion', a non-regulatory or voluntary approach. Montpetit argues that, despite evidence that the reduction of agricultural non-point-source pollution requires both regulatory and voluntary approaches, earlier success with non-regulatory soil protection programs and an institutionalized 'regulatory aversion' within the federal government help to explain the continued reliance on moral suasion in this area. Moreover, the chapter shows how Environment Canada's lack of capacity vis-à-vis Agriculture and Agri-Food Canada and the dynamics of federalism, which allows federal officials to avoid blame, also have reinforced this approach.

Heather Smith, in Chapter 15, adopts a foreign policy lens in her study of Canada's behaviour on climate change since the negotiation of the Framework Convention in 1992 and during negotiations on the 1997 Kyoto Protocol. Smith notes that, despite being a leader in the early stages of international negotiations on a climate change treaty, Canada transformed itself into a faithful member of a coalition committed to ensuring the adoption of 'the most cost-effective implementation possible' of the 1997 Kyoto Protocol. The chapter shows the interaction between international and domestic factors as it considers the influence of science, the US, the 'ideology' of globalization, the provinces, and industry on Canada's international behaviour. Smith also reveals the complexity of the domestic influences in her discussion of federal-provincial negotiations regarding greenhouse gas reductions and divisions within industry between those who are completely opposed to reductions and those who are strong proponents of market-based instruments such as emissions trading.

In Chapter 16, Robert Boardman examines the politics of species at risk. The federal government has made two unsuccessful attempts, in the Canadian Endangered Species Protection Act (CESPA) in 1996–7 and the Species at Risk Act (SARA) in 2000, to formalize arrangements governing its role in the protection of threatened wildlife species. These initiatives, he points out, have to be seen from the perspectives of the federal and provincial governments and in terms of the conservation programs of non-governmental environmental organizations. Given the ranges or migratory habits of many species, moreover, this environmental policy area has significant continental and international dimensions. These factors have continued to shape the activities and strategies of environmental groups as well as the policies of governments.

The final case study, by William Leiss and Michael Tyshenko, examines the 'fit' between the processes and products of the new biotechnology and current federal legislation, last amended over a decade ago. Chapter 17 provides a detailed explanation of 'genetic engineering', or the changing and moving of traits between different species of plants and animals, as well as an overview of the regulatory structure governing genetically engineered processes and products. The authors argue that assessing the risks associated with genetic engineering and emerging technologies presents new challenges for government departments, which must evaluate ever-increasing numbers of genetically modified products seeking approval for production and distribution to consumers. However, the broad, 'business-as-usual' definition of biotechnology included in current legislation, as well as its focus on the end products of biotechnology and not on the scientific and technological processes underlying these processes, has contributed to the increasing discrepancy between the pace of biotechnology innovation and the instruments used to regulate this activity. The authors thus argue for anticipatory public oversight by a specialized regulatory body at the national level to apply scientific and ethical criteria to evaluations of new biotechnology products and processes.

Biotechnology, non-point-source pollution, climate change, biodiversity, and smog are among the issues in the 'unfinished business' files of Canadian governments. Intergovernmental agreements, non-regulatory instruments, international conventions, 'networked' agencies, and co-management with First Nations are among the instruments Canadian governments have chosen to address these issues. Liberal economic ideals, low levels of public concern, centre-periphery inequalities, and continental integration are among the challenges facing those who want to protect the environment. Welcome to environmental policy-making in the twenty-first century.

Part One

Context

Starting point is Constitution
Act 1867 or the British N.A Act

Chapter 1

Legal Foundations of Canadian Environmental Policy: Underlining Our Values in a Shifting Landscape

Marcia Valiante

Environmental protection has come to be accepted as one of the fundamental values of Canadian society, at least on paper. International instruments, domestic policy documents, legislation, and court decisions abound with eloquent statements of commitment to biodiversity, sustainable development, and the health of future generations. Yet, efforts to implement those commitments reveal great uncertainty and disagreement over the pace and direction of environmental action.

This chapter looks at the legal context for Canadian environmental policy, with an emphasis on recent developments primarily at the federal level. Although necessarily selective, it is hoped that the discussion will help to build an understanding of the context in which environmental policy has been (and could be) developed. The legal landscape is the stage on which policy is carried out; it sets boundaries and rules for the debate and empowers a range of actors.

Powers and Limits

The usual starting point for a discussion of legal foundations of environmental policy is the Canadian Constitution Act, 1867 (formerly titled the British North America Act). In a federal state, plenary power to govern is distributed between governments and the legal constraint is on which level of government can undertake which actions. Once that is settled, the discussion can move on to an assessment of the substance of environmental policy, the actions that have and have not been taken, and the political constraints on further action.

Environmental matters in Canada revolve around shared jurisdiction. However, despite numerous court decisions, the boundary between federal and provincial jurisdiction remains uncertain. This legal uncertainty has important policy implications. The Constitution Act, 1867 does not expressly assign environmental matters to one or other level of government:

> environment, as understood in its generic sense, encompasses the physical, economic and social environment touching several heads of power assigned to the respective levels of government. . . . It must be recognized that the environment is not an independent matter of legislation

under the *Constitution Act, 1867* and that it is a constitutionally abstruse matter which does not comfortably fit within the existing division of powers without considerable overlap and uncertainty.[1]

Thus, it is impossible to say in general terms that either level of government has jurisdiction over air pollution or water pollution; one must look carefully at each enactment and judge its specific terms and factual context.[2]

Two types of powers under the constitution are relevant to environmental decision-making: proprietary powers and legislative powers. Proprietary powers are those giving governments ownership of lands, waters, resources, and facilities. At Confederation, public property was divided between the federal and provincial governments. Certain listed property, including canals, harbours, lighthouses, etc., was conveyed to the Dominion. The provinces retained the rest and s. 109 of the Constitution Act, 1867 emphasized that all 'lands, mines, minerals and royalties' located within the provinces continued to belong to them.[3] As owners of property, governments have the same control as any owner, including the power to sell or lease.

THE FEDERAL ROLE

Legislative powers are found in sections 91 and 92 of the Constitution Act, 1867. Federal powers include both specific subjects, including fisheries, navigation and shipping, 'Indians and lands reserved for the Indians', and federal works and undertakings, and broader 'conceptual' powers not limited to specific subjects, including 'Peace, Order and Good Government', taxation, the spending power, trade and commerce, criminal law, and the ability to enter into treaties with other countries.[4]

The federal power over 'seacoast and inland fisheries' has been relied on as authority not only for resource management measures (such as quotas, seasons, gear restrictions) but also for water quality measures. The Fisheries Act contains general prohibitions on disrupting fish habitat[5] and discharging 'deleterious substances' into water.[6] Use of the fisheries power has been extensively examined by the courts.[7] With respect to enactments to protect water quality, the Supreme Court of Canada has required that there be an explicit link between the proscribed conduct and actual or potential harm to fisheries.[8]

The power over navigation and shipping is the basis for the Navigable Waters Protection Act, which requires approval of the Minister of Transport for any obstruction in a navigable waterway (this includes most of the internal waters of Canada).[9] Although the statutory criteria do not address environmental concerns, the application of the Canadian Environmental Assessment Act to such decisions has expanded this power into a more explicitly environmental power.[10]

Much of the debate and uncertainty over the reach of federal jurisdiction has centred on the broader, conceptual powers and the extent to which they could support general environmental protection legislation. Most attention has focused on the residual power, the power to make laws for the 'Peace, Order and Good

Government of Canada' (or POGG). Two distinct aspects of this power have been recognized by the courts as grounding federal action: national concern and national emergency.

The national concern doctrine has been held to authorize some aspects of federal environmental law. The leading case, *R. v. Crown Zellerbach*,[11] clarified the test for application of the national concern doctrine and upheld the Ocean Dumping Control Act as falling within this doctrine. The doctrine applies both to 'new matters', such as aeronautics and nuclear power, that did not exist when the BNA Act was adopted in 1867, and to matters that started out as local or private within a province but have since become of national concern. To qualify as being of national concern, the matter must have 'attained a singleness, distinctiveness and indivisibility that clearly distinguishes it from matters of provincial concern and a scale of impact on provincial jurisdiction that is reconcilable with the fundamental distribution of legislative power under the Constitution.' In other words, the subject matter must have some defined boundaries (that is, more specific than just 'environmental protection'), and its assignment to the federal government must retain the prevailing balance of power between the two levels of government. As part of the analysis, one must consider what is known as the 'provincial inability test', that is, whether a province's failure to deal effectively with the matter within its borders would adversely affect interests beyond its borders. If so, this may signal a distinct matter requiring uniform legislative treatment.

A majority of the Supreme Court upheld the Ocean Dumping Control Act under the national concern doctrine. The majority defined the subject matter of the statute as 'marine pollution', which on the facts included dumping in provincial marine waters, but, because of its 'predominantly extra-provincial as well as international character and implications', held it to be 'a single, indivisible matter, distinct from the control of pollution by the dumping of substances in other provincial waters. [It] reflects a distinction between the pollution of salt water and the pollution of fresh water.' A strong dissent by Justice La Forest makes sense to anyone familiar with environmental theory: a division between salt and fresh water has little meaning in a complex ecosystem.

While this decision was seen at the time as a strong boost for federal legislative action, the Supreme Court has not relied on the national concern doctrine since. Thus, even though the 1988 Canadian Environmental Protection Act (CEPA) referred to toxic substances as a matter of national concern and the arguments in all four courts in the challenge to that legislation addressed the national concern doctrine, the Court upheld the federal toxic substances regime under another broad conceptual power: the criminal law power.[12]

This challenge arose in the context of a defence to the prosecution of Hydro-Québec for discharging polychlorinated biphenyls (PCBs) into the St Maurice River and for failing to report the discharge, contrary to the Chlorobiphenyls Interim Order, which had been adopted under CEPA.[13] The argument of Hydro-Québec at each stage of the litigation was that the Interim Order and the enabling provisions in CEPA were beyond federal authority. Three Quebec courts agreed. The Supreme Court of Canada in a closely divided decision disagreed, however, concluding that CEPA's toxic substance controls were valid as an exercise of the federal government's criminal law power. In doing so, the Supreme Court took a bold step in expanding notions of criminal jurisdiction.

Canadian courts have long held that the criminal power is very broad; so long as the form of the enactment was a prohibition coupled with penal sanctions and was enacted to achieve a legitimate public purpose, Parliament has been able to target whatever 'evils' it wishes, subject—since 1982—to the Charter of Rights and Freedoms. Since 1949, the legitimate purposes of criminal law have been recognized to be 'public peace, order, security, health, morality.'[14] It follows that, to the extent the CEPA provisions were similarly aimed at protecting public health, they would be valid.[15] However, the Supreme Court went further. All members of the Court agreed that protection of the environment itself, unrelated to human health effects, was a legitimate purpose of the criminal law. As Justice La Forest stated:

> the purpose of the criminal law is to underline and protect our fundamental values. While many environmental issues could be criminally sanctioned in terms of protection of human life or health, I cannot accept that the criminal law is so limited to that . . . . [T]he stewardship of the environment is a fundamental value of our society and . . . Parliament may use its criminal law power to underline that value. The criminal law must be able to keep pace with and protect our emerging values.[16]

Members of the Court disagreed only in regard to whether the form of the legislation was truly 'criminal'. The dissent focused on a dichotomy between laws that are 'criminal', in the sense that they specifically prohibit conduct and provide for penal sanctions, and those that are 'regulatory', in the sense that they empower an agency or official to exercise discretion in determining what activities to control and how. The Court had recently upheld a number of statutes containing a prohibition accompanied by a regulatory scheme that recognized exemptions, but the dissent expressed concern that the CEPA scheme not only contained no general prohibition but also had the potential, given its broad definitions of 'environment', 'toxic', and 'substance' as well as its comprehensive regulation-making powers, to go beyond a set of narrow, discrete controls and to address virtually every aspect of environmental degradation. This would, of course, interfere significantly in provincial jurisdiction.

The majority, by contrast, focused on the purpose of the provisions as ultimately restricting the number of substances to be controlled to those that are 'toxic in the ordinary sense'. This careful targeting through individual evaluation of substances 'avoids resort to unnecessarily broad prohibitions and their impact on the exercise of provincial powers.' Justice La Forest, given his dissent in *Crown Zellerbach*, was quite sensitive to the concern of encroachment on provincial jurisdiction. He emphasized that, by its nature, the criminal law power does not exclude provincial regulation of the same subject matter. By upholding these provisions as legitimately criminal, the Court has significantly pushed the 'regulatory' trend to a new plane.

The *R. v. Hydro-Québec* decision has powerful repercussions for future federal environmental law-making, in particular for the next Act entering the spotlight: protection of endangered species. Because environmental protection, regardless of its link to human health, is a legitimate objective of criminal law, and because targeted regulatory schemes are now a legitimate form of criminal law, there seems little doubt that an appropriately crafted federal endangered species statute could survive a challenge. The extent to which federal environmental jurisdiction can be hung on the POGG power remains uncertain, however. All of the Quebec courts and the dissent in the Supreme Court tested the CEPA provisions against the national concern test and found them wanting. The dissent characterized the purpose and sections of CEPA quite broadly[17] and then concluded that they lacked the requisite 'singleness, distinctiveness and indivisibility', although the judges did say that regulation of toxic substances could be divided up into pieces, some of which might then meet the test.[18] La Forest, for the majority, did not have to address the issue.[19]

Another issue with the *Hydro-Québec* decision is the poor fit between criminal jurisdiction and an administrative regime that is moving away from a focus on a 'command/penalty' model towards the use of economic instruments, alternative measures, negotiated outcomes, and voluntary initiatives.[20]

THE ROLE OF PROVINCES

Provincial legislative powers over environmental matters are sweeping. As a result, most environmental regulation happens at the provincial level. Provincial powers include authority to legislate with respect to the management of public lands and resources, non-renewable natural resources, forestry, electricity generation, municipal institutions, property and civil rights, and matters of a local or private nature.[21]

There are limits on provincial authority and provincial environmental statutes are certainly not immune from challenge.[22] One important limit is a territorial one: only matters within a province can be regulated. If there are interprovincial effects, an affected province cannot control them.[23] Another limit is that of 'interjurisdictional immunity', whereby the Crown and its agents may not be subject to legislation of another level of government.[24] For federally regulated or interprovincial undertakings, such as railways, the situation is more complex. The rule is that federally regulated undertakings are subject to provincial laws of 'general application', that is, those that apply generally to all relevant facilities or activities in the province, so long as the laws do not interfere with the management and control of the undertaking. For example, provincial air pollution laws can apply to railways, but only to those aspects that are ancillary to how the railways operate.[25] Another important limit occurs with respect to the taxation power: provinces are limited to direct taxation only. This aspect arose in a challenge to the Nova Scotia waste regulations that impose a deposit on beverage containers that is then paid into a fund used to support recycling and environmental awareness.[26] There the deposit was deemed valid because it was a 'charge' that was part of a regulatory scheme, not a tax.[27] This limit means that provinces must be careful in designing regulatory schemes that provide economic incentives or deterrents.

CO-OPERATION AND HARMONIZATION: RECONCILIATION OR REALIGNMENT?

The reality of uncertain boundaries between governments has prompted use of a wide range of adaptive techniques to avoid potential conflicts, referred to as 'co-operative' or 'executive' federalism.[28] Examples in the environmental sphere include co-ordinated legislation, delegation of administrative functions, intergovernmental consultation, joint processes, and intergovernmental agreements.

The most influential co-ordinating body is the Canadian Council of Ministers of the Environment (CCME). It is composed of the 14 environment ministers from the federal, provincial, and territorial governments and serves as a forum for discussion and consensus-based co-operative action.[29] For many years, the CCME has worked to develop co-ordinated approaches to a range of national environmental issues, including nitrogen oxides (NO_x) and volatile organic compound (VOC) emissions, management of toxic substances, hazardous waste management, water quality, contaminated site remediation, and packaging, among others.[30]

Since 1993, a priority of the CCME has been the development and implementation of a comprehensive program to harmonize environmental laws across the country. This culminated in an agreement, the Canada-Wide Accord on Environmental Harmonization, approved in January 1998 by all members of the CCME except Quebec. Three sub-agreements were also adopted.[31] The stated motivation behind the Accord was to reduce overlap and duplication, and the disputes that go with them, arising from shared jurisdiction over the environment. Yet, the Accord does not simply reduce overlap, it seeks to eliminate overlap entirely. The Accord sets about doing so by having Canadian governments agree on their 'respective roles and responsibilities' so that 'specific roles and responsibilities will generally be undertaken by one order of government only' and when one government has a responsibility, the other 'shall not act' in that role.[32] The Accord raises many issues for environmental policy, which are addressed in a detailed fashion by Kathryn Harrison in Chapter 7. For the purposes of this chapter, some of the legal issues are flagged.

Certainly, the central legal issue is whether this agreement is a de facto constitutional amendment. Many view the true motivation behind the Accord as the devolution of federal responsibilities to the provinces.[33] Whether the Accord accomplishes this devolution is as yet unclear, but a reasonable interpretation of the language of the agreement points towards that outcome. Even if the federal government nominally retains authority, there is a risk that a convention could emerge around its persistent failure to act, which would be hard to reverse later.

In a legal challenge to the Accord, the Canadian Environmental Law Association (CELA) skirted the constitutional issue and argued that other legal problems exist. In particular, CELA argued that the federal Minister of the Environment lacked authority to sign the agreements and, by signing, she 'fettered her discretion' by agreeing not to act on matters within federal authority.[34] On the first issue, the minister purported to sign the Accord under the authority of s. 7 of the Department of the Environment Act, which allows agreements with provinces with respect to the 'carrying out of programs for which the Minister is responsible'. The Federal Court read the meaning of 'programs' as broad enough to encompass policy-making initiatives such as those found in the Accord and sub-agreements. As well, the terms of the agreements fell within the minister's agreement-making authority under CEPA and CEAA. On the second issue, the Court refused to make a determination as to whether the minister had fettered her discretion. At this stage, the Court said, there is 'no specific factual situation' on which to base a conclusion. Thus, the argument was premature, and we will need to wait and see what actually happens before the validity of the minister's action can be assessed.

One of the most interesting aspects of this case was the argument put forward by the federal government that, not only do the Accord and sub-agreements not alter constitutional authority, they have no 'legal content' at all. In other words, they are 'statements of policy goals and . . . do not affect legal rights or have legal consequences. . . . The parties cannot be compelled to comply with the agreements and they cannot be prevented from acting within their respective jurisdiction, notwithstanding that such actions may contravene the agreements.' In response, CELA pointed out that, if the agreements are not binding, the entire exercise has been a 'charade' and the true nature of the Accord and the sub-agreements has been misrepresented to the provinces and the public. Certainly, the signatories and the Accord itself claim to have no effect on constitutional powers, although it does seem odd that the language of the Accord and its process of adoption would point towards a binding agreement if that was never the intention. This may explain why Quebec refused to sign the Accord until the federal government had actually amended its legislation.

THE ROLE OF FIRST NATIONS GOVERNMENTS

A significant change in the historic debate over the bilateral division of powers is under way as First Nations gradually gain recognition of their constitutionally protected rights and negotiate self-government and land claims agreements. This change will have impacts across the spectrum of public policy issues, including environmental protection. Certainly, recognition in s. 35(1) of the Charter of 'existing aboriginal and treaty rights' has had a major influence. Since 1982, most of the 'rights' cases and some of the treaty cases (including the well-known *Marshall* decision in 1999)[35] have focused on claims by First Nations to resources, particularly fish and game, but also to timber.

In the first case to address Aboriginal rights under the Charter, *R. v. Sparrow*,[36] and later in *R. v. Gladstone*,[37] the Supreme Court of Canada faced the controversial issue of who should get priority over a fishery resource, in *Sparrow* a rapidly shrinking one, once it was determined that an Aboriginal right existed. The Court determined that first priority should go to 'conservation', to ensure that the resource would continue to be available for harvest. Once conservation of the resource was assured, priority of access should go first to the Aboriginal food fishery. After that, allocation becomes more difficult. The Court refused to recognize that the Aboriginal commercial fishery should be able to exclude non-Aboriginal commercial fishers but that other objectives such as 'economic and regional fairness' and historical reliance on the resource should be weighed in the balance, in order to reconcile the place of Aboriginal societies within a larger Canadian society.[38]

Also addressed in these cases is the ability of the government to interfere with s. 35 Charter rights, for example, through its fisheries regulations. The test for justifying such interference requires the government to establish a valid legislative objective and an approach that respects the Crown's special obligations. At a minimum, meaningful consultation is always necessary; in some circumstances, consent is required. As Chief Justice Lamer stated in *R. v. Delgamuukw*:

> The nature and scope of the duty of consultation will vary with the circumstances. In occasional cases, when the breach is less serious or relatively minor, it will be no more than a duty to discuss important decisions. . . . Of course, even in these rare cases where the minimum acceptable standard is consultation, this consultation must be in good faith, and with the intention of substantially addressing the concerns of the aboriginal peoples whose lands are at issue. In most cases, it will be significantly deeper than mere consultation. Some cases may even require the full consent of an aboriginal nation, particularly when provinces enact hunting and fishing regulations in relation to aboriginal lands.[39]

Thus, because of their special status, the involvement of First Nations in decisions that affect their entrenched rights is profoundly different from, and judged by a much higher standard than, any other type of public or stakeholder consultation. This requires a fundamental shift in government administrative procedures.[40]

Another route bringing First Nations into environmental decision-making is under the terms of comprehensive land claims and self-government agreements. Fourteen such agreements have been finalized, with numerous others, primarily in northern Canada and British Columbia, at different stages of negotiation. These agreements are seen as 'modern treaties' and therefore have constitutional status. Starting in 1975 with the James Bay and Northern Quebec Agreement (JBNQA), all of the comprehensive land claims agreements contain provisions regarding the sharing of resource and development decisions.

The Nunavut agreement is perhaps the most structured example, but it serves to illustrate the trend.[41] Under the 1993 agreement, which formed the basis for the legislation establishing the new territory, several boards and tribunals were established, including the Nunavut Planning Commission, Water Board, Wildlife Management Board, and Impact Review Board. For each, membership is determined by a set formula, which allocates places to persons nominated by each of the territorial government, the federal government, and Inuit organizations. This formula ensures Inuit voices are heard on all resource and development decisions.[42]

There has been some difficulty with reconciling the environmental assessment provisions under these agreements with the parallel federal process under the Canadian Environmental Assessment Act and, in some cases, with a provincial process as well. For example, for the proposed Great Whale Project of Hydro-Québec, the second phase of its James Bay hydroelectric development, five impact assessment bodies reviewed components of the project before it was eventually halted. Quebec and the federal government had attempted to avoid duplication through an agreement that the Quebec process alone would suffice for all decisions. However, this agreement was challenged as being contrary to the JBNQA and the courts agreed.[43] In 1992, the Cree, the Inuit, and the two governments signed a memorandum of understanding for a joint assessment of the whole project as a way to resolve the issue.[44]

One of the problems with Great Whale was that, at the time the JBNQA was concluded, there was no binding federal environmental assessment process, so the development of such a process was not provided for in the agreement. However, even in later agreements that do address the overlap issue there has been confusion over how to avoid duplication of effort in the review of proposals that trigger more than one process. For example, under the Inuvialuit Final Agreement in the western Arctic there is no ability to substitute another process for the screening and review process of the Environment Impact Screening Committee (EISC) and the Environment Impact Review Board (EIRB). This means that a major project is likely to trigger both the agreement process and the CEAA. CEAA authorizes delegation of some tasks to bodies such as the EISC and EIRB and authorizes the minister to substitute EIRB review for panel review under the Act, but this has yet to be done. However, pursuant to a Memorandum of Understanding between the EIRB and the Minister of the Environment, this will be possible on a case-by-case basis.[45] For the Yukon First Nations that have entered into final agreements on self-government and land claims, it is expected that this issue will be settled in the Yukon Development Assessment Act, now being drafted.

First Nations not under similar agreements are in a somewhat different legal position; however, governments must still come to terms with the meaning of their constitutionally protected rights as interpreted by the courts. The new federal legislation, the Canadian Environmental Protection Act, 1999, does this by putting Aboriginal participation on a par with federal ministers and the provinces into the National Advisory Committee,[46] by enabling delegation of administration of the Act to a government or 'an aboriginal people',[47] and by requiring application of traditional Aboriginal knowledge to the identification and resolution of environmental problems.[48] Where this has *not* occurred, most significantly, has been in the CCME harmonization initiative. Failure to consult Aboriginal governments was one ground on which the House of Commons Standing Committee on Environment and Sustainable Development based its recommendation to delay adoption of the Accord.[49] While this recommendation was ignored at the time, the CCME has since pursued discussions with Aboriginal leaders to develop a formal relationship,[50] which will be a step towards complying with these new constitutional demands.

Measures and Trends

While a discussion of powers and limits is important to an understanding of Canadian environmental law and policy, the more significant question is, 'how are these powers being used?' The substance of Canadian environmental policy and its effectiveness in achieving environmental quality are examined elsewhere in this volume. For present purposes, discussion is limited to a review of recent federal legislative initiatives, emphasizing the tools of implementation and selected legal issues.

CANADIAN ENVIRONMENTAL PROTECTION ACT
The most important focus of recent federal law-making has been the adoption of the revised Canadian Environmental Protection Act, 1999, proclaimed in force on 31 March 2000. CEPA 1999 replaces the original 1988 Act with new provisions for the prevention and control of pollution. The original Act provided for a review of its effectiveness after the first five years but it took a further five years to put a new Act in place.[51]

The new legislation builds on the approach taken in the 1988 statute, expanding it without changing it dramatically. To understand how CEPA works, it is important to understand the context in which it is intended to function. Most importantly, it operates in the sensitive arena of shared federal and provincial jurisdiction. Given the narrow support for the Act's constitutionality in the *Hydro-Québec* case, it is hardly surprising that the federal government stayed close to the original version and continued the numerous requirements for consultation with and deference to the provinces prior to the taking of federal action. The legislation is also meant to be consistent with the Harmonization Accord and sub-agreements, particularly the Sub-Agreement on Standards, and with the Policy Statement for the Management of Toxic Substances.[52] Finally, CEPA is intended as residual legislation; it fills the gaps where other federal statutes fail to address an issue adequately.

One of the primary purposes of CEPA has been and continues to be the regulation of toxic substances.[53] CEPA 1999 contains expanded goals and objectives of the federal government, including pollution prevention, virtual elimination of persistent and bioaccumulative toxic substances, an ecosystem approach, the precautionary principle, co-operation with other governments, and biodiversity. Pollution prevention is flagged as the key purpose: 'protection of the environment is essential to the well-being of Canadians and . . . the primary purpose of this Act is to contribute to sustainable development through pollution prevention.'[54]

There was a great deal of debate among environmentalists, industry, and government over the meaning of these stock phrases, which reflected an underlying philosophical divide over the appropriate direction of federal policy. One illustration of this debate was the task of defining the precautionary principle, the principle from international environmental law that prevents scientific uncertainty from forming a legal impediment to regulatory action. The new provisions in CEPA 1999 are designed to adopt the language of the 1992 Rio Declaration; however, this language sparked weeks of heated debate. The central issue was whether uncertain science should postpone adoption of 'cost-effective measures' or adoption of any measures. Adding 'cost-effective' was seen as diminishing the range of potential measures. In the end, 'cost-effective' was included, but it is hard to see that it will make much difference to the government's power to act. The principle is set out in the preamble and, if a regulation adopted in conformity with it is challenged, it could assist a tribunal or court in interpreting the specific operative sections of the Act. However, because there is no guidance in the statute as to how much and what kinds of scientific evidence could justify a shift to a lesser standard, and because inclusion of 'cost-effective' language injects an uncertain range of issues into the balance, the outcome is unpredictable, making it difficult for the government to withstand a legal challenge to a regulation based on this provision. Governments thus far have not regulated when the science was quite uncertain and this provision is unlikely to encourage them to do so.

The regulation of toxic substances proceeds through a number of phases. First, information is gathered.[55] Second, substances are assessed to determine if they are toxic. To accomplish this, several lists are established: the Priority Substances List, for example, identifies substances that should be given priority for that assessment. Once a substance is on the list, the environment and health ministers have five years to make an assessment and reach a conclusion about toxicity. As well, two other lists are established, the Domestic Substances List (DSL)[56] and the Non-Domestic Substances List (NDSL).[57] The two ministers are required to categorize all substances on the DSL within seven years to identify which may have the potential for environmental harm.[58] The route for a substance on the NDSL and for any 'significant new activity' with a substance on the DSL is for the person proposing to use, manufacture, or import to supply certain information to the Minister of the Environment. The government then assesses the information to determine whether the substance is toxic prior to allowing its import, manufacture, or use in Canada.

The third phase is the action phase. The key to most actions under the Act is a finding that a substance is 'toxic'. The definition of 'toxic' is little changed from the earlier legislation; it includes harm to the environment, danger to the environment on which life depends, and danger to human life or health. If a substance is found to be toxic, it may be added to another list, known as the Toxic Substances List (TSL). With the 1999 legislation, it will now be the Governor-in-Council, rather than the ministers, who decides whether a substance will be added to the TSL. Only substances on the TSL can be the subject of regulations. Once on the list, new provisions require development of a regulation within two years.

Under both the earlier and the current CEPA, regulations to address every aspect of the life cycle of a toxic substance are possible, including quantities that may be manufactured, processed, used, or sold; the total, partial, or conditional prohibition on manufacture, use, processing, sale, offering for sale, import, or export of the substance or a product containing it; and release, storage, transportation, or disposal.[59] The breadth of these sections is what gave pause to the dissenters in the Supreme Court in the *Hydro-Québec* case as coming too close to traditionally provincial matters. However, the reality is that in CEPA's 12 years of existence, only 25 substances were found to be toxic and regulated. With the new legislation, deadlines are imposed, so the pace of assessment and regulation may quicken somewhat, although it is unlikely there will be great waves of regulations issuing from cabinet.

As well as life-cycle management, three new regulatory options are found in CEPA 1999: pollution prevention, virtual elimination, and economic instruments. Pollution prevention applies to substances declared to be toxic and is defined in a progressive way, stressing the avoidance or minimization of pollution and waste creation.[60] The Minister of the Environment acting alone may require specified persons to prepare and implement a pollution prevention plan with respect to specified activities.[61] The persons doing so need only report at specific intervals on what they are doing and whether they have accomplished what they set out to do. There is authority to require the submission of the plan to Environment Canada for purposes of assessing the actions being taken, but it appears that this will not likely be the normal practice.

Unfortunately, a great deal of discretion is vested in the minister to determine the appropriate parameters for such plans on a case-by-case basis, with no statutory guidance to help ensure consistency between companies, although there are provisions for the development of model plans and guidelines.[62] The approach is a middle ground between a completely voluntary system of ad hoc plans and a comprehensive mandatory system. The legislation certainly accepts that industry is the central designer of pollution prevention, but it fits that design into a minimal administrative framework. When developing regulations or instruments respecting preventive or control actions, the ministers are required to 'give priority' to pollution prevention. However, the Act allows pollution prevention to be used as an alternative to conventional regulations and allows the plans to fall outside the regulatory system, which will put them beyond public scrutiny and review. There is also a concern that the Act ignores existing and future voluntary pollution prevention initiatives. No mention is made of how these initiatives will be treated, how they will be monitored or evaluated, and whether there will be any public accountability.

The second new regulatory option, virtual elimination, will only be pursued for toxic substances posing the greatest threat to health and the environment, adopting into legislation the federal Toxic Substances Management Policy.[63] To qualify for this option, a substance must meet several criteria: it must be toxic under the statutory definition, and also must be 'inherently toxic', persistent and bioaccumulative, have long-term harmful effects, result primarily from human activity, and not be a naturally occurring radionuclide or inorganic substance.[64]

The definition of virtual elimination was one of the most controversial issues in both the House of Commons Standing Committee on Environment and Sustainable Development and Parliament. Debate focused on two key points: first, whether the focus should be on preventing the generation and use of target substances or simply on restricting their release into the environment, and, second, whether the amount to be released to the environment should reflect social, economic, or technical matters or just environmental or health risks. As with defining the precautionary principle, these seemingly minor points reflect a huge philosophical divide. At the end of the day, the meaning given to virtual elimination takes the less radical course: the ultimate reduction in release to the environment below a specified level of quantification, after taking into account information on 'relevant social, economic or technical matters'. Ironically, it is possible to ban the generation or use of a toxic substance under the ordinary regulation-making powers, but not under the virtual elimination powers.

When virtual elimination is the track taken for a substance, CEPA 1999 puts the onus on the user or producer to develop a virtual elimination plan. It seems that the targets in this plan can be incorporated into a regulation or control instrument; if they are, they become legally binding. If they are not, the legal status of the plan is unclear.

The third new regulatory option is the use of economic instruments and market-based approaches, specifically 'deposits and refunds' as well as 'tradeable units'.[65] These can be used as part of the control of toxic substances and in several other parts of the Act. The statute itself includes no guidance about when economic instruments would be appropriate for the control of toxic substances or what administrative controls would be necessary to ensure consistency and accountability. These details will be worked out in guidelines and regulations to be developed later.

Compliance was also an important focus of the CEPA review and the new Act contains a number of interesting innovations. Compliance became a hot issue because of a shift away from government enforcement, due to budget and staff cuts, towards voluntary initiatives by industry.[66] In a report by the House of Commons Standing Committee on Environment and Sustainable Development, Environment Canada officials revealed that, despite poor compliance rates in the absence of governmental regulation and inspection, there are only enough staff to enforce some federal regulations some of the time.[67] It was also reported that the federal government does not step in (and has perhaps lost its ability to do so) when provinces fail to enforce under authority delegated in federal-provincial agreements.

Reversing the trend with increased resources is an obvious answer to this situation. There are also some legal issues such as better drafting of regulations to make them enforceable. Prosecutions are always a last resort for a regulatory scheme, and CEPA 1999 includes a range of alternatives to prosecution that give regulators greater flexibility in achieving compliance and allow the public and the courts to play a role.

For the first time in a Canadian federal environmental statute, a clause allowing 'citizen suits', known as 'environmental protection action', was included over strong industry objection.[68] This permits an individual to bring a court action against a person who has committed an offence under the Act. Citizen suits are commonplace in US environmental statutes; in Canada, they have only been included in a few provincial and territorial statutes.

To bring an environmental protection action the person must first have applied to the Minister of the Environment for an investigation of an alleged offence and the minister either must have failed to conduct an investigation and present a report within a reasonable time or the minister's response to the investigation must have been 'unreasonable'.[69] An environmental protection action is a civil proceeding, not a criminal prosecution, so the standard of proof is the lesser civil standard of proof on the balance of probabilities.[70] The remedies available include a declaration, an order requiring the defendant to refrain from committing an offence or to do something to prevent the continuation of an offence, or an order to the parties to negotiate a plan to correct or mitigate the harm caused, but no money damages can be awarded to a plaintiff.[71] The court has the power to stay an action if it would be in the public interest to do so and costs may be awarded.

This action is modelled on a similar one in Ontario's Environmental Bill of Rights (EBR).[72] Unlike their American counterparts, these statutes have several very high hurdles that must be surmounted in order to get an action into a court and reach a decision. The combination of requiring significant environmental harm, going through the investigation application process, and showing either ministerial failure to respond to an investigation request or an unreasonable reaction by the minister makes it unlikely that many cases will even get before a court. Once there, the power to stay the proceedings and the wide range of defences available will mean even fewer cases will reach a resolution. In six years of existence, the EBR action has never been successfully used. However, the investigation sections have—and the existence of the citizen suit has had—an influence on the care with which the minister responds to an application for investigation.

The recently introduced Species at Risk Act, which died on the order paper with the fall 2000 election call, contained similar rights to apply for an investigation, but it did not include a citizen suit.[73] The backlash against 'litigiousness' espoused by industry in the Standing Committee hearings on CEPA was heard in this round and the right to enforce the Act through citizen action was dropped.[74]

CEPA 1999, also for the first time, authorizes the use of administrative orders, known as 'environmental protection compliance orders', as a tool for responding to contraventions of the Act.[75] Enforcement officers will now have the power to issue an order addressing a wide range of actions, from stopping operations that contravene the Act to restoring the environment. These orders will be appealable to a new set of review officers and contravention of an order is an offence under the Act. These orders, similar to those used at the provincial level, greatly expand the flexibility of enforcement officers under CEPA.

Another innovation in CEPA 1999 that seeks to facilitate compliance is a mechanism, known as 'environmental protection alternative measures', for diverting those committing offences under the Act away from prosecution and towards compliance.[76] These alternative measures are similar to those under the Criminal Code and the Young Offenders Act but have never been used outside the criminal context. The principle behind alternative measures is to give an appropriate offender a chance to come into compliance without the time and expense of a prosecution. Diversion is possible when charges are laid for certain offences and for offenders who meet a number of criteria, the most important of which pertain to compliance history. The Act contemplates that an agreement will be reached as to the actions to be taken, that once the agreement is approved by the court the charges will be stayed, and that once the terms of the agreement are fulfilled the charges will be dismissed.

Additional new provisions in CEPA 1999 facilitate public participation. A key component is the creation of an environmental registry for the posting of notices of environmental decisions, similar to the Ontario EBR registry. Overall, the new legislation allows for more flexible administration and a stronger focus on compliance rather than on enforcement in the narrow sense. The hallmarks of the new legislation are its strong statements of environmental values and sweeping powers for controlling toxic substances, tempered by its sharing of responsibility with provinces, industry, and the public.

CANADIAN ENVIRONMENTAL ASSESSMENT ACT

Environmental assessment (EA) is part of the law of provinces, territories, the federal government, and Aboriginal governments across Canada. The nature and application of EA processes vary widely from jurisdiction to jurisdiction. The federal process was the first in Canada, starting as a cabinet directive in 1973, which was used inconsistently. In 1984 it was modified and adopted under the authority of the Department of the Environment Act as the 'Environmental

Assessment and Review Process Guidelines Order'.[77] Originally, the government intended it to be an administrative directive to guide decision-making when projects had effects on areas of federal jurisdiction, but it was not viewed as legally binding. In a series of cases brought by environmental groups the courts eventually concluded that the Guidelines Order was legally binding, despite the federal government's arguments to the contrary.[78] However, the Guidelines Order would not apply in every case where a proposal would have an effect on a matter within federal jurisdiction; in addition, an 'affirmative regulatory duty', such as the issuance of an approval under statutory authority, must exist. As Harrison explains in Chapter 7, the federal government was forced into applying its own process in these cases, even to provincial government projects, thereby creating a great deal of political tension.

Even as litigation on the Guidelines Order was under way, the federal government was pursuing development of EA legislation, a process that took many years. In 1992, the Canadian Environmental Assessment Act was passed and given royal assent, but for political reasons it was not proclaimed in force until January 1995. Proclamation was accompanied by the entry into force of four regulations necessary to the Act's administration.

CEAA applies to projects where a federal authority is the proponent, provides financial assistance, disposes of federal lands as part of the project, or issues an approval from a prescribed list. Thus, the federal process does not just apply to federal projects; it can also apply to provincial or private projects and to projects either within or outside of Canada.

When CEAA applies, the relevant federal department is designated as the 'responsible authority'. The responsible authority is required to ensure the screening of the project to review its likely environmental effects. On the basis of the screening a determination is made by the responsible authority as to whether these effects will be 'significant' or not and, if significant, whether they can be mitigated.[79] For the vast majority of projects, the outcome of screening is a conclusion that the effects are not significant or that they can be mitigated. In those situations the project can proceed without further assessment. Where there is uncertainty about whether the project will have significant effects, where there will be significant effects but they may be justified, or where public concern is high, the next stage, panel review, occurs. Panel review is conducted as a rather informal public hearing. The outcome is a report containing recommendations to the responsible authority, which makes the ultimate decision about whether a project should proceed.

Many issues have arisen as implementation of CEAA has proceeded, some of which have been brought to courts to resolve. A five-year review of the Act is now under way and many of these issues are being openly debated in anticipation of possible amendments to the Act. The focus of the review is primarily on process and ways to streamline it. Two contentious issues with the potential to alter dramatically federal EA are efforts to harmonize CEAA with other processes and suggestions for limiting judicial review of EA decisions.

Harmonization, as earlier discussed, entails a rolling over of federal environmental decision-making, including EA. The Sub-Agreement on Environmental Assessment sets out a game plan for rationalizing the conduct of EA when two processes apply to a project, namely, that a lead party will take responsibility for conduct of the assessment and, in most situations, that lead will be a province. The reason for this rationalization is the fear of overlap, duplication, and inconsistency between federal and provincial processes, a fear of inefficiency, higher costs, and delay pushed by both industry and the provinces, despite clear evidence that duplication is not a problem.[80] For projects subject to two processes, CEAA already provides for co-ordination, delegation, or joint panel review and many projects have proceeded under these provisions. As the Canadian Institute for Environmental Law and Policy and others have pointed out, to turn every such project over to a provincial lead could result in an inadequate assessment and approval of projects with significant adverse effects, much as occurred with the Cheviot mine in Alberta.[81] For them, the push against duplication is a smokescreen for industries that do not want to go through proper EA and for provincial governments that want to minimize the role of the federal government in environmental decision-making. Despite these arguments, the trend is towards implementation of the Sub-Agreement.

A second legal issue of note in the five-year review is the request by industry to limit judicial review of EA decisions through addition of a 'privative clause' to the Act. Behind this proposal is a perception that a flood of litigation has resulted in courts interfering in the administration of the Act, sending it in inappropriate directions. Again, the facts do not support this perception,[82] and suspicions are running high on both sides of the debate. The purpose of a privative clause is to insulate a tribunal's decision from most court challenges. It would be unusual to use a privative clause for a tribunal in the nature of CEAA panels, which are ad hoc. The outcome would certainly be less litigation, but the courts have not been overly interfering. They have, however, been the only mechanism keeping the federal government to its clear statutory commitments.

Conclusion

This look at the shifting legal landscape for environmental policy reveals seemingly inconsistent trends. On the one hand, Canadian courts have repeatedly vindicated a central role for the federal government in environmental protection, interpreting the constitution generously and forcing federal compliance with its statutory and regulatory commitments. These decisions have opened the door to more comprehensive environmental legislation, including CEPA and CEAA. However, at the same time as it is being empowered to act boldly, the federal government is bent on sharing authority with provinces and territories through harmonization efforts and delegation of administration, with industry through voluntary initiatives, with First Nations through self-government and land claims agreements, and with the public through greater participation guarantees. As well, there is a desire, quite self-serving, by governments and industry to avoid litigation, whether prosecution or judicial review, on the grounds that it creates uncertainty and costs. It is hoped that these trends will not cancel each other out but that strong legal tools will be available and used when appropriate to achieve environmental protection.

Notes

1 *Friends of the Oldman River Society v. Canada (Minister of Transport and Minister of Fisheries and Oceans)*, [1992] 1 S.C.R. 3, at 64, per La Forest, J.

2 See A. Lucas, 'Harmonization of Federal and Provincial Environmental Policies: The Changing Legal and Policy Framework', in J.O. Saunders, ed., *Managing Natural Resources in a Federal State: Essays from the Second Banff Conference on Natural Resources Law* (Toronto: Carswell, 1986), 34.

3 Constitution Act, 1867, ss. 108, 109, 117. Other provinces eventually gained these same rights. See, generally, Peter W. Hogg, *Constitutional Law of Canada*, Looseleaf Edition (Scarborough: Carswell, 1997), ch. 28.

4 There are numerous sources for a detailed discussion of the division of powers. See ibid.; Roger Cotton and Alistair R. Lucas, *Canadian Environmental Law*, 2nd edn (Toronto: Butterworths, 2000), vol. 1, ch. 3; Rodney Northey, 'Federalism and Comprehensive Environmental Reform: Seeing Beyond the Murky Medium', *Osgoode Hall Law Journal* 29 (1989): 127–81.

5 Fisheries Act, R.S.C. 1985, c. F–14, s. 35(1).

6 Ibid., s. 36(3). Regulations adopted under the Fisheries Act to control water pollution include effluent regulations for chlor-alkali mercury, meat and poultry plants, metal mining, potato processing, petroleum refineries, and pulp and paper plants.

7 See Hogg, *Constitutional Law*, s. 29.5.

8 In *Fowler v. R.*, [1980] 2 S.C.R. 213, a Fisheries Act provision that prohibited the putting of any 'slash, stumps, or other debris' into water during logging operations was struck down because it failed to make this link. In contrast, the Court upheld the prohibition on the 'deposit of a deleterious substance of any type in water frequented by fish' as sufficient to make this link: *Northwest Falling Contractors v. R.*, [1980] 2 S.C.R. 292.

9 R.S.C. 1985, c. N-22, s. 5. This power has been delegated to the Canadian Coast Guard.

10 This was upheld by the Supreme Court of Canada in *Friends of the Oldman River Society v. Canada.*

11 [1988] 1 S.C.R. 401. As well, an earlier case in the Manitoba courts upheld regulations under the Clean Air Act on the basis of the POGG power: *R. v. Canada Metal* (1982), 12 C.E.L.R. 1 (Man. Q.B.).

12 The question stated for argument in the Supreme Court was whether the impugned provisions 'fall in whole or in part within the jurisdiction of the Parliament of Canada to make laws for the peace, order and good government of Canada . . . or its criminal law jurisdiction . . . or otherwise fall within its jurisdiction'. *R. v. Hydro-Québec*, [1997] 3 S.C.R. 213, para. 97.

13 Section 6(a) of the Interim Order (PC 1989–296) prohibited the release of more than one gram per day of PCBs into the environment from electrical equipment.

14 *Reference re Validity of Section 5(a) of the Dairy Industry Act*, [1949] S.C.R. 1, aff'd [1950] A.C. 179 (the 'Margarine Reference'). Thus, for example, provisions of the Food and Drugs Act and the Tobacco Products Control Act have been upheld under this power as aimed at the protection of public health. See *RJR-MacDonald Inc. v. Canada (Attorney General)*, [1995] 3 S.C.R. 199.

15 La Forest states as much: *R. v. Hydro-Québec*, para. 132.

16 Ibid., para. 127.

17 Ibid., para. 33.

18 Ibid., para. 77.

19 La Forest had written the compelling dissent in *Crown Zellerbach* to the effect that marine pollution was so interwoven with discharges to land, fresh water, and the atmosphere that assigning it to the federal government could eventually gut provincial power. Certainly a similar argument could fit the facts of this case, so it seems unlikely that the majority would have upheld the Act on this ground.

20 For detailed discussions of the impact of this decision, see Joseph F. Castrilli, '*R. v. Hydro Quebec*: The Criminal Law Power May Hinder the Future of Federal Protection of the Environment', *Criminal Reports* (5th) 9 (1997): 312–19; Sven Deimann, '*R. v. Hydro-Quebec*: Federal Environmental Regulation as Criminal Law', *McGill Law Journal* 43 (1988): 923–52; Jean Leclair, 'The Supreme Court, the Environment, and the Construction of a National Identity: *R. v. Hydro-Quebec*', *Review of Constitutional Studies* 4 (1988): 372–8.

21 For general discussions, see Hogg, *Constitutional Law*; Cotton and Lucas, *Canadian Environmental Law*.

22 Some cases challenging the constitutional validity of provincial environmental legislation include *R. v. TNT Canada Inc.* (1986), 37 D.L.R. (4th) (Ont. C.A.); *Re Canadian National Railway Co. et al. and Director under the Environmental Protection Act* (1991), 80 D.L.R. (4th) (Ont. Div. Ct.); *R. v. Canadian Pacific Ltd.*, [1995] 2 S.C.R. 1028, 1031.

23 *Interprovincial Cooperatives Ltd. and Dryden Chemicals v. R.*, [1976] 1 S.C.R. 477.

24 In *R. v. Eldorado Nuclear Ltd.* (1981), 34 O.R. (2d) 243 (Div. Ct), a federal Crown corporation was held to be immune from application of the Ontario Water Resources Act even though it had applied for permits thereunder. The Crown is not bound by a statute unless the statute expressly or by implication so states; while courts are hesitant to bind the federal Crown under provincial law, the opposite is not true, and Parliament can bind the Crown in right of a province. For example, Alberta argued that its Oldman River Dam project was immune from federal legislation, but the Supreme Court interpreted the context of the statute to find that the Crown in right of Alberta was bound: *Friends of the Oldman River Society v. Canada*.

25 In *R. v. Canadian Pacific Ltd.*, Ontario's Environmental Protection Act was allowed to apply to CP's methods of clearing rights of way; presumably it would not have applied to emissions from the engines operated along the rights of way.

26 *Cape Breton Beverages Ltd. v. Nova Scotia (Attorney General)*, 24 C.E.L.R. (N.S.) 319 (N.S.C.A.).

27 To reach this conclusion, it was necessary for the court to find that the amount of revenue collected would roughly match the uses to which it was being put and that any surplus would remain in the fund and not be used for other purposes.

28 Hogg, *Constitutional Law*, s. 5.8.

29 Similarly constituted councils have been established to address other environmental and resource issues, including fisheries, energy, forests, wildlife, and agriculture, and these councils sometimes meet jointly with the CCME to discuss issues of importance to both.

30 Detailed information on CCME accomplishments is found on their Web site: www.mbnet.ccme

31 The sub-agreements address inspections, standards, and environmental assessment.

32 Canadian Council of Ministers of the Environment, *Canada-Wide Accord on Environmental Harmonization*, adopted January 1998.

33 The recent history of environmental federalism and the underlying tensions and trends is charted in Kathryn Harrison, *Passing the Buck: Federalism and Canadian Environmental Policy* (Vancouver: University of British Columbia Press, 1996).

34 *Canadian Environmental Law Association v. Canada (Minister of the Environment)* (1999), 30 C.E.L.R. (N.S.) 59 (Fed. Ct., T.D.), aff'd (2000), 34 C.E.L.R. (N.S.) 159 (Fed. Ct.).

35 *R. v. Marshall*, [1999] 3 S.C.R. 456.

36 *R. v. Sparrow*, [1990] 1 S.C.R. 1075.

37 *R. v. Gladstone*, [1996] 2 S.C.R. 723.

38 The nature of this reconciliation is not necessarily consistent with First Nations' expectations of self-government nor with principles underlying their relations with the Crown. Nevertheless, the courts have staked out these limits.

39 *Delgamuukw v. The Queen*, [1997] 3 S.C.R. 1010, para. 168.

40 For example, in *Union of Nova Scotia Indians v. Canada (Attorney General)* (1997), 22 C.E.L.R. (N.S.) 293 (Fed. Ct., T.D.), the Federal Court held that an environmental assessment screening report reviewing a dredging project's impact on a traditional Aboriginal fishery was inadequate because it failed to follow the *Sparrow* test for justifying interference with Aboriginal rights.

41 *Agreement Between the Inuit of the Nunavut Settlement Area and Her Majesty the Queen in right of Canada*, signed in Iqaluit, 25 May 1993.

42 Similarly, under the recently finalized Nisga'a Agreement, Joint Fisheries Management and Joint Wildlife Management Committees are established with a balance in membership among the three parties. As well, the Agreement provides for the co-ordination of environmental assessment processes for projects on or affecting Nisga'a lands. Nisga'a Final Agreement, signed 27 April 1999 (by Nisga'a and BC representatives) and 4 May 1999 (by federal representatives), given legal effect through the Nisga'a Final Agreement Act, S.C. 2000, c. 7.

43 *Cree Regional Authority v. Robinson* (1991), 7 C.E.L.R. (N.S.) 201 (Fed. Ct., T.D.). For the Cree and the Inuit, this was particularly important because the agreement process addresses both social and environmental impacts, while the others are directed primarily to environmental impacts.

44 An agreement for a joint process was also used for Inco's Voisey's Bay mine in Labrador.

45 Canadian Environmental Assessment Agency, 'News Release: Federal Government and Inuvialuit Land Claim Organization Sign Environmental Assessment Agreement', 9 Mar. 2000. Also see 'Comments Concerning the *Canadian Environment Assessment Act* from the Perspective of the Environment Impact Review Board of the Inuvialuit Settlement Region', in Canadian Environmental Assessment Agency, *Five Year Review: Reports from Consultation Activities*, n.d., in which the EIRB recommends permanent substitution.

46 Canadian Environmental Protection Act, 1999, S.C. 1999, c. 33, ss. 6(2)(c), (3) and (4). The Committee will have representation from six Aboriginal governments, selected on a regional basis.

47 CEPA 1999, s. 9(1).

48 Ibid., s. 2(1). Also see s. 4.

49 Canada, House of Commons, Standing Committee on Environment and Sustainable Development, *Harmonization and Environmental Protection: An Analysis of the Harmonization Initiative of the Canadian Council of Ministers of the Environment*, Dec. 1997, Recommendation No. 2.

50 See discussion in John Fleming, *Canada-Wide Accord on Environmental Harmonization Two-Year Review: Consultation Paper*, prepared for the CCME, Feb. 2000, p. 4.

51 The review was conducted by the House of Commons Standing Committee on Environment and Sustainable Development starting in 1994, with a report in June 1995. A bill was introduced in 1996, but it died on the order paper when a federal election was called. Another bill was introduced into the new Parliament in March 1998. During the 18 months it took for the Standing Committee to review Bill C-32, several highly contentious issues arose leading to hundreds of proposed amendments. In the end, few of these were accepted by the government, due, many claim, to the intensive lobbying campaign by industry.

52 The Act (s. 2(1)(1)) provides that the 'Government of Canada shall . . . endeavour to act with regard to the intent of intergovernmental agreements and arrangements entered into for the purpose of achieving the highest level of environmental quality throughout Canada.'

53 CEPA also addresses a wide range of other issues, including ocean dumping, nutrient pollution, international air and water pollution, content of fuels, and vehicle, engine, and equipment emissions.

54 CEPA 1999, Declaration.

55 The Ministers of the Environment and Health are required to undertake and collect research on a wide range of environment conditions and health impacts. To assist them in carrying out these duties, the Minister of the Environment is empowered to compel anyone in Canada to provide specified information. One form this takes is the National Pollutant Release Inventory.

56 Domestic substances are those substances currently manufactured in, imported into, or used in commerce in Canada, now numbering more than 23,000.

57 Non-domestic substances are those substances in use elsewhere but not in Canada, numbering more than 43,000.

58 CEPA 1999, s. 74, requires a determination of which substances now in use are 'toxic or capable of becoming toxic' or that 'may present, to individuals in Canada, the greatest potential for exposure; or are persistent or bioaccumulative . . . and inherently toxic'.

59 Ibid., s. 93.

60 Pollution prevention is defined as 'the use of processes, practices, materials, products, substances or energy that avoid or minimize the creation of pollutants and waste and reduce the overall risk to the environment or human health'. Ibid., s. 3(1).

61 Ibid., s. 56.

62 Environment Canada has drafted *Guidelines for the Implementation of the Pollution Prevention Planning Provisions of the New Canadian Environmental Protection Act (CEPA)* (revised 4 Apr. 2000) and the *Pollution Prevention Planning Handbook* (24 May 2000) to guide implementation of these provisions. It is expected that pollution prevention plans will be used for substances declared toxic under the new Act but not normally for those declared such under the previous Act.

63 Environment Canada, *Toxic Substances Management Policy* (1995). See also *Persistence and Bioaccumulation Regulations*, SOR/2000–107, *Canada Gazette* Part II, 134, 7 (23 Mar. 2000): 607.

64 When a substance meets this test, it will be added to a Virtual Elimination List and a 'level of quantification' established. Then, the ministers can implement virtual elimination through virtual elimination plans, pollution prevention plans, regulations, or other instruments. See Environment Canada, National Office of Pollution Prevention, *Towards the Implementation of Virtual Elimination Planning Provisions under CEPA 1999*, 15 Dec. 1999.

65 CEPA 1999, s. 322.

66 This trend has occurred at both the federal and provincial levels. See Canadian Environmental Defence Fund, *Canada's Environmental Enforcement Report Card: A Failure to Act*, Dec. 1998.

67 House of Commons, Standing Committee on Environment and Sustainable Development, *Enforcing Canada's Pollution Laws: The Public Interest Must Come First!*, May 1998. Also see Environment Canada, *Enforcing Canada's Pollution Laws: The Public Interest Must Come First! The Government Response to the Third Report of the Standing Committee on Environment and Sustainable Development*, Oct. 1998.

68 CEPA 1999, s. 22.

69 Ibid. It is also required that the offence caused 'significant harm to the environment'.

70 Ibid., s. 29.

71 Ibid., s. 22(3).

72 S.O. 1993, c. 28, s. 84.

73 An Act Respecting the Protection of Wildlife Species at Risk in Canada, 2nd Session, 36th Parliament, Bill C-33, First Reading, 11 Apr. 2000, s. 93.

74 A citizen suit had been included in an earlier version of the bill.

75 CEPA 1999, s. 235.

76 Ibid., s. 296.

77 SOR/84–467.

78 *Friends of the Oldman River Society v. Canada.*

79 Canadian Environmental Assessment Act, S.C. 1992, c. 37. For some classes of projects, listed in one of the four regulations, screening is not carried out; rather the project requires comprehensive study. More than 99 per cent of projects subject to CEAA have been through screening only. Only 46 of 25,000 projects have required comprehensive study. Canadian Environmental Assessment Agency, *Review of the* Canadian Environmental Assessment Act: *A Discussion Paper for Public Consultation* (Dec. 1999), 25.

80 One study estimated that 98 per cent of projects under CEAA are not subject to any provincial EA process and fewer than 2 per cent are actually assessed by both levels. See Canadian Institute for Environmental Law and Policy, *Environmental Assessment and Mining: A Submission to the* Canadian Environmental Assessment Act *Five-Year Review Process*, 31 Mar. 2000. Also see Report of the Commissioner for Environment and Sustainable Development, May 1998, ch. 6.

81 CIELAP, *Environmental Assessment and Mining*. The Cheviot mine was reviewed by a joint Alberta-federal panel (with two Alberta EUB members and one federal member), which recommended approval. The Minister of Fisheries and Oceans issued the required authorization but it was quashed by the Federal Court on the grounds that the panel report failed to fulfil the requirements of CEAA as they relate to obtaining and considering information with respect to cumulative effects and consideration of alternatives. *Alberta Wilderness Assn. v. Cardinal River Coals Ltd.* (1999), 30 C.E.L.R. (N.S.) 175 (Fed. Ct., T.D.).

82 In five years, only 28 projects (out of an approximate total of 28,000) have been subject to judicial review. Some cases have yet to be decided, but in those that have been decided the EA was overturned only four times. Stewart Elgie, *Appendix 2—Detailed Review of Key Issues, Joint Submission by West Coast Environmental Law and Sierra Legal Defence Fund to the CEAA 5 Year Review*, 31 Mar. 2000.

Chapter 2

Policy Instruments and Implementation Styles: The Evolution of Instrument Choice in Canadian Environmental Policy

Michael Howlett

Contemporary governance, including that of the environment, takes place within a very different context from that of past decades. Many states have undergone a kind of 'hollowing out' process as various functions and activities traditionally undertaken by governments, from highway maintenance to psychiatric care, have been devolved to non- or quasi-governmental organizations.[1] Moreover, as modern societies develop larger and more numerous networks of interorganizational actors,[2] new policy tools are required to help co-ordinate and manage these increasingly complex entities.[3]

In the area of environmental regulation as well as a host of others, these processes challenge public administrators at the turn of the millennium.[4] In coming to terms with these challenges, many governments, including Canada's, have developed a renewed interest in policy implementation.[5] Policy analysts have begun to develop a renewed appreciation for the multiple, different types of policy instruments available to governments in policy design and the complex reasons behind their use in specific sectors and issue areas.[6]

Generally speaking, comparative implementation studies have shown that governments tend to develop specific implementation styles in areas they regulate.[7] These styles involve characteristic and long-lasting patterns in both the types of policy instruments chosen to implement policy as well as the manner in which they are implemented.[8] These styles combine various kinds of instruments into a more or less coherent approach to implementation that is consistently applied to particular sectors.[9]

As shall be argued below, Canadian environmental policy-making has evolved a distinct implementation style. Following a lengthy evolutionary process, by the mid-1960s Canadian environmental policy was implemented in a largely non-coercive manner through negotiations conducted between government regulators and regulated entities, usually industrial corporations generating pollutants or destroying habitat in the course of their production processes, over the enactment and enforcement of environmental standards.[10] This chapter examines the genesis of this style in earlier epochs and assesses recent developments that may presage its change.[11]

The chapter begins with a general discussion of policy tools and an introduction to the idea of implementation styles, including preferred combinations of procedural and substantial instruments. It then discusses historical patterns of instrument use in Canadian environmental policy, including the Common-Law Era (pre-World War II), characterized by the use of private legal remedies for environmental problems, and the Public-Law Era (post-World War II), characterized by the development of public regulatory regimes for environmental assessment and pollution/toxic regulation through bilateral industry-government negotiation. The contemporary use of substantive voluntary and market-based instruments, along with procedural instruments such as public and stakeholder consultation, is explored. The chapter concludes with a comparative assessment of the evolution of Canadian implementation styles vis-à-vis those of the United States and European Union.

Analysing Policy Implementation Styles: Distinguishing between Substantive and Procedural Instruments

Analytically, it is useful to distinguish among the several fundamentally different types of policy instruments contained in a government's implementation style. Specifically, we need to distinguish between instruments directly affecting the nature and quantity of goods and services produced and distributed in society, such as public enterprises or subsidies to businesses, and those tools indirectly affecting goods and services but that primarily affect decision-making or policy processes, such as public hearings or advisory committees.[12]

Substantive policy instruments are those directly influencing the provision of goods and services to members of the public or governments. They include a variety of tools or instruments relying on different types of governing resources for their effectiveness,[13] and numerous taxonomies and classification schemes have been developed to help categorize these instruments.[14] A useful way to classify these, however, is according to the type of governing resource upon which they rely. Although different interpretations of these exist, a commonly accepted schema is that originally set out by Hood, which distinguishes four basic resources: nodality or information, authority, treasure or finances, and administration or organization.[15] In Hood's model, the instruments governments use to affect or alter goods or services delivery are classifiable according to whether they are intended to effect changes in policy outputs or monitor the activities of societal policy actors and thereby contribute to more effective policy implementation. Taken together, this generates the eightfold taxonomy set out in Table 2.1.

Procedural policy instruments are different from substantive ones in that their impact on policy outcomes is less direct.[16] Rather than directly affecting the delivery of goods and services, their principal intent is to modify or alter the nature of policy processes at work in the implementation process.[17] A list of these instruments is provided in Table 2.2. These, too, can be classified by examining the nature of the governing resource each uses, while keeping in mind that they can be used either in a 'positive' or constructive manner to facilitate policy activities, or in a 'negative'

Table 2.1: A Taxonomy of Substantive Policy Instruments

	Governing Resource			
	Nodality	**Authority**	**Treasure**	**Organization**
Principle Use				
Effectors	Advice Training Advertising Education	Licences User charges Regulation Certification	Grants Loans Tax expenditures	Bureaucratic administration Public enterprises
Detectors	Reporting Registration	Census-taking Consultants	Polling Surveys	Record-keeping Policing

Source: Adapted from Christopher Hood, *The Tools of Government* (Chatham, NJ: Chatham House Publishers, 1986).

or obstructive fashion to impede or obstruct a policy process.

An implementation style can be thought of as being composed of a combination of substantive and procedural instruments. Hence, for example, the well-known implementation style found in many US policy sectors, dubbed 'adversarial legalism' by Robert Kagan, is composed of a preferred substantive instrument, regulation, and a characteristic policy process, judicial review, based on widespread, easily accessible legal procedures.[18]

Why a particular combination of procedural and substantive instruments is employed in particular sectors is a key question for the analysis of such styles. In the case of substantive instruments, Linder and Peters have argued that the features of the policy instruments themselves are important for selection purposes because some instruments are more suited to a task at hand than others.[19] Linder and Peters and other authors, however, note that instrument choice is not simply a technical exercise involving the matching of specific tools with specific problem

Table 2.2: A Resource-Based Taxonomy of Procedural Policy Instruments

	Governing Resource			
	Nodality	**Authority**	**Treasure**	**Organization**
Principle Use				
Facilitative	Hearings Inquiries Information release	Advisory group creation Consultations	Interest group funding Research and intervenor funding	Institutional restructuring Judicial review Administrative reform
Obstructive	Misleading information Propaganda	Banning groups and associations	Eliminating group or research funding	Administrative delay Information suppression

Source: Adapted from Michael Howlett, 'Policy Development', in Christopher Dunn, ed., *The Oxford Handbook of Canadian Public Administration* (Toronto: Oxford University Press, 2001).

situations, but that variables such as political culture and the depth of social cleavages have an influence on instrument selection.[20] Still others, like Hood, have noted that the organizational culture of the implementation agency, the nature of its links to clients and other agencies, and whether or not it has had experience dealing with similar problems also have significant potential impacts on instrument choices.[21]

This suggests that the choice of substantive policy instruments is shaped by the characteristics of the instruments, the nature of the problem at hand, past experiences of governments in dealing with the same or similar problems, the subjective preference of political and administrative decision-makers, and the likely reaction to the choice by affected social groups. Most significant for explaining a consistent preference for the use of a particular instrument over a wide range of contexts are the preferences of state decision-makers and the nature of the constraints within which they operate, since these persist over longer periods of time. States must have a high level of administrative capacity, for example, in order to use authority, treasure, and organization-based instruments in situations in which they wish to affect significant numbers of policy targets. While capacity is subject to dramatic change, it is unlikely to experience frequent rapid fluctuations over long periods of time. When a state has few of these resources, it will tend to use instruments like incentives or propaganda or to rely on existing voluntary, community, or family-based production and delivery.[22]

Although the literature on procedural policy instruments is less well developed, it also suggests that a key factor affecting instrument choice is government capacity to legitimize its decisions and actions.[23] That is, governments in modern democratic societies rely on social actors to deliver most goods and services and hence require that these actors consider government actions to be legitimate if substantive policy instruments are to be deployed effectively to alter target behaviour.[24] Also like substantive instruments, procedural policy instrument choice is affected by the size and complexity of the policy target.[25] Whether a government faces limited sectoral delegitimation or more widespread systemic delegitimation, for example, will affect the types of procedural instruments a government will employ.[26]

Hence, like substantive instruments, procedural instrument choice is affected by the nature of the constraints under which policy-makers operate and the type of target they are attempting to influence. Unlike substantive instruments, however, the relationship between instrument choices and constraints runs in the opposite direction. That is, while in the case of substantive instruments, a government facing a high level of resource constraints will tend to use less resource-intensive instruments such as nodality or treasure-based ones,[27] in the case of procedural instruments governments facing high levels of constraint, or high distrust, must take more aggressive, and resource-intensive, steps to counter the problem. As a result, in such circumstances they will tend to use more 'radical' or directive instruments that can substantially alter or restructure state-societal relations, such as bureaucratic or political reorganization.[28] Although numerous permutations and combinations are possible, putting these two types of instruments and key variables together leads to the model of basic implementation styles found in Table 2.3 below.

Governments facing a variety of resource and legitimation problems and dealing with large policy targets will tend to use low-cost instruments such as exhortation while restructuring or reforming basic policy institutions to alter the fundamental network structure of specific sectors and issue areas. This implementation style of *institutionalized voluntarism* can be seen in a number of cases, such as when the Canadian government established new structures to deal with official language policy and bilingualism while devoting substantial sums to advertising during the extended national unity crisis of the 1970–90 period.[29]

Faced with lower constraints and similarly large targets, governments tend to develop implementation styles based on the use of treasure-based tools, such as offering subsidies to producers of goods and services while extending recognition to specific interest groups in the form of specific kinds of consultations and advisory committees. In Canada, the use of this style of *directed subsidization* is very common and examples can be found in many policy areas.[30]

Given this analysis, it is to be expected that in situations where governments face precise targets under situations of high constraint, they will tend to use forms of authoritative substantive instruments, including such tools as regulation, along with procedural tools such as the extension of financial incentives to the formation and organization of specific policy actors. This results in an implementation style of *representative legalism*, one used in Canada recently in areas such as human rights and women's issues as governments created new regulations to deal with specific issues in these areas while extending funding to multicultural, human rights, and women's groups.[31]

Finally, in situations where they face low constraints and smaller targets, governments tend to use substantive organizational tools such as government cor-

Table 2.3: Basic Implementation Styles

	Nature of the Policy Target	
	Large	Small
Severity of State Constraints		
High	*Institutionalized Voluntarism* (Exhortation and institutional reorganization)	*Representative Legalism* (Regulation and financial manipulation)
Low	*Directed Subsidization* (Financial and recognition manipulation)	*Public Provision with Oversight* (Organization and information manipulation)

porations, public enterprises, or directly administered pubic service delivery, combined with procedural tools such as public hearings, reviews, and evaluations. Examples of this fourth implementation style of *public provision with oversight* are also found in many areas in Canada, such as radio and television broadcasting and, in the past, airline transportation.[32]

As this analysis suggests, implementation styles are not static, but will change as state capacity and target populations change. As shall be discussed below, a distinct preference for a hybrid implementation style of consultative legalism developed in the environmental sector in post-World War II Canada. This style emerged out of an earlier era characterized by the use of private, common-law environmental remedies as environmental issues became a focus of government and public concern. Although this hybrid style remains predominant today, in the 1990s limitations on government capacity in terms of both delegitimation and financial constraints, coupled with the continued expansion of policy targets, saw the style shift somewhat towards institutionalized voluntarism and directed subsidization.

Historical Pattern of Instrument Use in Canadian Environmental Policy

THE PRE-REGULATORY PRIVATE COMMON-LAW ERA

Until the 1960s, environmental concerns in Canada were dealt with in the private sphere and did not involve government actions.[33] A variety of common-law actions were available to private individuals to deal with what were generally considered to be purely private concerns, such as pollution or other damages to private property, which were generally classified as species of 'nuisance' actions.[34] Common-law court actions to correct a number of misdoings or torts respecting private property rights, such as nuisance, trespass, riparian rights, or negligence, were generally considered adequate to deal with negative environmental impacts stemming, in large part, from industrialization.[35]

Despite its longevity, however, this type of action proved to be inadequate for dealing with environmental issues as pressures on the environment grew during the last half of the twentieth century. Modern environmental grievances, such as air pollution or toxic discharges, often involved what is now termed 'non-point source' pollution for which strict liability was difficult, if not impossible, to assess.[36] Moreover, even if a single polluter could be identified, pollution and environmental damages increasingly tended to affect more than one individual and Canadian courts were very reticent to recognize a private individual's right to press public or common actions.[37] The courts historically reserved the right to initiate litigation ('standing') in such matters solely to aggrieved individual(s) while the right to pursue legal actions in the common good was restricted to governments.[38] For both reasons, by the post-World War II era, private nuisance actions were no longer significant deterrents to substantial environmental damage, as restricted standing for public actions and difficulties in determining liability in private cases prevented most issues from even entering the court system.

Not all legal avenues in this common-law era were purely private, of course. Towards the end of the period in the United States, for example, the courts allowed notions of a 'public trust' concerning common resources such as air or the seashore controlled by neither public nor private authorities, which citizens could then protect through recourse to the courts.[39] Although such resources certainly existed in Canada, Canadian courts refused to accord them special status, insisting that rights to their use existed in common law and could either be replaced by statute or litigated according to traditional common-law private actions.[40] A second avenue for quasi-public actions existed with respect to class action suits, the rules of which also were liberalized at this point in US judicial history.[41] Under English common law, however, class actions were viewed simply as multiple private actions, which could be heard more efficiently all at once. Thus, for a class action to proceed, there had to be a readily identifiable class of individuals with virtually identical grievances, for example, those involving nuisance or trespass alleged by multiple property holders along a railway line. In addition, those concerns had to meet the same minimum justiciability standards of private tort actions. Class actions were not allowed to substitute for public actions, which, once again, courts generally ruled could only be pressed by public authorities.[42] A third avenue, criminal charges, also existed in this period. Standing was not an issue in this area since individuals have long been able to lay criminal charges. The problem preventing the employment of criminal actions in environmental matters, however, is the burden of proof required for successful prosecution. For such cases to succeed, it was necessary to establish beyond a reasonable doubt that a guilty party possessed a guilty mind, or *mens rea,* at the time a crime was committed.[43] Given the difficulties associated with accomplishing this in environmental cases, the reality was that citizens could press charges in environmental cases but rarely did so.[44]

THE PUBLIC-LAW ERA AND THE DEVELOPMENT OF A CANADIAN ENVIRONMENTAL IMPLEMENTATION STYLE

The failure of the private law regime of environmental control to deal with large-scale and widespread environmental damage became more and more apparent as industrialization proceeded apace in Canada in the post-World War II era. As occurred in many other areas of social and economic life, this resulted in the supplementation of common-law legal devices by public-law regulatory regimes.[45] Over time, as this regime was extended and consolidated, a typical implementation style developed.

Although the environment was a late subject of regulation, by the end of the 1960s two distinct sets of statutory and quasi-statutory provisions had evolved as the basic framework for the new regime. One area was related to the regulation of the emission of toxic chemicals and industrial by-products into the air, water, and ground. This system involved the registration of specific toxins and control

over their production and discharge through a complex licensing system.[46] The
second pillar of the system involved the effort to mitigate or offset damages
caused by specific industrial and other projects, especially large-scale resource
projects. This was accomplished through the creation of federal, and later provincial, assessment 'guidelines' intended to assess initial environmental baseline
conditions and prescribe remedial or mitigative actions to project proponents in
order to minimize disruptions caused by construction and operation.[47]

Both of these developments were based on the use of a specific substantive
policy instrument: regulation. However, the implementation style that developed
in Canada at this time was heavily influenced by the use of a negotiative
approach to the development and enforcement of administrative standards.
Procedurally, the public law regime was based on compliance agreements with
polluters: a form of specialized recognition of industrial interests based on the
exercise of governmental procedural authority.[48] The result was a hybrid implementation style of consultative regulation falling somewhere between representative legalism and directed subsidization, a form of preferential regulation quite
different from the American system of adversarial legalism that developed at
around the same time.

The principal difference between the Canadian and American systems was the
general lack of citizen ability in Canada to overturn administrative decisions
through recourse to the courts.[49] In Canada, citizens and public interest groups
were prevented from influencing assessments and regulations through a combination of limited rules of standing and restricted grounds for judicial review of
administrative decisions.[50] In the US, the doctrine of the 'private attorney general'
provided citizens with the ability to pursue actions in the public good if so
authorized by congressional statute.[51] This practice lay at the heart of the National
Environmental Policy Act (NEPA), which authorized citizen-initiated reviews of
the application of environmental regulations.[52]

This was never the case in Canada. In civil cases involving public interests,
until quite recently, the general rule established 75 years ago by the Supreme
Court of Canada in *Smith v. Attorney General of Ontario*[53] was that only the public
attorney general could pursue cases pertaining to public grievances unless the
individual 'was exceptionally prejudiced by the wrongful act'. Thus, for the most
part, public actions remained the monopoly of the provincial or federal attorneys
general, who could undertake an action personally or through the appointment
of a private 'relator'.[54] Since the environmental regulations developed in this era
fall into the category of non-criminal public actions, prosecution of their violation
had to be supported by elected public officials.

In a series of cases decided in the 1970s and 1980s, the Supreme Court of
Canada did move to allow individual citizens greater access to the courts, but
only in very specific types of public actions. This affected environmental matters
but by no means opened the floodgates to citizens' suits as did the passage of the
NEPA in the US. In 1974, in *Thorson v. A.G. Canada*, the court liberalized stand-

ing in constitutional cases, a ruling that presaged the constitutionally entrenched right to litigate under the terms of the 1982 Canadian Charter of Rights and Freedoms.[55] The impact on environmental litigation of these changes in rules of standing governing constitutional cases, however, was negligible because there is no direct link between the Charter and environmental litigation. Although one Charter right (section 7) could be broadly interpreted as a right to a clean environment, it has not been so construed by the courts, which have restricted its application to questions of the due process of law.[56] More generally, Canadian courts have ruled that the Charter applies only to relations between citizens and governments, therefore excluding matters dealing, for example, with relations between employees and employers or between citizens and polluting companies.

While the constitutional aspects of *Thorson* had little impact on environmental litigation, the case was also used by the Supreme Court to provide greater judicial discretion in the definition of exceptional personal aggrievement set out in *Smith*. In 1986 in *Finlay v. Minister of Finance of Canada*, the Court clarified its ground rules for such private litigation in the public interest.[57] It argued that in exceptional circumstances, standing would be granted to private individuals to press public cases if: (1) the issue was 'justiciable', that is, could at least in theory be decided by a court; (2) the issue at the heart of the dispute was serious and not trivial or speculative; (3) the individual had a genuine interest in the issue based on personal interest or a strong interest based on involvement in a public policy process; and (4) there was no other reasonable means by which the action could be brought before the courts.[58] Environmental cases were among those to receive the benefit of subsequent judicial discretion in the area of standing. Cases such as *Canadian Wildlife Federation Inc. v. Canada (Minister of the Environment)*[59] and *Friends of the Oldman River Society v. Canada (Minister of Transport)*[60] broke new ground in Canadian environmental law and did so on the basis of cases brought before the courts under post-*Finlay* rules of standing. However, despite the significance of these cases, the fact is that standing in Canada has changed very little in most areas of law and, in the area of public law, remains subject to a very circumscribed judicial discretion.[61]

The second important procedural limitation on Canadian environmental law in this era concerned the limitations found in British parliamentary systems with respect to the role of the courts vis-à-vis legislation and especially the limited grounds provided for judicial review of administrative actions. In Canada, the courts followed British practice in that the central question to be decided in a review is whether or not an inferior court, tribunal, or agency has acted within its powers or jurisdiction.[62] If it has, and if it has also abided with key principles of natural justice and has not acted in a capricious or arbitrary fashion, then its decision will stand, subject to any existing statutory appeal provisions. In other words, in Canada, judicial review focuses primarily on issues or errors in law.[63] Since Canadian courts do not attempt to review cases on the facts, then as long as administrative agencies operate within their jurisdiction and according to principles of fundamental justice and due process, their decisions are unlikely to be overturned by the courts. Although changes at the federal and provincial levels in the late 1960s and 1970s specifically allowing for judicial appeals of many administrative decisions appeared to presage a greater scope for judicial review, the courts themselves proved very reticent to alter their behaviour.[64] In fact, the courts have consistently deferred to legislators in policy matters, including matters related to the environment.[65] Not surprisingly, this deference has resulted in a rather patchy, ad hoc approach to administrative law on the part of Canadian courts, but one still based on judicial self-restraint and unwillingness to become too closely involved in administrative decision-making.[66]

In the environmental area, this approach to administrative law and judicial review was manifest throughout the public law era. As noted in the preceding chapter by Valiante, in the course of deciding the *Canadian Wildlife Federation* case concerning the Rafferty-Alameda dam, the Federal Court held that federal environmental assessment guidelines passed by Order-in-Council in 1974 were in effect statutes and hence were legally binding on government departments. In subsequent cases, Canadian courts reviewed administrative and ministerial conduct in light of a mandatory environmental assessment process. However, while enthusiasts argued this amounted to a revolution in judicial conduct, analysis of the subsequent decisions revealed that only traditional criteria of judicial review were exercised. As Lucas argued:

> There has not been a general judicialization of federal environmental assessment. Apart from confirming the legally binding nature of the *Guidelines Order*, courts have not aggressively promoted environmental objectives. They have merely carried out their traditional judicial review role of ensuring the legality and fairness of administrative decisions. Although some judicial concern and even outrage at federal foot-dragging in environmental assessment is apparent, review has been according to established principles and remedial discretion has been exercised conservatively.[67]

Contemporary Canadian Environmental Policy Instrument Use in the 1990s: Portents of Change in Implementation Styles?

As Hawkins has suggested, in the 1960–90 period Canada developed all the elements of a 'compliance' system of environmental policy implementation in which recourse to penalties and coercion exists only as a very infrequently used last resort of administrators.[68] The Canadian environmental policy implementation style developed in this period was one of closed bargaining between government and business interests over the enactment of environmental standards, their implementation, and the level of compliance expected of corporate actors.

Because of the significance of industry to the Canadian economy, the historical dominance of single-industry production in many areas of the country, and the legacy of a staples economy, economic forces provided a significant constraint on regulation.[69] Regulation in the 1960–90 period was geared to the modification of business activity rather than to environmental protection per se. Industry, in the course of pursuing its own productive interests, has supplied much of the baseline data, up-to-date technical information concerning abatement technology, and cost-benefit analyses concerning production, pollution, and abatement costs, from which regulatory standards have been developed and applied. Industry's role in environmental regulation was cost-effective for governments, in that governments were not required to supply separate and potentially redundant information.[70] However, this system did not provide adequate protection of the environment from industrial and other activities.[71]

By the 1990s, as the scope of environmental issues and problems increased, Canadian governments began experimenting with a variety of new policy instruments, both procedural and substantive, in an effort to deal with the expansion of ecological and public environmental concerns.[72] While many of these instruments were expected to shift the general tenor of regulation from *ex post* mitigation to *ex ante* prevention and to legitimate that expansion, the results in practice were often disappointing.

EXPERIMENTATION WITH MARKET-BASED, CO-OPERATIVE, AND COMPREHENSIVE SUBSTANTIVE INSTRUMENTS

In the present era, experiments in substantive instrument use first involved a variety of proposals to replace regulation with market- and tax-based financial incentives.[73] Later in the 1990s, efforts were also made to promote industry self-regulation through a variety of co-operative and voluntary compliance arrangements.[74] These included programs such as the Canadian Industry Packaging Stewardship Initiative, the Voluntary Challenge and Registry Program created as part of Canada's response to the Kyoto Climate Change Convention,[75] and the Accelerated Reduction/Elimination of Toxics,[76] as well as sector-specific arrangements such as eco-labelling and certification in the forest sector.[77] In addition, several efforts were made to augment existing regulatory instruments, especially assessment processes, in order to develop and intensify their ability to predict and offset harmful effects of industrial and other projects.[78]

Not one of these experiments was successful. In the case of market-based financial instruments, declines in government fiscal capacity and the political emphasis placed on fighting the deficit led to their quick demise.[79] This was most readily apparent in the failure of numerous such proposals contained in the 1990 federal Green Plan to be seriously implemented.[80]

The emergence of an emphasis on co-operative or voluntary arrangements should also be seen in this light. That is, these proposals emerged in the context of a 'do-more-with-less' philosophy on the part of federal and provincial administrative agencies negatively affected by budget cuts in the mid-1990s.[81] Muldoon and Nadarajah have argued that 'significant practical problems have arisen in the application of voluntary initiatives', suggesting that 'such initiatives have been overrated as a policy instrument for moving us towards a sustainable environment.'[82] Very few of these arrangements were ever created and the difficulties in assessing their impact and efficacy, as well as legal issues concerning their status vis-à-vis existing laws, have led to few recent efforts towards their expansion.[83]

The expansion and extension of existing administrative arrangements and regulations during this time period were also problematic. The same difficulties with budget cuts, which led to calls for market-based and co-operative arrangements, undermined the extension of existing regulatory arrangements.[84] And, as Kennett has argued in the case of environmental assessments, there are distinct limitations to how far essentially *ex post* mitigative tools can be stretched to become *ex ante* ones.[85]

EXPERIMENTATION WITH MULTI-STAKEHOLDER AND TREATY-BASED PROCEDURAL INSTRUMENTS

More success appears to have resulted from the multiple experiments with procedural instruments also undertaken during this decade, although still not enough to alter significantly the fundamental nature of the Canadian environmental policy implementation style.

These experiments were generally oriented towards opening up the closed, bilateral system of government-industry consultations that characterized Canadian environmental policy-making in the public law era. The primary device used towards this end was the replacement of more or less informal bilateral consultations with more or less formalized multi-stakeholder ones.[86] These included the creation of government-industry-ENGO committees, such as the federal and provincial Round Tables on the Environment and Economy, as well as more specific provincial or local efforts, such as the Committee on Resources and the Economy land planning processes in British Columbia,[87] public consultations on such specific issues as waste disposal siting,[88] and public consultations in specific sectors such as mining or forestry.[89]

A second procedural device developed in this period was the intergovernmental treaty or 'framework agreement'. These involved the negotiation of non-binding federal-provincial agreements in a variety of areas, from assessments to toxic regulations, to minimize federal-provincial duplication and conflicts over jurisdictional issues related to environmental regulation. Such treaties had been negotiated in many countries,[90] and arrangements such as the Environmental Management Framework Agreement[91] and the Canada-Wide Accord on Environmental Harmonization[92] emulated international trends towards administrative decentralization of environmental responsibility as significant elements of federal powers were essentially transferred to the provinces.[93]

Like the experiments in substantive instruments described above, these procedural tools had less of an impact than originally expected. Many consultative bodies revealed major distances between participants and did not generate the cohesion and consensus that many administrators expected.[94] Nevertheless, although some have been abolished, it is now expected that major environmental decisions will involve some minimum level of public consultation, a significant change in implementation style from earlier eras.[95]

Conclusion

Under the public law regime, the preferred substantive instrument for environmental policy implementation has been bureaucratic regulation rather than information, treasure, or organization-based tools.[96] However, the context, style, and substance of the marketplace has tended to infiltrate much of the regulatory process. Compliance, for example, is usually approached in terms of market-based factors: profit margins, the economic viability of industry, employment patterns, and international competitiveness. Government grants to business also often underwrite compliance efforts, as devices such as subsidies for technological improvements enable industries to meet regulatory standards.

As far as procedural instruments are concerned, selective representation of affected interests continues to be the preferred approach of Canadian governments in determining and orienting policy-making processes. Although there have been some moves towards a multi-stakeholder approach and American-style pluralism, these remain very much within the overall implementation style of consultative legalism established in the early years of the public law regime.[97]

This Canadian implementation style remains quite distinct from that of the US.[98] Although there is some evidence that the US style is changing somewhat towards that of Canada,[99] this appears to be a case of what Unger and Van Waarden have termed 'strong' convergence, in which two countries move in tandem towards a third model, rather than a 'weak' case whereby one of two countries moves towards the other.[100] This interpretation is bolstered by the observation that many European countries also appear to be moving in similar directions.[101]

While this overall regulatory and administrative movement is often associated with the spread of a specific political-administrative ideology—the 'New Public Management' (NPM)[102]—the idea that this is solely responsible for convergence in the environmental sphere must be treated with caution. Although NPM has a fairly well-known set of policy prescriptions for downsizing bureaucracies and encouraging citizen participation in government,[103] many studies have questioned its direct link to specific policy reforms.[104] Rather, most studies point to general factors such as an improvement in the education of citizens,[105] the extension of industrialization and consumerism throughout the world,[106] and the expansion and lead of international organizations in the environmental sphere[107] as being the cause of policy convergence in this sector. This is not to say that NPM concepts have had no impact on this process, but rather, as Wilks and Doern, Kagan, and others have argued, simply to note that NPM principles are filtered through national and sectoral political and administrative arrangements that can blunt, deflect, or augment their impact.[108]

As a result, it should not be surprising that countries would exhibit both distinctive and convergent elements in their environmental policy implementation styles. The exact configuration of procedural and substantive instruments arrayed in a country's style will vary depending on the extent of that country's environmental difficulties and the degree to which their administrative resources and public opinion are challenged or congruent with these problems. However, generally speaking, the expansion of the environment as a policy target presages continual movement away from earlier implementation styles based on affecting smaller targets and towards those styles capable of dealing with larger issues. Although it has not yet solidified into a new style, this movement is well under way in Canada, as the experiments of the 1990s attest.

Notes

1 On these developments, see R.A.W. Rhodes, 'The Hollowing Out of the State: The Changing Nature of the Public Service in Britain', *Political Quarterly* 65, 2 (1994): 138–51.

2 On the intensification and expansion of interorganizational network structures, see Gerhard Lehmbruch, 'The Organization of Society, Administrative Strategies, and Policy Networks', in Roland M. Czada and Adrienne Windhoff-Heritier, eds, *Political Choice: Institutions, Rules, and the Limits of Rationality* (Boulder, Colo.: Westview Press, 1991), 121–55.

3 On networks and instrument choices generally, see Johan A. de Bruijn and Ernst F. ten Heuvelhof, 'Policy Networks and Governance', in D.L. Weimer, ed., *Institutional Design* (Boston: Kluwer Academic Publishers, 1995), 161–79; Erik-Hans Klijn, Joop Koppenjan, and Katrien Termeer, 'Managing Networks in the Public Sector: A Theoretical Study of Management Strategies in Policy Networks', *Public Administration* 73 (1995): 437–54.

4 Generally, see B. Guy Peters and Jon Pierre, 'Governance Without Government? Rethinking Public Administration', *Journal of Public Administration Research and Theory* 8, 2 (1998): 223–44.

5 Generally, see Neil Gunningham, Peter Grabowsky, and Darren Sinclair, *Smart Regulation: Designing Environmental Policy* (Oxford: Clarendon Press, 1998). On recent Canadian experiences see Susan Delacourt and Donald G. Lenihan, eds, *Collaborative Government: Is There a Canadian Way?* (Toronto: Institute of Public Administration of Canada New Directions—Number 6, 2000). On European experiences see Beate Kohler-Koch, 'Catching up with Change: The Transformation of Governance in the European Union', *Journal of European Public Policy* 3, 3 (1996): 359–80.

6 See Malcolm L. Goggin et al., *Implementation Theory and Practice: Toward a Third Generation* (Glenview, Ill.: Scott, Foresman/Little, Brown, 1990); Andrew Dunsire, *Manipulating Social Tensions: Collaboration as an Alternative Mode of Government Intervention* (Koln: Max Plank Institut fur Gesellschaftsforschung Discussion Paper 93/7, 1993); Leslie A. Pal, *Beyond Policy Analysis: Public Issue Management in Turbulent Times* (Toronto: ITP Nelson, 1997).

7 See Christoph Knill, 'European Policies: The Impact of National Administrative Traditions', *Journal of Public Policy* 18, 1 (1998): 1–28; Robert A. Kagan, 'Adversarial Legalism and American Government', *Journal of Policy Analysis and Management* 10, 3 (1991): 369–406.

8 On the notion of 'enforcement style' often used to characterize the latter aspect of the implementation process, see Keith Hawkins and John M. Thomas, 'Making Policy in Regulatory Bureaucracies', in Hawkins and Thomas, eds, *Making Regulatory Policy* (Pittsburgh: University of Pittsburgh Press, 1989), 3–30.

9 On sectoral and national styles, see Gary P. Freeman, 'National Styles and Policy Sectors: Explaining Structured Variation', *Journal of Public Policy* 5, 4 (1985): 467–96; Adrienne Heritier, Christoph Knill, and Susanne Mingers, *Ringing the Changes in Europe: Regulatory Competition and the Transformation of the State. Britain, France, Germany* (Berlin: Walter de Gruyter, 1996).

10 See Melody Hessing and Michael Howlett, *Canadian Natural Resource and Environmental Policy: Political Economy and Public Policy* (Vancouver: University of British Columbia Press, 1997); Ted Schrecker, 'Resisting Regulation: Environmental Policy and Corporate Power', *Alternatives* 13 (Dec. 1985); Kernaghan Webb and John C. Clifford, *Pollution Control in Canada: The Regulatory Approach in the 1980s* (Ottawa: Law Reform Commission of Canada, 1988).

11 On changes in regulatory styles in Canada, see G. Bruce Doern et al., 'Conclusion', in Doern, M.M. Hill, M.J. Prince, and R.J. Schultz, eds, *Changing the Rules: Canadian Regulatory Regimes and Institutions* (Toronto: University of Toronto Press, 1999), 389–406; Doern, 'The Interplay Among Regimes: Mapping Regulatory Institutions in the United Kingdom, the United States, and Canada', in Doern and S. Wilks, eds, *Changing Regulatory Institutions in Britain and North America* (Toronto: University of Toronto Press, 1998), 29–50.

12 Generally, see Michael Howlett, 'Managing the "Hollow State": Procedural Policy Instruments and Modern Governance', *Canadian Public Administration* 43, 4 (2001): 412–31. On the environment in Canada, see Howlett, 'Complex Network Management and the Governance of the Environment: Prospects for Policy Change and Policy Stability over the Long Term', in Edward Parson, ed., *Environmental Trends in Canada* (Toronto: University of Toronto Press, 2001).

13 These are quite well known and considerable attention has been paid to them in the policy literature. See B.G. Peters and F.K.M. van Nispen, eds, *Public Policy Instruments: Evaluating the Tools of Public Administration* (New York: Edward Elgar, 1998); Lester M. Salamon, ed., *Beyond Privatization: The Tools of Government Action* (Washington: Urban Institute, 1989).

14 For an overview of these classification efforts, see Evert Vedung, 'Policy Instruments: Typologies and Theories', in Marie Louise Bemelmans-Videc, Ray C. Rist, and Vedung, eds, *Carrots, Sticks and Sermons: Policy Instruments and Their Evaluation* (New Brunswick, NJ: Transaction Publishers, 1997); Michael Howlett, 'Policy Instruments, Policy Styles, and Policy Implementation: National Approaches to Theories of Instrument Choice', *Policy Studies Journal* 19, 2 (1991): 1–21.

15 Christopher Hood, *The Tools of Government* (Chatham, NJ: Chatham House Publishers, 1986).

16 These instruments have been much less systematically studied than substantive ones. See Michael Howlett, 'Legitimacy and Governance: Re-Discovering Procedural Policy Instruments', paper presented to the annual meeting of the British Columbia Political Studies Association, Vancouver, 1996; Roeland J.Veld, 'The Dynamics of Instruments', in Peters and van Nispen, eds, *Public Policy Instruments*, 153–62; W.J.M. Kickert, E.-H. Klijn, and J.F.M. Koppenjan, 'Managing Networks in the Public Sector: Findings and Reflections', in Kickert, Klijn, and Koppenjan, eds, *Managing Complex Networks: Strategies for the Public Sector* (London: Sage, 1997), 166–91.

17 See Andrew Dunsire, 'A Cybernetic View of Guidance, Control and Evaluation in the Public Sector', in F.-X. Kaufman, G. Majone, and V. Ostrom, eds, *Guidance, Control, and Evaluation in the Public Sector* (Berlin: Walter de Gruyter, 1986), 327–46; Evert A. Lindquist, 'Public Managers and Policy Communities: Learning to Meet New Challenges', *Canadian Public Administration* 35, 2 (1992): 127–59.

18 See Kagan, 'Adversarial Legalism'; Kagan and Lee Axelrad, 'Adversarial Legalism: An International Perspective', in P.S. Nivola, ed., *Comparative Disadvantages? Social Regulations and the Global Economy* (Washington: Brookings Institution, 1997), 146–202; Kagan, 'Should Europe Worry About Adversarial Legalism?', *Oxford Journal of Legal Studies* 17, 2 (1997): 165–83.

19 See Stephen H. Linder and B. Guy Peters, 'Instruments of Government: Perceptions and Contexts', *Journal of Public Policy* 9 (1989).

20 See Hans Th. A. Bressers and Laurence J. O'Toole, 'The Selection of Policy Instruments: A Network-based Perspective', *Journal of Public Policy* 18, 3 (1998): 213–39.

21 See Christopher Hood, 'Using Bureaucracy Sparingly', *Public Administration* 61, 2 (1983): 187–208; Hood, *The Tools of Government*.

22 See Michael Howlett and M. Ramesh, *Studying Public Policy: Policy Cycles and Policy Subsystems* (Toronto: Oxford University Press, 1995); Anne L. Schneider and Helen Ingram, 'Policy Design: Elements, Premises and Strategies', in S.S. Nagel, ed., *Policy Theory and Policy Evaluation: Concepts, Knowledge, Causes and Norms* (New York: Greenwood, 1990), 77–102.

23 Renate Mayntz, 'Legitimacy and the Directive Capacity of the Political System', in Leon N. Lindberg et al., eds, *Stress and Contradiction in Modern Capitalism* (Lexington, Mass.: Lexington Books, 1975), 261–74; Peter J. May et al., *Environmental Management and Governance: Intergovernmental Approaches to Hazards and Sustainability* (London: Routledge, 1997).

24 On legitimation, see David Beetham, *The Legitimation of Power* (London: Macmillan, 1991); Peter G. Stillman, 'The Concept of Legitimacy', *Polity* 7, 1 (1974): 32–56.

25 See Anne L. Schneider and Helen Ingram, 'Social Construction of Target Populations: Implications for Politics and Policy', *American Political Science Review* 87, 2 (1993): 334–47; Schneider and Ingram, 'Behavioural Assumptions of Policy Tools', *Journal of Politics* 52, 2 (1990): 511–29.

26 On the significance of the distinction between sectoral and generalized legitimation crises, see Claus Mueller, *The Politics of Communication: A Study in the Political Sociology of Language, Socialization and Legitimation* (New York: Oxford University Press, 1973). See also Jurgen Habermas, *Legitimation Crisis* (Boston: Beacon Press, 1975), Part III; Habermas, 'What Does a Legitimation Crisis Mean Today? Legitimation Problems in Late Capitalism', *Social Research* 40, 4 (1973): 643–67.

27 On the notions of the depletability or intensiveness of instrument resource use, see Hood, *The Tools of Government*.

28 See Eric A. Nordlinger, *On the Autonomy of the Democratic State* (Cambridge, Mass.: Harvard University Press, 1981).

29 See Jonathan Rose, 'Government Advertising in a Crisis: The Quebec Referendum Precedent', *Canadian Journal of Communication* 18 (1993): 173–96; Phil Ryan, 'Miniature Mila and Flying Geese: Government Advertising and Canadian Democracy', in S.D. Phillips, ed., *How Ottawa Spends 1995–96: Mid-Life Crises* (Ottawa: Carleton University Press, 1995), 263–86.

30 See M. Atkinson and W. Coleman, *The State, Business, and Industrial Change in Canada* (Toronto: University of Toronto Press, 1989).

31 See Sandra Burt, 'Canadian Women's Groups in the 1980s: Organizational Development and Policy Influence', *Canadian Public Policy* 16, 1 (1990): 17–28; Leslie A. Pal, *Interests of State: The Politics of Language, Multiculturalism, and Feminism in Canada* (Montreal: McGill-Queen's University Press, 1993). See also Peter Finkle et al., *Federal Government Relations with Interest Groups: A Reconsideration* (Ottawa: Privy Council Office, 1994).

32 For examples of such activities in the transportation and communications sector in the past, see J.E. Hodgetts, *The Canadian Public Service: A Physiology of Government, 1867–1970* (Toronto: University of Toronto Press, 1973).

33 On the early history of Canadian environmental regulation, see P.S. Elder, 'Environmental Protection Through the Common Law', *University of Western Ontario Law Review* 12 (1973): 107–71.

34 On the early development of Canadian nuisance law, see Jennifer Nedelsky, 'Judicial Conservatism in an Age of Innovation: Comparative Perspectives on Canadian Nuisance Law 1880–1930', in David H. Flaherty, ed., *Essays in the History of Canadian Law, I* (Toronto: University of Toronto Press, 1981), 281–322.

35 M.I. Jeffreys, 'Environmental Enforcement and Regulation in the 1980's: *Regina v. Sault Ste. Marie* Revisited', *Queen's Law Journal* 10, 1 (1984): 43–70; P.S. Elder, 'An Overview of the Participatory Environment in Canada', in Elder, ed., *Environmental Management and Public Participation* (Toronto: Canadian Environmental Law Research Foundation, 1975), 370–84.

36 See Carolyn Johns, 'Non-Point Source Water Pollution Management in Canada and the US: A Comparative Analysis of Environmental Policy Instruments and Institutional Arrangements', paper presented to the annual meeting of the Western Economics Association, San Diego, 1999.

37 John P.S. McLaren, 'The Common Law Nuisance Actions and the Environmental Battle— Well-Tempered Swords or Broken Reeds?', *Osgoode Hall Law Journal* 10, 3 (1972): 505–61. The similar English experience is outlined in Joel Franklin Brenner, 'Nuisance Law and the Industrial Revolution', *Journal of Legal Studies* 3, 2 (1974): 403–34.

38 See Thomas A. Cromwell, *Locus Standi: A Commentary on the Law of Standing in Canada* (Toronto: Carswell, 1986).

39 Joseph L. Sax, 'The Public Trust Doctrine in Natural Resource Law: Effective Judicial Intervention', *Michigan Law Review* 68 (1969–70): 475–566.

40 Constance D. Hunt, 'The Public Trust Doctrine in Canada', in John Swaigen, ed., *Environmental Rights in Canada* (Toronto: Butterworths, 1981), 151–94.

41 Arthur Miller, 'An Overview of Federal Class Actions: Past, Present and Future', *Justice System Journal* 4 (1978).

42 See Simon Chester, 'Class Actions to Protect the Environment: A Real Weapon or Another Lawyer's Word Game?', in Swaigen, ed., *Environmental Rights in Canada*.

43 Kernaghan Webb, 'On the Periphery: The Limited Role for Criminal Offense in Environmental Protection', in Donna Tingley, ed., *Into the Future: Environmental Law and Policy for the 1990's* (Edmonton: Environmental Law Centre, 1990), 58–69.

44 Kernaghan Webb, 'Between the Rocks and Hard Places: Bureaucrats, the Law and Pollution Control', *Alternatives* 14, 2 (1987): 4–13.

45 On the growth of the administrative state in Canada during this period, see Margot Priest and Aron Wohl, 'The Growth of Federal and Provincial Regulation of Economic Activity 1867–1978', in W.T. Stanbury, ed., *Government Regulation: Scope, Growth, Process* (Montreal: Institute for Research on Public Policy, 1980), 69–150.

46 See Kathryn Harrison and George Hoberg, *Risk, Science, and Politics: Regulating Toxic Substances in Canada and the United States* (Montreal and Kingston: McGill-Queen's University Press, 1994).

47 See Marie-Ann Bowden and Fred Curtis, 'Federal EIA in Canada: EARP as an Evolving Process', *Environmental Impact Assessment Review* 8, 1 (1988): 97–106; B. Mitchell and R. Turkheim, 'Environmental Impact Assessment: Principles, Practices, and Canadian Experiences', in R.R. Krueger and Mitchell, eds, *Managing Canada's Renewable Resources* (Toronto: Methuen, 1977), 47–66.

48 See Ted Schrecker, *Political Economy of Environmental Hazards* (Ottawa: Law Reform Commission of Canada, 1984).

49 See David Estrin, 'Environmental Law', *Ottawa Law Review* 7, 2 (1975): 397–449; John Swaigen, 'Environmental Law 1975–1980', *Ottawa Law Review* 12, 2 (1980): 439–88;

D.P. Emond, 'Environmental Law and Policy: A Retrospective Examination of the Canadian Experience', in Ivan Bernier and Andrée Lajoie, eds, *Consumer Protection, Environmental Law and Corporate Power* (Toronto: University of Toronto Press, 1985), 89–179.

50 See Michael Howlett, 'The Judicialization of Canadian Environmental Policy 1980–1990—A Test of the Canada-US Convergence Hypothesis', *Canadian Journal of Political Science* 27, 1 (1994): 99–127; Stewart Elgie, 'Environmental Groups and the Courts: 1970–1992', in G. Thompson, M.L. McConnell, and L.B. Huestis, eds, *Environmental Law and Business in Canada* (Aurora, Ont.: Canada Law Book, 1993), 185–224.

51 See Louis Jaffe, 'The Citizen as Litigant: The Non-Hohfeldian or Ideological Plaintiff', *University of Pennsylvania Law Review* 116 (1968).

52 Frederick R. Anderson, *NEPA in the Courts: A Legal Analysis of the National Environmental Policy Act* (Baltimore: Johns Hopkins University Press, 1973); Rowell S. Melnick, *Regulation and the Courts: The Case of the Clean Air Act* (Washington: Brookings Institution, 1983).

53 S.C.R., [1924] 331.

54 See Willard Estey, 'Public Nuisance and Standing to Sue', *Osgoode Hall Law Journal* 10 (1972): 563–82; Andrew J. Roman, '*Locus Standi*: A Cure in Search of a Disease?', in Swaigen, ed., *Environmental Rights in Canada*, 11–59.

55 1 S.C.R., [1975] 138. Sections 24(1) and 52(1) of the Constitution Act, 1982 allow citizens access to the courts to deal with infringements of their constitutionally protected rights. In 1976 the Supreme Court ruled in *McNeil v. Nova Scotia Board of Censors*, [1976] 2 S.C.R. 265, that a part of its earlier ruling in *Thorson* distinguishing between regulatory and legislative pronouncements in granting increased standing was unworkable. In 1981 it ruled in *Borowski v. Minister of Justice of Canada*, [1981] 2 S.C.R. 575, that constitutionality extended to violations of the (then) non-constitutionally entrenched Canadian Bill of Rights. On the Supreme Court standing 'trilogy' and 'quartet', see Ontario Law Reform Commission, *Report on the Law of Standing* (Toronto: Ministry of the Attorney General, 1989); Thomas A. Cromwell, *Locus Standi: A Commentary on the Law of Standing in Canada.*

56 Franklin Gertler, Paul Muldoon, and Marcia Valiante, 'Public Access to Environmental Justice', in Canadian Bar Association, *Sustainable Development in Canada: Options for Law Reform* (Ottawa: Canadian Bar Association, 1990), 79–97.See also Kent Roach, 'The Role of Litigation and the Charter in Interest Advocacy' in F. Leslie Siedel, ed., *Equity and Community: The Charter, Interest Advocacy and Representation.* (Montreal: IRPP, 1993) 159–88.

57 [1986] 2 S.C.R. 607.

58 W.A. Bogart, 'Understanding Standing, Chapter IV: *Minister of Finance of Canada v. Finlay*', *Supreme Court Law Review* 10 (1988): 377–97.

59 (1989), 3 C.E.L.R. (ns) 287.

60 (1992), 7 C.E.L.R. (ns).

61 Carl Baar, 'Judicial Activism in Canada', in K.M. Holland, ed., *Judicial Activism in Comparative Perspective* (London: Macmillan, 1991), 53–69.

62 Kenneth Kernaghan, 'Judicial Review of Administration Action', in Kernaghan, ed., *Public Administration in Canada: Selected Readings* (Toronto: Methuen, 1985), 358–73.

63 H.W.R. Wade, 'Anglo-American Administrative Law: More Reflections', *Law Quarterly Review* 82 (1966): 226–52.

64 On Canadian developments in the 1960s and 1970s, see Albert S. Abel, 'Appeals Against Administrative Decisions III: In Search of a Basic Policy', *Canadian Public Administration* 5, 1 (1962): 65–75.

65 On current Canadian practice, see R. Dussault and L. Borgeat, *Administrative Law: A Treatise* (Toronto: Carswell, 1990).

66 P.W. Hogg, 'The Supreme Court of Canada and Administrative Law, 1949–1971', *Osgoode Hall Law Journal* 11, 2 (1973): 187–223.

67 Alastair R. Lucas, 'Judicial Review of the Environmental Assessment Process: Has Federal Environmental Assessment Been Judicialized?', paper presented to the 6th CIRL Conference on Natural Resources Law, Ottawa, May 1993, 47.

68 In the US, meanwhile, the adversarial legalist system more closely resembled a 'penal' system in which coercion existed as the preferred tool of enforcement. See Keith Hawkins, *Environment and Enforcement: Regulation and the Social Definition of Pollution* (Oxford: Clarendon Press, 1984).

69 See Hessing and Howlett, *Canadian Natural Resource and Environmental Policy.*

70 For a rare cross-national empirical study attempting to assess the effectiveness of this Canadian 'negotiative' approach to implementation, see Kathryn Harrison, 'Is Co-operation the Answer: Canadian Environmental Enforcement in Comparative Context', *Journal of Policy Analysis and Management* 14, 2 (1995): 221–44.

71 See Murray Rankin and Peter Finkle, 'The Enforcement of Environmental Law: Taking the Environment Seriously', *University of British Columbia Law Review* 17, 1 (1983): 35–58.

72 On the role of international agreements and public opinion in expanding the Canadian environmental agenda at this point in time, see Glen Toner and Tom Conway, 'Environmental Policy', in G.B. Doern, L.A. Pal, and B.W. Tomlin, eds, *Border Crossings: The Internationalization of Canadian Public Policy* (Toronto: Oxford University Press, 1996), 108–42.

73 See G. Bruce Doern, ed., *The Environmental Imperative: Market Approaches to the Greening of Canada* (Toronto: C.D. Howe Institute, 1990); Allan M. Maslove, ed., *Taxes as Instruments of Public Policy* (Toronto: University of Toronto Press, 1994).

74 See Kathryn Harrison, 'Talking with the Donkey: Cooperative Approaches to Environmental Protection', *Journal of Industrial Ecology* 2, 3 (1998): 51–72; Harrison, 'Voluntarism and Environmental Governance', paper presented to the PRI/SSHRC Project on Trends—Environmental Section, University of British Columbia, Apr. 1999; Robert B. Gibson, ed., *Voluntary Initiatives: The New Politics of Corporate Greening* (Peterborough, Ont.: Broadview Press, 1999).

75 Elfreda Chang, Doug Macdonald, and Joanne Wolfson, 'Who Killed CIPSI?', in Gibson, ed., *Voluntary Initiatives*, 125–33; Robert Hornung, 'The VCR Doesn't Work', in Gibson, ed., *Voluntary Initiatives*, 134–40.

76 See Debora L. VanNijnatten, 'The ARET Challenge', in Gibson, ed., *Voluntary Initiatives*, 93–100.

77 Ben Cashore, 'Competing for Legitimacy: Globalization, Internationalization, and the Politics of Eco-Forestry Certification (Green Labeling) in the US and Canadian Forest Sectors', paper presented to biennial conference of the Association for Canadian Studies in the United States, Pittsburgh, 1999.

78 Richard Neufeld, 'The Pit and the Pendulum—The Search for Consistency in the Law Governing Environmental Assessment', *Resources* 67 (1999): 1–5; Steven A. Kennett, 'Cumulative Effects Assessment and the Cheviot Project: What's Wrong with This Picture?', *Resources* 68 (1999): 1–6. See also John Donihee, 'The New Species at Risk Act and Resource Development' *Resources* 70 (2000), 1–7.

79 On the deficit orientation of the decade, see Ronald Kneebone and Kenneth McKenzie, *Past (In)Discretions: Canadian Federal and Provincial Fiscal Policy* (Toronto: University of Toronto Centre for Public Management, 1999). On its effects on public service delivery.

80 On the components and failure of the 1993 Green Plan, see George Hoberg and Kathyrn Harrison, 'It's Not Easy Being Green: The Politics of Canada's Green Plan', *Canadian Public Policy* 20, 2 (1994): 119–37.

81 On the situation in Environment Canada, see G.B. Doern and Thomas Conway, *The Greening of Canada: Federal Institutions and Decisions* (Toronto: University of Toronto Press, 1994). For an example of the impact of cuts at the provincial level, see Anita Krajnc, 'Neo-Conservatism and the Decline of Ontario's Environment Ministry', *Canadian Public Policy* 26, 1 (2000): 111–28.

82 Paul Muldoon and Ramani Nadarajah, 'A Sober Second Look', in Gibson, ed., *Voluntary Initiatives*, 51–65.

83 See Alastair R. Lucas, 'Integrating Voluntary and Regulatory Environmental Management: The Legal Framework', *Resources* 64 (1998): 1–4; Harrison, 'Talking with the Donkey'.

84 See Kathryn Harrison, 'Retreat from Regulation: The Evolution of the Canadian Environmental Regulatory Regime', in G.B. Doern et al., eds, *Changing the Rules: Canadian Regulatory Regimes and Institutions* (Toronto: University of Toronto Press, 1999), 122–42.

85 See Steven A. Kennett, 'The Future for Cumulative Effects Management: Beyond the Environmental Assessment Paradigm', *Resources* 69 (2000): 1–7.

86 On the rise of multi-stakeholder processes in Canada, see George Hoberg, 'Environmental Policy: Alternative Styles', in M.M. Atkinson, ed., *Governing Canada: Institutions and Public Policy* (Toronto: Harcourt Brace Jovanovich Canada, 1993), 307–42. More generally, see Jody Freeman, 'Collaborative Governance in the Administrative State', *UCLA Law Review* 45, 1 (1997), 1–98.

87 See K.A. Graham and S.D. Phillips, eds, *Citizen Engagement: Lessons in Participation from Local Government* (Toronto: Institute of Public Administration of Canada, 1998).

88 See Michael Howlett, 'The Round Table Experience: Representation and Legitimacy in Canadian Environmental Policy Making', *Queen's Quarterly* 97, 4 (1990): 580–601.

89 Mary Louise McAllister and Cynthia Alexander, *A Stake in the Future: Redefining the Canadian Mineral Industry* (Vancouver: University of British Columbia Press, 1997).

90 See Pieter Glasbergen, 'Modern Environmental Agreements: A Policy Instrument Becomes a Management Strategy', *Journal of Environmental Planning and Management* 41, 6 (1998): 693–709; Peter Knoepfel, 'New Institutional Arrangements for a New Generation of Environmental Policy Instruments: Intra- and Interpolicy-Cooperation', in B. Dente, ed., *Environmental Policy in Search of New Instruments* (Dordrecht: Kluwer Academic Publishers, 1995), 197–233.

91 Steven A. Kennett, 'The Environmental Management Framework Agreement: Reforming Federalism in a Post-Referendum Canada', *Resources* 52 (1995): 1–5.

92 See P.C. Fafard and K. Harrison, eds, *Managing the Environmental Union: Intergovernmental Relations and Environmental Policy in Canada* (Kingston: Queen's University Institute of Intergovernmental Relations, 2000); Julie M. Simmons, 'The Canada-Wide Accord on Environmental Harmonization and Value Change Within the Department of the Environment', paper presented to the annual meeting of the Canadian Political Science Association, Sherbrooke, 1999.

93 Ted Schrecker, 'The Canadian Environmental Assessment Act: Tremulous Step Forward or Retreat Into Smoke and Mirrors?', *Canadian Environmental Law Reports* 5 (1991): 192–246; Alistair R. Lucas, 'Jurisdictional Disputes: Is "Equivalency" a Workable Solution?', in D. Tingley, ed., *Into the Future: Environmental Law and Policy for the 1990's* (Edmonton: Environmental Law Centre, 1990), 25–36.

94 L. Stefanick, 'Organization, Administration, and the Environment: Will a Facelift Suffice or Does the Patient Need Radical Surgery?', *Canadian Public Administration* 41, 1 (1998): 99–146.

95 Mark C. Baetz and A. Brian Tanguay, '"Damned If You Do, Damned If You Don't": Government and the Conundrum of Consultation in the Environmental Sector', *Canadian Public Administration* 41, 3 (1998): 395–418.

96 On regulation as the generally preferred policy tool in Canada, see G. Bruce Doern et al., 'Conclusion', in Doern et al., eds, *Changing the Rules*, 389–406.

97 See Panagiotis Karamanos, 'Voluntary Environmental Agreements: Evolution and Definition of a New Environmental Policy Approach', *Journal of Environmental Planning and Management* 44, 1 (2001), 67–84. On the limited nature of Canadian multi-stakeholder initiatives vis-à-vis the US, see George Hoberg, 'North American Environmental Regulation', in G.B. Doern and S. Wilks, eds, *Changing Regulatory Institutions in Britain and North America* (Toronto: University of Toronto Press, 1998), 305–27.

98 See Debora L. VanNijnatten, 'Participation and Environmental Policy in Canada and the United States: Trends Over Time', *Policy Studies Journal* 27, 2 (1999): 267–87; Alan S. Miller, 'The Origin and Current Directions of United States Environmental Law and Policy: An Overview' in Ben Boer, Robert Fowler, Neil Gunningham, eds, *Environmental Outlook: Law and Policy* (Sydney: The Federation Press, 1994), 17–37; and Michael E. Kraft 'US Environmental Policy and Politics: From the 1960s to the 1990s', *Journal of Policy History* 12, 1 (2000), 17–42.

99 George Hoberg, 'North American Environmental Regulation', in Doern and Wilks, eds, *Changing Regulatory Institutions*, 305–27; Michael Howlett, 'Beyond Legalism? Policy Ideas, Implementation Styles and Emulation-Based Convergence in Canadian and U.S. Environmental Policy', *Journal of Public Policy* 20, 3 (2000): 305–29.

100 Brigitte Unger and Frans van Waarden, 'Introduction: An Interdisciplinary Approach to Convergence', in Unger and van Waarden, eds, *Convergence or Diversity? Internationalization and Economic Policy Response* (Aldershot: Avebury, 1995), 1–35.

101 See Kenneth Hanf and Alf-Inge Jansen, eds, *Governance and Environment in Western Europe* (New York: Longman, 1998).

102 See, for example, Les Metcalfe, 'International Policy Co-ordination and Public Management Reform', *International Review of Administrative Sciences* 60 (1994): 271–90.

103 On NPM principles, see Christopher Hood, 'Contemporary Public Management: A New Global Paradigm?', *Public Policy and Administration* 10, 2 (1995): 104–17; Peter Aucoin, 'Administrative Reform in Public Management: Paradigms, Principles, Paradoxes and Pendulums', *Governance* 3, 2 (1990): 115–37.

104 See, for example, Patrick Dunleavy and Christopher Hood, 'From Old Public Administration to New Public Management', *Public Money and Management* 14, 3 (1994): 9–16; Hood, 'A Public Management for All Seasons?', *Public Administration* 69, (Spring 1991): 3–19.

105 Jon Pierre, 'Public Consultation and Citizen Participation: Dilemmas of Policy Advice', in B.G. Peters and D.J. Savoie, eds, *Taking Stock: Assessing Public Sector Reforms* (Montreal and Kingston: McGill-Queen's University Press, 1998), 137–63.

106 Bruno Dente, 'Introduction: The Globalization of Environmental Policy and the Search for New Instruments', in Dente, ed., *Environmental Policy in Search of New Instruments* (Dordrecht: Kluwer Academic Publishers, 1995), 1–20.

107 M. Janicke and H. Weidner, *National Environmental Policies: A Comparative Study of Capacity Building* (Berlin: Springer, 1997).

108 Stephen Wilks and G. Bruce Doern, 'Conclusions', in Doern and Wilks, eds, *Changing Regulatory Institutions*, 376–95; Robert A. Kagan, 'Should Europe Worry about Adversarial Legalism?', *Oxford Journal of Legal Studies* 17, 2 (1997): 165–83.

Chapter 3

Continuity and Change in the Canadian Environmental Movement: Assessing the Effects of Institutionalization

Jeremy Wilson

Most institutional biographies revolve around variants of the 'continuity despite change' theme. The history of the Canadian environmental movement is no exception. Most of the organizations that dominate the movement's political activities today have been central players since the 1970s or 1980s, and many of the descriptive generalizations applicable a decade or two ago still hold. Today, as in the past, the movement encompasses a sprawling collection of national, regional, and local organizations. Its diversity continues to be evident in both the range of issues covered and the variety of political strategies deployed. This diversity, along with the high commitment level of the movement's volunteers and paid staff, continues to be its main source of strength.[1] On the other side of the ledger, however, the movement still lacks the financial resources needed to respond effectively to many threats to the environment.

These and other elements of continuity cannot, however, mask obvious signs of change. Over the past decade, Canadian environmental organizations' issue foci have become more international and their interactions with counterparts in other countries more extensive. New technologies, particularly those associated with the Internet, have transformed the way organizations communicate with their members and design their campaigns. Local and regional groups continue to be very important, but compared to a decade or two ago, the public face of the movement now reflects more strongly the priorities and perspectives of large national organizations. The growing importance of these organizations, along with the course of maturation within them, has contributed to 'institutionalization'. More of the movement's advocacy and organizational maintenance work is now carried out by professional staff, and more organizations enjoy regularized access to the politicians and officials who guide environmental policy processes in Ottawa and the provincial capitals.

Institutionalization has been a major theme in accounts of the evolution of environmental movements in other parts of the industrialized world. While these accounts offer different judgements as to its consequences, some commentators contend that any benefits to movement effectiveness brought about by institutionalization are more than counterbalanced by significant costs and risks.[2] According to this indictment, too many environmental groups have been transformed from new social movement organizations into 'protest businesses'. As a result, it is argued, the environmental movement has lost some of its capacity for spontaneity and some of its taste for radical action. It has become more reliant on conventional tactics and more constrained by the imperatives of organization building and maintenance, particularly those connected to the need for continual large-scale fund-raising.

This chapter will assess the applicability of these concerns in the Canadian context. The chapter begins with an overview of the major organizations at the centre of the Canadian movement. It then surveys the large and ever-changing collection of local and regional groups that contribute so significantly to the movement's policy accomplishments. With the full scope of the movement in focus, the institutionalization indictment is then evaluated.

Eight National Environmental Organizations and Their Work

This section reflects on the characteristics and activities of a sample of Canada's largest environmental organizations. These groups, which we will refer to as 'the majors', are the Canadian Nature Federation (CNF), the Canadian Parks and Wilderness Society (CPAWS), the David Suzuki Foundation (DSF), Ducks Unlimited Canada, Greenpeace, the Nature Conservancy of Canada (NCC), the Sierra Club of Canada, and World Wildlife Fund Canada (WWF). This should not be taken as a complete list of *the* most important or accomplished organizations. In assembling this list, I have merely sought a sample that would provide a solid basis for generalizations about the characteristics of the organizations most prominent on the national political stage.

Although the organizational histories of these groups vary in length,[3] all can be considered well established. All have yearly budgets in excess of $1 million, with four reporting annual expenditures during the late 1990s of over $5 million.[4] All maintain professionally staffed central offices featuring a complex differentiation of functions, and several have chapter or branch offices across the country.[5] All devote considerable ongoing attention to fund-raising and to the maintenance of the organizational capacity needed to participate effectively in the policy process.

Each of our organizations would see itself as occupying a different niche in the overall effort to protect the Canadian environment. For example, the CNF regards itself as the national voice of Canada's naturalist community, and the WWF has a broad mission to conserve nature and ecological processes. Ducks Unlimited, which bills itself as 'Canada's Conservation Company', pursues its wetlands conservation programs through a 'pragmatic, non-confrontational and highly efficient approach',[6] while Greenpeace defines itself as a 'campaigning organization that uses non-violent, creative confrontation to expose global environmental problems.'[7] The NCC takes a 'quiet business-like approach', pursuing its goals through outright purchase or donations of land and through co-operative stewardship agreements with landowners.[8]

At any given time, each of these organizations is involved in a wide range of issues and projects. For example, in its 1998–9 list of highlights, the CNF noted, among other projects, its work to secure establishment of new national parks, its participation in the coalition of groups challenging the Cheviot open-pit coal mine near Jasper National Park, its efforts to discourage privatization and commercialization of national parks, its role in identifying and conserving Important Bird Areas, its work on endangered species issues, and its various education initiatives. The WWF runs complementary programs focused on endangered species, endangered spaces, wildlife toxicology, and the conservation of international wildlife and wild places. Both Ducks Unlimited and the NCC pursue a wide assortment of land acquisition and stewardship projects.

Considerable variation is also apparent in the approaches taken by the organizations stressing policy advocacy. All would no doubt endorse the view that effective advocacy work requires 'all-directional' lobbying[9]—close attention both to the government officials who make critical policy decisions and to the mass publics whose perceptions and passions define the political contexts that shape those decisions. Playing on both sides of this inside/outside divide requires some dexterity, forcing groups continually to weigh the risks that too great an emphasis on close consultation with officials might jeopardize efforts to galvanize public support.[10] Generally speaking, the organizations under consideration here have managed to find workable solutions to this and related dilemmas.

Organizations such as the WWF, CPAWS, and the CNF have built considerable capacity for lobbying officials in Ottawa and the provincial capitals. While their access to key policy-makers does vary across time and issues, individuals such as Monte Hummel of the WWF, Jim Fulton of the DSF, Harvey Locke and Mary Granskou of CPAWS, and Elizabeth May of the Sierra Club generally enjoy good access. In large part this is the result of the effort they and others in their organizations have invested in developing trusting relationships with key bureaucrats and politicians. These relationships also reflect the fact that a number of organizations have built highly respected scientific and technical capacity. For example, the WWF and the Sierra Club have made major contributions to the development of techniques for identifying gaps in the ecological representativeness of existing parks systems, using the results of their studies to support arguments for increased protected areas. Their expertise in technical fields such as geographic information system (GIS) mapping has often been drawn upon (and envied) by officials in government natural resource agencies. Ducks Unlimited's extensive inside work alongside officials from the Canadian Wildlife Service and provincial wildlife agencies is facilitated in part by research generated by Ducks Unlimited's Institute for Wetland and Waterfowl Research.[11]

As a result of these and related assets, the majors generally measure up well in terms of the two prerequisites essential for successful lobbying of government officials: door-opening ability and knowledge of the decision-making system. That is, these organizations demonstrate an ability to penetrate or hurdle the screens surrounding important decision-makers and a capacity to assess where and when the critical decisions in the lives of key issues are being made.

Environmental organizations lobbying inside the system have always appreciated the critical importance of linking these efforts to ones aimed at winning public support and persuading sympathizers to make their views known. Indeed, Canadian environmental organizations have traditionally put greater emphasis on outside lobbying than on direct lobbying of politicians and officials. This preference may have historical roots in environmentalists' distaste for the kind of politics involved in insider lobbying, as well as in their knowledge that efforts to win public support can serve an ancillary fund-raising function. Whatever the reason, some groups have traditionally operated on the belief that they can overcome inadequate access to decision-makers by demonstrating to politicians that significant numbers of voters care intensely about the issue in question. They understand that public interest groups are unlikely to move governments unless these groups can demonstrate they have the backing of significant numbers of voters. Ideally, organizations also want to be in a position to make a credible claim that these voters are (a) people the government party hopes to have on its side in the next election, and (b) people who feel passionate enough about the issue that they are likely to remember the government's response when that election rolls around.

As noted in Chapter 11 below, Canadian organizations' efforts to generate pressure on government have focused increasingly on international publics. During the 1990s, for example, a number of environmental groups joined campaigns aimed at persuading foreign consumers of Canadian timber products to demand higher standards of forest stewardship. In British Columbia, these campaigns are credited with a significant role in bringing about both a sharp reduction in the scale of logging in Clayoquot Sound on Vancouver Island and a pledge to end clear-cut logging from one of the province's major forest companies, MacMillan Bloedel (or after its 1999 takeover, Weyerhaeuser). By early 2000, international consumer pressures had forced Weyerhaeuser and other major BC companies to engage in negotiations with Greenpeace, the Sierra Club, and others over a moratorium on logging in parts of what environmentalists have dubbed the Great Bear Rain Forest, a major expanse of temperate rain forest on the province's mid-coast.

The methods environmental organizations use to push issues onto the agenda and win public support for their preferred problem definitions have evolved in response to new communications options. Many groups that formerly transmitted their messages using newsletters, mail-outs, slide shows, or free broadsheets now rely on (or augment their traditional methods with) e-mail lists or Web sites. There has been less change in the assessments of what constructions of issues are likely to resonate with significant constituencies. Whether it be delivered by broadsheet or Web site, the standard missive still relies heavily on photographs, with continuing emphasis on juxtaposing striking images of pristine nature against equally arresting images of the despoliation wrought by resource development. The typical package also continues to include testimonials from notables, with figures such as David Suzuki and Robert Bateman making frequent appearances to endorse a variety of campaigns.

Some groups have always disavowed emotional appeals in favour of hard, evidence-based arguments. Even those inclined to the former approach have increasingly recognized the importance of backing up their 'image-based' pitches with solid research. In general, the material circulated by groups such as those in our sample reflects greater research capacity than a decade ago. The work of the DSF provides an excellent example. Since its inception in 1990, it has generated an impressive series of research reports and books that analyse problems and advance solutions in its areas of interest. For instance, since 1997, its climate change project has turned out over a dozen reports, presenting high-quality research under titles such as *PowerShift: Cool Solutions to Global Warming* and *Taking the High Road: Sustainable Transportation for the 21st Century*.[12] These reports and the accompanying media releases have had positive effects on public discourse.

A number of groups also employ periodic 'report cards' as a way of focusing attention on issues and putting pressure on governments or companies deemed to be underperforming on the environmental front. For example, using an approach that illustrates the potential importance of international agreements as standard setters, the Sierra Club releases a yearly Rio Report Card on what (if any) progress federal and provincial governments have made towards meeting Canada's biodiversity and climate change commitments. The letter grades given jurisdictions are peppered with phrases such as 'forget the mega-project', 'clear cut failure', and 'most improved student'.[13] Similarly, the WWF releases annual ratings of the progress made by different jurisdictions in the achievement of the protected areas targets set out in its endangered spaces program. The WWF hopes that this and related tactics will put pressure on laggards. Provincial governments occasionally pick up grades that can be proudly displayed as badges of environmental sensitivity, but more often they find the ratings to be a source of embarrassment. In a variant of this strategy aimed at pressuring corporations rather than governments, Greenpeace released a 'toxic toys' report card reminding parents of the harmful additives present in some plastic toys.[14]

Reports like these will not, of course, have the desired impacts on public and government priorities unless they are amplified by the mass media. Canada's major environmental organizations have all acquired a sophisticated understanding of the factors shaping media coverage, including those deriving from the fact that reporters often do not have the background or time required to grasp fully the complex underpinnings of environmental problems. Generally speaking, the major groups' campaigns do attract coverage, although these organizations often have cause to complain about the media's failure to follow up on the issues highlighted. Like others involved in the political wars, environmental organizations find that most media outlets have a limited interest in stories lacking a dramatic narrative. And their experiences with the media provide plenty of support for the contention that the corporate-controlled (and advertising-dependent) media have little or no appetite for stories that trace environmental problems to the continued promotion of high-consumption lifestyles, economic growth, and the depletion of natural resource capital. Some organizations do try to circumvent media gates by buying advertising space. For example, during the spring of 2000, the DSF ran a series of ads in major BC papers challenging fundamental precepts underlying the province's approach to forest exploitation.[15] It goes without saying, however, that even well-established groups lack the financial resources needed to conduct extensive advertising campaigns.

Direct action tactics can be interpreted as serving various functions, including educational ones. Of the organizations in our small sample, Greenpeace is the only one that uses direct action. While its campaigns are not always confrontational, they certainly are planned with an eye for drama and symbolism. For instance, in the summer of 1998, Greenpeace activists placed 1,800 white crosses on the lawn of the Ontario legislature to symbolize the number of Ontarians it says die prematurely from the effects of air pollution each year.[16] The early and middle parts of Greenpeace's history were, of course, marked by even more dramatic tactics, and from the outset Greenpeace tried to ensure that its direct action initiatives generated the desired sort of media coverage. Greenpeace's use of the media has been the subject of considerable analysis, some of which has significantly advanced our understanding of the complicated symbiotic relationships linking social movement activists and media producers.[17] Since 1990, Greenpeace has put increased emphasis on the importance of backing up its dramatic gestures with persuasive science.

Some of the groups in our sample also devote significant resources to educational work aimed at creating awareness among children or in the general public. For instance, the CNF operates a community education program featuring components such as its magazine (*Nature Canada*), a Schools for Species educational package, a Project Feederwatch bird monitoring program, and a national Lady Beetle Survey.[18] Other examples include the WWF's Schools for Wildlife program, and Ducks Unlimited's Greenwing youth education program.[19] Most major groups have also sought to capitalize on the educational potential of the Internet, ensuring that those curious or concerned about issues have an increasingly easy time linking up with the organizations involved. Although initiatives such as these may not generate immediate pressure on policy-makers, they do at least indirectly increase the likelihood that future governments will face an environmentally aware and concerned citizenry.

Effective outside lobbying also depends on supporters expressing their views to politicians. Here the broadsheet to Web site transition has coincided with a shift away from reliance on exhorting supporters to sign petitions or write letters to cabinet ministers. Such methods are still used. For example, the aforementioned DSF ads included a clip-out form that could be used to ask the BC Premier to rethink the government's forest policies. This kind of approach, however, is increasingly augmented with ones reliant on new technology. By the end of the 1990s, for instance, major groups were trying out Web-site features that facilitate push-button faxes to targeted officials.[20] The advent of this and other possibilities in the realm of 'point and click' activism does raise questions about how politicians and officials evaluate displays of public concern generated in different ways. It is probably true that a Web page-facilitated fax will usually be given less weight than will a letter from a concerned citizen. Organizations using new methods of generating public response, however, hope that negative impacts of such discounting will be out-weighed by the increased volumes generated by the new procedures.

Although cost considerations mean that they are not in as strong a position to do so as some of their adversaries, a number of organizations also generate and use public opinion poll results in their efforts to persuade governments. For example, the WWF backed up its late 1999 pitch for increased wilderness protec-tion with poll results indicating that 91 per cent of Canadians believed in the importance of protecting an additional 40 million hectares.[21]

While the campaign for strong federal endangered species legislation has failed to achieve its goals, this effort has illustrated the environmental movement's diverse lobbying strengths. Led by prominent actors from organizations such as the CNF, the Sierra Legal Defence Fund, and the Canadian Endangered Species Campaign, the movement demonstrated strong capacity for both inside and outside lobbying during the long and difficult gestation period leading to the tabling of the ill-fated Species at Risk Act (SARA) in April 2000. A number of organizations participated expertly in the 1993 hearings conducted by the House of Commons Standing Committee on Environment and then in the multi-stake-holder consultative initiatives that followed.[22] Environmental lobbyists were cen-trally involved in the struggles that led the government to abandon its first attempt at legislation, Bill C-65, introduced in 1996. With the revival of the gov-ernment's quest for endangered species legislation following the 1997 election, environmentalists resumed intensive behind-the-scenes work. For a number of organizations, including the CNF and the Sierra Club, these latter efforts included participation with industry organizations such as the Canadian Pulp and Paper Association and the Mining Association of Canada in a group called the Species at Risk Working Group (SARWG). It explored the potential for compromise, paving the way for concessions by both sides.[23]

In the months leading up to the introduction of SARA, environmental lobbyists intensified efforts to sway the government on issues such as listing of endangered species by scientists rather than politicians, forceful habitat protection, strong funding for recovery efforts, and a meaningful federal government 'safety net' to counteract weak provincial conservation measures. Work during the winter of 1999–2000 illustrated many of the important strands that must be woven into a contemporary lobbying effort. Among other elements, the campaign encompassed media interviews and briefings (formal and informal) to ensure that the environ-mental line was prominently represented in journalists' reports of reaction to the government's proposals; development of briefing notes and detailed analyses that shaped the way spokespersons for environmental organizations across the country reacted to the bill; liaison with allies such as scientists, and negotiation with foes such as resource companies; meetings with MPs and staff from Environment Canada and other departments; and preparation of supportive documentation, including an important constitutional law opinion supporting a stronger federal stance on migratory species.

Throughout this period, the campaign's leaders devoted considerable attention to maintaining solidarity in the environmental camp. As it became apparent that SARA would give the movement some but not all of what it wanted, the more hawkish elements recognized the importance of counteracting the government's attempts to lure more moderate groups into endorsing the legislation.

Leaders of the lobbying effort also sought to generate pressure from south of the border. They helped organize an open letter to Prime Minister Jean Chrétien in which over 80 US environmental organizations expressed the view that US efforts to save endangered species would be wasted unless Canada adopted strong legislation. The position of the US groups was showcased for the media at an Ottawa press conference attended by figures such as the director of the US Endangered Species Coalition.[24] In addition, Canadian groups' meetings with White House staff and sympathetic members of Congress led to the issue being raised in upper-level meetings between politicians from the two countries.

These and other lobbying initiatives were underpinned by extensive efforts to educate the public and galvanize supporters into expressing their views. The CNF, the Sierra Club, and others regularly exhorted members to do so. By the final stages of the SARA campaign, those wishing to register a vote for strengthening the legislation had a number of avenues, including the easy one provided by the instant fax option of the Endangered Species Campaign available at their 'extinctionsucks' Web site.

The Prime Minister's decision to dissolve Parliament in October 2000 meant that SARA died on the order paper. The environmental coalition's campaign for strong legislation will resume once the new government settles into office. We can anticipate that the coalition's future campaigns will illustrate the strengths apparent in its efforts to date: its capacity for multi-dimensional lobbying, its ability to adapt strategy as issues move through the policy cycle, and perhaps more than anything, its resilience.

As our brief sketch indicates, the endangered species campaigns involved coordinated efforts by a network of organizations. It is in fact difficult to find any major contemporary environmental lobbying effort that does not involve a team of organizations. In some cases, co-operation is co-ordinated by campaign-specific structures. Examples include Nature Legacy 2000, which joins the WWF, the CNF, the NCC, and Ducks Unlimited in a nationwide initiative aimed at conserving wildlife and habitat on private and public lands, and the Partnership for Public Lands, which linked the WWF with allies such as the Wildlands League during Ontario's protected areas planning process in the late 1990s. In many other cases, the coalitions involved are informal and less structured. Most wilderness campaigns in BC, including the one that achieved preservation of a significant portion of Clayoquot Sound and the one currently working on protection of the Great Bear Rain Forest, have involved ad hoc alliances. Such coalitions often draw together mixes of large provincial or national groups and small local ones.

The close ties between Canadian endangered species campaigners and kindred American organizations are not at all unusual. Canadian groups have long enjoyed strong links to counterparts in other countries. Indeed, four of the groups under consideration here (the Sierra Club, Greenpeace, the WWF, and Ducks Unlimited) are parts of larger international families. Greenpeace has grown from its origins in Vancouver to become a $100 million (US) per year international complex encompassing more than two dozen national and regional offices.[25] In the other three cases, Canadian operations evolved out of organizations already established elsewhere. Each of these Canadian organizations is now fully independent, but the nature of ties to the international siblings (in some or all instances, 'cousins' might be more appropriate) varies. Some participate regularly or periodically in transborder revenue-sharing arrangements and/or co-ordinated campaigns, while others operate without any systematic reference to what their counterparts are up to in other countries.

Intra-organization linkages such as these are matched at any given time by scores of issue- or project-specific transnational alliances. In the bird conservation area, for example, the CNF links up with various Birdlife International partners in the Important Bird Areas program,[26] and Ducks Unlimited participates alongside numerous conservation organizations and agencies in initiatives such as the Western Hemisphere Shorebird Reserve Network and the North American Waterfowl Management Plan.[27] Greenpeace Canada, the Sierra Club, and other Canadian groups have worked closely with US organizations such as the Natural Resources Defence Council and the Rainforest Action Network to organize the market campaigns that have convinced Home Depot Inc. and other major companies to phase out purchases of wood products from BC's old-growth forests.[28]

Canadian groups have also begun to link up with American and Mexican allies to deploy the procedures laid out in Article 14 of the North American Agreement on Environmental Co-operation. This section allows complainants to launch submissions to the Commission for Environmental Co-operation (CEC) secretariat, claiming that one of the NAFTA countries is failing to enforce its environmental laws. The agreement provides no avenues for those questioning the quality of the laws themselves, and the Commission and its secretariat have limited means of forcing change where the complaints are found to have validity. Nonetheless, environmental advocates hope that favourable judgements from the CEC will embarrass governments into improving their performance. In a couple of recent examples, the DSF and allies filed a complaint alleging that Canada has failed to enforce effectively sections of its Fisheries Act that should govern logging in BC, while the Sierra Club joined a trinational coalition contending that in its regulation of logging operations, the US Fish and Wildlife Service fails to enforce the Migratory Bird Treaty Act.

The heavily networked character of contemporary campaigning is also apparent in a growing number of alliances between environmental groups and organizations from other sectors of the political map. The DSF, for example, recently joined the group that represents BC's doctors (the BC Medical Association) to launch a campaign aimed at increasing public awareness of the harmful effects of global warming and air pollution.[29]

Beyond what might be considered lobbying (even under an expansive definition), major organizations deploy a variety of other approaches in pursuit of their policy goals. Two are particularly important. First, contemporary Canadian environmental organizations increasingly use the court system. Although the discretionary nature of most provincial and federal environmental and natural resource legislation limits judicial possibilities, the movement has been very imaginative in capitalizing on the opportunities that do exist. In some considerable part the growing importance of this approach can be connected to the growth of public interest law organizations, particularly the Sierra Legal Defence Fund (SLDF). Along with a handful of similar organizations, it is dedicated to providing free or low-cost legal advice to groups and citizens pursuing important environmental issues. The SLDF (which is not related to the Sierra Club) is staffed by about a dozen lawyers. Its $3 million per year operations (1999) are funded by foundation grants and contributions from individual supporters. Each year it pursues several dozen cases in and out of court on behalf of a variety of clients, basing its choice of cases in part on its goal of developing a strong body of environmental law precedents. Its 1999 docket included cases relating to toxics, protected areas, biodiversity, and forestry.[30] One good example of its work was mentioned earlier. On behalf of the CNF, CPAWS, and others, the SLDF undertook action in the Federal Court that forced the federal government to undertake a new, more comprehensive environmental assessment of the proposed Cheviot coal mine near Jasper National Park. The SLDF also pursues cases pertaining to issues such as freedom of information and whistle-blowers' rights. These cases have broad implications for the protection and enhancement of citizen rights.

Second, as mentioned, the NCC and Ducks Unlimited focus on conserving or enhancing private land through purchase, establishment of conservation easements, or environmental improvement projects. Each year, Ducks Unlimited launches scores of initiatives directed at securing and enhancing wetland and upland habitat. In addition to purchasing land, it funds projects aimed at improving water management, promoting 'wildlife-friendly' grazing systems, and encouraging farmers to take marginal land out of production. It credits its programs with conserving 7.5 million hectares of Canadian waterfowl habitat since 1938.[31] Since 1962, the NCC has secured over 650,000 hectares of natural habitat.[32]

All of the activity synopsized above requires strong, well-funded organizations. Together, the eight organizations under analysis spend over $100 million per year.[33] This figure is skewed by Ducks Unlimited's large expenditures (over $60 million), but even if we leave it to the side, we still have several organizations operating multi-million-dollar annual programs.

Most of this money comes from individual contributions, transfers from international affiliates, or grants from foundations, governments, or corporations. The WWF illustrates successful diversification of revenue sources. In 1998–9, 15 per cent of its $12 million budget came from government grants, 6 per cent from foundations, 11.5 per cent from corporate donors, and 52.5 per cent from individual contributors. Revenue from sales of WWF products accounted for most of the remainder. WWF annual reports thank a long list of corporate, government, and foundation entities for large donations, recognizing companies such as Petro-Canada and Alcan Aluminum, government agencies such as Environment Canada and the Canadian International Development Agency, and foundations such as the Henry White Kinnear Foundation and the Richard Ivey Foundation.[34] The CNF provides another illustration of revenue diversification, drawing significant portions of its $2 million budget from several different sources. The DSF relied on foundation donations for 65 per cent of its 1999 revenues, but notes that it is committed to establishing a broad grassroots donor base.[35]

Since it does not accept funds from corporations or governments, Greenpeace relies heavily on individual contributors. Nearly 75 per cent of its 1998 revenues came from 'donor contributions', with about 8 per cent from bequests.[36] Greenpeace International contributed about 17 per cent, but the expenditure side of the ledger shows Greenpeace Canada returning more than half of this amount to the international council in 'support services'. Ducks Unlimited depends heavily on contributions from its American parent, but also harvests significant revenues from merchandise sales and its very active event-based fund-raising system.[37] In 1998–9, 900 volunteer-run events attracted 110,000 people and raised over $8 million.

In their quest for donations from individuals, most major Canadian environmental groups have adopted the elaborate procedures used by large public interest organizations across the rich world. Most have developed procedures to encourage bequests and have adopted direct-mail techniques to 'prospect' for new financial supporters or dun old ones. Like other groups depending on direct mail,[38] Canadian organizations have had to come to terms with several unhappy realities. Direct-mail solicitation is costly. To stimulate responses, organizations and their fund-raising consultants constantly experiment with different mail-out packages, as well as with lists of names either purchased or acquired through trades with other organizations. Response rates as high as 20 per cent have been reported,[39] but even well-designed campaigns rarely achieve rates over 3 or 4 per cent. Some organizations have concluded that the balance sheet for direct-mail campaigns climbs into the black only if significant portions of those enticed to contribute one year stay around to donate in successive years. Unfortunately, however, attrition rates among those attracted by direct mail tend to be quite high.

Not surprisingly, most groups dislike having to rely on direct mail. Most of the organizations under consideration have managed to assemble healthy lists of individual supporters,[40] and most claim to keep the portion of their total budget devoted to fund-raising to reasonable levels. For example, the WWF says that only 11.5 per cent of all its expenditures goes to fund-raising and administration.[41] The CNF reports that these categories account for just over 20 per cent of its budget,[42] while Greenpeace's reported fund-raising, finance, and administration costs represented about 32 per cent of its 1998 expenditures.[43] Nonetheless, all would like to expand their donor bases and wish there were satisfactory alternatives to direct mail. They recognize that a few dozen environmental (and other public interest) organizations are regularly contacting the same fairly narrow pool of potential donors, but they find it difficult to devise cost-effective ways of diversifying this pool.

These and related concerns figure prominently in arguments about the discontents and dilemmas attending institutionalization of the environmental movement. Before we can evaluate the applicability of these arguments in the Canadian context, we need to consider the sprawling reaches of the Canadian environmental movement as defined by the activities of smaller organizations.

The Cast of Thousands

It is difficult in a few pages to do justice to the diversity of the 'smaller groups' sector of the Canadian environmental movement. As well, the printed page is not the best medium through which to convey a sense of the dynamism that has characterized the evolution of this sector. Tens of thousands of Canadians participate in hundreds of small and medium-sized environmental organizations, and new organizations constantly spring up to channel Canadians' concerns into collective action. Much of this citizen energy is absorbed by groups working on local or regional issues, but many Canadians also participate with people from across the country in small organizations focused on particular issues of national or global scope.

At a conservative estimate, there are between 1,500 and 2,000 environmental organizations at work across Canada. Even a small sample from any of the lists maintained by the provincial environmental networks illustrates the great variety of these groups. For example, among the nearly 200 organizations in the Alberta network, we find everything from the Bow Valley Naturalists and the Society of Grasslands Naturalists to the Alberta Wilderness Association, Friends of the Whaleback, the Pesticide Working Group, the Foothills Recycling Society, and Wastewatchers Environmental Group.[44] Diversity is apparent whether we consider size, longevity, issue focus, or political approach. In terms of size, the groups in this small sample range from the six-member Pesticide Working Group to the 1,500–member Alberta Wilderness Association. Four of the other groups on this list have 100 members or fewer, typifying the membership totals reported by most of the local and regional organizations across the country. On the other hand, a few regional and provincial groups are more than medium-sized. The Western Canada Wilderness Committee (WCWC), for instance, reported a 1999 membership of over 26,000.[45]

Many of Canada's small and medium-sized environmental organizations are very well established. A large number of naturalist and outdoor recreation organizations predate the era of modern environmental politics, and some advocacy groups (such as Vancouver's Society Promoting Environmental Conservation) trace their origins back to the beginning of that era in the 1960s. Of course, Canadians with issue concerns or preferred approaches not covered by existing groups have never been reluctant to establish new organizations, not all of which survive for long.

The distinction among naturalist, outdoor recreation, and advocacy organizations captures some of the variation encompassed by the movement, but not all organizations involved in conserving the Canadian environment can easily be placed in one of these boxes. For instance, we certainly need another category to cover groups devoted primarily to activities such as operating recycling projects, managing nature sanctuaries or environmental education facilities, or restoring and enhancing natural areas. And no matter how extensive our schemata, we will need a residual category for 'square pegs', including the growing number of groups that link environmental concerns to health, economic, or social justice issues. A BC group known as Farm Folk/City Folk, for example, strives to promote a food production system that fosters good human and environmental health, seeking, among other things, to preserve farmland, promote farming practices that contribute to the health of the planet, protect the public's right to know where food comes from, and support local production of a diversity of foods.[46]

Each of the categories just mentioned encompasses groups of diverse orientations, foci, and approaches. The scores of small naturalist and outdoor recreation organizations across the country, for example, differ from one another in terms of how much attention they devote to activities that could be considered political and, when they do turn to political work, in terms of their *modus operandi*. Some restrict themselves mainly to educational work, while others frequently engage in direct lobbying.

Advocacy groups are particularly numerous and varied. This category includes hundreds of groups focused on saving or preserving particular areas, ecosystems, or species. The 500 groups making up the Ontario Environment Network include 16 'Friends of . . .' groups (for example, Friends of Temagami and Friends of the Spit) and another five 'Save . . .' organizations (for example, Save the Rouge Valley System). As well, scores of groups are devoted to particular environmental problem sets, including ones focused on pesticides, particular types of pollution, climate change, and urban transportation. The advocacy group category also includes many (the aforementioned Alberta Wilderness Association and Western Canada Wilderness Committee are good examples) that at any given time can be found working on several different issues. Extensive variation is also apparent in the approaches preferred by different advocacy groups. The range here is substantially greater than that found among the organizations surveyed in the previous section, running from groups that devote most of their energy to the careful homework required to develop scientifically respectable briefing material to those that deploy tactics such as tree sitting and road blockades in their attempts to preserve old-growth forests.

It is important, then, to realize that out beyond the dozen or so major organizations that dominate the images of the Canadian environmental movement conveyed by the national media, there exists a sprawling, ever-evolving, and thriving collection of smaller organizations. Canadians who become concerned about a particular threat are likely to find a group in their community or region already working on the problem. These organizations galvanize and absorb millions of hours of citizen energy every year, channelling incalculable amounts of information on problems, solutions, and people's anxieties, passions, and preferences into the processes that shape policy on the environment. Their impact must be taken into account in any assessment of the movement's health and prospects.

Has the Canadian Environmental Movement Become Too Institutionalized?

As noted in the introduction, a number of evaluations of American and European environmental organizations have fixed on the dilemmas and discontents arising from what is referred to as institutionalization. Equating institutionalization with bureaucratization, professionalization, and routinized politics, commentators express several concerns. Institutionalization, it is argued, may promote overcaution and inflexibility, for example, when fears of legal liability lead organizations to reject confrontation or where bureaucratic structures exert a bias towards certain issues or strategies.[47] Institutionalized groups are prone to stultification because they feature a large gulf between professional staff and 'vicarious activists', people who choose to donate money rather than time and energy, and thus, in essence, 'hire movement professionals to serve as a voice on their behalf.'[48] Expressing one version of the stultification thesis, Christopher Rootes acknowledges that professionalized groups have adapted well to a mass-mediated age but questions 'whether such adaptations ultimately weaken the capacities of [such groups] to effect the mass mobilizations from which the environmental movement's power initially derived and upon which it may ultimately depend.'[49] Similarly, Diani and Donati warn that 'under deteriorating political conditions, highly professional environmental lobbies might well prove unable to revert to that good, old weapon for excluded interests—contentious protest.'[50] Institutionalization also forces reliance on direct-mail fund-raising, which may encourage 'ambulance-chasing' environmentalism as well as the shunning or oversimplification of issues not deemed 'mediagenic'.[51] Reliance on direct mail discourages diversification of the support base, leaving too many groups 'overgrazing' the same affluent potential supporters and creating concerns about underemphasis of issues not salient to that particular demographic.[52] This dependence also makes groups vulnerable to swings in economic conditions and public attitudes.

Most elements of the indictment are captured by Jordan and Maloney's contention that large environmental organizations are better described as protest businesses than new social movement organizations: '"Members" have minimalist (and primarily financial) obligations. There is skilled professional stimulation of support that borrows from business practice. There is no internal democracy . . . [and organizations] seem just as affected by Michels' "iron law of oligarchy" as are political parties.'[53] Linking this argument to the oft-heard claim that interest groups have usurped many of the functions of parties, they offer the jaundiced view that 'People now appear to prefer to do very little in public interest groups as opposed to doing very little in political parties.'[54]

Does this indictment fit the Canadian experience? Has the Canadian movement been debilitated or disoriented by the problems alleged to accompany institutionalization? To unpack this issue we need to ask if large, established groups such as those considered above have encountered the problems said to attend institutionalization, and if so, whether these problems, on balance, have weakened these groups. We then need to consider whether any deficiencies uncovered are neutralized by the activities of smaller groups.

Have major Canadian environmental organizations experienced the sorts of problems said to attend institutionalization? Some elements of the indictment deserve to be taken seriously. Generally speaking, these groups do feature pronounced gulfs between professional staff, on one hand, and members or supporters, on the other. Both sides of this divide seem content with oligarchical management models. Several of the large organizations surveyed (for example, the Sierra Club, the DSF, and the CNF) do make considerable effort to involve volunteers, and some take pains to ensure at least a measure of internal democracy. Members of the Sierra Club, for instance, have a vote on who sits on the organization's board of directors. Nonetheless, opportunities for participation in decision-making are limited. Thus, while it would not be fair to characterize any of these groups as stultified, most could be said to be at least somewhat vulnerable to the sorts of problems highlighted by critics of institutionalization.

Another possible cause for concern is the fact that the fund-raising imperatives associated with institutionalization probably do exert constraining pressures of the sort noted. Reliance on direct-mail fund-raising leads over and over to the same doorsteps, creating overdependence on a fairly narrow slice of the demographic spectrum. Likewise, the quest for higher response rates creates pressure to design appealing mail-out packages. Resist as organizations may, pressures from the fund-raising side do exert some influence on decisions about issue foci and strategies. A case could be made that there is a connection between these factors and the movement's overall priorities, including the amount of attention paid to saving charismatic megafauna such as bears and to preserving landscapes valued by middle-class recreationists.

The life histories and daily practices of the majors, on the other hand, provide considerable grounds to dispute claims about the negative effects of institutionalization. First, they have overcome or resisted most of the tendencies and problems just noted. Several of our majors provide scope for supporters and members wanting to move beyond armchair participation. Opportunities to volunteer obviously do not translate automatically or easily into opportunities to participate in decisions, but leaders and members of large organizations such as these argue convincingly that the oligarchy here is of an open, benign brand.

Second, although arguments can be made about how middle-class values and concerns affect the majors' preoccupations, it does not follow that their work is narrow or unimportant. Together, these organizations continue to cover a wide range of issues, all of which can be defended as having important implications in terms of national and global environmental quality. Likewise, while most major Canadian environmental organizations favour political approaches on the less radical end of the spectrum, these approaches are valid and important parts of the full bag of tricks needed by a movement hoping to influence environmental policy and practice. Each of the majors can effectively defend its chosen approach as adding a necessary and valuable element to the mix.

A defence of the majors and their chosen developmental paths would also stress that institutionalization has some undoubted benefits. It promotes effective use of capacity, development of institutional memory, and the organizational stability needed to develop and maintain good access to decision-makers and strong relationships with sympathetic bureaucratic insiders. In these and other respects, institutionalization can be thought of as helping to ensure that organizations (and the causes they work for) will continue to benefit from present and past investments of political resources.

Finally, enlarging the focus to encompass the movement as a whole, we can say that any negative effects of institutionalization in large organizations are substantially counteracted by the work of smaller local and regional groups. The large organizations do occupy the conservative, cautious side of the spectrum. A movement composed solely of these groups might well be averse to experimentation, prone to stultification, and so on. Fortunately, though, there is much more to the movement than the majors. The hundreds of smaller organizations active across the country work on a wide assortment of issues, using a diverse set of strategies. They draw on the energy of people inclined to approaches other than those favoured by the majors, as well as the energy of a great many people who contribute to those large organizations but also want to participate in other ways.

In sum, the majors mobilize the resources of people who, because of preference or necessity, decide to participate mainly with their cheque books. The opportunities they provide for more active participation are somewhat limited, but when we consider the combination of these opportunities and those provided by smaller grassroots groups, it is difficult to sustain the argument that anyone wanting more than armchair participation in Canadian environmental politics will lack opportunities.

Conclusion

The Canadian environmental movement's greatest sources of strength continue to be its diversity and its highly committed membership. These and related attributes make for a mature, confident movement that covers more issues more authoritatively and assertively than it did a decade ago. The movement continues to do a better job of mobilizing and capitalizing on the political energy and talents of women and young people than do most other political organizations. It has skilfully exploited the potential for alliances with soulmates in other parts of the world and other parts of the Canadian political landscape. It has responded confidently and sure-footedly to both new technology and the changes in political constraints and opportunities associated with globalization.

Unfortunately, it is impossible to offer as positive an evaluation of the movement's accomplishments. No one can deny that its record is full of great achievements. The entire structure of federal and provincial laws governing the use of Canadian land, water, and air bears the strong imprint of environmental organizations. Indeed, it is difficult to imagine most of this legislation having been adopted in the absence of dedicated campaigning by the movement. The same point could be made about significant additions to the protected areas system, growing networks of urban bike routes, sharp increases in recycling infrastructure, or any number of other physical markers of environmental progress.

Despite all of its strengths and accomplishments, though, the movement has failed to bring about the kind of changes that most ecologists of the 1980s and early 1990s agreed were required by the end of the millennium. In Canada, as elsewhere across the developed world, the movement's greatest disappointments are in the area of agenda politics. It has had considerable success in pushing issues like species extinction and climate change onto public and government agendas. It has had less success with attempts to force governments and the public to face up to the source of these and other problems in the set of forces that continue to promote overconsumption and business-as-usual economic growth. Thus it was, to take one small but telling example, that the decade that was supposed to see the start of resolute action on CO_2 emissions became the decade in which SUVs took over the roads (and more to the point, the urban streets) of the nation. Too many Canadians who claim to be concerned about the environment are driving bigger and less efficient vehicles, building bigger homes, maintaining shopping habits that encourage environmental destruction throughout the developing world, and working as hard as ever to expand sectors of the economy that rely on destruction of natural capital and expansion of Canadian society's ecological footprint.

How the Canadian environmental movement will rate on a report card issued in 10 or 20 years will likely depend on whether, building on the successes of their forebears, environmental organizations in the years ahead can discredit the 'we can have our cake and eat it too' notions of environmental modernization that have been so successfully pushed by government, industry, and the media in the post-Brundtland, post-Rio world.

Notes

1 For my assessment of the movement's strengths and weaknesses *circa* 1990, see Jeremy Wilson, 'Green Lobbies: Pressure Groups and Environmental Policy', in Robert Boardman, ed., *Canadian Environmental Policy: Ecosystems, Politics, and Processes* (Toronto: Oxford University Press, 1992), ch. 6.

2 See, for example, Christopher Rootes, 'Environmental Movements: From the Local to the Global', *Environmental Politics* 8, 1 (Spring 1999): 1–12; Grant Jordan and William A. Maloney, *The Protest Business? Mobilizing Campaign Groups* (Manchester: Manchester University Press, 1997).

3 For example, the CNF and Ducks Unlimited both trace their roots back to the 1930s, while the DSF was set up in 1990.

4 Recent annual reports give these figures on annual spending: the CNF, 1999 expenditures of $2.4 million; CPAWS, 1997 expenditures of $1.2 million; the DSF, 1998–9 expenditures of $4.2 million; Ducks Unlimited Canada, 1998–9 expenses of $63 million; Greenpeace, 1998 expenditures of $6.0 million; the NCC, 1998 expenditures of $12.7 million; the Sierra Club of Canada, 1998 expenditures of $2.1 million (includes expenditures of its three chapters); the WWF, 1998–9 grants and expenditures of $11.9 million.

5 For example, CPAWS has 10 'grassroots' chapters across the country (see www.cpaws.org/chapters/indes.html), while the Sierra Club has chapters for BC, the Prairies, and eastern Canada, as well as a youth coalition (see www.sierraclub.ca). Ducks Unlimited has more than a dozen regional and field offices across the country (see Ducks Unlimited Canada, *1999 Annual Report*, 92).

6 Ducks Unlimited Canada, *1999 Annual Report*, 3.

7 Greenpeace Canada, *Annual Review 1998*, 15.

8 Covering letter from Sheri-Lynn Armstrong, received with Nature Conservancy of Canada, *Annual Report 1998*.

9 William P. Browne, 'Lobbying the Public: All-Directional Advocacy', in Allan J. Cigler and Burdett A. Loomis, eds, *Interest Group Politics*, 5th edn (Washington: Congressional Quarterly Inc., 1998), 343–64.

10 See Peter Rawcliffe, *Environmental Pressure Groups in Transition* (Manchester: Manchester University Press, 1998), 225. Rawcliffe sees this point in terms of the challenge of finding a balance between 'incorporation and autonomy within existing political and institutional frameworks'.

11 See Ducks Unlimited, *1999 Annual Report*, 11.

12 For the full list, see www.davidsuzuki.org/climatereports.htm. Accessed 1 June 2000.

13 For example, Sierra Club of Canada, '1999 Rio Report', at www.sierraclub.ca/national.rio. Accessed 12 Mar. 2000.

14 'Greenpeace issues industry report card on toxic toys', *Natural Life* 66 (Apr. 1999).

15 See 'These trees are worthless', *Vancouver Sun*, 7 Apr. 2000, A5; 'They have a stronger dollar and 3 times more jobs per tree. Maybe there's a connection', *Vancouver Sun*, 19 May 2000, A5.

16 Greenpeace Canada, *Annual Review 1998*, 5; see p. 9 of the same document for another example, this time by Greenpeace's toxic toy patrol.

17 For example, William K. Carroll and R.S. Ratner, 'Media strategies and political projects: a comparative study of social movements', *Canadian Journal of Sociology* 24, 1 (Winter

1999): 1–34; Stephen Dale, *McLuhan's Children: The Greenpeace Message and the Media* (Toronto: Between the Lines, 1996).

18 CNF, *1998–9 Annual Report*, 5.

19 WWF Canada, *1999 Annual Review*, 15; Ducks Unlimited, *1999 Annual Report*, 13.

20 See the Web site of the BC Endangered Species Coalition at www.extinctionsucks.com. See also Ian Mulgrew, 'The rise of point and click activism', *Vancouver Sun*, 17 Feb. 2000.

21 See WWF press release, 'World Wildlife Fund Urges BC Premier Dan Miller to Protect 1.5 Million acres of BC Wilderness to meet Commitments to Preserve Forests', 30 Nov. 1999.

22 William Amos, Kathryn Harrison, and George Hoberg, 'In Search of a Minimum Winning Coalition: The Politics of Species at Risk Legislation in Canada', in Karen Beazley and Robert Boardman, eds, *Politics of the Wild: Canada and Endangered Species* (Toronto: Oxford University Press, 2001).

23 See Robert Boardman, Amelia Clarke, and Karen Beazley, 'The Prospects for Canada's Species at Risk', in Beazley and Boardman, eds, *Politics of the Wild*. According to these authors, 'The SARWG experience thus represented a promising small-scale case study of accommodative politics.'

24 See 'Extinction law makes Canada "the weak link"', *Vancouver Sun*, 25 Feb. 2000, A10.

25 See Greenpeace International, *Annual Report 1998*, 'How Greenpeace Works', for an explanation of how the international (or 'Stichting') council is chosen, etc.

26 'CNF joins a new global partnership for bird conservation', *Nature Alert* 5, 2 (Spring 1995): 2.

27 See Jeremy Wilson, 'Science, Politics, and the Evolution of Western Hemisphere Migratory Bird Regimes', paper presented to the BC Political Science Association conference, 15 May 1999.

28 See, for example, Barrie McKenna, 'U.S. environmentalists swing axe at Canadian forest industry', *Globe and Mail*, 22 Jan. 2000, B1.

29 See DSF, 'Suzuki Foundation, physicians launch clear air project', news release, 24 Apr. 2000, at www.davidsuzuki.org/news_release_detail.asp?id = 100. Accessed 1 June 2000.

30 Sierra Legal Defence Fund, *1999 Annual Report*. The SLDF Web page is www.sierralegal.org.

31 Ducks Unlimited, *1999 Annual Report*, 5, 19.

32 The Nature Conservancy of Canada, *Annual Report 1998*, 'Report from the Chair', [first page].

33 All financial data from annual reports. See note 4.

34 WWF Canada, *1999 Annual Review*, 18.

35 Ernst & Young, 'Financial Statements: The David Suzuki Foundation', 31 Aug. 1999, 4.

36 Greenpeace Canada, *Annual Review 1998*, 14.

37 Ducks Unlimited, *1999 Annual Report*, 15, 21.

38 On the use of direct mail by environmental organizations and other public interest groups, see Paul E. Johnson, 'Interest Group Recruiting: Finding Members and Keeping Them', in Cigler and Loomis, eds, *Interest Group Politics*, 5th edn, ch. 2; Christopher J. Bosso, 'The Color of Money: Environmental Groups and the Pathologies of Fund Raising', in Allan J. Cigler and Burdett A. Loomis, eds, *Interest Group Politics*, 4th edn (Washington: Congressional Quarterly Inc., 1995), ch. 5; Jordan and Maloney, *The Protest Business?*, chs 4, 6.

39 See, for example, a reference by Monte Hummel of the WWF to a Canadian Wildlife Federation endangered species campaign drawing donations from 20 per cent of those contacted, cited in J. Alexander Burnett, 'A Passion for Wildlife: A History of the

Canadian Wildlife Service, 1947–1997', *Canadian Field Naturalist* 113, 1 (Jan.–Mar. 1999): 148–9.

40 For example, the CNF reports 40,000 supporters, the WWF 60,000, the DSF 24,000, and Ducks Unlimited 150,000. All figures are from recent annual reports.

41 WWF Canada, *1999 Annual Review*, 20.

42 CNF, *1998–99 Annual Report*, 7.

43 Greenpeace Canada, *Annual Review 1999*, 14. There has been considerable debate over Greenpeace's fund-raising costs. See, for example, Ian Mulgrew, 'Greenpeace Canada fights serious financial trouble', *Vancouver Sun*, 8 Sept. 1997, A1–A2.

44 The Alberta Environmental Directory is available at the Pembina Institute Web page (www.pembina.org).

45 Western Canada Wilderness Committee, '1999–2000 Members Report', 2.

46 See www.ffcf.bc.ca. Accessed 1 June 2000.

47 Rawcliffe, *Environmental Pressure Groups in Transition*, 111–12, 228.

48 JoAnn Carmin, 'Voluntary Associations, Professional Organisations and the Environmental Movement in the United States', *Environmental Politics* 8, 1 (Spring 1999): 102–3. See also Mario Diani and Paolo R. Donati, 'Organisational Change in Western European Environmental Groups', *Environmental Politics* 8, 1 (Spring 1999): 19; Donatella della Porta and Hanspeter Kriesi, 'Social Movements in a Globalizing World: An Introduction', in della Porta, Kriesi, and Rucht, eds, *Social Movements in a Globalizing World* (New York: St Martin's Press, 1999), 20.

49 Rootes, 'Environmental Movements: From the Local to the Global', 3.

50 Diani and Donati, 'Organisational Change in Western European Environmental Groups', 30.

51 Rawcliffe, *Environmental Pressure Groups in Transition*, 59–60; Jordan and Maloney, *The Protest Business?*, 186.

52 Bosso, 'The Color of Money', 114–16.

53 Jordan and Maloney, *The Protest Business?*, 190.

54 Ibid., 192.

Chapter 4

The Business Response to Environmentalism

Douglas Macdonald

By the mid-point of the twentieth century, the modern business corporation had become an organization highly skilled in detecting and influencing the ideas and behaviour of existing and potential customers. By and large, it could safely ignore other social groups. However, with the postwar expansion of the state and the articulation of new values by social movements that had gained sufficient political power to move their issues onto the policy agenda, that situation changed. As governments expanded their regulatory ambit, in both the economic and social spheres, the corporation had no choice but to focus on other societal actors and, most importantly, those policy-makers who were seeking to change its behaviour.

One of the first sectors to face this new external challenge was the tobacco industry. Throughout the 1950s, scientific evidence of the health effects associated with smoking had steadily increased.[1] These claims were given visibility and legitimacy in 1964, when a high-profile advisory committee to the Surgeon General of the United States reported that: 'Cigarette smoking is of sufficient importance in the United States to warrant immediate action.'[2] Cigarette sales immediately fell, although only for a brief period, and the Federal Trade Commission began to take steps to ban some forms of cigarette advertising. The six firms that dominated the American cigarette industry reacted both individually and collectively. Working together, in 1958 they established the Tobacco Institute, a trade association created to lobby governments by means of the élite contacts available to its first two directors, a former US ambassador and a former senator.[3] In an attempt to forestall the regulatory advertising restrictions, ultimately imposed in 1970, the Institute in 1964 developed the Cigarette Advertising Code, a form of voluntary self-regulation. While coming together to influence policy, each firm at the same time individually sought to benefit from this change in societal values by introducing new, 'safer' cigarettes, for instance, by adding filter-tips and highlighting their safety as an advertising theme, along with the traditional appeals to sophistication and taste.[4]

Although in this case the concern was for a product that harmed only the user (pollution in the form of second-hand smoke was not to become a policy issue for another 20 years), this early example nicely illustrates the basic options available to the firm that comes under external pressure as a result of new scientific knowledge and changing societal values. The firm can respond by changing its own behaviour, in this case product design and voluntary restrictions on advertising. It can also, however, work to change the ideas and behaviour of those, such as governments, exerting the pressure. These are the options that have faced resource and manufacturing industries in Canada since the emergence of the modern environmental movement in the 1960s. Environmentalism, and government policy responding to it, has demanded that corporations change the products they sell, such as packaging, cars, or pesticides; that they change production methods to generate less solid waste and toxic pollution; and, more recently, that some manufacturing inputs such as chlorine be completely eliminated. The firms involved have responded by significantly improving their environmental performance, but they have also actively reached into the policy process, strongly influencing both policy objectives and the means employed by governments to achieve them. This chapter explores both responses, with the focus on the latter. How have resource and manufacturing industries worked to influence the environmental policy intended to influence them?

The argument made here is that to answer that question we must first determine what objectives business is trying to achieve as it participates in the policy process. We cannot assume that the business interest is limited to profit alone. Although maximizing short-term profit is a fundamental goal of all firms, other goals, in particular the desire of polluters to regain social legitimacy, influence business behaviour as it interacts with governments and others. In responding to the concerns of environmentalism, business has attempted to achieve both objectives. By 'greening' its operations and products, the firm has forestalled regulatory pressure, reduced waste and inefficiency, and thus increased profit while improving its public image. When asked to make changes that more directly threaten the profit interest, however, such as eliminating an entire class of raw chemicals, business has balked. In those cases, instead of changing its own behaviour, business has employed élite-access lobbying to change the behaviour of governments.

Environmental Policy as Seen by the Firm

The subject addressed here is environmental policy-making, not business management. That process is viewed, however, through the eyes of the firm. From that vantage point, i.e., looking over the factory wall at the world outside, developments in scientific knowledge and changes in societal values are seen as having the potential for additional cost and forgone profit, but also opportunities for new marketing advantage. This approach to understanding organizational response to changes in the external environment is borrowed from Miles and others who are writing from the basis of two bodies of literature: the sociology of complex organizations and business management.[5] For them, unlike others who write on business, such as economists, the key issue is social legitimacy.[6] 'Because of the timing of the crisis, the tobacco industry became the first of the major US industries in modern times to have to confront head-on the now-widespread issue of corporate social responsibility.'[7]

Miles argues that the firm, because it is an organization embedded within the institutions and values of the society within which it functions, cannot simply ignore its critics.

> All complex organizations must contend with at least two fundamental aspects of organizational effectiveness: efficiency and legitimacy. Corporations in particular are both economic instruments that must bear the test of relative efficiency in some kind of market domain *and* social subsystems that perform roles for and within their embedding society.[8]

This search for legitimacy stems in part from the principal-agent problem, which means that, while shareholders may be exclusively interested in profit, they cannot fully control the actions of managers. Their values, including their desire for self-esteem, will lead them to adopt corporate strategies intended to gain respect in the eyes of others, even if some profit must be sacrificed. Marcus and his co-authors argue that, 'Although corporate advantage is the primary objective of the public affairs function, social legitimacy is an equally compelling consideration, which typically acts as a constraint on unbridled self-interest.'[9]

Business originally saw modern, postwar environmentalism as a set of alien values to be held at bay; 'most companies regarded environmentalists as enemies and environmental regulation as something to be fought off as long as possible and then complied with reluctantly.'[10] By the time of the 1992 Rio conference and creation of the World Business Council on Sustainable Development, this was no longer the case. Instead of engaging in the policy process with the objective of delaying the imposition of new regulatory standards, many corporations had moved 'beyond compliance', improving their environmental performance even when not mandated by law.[11] Why did this change take place? To answer that question, as stated above, we must examine the interest of the firm.

By and large, policy analysis looks to three variables: (1) interest, in terms of the economic or other benefits, such as identity, that policy actors pursue; (2) ideas, including scientific understanding and dominant values or goals such as individual liberty and human rights; and (3) institutions, defined as the rules and procedures that actors follow during the policy process.[12] Different approaches to policy analysis are distinguished in part by their relative focus on one or more of these three variables.[13] This discussion is intended to contribute to an understanding of the first variable, which, as Atkinson explains, is a method of understanding a given policy process by 'asking the simple question: who benefits?'[14] Although he discusses the political economy treatment of class interest, the subject is also the basis of pluralist studies of interest groups and of public choice analysis, which takes as its starting point individual pursuit of marginal utility. To understand a policy process by focusing on the variable of interest, however, we need to recognize that the actors involved may be pursuing multiple, and sometimes contradictory, objectives. Often, they not only seek self-interest but also want to contribute to the larger societal good.[15] Is this why business moved from the defensiveness of the 1960s and 1970s to the voluntary action of the 1990s?

Answering such a question and thus explaining this change in business strategy is of fundamental importance due to the simple fact of the enormous political power wielded by industry. Brooks and Stritch describe the power relationship this way: 'business occupies a privileged position in the politics of capitalist societies. This privileged position is based on a combination of the *cultural dominance* of business values, the *structural dependence* of governments on the behaviour of business, *élite linkages* and the *lobbying power* that business interests wield through pressure politics.'[16]

It is widely recognized that environmental policy-making in Canada, and elsewhere, is essentially a process of closed-door negotiation between regulators and the polluting industry in which the latter, having greater technical expertise, strong motivation, and ample opportunities for delay, holds the upper hand.[17] Environmentalists on occasion have managed to elbow their way into business-government negotiations, but they have not changed the basic power dynamic. These business advantages are augmented by the basic fact that Canada is a capitalist society in which the principal objective of all governments, regardless of party or ideology, is to facilitate the creation of wealth through investment of capital. Environmental policy is intended to mitigate some of the worst externalized effects of production, but it has never been carried out in a way to undermine that basic goal. Both the institutional process and context of ideas give business dominant power, and the interest it pursues as it participates in environmental policy-making, therefore, is of paramount importance.

The Firm as the Unit of Analysis

Before we can discuss the policy role of 'business', we need to define the term more precisely. Who is the policy actor? There are a number of possibilities. We might look primarily at the shareholders, who regularly move their investments among firms and, we are told, are able to influence policy by threatening capital flight. Alternatively, we might look at the corporation they invest in: a legally constructed entity, having rights and obligations essentially similar to an individual citizen. Within the firm, we might look exclusively at the chief executive officer, exercising his or her military-style, hierarchical powers from the lonely pinnacle of command. Perhaps, instead, we should look at the network comprised of all the relevant subunits within the firm, including senior management, public affairs, environmental management, product design, marketing, and labour, plus other firms, such as various suppliers and marketers, which collectively put a given product on the market and are, therefore, influenced by environmental policy. Finally, we might focus on the trade association, which is often the primary vehicle used by business to interact with governments.

From that list, the primary focus of this study is determined by the purpose to be achieved, that is, understanding the influence business brings to bear as provincial and federal governments set and, to greater or lesser degree, achieve environmental protection goals. Brooks and Stritch present the 'political interests of business' on a four-point spectrum, running from the most basic and commonly shared political objectives, such as 'social acquiescence to capitalism', through to specific interests, such as the search for government subsidies, which may be in conflict with the interests of other business actors.[18] The four points on their spectrum are: (1) capital as a whole; (2) sectoral or regional business interests; (3) industrial sectors; and (4) individual corporations.[19] Brooks and Stritch state that: 'At the most specific level of business-government relations, one finds the individual corporation.'[20] Following their lead, the business policy actor discussed here is the firm, with attention also paid to the trade associations firms create to pursue their shared policy interests.

When we look inside the black box of the firm, we must focus, given its hierarchical structure, on those who decide the environmental policy interest it will pursue: the CEO and relevant senior managers, who may work closely with some members of the board of directors. They, in turn, look for advice and technical guidance from those charged with public affairs and environmental management. The corporate public affairs department, which has expanded considerably in both resources and expertise during the past 50 years as new external pressures have come to bear on the firm, carries out three functions. It monitors events in the world outside the firm and internally relays its findings and analysis; it communicates with various external actors; and it seeks to influence the behaviour of external actors.[21] It would seem reasonable to assume that the internal organization of the firm will have an impact on the relative influence of the public affairs or environmental management department; either has more power if it reports directly to a vice-president rather than to several management levels below. Moreover, the relative power of the subunit will influence the extent to which the firm devotes resources to the attempt to influence governments and other policy actors, relative to other activities, such as product development or marketing.

The other aspect influencing the policy function of the firm is corporate culture, defined as the ideas held by those individuals within the organization. Inevitably, they will largely coincide with those held outside the firm, although to some extent they will be distinct. Schoenberge, seeking to explain the failure of some firms to pursue economic self-interest, says: 'the answer lies somewhere in the realm of corporate culture, which, in turn, is intimately involved in the production of corporate strategy.'[22] This chapter argues below that the business response to the external pressure of environmentalism changed between the 1960s and 1990s in part because of changes in the internal structure and culture of the firm and in part because of changes in the force of that external pressure.

The New Context for Environmental Policy

When the modern environmental movement first began to seek to influence business behaviour, for the most part it did so indirectly, by working through government. Environmentalists, largely by means of media exposure to generate public support, sought to bring enough pressure to bear on governments that they would pressure business, primarily by using the instrument of law. Although the newly created environment departments rarely used prosecution to enforce legal requirements, instead reserving it as a potential threat as they negotiated both standards and compliance, law was the policy instrument used. Thus, the initial policy process was as depicted in Figure 4.1.

Today, the resource or manufacturing firm no longer finds itself in that relatively simple world. Environmentalism has undergone a decline in political power in the 1990s. Environmentalists, however, are seeking to compensate for this decline in their ability to influence governments by applying pressure directly to customers. Moreover, the form and degree of regulatory pressure have changed. Finally, new non-governmental pressures, related both to production inputs and market demand, have emerged.

By the late 1980s, governments had moved to more active enforcement of law and were examining the potential use of various economic instruments. By century's end, however, regulatory pressure had been noticeably relaxed. Deregulation, initiated by federal and provincial governments in the mid-1990s, has meant both a change in policy instruments and significant reductions (in the order of one-third to one-half) in the size of the environment departments using them. Basic regulatory functions such as monitoring, inspections, and law enforcement have been reduced. Although law still provides the basis for the regulatory regime, for most new initiatives governments now rely on self-regulation, often codified in a memorandum of understanding with the relevant trade association and individual firms.[23]

While government pressure on the firm was lessening in the 1990s, the environmental concerns of those buying its products were on the rise. When McCain Foods recently responded to potential change in consumer demand and

Figure 4.1: Initial Environmental Pressure on the Firm

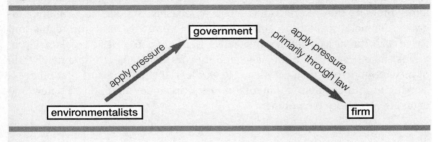

announced that it would no longer buy genetically modified potatoes, this had far more impact on the agricultural industry than any actions to date by biotechnology regulators. As Wilson points out in the preceding chapter, environmental campaigns increasingly target consumers. When environmentalists convince builders in Texas not to use BC old-growth forest by appealing to the green values of homebuyers, they can exert pressure on the BC forest industry while completely bypassing government. 'Attacking the market, rather than loggers directly, is proving to be a devastatingly effective tactic.'[24] In addition, the buying behaviour of individual consumers is influenced by labelling systems such as Eco-Choice.

Self-regulatory codes of conduct, such as the chemical industry's Responsible Care program, described below, or the International Organization for Standardization (ISO) 14000 Environmental Management System (EMS) are another form of external pressure. They offer the benefit of both cost savings from improved efficiency and a reduction in liability, since they can be employed in court as proof of due diligence. These programs require initial expenditure, however, and place the firm, which must demonstrate that it has met the standards embodied in the environmental management system, in a governance relationship with the certifying body. The Canadian Chemical Producers' Association acts as a proxy for the state when it uses the threat of expulsion to influence member firm behaviour. These voluntary standards developed by trade associations also have the potential to become incorporated into law. On at least one occasion in Canada, they have been mandated by a court.[25]

The firm's need for capital and insurance now also carries with it existing and potential environmental pressures. Ethical investors, some of whom buy shares to gain a voice at the annual meeting, do not yet make up a significant percentage of total shareholders but do have the potential to generate adverse publicity.[26] Sensing a new market, the auditing profession is moving to develop new ways of measuring and reporting environmental performance.[27] Banks, worried about their potential liability, require environmental audits and evidence of environmental management systems before lending. Those who sell environmental insurance impose similar conditions.[28]

We do not yet have data on the extent to which these non-governmental pressures (Figure 4.2) actually influence business environmental performance. Nor yet have governments actively investigated the new opportunities for regulatory pressure they afford. Government purchasing, support for labelling programs, financial regulation, and willingness to provide 'backdrop regulation' (used as a threat to convince free-riders to participate in self-regulatory programs) may some day be extensive and thus further transform this new world of mixed public-private governance. Regardless, the fact remains that business seeking to influence environmental policy must today function in a new and evolving regulatory environment.[29]

Options for Response

In response to these pressures, the firm has two basic options: to comply, completely or in part, or to attempt to change the pressure. Almost always, both options are pursued in tandem. In terms of the latter option, the firm must engage with three major sources of pressure: consumers, governments, and environmentalists. Changing consumer demand is met by new products and green marketing, including EMS certification, which other firms may require. Business seeks to influence government both through private, élite-access lobbying[30] and through participation in the public policy process, such as committee hearings and other forms of consultation.[31] In the environmental area, the primary form of business-government negotiation has always taken place at a relatively low level, as officials from the firm and environment department, who usually shared a similar technical expertise, discuss pollution abatement methods. Business has supplemented those discussions with others at a higher level as necessary, taking advantage of the contacts that political donations and class connections can provide. Business seeks to influence the actions of the environment movement by using both 'carrots' and 'sticks'. Financial support is provided to non-profits likely to advance pro-business views, while those in opposition are threatened with lawsuits.[32]

Business also uses advertising to make its policy case to the public. In the fall of 1997, for instance, as the federal and provincial governments were developing the Canadian position to be taken into the Kyoto climate change negotiations, the Canadian Association of Petroleum Producers, the Nuclear Association, and the Coal Association all made their arguments (as did the Suzuki Foundation) by means of full-page advertisements. In addition to paid advertising, business also does its best, as do environmentalists, to influence electronic and print news reporting.

Voluntary behaviour change, as illustrated above in the case of the cigarette manufacturers, may be prompted by a genuine concern to reduce the harm caused, but it is also likely to be part of a calculated strategy to influence those

Figure 4.2: Current Environmental Pressure on the Firm

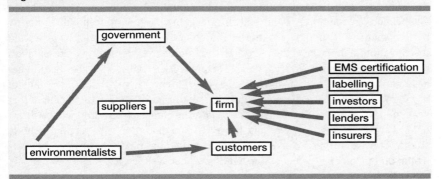

exerting pressure, most notably regulators. The firm offers up some behaviour change as a means of appeasing and forestalling those demanding a much greater degree of internalized cost. As we shall see, business increasingly began to adopt this option in the 1980s.

From Delay to Voluntary Behaviour Change

During the 1970s the major policy response of resource and manufacturing industries was to engage in technical negotiation with regulators in the new environment departments over the changes to be made in emissions to air and water. These discussions took place both on a case-by-case basis, as each firm negotiated separately the standards set forth in its regulatory permit, and on a sectoral basis. The major strategy used by the firms was private negotiation and lobbying. A picture of that strategy at play can be seen in efforts made by the Ontario Ministry of Environment over a 15–year period to reduce acid rain emissions from the Inco plant at Sudbury.

Throughout that period, Inco made no secret of its policy objective: it would only spend money on pollution control if doing so provided a net return through improved efficiency.[33] Although simple cost internalization was not something Inco was willing to do, it has always had an economic interest in developing more efficient means of separating ore from sulphur-laden rock, with the result that emissions had declined significantly, even before the firm was subjected to regulatory pressure. Throughout the acid rain policy negotiations, the basic question was always when Inco would make the necessary capital investment to achieve even more efficiency and pollution-reduction gains.

In 1970, an Ontario order required that the firm limit annual emissions to approximately 250,000 tonnes of sulphur dioxide per year by 1978.[34] Inco failed to meet the 1978 deadline and then, in the spring of 1980, the Ontario Minister of Environment announced plans for a new regulatory limit, capping emissions at their current level and requiring a reduction to approximately 640,000 tonnes per year by 31 December 1982. (This was well above the 1969 regulatory limit, which seems to have been nothing more than a pious hope. The 1982 limit was based on new technology the firm was currently investigating.)[35] The firm responded publicly by threatening litigation, based on the argument that such regulation was beyond the constitutional power of the province, and in private by arranging a presentation to the Ontario Premier and cabinet.[36] During this period it was also using élite access to put pressure on federal regulators in Environment Canada by means of northern Ontario MPs such as Judy Erola, then Minister of Mines.[37] By the fall of that year, the 1982 limit had been enshrined in law, the company had dropped the threat of legal action, and the Ontario ministry, for its part, had dropped a threat to require studies of even further reductions. Instead, that would be done, without any participation by Inco, by means of a federal-provincial task force.

In December 1982 the task force reported that Inco could bring its emissions down to as low as 18,250 tonnes per year, at a cost estimated to be somewhere between $519 million and $684 million. The external demand facing the company had now been explicitly stated: environmentalists as well as federal and Ontario environmental regulators wanted it to invest half a billion dollars or more to modernize and increase the efficiency of operations and thus reduce its acid rain emissions by well over 50 per cent. Inco responded by engaging in periodic closed-door negotiation with the regulators over the next two years.

At a meeting with Ontario ministry staff on 8 July 1983, Inco officials stated that the task force analysis was untrustworthy and that, in any case, it was only interested in 'new technology which would increase productivity while reducing emissions'.[38] Inco did give the impression, however, that it might be willing to move emissions down to 350,000 tonnes per year. Although it was not made public, that figure then became the basis for policy as the Inco reduction in the overall Eastern Canadian Acid Rain Program agreed to at the federal-provincial environment ministers' meeting of 5 February 1985. The Canadian program was announced on 6 March, without specifying reductions from individual sources. The figure was then made public by the firm itself, in a speech by Inco president Charles Baird on 24 April 1985, who presented it as the Inco contribution to the overall Canadian effort.[39]

A few months later, however, by the summer of 1985, a new Liberal government had taken power in Ontario and the firm was being pressured to reach a much lower limit of 150,000 tonnes. The firm balked in private negotiations and then used its familiar technique of élite access, going over the head of provincial Environment Minister Jim Bradley to appeal directly to Premier David Peterson. In late November 1985, news that the Ontario cabinet was being asked to approve the lower regulatory limit was leaked to the Toronto news media. On the morning of the cabinet meeting scheduled for 4 December, Inco's chairman and president had breakfast with the Premier. No decision was made at that day's cabinet meeting, and subsequent meetings were then held between Inco and ministry staff. Then, on 17 December Bradley announced that as part of the Ontario Count Down Acid Rain program, Inco would be required to reduce emissions to 265,000 tonnes by 1994.[40] By that date, the firm had put in place new technologies to modernize its operations at a cost of $600 million, met the regulatory requirement, and generated annual savings of $90 million per year through reduced labour costs.[41]

Throughout the process, Inco relied on direct lobbying, without offering voluntary behaviour change as a means of influencing the policy objective. Although it regularly issued press releases and other materials presenting its case to the public, it did not carry out any major advertising campaign. The first industrial sector to pioneer the use of these techniques, grounded in voluntary action, was the Canadian soft-drink industry.

For at least a hundred years before the emergence of modern environmentalism and the broad acceptance of a need to reduce, reuse, and recycle, soft drinks and all other beverages were sold in reusable containers—that was the cheapest option available to the manufacturers, who operated deposit-return systems without any urging by the state. By the 1960s, however, it had become cheaper for the industry to use throwaway metal containers rather than pay the costs of collecting, transporting, washing, and refilling glass bottles. Motivated both by concerns for pollution in the form of 'litter' and by the need to conserve resources, one of the major demands made by the nascent environmental movement was that the soft-drink industry return to the use of refillable containers.[42]

Responding to that pressure, a number of American states in the early 1970s passed 'bottle bills' requiring the use of refillable bottles. In 1971, BC and Alberta enacted regulatory requirements for deposits on non-refillable containers to give an incentive for the customer to take them to recycling centres. Ontario, in 1976, established a regulatory requirement that 75 per cent of the soft drinks sold in the province be in refillable containers. The initial response of the soft-drink industry in Ontario, which it follows to this day, was non-compliance. It took minimal steps to increase refillable sales to the required portion and has actively fought in the courts to block an attempted private prosecution.[43] By the early 1980s, allied with aluminum can manufacturers, the soft-drink industry had moved out of this defensive posture and was actively seeking to influence solid waste policy, working to make recycling, rather than reuse, the objective. The strategy used was financial support for the new blue box curbside recycling programs, which were then being established on an experimental basis, combined with life-cycle assessment studies suggesting that, when such things as energy and water used for washing bottles were taken into account, reuse was not necessarily the environmentally preferential option.[44]

By 1985 the industry had concluded a deal with the Ontario government, offering to pay one-third of the capital cost of the blue box program in exchange for a relaxation of the 1976 refillable ratio (which was not being enforced in any case). During the next 10 years the soft-drink industry expanded its alliance to include others who sold products in containers that might potentially become subject to regulatory demands for deposit-return reuse systems, most notably the grocery product manufacturers. The Canadian Industry Packaging Stewardship Initiative (CIPSI) program, which offered provincial governments subsidies for curbside recycling as an alternative to reuse policy measures, was proposed to a number of provincial governments. By 1994 such negotiations were under way in BC, Manitoba, Ontario, Quebec, New Brunswick, and Nova Scotia. By 1996 the industry had contributed $33 million towards the cost of curbside recycling in Ontario and had achieved its goal of forestalling any move towards mandatory deposit-return systems, at least in that province.[45] In 2000 a new organization, jointly administered by the soft-drink and grocery products industries, was developing yet another proposal for industry funding of municipally operated blue box programs in Ontario. Negotiations in the other provinces, however, had collapsed. Nevertheless, their curbside recycling costs are paid in part by the soft-drink and other relevant industries through various customer deposit systems.

Today, soft drinks in Canada are sold almost exclusively in recyclable rather than refillable containers. The policy debate centres not on reuse versus recycling, but on the question of how curbside recycling costs will be shared among governments, taxpayers, and the relevant industries. Thus, the soft-drink industry has achieved its basic objective of thwarting regulatory demands that it sell its product in refillable bottles.

During the 1980s the chemical industry also began to use voluntary action as a means of forestalling regulation. Like other contaminants, toxic chemicals, in the form of hazardous wastes emitted to air, water, or land and as chemical feedstocks, became subject to regulatory controls in the 1970s. (Chemicals prized for their lethal properties and used in pesticides or herbicides were also regulated, by means of a separate regime.) Chemical contamination as a threat to human health did not move fully to the forefront of environmental concern, however, until the Love Canal controversy in Niagara Falls, New York, during the late 1970s. Several years later, in December 1984, the accidental release of a pesticide gas by the Union Carbide plant in Bhopal, India, causing the death of several thousand people and severely injuring many more, ignited public concern and prompted voluntary action by the industry.

The Canadian chemical industry had first created a trade association to represent its collective policy interests in 1962. By the 1970s the Canadian Chemical Producers' Association (CCPA) had become one of the most sophisticated lobbyists in Ottawa, initiating the Business Association Interchange, an informal, monthly forum at which representatives of the major trade associations met in private, often with an invited bureaucrat or politician, to exchange the latest public policy intelligence.[46] In 1978, prompted by the explosion of a chemical factory at Seveso, Italy, the CCPA developed a set of principles intended to help its member firms prevent similar accidental chemical releases in this country. One-third of the membership adopted them, one-third refused, and the remaining third suggested changes to make the principles less stringent.[47] A year later these principles had been given the name Responsible Care, and after the Bhopal accident they were further developed as codes of conduct governing the storage, use, and transport of chemical stocks and hazardous wastes (they do not prescribe emission limits but instead list recommended operating systems). In 1986 the program was publicly unveiled and the trade association launched a major public relations campaign, using full-page newspaper and magazine advertisements intended to restore public confidence in the industry. In 1991 the principles were made a mandatory condition for membership in the CCPA and the Association then began a process, involving those living in local communities, to verify that member firms were in fact using the Responsible Care operating systems.[48]

The Responsible Care initiative, which has since been replicated by chemical industry trade associations in many other countries, is significant for several reasons. Even more than financial subsidy for curbside recycling, it represents a

significant development in the use of voluntary behaviour change, as a complement to direct lobbying, thus, combined with mass communications, providing a
three-pronged strategy to influence policy. In addition, it heralded the 1990s
policy shift from law-based regulation to voluntarism. In this process the trade
association has assumed a new role; not only does it seek to influence governments, it is also engaged in governing the behaviour of the member firms that
provide its annual revenues and manage its affairs.

Outside Canada, this trend to voluntary action took the initial form of development of environmental management systems for industrial sectors beyond the
chemical industry. Like Responsible Care, these systems specify operating proce-
dures rather than quantifiable pollution management objectives. The European
Eco-Management and Audit Scheme was announced in 1993, by which time the
ISO had begun work on the ISO 14000 Environmental Management System.[49] A
few years previously, at the second World Industry Conference on Environmental
Management, convened by the International Chamber of Commerce (ICC) at
Rotterdam in April 1991, 230 firms had signed a statement titled the ICC Business
Charter on Sustainable Development.[50] Ultimately, that initiative led to the cre-
ation of the World Business Council on Sustainable Development, an international
body with a mandate both to improve the environmental performance of business
and to participate in environmental policy development.[51]

The 1991 Business Charter sets out two themes. Based on the Brundtland definition of sustainable development as that which meets present needs without
compromising the ability of future generations to meet theirs, it argues that economic growth and environmental protection are complementary, not conflicting,
goals. The Charter then sets forth the essential role played by business in meeting
those twin objectives: 'versatile, dynamic, responsive and profitable businesses
are required as the driving force for sustainable economic development and for
providing managerial, technical and financial resources to contribute to the resolution of environmental challenges.'[52] By 1996, 46 Canadian firms and trade associations had formally endorsed the Business Charter.[53] A much larger number of
firms have developed their own statements of environmental principles and developed environmental management systems.

Within Canada, the next major step in voluntary action after Responsible Care
was taken in November 1990, when a group of environmentalists and business
officials met to discuss action beyond regulatory requirements that might be taken.
This meeting led to joint establishment of the New Directions Group.[54] Paul Griss,
co-ordinator of the process, has stated the business motivation for participating in
this way: 'Business is understandably not going to sit back and wait to be regulated.'[55] Working jointly with environmentalists, he suggests, was necessary to give
voluntary action credibility.[56] The New Directions Group drafted a position paper
on the reduction and elimination of persistent toxic chemicals, which in turn led
to a voluntary program for the Accelerated Reduction/Elimination of Toxics
(ARET). The program is co-ordinated by Environment Canada and has achieved

participation by companies representing 40 per cent of Canadian industrial production.[57] In September 1993, environmentalists withdrew from the process because of 'ARET's decision to focus on eliminating the release and not the use of substances'.[58] That same conflict over the policy objective of guarding against discharge of persistent toxic substances to air, water, or land (release) versus completely eliminating them from the production process (use) was to be repeated, in a much more vituperative fashion, several years later during review of the Canadian Environmental Protection Act.

During the course of the 1990s, business undertook a variety of other voluntary programs. In 1992 the automotive industry signed a memorandum of agreement with Environment Canada and the Ontario Ministry of Environment to establish a program for a 'verifiable reduction of persistent toxic substances as well as other environmental contaminants of concern used, generated or released by the participating member companies'.[59] On 20 January 1995 the Canadian Association of Petroleum Producers and Natural Resources Canada signed a memorandum of understanding setting out a program of voluntary action to reduce greenhouse gas emissions. The establishment of this program marked an important point in the conflict between two federal cabinet ministers, Anne McLellan, then Minister of Natural Resources, and Sheila Copps, then Minister of Environment and advocate of a regulatory approach to climate change. Copps lost and the Canadian climate change policy has since been based on voluntarism rather than law or economic instruments.[60] A number of analysts have pointed out that programs developed by business to forestall regulation are not truly 'voluntary' since they would not exist without the threat of government action. Regardless of the nomenclature, voluntary programs are now firmly established as an environmental policy instrument.

This does not mean, however, that business no longer whispers in the ear of the prince. While the oil industry has voluntarily offered to reduce its *own* emissions, it has relied on traditional, élite-access lobbying to prevent Canadian policy measures such as a carbon tax, which would significantly reduce the amount of their product used each year. Allied with provinces such as Alberta and functioning as part of The Climate Change Coalition, an international pressure group, the industry has worked hard to ensure that Canada relies only on voluntarism to reduce emissions.[61]

The other major use of old-fashioned, élite-access lobbying has come with efforts by the chemical industry, allied with other sectors, to forestall the incorporation of 'toxic use reduction' (defined as action to ban some chemical feedstocks or products and also referred to as 'sunsetting') into the Canadian Environmental Protection Act (CEPA). The major impetus for moving to eliminate completely some classes of chemicals came from the International Joint Commission (IJC) in its biennial reports on the implementation of the 1978 Great Lakes Water Quality Agreement (GLWQA). In its 1986 report the IJC suggested that some chemicals may have to be 'prohibited or replaced at their source if their

intrusion into the environment cannot otherwise be prevented.'[62] In 1992 it recommended that a number of specific substances, such as PCBs, DDT, dieldrin,
toxaphene, and mirex, be sunsetted and then went on to discuss problems associated with 'organochlorines': 'We know that when chlorine is used as a feed-
stock in a manufacturing process, one cannot necessarily predict or control which
chlorinated organics will result, and in what quantity. Accordingly, the
Commission concludes that the use of chlorine and its compounds should be
avoided in the manufacturing process.'[63] The IJC specifically recommended that
governments in Canada and the United States work with industry to 'develop
timetables to sunset the use of chlorine and chlorine-containing compounds as
industrial feedstocks.'[64]

These recommendations were a radical break from existing federal and provincial law, which is primarily intended to manage the discharge of dangerous chemicals into the environment as pollutants, rather than controlling their use as
inputs to the manufacturing process (the one exception is CEPA and its predecessor, the federal Environmental Contaminants Act, enacted in 1975, which dealt
with such things as the development and import of new chemical substances).
This policy objective of the effective containment of chemicals was something the
industry had been increasingly committed to since Bhopal and was working to
achieve through its voluntary program. In 1995, however, the concept of sunsetting classes of chemicals received its strongest endorsement yet when the House
of Commons Standing Committee on Environment and Sustainable Development
released its review of CEPA and suggested that, at least to some extent, chemicals
be regulated based on their inherent danger as well as likelihood of release.[65]
Immediately afterward, the Canadian Chemical Producers' Association, engaging
in public policy discussion, sent its response to cabinet members. The CCPA stated
that 'the Report takes an inappropriate, narrow toxic use reduction (TUR)
approach to pollution prevention focusing on preventing the generation and use
of substances.' The Association then proceeded to point to the apocalyptic consequences of environmentalism run mad: 'these recommendations could well
mean that most of the commercial substances used in Canada today would need
to be phased-out which clearly does not make sense.'[66]

In this instance, industry did not offer any voluntary behaviour change to pre-
empt regulation. Instead, it fell back on older methods and the lobbying battle
between environmentalists and industry raged in Ottawa for the next four years.
Writing in January 1997, the Mining Association of Canada and 10 other trade
associations used the same argument industry had first advanced 25 years earlier:
'we account for millions of jobs in communities across Canada, in a wide range
of resource based and manufacturing industries. We are writing to inform you of
our grave concerns'.[67] As well as making public submissions, the CCPA directly
lobbied MPs, with their campaign headed by former MP Claude-André LaChance.[68]
At the end of the day, industry had enough lobbying power, coming in part from
the services of paid lobbyists, to convince the Chrétien government to overrule

amendments proposed by the Standing Committee, on which Liberals formed a majority. Three Committee members, chairman Charles Caccia, Clifford Lincoln, and Karen Kraft-Sloan, voted against their government on final reading in the House. Caccia, as always, was blunt and 'accused the government of being convinced by the chemical industry to water down the bill.'[69]

Conclusion

Two questions were posed at the outset: (1) how does business work to influence federal and provincial environmental policy? and (2) why did business change from a strategy of defensiveness in the 1970s to voluntary action in the 1990s? In terms of the first, as we have seen, business works to influence government by élite-access lobbying, combined with other measures such as advertising intended to improve its media image, and on a number of occasions has also taken preemptive, voluntary action intended to forestall regulation. Why did it increasingly move to that strategy in the late 1980s? Although further research is required to give a definitive answer, it seems the answer is likely to be found in changes that took place both within the firm and in its external environment.

In the 1960s the internal organization of the firm was such that the public affairs and environmental management functions were small and far less influential than they would be 20 years later. Those subunits of the firm whose interests were best served, and which had the technical ability to develop a sophisticated, three-pronged strategy for responding to environmentalism, were unable at that time to influence the corporate policy interest. The other internal factor was the culture of senior management, consisting of values and assumptions held by middle-aged men who in no way shared the culture of environmentalism. Not surprisingly, they felt threatened and responded with defensiveness. It seems reasonable to assume that, 20 years later, corporate culture had changed to become more in tune with environmentalism, as a new generation of managers, exposed to environmental values from birth, moved into positions of influence. Seeking social legitimacy, they initiated the 'greening' of business.

These changes internal to the firm were matched by changes in the external pressure posed by environmentalism. In the 1960s, environmentalism had been very much a marginal social movement, advocating an extreme position of steady-state or declining industrial production. Given this radical fringe status, corporate managers presumably felt it could be safely ignored or given minimal attention. By 1990, however, that was no longer the case. Mainstream environmentalism had both moved to a more moderate stance and was far more securely grounded in the popular support that gave it political power. It had become something that business could not ignore.

This combination of factors internal and external to the firm brought about the change in strategy from defensiveness to policy activism and voluntarily accepted improvement in environmental performance. In part, no doubt, this was simply a rational attempt to forestall regulatory requirements that would have imposed even greater costs. It is also likely, however, that this was part of the search for social legitimacy that some analysts see as motivating business public policy. Legitimacy was not achieved, however, by fully complying with the demands of environmentalists. As we have seen, business was willing to make *some* changes but refused to make others, such as selling pop in refillable bottles or toxic use reduction, that more directly threatened profitability.

In the same way, the issue of climate change, once it is posed as a transportation and land-use issue, poses a threat to the basic economic interests of the oil and automotive industries. Cars manufactured today generate far less pollution per-mile driven than ever before. The automobile industry has also come to pursue a policy interest of co-operation with governments in the regulation of both per-mile pollution and pollution generated during car production, the latter, as discussed above, to be done on a voluntary basis. On the other hand, it has worked with the oil industry to engage in defensive lobbying on the issue of climate change. Effective policy measures to reduce fossil fuel emissions, such as the increased land-use density needed to make transit systems viable, would result in a reduction in the total number of miles driven each year and, therefore, cars and gasoline purchased. Neither of these sectors has proposed voluntary measures to achieve that objective.

The conclusion to be drawn is that business has primarily worked to achieve social legitimacy by making those behaviour changes that are already in accordance with its own value of increased efficiency. When the goal of legitimacy has clashed too strongly with the fundamental objective of the firm, profit maximization, legitimacy has had to take second place.

These findings have implications for both applied environmental policy-making and academic understanding of that process. In terms of theoretical understanding, they point to the need for a more sophisticated conceptualization of the interest of policy actors. We must do more to distinguish among *degrees* of interest, the differing motivations associated with marginal and fundamental external threats, and the way this differing level of motivation influences the policy strategy chosen. Second, the connection between self-interest and contribution to the larger good must be carefully considered in each case. It seems reasonable to assume that policy actors seek both, but to determine how they balance the two goals when they are in contradiction we must examine specific cases, opening up the black box of the interest group, government department, or firm to determine how each establishes its policy objective.

In terms of applied policy, these findings highlight the challenge of the transition to sustainability. Something akin to the goal of a permanent cap on production and associated stabilization of energy and material use will never be achieved through the existing corporate internalization of environmental values or the now weaker external pressure of governmental regulation. These must be accompanied and strengthened by other external changes, particularly in market demand, which bring about a transformation of corporate economic interest. Given the political power of business, fundamental challenges such as resource and fossil fuel consumption and proliferation of persistent toxic chemicals will only be met when it truly is more profitable, because of changes in demand, to use reusable packaging and containers, to sell renewable energy, and to use feedstocks other than chlorine. That can only be done if we move beyond the notion, now represented by 'sustainable development', that the environmental problem is nothing more than a lack of efficiency. Some new form of external pressure, which may start at the fringe but must ultimately be grounded in public support, will be needed to bring about another generation of change in the profit and social legitimacy interests of the firm.

Notes

1 Robert H. Miles and Kim S. Cameron, *Coffin Nails and Corporate Strategies* (Englewood Cliffs, NJ: Prentice-Hall, 1982). See also Richard McGowan, *Business, Politics, and Cigarettes: Multiple Levels, Multiple Agendas* (Westport, Conn.: Quorum Books, 1995).

2 Public Health Service, *Smoking and Health: Report of the Advisory Committee to the Surgeon General of the Public Health Service* (Washington: US Department of Health, Education and Welfare, 1964), quoted in Miles and Cameron, *Coffin Nails*, 41.

3 Ibid., 67.

4 Ibid.

5 Representative works are C. Perrow, *Complex Organizations: A Critical Essay* (Glenview, Ill.: Scott, Foresman, 1979); A.D. Chandler, Jr, *Strategy and Structure: Chapters in the History of the American Industrial Enterprise* (Cambridge, Mass.: MIT Press, 1962).

6 For an example of that literature, which assumes profit maximization to be the only interest of the firm, see Dennis W. Carlton and Jeffrey M. Perloff, *Modern Industrial Organization* (New York: HarperCollins, 1990).

7 Miles and Cameron, *Coffin Nails*, xiii.

8 Ibid., 21.

9 Alfred A. Marcus, Allen M. Kaufman, and David R. Beam, *Business Strategy and Public Policy: Perspectives from Industry and Academia* (New York: Quorum Books, 1987), 7.

10 Frances Cairncross, *Green Inc.: A Guide to Business and the Environment* (Washington: Island Press, 1995), 178.

11 Carl Frankel, *In Earth's Company: Business, Environment and the Challenge of Sustainability* (Gabriola Island, BC: New Society Publishers, 1998).

12 See Leslie A. Pal, *Public Policy Analysis: An Introduction*, 2nd edn (Scarborough, Ont.: Nelson Canada, 1992); G. Bruce Doern and Richard W. Phidd, *Canadian Public Policy: Ideas, Structure, Process*, 2nd edn (Scarborough, Ont.: Nelson Canada, 1992).

13 Howlett and Ramesh list the following six schools: public choice; Marxism; neo-institutionalism; welfare economics; pluralism/corporatism; and statism. Michael Howlett and M. Ramesh, *Studying Public Policy: Policy Cycles and Policy Subsystems* (Toronto: Oxford University Press, 1995), 19.

14 Michael M. Atkinson, 'Introduction: Governing Canada', in Atkinson, ed., *Governing Canada: Institutions and Public Policy* (Toronto: Harcourt Brace Jovanovich, 1993), 2.

15 Jane Mansbridge, ed., *Beyond Self-Interest* (Chicago: University of Chicago Press, 1990).

16 Stephen Brooks and Andrew Stritch, *Business and Government in Canada*

(Scarborough, Ont.: Prentice-Hall, 1991), 16.

17 See Roger Cotton and Kelley M. McKinnon, 'An Overview of Environmental Law in Canada', in Geoffrey Thompson, Moira L. McConnell, and Lynne B. Heustis, *Environmental Law and Business in Canada* (Aurora, Ont.: Canada Law Book, 1993). Cotton and McKinnon correctly identify Andrew Thompson as the first to characterize environmental protection as a process of business-government negotiation. See Andrew Thompson, *Environmental Regulation in Canada: An Assessment of the Regulatory Process* (Vancouver: Westwater Research Centre, 1980).

18 Brooks and Stritch, *Business and Government in Canada*, 11.

19 Ibid.

20 Ibid., 12.

21 Andrew B. Gollner, *Social Change and Corporate Strategy: The Expanding Role of Public Affairs* (Stamford, Conn.: IAP, 1983); James E. Post, Anne T. Lawrence, and James Weber, *Business and Society: Corporate Strategy, Public Policy, Ethics*, 9th edn (Boston: Irwin/McGraw-Hill, 1999).

22 Erica Schoenberge, *The Cultural Crisis of the Firm* (Oxford: Blackwell, 1997), 113.

23 See Robert B. Gibson, ed., *Voluntary Initiatives: The New Politics of Corporate Greening* (Peterborough, Ont.: Broadview Press, 1999).

24 Barrie McKenna, 'US environmentalists swing axe at Canadian forest industry', *Globe and Mail Report on Business*, 22 Jan. 2000, 1.

25 In *R. v. Prospec Chemicals* an Alberta court in 1996 required as part of its sentence that the firm obtain ISO 14000 certification. See Kernaghan Webb, 'Voluntary Initiatives and the Law', in Gibson, ed., *Voluntary Initiatives*, 33.

26 For instance, see Taskforce on the Churches and Corporate Responsibility, *Is Corporate Canada Ready for Its Responsibilities in the Global Economy?* (Toronto, 1 May 2000).

27 Greg Judd, 'Environmental Accounting and Reporting Practices', in Brett Ibbotson and John-David Phyper, *Environmental Management in Canada* (Toronto: McGraw-Hill Ryerson); Alan Willis, 'Counting the Costs', *CA Magazine* (Apr. 1997).

28 Stephan Schmidheiny and Federico J.L. Zorraquín, *Financing Change: The Financial Community, Eco-efficiency and Sustainable Development* (Cambridge, Mass.: MIT Press, 1996).

29 This was one of the major conclusions of a 1999 discussion of the subject. Trent Environmental Policy Institute Paper Number 1, *Business as an Environmental Policy Actor: A Roundtable Discussion Amongst Academics and Environmental Professionals*, Proceedings, Trent University, 29–30 Oct. 1999.

30 See the analysis of lobbying techniques in Brooks and Stritch, *Business and Government in Canada*; Clinton Archibald and Giles Paquet, 'Lobbying as Amphiboly: A Canadian Perspective', in Alain Gagnon and Brian Tanguay, eds, *Canadian Parties in Transition*, 2nd edn (Scarborough, Ont.: Nelson Canada, 1996). For an account of the emergence of public affairs consulting companies, see John Sawatsky, *The Insiders: Government, Business, and the Lobbyists* (Toronto: McClelland & Stewart, 1987).

31 For multi-sectoral consultation in the environmental field, see Lorna Stefanick, 'Organization, administration and the environment: will a facelift suffice, or does the patient need radical surgery?', *Canadian Public Administration* 41, 1.

32 Sharon Beder, *Global Spin: The Corporate Assault on Environmentalism* (Foxhole, UK: Green Books, 1997).

33 At a meeting with environmentalists on 20 December 1983, Inco officials stated they were only interested in pollution-control measures that were 'cost-effective'. See Doug Macdonald, 'Policy Communities and the Allocation of Internalized Cost: Negotiation of the Ontario Acid Rain Program, 1982–1985', Ph.D. thesis (York University, 1997), 240. In a press release dated 24 April 1985, Inco stated it was looking for 'means to

reduce emissions at our operations in the most cost effective way'. Inco Media Information, 'Inco Chairman Commits to 70 per cent Reduction in Sulphur Dioxide Emissions at Sudbury by 1994', 24 Apr. 1985.

34 Sulphur dioxide emissions in 1965 were 2,250,000 tonnes. Inco news release, 'Background: Emissions in Canada', Mar. 1984.

35 Macdonald, 'Policy Communities'.

36 Ibid., 156.

37 Ibid.

38 Tom Brydges, Ministry of Environment, to Walter Giles, assistant deputy minister, 2 Aug. 1983, providing a record of the 8 July discussion. Quoted in Macdonald, 'Policy Communities', 220.

39 Inco Media Information, 'Inco Chairman Commits to 70 per cent Reduction'.

40 All of this is based on Macdonald, 'Policy Communities'.

41 Inco, 'Our new flash furnace in theory/in practice', brochure, undated.

42 Doug Macdonald, *The Politics of Pollution: Why Canadians Are Failing Their Environment* (Toronto: McClelland & Stewart, 1991), 207–12.

43 Personal communication, Gord Perks, Toronto Environmental Alliance, 10 Nov. 2000.

44 Recycling Development Corporation, *Deposits as a Waste Management Tool: A Review of the Literature and Experiences*, prepared for the [Ontario] Waste Reduction Advisory Committee, June 1991.

45 Remarks by Stuart Hartley, Ontario Soft Drink Association, to the Recycling Council of Ontario, 4 Oct.1996.

46 Sawatsky, *The Insiders*, 181–3.

47 J. Arthur O'Connor, *Doing the Right Thing*, Canadian Chemical Producers' Association, undated, 8.

48 See John Moffet and François Bregha, 'Responsible Care', in Gibson, ed., *Voluntary Initiatives*; Neil Gunningham, 'Environment, Self-Regulation and the Chemical Industry: Assessing Responsible Care', *Law and Policy* 17, 1 (Jan. 1995).

49 Saeed Parto, 'Aiming Low', and Jennifer Clapp, 'Standard Inequities', in Gibson, ed., *Voluntary Initiatives*.

50 Jan-Olaf Willums and Ulrich Goluke, *From Ideas to Action: Business and Sustainable Development* (Oslo: ICC Publishing, 1992).

51 Matthias Finger and James Kilcoyne, 'Why Transnational Corporations are Organizing to "Save the Global Environment"', *The Ecologist* 27, 4 (July-Aug. 1997).

52 Ibid., 322.

53 Personal communication, Barbara Fischer, Canadian Council for International Business, 3 Feb. 1997.

54 Paul Griss, 'The New Directions Group Position', in Gibson, *Voluntary Initiatives*.

55 Paul Griss, 'ENGOs and Business: Partners for a Sustainable Future', *Ecodecision* (Autumn 1996): 41.

56 Ibid.

57 Debora L. VanNijnatten, 'The ARET Challenge', in Gibson, ed., *Voluntary Initiatives*. ARET was modelled on the US EPA 30/50 challenge program, in which government invited business to meet reduction targets 'voluntarily'.

58 Canadian Environmental Law Association and Ontario College of Family Physicians, *Environmental Standard Setting and Children's Health* (Toronto, 2000), 208.

59 Third Progress Report from the Task Force of the Canadian Automotive Manufacturing Pollution Prevention Project, June 1995, 1.

60 Doug Macdonald, Nancy Palardy, and Heather Smith, 'Firms, international regimes and instrument choice: Lessons from Canadian implementation of the Rio Climate Change Convention', paper presented at the Conference of the Canadian Society for Ecological Economics, McMaster University, Hamilton, 6 Oct. 1997; Doug Macdonald and Heather Smith, 'Promises Made, Promises Broken: Questioning Canada's Commitments to Climate Change', *International Journal* 55, 1 (Winter 1999–2000).

61 Macdonald and Smith, 'Promises Made, Promises Broken'.

62 International Joint Commission, *Third Biennial Report under the Great Lakes Water Quality Agreement of 1978 to the Governments of the United States and Canada and the States and Provinces of the Great Lakes Basin*, 31.

63 International Joint Commission, *Sixth Biennial Report*, 29.

64 Ibid., 30. For the argument that chlorine should be eliminated as a manufacturing input, see Joe Thornton, *Pandora's Poison: Chlorine, Health and a New Environmental Strategy* (Cambridge, Mass.: MIT Press, 2000).

65 For a discussion of the distinction between 'risk assessment', which calculates likelihood of release and exposure of organisms, and 'hazard assessment', which looks to inherent properties of the substance, see William Leiss, 'Governance and the Environment', in Thomas J. Courchene, ed., *Policy Frameworks for a Knowledge Economy: Proceedings of a Conference Held at Queen's University 16–17 November 1995* (Kingston: Queen's University, 1995).

66 CCPA, *It's Our Health!—CEPA Revisited*, Preliminary CCPA Submission and Analysis of the Report of the House of Commons Standing Committee on Environment and Sustainable Development, June 1995, July 1995.

67 C. George Miller, president, Mining Association of Canada, to Hon. Charles Caccia, MP, 29 Jan. 1997. The co-signatories were the Canadian Association of Petroleum Producers; Canadian Chamber of Commerce; Canadian Chemical Producers Association; Canadian Electricity Association; Canadian Fertilizer Institute; Canadian Manufacturers of Chemical Specialties Association; Canadian Petroleum Products Institute; Canadian Pulp and Paper Association; Canadian Steel Producers Association; and the Centre patronal de l'environnement du Québec.

68 Transcript, Richard Paton, president, CCPA, interviewed by Michael Enright, *This Morning*, CBC Radio One, 9 Nov. 1999; Hugh Winsor, 'Ex-Liberal spearheads industry's bid against bill', *Globe and Mail*, 26 Apr. 1999.

69 Laura Eggerston, 'Controversial environment bill passed by House', *Toronto Star*, 2 June 1999.

Chapter 5

Aboriginal Peoples and Environmental Policy in Canada: No Longer at the Margins

Greg Poelzer

It is increasingly clear that Aboriginal peoples are central to environmental policy and politics in Canada. Court decisions over the past two decades have empowered Aboriginal peoples and their communities to exercise their legal and constitutional rights, especially over resource and land use. The federal and provincial governments can no longer ignore Aboriginal interests. However, the emerging role that Aboriginal peoples and communities play in shaping environmental policy and resource management is far from monolithic. In some instances, they have allied with environmental groups against government and industry in pursuit of conservationist objectives. In other instances, Aboriginal communities have collaborated with government to establish parks. Aboriginal leaders and communities have even worked with government to promote resource development in opposition to environmental groups. Finally, some Aboriginal communities have engaged in economic activities and cultural practices in direct opposition to the policy objectives of environmentalists and/or government.

To understand these diverse roles that First Nations play in environmental policy in Canada, this chapter begins with a brief discussion of current approaches to understanding Aboriginal peoples and environmental policy. It then outlines some of the key reasons First Nations have moved towards the centre of environmental and resource policy communities. Finally, the chapter examines several case studies that demonstrate the complexity of First Nations and environmental policy-making in Canada.

Understanding First Nations' Role in Environmental Policy: A Political Community Approach

Few would question the increasing influence of First Nations over environmental policy, but there are different views on what this influence means and on the nature of First Nations' roles in shaping environmental policy. One approach suggests that the interests of environmentalists and First Nations are largely compatible, if not the same, and that alliances between environmentalists and First Nations over specific environmental issues represent the new politics based on post-material values. Far too many cases, however, demonstrate that the policy agendas of First Nations and environmentalists are often in conflict. Most scholars recognize that Aboriginal peoples' environmentalism is often part of broader concerns with obtaining Aboriginal title to lands and resources as well as seeking rights to govern those lands and resources.[1]

A much more useful approach to the study of Aboriginal peoples and environmental policy is found in Melody Hessing and Michael Howlett's *Canadian Natural Resource and Environmental Policy*. The authors approach the study of natural resource and environmental politics from a policy subsystem framework. The policy subsystem is composed of: (1) the larger policy community comprised of those actors who have an interest in, or who are impacted by, government policy in a particular sector, and (2) the more tightly knit policy network consisting of those actors who participate more directly and regularly in the formulation of policy in that sector. Within the resource and environmental policy subsystem, the authors suggest that Aboriginal peoples are one of the five major actors; the other actors include government, business, labour, and environmental groups.[2] Hessing and Howlett classfiy these five actors into two distinct sets of categories. The first set divides societal and state actors; state actors include those individuals in legislative, judicial, executive, and administrative branches of government. The second set distinguishes societal actors on the basis of productive and non-productive interests. Actors with productive interests are those who have a direct material interest in government policy in a particular sector. Hessing and Howlett suggest that First Nations are societal actors with non-productive interests. The utility of Hessing and Howlett's approach lies in the distinctions it makes between state and societal actors as well as between productive and non-productive interests. However, the substantive application of their approach to First Nations and environmental policy requires further refinement.

First Nations are political communities, not merely societal actors. First Nations are distinct from, albeit intertwined with, the larger Canadian and provincial political communities and, accordingly, possess their own state and societal actors. First Nation governments, i.e., executives, legislative bodies, and administrations, make policy on environmental and resource issues every day across Canada, although their power to do so is often quite limited. With the exception of the Nisga'a in BC, who have just negotiated a true self-government agreement with the federal and provincial governments, the decision-making authority of First Nations governments is delegated, but that does not make their actions and consequences any less real. Moreover, First Nation societal actors vary greatly in their interests. For example, some Aboriginal people operate their own logging companies and thus have a direct material interest in environmental and resource policy. Other Aboriginal actors in the same community are involved in health care or education and therefore do not. First Nations, accordingly, are not similar to business, labour, or environmentalists in policy communities and networks. Instead, First Nations are much more analogous to provinces, in particular, Quebec, which has additional cultural policy imperatives above and beyond those of its provincial counterparts.

Another approach is found in Edward Morawski and George Hoberg's analysis of forestry and Aboriginal policy in Clayoquot Sound. Morawski and Hoberg argue that policy change can occur from the intersection of distinctive policy regimes.[3] A policy regime approach includes the organizational components of policy communities and policy networks, but adds to it 'both normative and empirical ideas that provide the organization arrangement with legitimacy—a triad of actors, institutions, and ideas'.[4] Morawski and Hoberg note that, in the 1990s, a critical combination of factors led to the convergence of forest and Aboriginal policy regimes and, consequently, to radical policy changes in the management of Clayoquot Sound. The strength of their study lies in the analysis of the role that First Nations played in transforming environmental and resource policy. In particular, First Nations' relationships with government and environmental groups changed as a result. However, it is less clear that this was the result of the intersection of two distinct policy regimes.

First Nations are distinct political communities, but they are not reducible to one policy regime. This is not to argue that an Aboriginal policy regime does not exist. Arguably, a Quebec policy regime exists, too, which is concerned with that

Figure 5.1: The Policy Community

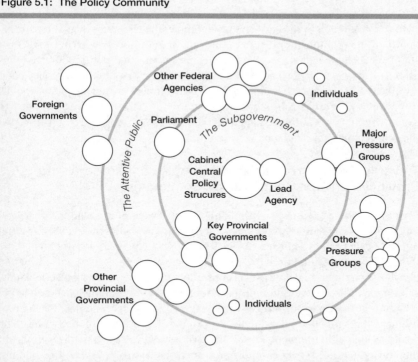

Source: A. Paul Pross, 'Pressure Groups: Talking Chameleons', in Michael S. Whittington and Glen Williams, eds, *Canadian Politics in the 1990s*, 3rd edn. (Scarborough, Ont.: Nelson Canada, 1990), 301.

province's place within the constitutional and political framework of Canada. Like Quebec and other provinces, however, First Nations are involved in multiple policy regimes (education, health, environment, and so on). From this perspective, an equally cogent argument can be made that First Nation communities in Clayoquot Sound and elsewhere are but one of the actors in environmental and resource policy regimes along with federal and provincial governments and various societal actors. The role that First Nations play varies, as Morawski and Hoberg outline. Sometimes First Nations occupy a position at the margins of environmental policy communities, while at other times they move to the centre, as in the case of Clayoquot Sound with the creation of a management board based on equal First Nation and provincial membership. To use Pross's model of a policy community (see Figure 5.1), First Nations may lie near the outside of the policy community closer to the attentive public, or First Nation state actors may themselves constitute the subgovernment that is forming policy. In the case of Clayoquot Sound, it could be argued, in contrast to Morawski and Hoberg, that it was not an intersection of policy regimes but rather simply that one of the actors, the Nuu-chah-nulth First Nation, had more resources to affect the policy outcome of that particular environmental and resource policy issue.

In the discussion of the case studies to follow, the chapter adopts the perspective that First Nations are distinct political communities possessing their own state and societal actors as well as diverse productive and non-productive interests. As such, First Nations across Canada participate in a number of policy communities and regimes, among which environmental and resource policy communities are acquiring increasing importance. First, however, we need to examine why First Nations have moved dramatically from the margins towards the centre of environmental policy communities.

Towards the Centre: Aboriginal Peoples and Federal and Provincial Environmental Policy Communities

For most of Canada's history, Aboriginal peoples were at the margins of policy-making that affected their lands, resources, and environment. Many of the significant decisions impacting on the lives of Aboriginal peoples occurred with little thought of, or consultation with, those affected. While it is true that Aboriginal peoples sometimes shaped the decisions affecting the selection of reserve lands, as in parts of Saskatchewan, and, in the case of the Alberta Métis, succeeded in obtaining a land base to protect their way of life against encroaching natural resource and agricultural development, the opposite was more often the case. The combination of environmental disasters at Grassy Narrows is a tragic example. In the late 1960s the Ojibwa communities of Grassy Narrows and White Dog not only bore the major disruptions of community relocations caused by hydroelectric dam development, but also suffered the destruction of subsistence and commercial fisheries caused by mercury poisoning from discharge from a pulp mill in

Dryden. The consequences of these two events, documented in Anastasia Shkilnyk's *A Poison Stronger than Love*, played colossal roles in undermining the well-being of these two northern Ontario reserves.[5] In both cases, Native people were not central to the resource and environmental policy decisions that had so profoundly affected them. By the end of the 1960s this began to change.

The movement of Aboriginal peoples from the margins towards the centre of environmental and resource policy communities is the result of a combination of factors. First, Canada, along with other Western countries, emerged from the experiences of World War II as a society permitting greater dissent. In Canada, Prime Minister John Diefenbaker's 1960 Bill of Rights and the Quiet Revolution in Quebec reflected the profound social and political changes occurring in Canadian society. For Aboriginal peoples, these developments were reflected in significant changes in government policy. In 1950, status Indians in Canada were given the franchise in federal elections. Very significantly, the 1927 provisions of the Indian Act making it illegal for Indians to organize politically or to retain lawyers to pursue land claims were eliminated in 1951. Then, the Hawthorn Report of 1966 advocated a 'citizens plus' approach towards Aboriginal peoples. These changes permitted greater opportunity for Aboriginal political activism, which came to the fore with the federal government's 1969 White Paper on Indian policy, which proposed the winding down of the Indian Act and that all Canadians, Natives included, be treated equally before the law. After concerted and well-organized Aboriginal protest, Ottawa withdrew the White Paper proposals two years later.

Second, the international arena assumed a far greater role in influencing domestic policy issues. The creation of the United Nations provided Aboriginal peoples in Canada and elsewhere with a forum to raise issues concerning their relations with the states that dominated them. Documents such as the Universal Declaration of Human Rights and, later, the International Labour Organization's Convention on Indigenous Peoples provided further ammunition. Aboriginal organizations were quick to exploit these opportunities to elicit external support to pressure the Canadian government to change its policies affecting Aboriginal interests. Aboriginal leaders not only linked with other indigenous organizations around the world, but also entered the international stage through the United Nations and other institutions to publicly embarrass the Canadian government for its treatment of Aboriginal peoples. In the 1980s and 1990s the international stage would prove to be even more effective when linked with other Aboriginal or environmental organizations, as the case of the proposed expansion of the James Bay hydroelectric project demonstrated.

Third, by the end of the 1960s Aboriginal organizations themselves were better organized and possessed greater resources than at any time in the past. A small but growing well-educated Aboriginal élite, which counted lawyers among their ranks, emerged with the capability to challenge federal and provincial governments. The most prominent organization was the National Indian Brotherhood, later to become the Assembly of First Nations. In 1972, the National Indian

Brotherhood produced a document, *Aboriginal People of Canada and Their Environment*, that was highly critical of federal and provincial government environment and resource policy, particularly where it adversely affected the interests of Aboriginal peoples.[6] This formulation of a national Aboriginal perspective on environmental and resource policy was relatively new and followed on the footsteps of Aboriginal reaction to the 1969 White Paper. At the same time, regional organizations proved to be no less capable of pursuing Aboriginal interests that affected lands, resources, and the environment. The Dene, Nisga'a, and James Bay Cree emerged in the 1970s as increasingly powerful and skilled in their dealings with federal, provincial, and territorial governments. This modern Aboriginal leadership demonstrated their skills during debates over two proposed mega-projects in the 1970s, the proposed Mackenzie Valley pipeline and the James Bay hydroelectric development.

The final factor profoundly shaping the role of First Nations in environmental and resource policy has been legal and constitutional change. Since 1973, the courts have proven to be one of the key instruments for First Nations in securing their claims to Aboriginal legal rights to ownership and control over land and resources. Although none of the individual court cases has been a decisive win, each partial victory has added a layer of armour in the defence of Aboriginal claims. The Nisga'a, for instance, did not win the *Calder* case in 1973, but the split decision of the Supreme Court of Canada did lend significant credence to the view that Aboriginal people have a legal rights basis for claims to Aboriginal land title. This led to fundamental changes in federal government policy and to the development of comprehensive land claims negotiations. Subsequent court decisions, such as *Guerin* (1984), *Sioui* (1990), *Sparrow* (1990), *Delgamuukw* (1997), and *Marshall* (1999), some of which are discussed in detail in Chapter 1 by Valiente, have further strengthened the legal basis of Aboriginal rights, and not only to land title. They also strengthened Aboriginal rights to resources such as forests and fisheries, even extending priority rights to Aboriginal users ahead of others once conservation needs have been met. These court cases further created higher thresholds for federal and provincial governments to infringe on Aboriginal rights where there is extant Aboriginal interest in land or resources. Moreover, particularly in the recent *Delgamuukw* decision, federal and provincial governments have a clear legal duty to consult First Nations on development that affects land, resources, and the environment. As Valiente explains, governments are in the process of building Aboriginal participation into their various environmental structures and processes. It is important to understand, as well, that court cases since 1982 have even greater significance as they must now take into account the Constitution Act, 1982, which explicitly recognizes Aboriginal rights in sections 25 and 35. Thus, many court decisions are defining Aboriginal rights that are understood to have constitutional protection.

Together, these four factors—the emergence of a dissent-permitting society, international pressure, more effective Aboriginal political organization, and legal and constitutional change—have moved First Nations from the margins of environmental and resource communities toward the centre. Below, through an examination of several recent cases, this chapter explores the new realities of Aboriginal peoples and environmental policy-making in Canada.

First Nations and Environmental Groups Allied Against Resource Development: The Case of the James Bay Cree

For many Aboriginal communities, especially those located in remote or northern areas of Canada, environmental and resource issues are of paramount concern because hunting, trapping, and fishing still play important roles in community life. It would be a mistake to assume that First Nations are politically active in environmental and resource policy solely for the purpose of controlling natural resources and extracting resource rents for their communities. Natural resource development can have devastating effects on Aboriginal subsistence economies, as events at Grassy Narrows demonstrate. In their efforts to protect their lands from the encroachment or expansion of resource development, First Nations often will ally with environmental groups. The effort of the James Bay Cree to stop the expansion of the James Bay hydroelectric development is a recent example.

On 18 November 1994, Quebec Premier Jacques Parizeau announced that the $13.3 billion Great Whale hydroelectric project was postponed indefinitely. The news was dramatic. Just over two decades earlier, in 1971, the Quebec government had announced the massive, multi-billion-dollar hydroelectric project on the river drainage system of James Bay. Hydroelectric power was to be a pillar of Quebec's future economic and political development. The first phase was largely complete by the mid-1980s. In March 1989, Hydro-Québec announced that the Great Whale project (James Bay II) was to commence in 1991 and to begin operations as early as 1998. The project was enormous; it would flood an area of 3,400 square kilometres and divert five major rivers. The project would produce 3,212 megawatts of power and create 66,700 direct and indirect jobs.[7] In April 1989, in anticipation of the completion of the Great Whale project, Quebec Premier Robert Bourassa signed a historic, $17 billion, 1,000 megawatt contract with New York Governor Mario Cuomo. Five years later, both the contract and the hydroelectric project would be cancelled. The ability of the James Bay Cree to alter the policy outcome of a resource development project of such enormous scale and provincial importance demonstrates how far First Nations have moved towards the centre of environmental and resource policy communities.

During the planning stages of the original 1970s James Bay project, the Cree bands of northern Quebec were not successful in stopping hydroelectric development, but they did make significant strides in mitigating its effects and shaping future development. The eight Cree communities, along with northern Quebec Inuit, worked together to challenge the provincial government. The federal government, despite having a fiduciary responsibility to the Cree and Inuit, largely chose to remain on the sidelines, arguably in an attempt not to alienate the Quebec government. Notwithstanding the lack of initial involvement from Ottawa, the Cree and Inuit (as the Nisga'a had done in the 1973 *Calder* case) used the court system to advance their policy interests and filed an injunction to halt the project. Although the Quebec Court of Appeals suspended a lower court's decision to grant an injunction, the Quebec government did not want to risk further court decisions at the Supreme Court of Canada level.[8] Instead, Quebec opted to negotiate and conclude the historic James Bay and Northern Quebec Agreement of 1975 with the federal government and the Cree. This first 'modern' treaty provided for landownership, advisory environmental and resource co-management, local and regional self-government, and monetary compensation for the Cree. The agreement was groundbreaking; nevertheless, the hydroelectric project proceeded.

Why were the First Nations successful in stopping the Great Whale project two decades later? Several factors were radically different in 1989 as compared with 1971: first, the Cree political community had evolved in fundamental ways as a consequence of the James Bay Agreement and hydroelectric development; second, the federal government played a much more interventionist role; third, the Cree actively sought alliances with societal actors of the dominant society, namely environmental groups; and, fourth, the Cree relied heavily on international pressure to determine domestic policy outcomes.

The James Bay Agreement and the hydroelectric development changed the Cree political community, both state and societal actors. Prior to the James Bay project, the Cree communities of northern Quebec, who were subject to the provisions of the Indian Act, existed largely independent of one another. The creation of the Grand Council of the Cree (of Quebec) in 1974, established in response to the imperatives of the hydroelectric development, marked initial efforts to create meaningful regional political organization and identity. The James Bay Agreement provided for municipal-style, local self-government of the eight Cree communities and regional self-government through the Cree Regional Authority. It is hard to overstate the importance of these structures. The institutions of local and regional self-government provided far greater authoritative and fiscal resources both to build a regional Cree identity and to engage the Quebec government over environmental and resource policy. In March 1989, when the James Bay Cree announced that they would fight the Great Whale project, the Quebec government faced a far more formidable adversary than it had in the early 1970s. As the Cree would demonstrate, the question of who was the legitimate subgovernment in the environmental and resource policy community for northern Quebec became highly contested.

Cree state actors were not the only ones to experience change. The interests of Cree community members also evolved as a consequence of the impact of the initial hydroelectric development and the James Bay Agreement. The social impact of the initial hydroelectric development is hard to underestimate. To be sure, there were real benefits. Increased Cree control over health and education, the Income Security Program for Cree hunters and trappers, and the emergence of a regional political identity giving new strength to Cree social and political expression were welcome developments. However, the hydroelectric development was not all positive. Flooding caused by the dams forever submerged traditional hunting and trapping grounds and also increased levels of methyl mercury in fish, an important staple of the Cree. The control of river flow reversed the natural cycle of high and low water levels in order to maintain adequate generation of power, which led to the drowning in 1984 of 10,000 caribou. Communities also faced major social dislocation. Community relocation from Fort George to the new settlement of Chisasibi and road construction linking the north to the south contributed to increased social pathologies.[9] The shared experience of the social and environmental impacts of the James Bay project galvanized Cree community members to oppose further development. Although some Cree business leaders were initially supportive of the proposed Great Whale project in 1989 and argued that it would create an economic boom, the clear majority was against it.[10] The overwhelming support of Cree community members to pursue non-productive environmental interests was an important resource in legitimizing the claims of Cree state actors against the Quebec government. If Cree members were willing to negotiate with Hydro-Québec in the 1970s, they were no longer willing in 1989.

A key state actor to change its role was the federal government. In contrast to its more hands-off approach during the initial project, the federal government became more interventionist. By 1989, environmental issues had become mainstream and federal environmental policy interests, along with its administrative apparatus, were more clearly developed. The Quebec government initially wanted to proceed with work on the Great Whale project and indicated that an environmental impact assessment would be conducted under provincial guidelines rather than those of the James Bay Agreement.[11] However, then federal Environment Minister, Lucien Bouchard, threatened a unilateral federal environmental review.[12] Quebec proposed to split the review into two stages, one for roads and infrastructure, the other for the dams and powerhouses. The federal government began to flip-flop, but the Cree Regional Authority, using the federal court system, forced Ottawa to uphold the provisions of the James Bay Agreement and its corresponding responsibilities. The federal government was thus committed to an independent review of the project. By 1992 the federal government, Quebec, the Cree, and the Inuit agreed to a memorandum of understanding to co-ordinate their reviews of the project. Whether it wanted to or not, the federal government was directly involved.

The involvement of the federal government in the environmental review process had the consequence of providing more time for the Cree to engage in their most important tactic: forging alliances with environmental groups and building international pressure against the project. The Cree interest in stopping the Great Whale project aligned with the interest of major environmental groups, both in Canada and abroad. During the campaign against the project, the Cree were able to gather the support of Greenpeace, the Sierra Club, and the Audubon Society, to name but a few. The Cree also enlisted the support of celebrities with known environmentalist sympathies to support their cause, with Robert Kennedy Jr being the most prominent example.

The alliance with environmental groups in garnering international support against the project proved to be decisive in the final outcome. Overall, the Cree spent $8.2 million on a sophisticated campaign. Although a large portion of this was spent on hiring energy experts and lawyers to fight court cases, a significant portion of the sum was spent on travel to Europe and the United States as well as on public relations in the United States, $200,000 alone being paid to Hill & Knowlton, a public relations company.[13] The public relations campaign aimed to demonstrate the colossal harm to the environment, and thus to the Cree, that would result from the hydroelectric project. The alliance between First Nations and environmental groups was manifest unabashedly on 21 October 1991, when Greenpeace USA ran a full-page advertisement against the project in the *New York Times* that was signed by the Grand Council of the Cree. According to Robert Mainville, a lawyer working for the Cree during this campaign, the provocative ad created adverse reaction in Quebec, so attention on influencing public opinion was directed to the United States.[14] Other avenues included prominent environmental and geographic magazines. The five-year campaign, with the assistance of environmentalist networks, sought to bring pressure on state legislatures, utility authorities, and others who had a financial interest in Hydro-Québec. The campaign did not go unnoticed. In April 1994, Matthew Coon Come, Chief of the Grand Council of the Cree, to his surprise, was awarded in New York the Goldman Environmental Prize (worth $60,000) for his efforts.[15]

The outcomes of the campaign were significant. Notwithstanding the support the Quebec government enjoyed from its societal actors, especially business and labour, and notwithstanding efforts to mitigate the damage of the Cree campaign through its own public relations efforts and a 5,000–page study supporting the project at a cost of $256 million, the Cree had won. A campaign to enlist American colleges and universities to divest themselves of Hydro-Québec bonds yielded Dartmouth College and Tufts University.[16] The states of Rhode Island, Vermont, Massachusetts, and New York all cancelled power contracts with Quebec. To be sure, a major reason for these cancellations was the reduced need for power, but there was little doubt that the Cree campaign had made its impact. The New York Power Authority president stated: 'We don't need the power, the price is too high and there are unresolved environmental questions in Quebec.'[17] The NYPA also noted that 'cancelling this contract assures that we will in no way be contributing to construction of new power projects in northern Quebec for which environmental reviews have not been completed.'[18] Without these multi-billion-dollar American contracts, the Great Whale project had no future. In November 1994, the Quebec government announced that the project was dead.

The James Bay case clearly demonstrates the central role that First Nations can play in environmental and resource policy communities. The authoritative and fiscal resources that First Nations state actors are able to deploy to organize campaigns and build alliances with societal actors domestically and abroad can prove to be decisive in shaping policy outcomes. However, as the next case demonstrates, First Nations and environmentalists do not always share the same policy interests.

First Nations and Government Allied Against Environmentalists: The Case of the Nuu-chah-nulth

The commonly held view of First Nations as non-productive societal interests who are invariably allied with environmentalists against business and state actors pursuing productive interests is quickly challenged when we examine the case of Clayoquot Sound. First Nations vociferously supported sustainable logging in Clayoquot Sound and publicly criticized environmental groups, most notably Greenpeace. In fact, the Nuu-chah-nulth not only ended up allying with the government of British Columbia, but also became part of the subgovernment responsible for overseeing environmental and resource policy in that area.

Clayoquot Sound, located on the west coast of Vancouver Island, was the focus of considerable national and international attention in the early 1990s. Environmentalists, pursuing a preservationist agenda, sought to cease all logging operations in one of the most beautiful, old-growth, coastal rain forests on the Northwest Coast. The intensity of the conflict between environmentalists and government, industry, and labour led to a massive civil disobedience campaign resulting in the arrest of 800 protestors.[19] Environmentalists not only engaged in domestic action, but also mounted a massive international campaign to pressure European governments, businesses, and consumers to stop purchasing BC forest products. Reportedly, a few German publishers, including *Der Spiegel*, were no longer going to purchase BC forest products. Members of the European Parliament were considering a boycott of BC forest products. The stakes were significant, as approximately 10 per cent of BC forest products are destined for Europe, representing $1.6 billion.[20]

If environmentalists had concerns over development in Clayoquot Sound, First Nation interests were even stronger, as this was the traditional territory of the Nuu-chah-nulth. Before Clayoquot Sound became the current focus of some environmentalists, the Nuu-chah-nulth had already engaged the provincial government over logging on First Nation territories in the area. In 1985, the Clayoquot and Ahousat bands sought and won an injunction to suspend the logging operations of MacMillan Bloedel on nearby Meares Island.[21] The BC Court of Appeal halted logging on the island until First Nation land title issues were resolved. The effect of this decision was to place an additional card in the hands of First Nations when dealing with government and industry over environmental and resource policy on contested lands.

On the surface, it appeared that there was potential for an alliance between First Nations and environmentalists against resource development, this time with respect to forestry. However, First Nations had a separate environmental and resource policy agenda. Referring to the broader context within British Columbia, Hoberg and Morawski observed that: 'Despite initial cooperation between environmentalists and aboriginal peoples, First Nations maintained an independent position throughout the period' of transition in the forestry regime.[22] As distinct political communities, First Nations have their own productive and non-productive interests. In Clayoquot Sound, environmentalist and First Nation interests would collide.

In an attempt to address the diverse concerns surrounding logging in Clayoquot Sound, the BC government created a sustainable development steering committee representing the different stakeholders. This effort failed. In April 1993, the government unilaterally announced a significant decrease from 81 to 45 per cent in the area available to logging activities, along with a sizable decrease in the allowable annual cut, from 900,000 to 600,000 cubic metres.[23] Neither environmentalists nor First Nations welcomed the announcement, but for different reasons. Environmentalists were upset because logging would continue; First Nations were dismayed because they were not involved in the process.

To address the controversy generated by its decision, the government took two steps that fundamentally changed the role of the Nuu-chah-nulth in the environmental and resource policy regime of Clayoquot Sound. First, it created a Scientific Panel for Sustainable Forest Practices in Clayoquot Sound, which was to produce recommendations on managing the area. Significantly, the panel included four Nuu-chah-nulth representatives. In July 1995 the government announced that it would adopt all of the panel's recommendations. Second, negotiations between the provincial government and the Nuu-chah-nulth led to an Interim Measures Agreement signed in March 1994. This agreement provided for the creation of a Central Regional Board with equal representation from the province and the Nuu-chah-nulth, two co-chairs, one from each side, and the requirement of a double-majority vote on decisions rendered by the Board. Although de jure the cabinet retained final authority in cases of dispute, de facto the Nuu-chah-nulth had acquired co-management powers over environmental and resource policy in Clayoquot Sound and, thus, had become part of the sub-government in that policy community.

Notwithstanding these steps, Greenpeace continued its massive campaign in Europe against BC logging practices in general and against logging in Clayoquot Sound in particular. By early 1994, the BC government began a counteroffensive. This time, however, the provincial government had gained a powerful ally: First Nation political communities. In February, the Harcourt government initiated a campaign to counter the damage caused by Greenpeace in Europe. Premier Mike Harcourt went to Europe with an entourage of 14 people, including business and labour representatives. However, the most effective spokesperson was George Watts, who had been the chief of the Nuu-chah-nulth Tribal Council (representing some 14 bands) for some 23 years. The role of First Nation representation proved decisive in turning the tide in Europe.

Environmentalists may have expected First Nations to pursue non-productive interests; they were wrong. The Nuu-chah-nulth instead came out in favour of sustainable logging in Clayoquot Sound. Before the entourage left for Europe, George Watts stated these interests clearly: 'We don't need to displace people. We just need to get into partnerships so we can generate wealth. It is time for us all to recognize this, to allow Indian people to get into forestry in order to generate wealth.'[24] First Nation pursuit of productive interests was understandable. The Nuu-chah-nulth village of Ahousat, for example, had a median income of $9,300, whereas the nearby logging towns of Tahsis and Gold River had median incomes of $37,400 and $36,100.[25] First Nation participation in and control over forestry were important to community well-being.

In Europe, and to the shock of environmentalists, George Watts caustically attacked the environmental movement and defended the First Nation right to pursue productive interests. In Germany, Watts tied the consequences of earlier campaigns by environmentalists to stop the fur trade to Greenpeace's current efforts to stop logging.

> Entire communities were dependent on that fur trade and those communities are the ones you see in the paper where young children are sniffing gasoline and have a higher rate of suicide amongst children. I don't want your welfare . . . I just want to get my people back to work. . . . Most of our people get up in the morning and think about how the hell they are going to be fed and put clothes on their back. They don't have the luxury of sitting in some bloody office dreaming about what the environment should look like.'[26]

In defence of the right of First Nation state actors to manage as they saw fit, Watts further stated at a meeting in Great Britain, 'We are not going to negotiate with Greenpeace and the environmental movement about what we are going to do on our land in BC and Canada.'[27] The statement foreshadowed events to come.

In 1996, Nuu-chah-nulth state actors and Greenpeace were again at loggerheads. In June of that year, with the approval of the Central Regional Board, logging resumed in Clayoquot Sound. The anticipated annual cut was only 147,000 cubic metres (down from 900,000 in 1991). Nevertheless, Greenpeace was opposed and set up a blockade without informing the Nuu-chah-nulth, which drew their ire. In response, Francis Frank, co-chair of the Nuu-chah-nulth central regional chiefs, reported, 'We have formally asked [Greenpeace activist] Tzeporah Berman to request the ship *Moby Dick* to move out of our territory.' Nelson Keitlah, fellow co-chair of the central regional chiefs, stated further: 'Logging is changing in Clayoquot Sound and we are part of that change. . . . We feel put off by people coming here who have literally nothing at stake.'[28] The incident damaged Greenpeace's public relations and the organization withdrew its blockade. Greenpeace activists Karen Mahon and Tzeporah Berman justified their action in an editorial in a major BC newspaper: 'the Nuu-Chah-Nulth chiefs approved the logging we were protesting. . . . So this time we made the difficult decision not to inform a First Nation of our actions.' Significantly, the activists acknowledged the subgovernment role that the Nuu-chah-nulth now played in the policy community: 'We respect the Nuu-Chah-Nulth in their emerging governance role. . . . But, as with any government, we reserve the right to disagree with the decisions that cause irreparable ecological harm.'[29]

The Clayoquot Sound case is revealing for several reasons. First, as in the case of the James Bay project, it demonstrates that First Nations are no longer at the margins of environmental and resource policy communities that have critical importance to larger provincial economies. Second, it shows that First Nations are not just influential, but may actually form part of the subgovernment of environmental and resource policy communities. Finally, in contrast to the James Bay case, Clayoquot Sound demonstrates that First Nations sometimes pursue productive interests, even in ecologically sensitive areas, and that these interests will place First Nations in an adversarial position to domestic and international environmental groups.

Environmental Conflicts on First Nations Lands: The Case of the Stoney Nation of Morley, Alberta

In January 1995 the media began reporting that intensive clear-cutting was occurring on the Stoney Indian Reserve in southwestern Alberta. The media reports were shocking. It was not merely that members of a First Nation community were engaged in clear-cutting, a practice widely condemned by environmentalists. First Nations, after all, were supposed to be more environmentally conscious than the dominant Canadian society. It was also that the purported rate of clear-cutting was well beyond a level of sustainability; initial reports suggested that the level of cutting was 10 times the recommended annual cut for the reserve. To make matters worse, the intensive clear-cutting was occurring near one of the most scenic areas of Canada (the Stoney Reserve is located between Banff National Park and Calgary, some 60 km west of Calgary). The stereotype associated with the forest industry—short-term profit first, the environment second—was now being played out by a First Nation community. In the end, the environmental consequences of the clear-cutting forced the Canadian and Alberta governments to intervene and halt logging activities on the reserve.

Perhaps more starkly than any other recent case, this demonstrates the complex role of First Nations in environmental and resource policy. It demonstrates that First Nations possess state and societal actors and that, internally, societal actors in First Nation communities possess both productive and non-productive interests. To begin, the issue of clear-cutting occurred on First Nation lands under the immediate jurisdiction of a First Nation government. In fact, the federal and provincial governments appeared reluctant to intervene in the resource and environmental management of the reserve and usurp the authority of the First Nation government. Internally, the First Nation community was divided between societal actors who pursued productive interests in terms of logging or facilitating logging and those who represented non-productive interests opposed to the logging.

During 1994–5, British Columbia experienced a shortage of wood supply, particularly for the pulp and paper industry. As the laws of supply and demand would dictate, the shortage caused wood prices to climb. It also sent British Columbia mills in search of a supply beyond provincial boundaries. Given its proximity to the BC border, Alberta was a natural supply source. Logs on Crown land cannot be exported to mills beyond Alberta's borders, although logs on private land can. A number of private landowners in Alberta began harvesting their own woodlots to feed the increasing demand in British Columbia. BC operations were willing to pay twice the going price in Alberta for logs. But private landowners were not the only ones seeking a piece of the timber boom. Members of several Indian reserves in southern Alberta began logging in earnest, but given the scale of their clear-cutting, the Stoney Reserve at Morley, Alberta, received the most attention.

A Canadian Forestry Service study had estimated that the annual allowable cut on the reserve should be 19,000 cubic metres a year. Observers estimated that during the three months prior to February 1995, between 50 and 200 trucks a day were leaving the Stoney Reserve, each carrying an estimated 25 to 40 cubic metres of wood on any given day. By the time the federal and provincial governments halted the logging on the reserve, some estimated that up to 525,000 cubic metres of timber had left the reserve.[30] The actual cut may never be precisely known, but all estimates were that it was clearly extensive. On the receiving end, BC mills confirmed significant increases in their supply of timber from the Stoney Reserve. One mill in Golden estimated that 15 to 20 per cent of its deliveries came from the Stoney Reserve.

The environmental consequences of the clear-cutting were described as 'devastating', and 'an environmental disaster'. The scale of the logging raised three primary concerns beyond the forest ecosystem on the 39,000–hectare reserve. First, some raised concern over potential damage caused by runoff pollution to the Bow River, the primary water supply of the city of Calgary. Second, provincial officials noted concerns as the weakened timber stands on the reserve posed a risk to increased infestations that could spread to adjacent provincial timber stands. Finally, the volume of slash left behind presented a very real fire hazard to forests both on and off the reserve.

To understand the events and outcomes of the environmental debacle on the Stoney Reserve, it is essential to identify the actors, their institutional constraints and opportunities, and the normative context in which these actors operated. The primary state actors involved in decision-making over logging on the reserve included the chiefs and council, as well as Indian Affairs in Ottawa.[31] The primary First Nation societal actors who represented productive and non-productive interests were the members of the Stoney First Nation, who were either involved in the logging or opposed to it. Finally, an outside environmentalist group played an important role in the unfolding of the events.

The first actor to bring to light the intensive clear-cutting was the Rocky Mountain Ecosystem Coalition. The organization's executive director, Mike Sawyer, contacted the federal Department of Indian Affairs in October 1994 to alert the department of the logging activity. The initial response was that the cutting permits issued were in order. The Rocky Mountain Ecosystem Coalition, however, continued to press Indian Affairs and even threatened to take court action in an effort to stop logging on the reserve. The activities of the environmental group to publicize the clear-cutting bore fruit, as not only did provincial and national media cover the story but MPs from Alberta challenged the federal government in Parliament. The mounting public pressure, among other factors, left little choice but for the Minister of Indian Affairs to halt the logging in early February 1995.

Legal authority over lands and resources on Indian reserves in Canada ultimately rests with the Minister of Indian Affairs, although practical governance is more complex. The Indian Act sets out provisions for the management of timber resources on Indian lands: a permit from the Minister is required to harvest any forest resources. Forests on Indian lands are further governed under the Indian Timber Regulations. However, the practicality of these provisions and regulations means that their enforcement is extremely variable across Canada. Claudia Notzke suggests that in the 'Prairie Provinces and in Quebec they do not appear to be applied at all.'[32] As a consequence, First Nations often have increasingly greater power to manage timber resources on reserve lands. This observation is reflected in comments made by Marcel Boutet, director of lands and trusts for Indian Affairs in Alberta, regarding the monitoring of timber permits on the Stoney Reserve: 'We permit [issue timber permits] at the request of the bands. . . . We just don't have the manpower to continually monitor what's going on.'[33] The reality that Indian Affairs concedes de facto the everyday authority to monitor timber resources to First Nations is reflected in the comments by Bryan Scully, a spokesperson for Indian Affairs in Edmonton: 'If cutting is occurring at an unsustainable rate, Indian Affairs doesn't have the power to stop it. . . . That's the band's responsibility. . . . Our department has been told the band is investigating allegations of overcutting.'[34] Although Indian Affairs may not have exercised its authority on a day-to-day basis, it eventually did use its authority de jure to bring a halt to logging.

Within the Stoney Reserve, societal actors were divided. Many benefited directly from the logging boom. One BC log buyer reported that he paid some individuals monthly cheques as high as $200,000. According to one CTV report there was widespread support for increased logging on the reserve. One resident, Lawrence Two Youngmen, commented: 'The majority of people here we are unemployed and they wanted to make a few extra dollars to have, ah, something on the dinner table.'[35] But not all residents of the reserve agreed with the clear-cutting. Rachel Snow, daughter of a former chief, stated that 'Brothers and sisters are fighting against each other. Families are clashing. . . . And what's this business about Indians being stewards of the land. Money has become our god. We're just as awful as non-native people if we think like this.'[36] Another Stoney First Nation member, Trina Daniels, observed: 'People are quitting their jobs and quitting university to come home and protect what's on their land. . . . Neighbors are fighting because one guy take the logs from another guy's yard.'[37] Later in 1995, some members even erected blockades to prevent further logging on the reserve.

Events at the Stoney Reserve raise questions about the role of First Nation, provincial, and federal state actors. The initial hesitancy of Indian Affairs to intervene in the situation is understandable. Indian Affairs has increasingly devolved authority to First Nations over the past two decades and, with the federal government's policy on the inherent right to self-government, any actions usurping First Nation governing authority would naturally fly in the face of that policy. Predictably, some First Nation reaction to the intervention of Indian Affairs was critical. Andrew Bear Robe, executive director of the Calgary Aboriginal Awareness Society, argued that: 'In this day and age, it's really out of character for Indian Affairs to step heavily on the Stoneys—in light of the national commitment to self-government and the settlement of native land claims.' Moreover, he expressed the view that, with constitutional change in the 1980s, there was a recognition of an 'inherent right to self-government . . . the tribal chief and counsel [sic] are the governing bodies on reserve. . . . They are responsible for putting in place a forestry management regime. People should no longer call in Indian Affairs.'[38] Although expressing concern about the situation, the Alberta government for the most part took a hands-off approach, arguing that the problem fell under federal jurisdiction. It is important to note that both First Nation reaction and federal government hesitancy to intervene clearly underscore the reality that First Nation governments more than ever operate as state actors in their own right in environmental and resource policy, as well as other policy sectors.

The acknowledgement of First Nation governments as state actors distinct from federal and provincial governments was manifest in the policy outcomes of the clear-cutting aftermath. Although the Stoney First Nation initially launched a lawsuit against the federal government for negligence in its fiduciary responsibility to manage Indian lands and resources, both parties, albeit with a heavy hand from Indian Affairs, agreed to the solutions. The cleanup of the clear-cutting cost over $1 million. This cost was borne by the Stoney First Nation from the royalties and stumpage fees it had collected during the harvesting. Responsibility for cleaning up the mess, managing logging operations, and developing a forest management plan fell to the Stoney Natural Resource Committee. By allowing the clear-cutting to take place on such a large scale, the Stoney First Nation government had a significant part in the problem; it also played a central role as subgovernment state actor in the policy outcomes.

The Morley case is instructive for other reasons as well. First, it challenges the assumption that, simply because individuals or communities are Aboriginal, it necessarily follows that they hold conservationist environmental values. In other words, this case challenges the stereotype, albeit a benign assumption, that First Nations are inherently better stewards of the environment than the dominant society. Empirically, this may often be the case. Yet it is a stereotype, and one that ought not to be automatically assumed by scholars and policy-makers alike. Second, the case demonstrates the unintended consequences that Canadian federalism can have on Aboriginal peoples and environmental policy. The proximate cause of the clear-cutting emanated from the different forestry practices of two neighbouring provinces. The spillover of changing forestry policy in British Columbia had profound effects on the environmental policy of a First Nation in Alberta.

Conclusion

First Nations no longer are at the margins of environmental and resource policy communities in Canada. As the cases above demonstrate, First Nations are political communities in their own right and, accordingly, possess their own state and societal actors. The role that First Nations play in shaping environmental policy is diverse. In some instances, such as James Bay, First Nations pursue non-productive interests. In other instances, such as Clayoquot Sound and the Stoney Reserve, productive interests are at the fore. Moreover, as the cases demonstrate, First Nations and environmentalists are not inherently natural allies. In each of these cases, however, First Nation state actors proved central to determining policy outcomes.

We should expect increasing prominence in the future role that First Nations will play in environmental policy communities, particularly with the election of Matthew Coon Come as Grand Chief of the Assembly of First Nations. Recent developments such as the Nisga'a Agreement of 1999, creating for the first time in Canada an Aboriginal third order of government, and the *Marshall* decision, extending Aboriginal rights to Aboriginal fishers in the Maritimes, give greater authority to First Nation political communities to shape decisions affecting the environment and resources of First Nation territories. How these increased authorities are interpreted, as the current lobster dispute between the federal government and the Mi'kmaq of the Burnt Church Reserve in New Brunswick demonstrates, will often prove contentious. However, contention between political communities in a federal polity is not necessarily unhealthy, as conflict often leads to resolution and accommodation between distinct political communities. Environmental and resource policy, therefore, may well prove to be an important arena in achieving accommodation of First Nation political communities within Canada.

Notes

I would like to express my thanks to my colleagues, Tracy Summerville, for her invaluable input in framing the argument of the chapter, and Joanne Matthews, for her assistance in obtaining essential resource materials. All shortcomings and errors are mine.

1 See, for example, Kathryn Harrison, 'Environmental Protection in British Columbia: Postmaterial Values, Organized Interests, and Party Politics', in R.K. Carty, ed., *Politics, Policy, and Government in British Columbia* (Vancouver: University of British Columbia Press, 1996); George Hoberg, 'The Politics of Sustainability: Forest Policy in British Columbia', in Carty, ed., *Politics, Policy, and Government in British Columbia*; Claudia Notzke, *Aboriginal Peoples and Natural Resources in Canada* (North York, Ont.: Captus University Publications, 1994).

2 Melody Hessing and Michael Howlett, *Canadian Natural Resource and Environmental Policy* (Vancouver: University of British Columbia Press, 1997), 147.

3 George Hoberg and Edward Morawski, 'Policy Change Through Intersection: Forest and Aboriginal Policy in Clayoquot Sound', *Canadian Public Administration* 40, 3 (Fall 1997).

4 Ibid., 389.

5 Anastasia M. Shkilnyk, *A Poison Stronger Than Love: The Destruction of an Ojibwa Community* (New Haven: Yale University Press, 1985).

6 National Indian Brotherhood, *Aboriginal People of Canada and Their Environment*, rev. edn (Ottawa: National Indian Brotherhood, 1973).

7 Jack Aubry, 'The beaching of a Whale: The Crees spent $8.2 million to fight the Great Whale project on environmental grounds', *Ottawa Citizen*, 26 Nov. 1994, B3.

8 Toby Morantz, 'Aboriginal Land Claims in Quebec', in Ken Coates, ed., *Aboriginal Land Claims in Canada: A Regional Perspective* (Toronto: Copp Clark Pitman, 1992), 112.

9 Ronald Niezen, 'Power and Dignity: The Social Consequences of Hydro-Electric Development for the James Bay Cree', *Canadian Review of Sociology and Anthropology* 30, 4 (Nov. 1993).

10 Graeme Hamilton, 'Power to the People: Cree battle for North was won in the South', *Montreal Gazette*, 26 Nov. 1994, B1.

11 Evelyn J. Peters, 'Native People and the Environmental Regime in the James Bay and Northern Quebec Agreement', *Arctic* 52, 4 (Dec. 1999): 401.

12 Kathryn Harrison, *Passing the Buck: Federalism and Canadian Environmental Policy* (Vancouver: University of British Columbia Press, 1996), 149.

13 Hamilton, 'Power to the People'.

14 Ibid.

15 'Cree chief is awarded $60,000 environmental prize; Efforts cancelled dam project', *Hamilton Spectator*, 21 Apr. 1994, D11.

16 Hamiton, 'Power to the People'.

17 Kevin Dougherty, 'New York cancels US$5B Quebec deal', *Financial Post*, 30 Mar. 1994, 3.

18 Ibid.

19 Hessing and Howlett, *Canadian Natural Resource and Environmental Policy*, 116.

20 Eric Reguly, 'Harcourt Hounded: Environmentalists storm out of talks in London', *Financial Post*, 5 Feb. 1994, 7; 'Logging group scores a round', *Toronto Sun*, 7 Feb. 1994, 29.

21 Frank Cassidy, 'Aboriginal Claims in British Columbia', in Coates, ed., *Aboriginal Land Claims in Canada*, 21.

22 Hoberg and Morawski, 'Policy Change Through Sector Intersection', 394.

23 Ibid., 399.

24 Tony Wanless, 'Natives seek piece of pie: Land claims not a threat, loggers told', *Vancouver Province*, 14 Jan. 1994, A47.

25 Stewart Bell and Gordon Hamilton, 'Treaties in the Making', *Vancouver Sun*, 15 Dec. 1994, SR1.

26 'Stay out of native affairs, Greenpeace told', *Halifax Daily News*, 3 Feb. 1994, 39.

27 Keith Baldrey, 'Greenpeacers arrested outside of B.C. House', *Vancouver Sun*, 5 Feb. 1994, A2.

28 'Leave us alone, Greenpeace told', *Edmonton Journal*, 22 June 1996, A9.

29 Karen Mahon and Tzeporah Berman, 'Why Greenpeace didn't tell the Clayoquot chiefs of its protest', *Vancouver Sun*, 29 June 1996, A19.

30 The Rocky Mountain Ecosystem Coalition estimated 500,000; *Windspeaker*, a leading Aboriginal newspaper, reported an estimate of 525,000 cubic metres; Marcel Boutet, director of lands and trusts for Indian Affairs in Alberta, placed the estimate at about 5,000 loads.

31 The Stoney government consists of 12 council members and three chiefs (one for each band). See Tom Flanagan, *First Nations? Second Thoughts* (Montreal and Kingston: McGill-Queen's University Press, 2000), 89.

32 Notzke, *Aboriginal Peoples and Natural Resources in Canada*, 88.

33 Vicki Barnett, 'Band told to clean up log mess', *Calgary Herald*, 9 Feb. 1995, A1.

34 'Clearcutting on reserve "a mess"', *Edmonton Journal*, 29 Jan. 1995, A8.

35 CTV National News, 7 Feb. 1995.

36 Vicki Barnett, 'Logging chaos curbed: Lucrative timber selloff splits Stoney Indians', *Calgary Herald*, 8 Feb. 1995, A1.

37 Vicki Barnett, 'Some members of the Stoney tribe say cutting has not been stopped', *Calgary Herald*, 9 Mar. 1995, B6.

38 Gordon Jaremko, 'Natives charge double standard', *Calgary Herald*, 27 Feb. 1995, A1.

Chapter 6

Environment Canada as a Networked Institution

G. Bruce Doern

This chapter examines Environment Canada's evolution in recent years into a more networked and less hierarchical form of institution, 'reinvented' through design and default by the imperatives of fiscal pressures, the dynamics of defining and operationalizing sustainable development, the changing nature of science-based governance, and the broad reconfiguration of its stakeholder politics inside and outside the parameters of the state. The chapter is institutionally focused in that it covers some basic realities that confront the Minister of Environment and the deputy minister. Institutional analysis means that Environment Canada must be seen as an amalgam of laws, political and bureaucratic players, and organizations with cultures and histories. These elements are interacting in increasingly networked ways with diverse interests and epistemic communities that hold strong contending views about what has been done and needs to be done about the greening of Canada in an increasingly interdependent world.[1] Environment Canada is a complex and changing institution and, thus, this chapter can provide only a partial and necessarily selective look at its institutional evolution.

The Central Thesis

My central thesis is that Environment Canada is increasingly a more networked institution. Hierarchy, networks, and markets are three of the main ways in which any complex human task can be organized, and in arguing that Environment Canada is more networked one certainly cannot claim that hierarchy ever disappears as an institutional feature. Environment Canada is still a form of bureaucratic hierarchy functioning within a larger and quite complex hierarchy, the government of Canada. However, it has had to reconfigure itself into a much more networked institution relative to its shape and form in the 1970s and 1980s. It is networked in the sense that it has had to develop more complex relations based on trust and exchange, a greater reliance on partnership and joint funding, and more complex networks of persuasion and cajoling within the federal government. Four factors have helped produce this change, only some of which can be said to flow from environmental policy and politics per se. These factors include: the New Public Management or reinvented government; budget and personnel reductions that had their own direct impacts but also reinforced the reinvention ethos; the emergence of the 'innovation policy paradigm' in federal microeconomic policy; and the need to institutionalize the 'sustainable development paradigm' at the core of environmental policy. Each of these factors is highlighted and then drawn out further in subsequent sections.

The first factor is the growth of ideas and practices centred on the New Public Management (NPM) and/or 'reinvented' government. NPM is very much seen in relation to the weakness and decline of traditional hierarchical and bureaucratic government.[2] These ideas are partly the product of debates about the role of government and the nature of bureaucracy, but they are also crucially and increasingly entwined with the implications of governing through, and with, the new information technologies and, thus, with new forms of digital democracy.[3] Moreover, the NPM and reinvention ethos essentially argued that public service bureaucracies had to focus much more on service, customers, and the quality of service and downplay their historic focus on top-level policy development roles. Such structures, in short, needed to look 'down and out' rather than 'up and in'. Accountability concepts also had to be changed, with more focus on managerial matrices and performance and results, less on bureaucratic lines of authority.

A second factor causing the shift to more networking was federal budget cuts. In essence, these cuts required Environment Canada and many other federal departments to seek out partners (inside and outside the state) with money, human resources and expertise, ideas, and sources of legitimacy as well as support.

The third factor is the articulation of an innovation policy paradigm. Innovation policies have in many ways supplanted traditional industrial and microeconomic policy.[4] For example, the Chrétien government made innovation the central concept in its main microeconomic policy paper, *Building a More Innovative Economy*.[5] Evolving out of free trade, the globalization of production, the revolution in telecommunications and computers, and capital and financial mobility, the dominant view inherent in innovation policies was that liberalized markets were the best economic route for governments to follow. Yet, also a part of this view was the notion of innovation being generated and fostered by an even larger *national system of innovation*. As de la Mothe has stressed:

> an 'innovation system' approach allows us to move towards more accurate depictions of how knowledge actually leads to growth, underpins our economic and social union, and how institutions adapt to rapidly changing circumstances. This embraces the reality that no institution— firm, research lab or government agency—can 'know it all' or 'do it all.'[6]

The innovation policy paradigm thus argued for the need for quite complex systems of understanding about how innovation worked as an interplay among firms, the state, and researchers in the scientific and technical community.

Last but far from least, the need to institutionalize the paradigm of sustainable development compelled the need for more fluid and flexible forms of networked activity.[7] As we see further below, sustainable development meant that Environment Canada had to spearhead a preventive and intergenerational approach to all forms of decision-making within and outside the state. It is axiomatic in this approach that Environment Canada needed support from the rest of the government and all sectors of society and could never do it alone or simply by regulatory fiat. Sustainable development requires a complex set of organizations with the capacity to learn, and, hence, innovating institutions were necessarily linked to the even larger innovation policy paradigm referred to above.

Mandate and Structure

Environment Canada's departmental *vision* is that it wants 'to see a Canada where people make responsible decisions about the environment; and where the environment is thereby sustained for the benefit of present and future genera-tions.'[8] Its *mandate* is:

> to preserve and enhance the quality of the natural environment, includ-ing water, air and soil quality; conserve Canada's renewable resources, including migratory birds and other non-domestic flora and fauna; con-serve and protect Canada's water resources; carry out meteorology; enforce the rules made by the Canada-United States International Joint Commission relating to boundary waters; and coordinate environmental policies and programs for the federal government.[9]

Its *mission* is 'to make sustainable development a reality in Canada by helping Canadians live and prosper in an environment that needs to be respected, pro-tected and conserved.'[10] In earlier eras, these aspirations would have been described as mere objectives or purposes, but in the era of reinvented, business-like government, visions, mandates, and missions are the new nomenclature. The manner in which the department currently describes itself is an important politi-cal and institutional starting point for understanding change.

Environment Canada's statutory authority flows from major legislation such as the Department of Environment Act, Canada Water Act, Canada Wildlife Act, Canadian Environmental Assessment Act, Canadian Environmental Protection Act, and a number of other laws (14 Acts in total that are its own responsibility). The department and its minister also formulate policy and regulate jointly with other ministers and departments under the auspices of several other laws, includ-ing the Fisheries Act. Numerous regulations also flow from parent statutes and, moreover, the department's activities are driven by an ever-growing number of international agreements.

Environment Canada describes its structure as a matrix management approach in that there are five headquarters or organizational units (and five regional oper-ations), which are crosscut by four 'business lines'. The organizational units are responsibility centres that manage resources and are responsible for the delivery of results. Four of these are functional, in that they deal with the minister and deputy minister, corporate services, policy and communications, and human resources. Three of the units, the Meteorological Service of Canada (MSC), the Environmental Conservation Service (ECS), and the Environmental Protection Service (EPS), are directly program-oriented services. While science underpins each service, the broader research science and monitoring tend to reside in the MSC and ECS, with EPS having a more operational science function tied to direct regulation (see more below). The business lines are broader groupings of activity intended to ensure that the department's activity is 'defined in a national context and delivered in a client-centred manner respecting regional differences; makes results the focus of departmental planning and reporting; and provides a shared strategic context for department-wide expenditure management.'[11]

The three program-related business lines are currently described by the department as: a clean environment (inspections and enforcement; dangerous chemicals; environmental impact assessments; environmental technology advancement); weather and environmental prediction (public, marine, and sea forecasts; aviation forecasts, etc.); and natural heritage (migratory birds; habitat; plant and animal species at risk; community initiatives). The department also states that its science 'is the foundation of each of its businesses' and that it dedicates 81 per cent of its budget and 60 per cent of its workforce to 'science and technology related activities'[12]. The department's core staff is composed of approximately 4,700 persons located in 100 communities, and its budget in 2000–1 was $700 million.

This bare-bones institutional description conveys, it may be said, too much of the organization chart mentality. However, the manner in which Canada's core environmental agency describes itself and fashions its basic structure is quite crucial. For our purposes, it already suggests multiple pathways for policy, implementation, and science-based governance, which require integration and can generate collisions and conflict over mandates within the department. The matrix of four main functional organizations referred to above interacting with business lines to deliver on results over a continent-wide territory (not to mention global obligations) suggests from the outset a complex agenda and sets of processes and management requirements. Such matrices are already a form of lessened pure hierarchy. Also, Environment Canada's regional operations are extensive and include several research institutes, and the department maintains complex and difficult science and policy relationships with other federal departments. These relations expand exponentially the more that the systematic policy approach of sustainable development is translated from words into action. This is because the decisions of these other ministries must be influenced at the earliest stages of decision-making.

Historical Evolution

Environment Canada's current mandate and future challenges must be placed briefly against the historical backdrop of the department and of environmental politics and economics.[13] The pattern here is one of a double dose of 'rise and fall' in political fortunes and levels of basic political saliency in the context of a quite steady long-term growth trajectory in the underlying importance of environmental matters and of concern about sustainable development.[14] The first rise occurred in the 1970s, followed by a fall in institutional clout during the1980s. Environment Canada enjoyed a decade of birth and expansion in the 1970s, with a heady confidence in its mandate and science, backed by the growth of environmental non-governmental organizations or ENGOs. From the late 1970s until about 1988, a long decline occurred, largely evidenced by a policy of weak regulatory enforcement, deference to real or imagined provincial jurisdiction, and opposition within the federal government from resource departments and their allied business interest groups.[15]

The duration of the second dose of rise and fall, but starting from a higher base point in the longer-term trajectory, encompassed the last decade. Environment Canada's sense of place in national priorities reached its zenith with the announcement of the $3 billion Green Plan in 1990. This elevated position was underpinned by several contributing forces and ideas that included: some newsworthy natural disasters in the late 1980s; the ascendancy of evidence and debate about global warming; and the articulation of the philosophy of sustainable development by the Brundtland Commission and then its endorsement by G-7 leaders at their 1988 Toronto Summit. A new federal assertiveness was in evidence during this period, backed by opinion polls that strongly supported both the environment as a national priority and federal leadership. Arguably, this period peaked or ended with the Rio Earth Summit in 1992 but included the important acid rain agreement with the United States.[16]

The most recent decline occupies the period since 1992.[17] Cuts in the Green Plan began to occur almost immediately, but the dominant impetus for the decline in the environment as a perceived political priority came from the recession of the early 1990s and initiatives to manage the growing federal deficit. These initiatives took the form of a major governmental reorganization in 1993 and the introduction of Program Review in 1994. The cumulative consequences and effects of the latter's multi-year cuts extend right to the present. The net effect of the various phases of Program Review was that Environment Canada absorbed a budget cut of over 31 per cent and lost almost 23 per cent of its personnel.[18] The department in 1993 had just lost Parks Canada, which was transferred to the newly formed Department of Canadian Heritage, and it was also engaged in reorganizing its regional personnel into five integrated regions. The last period of decline was somewhat different from the first in that it was largely a resource decline, but it was combined with major reorganization. Meanwhile, however, the department's mandate had in fact grown, as had its statutory base. These enlarged responsibilities had emerged from the development of legislation, such as the Canadian Environmental Protection Act (CEPA) and the Canadian Environmental Assessment Act, as well as from post-Rio obligations on matters such as global warming and biodiversity. Parliament has further deepened the mandate in 1999 through a revised CEPA in the context of continuing resource constraints. The federal Commissioner of the Environment and Sustainable Development drew particular attention in his first report to Parliament in 1997 to what he called a serious 'implementation gap'.[19]

Ministers and Agendas: Nobody Stays For Long

At the apex of Environment Canada, institutional change is centred on relations between a changing set of ministers and the department as a whole. Their interactions and respective views and needs largely determine what the green agenda is, or at least how it will be expressed as a vision and set of policy statements. They, in turn, are each reviewing in their own ways the larger political and economic demands and pressures emanating from the main elements of Environment Canada's policy community: business, the ENGOs, the provinces, international and global interests, public opinion, and other federal departments.

In any examination of ministers, the most compelling fact is that, in its 29 years of existence since 1971, Environment Canada has had 21 ministers—an average tenure of only 1.4 years. In short, ministers do not stay for long. In the overall process of dual ups and downs these ministers came and went, some contributing to and some simply riding the environmental waves in whatever direction they were already going.[20] In the seven-year Chrétien Liberal era since 1993, there have been four ministers—Sheila Copps, Sergio Marchi, Christine Stewart, and David Anderson—with an ever so slight improvement in length of tenure and familiarity with the environmental reigns of power. In contrast, in the same seven-year period, Canada had but one Minister of Finance and one Minister of Industry to anchor the key economic portfolios of power and policy-making.

In the Chrétien era to date there have been five different deputy ministers in Environment—Nick Mulder, Len Good (twice in the job), Mel Cappe, Ian Glen, and Allan Nymark. Nymark and Good brought their perspectives as economists to the portfolio and, along with Cappe, their other cumulative experiences in previous postings in other departments and agencies, such as Energy, Mines and Resources (now Natural Resources Canada), Industry Canada, Treasury Board, and Health Canada. In this grouping of deputy ministers, the larger instinct has been to move towards a greater reliance on economic incentives and partnership activity in environmental policy and governance. This movement has not been stridently expressed because, in many respects, the management of Environment Canada has been intermingled and jarred by other imperatives that drove its agenda within the government of Canada. These were reflected in the influences of new or even unique pressures on Environment Canada agenda-setting from the centre, in the form of the Liberal Red Book (1993 and 1997), the Program Review (1994–5), and related pressures, as well as ideas about reinventing government with a new sensitivity to service delivery and alternative delivery mechanisms. As the new century began, Environment Canada agenda-setting and management also began to be influenced by the new politics of budgetary surpluses and the end of the deficit era. Each of these is highlighted very briefly below in the context of ministerial turnover and change. One also needs to be mindful of the fact that, despite these dynamics, Environment Canada's mandate throughout this period has been constantly expanding, in part because public awareness of environmental issues and support for solutions, including a strong federal role, has been expanding.

The first three ministers of the Chrétien era were all essentially constrained by the imperatives of Program Review and then its lingering consequences, which came in the form of the aforementioned severe budget and personnel cuts. Other issues about their tenure, however, also limited the possibility of sustained political leadership. Sheila Copps was simultaneously Deputy Prime Minister and, hence, not always fully engaged in the Environment file. Though she was a senior minister, she was followed into the job first by Sergio Marchi and then by Christine Stewart. Both entered the portfolio as more junior ministers and thus lacked the political clout to sell initiatives or to garner support in a period when deficit reduction was the overwhelming top priority.

Some aspects of David Anderson's stewardship are of interest in the context of this chapter and in illustrating how ministers face moments of opportunity. First, Anderson came to Environment Canada from a previous stint as Minister of Fisheries and Oceans, where he had absorbed considerable criticism regarding the collapse of fish stocks (in different ways on both the east and west coasts). Arguably, this steeled his determination to make up for lost ground in the Environment portfolio. To this end, he made firm statements early on about the need for green taxes[21] and for reductions in greenhouse gas emissions. Second, as a minister from BC and senior cabinet minister, he entered the portfolio not only in the run-up to an election but also at a time when federal budgetary surpluses were available for the bidding. He was the first federal Environment Minister since Lucien Bouchard in 1988–9 who, it seemed, could afford to think more optimistically about Environment Canada and the greening of Canada. Certainly, Anderson's early tenure showed an effort to articulate a more comprehensive view:

> we are seeing broadly-based momentum toward a new architecture of environmental management. Canadians are more attuned to action moving beyond the symptoms to addressing root causes; and they understand and appreciate approaches which focus on rewarding personal and corporate responsibility up front rather than emphasis on regulations and enforcement after the fact. It is an architecture on which Canada can be a world leader in bringing science and innovation to bear on our challenges.[22]

His actual policy successes have been limited, however. While Anderson was able to get an agreement with the Americans aimed at reducing the cross-border flow of smog, federal endangered species legislation and a federal-provincial greenhouse gas reduction plan (to meet the country's commitments under the Kyoto Protocol) did not materialize. Back in cabinet and at the helm of Environment Canada after the 2000 federal election, he now has a second chance to push a green agenda.

The 2000 federal Budget Speech announced that from 1999–2000 to 2002–3, the federal government would invest '$700 million to enable Environment Canada and its partners to address environmental priorities'.[23] These initiatives include the Green Municipal Enabling Fund and the Green Municipal Investment Fund, as well as one for the Great Lakes basin. They also contain funding in support of the Protection of Species at Risk and, on the tax side of the ledger, an Ecological Gifts Program to allow for a reduction of capital gains tax on donations of ecologically sensitive lands. Other funds have been established to promote innovation and enhance science capacity, including the Sustainable Development Technology Fund and the Canadian Foundation for Climate and Atmospheric Sciences.[24]

This brief glimpse into the ministerial realm of Environment Canada cannot do justice to other particular initiatives that any given minister might launch and feel strongly about. The 'changing architecture' line of argument is also something that other previous ministers in the last decade have found their own similar ways of expressing. Every minister, and Environment Canada as a whole, has faced the dilemmas of talking about and seeking the desired mixes of regulation and part- nered networked changes and forms of induced behaviour. Nor are budgetary losses or gains themselves an unambiguous sign of institutional performance. A brief look at interdepartmental green politics in the context of sustainable devel- opment brings this fact out more starkly.

Interdepartmental Politics and the Changing Lobby From Within

Environment Canada has always had to battle with the lobby from within. Other federal departments with largely industrial clientele or that were pro-business in their mandates were historically viewed, in two senses, as an anti-environmental lobby from within. First, departments such as Industry Canada and Natural Resources Canada had their own interests to pursue in the inevitable internal struggle for political attention, resources, and capacity. They were competitors with Environment Canada. Second, these departments represented industrial views within the state. As long as Environment Canada was primarily an 'end-of- pipe' department with ambitions to regulate key industries such as pulp and paper and the energy industry, it was in a state of permanent tension and conflict with these departments. This snapshot of early interdepartmental postures does not mean that no discussion or co-operation occurred across departmental lines, but they were the exception rather than the rule.

In recent years, the core instinct for opposition in principle and in practice has been altered by the paradigm shifts examined above and by some institutional- ized forms of learning and change. First, the paradigm of sustainable development has been endorsed at a government-wide level as a part of national policy.[26] Furthermore, in many senses, because it is a preventive approach paradigm, it requires more non-regulatory instruments of governance and depends on a department such as Environment Canada being able to influence the policies and decisions of its fellow departments at much earlier stages in the decision process than had earlier been the case. This does not mean that sustainable development has been practised as such, but it has been institutionalized to some extent. A further impetus to institutionalization emerged in the creation of the Commissioner of the Environment and Sustainable Development, whose role within the Office of the Auditor General of Canada is to scrutinize and report regularly on the extent to which all departments are developing and implementing sustainable development strategies (and other environmental measures). Again, this institutional presence does not guarantee changed behaviour, but it does create pressure for change simply because departments have to report regularly in a more public manner.

If these features begin to 'open the doors' of interdepartmental politics, at least two other elements of change suggest that Environment Canada and other pro-green forces may be pushing against interdepartmental doors that are being left more open by the erstwhile lobbies from within. A brief look at Industry Canada and Natural Resources Canada shows how both changes can be linked to the innovation policy paradigm and to budgetary politics.

With regard to Industry Canada, the potential for more open doors is centred on the fact that the federal government's lead department for microeconomic policy has been the chief architect of the need for an innovation policy paradigm, rather than old-style industrial policy. It is far more inclined than it once was to see progressive environmental and sustainable development policy as a potential source, and indeed cause, of innovation.[27] Moreover, from the early 1990s on, Industry Canada could no longer function as if the industry sectors in its policy community were homogeneous vis-à-vis core environmental politics.[28] Its industrial clientele increasingly included, at a minimum, four different kinds of industry-environment clusters. First, the department did, of course, have polluters in industries such as pulp and paper and chemicals, but even these were more conscious than before of the need for change. Second, it had industries such as telecommunications and software that saw themselves as essentially clean and non-polluting. Third, new environmental industries (and an Industry Canada branch of the same name) were seen as innovative and oriented towards the 'new economy', and some of these thrived on the existence of tough regulation. And finally, though well beyond Industry Canada's own bailiwick, financial and insurance industries were increasingly active in matters of greening because part of their job was to ensure that firms did not have environmental liabilities.

What have been the equivalent, more 'open-door' impulses in a department such as Natural Resources Canada? At first glance, they would not seem to be much more than a crack in the doorway. After all, in the test case of climate change policies and global warming, it would appear that the instinct of Natural Resources, urged on by Alberta and other key energy provinces, is to defend the oil and gas industry and to avoid or slow down precipitous post-Kyoto targets. This is still undoubtedly true, although even here in institutions such as the Climate Change Secretariat, which is quite multi-departmental in nature, there is a new core institutionalized link between Natural Resources Canada and Environment Canada.

Moreover, other influences are at play. Natural Resources Canada was formed in 1993 to become a more integrated arena for dealing with natural resources.[29] This meant bringing federal forestry policy and services under one roof with sectors such as oil, gas, and mining. While these separate sectors still have a strong tendency to function as separate fiefdoms within the Natural Resources ministry, one feature of recent thinking has caused change within the department. This is the view that too many parts of the rest of the federal government were beginning to lump all of the industries within the department's domain as being a part of the 'old economy' of Canada's natural resource-dominated past, rather than its 'new economy' centred on knowledge and innovation. At the insistence of both its minister, Ralph Goodale, and key parts of its resource industries, Natural Resources has sought to reassert that the natural resource industries have always been innovative (and global). As a result, the department's own presentation of its mandate and mission focuses on the innovation paradigm and, furthermore, links it closely to sustainable development.[30]

Some of this embrace of the new paradigms is also undoubtedly budget-related. These departments also faced heavy cuts in the 1990s and hence needed to seek out each other in more co-operative ways than had been the norm in earlier eras. For example, a memorandum of understanding was reached on science and technology policies and resource strategies for sustainable development among several federal departments.[31]

None of the points made above is intended to argue that a new heyday of sustainable development and economy-environment integration has arrived in some perfect form. Far from it. There is still a lobby from within that Environment Canada must deal with and seek to influence. Yet there are shifts in thinking, and forms of institutionalization have been put in place that have the potential for inducing and requiring further change and that show, for our purposes, that Environment Canada is a more networked institution.

The Changing Nature of Science-Based Governance

Environment Canada has to practise, and be seen to practise, increasingly complex and changing forms of science-based governance.[32] Its role as a changed twenty-first century institution cannot be separated from these imperatives. Environment Canada's most comprehensive philosophical statement about its overall science role can be found in a 1996 document, where it was tied to the broader federal government review of science and technology then being completed as part of Program Review. Environment Canada maintained that its approach to science was consistent with the federal government's seven science and technology (S&T) principles. First, it would increase the effectiveness of federally supported research and training through peer review and a market test of relevance. Second, it would increasingly capture the cost-risk and knowledge-sharing benefits of partnership with universities, business, and other governments. Third, it would emphasize preventive approaches and sustainable development, as discussed above. Fourth, it would adopt policies, practices, and regulatory approaches that encourage innovation. Fifth, it would extend information networks as part of the infrastructure of the knowledge economy. Sixth, international S&T linkages would be strengthened. And finally, a greater science culture would be fostered.

As a mid-1990s statement, echoed by other statements since, these aspirations, while often quite problematical, are undoubtedly in keeping with the perceived realities of 'green science' at the millennium. At least half of these statements would not and did not find expression a decade earlier. But science in the overall departmental context is necessarily only the beginning. Environment Canada is also a holding company of diverse services and program providers and, therefore, has a number of different pathways for science to travel as it interacts with policy and is, in turn, influenced by it.

As defined by Environment Canada, science includes research, monitoring and assessment, technology and indicators development, and reporting activities. For some science managers in Environment Canada, these kinds of science are compressed into two broad kinds: research science and assessment and monitoring, with the latter centred on the strict analysis of samples and other data. The former is cast as a less reactive kind of science than the latter, in that it involves a process whereby researchers identify longer-term issues and problems and mount research programs to predict effects and, ultimately, to inform possible policy and regulatory responses. An example of this kind of research science is that which identified and tracked acid rain or, perhaps less well known, persistent organic pollutants (POPs). With the advantage of hindsight, one can see that this type of 'patient research science' can extend over a 10–15-year cycle and, of course, it eventually will generate the need for ongoing science monitoring.

Assessment and monitoring are ostensibly more routine. Or these functions may be needed to respond to real and perceived environmental problems, events, spills, and other occasions when ministers or communities need information about such problems and about whether or not the government has these problems, in some sense, under control (politically, environmentally, or both). This kind of science can be likened to science 'on demand'. Scientific monitoring capacity is also needed for ongoing environmental indicators and reporting and accountability, and for informing citizens about the state of national, local, regional, and even neighbourhood environmental issues.

In the last decade, the nature of science in Environment Canada has undergone five changes that affect the nature of both of these broadly defined kinds of science and the relationships between the two. (1) Science has to be conducted and managed, broadly speaking, with less money and internal personnel. (2) There is now a much more concerted effort to match closely science and policy. In short, there is more pressure for 'science on demand'. This need flows from the hard budget constraint but is also due to the expanded mandates referred to above and is required for accountability. (3) There is less 'freedom to roam' in launching new research initiatives based on the instincts of Environment Canada scientists, as opposed to the dictates of existing policies and commitments. In these terms, there is less room for 'patient science'. (4) There is simply much more global science, both because the scale of environmental problems is global and because modern computerized and Internet technologies put Environment Canada scientists in touch on a daily basis with scientists and science throughout the world. (5) With regard to monitoring science, there is a shift away from repeated measuring activity (such as regular measurements over a 12–month period) to the use of statistical sampling approaches. Though this may partly stem from budget cuts, it also results from quite genuine views in compliance and monitoring theory (including financial auditing) that less routine and bureaucratic approaches can work just as well, especially in the information age.

Each of these five changes is important and daunting enough, but they are all layered on top of yet other features of science in the environmental realm that form part of Environment Canada's history, its current institutional memory, and its organizational and cultural makeup. These elements do not simply go away and they are each partly driven by inherent tensions within each element. These elements include: the previously mentioned cleanup versus sustainable development concepts of environmental policy and regulation; the perceived historical need to 'out-science' other countries, especially the United States on bilateral problems; and the varying concepts of risk-management practised, if not always enunciated, by Environment Canada.

The remediation versus prevention tensions are of long standing in Environment Canada. The very definition of the department in 1970 centred on those who advocated a systemic resource management approach (the precursor to the 1980s sustainable development concept) versus those who saw the greater need being an end-of-pipe cleanup approach. The latter won the day in the 1970s.[33] When sustainable development emerged as an articulated concept in the late 1980s, the former gained a greater foothold. But a tension remained, often with new ministers (and remember, there are *always* new ministers) who wanted a tougher line taken with polluters. The sustainable development model is always more subtle, multi-faceted, knowledge-based, and inchoate. It achieves by 'preventing', which means that it ultimately trades in a world of non-events, that is, things that do not happen and that cannot be 'announced', only obliquely 'reported on'. It does not make for good media-driven politics or the proverbial 30–second sound-bite. The more that

Environment Canada becomes a sustainable development department, the more its science may become less explicitly noticeable, though still remaining essential. Meanwhile, science in support of end-of-pipe remedial regulatory action often has to be explicit, specific, or local, and it must be administratively causal science if blame is to be legally apportioned and assigned to firms or other polluters.

The desire to 'out-science' may seem paradoxical given the greater than ever need for global sharing and co-operation in environmental science. Yet it has been an important part of the attitude towards, and pride in, science at Environment Canada. Given early bilateral problems such as Great Lakes pollution and acid rain, and given the asymmetry of political power between Canada and the US, Environment Canada always felt that its counterweight to US political might had to be very good science, indeed, better science than the Americans might assemble. There was considerable sense in this view and its legacy is still present in Canada's approach to other problems since then, even when these are increasingly multilateral and global in character. Canada's leadership on the science on the ozone layer, which led to the 1987 Montreal Protocol, reflected this need for science as a crucial power base. To have a voice that will be heard at the growing number of international tables, a small or medium-sized country has to bring a good science-based view or else it will simply not be a credible player in complex negotiations.[34]

The third and final long-term element that characterizes science in Environment Canada is the department's varying views of risk and risk management. These views are varied in that they are both stated and unstated, and they vary across the department's mandate areas. In addition, Environment Canada's main interest groups—the ENGOs and business—also have diverse views about risk. In its early water pollution regulatory programs, the preferred approach in Canada (and in many other countries) was to require firms to minimize end-of-pipe effluents consistent with the 'best practicable technology', rather than to promulgate more precise standards regarding assimilative capacities in particular bodies of water. This was a strategy more akin to preventive risk management.

Interestingly, as noted earlier, Environment Canada perceives its job as being to help Canadians 'reduce risk', rather than to manage risks and benefits. Environment Canada has adopted the precautionary principle as a concept from the Rio Summit to underpin sustainable development. It is a feature of laws such as CEPA (especially regarding the screening of new substances). The precautionary principle is itself vague, but in general it implies that action should be taken to prevent environmental damage even if there is uncertainty regarding its possible cause and possible extent. According to this view, 'the environment should not be left to show harm before protective action is taken; scientific uncertainty should not be used as a justification to delay measures which protect the environment.'[35] One implication of this view is that one does not need complete scientific proof to practise the principle. As Jordan and O'Riordon argue, the use of the precautionary principle may be more propitious in recent years because of a broad critique about science in environmental policy and regulation. They argue that the 'science of assimilative capacity, predictive modelling and compensatory investment to offset the loss of ecological resilience is being challenged.'[36] This and other criticisms have led to the view that, 'at the very least, science should evolve into a more applied, interdisciplinary, format for coping with environmental threats, and that it should be seen as a tool for a more open and participatory culture of decision taking.'[37]

Environment Canada's main public statements stress the sustainable development concept rather than the precautionary principle, but they do show a greater acceptance of the applied interdisciplinary nature of contemporary environmental threats and policy challenges. The department is careful, however, not to endorse the implied view that one does not need science. Even to engage in precautionary practices, one needs good science and one needs far more networked modes of institutional development.

Conclusion

This chapter has shown how and why Environment Canada has become a more networked institution and has had to reconfigure itself away from earlier instincts for hierarchy. Four main factors have influenced this transformation: the pressures of the New Public Management or reinvented government; the imperatives of budget and personnel cuts; the emergence of the innovation policy paradigm; and the need to institutionalize the sustainable development paradigm. These factors are, of course, also tied to other larger pressures from Environment Canada's policy community examined in other parts of this book.

Environment Canada's change in mandate and its growing responsibilities under a sustainable development and innovation rubric have been set in a context of severe budget cuts, which partly immobilized the first three Environment ministers of the Chrétien era. Only in the recent tenure of David Anderson have new resources emerged to fund new networking initiatives. However, an era of actual or potential budgetary surpluses does not change the underlying realities. There will never be enough money and no regulatory machine can ever solve the inherent demands of both sustainability and innovation, which are now central to the Environment Canada mandate.

The discussion of interdepartmental politics has also shown that some key former sources of instinctive opposition to environmental policy, or at least non-co-operating stances, are now governed by newer, amended instincts. The brief look at Industry Canada and Natural Resources Canada suggests that the industrial lobby from within has changed to some extent. To be sure, opposition and skepticism remain, but there also is some evidence of these other internal domains being influenced by their own embrace (at least in stated policy mandates) of aspects of both the sustainable development and innovation policy paradigms.

The analysis of the changing nature of science-based governance also shows that Environment Canada's functions need to be seen with a quite subtle set of notions about what kinds of science, technology, and innovation must underpin regulatory and non-regulatory approaches to action. The tension between 'patient science' and 'science on demand' captures some of these realities, but it also shows how difficult and complex networked science is and will increasingly be.

At the dawn of the twenty-first century, Environment Canada is undoubtedly destined for more periods of ups and downs, in part because it is but one policy and institutional realm in a larger national and governmental agenda, not to mention the global agenda. This chapter has not evaluated Environment Canada's performance as such, but rather has commented on its overall trajectory of change as an institution. In this regard, its transformation towards a more networked entity makes broad sense, but in itself this does not guarantee success or a greener Canada.

Notes

1 See G. Bruce Doern and Tom Conway, *The Greening of Canada: Federal Institutions and Decisions* (Toronto: University of Toronto Press, 1994); Canada, *1998–99 Estimates: Part III Environment Canada* (Ottawa: Public Works and Government Services Canada, 1998).

2 See Peter Aucoin, *The New Public Management: Canada in Comparative Perspective* (Montreal and Kingston: McGill-Queen's University Press, 1997).

3 See Christine Bellamy and John A. Taylor, *Governing in the Information Age* (Buckingham: Open University Press, 1998).

4 See Bruce Doern and Markus Sharaput, *Canadian Intellectual Property: The Politics of Innovating Institutions and Interests* (Toronto: University of Toronto Press, 2000).

5 Industry Canada, *Building a More Innovative Economy* (Ottawa: Industry Canada, 1994).

6 John de la Mothe, 'Government Science and the Public Interest', in Bruce Doern and Ted Reed, eds, *Risky Business: Canada's Changing Science-Based Regulatory Regime* (Toronto: University of Toronto Press, 2000), 34.

7 See William Leiss, 'Governance and the Environment', in Thomas J. Courchene, ed., *Policy Frameworks for a Knowledge Economy* (Kingston: John Deutsch Institute for the Study of Economic Policy, 1996); Glen Toner, 'Canada: From Early Frontrunner to Plodding Anchorman', in William M. Lafferty and James R. Meadowcroft, eds, *Implementing Sustainable Development: Strategies and Initiatives in High Consumption Societies* (Oxford: Oxford University Press, 2000), ch. 3.

8 http://www.ec.gc.ca/introec/index_e.htm. Accessed 16 May 2000.

9 Ibid.

10 Ibid.

11 Canada, *1998–99 Estimates*, 7.

12 http://www.ec.gc.ca/introec/keyfacts.htm. Accessed 16 May 2000.

13 See M.P. Brown, 'Organizational Design as Policy Instrument: Environment Canada in the Canadian Bureaucracy', in Robert Boardman, ed., *Canadian Environmental Policy: Ecosystems, Politics, and Process* (Toronto: Oxford University Press, 1992), ch. 2.

14 See Doern and Conway, *The Greening of Canada*; Glen Toner, 'Environment Canada's Continuing Roller Coaster Ride', in Gene Swimmer, ed., *How Ottawa Spends 1996–97: Life Under the Knife* (Ottawa: Carleton University Press, 1996), 99–132; Glen Toner, 'The Green Plan: From Great Expectations to Eco-Backtracking . . . to Revitalization?', in Susan Phillips, ed., *How Ottawa Spends 1994–95: Making Change* (Ottawa: Carleton University Press, 1994), 229–60.

15 See Brown, 'Organizational Design'; Kathryn Harrison, *Passing the Buck: Federalism and Canadian Environmental Policy* (Vancouver: University of British Columbia Press, 1996); George Hoberg, 'North American Environmental Regulation', in G. Bruce Doern and Stephen Wilks, eds, *Changing Regulatory Institutions in Britain and North America* (Toronto: University of Toronto Press, 1998), 305–27.

16 See Toner, 'Environment Canada's Continuing Roller Coaster Ride'; Harrison, *Passing the Buck.*

17 See Lorna Stefanick and Kathleen Wells, 'Staying the Course or Saving Face?: Federal Environmental Policy, Post-Rio', in Leslie A. Pal, ed., *How Ottawa Spends: 1998–99* (Toronto: Oxford University Press, 1998), 243–70.

18 Canada, *Environment Canada's Science and Technology: Leading To Solutions* (Ottawa: Minister of Supply and Services Canada, 1996), 4. See also Toner, 'Environment Canada's Continuing Roller Coaster Ride'.

19 See *Report of The Commissioner on the Environment and Sustainable Development to the House of Commons* (Ottawa: Minister of Public Works and Government Services, 1997).

20 See Doern and Conway, *The Greening of Canada.*

21 See Andrew Duffy, 'Anderson Opens Door to Green Taxes', *Ottawa Citizen*, 23 Mar. 2000, 3.

22 See Hon. David Anderson, ' The Clean Air Challenge', Speaking Notes for Speech at Hart House, University of Toronto, 21 Mar. 2000, 2.

23 Environment Canada, *Overview: Environment Canada and Budget 2000* (Ottawa: Environment Canada, 2000), 1.

24 Ibid., 1–2.

25 Several departments could be examined in this context, including Agriculture and Agri-food Canada, Transport Canada, and Fisheries and Oceans Canada. In this chapter we look briefly only at Industry Canada and Natural Resources Canada. See Doern and Conway, *The Greening of Canada.*

26 See Toner, 'Canada: From Early Frontrunner'.

27 Doern and Sharaput, *Canadian Intellectual Property.*

28 See Trent Environmental Policy Institute, *Business as an Environmental Policy Actor*, Roundtable Proceedings and Associated Documents, 1999.

29 See G. Bruce Doern, 'The Formation of Natural Resources Canada: New Synergies or Old Departmental Fiefdoms', paper prepared for Workshop on the Reorganization of the Federal Government, Canadian Centre for Management Development, 15 Mar. 1995.

30 See Canada, *Natural Resources Canada: 2000–2001 Estimates* (Part III) (Ottawa: Public Works and Government Services, 2000).

31 See Canada, *1996–97 Annual Report on the Memorandum of Understanding Among the Four Natural Resources Departments on Science and Technology for Sustainable Development* (Ottawa: Minister of Public Works and Government Services Canada, 1997).

32 See Doern and Reed, eds, *Risky Business.*

33 See Doern and Conway, *The Greening of Canada.*

34 See Bruce Doern, *Green Diplomacy* (Toronto: C.D. Howe Institute, 1993).

35 Andrew Jordan and T. O'Riordan, 'The Precautionary Principle in UK Environmental Policy Making', in Tim S. Gray, ed., *UK Environmental Policy in the 1990s* (London: Macmillan, 1995), 59.

36 Ibid., 61.

37 Ibid.

Chapter 7

Federal-Provincial Relations and the Environment: Unilateralism, Collaboration, and Rationalization

Kathryn Harrison

Federal-provincial relations concerning the environment have witnessed considerable turmoil and change in the last 10–15 years. After a prolonged period of relatively harmonious intergovernmental relations during the 1970s and 1980s, tensions emerged in the late 1980s and early 1990s. Federal and provincial governments disagreed over such matters as the federal government's new Canadian Environmental Assessment and Canadian Environmental Protection Acts and the federal government's role in environmental assessment of major projects, including the Rafferty-Alameda Dam in Saskatchewan, the Oldman River Dam in Alberta, and the Great Whale hydroelectric project in Quebec. At the limit, in the Rafferty-Alameda case, Canadians witnessed the unseemly spectacle of federal and provincial ministers challenging each other's version of a backroom deal in court.[1] Since the early 1990s, however, both federal and provincial governments have sought to restore harmony to the environmental field. This last period culminated in January 1998 when the federal government and all territories and provinces except Quebec signed the Canada-Wide Accord on Environmental Harmonization. The Accord promises to provide a template for federal-provincial relations and national environmental policy-making for the foreseeable future.

It is worth noting that this recent evolution from co-operation to conflict and back again was, in many respects, a replay of developments from the late 1960s to the 1980s. The pendulum between co-operative and conflictual federal-provincial relations has thus completed two cycles. The purpose of this chapter is to examine these trends more closely and to consider the desirability of our current trajectory. The next section will review theoretical arguments for centralization and decentralization of environmental policy and for alternative models of intergovernmental relations. Thereafter, the history of federal-provincial relations concerning the environment will be reviewed, with particular attention to national standard-setting under the new Canada-Wide Accord. The concluding section will revisit arguments about the risks and promise of Canadian governments' current approach to intergovernmental co-operation.

The Theory of Federalism and Environmental Policy

Political theorists have long debated the wisdom of centralization and decentralization in federal political systems. The merits of federal vs provincial responsibility for environmental protection and conservation continue to be highly salient in Canada today. Before considering the arguments offered by both sides, we should note that policy-making with respect to the environment is guided by multiple and sometimes competing objectives, including not only preventing risks to human health and the environment, but also minimizing costs to taxpayers and regulated interests, ensuring equity among those affected by environmental policies, and promoting democratic accountability. This multiplicity of objectives complicates debates concerning institutional arrangements, since different participants in policy debates tend to weigh these various objectives differently.

Those who favour federal leadership typically emphasize the presence of economies of scale in studying environmental problems and developing technically complex solutions.[2] Given the considerable investment required to devise environmental standards, they argue that it is more cost-effective for taxpayers to pay for the federal government to do so once, rather than for provincial governments to repeat the exercise 10 times. Proponents of a strong federal role also emphasize equity in arguing that only the federal government can ensure consistent national standards of environmental quality. Federal leadership may also offer environmental benefits, since only the federal government has constitutional authority to address interprovincial spillovers of pollutants, and it arguably also carries greater credibility in negotiations concerning international spillovers. Another common argument for environmental benefits is that federal responsibility is necessary to avoid a 'race to the bottom' that could emerge if provincial governments compete to attract industry by lowering their environmental standards.[3] Finally, some have argued that federal responsibility for the environment is more democratically accountable, since the federal government is in a better position to resist the demands of regionally dominant interests.[4] This argument has particular resonance in the Canadian context, where the provinces as owners of Crown resources have historically enjoyed close relationships with resource extraction industries.[5]

Each of these arguments is met by a counter-argument from those who advocate provincial leadership with respect to the environment. Rather than economies of scale, proponents of a lead role for the provinces emphasize diseconomies of scale in arguing that provincial governments better understand local problems and can thus devise more effective solutions tailored to local circumstances. They also argue that there is little or no empirical evidence to support speculation about races to the bottom. Environmental control costs typically represent only a very small percentage of business's costs,[6] and, consistent with this, statistical analyses of business location decisions among American states find no evidence of a relationship between environmental compliance costs and investment decisions.[7] Proponents of provincial responsibility also counter that it is more equitable to allow individual provinces to make decisions with respect to their own resources. Moreover, to the extent that the residents of some provinces support more aggressive environmental policies than their neighbours in other provinces, diverse provincial environmental policies will better satisfy voters' preferences and thus promote democratic accountability.[8] It is also sometimes argued that provincial governments are 'closer to the people' and thus better able to discern voter preferences than a distant federal government, though given the size and population of many Canadian provinces this argument can easily be overstated.[9] Finally, there is a claim that provincial diversity facilitates policy innovation and diffusion (in effect, an argument that '10 heads are better than one').[10]

Whatever the *ideal* allocation of responsibilities for the environment between the federal and provincial governments, the *reality* is one of overlapping jurisdiction, as discussed by Valiante in Chapter 1. Provincial governments have clear and extensive authority to manage natural resources and protect the environment, albeit only within their own borders. The extent of federal authority is less clear, but has been interpreted generously by the Supreme Court in a series of decisions over the past 15 years. The question is thus not simply which level of government should be responsible for the environment, but rather, what is the most appropriate relationship between federal and provincial governments in light of their overlapping authority?

Three models for the federal-provincial relationship have emerged, though in practice the distinctions between them are complicated by combinations of approaches.[11] The first model is that of unilateralism by both orders of government. Advocates of this approach accept, indeed embrace, overlapping constitutional authority. They stress that if federal and provincial governments are both involved in environmental policy, they can better keep an eye on each other's activities, which is particularly important since Canadian governments are themselves often proponents of major resource developments. Federal and provincial governments can also back each other up. In other words, if one order of government fails to do the job, there is at least a chance that the other will come through.[12] Finally, some have argued that democratic accountability is enhanced by overlap, which promotes healthy competition among jurisdictions seeking to impress the same voters.[13]

In response, however, critics of unilateralism emphasize the costs of duplication, not only for taxpayers who foot the bill twice but for industries that may face inconsistent reporting requirements or regulatory decisions. Critics question whether overlapping responsibility will ensure backup or merely facilitate buck-passing. Finally, critics also raise the prospect of unseemly conflicts between federal and provincial governments, which can have repercussions well beyond the environmental policy sphere. In response, those who favour unilateralism argue that the conflicts among Canadian governments over the environment in the past have often yielded stronger environmental protection, as when projects that have already been approved by one order of government have been forced by the other order of government to undertake additional measures to mitigate environmental impacts.[14]

The other two models for the federal-provincial relationship are predicated on co-operation in different forms. Examples of the first, collaboration, include joint environmental assessments (with or without joint decisions with respect to project approvals) and joint development of harmonized environmental standards. The benefits of this model include enhancing decision-making by both orders of government through sharing of information and expertise, and minimizing policy conflicts by working through inconsistencies in advance. In theory, such benefits can be achieved with limited impacts on policy-making autonomy, since participating governments typically maintain their independence with respect to implementation of joint decisions. However, critics of collaboration are less sanguine about restrictions on autonomy in light of the fact that joint decision-making invariably relies on a decision rule of consensus.[15] This can result in a 'joint decision trap', in which each participant's opportunity to veto any decision is a formidable obstacle to progress.[16] Moreover, joint decision-making can be biased towards the status quo since the opportunity to block a decision is more valuable to (and thus more likely to be exercised by) those who favour the status quo than to those who favour policy change. For this reason critics often argue that joint federal-provincial decision-making will tend towards the 'lowest common denominator'. Finally, joint decision-making raises potential problems with accountability to the extent that governments are deferring to a collective body not directly accountable to voters.[17]

The third model for the federal-provincial relationship is rationalization. Rather than co-operating by working together, federal and provincial governments may co-operate by divvying up their activities to eliminate overlap and duplication as much as possible. Rationalization may entail allocating responsibility for different aspects of environmental policy (e.g., research, environmental assessment, standard-setting, enforcement) to different orders of government and/or allowing for a different division of federal and provincial responsibilities in some provinces than others. Rationalization is often depicted as an opportunity to take advantage of the strengths of both federal and provincial governments, thus capturing the 'best of both worlds'. For instance, the federal government could take the lead with respect to interprovincial spillovers and environmental regulation of products that are marketed nationally, such as automobiles, while the provinces could take responsibility for regional problems with which they are more familiar. Rationalization also offers cost savings through reduction of overlap and duplication. The potential drawbacks of this approach are the flip side of unilateralism: loss of backup of one government by the other, with an attendant risk of gaps in coverage and loss of mutual oversight. The theoretical benefits of rationalization also beg the question of which government is best at, and thus should get responsibility for, which activities. The benefits of rationalization will thus turn to a large degree on the capacity and political will of governments to fulfil their assigned responsibilities pursuant to a particular federal-provincial agreement. Interdelegation of responsibilities between federal and provincial governments may also complicate accountability.

It is noteworthy that the positions of different participants in debates about federal-provincial arrangements revolve around not only the theoretical strengths and weaknesses of each of the three institutional arrangements summarized above, but also the degree to which each is perceived as leading to centralization or decentralization in practice. Unilateralism tends to be favoured by those who support a strong and independent federal government role, since they see the alternative approaches of joint action and rationalization as at best delaying and at worst restricting the scope of federal involvement. The most vocal advocates of this argument are Canadian environmentalists, who have historically looked to the federal government to promote consistent national standards and to resist provincial concessions to resource industries.[18] Environmentalists tend to depict collaboration and rationalization as devolution in disguise, which will inevitably yield either patchwork standards or consistent ones set at the lowest common denominator.

Both collaboration and rationalization, in contrast, typically receive strong support from governments and business. Politicians and bureaucrats are motivated to avoid embarrassing public conflicts as well as to conserve scarce resources by avoiding duplication. However, as discussed below, their motives may on occasion have less to do with 'good environmental policy' than with 'good politics'. Most Canadian industries have historically emphasized the need for rationalization to achieve a 'one-window' approach to environmental policy, or, failing that, collaboration to avoid inconsistencies and 'bidding wars'. It is noteworthy, though, that many industrial sectors have historically expressed a strong preference not just for a 'single window', but for a window staffed by the provinces.[19] One can speculate that this is because they perceive a closer relationship with provincial governments or that they expect to gain concessions by pitting provincial governments against each other, the very reasons that environmentalists favour federal involvement.

The Evolution of Federal-Provincial Relations Concerning the Environment

Prior to 1970 there was little federal-provincial interaction concerning the environment. With the exception of fisheries, natural resources and their conservation typically were considered provincial matters by federal and provincial governments alike. Federal politicians resisted occasional calls to address environmental problems by arguing that resource management was a provincial matter. However, when unprecedented public concern for the environment emerged in the late 1960s, the federal government reconsidered its jurisdiction. It asserted an independent role in the environmental field in passing five new environmental statutes, including the Canada Water Act, the Fisheries Act Amendments, and the Clean Air Act in the span of just three years from 1969 to 1972. At the same time, provincial governments were also responding to public demand by writing their own new environmental statutes.

Although various authors have characterized this period as one of unilateralism and federal-provincial conflict,[20] it is noteworthy that the federal government clashed only with the four most populous provinces. The flashpoint was the federal government's Canada Water Act. While Quebec and British Columbia registered objections on constitutional grounds, Alberta and Ontario objected to the federal government's proposal to set discharge standards or fees on a watershed basis, which conflicted with the provinces' preference for uniform discharge standards. In fact, during this period there was a high degree of provincial support for a strong federal government role in setting national standards.

In an effort to restore intergovernmental harmony, the federal government and the provinces rejuvenated the existing Canadian Council of Resource Ministers, renaming it the Canadian Council of Resource and Environment Ministers (CCREM). CCREM and its contemporary successor, the Canadian Council of Ministers of the Environment (CCME), are unusual among intergovernmental councils in that the federal government, the provinces, and, more recently, the territories participate as equals, with the chair rotating annually among them. It also has an independent secretariat funded jointly by the member governments. Although the Council has no constitutional authority, it serves as the central forum for discussion, debate, and co-ordination among federal and provincial governments with respect to the environment.

By the early 1970s, public attention to the environment had subsided as quickly as it had emerged.[21] Federal and provincial governments alike faced the challenge of implementing their new environmental laws in a climate of budgetary retrenchment and public inattentiveness to environmental issues. They responded by rationalizing their activities. CCREM was instrumental in drafting bilateral federal-provincial accords, which were signed by the federal government and seven provinces in 1975. These first-generation accords established a one-window approach in which the provinces were responsible for implementing both their own and federal standards, while the federal government's role was to develop national environmental quality and discharge standards. The federal government agreed to refrain from directly enforcing its own standards as long as the provinces were doing the job.

There is no question that federal-provincial harmony was restored under these accords. However, it is more difficult to identify environmental benefits. Although provincial enforcement of federal standards was uneven at best and non-existent at worst, only rarely did the federal government intervene.[22] A similarly deferential approach was taken by the federal government in Quebec, British Columbia, and Newfoundland, the three provinces that did not sign bilateral accords. Over time, the federal government even withdrew from its national standard-setting function, issuing no new discharge standards for air or water between 1979 and 1992.[23]

The degree to which this dismal record of policy development and implementation is attributable to the accords is debatable, however. One can argue that the federal-provincial accords merely reflected an underlying compatibility of policy objectives: neither order of government was keen to pursue aggressive environmental regulation during this period.[24] However, the accords arguably provided a federal government looking for a way to evade politically difficult regulatory responsibilities with a convenient exit from the field. Thus, during the 1970s and early 1980s the provinces once again became the lead players in the environmental field, with the federal government playing a supporting role of providing research and ambient environmental monitoring.[25]

Intergovernmental tensions did not re-emerge until the federal government reasserted a unilateral role in the environmental field with the passage of the Canadian Environmental Protection Act (CEPA) in 1988. With concern for the environment rising in public opinion polls, CEPA represented a significant departure from past federal environmental policy by promising unilateral federal standard-setting and enforcement. As the federal Environment Minister at the time, Tom McMillan, boldly stated, 'we do have authority and the federal government intends to exercise it. We do not intend to do it by committee.'[26] Provincial opposition was led by Quebec, Ontario, Alberta, and British Columbia, the same four provinces that had opposed the Canada Water Act 20 years earlier. Although the federal government responded to provincial objections by authorizing federal regulations to be waived if a province establishes equivalent regulations of its own, it attached stringent conditions to doing so in order to promote consistency with national standards.

Intergovernmental tensions were further exacerbated by the federal government's development of its Green Plan, a high-profile spending program launched at the peak of this second wave of public interest in the environment. Although provincial governments feared a 'power grab' by the federal government, they were generally reassured when the resulting Green Plan was primarily a spending (as opposed to regulatory) document.[27] Disagreements over CEPA and the Green Plan paled in comparison to those that emerged concerning environmental assessment, however. In 1989, environmentalists successfully sued the federal government, forcing it to perform an environmental assessment of the Rafferty-Alameda Dam project in accordance with its own Environmental Assessment and Review Process (EARP) Guidelines Order. The federal government had always considered the EARP Guidelines Order to be discretionary and, as in other areas of environmental policy, had deferred to the provinces rather than performing its own environmental impact assessments. It was thus a surprise, not least to the federal government itself, when the Federal Court ruled that Ottawa, however unintentionally, had created non-discretionary duties for itself and would thus be required to perform federal environmental assessments under conditions specified in the Guidelines Order. In the face of that decision, the federal government was forced to conduct assessments of dozens of projects it previously would have deferred to the provinces.

The Rafferty-Alameda case had profound implications for federal-provincial relationships in the environmental field. However, it is noteworthy that the ensuing conflicts were not just about which level of government could do a better job of protecting the environment. Rather, the newly assertive federal role in environmental assessment brought to the fore a potential tension between a strong federal role in protecting the environment and the provinces' role in promoting economic development through exploitation of their natural resources. As one provincial official explained in the wake of the Court decisions, 'The bottom line here is not environmental protection, it's economic development.'[28]

Intergovernmental tensions were exacerbated by the fact that the federal and provincial environment ministers could no longer retreat behind the closed doors of the CCME to resolve their differences. In granting citizens enforceable claims to federal actions, the courts had effectively empowered private litigants to drive a wedge between federal and provincial governments. As one provincial official bitterly complained at the time, 'as it now stands, it's no longer a matter between us and them. It's up to third parties who walk in off the street and demand an environmental assessment.'[29]

When the federal government proposed the Canadian Environmental Assessment Act to replace the EARP Guidelines Order, the new statute drew unanimous opposition from the provinces. In drafting the Act, the federal government sought to regain control of its agenda from the courts by specifying the conditions under which environmental reviews would be required. However, in the face of unprecedented public concern for the environment, it did not retreat from its new-found role in the environmental assessment field. Amendments proposed by the provinces that would have restricted the scope and frequency of federal environmental reviews within provincial borders were rebuffed by both cabinet and the House of Commons committee considering the bill, which passed in 1992.

In the environmental field, this second period of heightened public concern thus saw unilateral legislative and, in some cases, regulatory activity, which gave rise to considerable federal-provincial conflict. By the early 1990s, however, public attention had again subsided and the federal and provincial governments were seeking to repair relations. Efforts to restore harmony proceeded in two stages.[30] In the first, the intergovernmental council, which had atrophied since the mid-1970s, was revitalized and renamed the Canadian Council of Ministers of the Environment. The CCME initially sought to promote federal-provincial collaboration as an alternative to unilateralism. In 1990, the ministers signed a multilateral agreement to co-operate, the 'Statement on Interjurisdictional Cooperation', which was followed in 1991 by a statement of environmental assessment principles.[31]

CCME documents of this period invariably emphasized 'partnership', the assumption being that both federal and provincial governments would continue to be involved in the field and that they should thus work together to promote consistency. It is significant that the impetus for collaboration came from the provinces, in particular those provinces most sensitive to federal 'intrusion' with respect to provincial natural resources. In the wake of the Supreme Court's *Crown Zellerbach* decision (discussed by Valiante in Chapter 1), in which the Court for the first time found federal environmental authority under the 'Peace, Order and Good Government' power, these provinces reverted to a second-best strategy of preventing federal unilateralism by immobilizing the federal government with consultations. As one of the architects of the Statement on Interjurisdictional Cooperation explained, 'if some guy moves into your basement and you can't evict him, you at least try to keep him in the basement.'[32]

In contrast, in the second stage of efforts to restore intergovernmental harmony, the CCME increasingly emphasized rationalization rather than collaboration. In 1993, at a time when both federal and provincial environment ministers were confronting deep cuts to their budgets, waning public attention to the environment, and pressure from investors anxious about the prospect of overlapping federal and provincial requirements, the CCME launched a 'harmonization initiative' with the goal of eliminating overlap and duplication. Interestingly, the impetus for this initiative came from the federal government.[33] It would seem that the unwelcome tenant was ready to move out voluntarily, and the provinces were quite happy to reclaim their basements.

In November 1995, a draft Environmental Management Framework Agreement (EMFA) and 10 accompanying schedules concerning different aspects of environmental policy (e.g., environmental assessment, environmental quality monitoring, regulatory enforcement) were released for public comment.[34] In many respects, the EMFA echoed the bilateral accords of the 1970s in promoting one-window delivery of environmental programs. As in the 1970s, it envisioned that the provinces would take the lead in implementing both their own and national standards, with the federal government taking the lead on federal lands and in matters concerning international boundaries. However, the EMFA also envisioned more far-reaching changes than the first-generation accords of the 1970s. The draft agreement proposed 'national' discharge standards developed jointly by federal and provincial governments as an alternative to 'federal' standards, thus redefining the federal government's role from one of primary responsibility for setting national standards to mere participation as one of 13 governments seeking consensus on national standards.

The EMFA was shelved after a national consultation workshop in January 1996 revealed strong opposition from both environmentalists and First Nations.[35] However, when the environment continued to emerge as an irritant in discussions among first ministers, the Prime Minister's Office directed Environment Canada to resume negotiations with a goal of delivering results by the end of the year. The fast-track approach was successful, yielding approval in principle of the Canada-Wide Accord on Environmental Harmonization at the November 1996 CCME meeting.

Opposition to the EMFA simply shifted to the Accord. Over 90 environmental groups issued a joint statement urging the federal government to reject the Accord, depicting it as an 'abandonment of the federal role' in environmental protection.[36] Opponents raised the spectre of national standards set at the lowest common denominator, a race to the bottom among the provinces given discretion to implement those standards, and transformation of the CCME into a new but unaccountable third order of government. (It is illustrative of the differences between the CCME and a democratically accountable government that a CCME official interviewed for this chapter declined to release information on the CCME's budget on the grounds that 'CCME is a non-profit corporation under law, so its financial affairs are its own.'[37]) Supporters of the Accord in turn emphasized the benefits of promoting consistency of standards and approaches between the provinces and federal government, cost savings from elimination of duplication, and opportunities to identify and fill gaps by working together.

The debate drew to a head before the January 1998 CCME meeting, at which the ministers planned to formally sign the Accord and sub-agreements setting out the respective roles and responsibilities of each level of government in the areas of monitoring, setting standards, and environmental assessment. Even the House of Commons Standing Committee on the Environment and Sustainable Development issued a report in December 1997 calling on the federal cabinet to delay signing the Accord until consultations could be pursued with Aboriginal peoples and further studies on the extent of gaps, overlap, and duplication could be done.[38] Opponents of the Accord found some support within the federal cabinet, which reconsidered its support for the Canada-Wide Accord in the final days leading to the January 1998 CCME meeting. However, despite these last-minute machinations, the federal government elected to maintain its course, joining nine provinces and the two territories in signing the Accord and sub-agreements. The new Nunavut territorial government subsequently signed on to the Accord in June 2000. Quebec alone has declined to sign the Accord in the absence of additional reassurance of the federal government's commitment to avoiding overlap in the form of amendments to federal environmental legislation.

The basic premise of the Canada-Wide Accord remains the same as that of the EMFA: rationalized implementation of standards developed through federal-provincial consensus, though those standards are now referred to as 'Canada-wide' rather than 'national'. However, the Accord reflects a strategy of more modest scope (at least initially) and greater flexibility than the EMFA. Rather than seeking consensus at the outset on a massive package of 11 schedules, a strategy that sank the EMFA, the ministers chose to proceed incrementally with a plan to build on the first three sub-agreements over a number of years. Moreover, in place of the EMFA plan to redefine federal and provincial roles once and for all, with the same roles for all provinces, there is an acknowledgement that a different division of federal and provincial/territorial responsibilities may be needed for different environmental problems or in different jurisdictions. The sub-agreement on standards, for example, envisions that individual governments will develop implementation plans for particular Canada-wide standards and that those plans need not be uniform across jurisdictions. The sub-agreements make it clear that the provinces will take the lead in most circumstances.[39] In response to criticisms about accountability, federal and provincial governments stress that no jurisdiction could be compelled to sign on to any Canada-wide standard; each government retains its full constitutional and legal authority to act unilaterally should it choose to do so.

Another important difference from the 1970s accords and the aborted EMFA was a subtle change in the definition of standards. The standards sub-agreement states that the primary focus will be on developing uniform Canada-wide standards for ambient environmental quality, rather than discharge or product quality standards. The distinction is not merely semantic. In light of different concentration of sources and varying dispersion patterns in different regions, consistent *environmental quality* standards might be expected to yield inconsistent *discharge* standards in different provinces. In any case, there is no expectation that a 'lead government' would have to develop enforceable discharge standards at all, since the sub-agreement guarantees each jurisdiction complete flexibility to adopt the approach it considers most appropriate to achieve a shared environmental quality goal, including voluntary programs. This reduced emphasis on uniform discharge regulations represents a significant departure from federal and provincial governments' historical emphasis on national discharge standards as a means to prevent 'races to the bottom'.

This brief overview of over three decades of policy development indicates that the intergovernmental pendulum has completed two full cycles between conflict and co-operation. Federal and provincial governments have moved from unilateralism in the late 1960s, to rationalization between the early 1970s and late 1980s, to unilateralism again in the late 1980s, followed by collaboration and, most recently, renewed rationalization. Intergovernmental conflicts have been most common, not coincidentally, during the two periods of unilateralism. Co-operation has tended to prevail during periods of joint decision-making and rationalization. However, it seems less likely that this is because collaboration and rationalization promote intergovernmental co-operation than that they are products of a prior will among federal and provincial governments to co-operate.

An obvious question is how one can account for this high degree of variation over time since the advantages and disadvantages of the three models for intergovernmental relations have not changed. The foregoing discussion places considerable emphasis on cyclical trends in public attention to environmental issues over recent decades, which I have argued elsewhere has a profound effect on the balance of federal and provincial roles and on the nature of federal-provincial relations with respect to the environment.[40] The environment has risen to the top of the polls twice in recent memory, and it was during these two periods, in the late 1960s and late 1980s, that Canadian governments have been most inclined to interpret their jurisdiction broadly and to assert it unilaterally. However, when public attention has moved on to other issues, federal and provincial governments have had fewer incentives to seek political credit by pursuing aggressive environmental protection measures. Although the public may still react favourably to environmental initiatives during such periods, a government's performance on environmental issues is unlikely to be foremost in voters' minds when they enter ballot booths preoccupied by other concerns. On the other hand, opponents of strong environmental measures—including regulated industries that stand to pay the price for a cleaner environment—do not let down their guard even during lulls in attention to the environment by the broader public. Thus, as public attention to the environment waxes and wanes, so, too, do the political incentives for unilateralism.

This shift in political incentives can have quite different implications for federal and provincial governments. During lulls in public attention to the environment, the federal government might be expected to retreat by deferring to the provinces, effectively 'passing the buck' for the politically difficult task of protecting the environment. The provinces, on the other hand, while not necessarily any more eager to pursue strong environmental policies, tend to be keen to maintain their environmental authority, since it is the flip side of their authority to develop Crown resources. As a result, during periods of lower salience of environmental issues one can anticipate greater federal-provincial co-operation as well as devolution of at least some federal responsibilities to the provinces. The implication of this is that the reasons for the shifting balance of federal and provincial roles and for adoption of different intergovernmental arrangements over time may owe less to theoretical debates about the strengths and weaknesses of alternative federal-provincial models than to shifting political winds, all the more reason to scrutinize carefully the efficacy of federal-provincial agreements.

The Canada-Wide Standard-Setting Process

In signing the Canada-Wide Accord in 1998, the federal, provincial, and territorial environment ministers directed their officials to begin developing national standards for six priority substances, to negotiate four more sub-agreements, and to devise annexes to the Accord concerning public participation and Aboriginal involvement.[41] A public participation annex was subsequently approved by the CCME in September 1998. At the same meeting, the ministers met for the first time with Aboriginal leaders and agreed to work together to develop principles for Aboriginal involvement in CCME processes. In June 2000 the ministers accepted in principle the wording of a new sub-agreement that added enforcement to the existing inspections sub-agreement.

In the three years since the Accord was signed, however, most of the activity within the CCME has concerned development of Canada-wide standards.[42] The standards sub-agreement also warrants careful scrutiny since it is the feature of the Accord that could have the most dramatic implications for national environmental policy-making in Canada. As noted above, the sub-agreement envisions collaboration in setting 'Canada-wide' (as opposed to 'federal') standards, followed by rationalized implementation of those standards. The lead government, normally expected to be the province or territory, is to be given discretion in determining how it will achieve an agreed-upon Canada-wide standard. As foreseen by the inspections and enforcement sub-agreement, that lead government will also take primary responsibility for enforcement of any regulatory standards.

A two-year review of the Canada-Wide Accord conducted by the CCME in June 2000 concluded: 'There is general recognition that the two years since the Accord was signed have led to progress in agreements among jurisdictions, but little impact on the environment.'[43] That is not surprising given the relatively short time frame since the Accord was signed. There has, however, been sufficient progress in standards development to draw some preliminary conclusions about the nature and direction of the Canada-wide standards process.

At the June 2000 meeting of the Council, ministers from all jurisdictions but Quebec ratified the first Canada-wide standards concerning ambient particulate matter (PM) and ground-level ozone, mercury from incinerators and metal smelting, and benzene from various sources.[44] At the same time, several other standards were accepted in principle, with the expectation that they will be ratified at the next CCME meeting.[45] This is an impressive record of achievement in less than three years, given that it takes most jurisdictions several years to develop new standards. Two caveats are in order, however. First, the rapid progress in developing the first few Canada-wide standards to a large degree reflects the ability of the CCME development committees to piggyback on policy development initiatives already undertaken by individual jurisdictions, particularly the federal government.[46] Indeed, progress in developing Canada-wide standards in many respects reflects a transfer of federal programs to the CCME. Second, it should be noted that adoption of a Canada-wide standard by the CCME is typically several steps removed from voluntary programs or regulations being adopted by individual jurisdictions. This is especially true with respect to ambient standards, such as the PM/ozone standard, which demand that the responsible jurisdiction devise a package of control measures to achieve the standard. However, as discussed below with respect to the dioxin/furan case, considerable policy development work can remain even when consistent national discharge standards are proposed.

It is worth noting, particularly in light of long-standing criticisms of federal-provincial bodies for excluding the public, that the CCME has undertaken extensive consultations in support of each of these new Canada-wide standards. In the three years since the Accord was signed, the CCME has sponsored 22 national stakeholder consultations.[47] It remains the case, however, that deliberations of the committees in which decisions are actually made, including the Council itself, are private. (This is also true, of course, in regard to cabinet decision-making within individual jurisdictions.)

Closer examination of the standards produced thus far by the dioxins and furans development committee yields further insight. Thus far, the committee has developed Canada-wide standards for two of six source sectors identified as a priority—incineration and pulp mill boilers, which together account for 25 per cent of atmospheric releases nationally. The proposed standards will result in a reduction of dioxin and furan releases of roughly 75 per cent from these two sectors. In both cases, the CCME committee set standards for emissions from the stack to be achieved by 2006.[48]

Recalling that the standards sub-agreement combines collaborative standard-setting with rationalized implementation of standards, it is useful to consider how each of these stages of the process fares relative to the theoretical strengths and weaknesses of the collaboration and rationalization models discussed previously. Proponents of collaboration emphasize the advantages of consistency, which can yield important cost savings to the private sector in the case of federal-provincial overlap and prevent an interprovincial race to the bottom in the absence of federal government involvement. Detractors, on the other hand, speculate about potential delays in decision-making and standards set at the lowest common denominator. The consensual standards set thus far do promise a high level of consistency Canada-wide, though it is difficult to assess what degree of duplication and thus what costs would have emerged in the absence of the Accord. It is noteworthy that the committee has promoted consistent *discharge* standards, rather than ambient standards that could have led to inconsistent discharge standards. In fact, the same approach has been taken for most of the standards ratified or accepted in principle to date, despite the emphasis of the standards sub-agreement on ambient standards.

It is difficult to assess whether standards were set at the lowest common denominator, since deliberations of the federal-provincial committee that developed and the Council of Ministers that approved the standards are confidential. On the one hand, the proposed standards will require very real investments from the affected sectors and will result in significant reductions of dioxin and furan releases. On the other hand, the proposed standards will not achieve 'virtual elimination', which is ostensibly the CCME's objective for persistent and bioaccumulative toxicants, including dioxins and furans. The proposed standards are, in fact, quite traditional end-of-pipe standards based on the demonstrated performance of affordable control technologies.

With respect to the question of lowest-common-denominator standards, it is relevant that when the committee began its work, dioxins and furans had already been scheduled for virtual elimination under the federal Toxic Substances Management Policy, an objective that was subsequently incorporated in the Canadian Environmental Protection Act when it was revised in 1999. This credible threat of unilateral federal action had important implications for federal-provincial negotiation of Canada-wide standards. As noted above, the argument that a joint decision trap will yield a decision at the lowest common denominator rests on the assumption that the status quo will prevail in the absence of consensus. In the dioxin case, however, it was widely accepted that the status quo would not prevail in the absence of a federal-provincial agreement. The very real threat of federal unilateralism thus was an important factor in moving some provinces towards acceptance of the proposed standards.[49] Would-be laggards were more reluctant to block consensus, given the explicit threat of the federal stick.

Despite this, it is noteworthy that the negotiation process, while not pulling all jurisdictions down to the lowest common denominator, has done little thus far to pull up the most recalcitrant province. The incineration sector, to which one of the two Canada-wide dioxins standards developed thus far applies, conveniently excludes municipal waste incinerators in Newfoundland. Given the difficulty of establishing landfills on 'the rock', local communities in Newfoundland have long relied on conical waste combusters. These low-tech incinerators contribute roughly 40 per cent of national releases of dioxins to the air, and those releases are concentrated in a small province, thus exacerbating potential health risks. Yet despite pressure from other governments for Newfoundland to match their own efforts, the Newfoundland government thus far has offered only a commitment to '*review* the use of conical waste combusters' and to '*consider* a phase-out strategy'.[50]

With respect to rationalization of implementation, advocates stress the cost savings associated with eliminating duplication. Critics, on the other hand, fear a loss of accountability and anticipate a patchwork of standards at best and a race to the bottom at worst. There is no question that the Canada-wide standards developed for dioxins and furans thus far greatly reduce the prospects of overlapping federal and provincial standards. As anticipated, they do so by delegating the lead role in implementing agreed-upon national standards to the provinces. It is noteworthy that the standards developed include numerical standards, deadlines for compliance, and public reporting commitments for individual jurisdictions, none of which were included in the first-generation accords.

The flexibility with which individual provinces can fulfil their implementation obligations is cause for concern, however. In the 'initial set of actions' document that accompanied the draft dioxin standards, few provinces were specific as to whether they would pursue regulatory or voluntary control measures. Indeed, most provinces were surprisingly noncommittal with respect to their compliance strategies for these agreed-upon Canada-wide standards, offering only to 'develop implementation plans' (Canada), 'review options for implementation' (Manitoba), make 'determined efforts' (Northwest Territories), and 'endeavour to form partnerships with the affected facilities' (Saskatchewan).[51] This is particularly troubling in light of the widespread failure of provinces to adhere to national standards they had committed to implement under the accords of the 1970s.[52] Moreover, as critics and legal analysts of the Accord alike have emphasized, provincial governments are in any case not legally bound to uphold Canada-wide standards that they commit to under the sub-agreement.[53]

With respect to accountability, it is striking that the CCME has offered no consistent philosophy for setting Canada-wide standards. The CCME promises only that some combination of health and environmental risks, technological feasibility, and socio-economic costs of control will be considered in setting Canada-wide standards. Indeed, the CCME acknowledges that the manner in which these factors are weighed will vary from standard to standard.[54] In the absence of either more explicit principles for standard-setting or more complete explanation of the basis for particular standards, it will be difficult for Canadians to hold the CCME or any of its member governments accountable for the Canada-wide standards they set. To be fair, though, the discretionary enabling statutes historically adopted by Canadian parliamentary governments also typically decline to offer a principled basis for standard-setting.

In summary, the first dioxin and furan Canada-wide standards have achieved a high level of interjurisdictional consistency with respect to numeric standards and also promise to eliminate duplication with respect to implementation. However, little progress has been made to date with respect to the sector that contributes the largest proportion of dioxin releases to air, conical waste burners in Newfoundland, largely because the Canada-wide standard-setting process emphasizes discretion at the provincial level. Moreover, the quite general commitments offered by most provinces thus far raise questions about how consistently those numeric standards will be implemented in practice.

It is, of course, possible that the CCME's experience with dioxins and furans is unrepresentative of other current or future priorities for Canada-wide standards. Criticism of the PM/ozone standard is discussed by VanNijnatten and Lambright in Chapter 13. The CCME's two-year review of the Canada-Wide Accord also reports a consensus among stakeholders that 'the current and anticipated results from the [PM/ozone] initiative will not meet the objectives of the initiative or the Accord.' Federal and provincial ministers accepted in principle both numeric particulate matter and ozone standards and a deadline of 2015 at their fall 1999 meeting. Both federal and provincial officials interviewed used the phrase 'lowest common denominator' in referring to these proposed standards, which is consistent with the fact that 2015 was the latest possible deadline discussed in materials prepared for public consultations on the PM/ozone standard. However, before the Canada-wide standard could be ratified in June 2000, the federal minister launched a campaign to tighten the deadline to 2010. Although he encountered stiff resistance from Ontario, the minister was ultimately successful in convincing his provincial colleagues and achieving the requisite consensus on the earlier deadline. However, one wonders what would have happened had contamination of drinking water in Walkerton, Ontario, not put the environment back on the front pages immediately before that June 2000 CCME meeting.

In contrast to PM/ozone, federal and provincial officials interviewed consider the dioxin and furan standards a success story. The CCME committees and the ministers themselves may have been more willing to pay a price to reduce dioxin and furan discharges in light of the high level of public concern historically associated with dioxins. Moreover, as noted above, the fact that the dioxin standard-setting exercise was played out against a backdrop of a federal commitment to virtual elimination may have created greater upward pressure on provincial negotiators than will be the case for other Canada-wide standards. Finally, the fact that the dioxin committee was not established until January 1999, after most other development committees were already up and running, meant that they were able to benefit from their colleagues' experience.[55]

Conclusion

Over the past three-and-a-half decades, there have been two distinct periods of intergovernmental conflict concerning the environment. In the late 1960s and again in the late 1980s, federal and provincial governments both undertook extensive policy reforms in response to heightened public concern for the environment, and in so doing occasionally stepped on each other's toes. They soon restored harmony, however, through collaboration and rationalization of their activities. Federal-provincial co-operation thus prevailed over most of this period.

While intergovernmental harmony is often presented as an unqualified good, it is by no means clear that such co-operation has contributed to stronger environmental protection and conservation in Canada. One can argue that the first generation of accords merely provided the federal government with a credible justification to withdraw from the field while allowing provincial governments, protective of their authority to manage natural resources, to reclaim their lead role in the environmental field. Neither order of government lived up to its environmental commitments in the 1970s and early 1980s. While it is likely that the first-generation accords did allow the federal government to save money by reducing its environmental activities (or by not increasing them to the degree that would have been required to enforce its own standards), the obvious question is: 'at what cost to the environment?'

It is tempting, particularly in a chapter on intergovernmental relations, to attribute this environmental policy failure to federal-provincial arrangements. However, while it is true that federal and provincial governments are more inclined to question the environmental impacts of each other's activities during periods of unilateralism, to a large degree this reflects the fact that unilateralism prevails when environmental protection is a higher priority for both federal and provincial governments. Similarly, federal and provincial governments are more inclined to work out co-operative arrangements when they are under the least public scrutiny and have committed the fewest resources to their environmental programs. Intergovernmental arrangements are thus but one factor, and arguably not even the most important one, influencing the efficacy of environmental programs. However, the environmental policy failure that occurred under the regime of the 1970s accords does reveal that intergovernmentalism is by no means a panacea; federal-provincial accords and sub-agreements are no substitute for political will.

Past experience thus provides cause for concern regarding the direction federal and provincial governments have taken under the Canada-Wide Accord on Environmental Harmonization. Rationalized implementation of national standards failed quite miserably last time. And there are preliminary indications that some provincial governments are less than enthusiastic with respect to implementing

Canada-wide standards this time around. Moreover, although federal and provincial governments have not formally pursued consensus standards as an alternative to federal standards before, the dynamics of informal federal-provincial negotiations concerning federal standards in the past suggest that there is a tendency to defer to the weakest provinces.[56] Recent experience in setting Canada-wide standards for dioxins/furans and PM/ozone confirms this pressure towards the lowest common denominator, though that was overcome in the dioxins case by isolating the laggard province (unfortunately, the one facing the greatest environmental risks), and in the ozone case through a combination of federal leadership and the timing of an environmental tragedy.

Some potentially important differences between the new Canada-Wide Accord and the first generation of accords are already evident, however. First, federal environmental statutes since the late 1980s have become more specific with respect to duties, deadlines, and mechanisms for citizen participation (though they are still far more discretionary than comparable US statutes). It will thus be more difficult for the federal government to retreat should it be inclined to do so. Second, the CCME has learned valuable lessons since the 1970s, and has attached firm deadlines and detailed reporting requirements to its intergovernmental standards. As a result, it will be easier for federal and provincial governments to hold each other accountable for their commitments. Third, the CCME has made a concerted effort to provide opportunities for public input to its deliberations in recent years. Environmental groups with both a place at the table and access to individual jurisdictions' reports to the public will be in a much stronger position to hold both orders of government to account should their commitment to Canada-wide standards wane in the future. Fourth, some key industrial sectors in recent years have become more receptive to, and in some cases even demanding of, credible national standards in order to protect their reputations with environmentally conscious consumers in international markets. These sectors thus may join with environmentalists in pressing for consistent application of national standards. Fifth, newly created environmental watchdogs at both the federal and provincial levels, including the federal Commissioner for Sustainable Development, have emerged as high-profile internal critics when governments do not deliver on their commitments. And finally, the events in Walkerton in the spring and summer of 2000 are a tragic reminder that public attention to the environment can quickly reignite, placing sudden demands on federal and provincial politicians alike. One can only hope that other mechanisms of accountability will work well enough to prevent such tragedies in the future.

Notes

1 Ross Howard and David Roberts, 'De Cotret Denies Making Deal with Saskatchewan on Dams', *Globe and Mail*, 13 Oct. 1990, A1; David Roberts, 'Minister "Didn't Care" if Dam Panel Quit', *Globe and Mail*, 2 Nov. 1990, A1.

2 Jerry L. Mashaw and Susan Rose-Ackerman, 'Federalism and Regulation', in George C. Eads and Michael Fix, eds, *The Reagan Regulatory Strategy* (Washington: Urban Institute Press, 1984), 118.

3 Kathryn Harrison, 'The Regulators' Dilemma: Regulation of Pulp Mill Effluents in the Canadian Federal State', *Canadian Journal of Political Science* 29, 3 (1996): 469–96.

4 Richard B. Stewart, 'Pyramids of Sacrifice? Problems of Federalism in Mandating State Implementation of National Environmental Policy', *Yale Law Journal* 86 (1977): 1196–272.

5 Larry Pratt and John Richards, *Prairie Capitalism: Power and Influence in the New West* (Toronto: McClelland & Stewart, 1979); Jeremy Wilson, 'Wilderness Politics in B.C.: The Business Dominated State and the Containment of Environmentalism', in W.D. Coleman and G. Skogstad, eds, *Policy Communities in Canada: A Structural Approach* (Mississauga, Ont.: Copp Clark Pitman, 1990), 141–69; S. Holtz, 'The Public Interest Perspective', in D. Tingley, ed., *Environmental Protection and the Canadian Constitution: Proceedings of the Canadian Symposium on Jurisdiction and Responsibility for the Environment* (Edmonton: Environmental Law Centre, 1987).

6 World Trade Organization, *Trade and Environment*, Special Studies 4 (Geneva: WTO, 1999).

7 Arik Levinson, 'The Missing Pollution Haven Effect: Examining Some Common Explanations', *Environmental and Resource Economics* 15, 4 (2000): 343–64. Others counter that the threat of capital flight may have greater resonance with regulators in jurisdictions desperate for jobs, in industries with higher pollution control costs, or with respect to failing individual facilities. Thus, evidence exists of regulatory reluctance (if not downward competition) in provinces with single-industry towns and marginally competitive older factories. See Harrison, 'The Regulators' Dilemma'.

8 A related argument is that decentralized policy-making better satisfies voters since citizens have the option of 'voting with their feet' by moving to a jurisdiction offering a package of policies more consistent with their preferences. See C.M. Tiebout, 'A Pure Theory of Local Expenditures', *Journal of Political Economy* 64 (1956): 416–24.

9 With respect to strategic use of this argument by provincial governments, see Kathryn Harrison, *Passing the Buck: Federalism and Canadian Environmental Policy* (Vancouver: University of British Columbia Press, 1996), 137–8.

10 P.E. Trudeau, 'The Practice and Theory of Federalism', in Michael Oliver, ed., *Social Purpose for Canada* (Toronto: University of Toronto Press, 1961). An oft-cited example of this argument is former United States Supreme Court Justice Louis Brandeis's reference to the states as 'little laboratories of democracy'.

11 Kathryn Harrison, 'Intergovernmental Relations and Environmental Policy: Concepts and Context', in Patrick C. Fafard and Kathryn Harrison, eds, *Managing the Environmental Union: Intergovernmental Relations and Environmental Policy in Canada* (Kingston: Institute of Intergovernmental Relations, Queen's University and Saskatchewan Institute of Public Policy, 2000), 3–19.

12 Peter Nemetz, 'The Fisheries Act and Federal-Provincial Environmental Regulation: Duplication or Complementary', *Canadian Public Administration* 29 (1986): 401–24; Kernaghan Webb, 'Gorillas in Closets? Federal-Provincial *Fisheries Act* Pollution Control Enforcement', in Fafard and Harrison, eds, *Managing the Environmental Union*, 163–203.

13 Albert Breton, 'Supplementary Statement', *Report of the Royal Commission on the Economic Union and Development Prospects for Canada*, vol. 3 (Ottawa: Minister of Supply and Services Canada, 1985), 493.

14 The history of federal-provincial conflicts concerning the Rafferty-Alameda Dam, the Al-Pac pulp mill, and Hydro-Québec's proposed Great Whale project are reviewed in Harrison, *Passing the Buck*, ch. 6.

15 That governments typically insist on consensus in joint decision-making is not surpris-

ing if one considers that they have little incentive to enter voluntarily into collaborative arrangements that authorize other governments to impose decisions on them without their consent.

16 Fritz Scharpf, 'The Joint-Decision Trap: Lessons from West German Federalism and European Integration', *Public Administration* 66 (1988): 239–78.

17 K.L. Clark and M.S. Winfield, *The Environmental Management Framework Agreement— A Model for Dysfunctional Federalism? An Analysis and Commentary*, Brief 96/1 (Toronto: Canadian Institute for Environmental Law and Policy, 1996).

18 Harrison, *Passing the Buck*, 125; Patrick C. Fafard, 'Groups, Governments and the Environment: Some Evidence from the Harmonization Initiative', in Fafard and Harrison, eds, *Managing the Environmental Union*, 81–101.

19 Harrison, *Passing the Buck*, 64, 95–6.

20 James W. Parlour, 'The Politics of Water Pollution Control: A Case Study of the Formation of the Canada Water Act, Part I: Comprehensive Water Resource Management', *Journal of Environmental Management* 12 (1981): 31–64; O.P. Dwivedi and R. Brian Woodrow, 'Environmental Policy-Making and Administration in Federal States: The Impact of Overlapping Jurisdiction in Canada', in William M. Chandler and Christian W. Zollner, eds, *Challenges to Federalism: Policy-Making in Canada and the Federal Republic of Germany* (Kingston: Institute of Intergovernmental Relations, Queen's University, 1989).

21 Trends in public opinion from 1968 to 1996 are discussed in Harrison, *Passing the Buck*, chs 4–6.

22 Lynne B. Huestis, 'Policing Pollution: The Prosecution of Environmental Offenses', working paper, Law Reform Commission of Canada, Sept. 1984; David Estrin, 'Mirror Legislation', in Tingley, ed., *Environmental Protection and the Canadian Constitution*; Harrison, *Passing the Buck*, 106.

23 Harrison, *Passing the Buck*, 101–2.

24 Grace Skogstad and Paul Kopas, 'Environmental Policy in a Federal System: Ottawa and the Provinces', in Robert Boardman, ed., *Canadian Environmental Policy: Ecosystems, Politics, and Process* (Toronto: Oxford University Press, 1992), 43–59.

25 A.R. Thompson, *Environmental Regulation in Canada: An Assessment of the Regulatory Process* (Vancouver: Westwater Research Centre, 1980).

26 House of Commons, *Minutes of Proceedings and Evidence of the Legislative Committee on Bill C-75*, 3 Feb. 1988, 14:18.

27 George Hoberg and Kathryn Harrison, 'It's Not Easy Being Green: The Politics of Canada's Green Plan', *Canadian Public Policy* 20 (1994): 119–37.

28 Confidential interview.

29 Confidential interview.

30 Kathryn Harrison, 'Prospects for Intergovernmental Harmonization in Environmental Policy', in D.M. Brown and J. Heibert, eds, *Canada: The State of the Federation, 1994* (Kingston: Institute of Intergovernmental Relations, Queen's University, 1994).

31 Canadian Council of Ministers of the Environment (CCME), 'Statement of Interjurisdictional Cooperation on Environmental Matters', Mar. 1990; CCME, 'Cooperative Principles for Environmental Assessment', May 1991.

32 Confidential interview.

33 Harrison, 'Prospects for Intergovernmental Harmonization'.

34 The EMFA was accompanied by 10 schedules, concerning education, standards, legislation, policy, emergency response, research, inspection, enforcement, international negotiations, and state of environment reporting. An eleventh schedule, on environmental assessment, which had been a source of contention between the federal government

and the provinces, was never released.

35 The business community, though generally supportive, was less engaged than opponents of the EMFA. See Fafard, 'Groups, Governments and the Environment'.

36 Martin Mittelstaedt, 'Pollution foes attack federal plan', *Globe and Mail*, 20 Nov. 1996, A8.

37 Confidential interview.

38 House of Commons Standing Committee on Environment and Sustainable Development, 'Harmonization and Environmental Protection: An Analysis of the Harmonization Initiative of the Canadian Council of Ministers of the Environment', Dec. 1997.

39 Sections 6.8 and 6.9 of the standards sub-agreement set out the main functions of federal and provincial/territorial governments. The primary roles of the federal government include providing scientific and technical support, implementing agreed-upon measures at international borders and on federal lands, and implementing standards for products traded in interprovincial or international commerce. The provinces are assigned responsibility for requiring action from industry and other sectors contributing to environmental problems within their borders. The draft inspection and enforcement sub-agreement, which the CCME expects to finalize in 2001, sets out a comparable division of responsibilities between the federal and provincial/territorial governments in sections 4.1.1 and 4.1.2.

40 Harrison, *Passing the Buck*.

41 The priority substances for national standards are mercury, particulate matter, benzene, dioxins and furans, petroleum hydrocarbons in soil, and ground-level ozone. Sub-agreements for enforcement, research and development, emergency response, and environmental monitoring were planned, but the CCME has subsequently elected to pursue an alternative strategy with respect to monitoring in recognition of the extensive role of the private sector in performing environmental monitoring.

42 With respect to the environmental assessment sub-agreement, several bilateral federal-provincial agreements have been concluded. However, most of these merely update previous agreements and do not represent a significant change in direction from the collaborative arrangements put in place in the mid-1990s.

43 CCME, 'Two-Year Review of Canada-Wide Accord on Environmental Harmonization', June 2000.

44 The Quebec government has indicated that it will act in a manner consistent with other jurisdictions with respect to the Canada-wide standards adopted thus far, even though it is not a signatory to the Accord and its sub-agreements. CCME, 'Record of Achievement, Council of Ministers Meeting, 5–6 June 2000', 17 Aug. 2000.

45 The standards accepted in principle concern dioxin and furan releases from medical, hazardous, and municipal waste incineration, dioxin and furan releases from pulp mill boilers, mercury from fluorescent lamps and dental wastes, and petroleum hydrocarbons in soil. The following Canada-wide standards are still under development: mercury releases from electric power generation; dioxin and furan releases from iron and steel processing, residential wood stoves, and conical waste burners; and a second-phase standard for benzene in air.

46 For instance, the benzene standard builds on an ongoing federal 'strategic options process' for the petroleum industry under CEPA, a dioxin inventory was nearing completion by a federal-provincial committee established under CEPA before the Canada-wide standards process was launched, dioxin/furan standards for the steel industry will also benefit from a CEPA strategic options process, and the PM/ozone committee was able to piggyback on earlier federal, provincial, and CCME initiatives with respect to ozone.

47 CCME, 'CCME Consultation Calendar', http://www.mbnet.bc.ca/ccme/. Accessed 29 Aug. 2000. This figure excludes consultations with technical advisory bodies, as well as conference calls by advisory groups established by individual standards development committees. There are several of these groups, since the development committees for

most of the six priority Canada-wide standards have divided their work by creating sub-committees to address different sources (e.g., dioxins and furans from pulp and paper boilers, steel manufacturing, residential wood stoves, etc.). Many of these subcommittees have established their own stakeholder advisory bodies. In the dioxins/furans case, there is also a multi-stakeholder committee at the development committee level, with which the committee consults concerning the consultation process!

48 Emission standards for pulp and paper mill boilers have been set at 100 pg/m³ and 500 pg/m³ for new and existing boilers, respectively. For the incineration sector (excluding conical waste burners in Newfoundland), standards were set at 80 pg TEQ/m³ for all sources except existing sewage sludge incinerators, which were allowed up to 100 pg/m³.

49 Confidential interview.

50 Emphasis added. The dioxin/furan case is unusual in that there are two source categories confined to a single province: conical waste burners in Newfoundland and pulp and paper mill boilers in British Columbia. (Although mills in other provinces also have boilers, only in BC are logs transported by sea to the mills, thus introducing chlorine to the wood from the sea salt, which can react to form dioxins during combustion.) The contrast between the two provinces is quite striking. While Newfoundland has dragged its heels, the BC government took the lead in developing standards for air emissions from the pulp and paper sector, yielding one of the first Canada-wide standards for dioxins. The difference is understandable if one considers that the pulp and paper industry in BC is particularly sensitive to the dioxin issue, having been taken by surprise in the 1980s by both the discovery of dioxins in their mills' releases and the political furor that ensued. The industry was thus willing to work with the province and other stakeholders to develop a strategy to reduce its releases (though it did not volunteer to eliminate them entirely). In contrast, conical combusters in Newfoundland are owned and operated by municipalities, many of them impoverished. While BC residents might clamour for the privately owned mills in their communities to clean up their releases, there does not appear to be comparable pressure from Newfoundland taxpayers, who would have to pay the tab for cleanup of their own public facilities.

51 CCME, 'Canada-wide Standards for dioxins and furans, Initial Set of Actions', accepted 6 June 2000 for endorsement in Nov. 2000.

52 In the 1970s and 1980s, provincial governments often simply ignored national standards in setting permit requirements for sources within their jurisdictions. For instance, a comparison of provincial permits for the pulp and paper industry with federal regulations in five provinces (comprising 90 per cent of mills nationally) in 1987 revealed that only 40 per cent of provincial permits met federal standards. Kathryn Harrison, 'Passing the Buck', Ph.D. thesis (University of British Columbia, 1993), 376–81.

53 Alastair R. Lucas and Cheryl Sharvit, 'Underlying Constraints on Intergovernmental Cooperation in Setting and Enforcing Environment Standards', in Fafard and Harrison, eds, *Managing the Environmental Union*.

54 CCME, 'Canada-wide Standards—Overview', June 2000.

55 In particular, committee members concluded that if consensus is sought too soon, at the level of the technical committee, the resulting standards tend to be weaker; they have found senior officials and their ministers more willing to make sacrifices in pursuit of broader objectives.

56 Harrison, 'The Regulators' Dilemma'.

Chapter 8

The Bumpy Journey Ahead: Provincial Environmental Policies and National Environmental Standards

Debora L. VanNijnatten

Even as this chapter is being written, the provinces and the federal government are busily formulating national standards under the auspices of the Canadian Council of Ministers of the Environment (CCME) and within the framework of the 1998 Canada-Wide Accord on Environmental Harmonization. As Harrison notes in the preceding chapter, the current period is one of relative harmony in federal-provincial relations, as governments go about the business of 'rationalizing' their respective roles and responsibilities in terms of environmental protection in Canada. Harrison also points out that, under the Accord's sub-agreements, the provinces will take the lead in most circumstances. Thus, the prospects for achieving nationally consistent 'Canada-wide' standards under the Accord will depend on the commitment and capacity of the provinces to pursue the goals set out in these standards.

What is *not* known at present is how great the differences among provinces actually are with regard to their approaches to environmental protection, the policies they employ to give substance to this approach, and the extent to which they are committed to following through with these policies. Do the provinces differ? What are the implications of these differences (to the extent they do exist) for realizing nationally consistent environmental policies across provinces? In other words, how difficult a task will harmonization be? A major obstacle to answering such questions is that very little comparative information on the provinces exists with regard to environmental protection policies. In contrast with the United States, where the federal government, a variety of interstate bodies, academics, and even industry associations make a practice of studying state policies comparatively, such work is rarely undertaken in Canada.

This chapter constitutes a preliminary attempt to fill this gap in our knowledge of the environmental protection regime in Canada by comparing the provinces in two broad areas: environmental policy outputs, and what is referred to here as 'commitment to implement'. The chapter sets the context by first providing an overview of recent developments in provincial environmental protection frameworks and then examines provincial policies in a representative range of areas on selected indicators: environmental assessment, air quality, solid waste management, endangered species protection, and protected areas. Although differences in provincial policies do exist, these differences could not be characterized as stark.

More significant is the finding that there are important differences in the levels of commitment to implement displayed by the provinces, as measured through a comparison of public and private expenditures on environmental protection and natural resource management, numbers of personnel associated with certain environmental protection tasks, and enforcement activities. Overall, certain western provinces show relatively high commitment levels, Ontario and Quebec show minimal commitment, and a mixed pattern exists in the Maritime provinces. This has obvious implications for the actual attainment of Canada-wide standards set collaboratively by the CCME but implemented by individual provinces.

Recent Developments in the Provinces

As a result of both constitutional mandates and political realities, Canadian provincial governments are more powerful and more independent than are, for example, American state governments in most areas of environmental protection. This is not to say that there are no significant federal laws, as pointed out by Valiante in Chapter 1. However, provincial laws provide much of the basis for environmental regulation in Canada. Tracking provincial environmental laws and regulations is a complex task. Some provinces include most environmental protection tasks under one framework Act, while others have separate statutes governing discrete environmental protection tasks. Still others mix environmental protection responsibilities under a number of laws that may not directly refer to these tasks. Moreover, many provinces have undertaken major overhauls of their environmental regimes in recent years, generally in the direction of consolidating existing environmental legislation into much larger 'omnibus' statutes. The other major developments at the provincial level have involved extensive departmental reorganizations, significant environmental budget reductions, and deregulation.

At the beginning of the 1990s Ontario was seen as being at the forefront of environmental regulation and enforcement. Indeed, in 1990, *Maclean's* bestowed on Ontario the highest mark—a 'B'—in its assessment of provincial environmental performance.[1] The runner-up was Prince Edward Island ('B-'), followed by British Columbia and Quebec ('C + '), then Manitoba, Saskatchewan, New Brunswick, and Newfoundland ('C'), and finally, Alberta ('C-') and Nova Scotia ('D'). In particular, the assessors cited Ontario's record for 'enforcing strong laws, including measures to limit acid rain', and, despite some weaknesses, its overall environmental performance was characterized as being 'ahead of other provinces'.[2]

Things appeared quite different in Canada's largest province towards the end of the decade. While the early 1990s brought New Democratic initiatives such as the Environmental Bill of Rights, the Municipal Industrial Strategy for Abatement focusing on point-source water pollution, a ban on incineration, and a focus on waste reduction, changes brought about by the Progressive Conservative government in Ontario since its election in 1995 have been far-reaching. Shortly after taking up the reins of government, the Conservatives initiated two regulatory review processes, one under the auspices of an eight-member 'Red Tape Commission' and another within the Ministry of Environment and Energy (Ministry of Environment, as of 1997).[3] The MOEE reviewed all regulations under nine environment-related statutes,[4] while the Commission made even broader recommendations to the ministry on how to reduce unnecessary regulatory barriers to economic activity. In mid-1996, the ministry released preliminary proposals for reforming 80 of Ontario's environmental and energy-related regulations, which were then revised in response to public input.[5]

As a result, major amendments were made to almost every piece of environmental and natural resources legislation. Only the Environmental Bill of Rights remained untouched.[6] Five environmental agencies were eliminated and three[7] were amalgamated into a new Environmental Appeals Tribunal. At the same time, the Environment Ministry's budget and staff were subjected to deep cuts; over the period 1994–5 to 1998–9, the ministry's operating budget was reduced by 45 per cent, with a net loss of 30 per cent of its staff.[8] This led many to question how Ontario's environmental regime could remain effective with such depleted resources. In 1996, in her annual report, Ontario's Environmental Commissioner characterized the extent and scale of change as 'daunting' and declared that many of the changes had been made without any assessment of their environmental impacts. Successive annual reports by the Commissioner, as well as by the Canadian Institute for Environmental Law and Policy, have tracked these changes in detail and together provide a critical picture of environmental regulatory change in the province.

Alberta has followed a trajectory similar to that of Ontario, although it chose this path somewhat earlier. In Alberta in the early 1990s, nine existing environmental statutes were integrated into one Act 'to provide an overall framework for environmental protection and enhancement'.[9] Only the province's Water Resources Act, historically the subject of considerable controversy, remained independent of the new omnibus legislation. The province also undertook a comprehensive review of its environmental regulatory regime in order to achieve a more streamlined and efficient regulatory process, to integrate ministry regulatory activities through a 'one-window' approval process, to minimize costs to individuals and industry, and to eliminate regulatory overlap and duplication.[10] However, many regulatory requirements for approvals were eliminated, some regulations were consolidated, and the Departments of Forestry, Lands and Wildlife, Environment, and Recreation and Parks were amalgamated. Moreover, significant budget reductions also occurred as part of the Alberta government's deficit reduction strategy; beginning in 1993, a 30 per cent budget cut was administered, with 1,500 staff to be cut by 2000.[11] The budget figures have rebounded slightly, however.

In comparison, the last decade has seen quite different developments in British Columbia. While Ontario seemed to build up its regulatory regime in the early 1990s and then put on the brakes mid-decade, British Columbia continued its expansion over this period. In 1991, the province's incumbent government released 'Environment 2001', a strategic document intended to guide a comprehensive revision of legislation relating to water and air quality, wildlife and resource management, pesticides management, and environmental assessment.[12] Indeed, British Columbia has outpaced other provinces over the last decade in terms of new, sometimes far-reaching initiatives in virtually all areas of environmental policy, including forest and natural resource management, parks and protected areas, air and water emissions, solid waste reduction, and non-point-source pollution (an especially challenging problem). The province also has been active in terms of considering alternative policy instruments, such as emissions trading regimes for greenhouse gases and 'tax shifting' towards polluting activities.[13]

Quebec has undertaken piecemeal, more minor revisions to its environmental protection regime over recent years. Policy revisions were initiated during this period with respect to underground water, soil, pesticides, atmospheric emissions, and hazardous materials. Along with all other provinces, Quebec also formulated new regulations on contaminated lands and ozone-depleting substances. In 1997, the government adopted the Regulation Respecting the Reduction of Pollution from Agricultural Sources, which replaced an earlier, narrower regulation.[14] In addition, after years of discussion, Quebec overhauled the waste management provisions in the province's Environment Quality Act to give the government more effective control over the production and elimination of waste and to place greater emphasis on waste reclamation.

Changes to the environmental protection regimes in Saskatchewan and Manitoba during the 1990s were less comprehensive than those in BC, Ontario, and Alberta. In mid-1997, Manitoba introduced a revised Sustainable Development and Consequential Amendments Act, which enshrined in law the government's commitment to sustainable development and contained many initiatives designed to realize this commitment. Several recommendations with regard to environmental assessment, resource allocation, and land-use planning have resulted from a committee set up to implement the legislation. Moreover, in late 1999 the Environment, Energy, and Natural Resources departments were consolidated to form a new Ministry of Conservation. In Saskatchewan the focus in recent years has been on the petroleum industry, specifically the management of waste oil, as well as agricultural practices and the protection of forest lands. Saskatchewan and Manitoba have also signed an accord on environmental co-operation to maximize the effectiveness of their environmental management activities.[15]

As one official in Nova Scotia put it, environmental policy in that province has been 'a constantly moving target'. As of 1993, environmental protection in the province was carried out via 16 statutes and 44 sets of regulations, all administered by the Department of Environment.[16] In 1993–4 the incumbent government undertook a comprehensive review of existing legislation, with the result that these statutes and regulations were consolidated into a single Environment Act in 1995. The new Act emphasized public involvement, monitoring and enforcement, industry and community stewardship, and the development of local environmental technologies.[17] The 1995 Act had been scheduled for review in 2000 and public input was being solicited beginning in 1999 on three aspects in particular: how better to define 'adverse' environmental effects, remediate contaminated sites, and conduct environmental assessment. However, shortly thereafter, a massive reorganization of government and its activities was initiated by the newly elected Conservative government, whose focus was on reducing the size of government, devolving services to communities, and providing 'value for money'.[18] As part of these changes, the Department of Environment currently is being merged with Labour to become the Department of Environment, Labour and Regulatory Affairs.

New Brunswick, Newfoundland, and PEI have recently undertaken reforms to their existing environmental protection regimes. New Brunswick's main environmental legislation, the Clean Environment Act, was passed in the 1970s and exhibits a number of features of that era, namely an emphasis on remedial and media-specific measures as well as minimal opportunities for public involvement.[19] New measures to improve air and water quality and new solid waste management policies were under discussion during the latter half of the 1990s, with a new Clean Air Act released during this period. At the end of 1996, New Brunswick's Department of the Environment was reorganized into four new sections (corporate service, environmental quality, regional services and enforcement, and assessment and approvals) to integrate better the environmental assessment and approval processes.[20] Newfoundland, meanwhile, initiated an overhaul of all provincial environmental legislation in 1997, with six environmental statutes consolidated into one new Environmental Protection Act. Reforms to the province's Environmental Assessment Act and new hazardous waste regulations also have been under discussion for some time. In PEI, changes to the environmental protection regime have been moderate and gradual. Drinking water quality, agricultural practices and non-point-source pollution, protection of natural areas, and waste management have figured prominently in reform initiatives. Moreover, a new Department of Fisheries, Aquaculture and Environment was created on 1 May 2000, which assumed the responsibilities of portions of the former Departments of Fisheries and Tourism, and Technology and Environment.

Perhaps not surprisingly given the budgetary climate, many provinces began to show a distinct preference beginning in the mid-1990s for voluntary or non-regulatory instruments as a way of addressing pollution concerns. In both Ontario and Alberta, regulatory reviews were conducted with a view to achieving the objectives of existing regulations through non-regulatory mechanisms wherever possible.[21] As a result, numerous tasks were transferred to the private sector. For example, in Alberta, coal and oil sands exploration no longer requires government approval, as the operator is expected to adhere voluntarily to Environmental Protection Guidelines issued by the Environment Ministry. Moreover, in the fall of 1996, codes of practice were developed to replace formal approvals for low environmental impact activities. In Ontario, self-monitoring and enforcement are now the norm in the forestry, petroleum, commercial fisheries, and aggregates industries.[22] In November 1996 the Quebec government adopted a policy whereby ministers who wanted to submit a draft regulation to cabinet must complete an 'impact study'. This study was to focus on the impact on business of the proposed regulation, conduct a cost-benefit analysis, and demonstrate that the problem addressed by the regulation could not be dealt with using non-regulatory methods.[23] While British Columbia also set up a 16-person task force during this period to make recommendations on cutting red tape and streamlining and eliminating unnecessary government legislation, processes, and regulations, this province has seemed generally more reluctant to embrace voluntary approaches.

Thus, the past decade, and especially the last five years, has been a time of great change, and often upheaval, with respect to environmental protection in the provinces. Those provinces that have undergone far-reaching changes, such as Ontario and Alberta, have moved in very similar directions. Nova Scotia, which appeared to have chosen a very different path mid-decade, may now be heading down this same road. British Columbia also has undertaken significant changes to its environmental regime, but more in the direction of expansion on a broad range of fronts with less emphasis on deregulation and voluntarism. Changes have been less comprehensive in the other Maritime provinces, Saskatchewan, and Manitoba. Given these various trajectories, how similar or different are the provinces with respect to their environmental policies and their commitment actually to implement these policies?

Provincial Environmental Policies

This section provides a selective overview of provincial policy outputs in a range of areas, which yields some initial insights into activities in the various jurisdictions. The picture that emerges is not one of radically varying standards and processes across the country. Moderate differences do exist, specifically in air quality, endangered species protection, and parks/protected areas, while the provinces appear to be more similar with regard to environmental assessment and solid waste reduction policies.

Environmental Assessment

Environmental assessment (EA) increasingly has been employed as a way of identifying, evaluating, and mitigating possible environmental impacts of new developments, and both the federal and provincial governments have responsibilities with regard to EA. Harrison notes that, in response to litigation over the Rafferty-Alameda and Oldman dams as well as proposed federal environmental assessment legislation (which became the Canadian Environmental Assessment Act in 1995), a number of the provinces revamped their own EA processes.[24] Whereas in 1985 only four provinces (New Brunswick, Quebec, Ontario, and British Columbia) had specific EA regulations,[25] all provinces now have legislated requirements. Ontario's Environmental Assessment Act was, in fact, the first legislated EA process in Canada.[26]

Provincial EA policies are relatively similar with respect to how 'adverse' or 'environmental' impacts are defined.[27] More important for comparing EA policies is the amount of discretion exercised by officials at various stages of the process. Overall, discretionary decision-making is characteristic of EA processes in all provinces, though to varying degrees. In some provinces, such as PEI, Newfoundland, and New Brunswick, decisions about the application of the EA process and the exemption of projects is largely discretionary. In New Brunswick, officials determine whether an assessment is necessary for any government-sponsored, municipal, or private project only after the proponent registers the project. Newfoundland's Environmental Assessment Act applies to 'undertakings', defined as 'an enterprise, activity, project, structure, work, policy, proposal, plan or program that may, *in the opinion of the Minister*, have a significant environmental impact'.[28]

Other provinces, such as Nova Scotia, Alberta, Ontario, and Quebec, require some projects to undergo an EA while others may be exempted. Nova Scotia regulations divide proposed projects into those that require an EA (energy-related activities, major industrial facilities, transportation corridors, and waste management projects) and those that do not (industrial facilities, mining, and highway construction projects).[29] In Alberta, pulp mills, oil refineries, and large dams are required to undergo an environmental assessment process while other projects may not. In both Alberta and Ontario, environmental assessment panels have some powers to make such decisions, although final authority rests at the ministerial level. Ontario's new Environmental Assessment and Consultation Improvement Act awards considerable discretionary power to the minister; as one observer has noted, 'The most salient feature of the EA reforms is the enhanced degree of discretion in the Minister of the Environment over whether any process need be followed and what its components will be in individual cases.'[30] In addition, Ontario is the only province whose assessment processes automatically apply only to public-sector projects, although the government may decide to designate 'major commercial or business enterprises or activities or proposals' as subject to environmental assessment.[31]

BC and Saskatchewan appear to have built somewhat less discretion into the initial decision concerning whether EA is warranted, although more discretion is exercised in the conduct of the process itself. BC sets out a broad range of activities that are automatically subject to an EA in its Reviewable Projects Regulation, i.e., projects involving 'the construction, operation, dismantling and abandonment of new facilities and the modification, dismantling or abandonment of existing facilities'.[32] However, changes instituted in 1998 mean that smaller development processes are subject to ministry review and permitting processes rather than a full EA.[33] The Saskatchewan process requires that any project defined as a 'development' must undergo an EA and, in a manner similar to BC, the definition of 'development' is quite encompassing.[34]

In addition, whether or not public participation is required at various stages of the assessment process, as well as the type of participation offered, differs among provinces. These participatory patterns tend to magnify the discretionary nature of a particular EA process. All provinces provide the public with 'non-interactive' participatory opportunities, such as the right to review and comment on written material provided by the proponent on some type of registry, often over successive stages in the process. Some provinces, specifically Manitoba, New Brunswick, Nova Scotia, and Newfoundland, encourage (but do not require) proponents to consult with interested stakeholders while preparing an EA document. In Ontario, proponents are required to consult with the public to ensure that environmental issues are identified and resolved early in the process. Prior to the arrival of the Harris Conservatives, Ontario ran a pilot project for intervener funding in Environmental Assessment Board hearings, and proponents also were encouraged to fund participants in prehearing stages.[35] As of 1996, administrative changes eliminated this funding and encouraged interveners with similar interests to co-operate in the process.

Provinces also may encourage participation in formal hearings.[36] Some, such as Manitoba, Saskatchewan, PEI, and Newfoundland, may conduct hearings at the minister's discretion. In New Brunswick, however, hearings are a mandatory part of the process. Public hearings or meetings may be held in British Columbia, Ontario, and Alberta if the relevant EA board decides this is appropriate. British Columbia's Environmental Assessment Act also allows for the establishment and use of public advisory committees if the ministry decides this is warranted.[37] Quebec has an Office for Public Hearings on the Environment, an independent public consultation agency under the authority of the Minister of Environment and Wildlife, which may conduct public hearings upon the request of proponents. For its part, Nova Scotia's Environment Act provides for the resolution of particularly controversial EA issues through the voluntary use of alternative dispute resolution.

AIR QUALITY
As noted in Chapter 13 of this volume, the provinces actually establish air quality standards for air pollutants within their boundaries. The federal government sets science-based guidelines for ambient levels (in the surrounding atmosphere) of 'criteria' air pollutants (ozone, SO_2, NO_2, volatile organic compounds or VOCs, CO), but these are non-binding. The provinces do tend to fashion their policies in a manner consistent with these national objectives, however. Provincial ambient air standards, as compared with emission standards for point sources (e.g., industry), which are not examined here, are intended to measure the amount of pollutants present in the air over shorter as well as longer time periods. One-hour standards tend to be looser in order to account for occasional emission peaks, while 24-hour and annual standards account for chronic emission levels.

A comparison of provincial SO_2, NO_2, O_3 (ozone), and CO standards (Tables 8.1–8.4) shows that although provinces generally abide by federal maximum 'desirable', 'acceptable', and 'tolerable' guidelines, they differ in the degree to which they have chosen the 'desirable' or 'tolerable' ends of the standards spectrum. Ambient NO_2 and O_3 standards show only minimal differences among the provinces. British Columbia has no NO_2 standards, although its 'draft' O_3 standards are the most stringent. It should also be noted that New Brunswick and PEI have no O_3 standard. Ambient SO_2 standards tend to be more stringent in the western provinces (with the exception of Manitoba) and become less stringent as one moves eastward. Quebec is an outlier here, with an SO_2 one-hour standard two times higher than Ontario's and four times higher than that of the western provinces. The western provinces also tend towards the maximum 'desirable' end of the CO spectrum, while Ontario, Quebec, and the Maritime provinces tend towards the maximum 'acceptable' end.

One potential reason for differences among provincial policies is that some types of air pollution are problematic only in certain regions of the county. Smog incidences, for example, are more intense in central/eastern Canada and on the west coast. This is not a sufficient explanation for provincial policy differences in this particular area, however, especially considering the varying management approaches adopted by those provinces with more serious smog problems, such as British Columbia, Ontario, and Quebec. For example, British Columbia undoubtedly has been the 'policy entrepreneur' province in terms of vehicle emissions,

Table 8.1: Ambient Sulphur Dioxide Standards, 1999

	1-Hour Average (micrograms per cubic metre)	24-Hour Average (micrograms per cubic metre)	Annual Average (micrograms per cubic metre)
Fed. Guideline	Max. desirable: 450	150	30
	Max. acceptable: 900	300	60
	Max. tolerable: / *	800	/
BC**	Level A: 450	160	25
	Level B: 900	260	50
Alta	450	150	30
Sask.	450	150	30
Man.	900	300	60
Ont.	690	275	55
Que.	1,310	288	52
NB	900	300	60
NS	900	300	60
PEI	900	300	60
Nfld	900	300	60

* / indicates no standard.

** Level A = desirable goals, Level B = acceptable interim objectives.

Source: Table reproduced from Alberta Environmental Protection, *A Comparison of Alberta's Environmental Standards*, Mar. 1999.

Table 8.2: Ambient Nitrogen Dioxide Standards, 1999

	1-Hour Average (micrograms per cubic metre)	24-Hour Average (micrograms per cubic metre)	Annual Average (micrograms per cubic metre)
Fed. Guideline	Max. desirable: /*	/	60
	Max. acceptable: 400	200	100
	Max. tolerable: 1,000	300	/
BC	/	/	/
Alta	400	200	60
Sask.	400	/	100
Man.	400	200	100
Ont.	400	200	/
Que.	414	207	103
NB	400	200	100
NS	400	/	100
PEI	400	/	100
Nfld	400	200	/

* / indicates no standard.

Source: Table reproduced from Alberta Environmental Protection, *A Comparison of Alberta's Environmental Standards,* Mar. 1999.

Table 8.3: Ambient Ozone Standards, 1999

	1-Hour Average (micrograms per cubic metre)	24-Hour Average (micrograms per cubic metre)	Annual Average (micrograms per cubic metre)
Fed. Guideline	Max. desirable: 100	30	/
	Max. acceptable: 160	50	30
	Max. tolerable: 300	/*	/
BC	Max. acceptable: 100	30	/
('draft' standards)	Max. tolerable: 160	50	30
Alta	160	50	/
Sask.	160	/	/
Man.	160	50	30
Ont.	165	/	/
Que.	157	/	/
NB	/	/	/
NS	160	/	/
PEI	/	/	/
Nfld	160	50	30

* / indicates no standard.

Source: Table reproduced from Alberta Environmental Protection, *A Comparison of Alberta's Environmental Standards,* Mar. 1999 (with some modifications).

Table 8.4: Ambient Carbon Monoxide Standards, 1999

	1-Hour Average (milligrams per cubic metre)	24-Hour Average (milligrams per cubic metre)	Annual Average (milligrams per cubic metre)
Fed. Guideline	Max. desirable: 15	6	/
	Max. acceptable: 35	15	/
	Max. tolerable: /*	20	/
BC	Level A: 14.3	5.5	/
	Level B: 28.0	11	/
Alta	15	6	/
Sask.	15	6	/
Man.	35	15	/
Ont.	36.2	15.7	/
Que.	34	15	/
NB	35	15	/
NS	34.6	12.7	/
PEI	35	15	/
Nfld	35	15	10

* / indicates no standard.

Source: Table reproduced from Alberta Environmental Protection, *A Comparison of Alberta's Environmental Standards,* Mar. 1999.

which contribute to the buildup of smog-precursors (see Table 8.5). The province introduced the country's first vehicle emissions inspection system, AirCare, in 1992, five years before Ontario's Drive Clean Program,[38] and it has expanded the program to encompass trucks, buses, and diesel-powered vehicles. Both Quebec and Alberta are operating voluntary emissions testing as pilot programs. BC also has been the only province to adopt California's Low Emission Vehicle Program standards, the most stringent in North America, the only province with firm targets for zero-emission vehicles, and the first province to set standards for particulate matter (in the absence of any federal guidelines). Ontario has more recently introduced interim particulate standards. Quebec appears to lag behind its large-province counterparts somewhat in terms of air quality policy development.

Table 8.5: Vehicle Emissions Inspection and Maintenance Programs, 1999

Steady-State Testing	Evaporative Testing/ Visual Inspection	None (or Voluntary Testing)
BC, Ont.	NB	Alta, Man., Nfld, NS, PEI, Que., Sask.

Sources: Environment Policy & Law; Manufacturers of Emission Controls Association; provincial Web sites.

SOLID WASTE MANAGEMENT

The provinces deal with the transport, treatment, and disposal of solid waste. Each province even develops its own definition of waste; 'solid waste' is a commonly used classification although its meaning may differ slightly by province.[39] In the 1990s the provinces actively sought to deal with rising amounts of waste and decreasing landfill space.[40] Provincial waste reduction initiatives have included the expansion of recycling, container deposit, composting, and product stewardship programs, although these programs have taken somewhat different forms in different jurisdictions. British Columbia has long been recognized as a solid waste reduction leader and Nova Scotia has more recently instituted a variety of programs requiring waste reduction.

As of 1997, all provinces provided household access to recycling, either through curbside programs or depots. However, some provinces (Alberta, British Columbia, PEI, and Nova Scotia) had a mandatory recycling goal of 50 per cent by 2000, as endorsed by the CCME, while the others made this a preferred 'target' (Table 8.6). Moreover, while some provinces, such as Alberta, British Columbia, and Manitoba, had the authority to ban specific materials from landfills for the purpose of encouraging waste reduction, others did not. Nova Scotia has more recently instituted a series of landfill bans on a wide variety of beverage containers, packaging, and compostable waste. A number of provinces ban scrap tires from landfills.

With one exception, Ontario, provinces have required producers to take responsibility for beverage container waste. As a result, deposit programs have expanded from coast-to-coast, especially over the 1992–8 period.[41] British Columbia has the oldest deposit-refund system in North America (now 30 years old), which has been continually expanded. In terms of the general nature of their deposit systems, as of 1999 six provinces had 'all-but-milk' (ABM) container deposit systems and four had partial systems (Table 8.7). Provinces differed, however, in whether they used a 'return-to-retail' or 'universal depot' approach and in the actual deposit rates set on containers. In all 10 provinces (most recently also Quebec), beer containers are collected via deposit-return systems because of either government mandate or industry self-regulation.[42] In Alberta, the province has begun a unique milk jug recycling program, the first of its kind in North America.

With regard to composting, three provinces (British Columbia, New Brunswick, and Nova Scotia) have regulatory composting standards, two (Ontario and Quebec) have interim guidelines, three (Alberta, Saskatchewan, and Manitoba) adhere to CCME Guidelines for Compost Quality, and two (PEI and Newfoundland) have no standards.[43] Moreover, a number of provinces have undertaken initiatives specifically designed to encourage industry product stewardship, although Manitoba's is the most formalized. The province's Multi-Material Stewardship Regulation and Waste Reduction and Prevention Strategy are targeted at diverting a wide range of packaging and other wastes.

Table 8.6: Mandatory Recycling Goal and Power to Ban, 1997

	Mandatory Recycling Goal of 50% by 2000	Power to Ban Any Package from Landfill
YES	Alta, BC, NS, PEI	Alta, BC, Man., Ont.
NO	Man., NB, Nfld, Ont., Que., Sask.	NS, NB, Nfld, PEI, Que., Sask.

Sources: Environmental Policy & Law; State Laws Recycling Update, 1997.

Table 8.7: Deposit Programs, 1999

All but Milk	Partial
Alta, BC, NB, Nfld, NS, Sask.	Man., Ont., PEI, Que.

Sources: Environmental Policy & Law; Container Recycling Institute; Alberta Bottle Deposit Association; provincial Web pages.

ENDANGERED SPECIES

One environmental issue that has proven controversial and difficult to address in Canada is the protection of endangered species and habitat. As Boardman and others discuss in this volume, the federal government has made a number of attempts over the past few years to formulate national endangered species legislation. Yet each attempt has foundered on the shoals of provincial opposition, with the provinces arguing that federal action in this field is simply a duplication of existing provincial policies. In fact, half of the provinces (Ontario, Quebec, New Brunswick, Nova Scotia, and Manitoba) have specific endangered species legislation. The other provinces address aspects of endangered species and habitat protection in general wildlife and other environmental legislation. For example, BC's Wildlife Act covers game animals, raptors, and other vertebrate species, its Forest Practices Code Act addresses vertebrates, invertebrates, and plants 'at risk' from impacts due to forestry and grazing activities, and its Ecological Reserves Act, along with the Parks Act, provides protection for all species within park borders.

In October 1996 the federal and provincial governments agreed in principle on a National Accord for the Protection of Species at Risk. The National Accord contained 14 criteria that together were intended to provide the basis for the protection of endangered species across Canada. These criteria included a commitment on the part of all jurisdictions to: provide an independent process to assess the status of species; legally designate species as endangered or threatened; provide immediate legal protection for these designated species; provide protection for the habitat of these species; ensure multi-jurisdictional co-operation for cross-border species through recovery plans; and consider the needs of species at risk as part of the environmental assessment process.[44]

Every year since the formulation of the Accord, the Canadian Endangered Species Coalition has published a 'Report Card' that assesses the progress of all jurisdictions in achieving the National Accord criteria.[45] Provincial performance on selected criteria is provided in Table 8.8. The highest mark awarded by the Coalition in its 2000 Report Card, a 'C + ', went to Nova Scotia. Nova Scotia's relatively new Endangered Species Act (1999)[46] contains legislative requirements in four of six criteria and discretionary legislative (optional) provisions for the other two criteria. By contrast, British Columbia, which possesses no legislative requirements at all for three of the criteria and discretionary provisions for the other three, received the lowest mark, an 'F'. Almost all provinces do poorly in terms of co-operating across borders to protect species, although almost all provide immediate legal protection for species once they are designated to be at risk (often a controversial activity in itself), as well as protection for critical habitat.

Table 8.8: Provincial Achievement of National Accord for Protection of Species at Risk Criteria, 2000

Element of Accord	Legislative Requirement	Legislative, but Discretionary	Non-legislative Provision Mechanisms	No Provision
Independent process to assess species status	Alta, Man., NS	PEI, Sask.	NB, Ont., Que.	BC, Nfld
Legal designation of species as endangered	NS	Alta, BC, Man., NB, Ont., PEI, Que., Sask.		Nfld
Immediate legal protection for endangered species	Man., NB, NS, . Ont., PEI, Que., Sask.			Alta, BC, Nfld
Protection for habitat of endangered species	Man., NB, Ont., PEI	Alta, BC, Nfld, NS, Que., Sask.		
Multi-jurisdictional co-operation for cross-border species	NS	Sask.	Ont., PEI	Alta, BC, Man., Nfld, NB, Que.
Species at risk considered in EA process		Alta, BC, Man., Nfld, NB, NS, Ont., PEI, Que., Sask.		

Source: Canadian Endangered Species Coalition, 2000 Report Card.

PARKS/PROTECTED AREAS

The preservation of natural areas is important for maintaining ecological processes, protecting wildlife and biological diversity, and preserving special geographical features. All provincial governments establish parks and protected areas, and all have in recent years formulated strategies to increase the amount of protected area. While provinces often categorize parks and protected areas in very different ways, and they allow different recreational and commercial activities in these areas, one measure of comparison is the amount of area actually under protection (Table 8.9).

The percentages listed in Table 8.9 reveal significant differences among the provinces. Provinces such as British Columbia, Alberta, Manitoba, Ontario, and Nova Scotia have made significant progress towards reaching the United Nations recommended target of setting aside 12 per cent of lands within a jurisdiction. With its Lands for Life program (not accounted for in these figures), Ontario's protected land surface will be further expanded. Quebec and the other Atlantic provinces have made less progress it would seem.

Table 8.9: Protected Lands

	% of Provincial Lands Protected, 1999
BC*	11.2
Alta	9.9
Sask.*	6.0
Man.	8.1
Ont.	8.8*
Que.	4.2**
NB	1.3
NS	8.2
PEI	4.1
Nfld	1.8

* Does not include Ontario's Lands for Life Program, which would bring the total figure closer to 12 per cent.
** The majority of Quebec's protected areas are under 'interim' protection only, according to the WWF.
Source: World Wildlife Fund Endangered Spaces Campaign, 1999.

ASSESSMENT OF POLICY DIFFERENCES

There are some moderate differences among the provinces in terms of the limited number of environmental policy indicators surveyed above, although on most indicators these differences could not be characterized as stark. All provincial EA processes are discretionary to some extent (especially when compared with American states), with processes in the Atlantic provinces, Manitoba, and Ontario being somewhat more discretionary. Nova Scotia is an Atlantic exception, as it more resembles provinces such as Quebec and Alberta. British Columbia's EA process appears to be the least discretionary. With regard to solid waste reduction, all provinces have engaged in reduction initiatives, with the expansion of deposit, recycling, and composting programs from coast to coast. Here, British Columbia is out in front along with Nova Scotia, while Ontario and Quebec are lagging. It is difficult to characterize groups of provinces in terms of stringency in this area, however. On endangered species, none of the provinces perform overly well, although Nova Scotia appears to be a frontrunner, with British Columbia and Newfoundland considerably behind and the other provinces grouped somewhere in the middle. Here, too, there do not appear to be any regional trends.

All of the provinces set air quality standards in accord with federal objectives. There are only minimal differences among the provinces with regard to NO_2 and O_3 standards, with SO_2 and CO standards being somewhat more stringent in the western provinces. One might argue here that these differences can be accounted for by the air pollution problems in the provinces themselves, i.e., central Canadian provinces would find air quality standards more difficult to meet due to the concentration of people and industry. However, with regard to vehicle emissions, British Columbia has adopted the most stringent programs, followed by Ontario, with the other provinces trailing behind. Concerning the amount of park and protected areas, the western provinces and Ontario fare relatively well on the indicators provided. New Brunswick and Newfoundland have made less progress on this indicator, Nova Scotia and Quebec more so.

Overall, there is a slight trend towards increased stringency as one moves westward, although there are numerous exceptions to this. British Columbia seems to be a leader on a number of indicators, while in Saskatchewan and Manitoba the record is more mixed. Nova Scotia has more stringent policies than its Atlantic counterparts, indeed, than other provinces generally, in a number of areas, while Ontario and Quebec appear less activist on a number of indicators.

Commitment to Implement

Comparing environmental policies provides only part of the total environmental protection picture in Canada's provinces. Even if differences among provincial policies are minimal, which appears to be the case in the limited number of areas surveyed above, this tells us little about the willingness and capacity of provinces to implement these policies. This section explores the 'commitment to implement' displayed by the provinces across a range of measures. Measuring public expenditure levels in all provinces provides some indication of their commitment to undertake environmental protection.[47] In addition, private expenditures on environmental protection may be related to regulatory controls instituted by public authorities. Further, we need to compare the number of personnel engaged in environmental protection and natural resource management tasks as a percentage of total provincial employment levels. Finally, some enforcement statistics are telling, as the willingness to enforce existing legislation and standards also indicates the degree to which environmental protection is a priority in a given jurisdiction.

POLLUTION ABATEMENT AND CONTROL EXPENDITURES

Comparing environmental expenditure data for the provinces presents certain methodological challenges. Provinces tend to organize environment-related functions in different ways; for example, while some separate environmental protection and natural resource management activities, others (especially the smaller provinces) combine them. Thus, expenditures are allocated differently among departments and within budgets. For some years, Statistics Canada calculated comparable public and private pollution abatement and control (PAC) expenditures[48] for all provinces, thereby making this task considerably easier. This section provides some comparison of 1994–5 Statistics Canada figures for private and public PAC, the last set available, and then provides more recent environmental protection and natural resource management expenditure data for 1998–9. These 1998–9 expenditures are, for most provinces, ministry budgets and thus provide somewhat different expenditure measures from the PAC data.[49]

In terms of per capita provincial expenditures on pollution abatement, the provinces spent relatively similar amounts on environmental protection in 1994–5, although there is some variation (Table 8.10). Newfoundland was a marked outlier, spending less than 40 per cent of the national average. Among the remaining provinces the differences are not insignificant; for example, Manitoba would have had to spend two-thirds again as much to match public PAC expenditures in BC.

Levels of investment in PAC by private interests within provinces also can be regarded as a measure, though admittedly inexact, of regulatory commitment by governments.[50] More significant differences existed among the provinces in 1994–5 in terms of private PAC expenditures than is the case with public PAC expenditures. Even ignoring PEI, which is a marked outlier in this respect, private PAC expenditures in the high expenditure provinces (New Brunswick, Alberta) were three to four times higher than those in the low expenditure provinces (Manitoba, Nova Scotia). It is interesting to note that private PAC expenditures are similar in the most populous and heavily industrialized provinces (Ontario, BC, and Quebec), but that these expenditures are higher in Saskatchewan, Alberta, and New Brunswick, sometimes by a significant margin. Differences in private PAC expenditure among the Atlantic provinces are also notable.

Table 8.10: Public and Private Pollution Abatement and Control, 1994–1995

	Public PAC ($ per capita)	Private PAC ($ per capita)
BC	186.8	155.3
Alta	139.3	249.7
Sask.	156.5	203.3
Man.	113.2	87.0
Ont.	161.7	140.0
Que.	163.1	147.4
NB	176.3	244.4
NS	175.8	68.3
PEI	178.8	16.4
Nfld	57.9	92.8

Sources: Statistics Canada, *Environmental Expenditures in the Business Sector 1995,* 16F0006XIE, Ottawa, July 1998; Statistics Canada, Catalogue no. 11–528–XPE; CANSIM 2000.

Table 8.11 cross-tabulates private and public PAC expenditures per capita by province, thus suggesting the commitment of various governments to pollution abatement and control (total PAC expenditures) as well as their preferred policy instruments in achieving those goals, i.e., direct public expenditure (public PAC) versus public regulation of private production (private PAC). Provinces can be divided on the basis of total combined public and private PAC expenditures into high expenditure units (over 130 per cent of Canadian per capita expenditures), medium expenditure units (greater than 70 per cent but lower than 130 per cent of Canadian per capita expenditures), and low expenditure units (under 70 per cent of Canadian per capita expenditures). Dividing provinces as such demonstrates differences in terms of the overall commitment of provinces to pollution control and abatement. Although a significant number of provinces are grouped in the 'medium' expenditure category, there are provincial examples in all but one category.

Moreover, provinces can be divided on the basis of the extent to which total expenditures on PAC in the province are based on public or private expenditures, i.e., whether provinces attempt to achieve their pollution abatement and control goals primarily through direct spending or through regulation requiring private expenditures. Provinces can be divided into units where PAC expenditure is primarily public (where over 60 per cent of PAC expenditures are public), mixed systems (where public PAC expenditures represent between 41 to 59 per cent of total expenditures), and primarily privately funded systems in which public expenditures make up less than 40 per cent of total expenditures. Here, provinces are represented in each category, although they are most heavily represented in the mixed public category. New Brunswick is close to being in the private category.

What is perhaps most interesting is the pattern evident when the two measures

Table 8.11: Provincial PAC Expenditure and Private PAC Investment, 1995

Expenditures	Primarily Public (> 60% of total expenditures are public)	Mixed	Primarily Private (< 40% of total expenditures are public)
High (>130% of total Canadian expenditures per capita)		NB	Alta
Medium	NS	Ont., Que., Sask., BC	
Low (<70% of total Canadian expenditures per capita)	PEI	Man.	Nfld

Sources: Statistics Canada, *Environmental Expenditures in the Business Sector 1995*, 16F0006XIE, Ottawa, July 1998; Statistics Canada, Catalogue no. 11–528–XPE; CANSIM 2000.

are combined. Here, only two provinces (Nova Scotia and Prince Edward Island) have primarily publicly funded PAC systems, though their expenditure levels are medium or low. In only one province, Alberta, are PAC expenditures high while also being primarily privately funded.[51] Also, only in Newfoundland are PAC expenditures low and primarily privately funded, i.e., where regulation may be the primary instrument of pollution abatement and control policy but this regulation tends to be weak. Ontario, Quebec, British Columbia, and Saskatchewan all exhibit mixed public and private expenditure systems with medium expenditure levels.

The 1998–9 expenditure figures, which include expenditures on both environmental protection and natural resource management (Table 8.12), reveal some interesting trends. With the exception of New Brunswick, public expenditure figures decline as one moves from west to east. The western provinces, especially British Columbia and Alberta, have the highest per capita expenditures, with Saskatchewan and Manitoba following. However, Manitoba's proportionally high natural resource expenditures are responsible for the province's better showing overall and mask its low environmental protection expenditures, which are on par with those in Nova Scotia. This shows some consistency with the picture of public PAC expenditures presented above for 1994–5, keeping in mind that the data include different types of expenditures. The most remarkable finding in this 1998–9 comparison is the low per capita expenditures in Ontario and Quebec, which appear more similar to expenditures in the Maritime provinces than those in the western provinces. Per capita expenditures in Canada's two largest provinces are one-third those in British Columbia and Alberta, and it is worth noting here that the ratios of environmental protection to natural resource management expenditures in these four provinces are not out of line with each other.

Table 8.12: Provincial Environmental Expenditures, 1998–1999

	Environmental Protection ($ thousands)	Natural Resource Management ($ thousands)	Total Environment-Related ($ thousands)	Per Capita Expenditures ($)
BC	175,439	478,089	653,528	199.1
Alta			490,974	192.9
Sask.			165,469	167.3
Man.	13,907	136,799	150,706	138.0
Ont.	160,000	521,000	681,000	67.5
Que.	179,000	369,000	548,000	79.5
NB	24,627	77,501	102,128	141.1
NS	15,480	59,749	75,229	77.0
PEI*			7,746	59.7
Nfld	4,669	14,191	18,860	33.2

* The PEI figures are for the 1999–2000 fiscal year.
Sources: Provincial government estimates; CANSIM 2000.

New Brunswick is an outlier among the Maritime provinces and appears more similar to Saskatchewan and Manitoba.

NUMBERS OF PERSONNEL

When examining the number of environment and natural resource personnel as a percentage of total government employment in the provinces (Table 8.13), the western provinces also figure prominently. British Columbia has the highest numbers of personnel, followed by Alberta and Saskatchewan, and then Nova Scotia and New Brunswick. Here, too, Ontario and Quebec fall in the lower category, with approximately one-third the number of personnel in BC and one-half that of the other western provinces. Again, it is worth noting that the ratio of environmental protection to natural resource management personnel in British Columbia, Ontario, and Quebec is roughly similar. Only Manitoba, PEI, and Newfoundland have fewer personnel than Ontario and Quebec.

ENFORCEMENT ACTIVITIES

The level and nature of enforcement activity also vary across the provinces. Comparing enforcement activities presents its own difficulties as some provinces, especially the western provinces and Ontario, provide detailed information readily available to the public (on Web sites or annual reports) while others do not. With the exception of New Brunswick, the Maritime provinces generally do not calculate and make available enforcement statistics in the same way as other

Table 8.13: Provincial Environmental Personnel, 1999–2000

	Environmental Protection	Natural Resource Management	Total or Functions Combined	As Percentage of Total Government Employees
BC	2,081	4550	6,631	33
Alta			3,607	15
Sask.			1,211	15
Man.			181	1.7
Ont.	1,501	3,400	4,901	9.7
Que.	1,414	3,246	4,660	7.9
NB	170	800	970	10.7
NS	236	932	1,168	12
PEI			90	3
Nfld*	89			1.1

* Newfoundland's personnel numbers are very difficult to calculate, as some staff performing environmental functions are in other departments. For example, enforcement staff are housed in the Government Service Centre, not in the Ministry of Environment and Labour. Thus, only the number for the latter department is used here. It should be recognized that this number is underestimated.

Sources: BC Ministry of Environment, *Lands and Parks Business Plan 1999–2000;* BC Ministry of Forests, *Annual Report;* Saskatchewan Environment and Resource Management—Budget; Ontario Ministry of the Environment, *Business Plan 2000–2001;* Ontario Ministry of Natural Resources, *Business Plan 2000–2001;* departmental Web sites and e-mail/telephone information requests for other provinces.

provinces. Moreover, while some provinces separate environmental protection and natural resource enforcement activities, others combine these measures. Thus, two tables (Tables 8.14 and 8.15) have been created to take this fundamental difference into account. The figures provided here can only give a general indication of provincial enforcement activity and no data were available for Quebec, PEI, and Nova Scotia.

From the limited information that is available, Alberta, British Columbia, Nova Scotia, Saskatchewan, and Ontario appear to be at least relatively active. Alberta's (and probably Saskatchewan's) figures are inflated as compared with the other provinces, as natural resource (including forests) enforcement activities are combined with those under environmental protection legislation. Nevertheless, a look at Alberta's impressively detailed *Enforcement Activities: Annual Report* indicates that the province is indeed quite active in this regard. British Columbia's figures tell only part of the story, as forestry statistics are not included in the figures provided and the province has made amendments to ticketing regulations that give enforcement officers the option of issuing tickets on the spot for more than 50 environmental offences, rather than pursuing formal charges and court action.[52] British Columbia has also levied some of the largest fines; for example, in the fall of 1999 the province fined a businessman $90,000 for spilling PCB-contaminated

Table 8.14: Provincial Environment/Natural Resource Enforcement Activities, 1998–1999

	Charges	Convictions	Penalties ($)
BC (for 1999–2000)	649		223,666
Alta	4,890	2,643	1,723,982
Sask.	2,725	2,222	
Man.	165	153	80,790

Sources: Alberta Environment, *Enforcement Activities: Annual Report April 1, 1998–March 31, 1999;* Saskatchewan Environment and Resource Management, *Enforcement Activity Report 1999;* Manitoba Conservation, *Enforcement Statistics,* http://www.gov.mb.ca/environ/prgareas/enforce.html; BC Ministry of Environment, Lands and Parks, Enforcement and Emergencies Branch, Charges and Penalties Summary Under Environmental Protection Legislation, http://www.elp.gov.bc.ca/eeeb/charges/102199charges.html

Table 8.15: Provincial Environmental Enforcement Activities, 1998–1999

	Charges	Convictions	Penalties ($)
Ont.	805	414	863,840
NB	23 (+13 min. orders)		9,364
Nfld	47	7	16,700

Sources: M. Winfield and G. Jenish, *Ontario's Environment and the Common Sense Revolution: A Four Year Report* (Toronto: Canadian Institute for Environmental Law and Policy, Sept. 1999); New Brunswick Department of Environment, *1998–99 Annual Report;* personal communication from Government Service Centre, Government of Newfoundland and Labrador; Saskatchewan Environment and Resource Management, *Enforcement Activity Report 1999.*

oil in the Fraser River.[53] While comparable figures for Nova Scotia are not available, it should be noted that 60 per cent of the Department of Environment's budget has been allocated to inspection, monitoring, and enforcement.[54]

Observers have been particularly concerned about enforcement in Ontario after such deep budget and personnel cuts. In 1997 the Harris government laid off 186 environmental inspectors, investigators, and pesticide monitors.[55] In 1998, the province's Environmental Commissioner proclaimed that the government's budget cuts had 'hobbled' Ontario's ability to enforce environmental regulations. She noted: 'There is very little point to having world-class regulations and high standards unless the ministries . . . have the staff, resources and the commitment to enforcement, monitoring and reporting.'[56] However, in late 1998, Ontario introduced the Environmental Statute Amendment Act, which increased the fines for infractions, gave the courts more authority to impose jail sentences, and gave ministry offices more powers of investigation and seizure. Yet, the enforcement staff has not been increased, and the Canadian Institute for Environmental Law and Policy has noted that charges and penalties in Ontario are at their lowest levels since 1986–7.[57]

Manitoba, New Brunswick, and Newfoundland appear to be less active with regard to enforcement. However, Newfoundland amended its Environment Act in 1999 to set higher penalties for environmental offences in an attempt to bring the province into line with its counterparts in this area. Its enforcement statistics also appear to show a certain degree of proactiveness.

ASSESSMENT OF PROVINCIAL COMMITMENT
It is evident from the above glimpse at per capita expenditures, personnel, and enforcement data that considerable differences exist among the provinces with regard to their commitment to implement environmental policies. The overall picture afforded by the three measures of provincial commitment to environmental protection is one of western leadership. British Columbia and Alberta have maintained high per capita expenditures and appear to have encouraged at least medium levels of industry investment in PAC (high levels in the case of Alberta) as of mid-decade. British Columbia has made the largest investment in personnel, with Alberta among a 'second tier' of provinces. Both provinces also appear relatively active in terms of enforcement activity.[58] Saskatchewan measures up reasonably well in terms of expenditures and enforcement, while Manitoba has invested relatively less in environmental protection expenditures and did not appear to encourage industry PAC investment, at least in the mid-1990s. Moreover, Manitoba has fewer personnel relative to total government employment than all other provinces except PEI and Newfoundland, and its level of enforcement activity could probably be characterized as moderate.

Ontario and Quebec do *not* exhibit high levels of commitment to environmental protection, at least in terms of the measures examined here. Their per capita public and private PAC expenditures seemed relatively similar to those in British Columbia and Saskatchewan in 1994–5, but their 1998–9 environmental protection and natural resource management expenditures are among the lowest, similar to those in Nova Scotia and PEI. Personnel numbers are also significantly behind those in the western provinces and on par with those in Atlantic Canada. It is more difficult to make conclusions on the basis of the available enforcement data, although Ontario appears to be less active in this area than it was even in the mid-nineties.

The picture in the Atlantic provinces is more mixed. New Brunswick's public and private per capita PAC expenditures were high in 1994–5 and its 1998–9 environmental protection and natural resource management expenditures also hold up to those in Saskatchewan and Manitoba. New Brunswick's personnel numbers are on par with those in Ontario and it does exhibit some level of enforcement activity. Nova Scotia's expenditures, characterized as medium in 1994–5, are now quite low, although its personnel numbers (on par with those in New Brunswick and thus Ontario) and its commitment to enforcement are more promising. Newfoundland and PEI exhibit low levels of commitment in terms of expenditures and personnel, although Newfoundland is renewing its efforts in the area of enforcement.

Conclusion

This overview indicates that differences in provincial policies are moderate. On the other hand, more significant differences *do* exist in the levels of provincial commitment to environmental protection through their expenditures, staffing levels, and enforcement activities. Thus, while provincial policies may appear to be relatively similar on the surface (especially in environmental assessment and solid waste reduction, probably less so in endangered species protection, air quality, and parks/protected areas), the commitment and the capacity of the provinces to implement these policies differ greatly. For example, while Nova Scotia appears to have moved from its 'D' position in 1990 to being in many ways an environmental policy leader in 2000, it is not clear that the province has the necessary resources to realize the policy commitments it has made. Recent downsizing activities in the province darken the picture even further. Ontario, the leader in 1990 with a 'B', does not appear to possess either the policies or the commitment to be an environmental policy leader a decade later. In British Columbia, the situation seems somewhat brighter.

These realities should give pause to those who argue that intergovernmentalism will result in the construction of an effective national environmental protection framework, where none existed before. The provinces appear to exhibit varying degrees of willingness to regulate environmental protection and their environmental policies are by no means homogeneous. While intergovernmental accords may set out guidelines for provincial action, implementation and enforcement remain subject to the environmental proclivities and commitment of the provinces.

Notes

1 The assessment was based on six indicators: environment ministry budget, number of inspectors, number of convictions for environmental offences, energy consumption, tap-water regulations, and environmental assessment procedures. 'Mixed Results: All 10 provinces have room to improve', *Maclean's*, 17 Sept. 1990, 72–3.

2 Ibid.

3 L. Griffiths and T. Hussain, 'Cutting the Red Tape', *Hazardous Materials Management* (Apr.-May 1996): 13.

4 These include the Environmental Protection Act, the Ontario Water Resources Act, the Environmental Assessment Act, the Environmental Bill of Rights, the Niagara Escarpment Planning and Development Act, the Pesticides Act, the Ontario Energy Board Act, the Power Corporation Act, and the Energy Efficiency Act.

5 Government of Ontario, *Better, Stronger, Clearer: Environmental Regulations for Ontario* (Toronto, Nov. 1997).

6 M. Winfield and G. Jenish, *Ontario's Environment and the Common Sense Revolution: A Four Year Report* (Toronto: Canadian Institute for Environmental Law and Policy, Sept. 1999), Highlights.

7 Environmental Appeal Board, Environmental Assessment Board, and Niagara Escarpment Office.

8 Winfield and Jenish, *Ontario's Environment and the Common Sense Revolution*, 1–4.

9 Alberta Environment, *Summary of the Proposed Alberta Environmental Protection and Enhancement Act*.

10 Alberta Environmental Protection, 'Alberta Environmental Protection Releases Regulatory Reform Action Plan', press release, 6 Nov. 1995.

11 Paul Muldoon and Ramani Nadarajah, 'A Sober Second Look', in Robert B. Gibson, ed., *Voluntary Initiatives: The New Politics of Corporate Greening* (Peterborough, Ont.: Broadview Press, 1999).

12 BC Environment, 'Environment 2001 Charts B.C. Environment's Agenda', news release, 9 Aug. 1991.

13 See Dale Marshall, *Shifting Ground: A CCPA-BC Policy Brief on the Potential and Limitations of Environmental Tax Shifting* (Vancouver: Canadian Centre for Policy Alternatives, 2000).

14 *Environmental Law & Policy* 8, 5 (Aug. 1997): 577.

15 Ibid., 8, 8 (Nov. 1997): 611.

16 Nova Scotia Department of the Environment, *2000/2001 Business Plan*, 1.

17 Ibid.

18 Nova Scotia Government, 'The Course Ahead: Backgrounder': http://www.gov.ns.ca/prio/courseahead2000/index.html

19 N.J. Brennan, 'Impediments to Environmental Quality and New Brunswick's Clean Environment Act: An Argument for a New Statute', *Journal of Environmental Law and Practice* 7, 1 (1997): 98–9.

20 *Environmental Law & Policy* 7, 9 (Dec. 1997): 472.

21 Griffiths and Hussain, 'Cutting the Red Tape', 14; Alberta Environment, *Details of Regulatory Reform Initiatives*, 1995.

22 Winfield and Jenish, *Ontario's Environment and the Common Sense Revolution*, Highlights.

23 *Environmental Law & Policy* 7, 12 (Mar. 1997): 513.

24 K. Harrison, *Passing the Buck: Federalism and Canadian Environmental Policy* (Vancouver: University of British Columbia Press, 1997), 154.

25 R.J. Malvern et al., *A Reference Guide to Environmental Legislation in Canada*. Prepared by Environmental Studies and Assessments Department, Design and Development— Generation Division, Ontario Hydro, Report #85438, Dec. 1985.

26 M. Valiante, 'Evaluating Ontario's Environmental Assessment Reforms', *Journal of Environmental Law and Practice* 8 (1999): 217.

27 For example, BC's process provides for an assessment of 'the environmental, economic, social, cultural, heritage and health effects of all reviewable projects', while New Brunswick's regulations refer to 'both socio-economic and bio-physical impacts'. Similarly, Alberta's process focuses on 'environmental, social, economic and cultural consequences'. Saskatchewan's EA process considers potential environmental effects 'upon the land, water, air, living organisms, and the interacting natural systems that connect these components to the earth', as well as on 'human health and socio-economic conditions, physical and cultural heritage and on the current use of lands and resources for traditional purposes by aboriginal peoples'. Nova Scotia's definition of environmental effects considers biophysical changes as well as changes in socio-economic conditions, environmental health, physical and cultural heritage, the human 'built' environment, and structures of historical, archaeological, paleontological, or architectural significance. Ontario's new Environmental Assessment and Consultation Improvement Act also defines 'environment' in an inclusive and complex fashion.

28 Ministry of Environment and Labour, *Guide to Environmental Assessment*: http://www.gov.nf.ca/env/Env/EnvAssess/guide_to_ea.asp (emphasis added).

29 Nova Scotia Department of the Environment, *Environmental Assessment*: http://www.gov.ns.ca/envi/dept/ess/ca/index.htm#EA

30 Valiante, 'Evaluating Ontario's Environmental Assessment Reforms', 263.

31 Environmental Assessment and Consultation Improvement Act 3 (b).

32 Province of British Columbia, Environmental Assessment Act: http://www.eao.gov.bc.ca/guide/intro.thm#features

33 *Environmental Law & Policy* 9, 8 (Nov. 1998): 755.

34 Saskatchewan Environment and Resource Management, *The Environmental Assessment & Review Process*: http://www.gov.sk.ca/serm/www/assess/process.htm

35 Valiante, 'Evaluating Ontario's Environmental Assessment Reforms', 258–9.

36 Commission on Environmental Co-operation, 'Environmental Impact Assessment: Law and Practice in North America', *North American Environmental Law and Policy Series* (Winter 1999): http://www.cec.org

37 BC Environmental Assessment Office, 'New Environmental Assessment Act Becomes Law in BC': http://www.eao.gov.bc.ca/Proclaim.htm

38 In fact, Ontario's Drive Clean Program was not activated until the spring of 1999.

39 OECD Environmental Performance Reviews, 77.

40 At the intergovernmental level, the provinces, along with industry and environmental representatives, set up a National Packaging Task Force under the auspices of the CCME, which formulated guidelines for reducing packaging waste. The Task Force also challenged industry to achieve voluntarily a 50 per cent reduction in packaging waste sent to landfills by 2000—a target that has been met. See Canadian Council of Ministers of the Environment, *National Packaging Results: Canada Exceeds Target To Reduce the Amount of Packaging Sent For Disposal Four Years Ahead of Schedule*: http://www.ccme.ca/ccme/le_about/leg_communiques/leg3.html. Accessed 20 June 1998.

41 Container Recycling Institute, 'Beverage Container Reuse and Recycling in Canada': http://www.container-recycling.org/page66.htm. Accessed 28 Nov. 2000.

42 Ibid.

43 Composting Council of Canada, 'Composting Regulations and Guidelines Across Canada': http://www.compost.org/

44 Environment Canada, *National Accord for the Protection of Species at Risk* (Ottawa, Oct. 1996).

45 Canadian Nature Federation, 2000 Endangered Species Report Card. http://www.cnf.ca/report_2000/report_card_.html. Accessed 28 Nov. 2000.

46 *Environmental Law & Policy* 7, 10 (Jan. 1997): 487.

47 One could argue that as population, levels of industrialization, and the nature of environmental problems differ among the provinces, one *should* expect differences in environmental expenditures. While these factors may explain some interprovincial variations, this is not a sufficient explanation for the extent and nature of provincial differences, as is evident is this section.

48 Public PAC expenditures include capital and operating expenditures on pollution control, sewage and waste collection and disposal, environmental protection, and environmental services. Private PAC expenditures include capital and operating expenditures on end-of-pipe and integrated processes.

49 All data are calculated as per capita expenditures for comparability.

50 This is based on the assumption that most private investment on pollution abatement and control is in response to (or in anticipation of) government regulatory requirements.

51 New Brunswick is also high in terms of expenditures and is close to falling into the primarily private category, with private PAC comprising just under 60 per cent of all PAC expenditures.

52 *Environmental Law & Policy* 7, 12 (Mar. 1997): 515.

53 Ibid., 10, 7 (Oct. 1999): 900.

54 Nova Scotia Department of the Environment, *2000/2001 Business Plan*, 2.

55 *Environmental Law & Policy* 7, 12 (Mar. 1997): 513.

56 Office of the Environmental Commissioner, *1997 Annual Report*.

57 Winfield and Jenish, *Ontario's Environment and the Common Sense Revolution*, Highlights.

58 One should take into account British Columbia's changes to enforcement here.

Chapter 9

Canadian-American Environmental Relations: A Strategic Framework

George Hoberg

Canadian environmental policy-makers confront formidable challenges managing relations with the United States. The two countries share a continental ecosystem consisting of a shared air mass, a remarkable system of freshwater lakes, and other shared resources. Due to its size and the nature of environmental flows, the US exports a significant amount of its pollution to Canada. These bilateral issues have been joined by an increasingly complex array of international environmental issues, such as stratospheric ozone depletion, global warming, biodiversity, and forestry. Economic integration and trade agreements have spawned numerous and varied links between environmental policy and trade. In addition, US environmentalists have taken an increasing interest in environmental conditions in Canada.

This chapter provides a strategic framework for analysing Canadian-American environmental relations. The first section provides an analysis of the mechanisms of US influence on Canadian environmental policy, while the second examines the institutional differences between the Canadian and US systems of government and what these differences imply for environmental relations. The third section then provides an overview of recent trends affecting US environmental policy and politics and their implications for Canada. Finally, the chapter ends with a discussion of the strategic options for addressing Canada's environmental relations with the US.

While specific environmental issues or conflicts may arise in the discussion below, the purpose of the chapter is not to provide a survey of particular environmental issues but to present a broader framework for understanding issues as they arise.

Six Mechanisms of US Influence

Canada and the US share a social, cultural, economic, and biophysical environment. There are, accordingly, a number of avenues by which developments in the US can influence Canadian domestic or international environmental policy.

Perhaps the most direct mechanism of influence is the physical one, in which economic activities in the US produce environmental problems that spill over into Canada. These can occur at quite different scales: locally, in the case of emissions or effluents into shared resources along the border (the Great Lakes, St Lawrence River, etc.), at a more regional scale (acid deposition or ground-level ozone), and even on the global scale (climate change).

US actions and policies also can have a significant influence on Canada simply as an example. Policy development frequently occurs through 'emulation', as one country evaluates the experience of another country. Given the proximity, size, and dynamism of the US, it is only natural that this country serves as a frequent model for policy development. There are two types of emulation. In *élite-driven emulation*, government officials learn from the experience of other countries. In *activist-driven emulation*, activists in one country use the experience of another country to pressure their own government to take action. This process can be referred to as 'shaming', in the sense that it typically is based on the logic that 'if policy X is good enough for Americans, it is good enough for Canadians.' There are many examples of activist-driven emulation in Canadian environmental politics, the most recent prominent case being the debate over legislation to protect endangered species. This 'shaming' strategy is also used by some international institutions, such as the NAFTA Commission on Environmental Co-operation in its *Taking Stock* reports and the UN Commission on Sustainable Development in its reports, which seek to use cross-national disparities in environmental performance to motivate the laggards. Of course, emulation is frequently partial, as policy-makers or advocates pick and choose which aspects of a policy they like and then tailor these to their own interests or domestic circumstances. Emulation also can be negative, relying on the argument that 'we want to avoid the American experience.' An example of negative emulation in environmental relations would be the widespread Canadian desire (not shared by some environmentalists) to avoid the adversarial legalism so rampant in US environmental policy.

American influence could also emerge through diplomacy or the use of international institutions such as the International Joint Commission (IJC), the North American Agreement on Environmental Co-operation (NAAEC), and the consultative bodies of the various multilateral environmental agreements.

Trade agreements may provide an avenue for US influence in three ways. First, trade agreements promote the harmonization of environmental standards (such as pesticides in the NAFTA context). Second, they open Canadian environmental policies to challenge by competitors on the grounds that they provide unfair subsidies or are a non-tariff barrier to trade. Environmentalists are extremely concerned that international trade agreements will be used to trump domestic environmental standards.[1] It is true that the World Trade Organization (WTO) may increase the evidentiary burden on governments not accustomed to providing detailed rationales to support their regulations. The WTO does require that regulations calling for more than international standards have to be justified by risk assessments. However, the WTO and its rationales for dispute settlement decisions make it clear that governments have the right to set their own level of protection. WTO rules leave a great deal more room for domestic regulations, even those with considerable trade implications, than is widely believed.[2] Third, while most of the provisions in NAFTA are very similar to those of the WTO, NAFTA does contain a distinctive 'investor suit' provision that might allow foreign firms to demand compensation for regulations that reduce the value of their investments in Canada, the MMT and Sun Belt cases being recent examples.[3]

In addition to the more direct pressure through trade agreements, economic integration also can create pressures on Canadian environmental policy. Two out of every five economic transactions in Canada is with a foreign country, and one of every three is with the United States. Indeed, 84 per cent of Canadian exports are destined for the US. Pressures towards harmonization of standards may occur as a result of the costs that environmental regulations impose on firms competing in international markets. Firms are likely to lobby their governments to reduce regulatory burdens, creating the potential for a 'race to the bottom', in which each nation attempts to create a competitive advantage for its firms by weakening environmental standards. This dynamic can be countered by the so-called 'California effect', where stringent regulations in large markets spill over into smaller ones, pulling the laggards up.[4] Canada has experienced this in the case of automobile emissions and other pollutants, where tight US standards have helped strengthen Canadian standards.[5] Moreover, some industries may be subjected to 'green consumerism', where pressures in the international marketplace encourage firms to move beyond government standards. The forest industry is probably the best example of this phenomenon.[6]

A final mechanism of influence would be cross-border lobbying, as US environmental groups or international environmental groups with strong US affiliations put pressure on Canadian governments to act. This influence has been apparent over the past decade in the case of the Great Whale hydroelectric project in Quebec, BC forestry, and, most recently, endangered species.[7] Cross-border lobbying, as Wilson notes in Chapter 3, occurs through direct lobbying by the US groups, close alliance between Canadian and US groups, and US foundation support for Canadian groups.

There are three noteworthy aspects about these mechanisms. First, some of these influences are clearly negative, such as the export of pollution across the border, but some can be more positive for the environment, such as when aggressive US regulations facilitate policy development in Canada or US market pressures or opportunities spur environmental innovation. Second, these mechanisms of influence can frequently occur in combination. For example, transborder pollution often leads to diplomacy, and many recent cross-border lobbying efforts have been channelled through economic pressures. Finally, different mechanisms may create different levels of concern for Canadian policy-makers.

Comparison of Policy Regimes

Despite many social, cultural, and economic similarities between Canada and the United States, policy-makers in the two countries address environmental problems within quite different political systems. Canadian government has its roots in the mother country of Great Britain, from which it has adopted the

Westminster-style parliamentary system. Governments in the US have their roots in a revolution against the eighteenth-century form of that British system, creating a distinctive system of 'separation of powers' and 'checks and balances'. These deep macropolitical differences have profound consequences for how policy is made in the two countries. An understanding of Canadian-American environmental relations requires an understanding of these differences.

In the US, Congress plays a very powerful role. The US system of separation of powers and checks and balances is profoundly different from the Westminster-style of government in Canada. In Canada, the legislative and executive branches are combined. The cabinet and the Prime Minister (or Premier) are selected from the party with the most seats in the legislature, or the majority party. This fact, combined with exceptionally strong party discipline, means that the political executive (cabinet), and in particular the leader, dominates policy-making and there is virtually no significant role played by the legislature independent of the cabinet.[8] In the US, the political executive is elected separately from the Congress and, in fact, the constitution explicitly prohibits members of Congress from serving in the cabinet. This separation of electoral bases creates the possibility that one or both houses of Congress will be dominated by a party different from that of the President. This possibility has become the normal state of affairs since 1968 (see below). Even when the houses are controlled by the same party, an independent role for Congress is ensured by the tradition that members of Congress serve their geographical districts first and not their party.

This powerful congressional role manifests itself in several ways. First, Congress dominates the legislative and budgetary processes. Presidents have a big impact on legislation by introducing bills,[9] through selective use of the veto threat, and through their responsibility for the conduct of foreign affairs. However, Congress plays a dominant and independent role.

Second, the separation of powers between the branches creates an institutional distrust that means Congress is not willing to delegate much discretionary authority to the executive branch. In Canada, legislation generally provides broad grants of authority, but almost never binds the Crown to perform any particular task. In the US, legislation typically contains a broad range of devices that specify particular standards and procedures. To take perhaps the most extreme example, automobile emissions standards are written into the actual text of the Clean Air Act rather than delegated to the Environmental Protection Agency (EPA) to establish. And virtually every statute has a vast array of required procedures and deadlines that, if they are not followed, give environmental groups an opportunity to sue. Thus, Congress, acting independent of the executive, plays a far more important role in determining the actual substance of environmental policy in the legislative process than in the case of Parliament in Canada.

Third, the active congressional role does not end once the exhaustive process of enacting legislation is completed. Congress continues to play a vigilant oversight role. Congressional oversight can take the form of hearings at which members can question or castigate responsible agency officials, requests for investigations by the General Accounting Office, or longer-term investigations by bodies like the National Academy of Sciences. Because of congressional control (shared with the President) over appointments,[10] statutory mandates, and especially agency budgets, these oversight activities influence agency behaviour.

Fourth, Congress also plays a very important role in the budgetary process. Formally, there is a distinction between the legislative or 'authorizing' process, such as passing new Clean Air Act amendments, and the 'appropriations' process, such as budgeting EPA to spend money to implement the Act. Two-thirds of the US federal budget is made up of entitlement programs and other forms of 'direct spending' that require no specific annual appropriations. The rest of government spending, including all environmental programs, is funded by 13 annual appropriations bills. (Funding for EPA is incorporated into the bill funding the Departments of Veterans Affairs and Housing and Urban Development, and independent agencies.) In practice, this distinction between legislation and budgeting is frequently blurred. 'Appropriations riders' refer to the practice of attaching specific language to spending bills that alter substantive law in one way or another, e.g., by prohibiting the spending of money on a specific activity or by creating a new exemption from a regulatory requirement.[11] 'Earmarking' is the practice of inserting in appropriations bills (or accompanying reports) specific language that sets aside funds within a broader account for a more specific purpose. Relevant examples of these phenomena will be described below.[12]

The different roles of legislatures in the policy process mean that the relationship between the government departments responsible for environmental protection and the political process is quite different. Environment Canada is a cabinet department, formally responsible to the legislature through the Minister of the Environment. Because of the limited independent role of the Parliament, however, the cabinet dominates the department's political environment. The US Environmental Protection Agency is a different type of agency in a different political environment. It is not a cabinet agency, like the US Departments of State, Interior, or Agriculture. It is an 'independent agency'. The distinction between the EPA's status and other cabinet departments is modest, however. It does mean that the head of the EPA (the Administrator) has no seat at the cabinet table, but in the US system the cabinet has no formal role and precious little informal role.[13] As an independent agency, the EPA reports directly to the President, but because of the complex array of congressional mandates it is authorized to implement and because of its need for annual budgetary appropriations, the EPA must remain responsive to Congress as well as the President.

Because of the importance of Congress, it is necessary to understand the legislative process. Clearly, this is not the place for a primer on how a bill becomes a law,[14] but several crucial features bear emphasis. Power is fragmented and there are a number of points where action can be vetoed. The House and the Senate play equal roles (although some functions are reserved for each chamber) and the agreement of both chambers is necessary for anything to go forward. Most of the real work is done in committees, the main point of access for those seeking to influence legislation. Over the past decade, party leaders have begun to play a more powerful role with respect to committees, but the latter are still exceptionally important. If a bill manages to survive the committee stage, it still must be approved on the floor in the context of a much greater diversity of legislative interests. In the Senate, this is particularly challenging, because the rules there allow for filibusters by those opposing legislation. Because it takes 60 senators to 'invoke cloture', i.e., cut off a filibuster, a relatively small group of senators can thwart action.

If the bill is successful in passing through both chambers, differences are ironed out in a 'conference committee', a temporary joint committee of relevant members of both chambers. If agreement is reached, the bill is then returned for ratification to the floors of both chambers (no amendments allowed) and, if that succeeds, sent to the President for signature. If the President vetoes the bill, Congress can overturn the veto with two-thirds majorities in *both* chambers. Because of that exacting standard, presidential vetoes are an exceptionally successful tool. The effect of this complex process is that *it requires extraordinary majorities to accomplish any legislative change.*

Political scientists studying legislative output have been surprised to find little difference in the productivity of Congress between periods of split and unified party control of the branches. The main reason for this is that the multiple veto points in the process mean that any coalition for action needs to attract an extraordinary majority. In terms of the probability of legislative change, the most important things to understand are the 'magic numbers' of 60 and 67. In a period of split party control, legislation needs to attract the support of 67 per cent of both chambers so that it can overcome a presidential veto. When one party controls both branches, things are not that much easier, as legislation still needs the support of 60 senators to overcome a filibuster. These realities make the pervasive sense of stalemate easier to understand.

Another profound difference between Canada and the US is the role of the courts. This results, in part, from different traditions in the judiciary, but more importantly from the institutional difference in legislative structures. Because legislation in Canada is written by the government party, there is little incentive to include provisions that 'fetter the Crown'. As a result, litigation over environmental issues in Canada is relatively rare. Two exceptions have been the area of environmental assessment, where non-discretionary duties were built into the policy,[15] and cases that raise constitutional questions about the division of power.

In contrast, in the US, the Congress distrusts the President, so it writes very detailed, 'action-forcing' statutes, which also contain provisions authorizing citizens to sue the agency (and sometimes polluters) for non-compliance. These statutes give interest groups a legal cause of action if the administration does not fully comply with deadlines and directives specified in the statute. As frustrating as it is for many, litigation is a normal, fundamental part of the US policy process. About one-third of the significant rules enacted by the EPA end up in court.[16] The Clean Air Act is a classic example. Most major rules are challenged in the courts by industry, environmentalists, or frequently both. The legalistic structure even provides opportunities on occasion for foreign governments such as Canada to sue the US.

Moreover, interest groups play a more important role in the US, in part because the institutional process gives them a large number of access points. For example, they can lobby Congress (through either branch), appeal directly to the EPA (or over its head to the President), pursue change through state governments, or take agencies to the courts. Interest groups frequently write legislation offered by members of Congress. While the role of industry groups is relatively similar in the two countries, environmental groups play a far more influential role in the US policy process. This results in part from their size, wealth, and sophistication. Drawing from a much wider base of population and financial support (much of it from philanthropic foundations, which are uncommon north of the border), US environmental groups have much more formidable analytical capacities than their Canadian counterparts. The legalism of the US system also gives environmentalists a significant power resource. Canadian environmentalists can lobby and attempt to mobilize the public, but generally they do not have formidable legal weapons. In the US, much of the environmental agenda is dictated by what issues environmentalists pursue in the courts.

While certainly daunting in its complexity, the combination of this greater role of Congress and the courts means that the policy process is far more open and accessible. A combination of statutory requirements and the need to defend against future judicial review means that agencies provide far more extensive public rationales for their rules than is the case in Canada. For Canada, this has the advantage of easing access to information about issues that may be of interest.

Despite initial intentions, the division of powers in Canada has evolved into a far more decentralized system than that of the US. For the most part, the Canadian federal government has been hesitant to play a strong role in setting standards and has chosen to play a more supportive role in research and facilitation of federal-provincial consensus on national standards. The US federal government plays a much larger role in setting national standards for a broader set of environmental issues. In addition, the US federal government has done so in a way that is much more hierarchical with respect to state governments. Federal legislation usually dictates outcomes but relies on state government implementation. However, state participation is often coerced rather than voluntary. This is exemplified by the Clean Air Act, through which the federal government establishes air quality and new source standards, but relies on the states to implement them. States are offered carrots in the form of financial support for state pollution control administration, and are threatened with sticks such as a ban on permitting new sources and loss of highway grants. This larger federal role has been quite resilient, despite the rise and fall of devolutionary movements over the past several decades. In contrast, the role of the Canadian federal government has fluctuated more in response to political conditions.[17]

Finally, the United States has generally relied on harder policy instruments in the environmental arena. It has been more willing to use command-and-control regulations to pursue environmental objectives, with legally mandated punitive measures for non-compliance.[18] This difference is revealed in both the type of policy instruments used and the style of enforcement, which tends to be more coercive in the US. Both countries have shown an increased interest in both market-oriented and co-operative approaches towards environmental policy in recent years, but the US is doing so from a baseline of a much more coercive tradition. The US approach also is likely to be more resilient in the face of the fluctuating priorities of the public and agencies.[19]

Trends in US Policy and Politics

Historically, the US has relied on command-and-control regulation, despite decades of criticisms by economists that taxes and marketable permits were a superior approach.[20] The economic argument is finally winning adherents, however. The major breakthrough was clearly the sulphur dioxide reduction program embodied in the 1990 Clean Air Act that created a very successful trading program for emission permits. A revealing indicator of the influence of market-based instruments is the debate over how to reduce greenhouse gas emissions. There is no discussion of any sort of uniform technology-based approach. Rather, the debate is over what type of incentive-based system, taxes or marketable permits, is likely to be most effective and politically marketable.[21] The US has developed considerable practical experience and an enormous amount of research on this issue, from which Canada could benefit in the redesign of existing programs or implementation of new programs.

The US also has shown increasing interest in 'challenge' programs, required reporting of emissions, and other programs designed to achieve voluntary environmental improvements. These programs are also popular in Canada, so there is a significant opportunity for cross-national learning. The difference between the two countries, however, is that in the US these programs are established within the context of a more rigorous regulatory framework. Indeed, voluntary programs may be more effective when used as a complement to traditional regulatory programs rather than as a replacement for them.[22]

As noted above, the federal division of powers in the US allows for a far more centralized environmental policy than in Canada. However, the trend in the US appears to be towards greater decentralization, reflecting a system-wide trend of greater assertiveness and innovation by state governments.[23] Some of the most important trends of the 1980s and 1990s emerged from state initiatives. Innovation can occur either in the creation of new programs with no federal precedent (such as disclosure requirements) or state decisions to go beyond the requirements of federal rules (such as California's automobile emission control requirements). Generally, federal environmental programs act as floors, allowing states to adopt more stringent standards. California is widely regarded as the most progressive state, so much so that one scholar has coined the term 'California effect' to refer to how the requirements of large and green jurisdictions can, through the sheer force of market attraction, pull up the standards of other jurisdictions. Michigan, Minnesota, New Jersey, and Massachusetts have also been credited with significant initiatives. Thus, monitoring US trends requires not just a focus on the federal level, but also an awareness of major initiatives in the states.[24]

PUBLIC OPINION: HIGH SUPPORT, LOW SALIENCE

Since the late 1960s, US opinion towards the environment has been characterized by a pattern of high 'support' but low 'salience,' with two exceptional bursts of salience that had extraordinary consequences.[25] Support measures basic attitudes towards the environment, such as how seriously people take environmental problems and how supportive they are of measures to address those problems, including how much they are willing to trade off other concerns, such as jobs. Polling has consistently shown very high support for environmental protection and surprisingly large numbers of respondents willing to support tough environmental controls, even if it costs jobs. For example, an April 1999 Gallup Poll asked the following question:

> Which of these statements come closer to your point of view: (1) Protection of the environment should be given priority, even at the risk of curbing economic growth, or (2) Economic growth should be given priority, even if the environment suffers to some extent?

Sixty-seven per cent of the respondents selected the first option, 28 per cent selected the second. From 1984 through 1999, the percentage of pro-environment responses to this Gallup question has ranged from 61 per cent to 71 per cent.[26] Salience is a different kind of measure of public opinion. It tries to measure how important an issue is to the public, usually framed as a response to the question, 'What do you see as the most important problem facing the nation?' When an issue is highly salient, it means voters are likely to make their choices based on how parties and candidates perform on that issue, which forces politicians to pay attention. When the issue is of low salience, politicians are more likely to think they can afford to ignore it. The environment has been a somewhat paradoxical issue, because it receives a great deal of support but is usually low in salience.

There were two major exceptions to this low salience: once around 1970, and once around 1990. At these times, environmental issues became 'top-of-mind' issues and dominated the media and the public agenda. Politicians were responsive in terms of major new programs. Both bursts of attention were followed by sharp declines in salience within a year. At present there is little evidence of a renewed burst of salience. A July 2000 *New York Times*/CBS poll showed 2 per cent of respondents selecting the environment as the most important problem, while an ABC/*Washington Post* poll at the same time showed the environment as tied for eighth among issues considered 'very important' to voters in the 2000 presidential election (Figure 9.1).[27]

During bursts of salience, politicians are forced to address environmental issues. During periods of low salience, Republicans have twice tried dramatic moves to weaken environmental policy: in the first several years of the Reagan administration and in the wake of the 1994 congressional elections. In both cases, a significant public backlash forced Republicans to retreat from their plans.

The major question regarding public opinion is whether we might be poised for another burst in salience. While a sample of two is not much to go on, there is a distinctive pattern behind the 1970 and 1990 bursts. Both resulted from a combination of long periods of economic prosperity and dramatic focusing events that drew attention to the issue.[28] The first condition was clearly in place in the United States in the mid- and late 1990s (although this appears to be changing now). Prosperity is probably a necessary condition, because it means people feel they can afford to be concerned about lifestyle issues as opposed to more basic economic concerns about employment and income security. It is not a sufficient condition, however. One or more major focusing events, e.g., a Chernobyl or *Exxon*

Figure 9.1: ABC News/Washington Post Poll on Important Issues in Decision on Who to Vote for in 2000 Presidential Election (taken 20–23 July 2000)

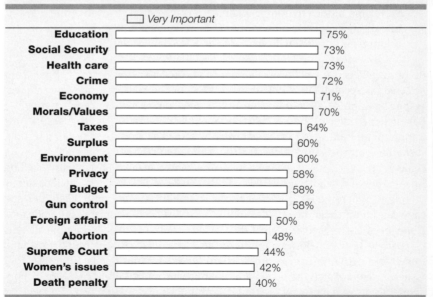

Source: http://www.pollingreport.com/prioriti.htm

Valdez disaster, could thrust the issue back to the top of the public minds. Policy-makers would be well advised to have strategies in place for how to ride the wave should it begin to break.

DIVIDED GOVERNMENT AND ENVIRONMENTAL POLICY IN THE 1990S

Since 1968, the dominant pattern of American elections has been 'divided government', that is, with the presidency being held by one party and at least one branch of Congress being held by the other party. From 1968 to 2000, this pattern has held 81 per cent of the time, the only exceptions being the four years of the Carter presidency (1976–80) and the first two years of the Clinton presidency (1993–4). The dominant pattern during this period was a Republican President and a Democratic Congress. But Clinton managed to pick the lock on the presidency in 1992, and in an event that stunned all political observers the 1994 elections swept Republicans into majorities in both the House and the Senate for the first time since 1954. From 1994 to 2000 a new pattern of Democrats in the White House and Republicans in Congress emerged.

Partisan control clearly makes a difference, because Democrats tend to be far more pro-environment than Republicans. Table 9.1 shows the differences in scores, with 100 being 'perfect', compiled by the League of Conservation Voters, which is based on analysis of congressional voting decisions.

Voters also recognized this difference. In a November 1999 *New York Times*/CBS poll, the environment was tied with health care as the issue on which the Democrats had the biggest advantage over Republicans.[29]

Environmental policy in the 1990s has been extremely divisive. The decade began with an extraordinary accomplishment and ended with a legacy of gridlock and inaction. The 1990 Clean Air Act, which included a significant acid rain reduction program of benefit to Canada, showed that the system is still capable of producing significant environmental legislation, but that it requires very special conditions. The acid rain issue had been festering for a decade and a number of other aspects of the Clean Air Act needed change, but the Reagan administration was very resistant. One of the ways that President George Bush sought to distinguish himself as 'kinder and gentler' than former President Ronald Reagan was his 1988 campaign commitment to become 'the environmental President'. While

Table 9.1: League of Conservation Voter Scores

	House		*Senate*	
	Democrats	Republicans	Democrats	Republicans
1998	84	24	72	12
1996	74	20	84	13
1994	68	19	75	19

Source: http://www.lcv.org/scorecards/index.htm

Bush generally had a poor environmental record, particularly on international issues (recall Rio), he staked his commitment on revising the Clean Air Act. He was successful for two reasons: first, sufficient congressional support was mustered by Senate Majority Leader George Mitchell, a tireless advocate of clean air, and, second, a major burst in the salience of environmental issues in 1989 and 1990 made both parties want to have a positive environmental record.[30]

Despite the emergence of unified government with the election of Bill Clinton in 1992, little legislative action occurred on the environment in the first two years, as the system focused on the budget, health care, and welfare reform. The dynamics changed dramatically after the stunning 1994 congressional elections swept Republican majorities into both houses of Congress. Part of Newt Gingrich's 'Contract with America' involved dramatic reforms to regulation to reduce costs. But when Congress began moving on the issue, it was confronted by the same kind of public backlash that met Reagan's efforts to roll back environmental policy in his first few years in office. In both cases, Republicans fell into the 'salience trap', mistaking their victories as mandates to reverse environmental policy.

After the first session of the 104th Congress (1995), the Republicans retreated from their efforts to reform environmental laws. They adopted the more furtive strategy, however, of undercutting regulation by defunding environmental agencies and attaching riders to appropriations bills that hamstrung agency implementation of their environmental mandates. These initiatives provoked high-level tensions between Congress and Clinton, and were part of the mix of factors that caused the budgetary gridlock that shut down the government for a period in late 1995 and into 1996. Clinton won the public relations battle over the shutdown, and Congress backed off from its efforts to defund environmental agencies.[31]

However, Congress has clung to its strategy of attaching riders to appropriations bills, denounced as 'policy by stealth' by critics in the administration and elsewhere. As described above, the substance of policy is supposed to be made in the so-called 'authorizing' of statutes (such as the Clean Air Act or Endangered Species Act), but the gridlock over statutory change creates pressures for the expression of congressional policy input that get channelled into the budgetary process. Appropriations bills, the 13 money bills that provide the funding for specific agencies, are attractive vehicles because they have to be passed every year in order to fund the government. While there are many examples of such riders in the environmental area, one of the most prominent is the rider for the 1998–9 fiscal year (re-enacted for 1999–2000)[32] that prevents the administration from spending any money on any new programs to implement the Kyoto Protocol on climate change.[33] Because it is far less public and visible, the increased reliance on this strategy creates new challenges for those attempting to monitor environmental provisions through the legislative process. Fortunately, US environmental groups have learned to be very vigilant in observing this practice.[34]

IMPLICATIONS OF THE 2000 ELECTIONS

The extraordinary elections of the year 2000 have left the US body politic evenly divided and sharply polarized. Nonetheless, Republicans control the presidency, the House, and the Senate for the first time since 1954. George W. Bush's contested victory gives the presidency back to the Republicans, but the conflicts over the election weakened any mandate for change that he can claim. Republicans have a razor-thin edge in the House and control the evenly divided Senate only because the Republican Vice-President casts the tie-breaking vote.

Despite their narrow advantage, Republicans will control both the administrative and the legislative agenda. Bush's record in Texas and his statements in the campaign suggest that he is unlikely to pursue any major new environmental initiatives and that he would focus on reforming existing programs to increase the role of voluntary and market measures. Because the Democrats hold 50 seats in the Senate and thus can easily filibuster any anti-environmental bills, it is unlikely that there will be any major statutory changes to relax environmental controls. But environmentalists will be constantly on the defensive. In addition, Republican control over administration and enforcement might produce some significant changes in policy. And it is unlikely that a Bush administration will take any international leadership in environmental policy. Canada should expect much less co-operation on bilateral and multilateral environmental issues. It is most likely that the US agenda will be oriented towards reducing the costs of environmental programs, which strengthens the hand of those resistant to the green agenda north of the border.

Strategies for Influencing the United States

The wide variety of mechanisms by which bilateral issues with the US might emerge creates a real challenge for Canadian environmental policy-makers. The cross-border flow consists not just of pollutants, but also of economic costs and policy models. In some cases, US influence creates a real threat to the Canadian environment, either directly through transborder pollution or indirectly by constraining Canadian policy capacities. In other cases, US influence has a positive impact on the Canadian environment. Canadians concerned about domestic environmental protection might actually welcome some forms of influence.

To the extent that Canada wants to influence US policy, there are six potential options: working-level arrangements; direct diplomacy; using bilateral and multilateral institutions; getting our own house in order; fostering analytical capacity and communication; and mobilizing support within US civil society. Each of these strategies, summarized in Table 9.2, has its own advantages and disadvantages.

WORKING-LEVEL ARRANGEMENTS

On any issue of trade or transboundary pollution, it makes sense to rely first and foremost on the many working-level arrangements that already exist between officials to share information and address differences. This has the advantage of focusing arguments directly on issues of concern and may be the most efficient means of resolution. However, technical working arrangements are unlikely to be able to resolve issues where any significant political conflict exists.

DIRECT DIPLOMACY

When working-level arrangements are not adequate to resolving conflicts, direct diplomacy is typically the next choice. Diplomacy also has the advantage of directly focusing Canadian arguments on issues of greatest concern. The major disadvantage of this approach, however, is US parochialism. US policies are over-whelmingly influenced by domestic politics and Canadians do not vote in US elections. This is especially true of Congress. While on many issues of foreign policy, the President and other officials have significant room to manoeuvre, they tend to be far more constrained on issues with direct domestic implications in the US, and virtually all bilateral environmental issues have domestic implications.

The 1990 Clean Air Act amendments are a classic example. Despite the over-whelming support for the Canadian position in both international law and basic ethics, none of the major accounts of the enactment of the acid rain reduction program credit Canadian arguments with any significant role.[35] Canadian argu-ments lent some very modest strength to the arguments of environmentalists and their allies, and Bush's desire for good relations with Canada may have increased

Table 9.2: Strategies for Influencing the US

Strategy	Advantages	Disadvantages
Working-level arrangements	• Direct • Focused • Quiet	• Limited to issues where political conflict is minimal
Direct diplomacy	• Above board • Direct • Focused	• US parochialism
International institutions	• Slight increase in legitimacy over direct diplomacy	• US parochialism
Put our own house in order	• Strengthens moral case • Promotes domestic environmental agenda	• Potential for overkill (unwarranted expense)
Mobilize US domestic support	• Taps into source of incentive for US policy	• Indirect • Risks accusations of foreign meddling
Foster analytical capacity	• Strengthens arguments within US domestic arena • Domestic Canadian benefits • International prestige	• Indirect • Costly

his interest in seeing the issue through.[36] But both in the White House and far more so on Capitol Hill, the domestic configuration of interests within the US determines environmental policy.

In the more recent regulatory controversies over regional ground-level ozone transport, an issue in which Canada again has a direct stake based on both international law and basic ethics, Canada receives no mention in the exceptionally extensive documentation supporting EPA decision-making.[37] Of course, influence does operate in the opposite direction, from the US to Canada, as Chapter 13 in this volume demonstrates. But even when core environmental programs are in crisis, the EPA declines to refer to Canadian arguments and interests to buttress its arguments. If Canadian interests are relevant, American decision-makers hide it well.

USING BILATERAL, REGIONAL, OR MULTILATERAL FORUMS

There are many opportunities to use international forums to attempt to influence US policy. The International Joint Commission (IJC) and Great Lakes bodies are clear examples in the bilateral context, the NAAEC in the regional context. These institutions have an advantage over bilateral diplomacy because they have a status independent of Canadian national interests and, in the regional or multilateral context, they can marshal the support of other countries. However, these institutions face the same resistance from US parochialism. Reports and actions of such forums are more likely to be influential if they are picked up and used by domestic interests in the US.

GETTING OUR OWN HOUSE IN ORDER

Canada may also have to take the more costly step of leading by example. Again, the acid rain case is relevant. In the US context, the Canadian arguments would have had even less weight if Canada had not taken a major initiative on its own. It will be difficult to persuade reluctant US politicians if Canada is not complying with the same (or more stringent) standards it is asking the US to enact. In Canadian diplomacy there is little more than the moral force of arguments, and the moral advantage requires leading by example. This strategy has the added benefit of using bilateral issues to leverage more domestic environmental protection in Canada. The disadvantage is that it puts Canada in something of an awkward position when domestic environmental conditions might not justify as stringent limitations (e.g., automobile emission controls). Canada might find itself implementing costly standards in the ultimately fruitless hope of encouraging US co-operation.

MOBILIZING US DOMESTIC SUPPORT

The key to the heart of any American politician is constituent support. Thus, a major avenue for potential influence is indirectly through US interest groups. While US environmental groups are exceptionally resourceful compared to their Canadian counterparts, they are always looking for ways to strengthen their legal, factual, and political arguments. Canadian officials and interest groups can take advantage of this desire. The risk of this strategy is the potential for backlash against foreign manipulation of domestic US politics. Despite Canada's clear stakes in the acid rain battle, that accusation emerged on several occasions in the 1980s.

FOSTERING ANALYTICAL CAPACITY

Perhaps the most effective strategy might be to foster the analytical capacity on the problems at stake and to communicate that analysis effectively. Canada has already developed a stellar reputation for its global climate modelling. If it could extend that prestige to other areas of analysis, Canadian concerns could find their way into US politics through the use of Canadian analysis by those seeking the strongest factual arguments to strengthen their position. Again, the disadvantage of this strategy is its indirectness and its potential to distort the allocation of financial and analytical resources. But if there are areas where investment in analysis would yield domestic payoffs as well, this approach might yield significant dividends. Within domestic Canadian politics, the approach is also consistent with a renewed emphasis on strengthening research and development and the scientific community more generally. The Internet should make the communication aspects of that strategy relatively inexpensive.

Clearly, these strategies are not mutually exclusive. In fact, on issues of importance (e.g., ground-level ozone) it makes sense to pursue all of them simultaneously. But in choosing how to allocate resources, one should always keep in mind the inherent limits on Canadian influence or, for that matter, the influence of any foreign country on US policies. In 1968, during his first official visit to Washington, Trudeau said that living next to the United States is like a mouse sleeping next to an elephant. Thirty years later, there have been dramatic changes in environmental policy and politics and breathtaking innovations in communications. Yet the distribution of power between the countries has not changed in any fundamental way. It is not impossible for a mouse to influence an elephant, but it is wise to choose strategies with caution and to be realistic about their impact.

Notes

1 See, for example, National Wildlife Federation, *What's Trade Got to Do With It? A Guide to Trade Policy and Saving the Environment* (Washington: National Wildlife Federation, 1999); Steven Shrybman, *The World Trade Organization: A Guide for Environmentalists* (Vancouver: West Coast Environmental Law Association, 1999). Available at http://www.vcn.bc.ca/wcel/trade/

2 George Hoberg, 'Trade, Harmonization, and Domestic Autonomy in Environmental Policy', *Journal of Comparative Policy Analysis* (forthcoming); Padideh Ala'I, 'Free Trade or Sustainable Development? An Analysis of the WTO Appellate Body's Shift to a More Balanced Approach to Trade Liberalization', *American University International Law Review* 14, 4 (1999): 1129-71; Robert Howse and Donald Regan, 'The Product/Process Distinction—An Illusory Basis for Disciplining Unilateralism in Trade Policy', *European Journal of International Law* 11, 2 (2000): 249-89.

3 Howard Mann and Howard von Moltke, 'NAFTA's Chapter 11 and the Environment: Addressing the Impacts of the Investor-State Process on the Environment' (Winnipeg: International Institute for Sustainable Development, 1999). In the MMT case, the Canadian federal government sought to ban the sale of this manganese-based gas additive on the grounds that the substance was toxic, although the science was uncertain. The government backed off this decision when the major US supplier, Ethyl Corp., initiated proceedings under NAFTA's investor-suit provisions to sue the Canadian government for compensation of lost investment. In the case of Sun Belt Water Co., this California company initiated a suit against the BC government, using the same NAFTA clause, after its licence to draw and export water from the province was revoked.

4 See David Vogel, *Trading Up* (Cambridge, Mass.: Harvard University Press, 1995).

5 See Chapter 13 for a detailed discussion of the US influence on Canadian air quality policy.

6 See Wilson (Chapter 3) and Cashore and Bernstein (Chapter 11) in this volume.

7 For detailed discussion of these cases, see Chapter 5 (James Bay), Chapter 11 (BC forestry), and Chapter 16 (endangered species).

8 Donald Savoie, *Governing from the Centre: The Concentration of Power in Canadian Politics* (Toronto: University of Toronto Press, 1999).

9 The President can't technically introduce legislation but it is never difficult to get a member of the party in Congress to introduce an administration bill.

10 While not separated out here, the appointment process is another avenue for congressional influence. The President appoints high-level officials, usually ranging from the secretary or administrator to the next two levels down in the agency, but approval is required by a simple majority of the Senate.

11 An appropriations rider is a subset of the broader category of legislative riders, a term usually referred to when unrelated amendments are attached to another piece of legislation. This practice is a clear violation of House rules but is allowed in the Senate. In the appropriations context, riders are usually more related to the substantive aspects of the spending measure, but they still are considered a violation of the principle of the separation of the authorization and appropriations processes. They persist when, for political reasons or lack of awareness, authorizing committees or other members do not object.

12 Congressional Research Service, *The Congressional Appropriations Process: An Introduction*, 11. Available at http://www.house.gov/rules/crs_reports.htm

13 For an amusing perspective, see Robert Reich, *Locked in the Cabinet* (New York: Knopf, 1997).

14 Project Vote Smart has one such primer: http://www.vote-smart.org/ce/congresstrack/billtolaw.phtml?titlehead = How + a + Bill + Becomes + a + Law&checking =

15 See discussions by Harrison, Chapter 7, and Valiente, Chapter 1, concerning environmental assessment.

16 Cary Coglianese, 'Assessing Consensus: The Promise and Performance of Negotiated Rulemaking', *Duke Law Journal* 46 (1997): 1255–1350.

17 Kathryn Harrison, 'The Origins of National Standards: Comparing Federal Government Involvement in Environmental Policy in Canada and the United States', in Patrick Fafard and Harrison, eds, *Managing the Environmental Union* (Kingston: Queen's University School of Public Policy and Saskatchewan Institute for Public Policy, 2000), 49–80.

18 George Hoberg, 'Governing the Environment: Environmental Policy in Canada and the United States', in Keith Banting, Hoberg, and Richard Simeon, eds, *Degrees of Freedom: Canada and the United States in a Changing Global Context* (Kingston and Montreal: McGill-Queen's University Press, 1997), 341–88; George Hoberg and Kathryn Harrison, 'It's Not Easy Being Green: The Politics of Canada's Green Plan', *Canadian Public Policy—Analyse de Politiques* 20 (June 1994): 119–37.

19 Harrison, 'The Origins of National Standards'.

20 This section does not review trends in environmental conditions and programs specifically. The most comprehensive survey of the effectiveness of US environmental programs, at least for pollution control, is J. Clarence Davies and Jan Mazurek, *Pollution Control in the United States* (Washington: Resources for the Future, 1998). Paul Portney, president of Resources for the Future and a leading observer of US environmental policy, claims 'it is virtually inconceivable that ambient environmental conditions in the United States, as well as in most other western democracies, will not continue to improve in the decades to come.' Portney, 'Environmental Problems and Policy: 2000–2050', *Journal of Economic Perspectives* (forthcoming).

21 Ibid.

22 Kathryn Harrison, 'Talking with the Donkey', *Journal of Industrial Ecology* 2, 3 (1988): 51–72.

23 Barry Rabe, 'Power to the States: The Promise and Pitfalls of Decentralization', in Norman J. Vig and Michael E. Kraft, eds, *Environmental Policy*, 4th edn (Washington: Congressional Quarterly Press, 1999); Harrison, 'The Origins of National Standards'; Portney, 'Environmental Problems and Policy'.

24 One such effort to do so in the case of climate change is Barry Rabe, 'Greenhouse and Statehouse: American State and Canadian Provincial Capacity to Address Global Climate Change', paper presented at the 15th Biennial Conference of the Association for Canadian Studies in the United States, Pittsburgh, 17–21 Nov. 1999. Rabe concludes that 'the conventional wisdom on the perceived virtues of environmental regulatory decentralization is sorely tested by the recent experience of American states and Canadian provinces in relation to greenhouse gases and climate change.'

25 Riley Dunlap, 'Public Opinion and Environmental Policy', in James Lester, *Environmental Politics and Policy: Theories and Evidence* (Durham, NC: Duke University Press, 1989), 87–134; Christopher Bosso, 'Environmental Groups and the New Political Landscape', in Vig and Kraft, eds, *Environmental Policy*, 55–76.

26 The Gallup Organization, 'Environmental Concern Wanes in 1999 Earth Day Poll'. Available at http://www.gallup.com/poll/releases/pr990422.asp

27 http://www.nytimes.com/library/national/072500poll-results.html. For a compilation of issue priority polls, see http://www.pollingreport.com/prioriti.htm

28 George Hoberg, 'Environmental Policy: Alternative Styles', in Michael Atkinson, ed., *Governing Canada: State Institutions and Public Policy* (Toronto: HBJ-Holt Canada, 1993), 307–42.

29 http://www.nytimes.com/library/national/111099poll-results.html

30 Gary Bryner, *Blue Skies, Green Politics: The Clean Air Act of 1990 and Its Implementation* (Washington: Congressional Quarterly Books, 1995).

31 A nice overview of congressional action (or inaction) during this period can be found in Michael Kraft, 'Environmental Policy in Congress: From Consensus to Gridlock', in Vig and Kraft, eds, *Environmental Policy*, 121–44.

32 This rider is available on-line at
http://thomas.loc.gov/cgi-bin/query/D?c106:1:./temp/ ~ c106jYnBDx:e104041:

33 Michael J. O'Grady, 'Going Nowhere Fast: The Environmental Record of the 105th Congress', *ELR News & Analysis* 29, 2 (Feb. 1999): 10085–10103.

34 For example, the Natural Resource Defense Council Web site tracks these initiatives. See http://www.nrdc.org/field/state.html

35 Bryner, *Blue Skies, Green Politics*; Richard E. Cohen, *Washington at Work: Back Rooms and Clean Air* (New York: Prentice-Hall, 1994).

36 These observations are based on the author's own analysis as well as personal communications with Gary Bryner.

37 The 691 pages of the 'NOx SIP call' rule do not contain a notice of Canadian interests; 424 pages of the 'final action on Section 126 petitions' contain no mention of Canada. The July 1997 Ozone NAAQS (National Ambient Air Quality Standard) final rule contained one mention of Canada but only in the context of a health study. The 29 Oct. 1999 proposed reinstatement of a one-hour standard did not include a mention of Canada. All of these documents are accessible at http://www.epa.gov/airlinks/

Chapter 10

Milk-and-Potatoes Environmentalism: Canada and the Turbulent World of International Law

Robert Boardman

International environmental law has become a more entrenched feature of international politics. This rapidly growing world of rules and rule-making, norms and governance is now much more complicit with trade policy, and, through the growth of compliance mechanisms, more intrusive and demanding in its claims on states than was true a decade ago. This chapter looks at the significance of these systemic developments and at the capacities of Canada's external policies to influence them. After discussing the nature of international law, the chapter turns to three international settings of environmentalism: multilateral environmental agreements; the growing interconnections among trade and environment issues as a result of the North American Free Trade Agreement (NAFTA) and the World Trade Organization (WTO); and the effects of international environmental developments on Canada's bilateral relations with other states, and particularly in relation to the European Union (EU), Japan, and developing countries. Canada-US bilateral relations are dealt with in Chapter 9, while Canadian policies specifically in relation to the international climate change regime are discussed in Chapter 15.

Environmental Governance and the State System

The internationalization of environmental policy in recent decades is a result of three interrelated sets of factors. First, many environmental problems have increasingly been recognized as transnational in character. Pollutants and hazards spill over borders, for example, in rivers and in trade flows. The boundaries of states have not usually been determined by ecological processes. The Canada-US border intersects nine ecological regions, several mountain ranges, and different types of forests, as well as two coastal plains and the Great Lakes.[1] Responses to many problems, from the spread of disease vectors in sub-Saharan Africa to the cyanide spill on the Danube in 2000, cannot be contained within particular polities. Transborder collaboration is thus a prerequisite for sustained and effective environmental policy. Further, several core issues transcend particular bilateral settings and international regions. The consequences of depletion of the ozone layer, climate change induced by economic activities, and the complex interactions among the oceans and atmosphere affect all countries. As Hurrell and Kingsbury have observed, 'it is this global character that is the most distinctive feature of the present era.'[2]

Second, national responses to environmental problems are now formulated in complex transnational networks comprising states and non-state actors. National governments remain significant players in these changing mixes. Law-making processes, for example, retain much of their classical state-based character. The territorial organization of the international system both reflects and constitutes historical conceptions of sovereignty, the rights of states, and the bases of political community. States continue to regulate trade and influence the direction of capital flows. These activities shape international environmental politics in fundamental ways. In the agreements of the 1990s, however, we see internationally defined obligations and the presence of shifting mosaics of governance players exerting a greater pull on governments. Internationalization, according to Schreurs and Economy, 'reflects the efforts by international actors and institutions to reach down into the state to set domestic policy agendas and influence policy formation and implementation processes.'[3] This process has also energized domestic politics. As shown in Canadian responses to the 1997 Kyoto Protocol on climate change and the negotiations on the Biosafety Protocol of the Convention on Biological Diversity (CBD) in 1999–2000, the making and implementation of international legal instruments affects domestic interests. Clashes of interest also structure the alignments of states. An important factor for Canada in the 1990s was a polarization on several key issues between the US and the EU, a product of often profoundly different views of the trade-and-environment architecture of global governance. Canada was among the countries, led by the US, pressing for WTO examination of the rules on trade in products containing genetically modified organisms in the preparations for the Seattle meetings in 1999, but strong opposition from Brussels in effect vetoed this.

The games of international rule-making have nonetheless become open to other kinds of actors than states. Companies have interests that extend transnationally. Many have a stake in international environmental policy developments and lobby institutions directly and through industry associations. The World Health Organization (WHO) regularly consults with pharmaceutical companies on some issues, while others, including tobacco companies, have engaged in campaigns to discredit the agency's programs in developing countries. A common theme taken up by corporations has been the need for greater harmonization of environmental rules, partly to make markets less vulnerable to the campaigns of non-governmental organizations (NGOs). The Global Environmental Management Initiative is one such grouping that has argued on behalf of a group of multinational corporations in favour of higher environmental standards.[4]

Environmental groups have also become more influential. They contribute to agenda-setting, help monitor international agreements and publicize defectors and stragglers, educate publics, and collect and disseminate data. During the 1990s NGOs steadily expanded their capacities to influence United Nations (UN) multilateral conferences, both directly and through the organization of parallel non-governmental forums.[5] Some have become skilled in the art of developing relations with sympathetic states or agencies, as in the collaboration between NGOs and parts of the Department of Foreign Affairs and International Trade (DFAIT) that led to the anti-personnel mines agreement of 1997. Many groups also retain options of extra-institutional protest, as in Greenpeace's traditional activities against whaling and nuclear power and the support various environmental groups lent to anti-globalization protests in Seattle and other cities in 1999–2000.

Intergovernmental organizations (IGOs), the other element in this non-state mix, are creatures of the states that constitute their memberships and provide them with funding, personnel, and policy support. But they are also capable of manoeuvring autonomously to effect change. These have become more significant as sources of the agreements and norms that influence the environmental policies of national governments.[6] There are multiple sources of environmental initiative, as well as multiple veto points, in the international system. Those important for Canada include the UN and its multilateral conferences, its regional institutions (particularly the Economic Commission for Europe [ECE]), and the intergovernmental agencies linked to it (such as the International Maritime Organization on marine pollution). IGOs and conventions provide government agencies and NGOs with a growing and ceaseless annual round of meetings of working groups, regional groups, conferences of parties, and preparatory and negotiating committees for new agreements and conferences. Debates on ways to expand the political clout of intergovernmental environmentalism are endemic to these activities. Many critics have argued for a restructuring of the UN system to give greater prominence to sustainable development issues. The rise and environmental policy significance of the WTO in the 1990s highlighted the relative weakness of many environment-related IGOs and led to renewed debate on the prospects for some form of world environmental organization.[7]

A third set of factors stems from processes of economic globalization. These raise major questions about the capacities of states.[8] First, economic change reinforces minimalist conceptions of the appropriate roles of governments (and, except for trade-policy bodies, of IGOs). Concepts of environmentalism grounded in interventionist states have been largely discredited. Regulatory or command-and-control strategies have given way to a diversity of more market-friendly mechanisms such as tradable pollution permits. Second, the dynamics of trade liberalization also lead to pressures for greater harmonization, or at least steps to reduce significant disparities among the environmental standards of jurisdictions. The objection here is not so much to regulation itself but to the spread of widely different standards among jurisdictions and sectors on the grounds that these can have trade-distorting effects. The Agreement on Technical Barriers to Trade negotiated in the Uruguay Round of the GATT (General Agreement on Tariffs and Trade, the predecessor regime to the WTO), for example, aimed to encourage though not to require states to adopt international standards in environment-related areas. Differences among standards are tolerable in trade regimes so long as governments do not by this means discriminate between domestic and foreign economic actors.

Of the underlying principles of international environmental agreements, two are both fundamental and at the same time politically controversial. The precautionary principle, VanderZwaag has written, has become 'an evolving norm of international environmental law'[9], as well as one with 'hesitant acceptances' in Canadian environmental law. It emphasizes the fact of scientific uncertainty on many environmental issues, but argues against this fact becoming a rationale for failure to take preventive action. The onus is on proponents of development projects to defend these against environmental impact and other criteria. Trade agreements, by contrast, including NAFTA, tend to operate in the reverse direction. They place the burden of proof instead on the producers of environmental rules to justify these against trade-restriction criteria. Second, many international instruments, echoing Principle 21 of the UN Conference on the Human Environment (UNCHE) Declaration of 1972 and various formulations since, draw on classical notions of sovereignty to maintain that states have a 'sovereign right' to develop their natural resources. This is subject, however, to the rule that they also have an obligation not to cause environmental damage outside their borders, or a duty to inform others of possible transboundary consequences of domestic actions. Even so, this qualification is sometimes overshadowed by more insistent defences of sovereign rights by developing countries, for example over tropical forests, that constrain the pursuit of international environmental agreements.

The growing international dimension of environmental policy, then, comprises formal agreements, accepted norms, looser obligations contained in IGO resolutions and other forms of soft law, and the continuing activities of international institutions.[10] Conventions have expanded considerably in number, scope, and complexity. Those since the mid-1980s have included agreements with far-reaching implications for economies and national policies. Canada's involvement began with the 1906 boundary waters agreement with the US; the pace of Canadian responses to international agreements accelerated in the 1940s and then again during the 1960s.[11] A recent Organization for Economic Co-operation and Development (OECD) classification groups environmental agreements into those on atmospheric pollution (19 major agreements in recent decades), inland water pollution (19), fisheries (22), flora and fauna (26), nuclear issues (21), and marine pollution (62).[12] 'Soft' instruments include the resolutions and declarations of IGOs and multilateral conferences. Both the Stockholm (1972) and Rio (1992) conferences were associated with influential statements of global environmental principles. A non-binding statement of principles on the world's forests, adopted at the 1992 summit, led to several years of international efforts, in which Canada took a lead, aimed at a formal agreement.

Convention-making processes recognize sovereignty and state power. Some types are focused around an institution, such as the International Maritime Organization. Others are the products of multilateral negotiating sessions convened for that purpose. Many depend at key points on the initiatives of supporting states. Many also have a lengthy 'pre-history'. The 1997 Kyoto Protocol has been described as the result of 'decades of scientific research and many years of economic and political analysis'.[13] In some, such as the UN Convention on the Law of the Sea, sheer complexity and multiple conflicting interests make for protracted preparatory and negotiating sequences. The Convention on Biological Diversity in 1992 was shaped by several sets of interests represented by the proponents of parks and protected areas, debt-for-nature agreements, a global environmental fund, sustainable use of resources, farmers' rights, and bio-prospecting.[14] The typical pattern is for countries to negotiate a convention, decide whether or not to sign, and then make key decisions on ratification at a later stage according to their respective constitutional rules. Agreements normally enter into force internationally when a defined number of states have acceded. As with key marine pollution agreements, these may then be subject to change through formal amendments in subsequent negotiating rounds. Some, such as the Convention on International Trade in Endangered Species (CITES) of 1973, contain technical appendices that are the focus of negotiations at regularly scheduled conferences of the parties (COPs). An increasingly common approach, as in the Vienna Convention for the Protection of the Ozone Layer (1985) and the Framework Convention on Climate Change (FCCC) of 1992, is for the agreement itself to define a broad framework of principles, goals, and institutional machinery, with the specifics of timetables and other matters being left for later negotiations in protocols.

Canada and International Environmental Agreements

Canada has a varying stake in these agreements. Some international conventions are restricted in scope to particular regions. Several, for example, have historically been structured around transborder problems in Europe, such as those of rivers. According to one estimate, Canada has signed or endorsed more than 230 international environmental instruments.[15] In some, such as the recent agreements on climate change, biodiversity, and transboundary pollutants, important private-sector interests are affected. However, the criteria for Canada's engagement with international environmental agreements have historically not been restricted to narrow conceptions of self-interest. In Canadian foreign policy of the classical mould, definitions of enlightened self-interest produced commitments to international institutions and placed intrinsic values on governance by multilateralism. Environmental policy rationales have also glided into larger foreign policy conceptualizations, such as those of comprehensive security arising out of European debates in the 1980s and Ottawa's human security agenda of the second half of the 1990s.

Canada has a limited capacity to influence systemic developments in a world of 190–plus states, numerous IGOs and NGOs, and large-scale structural features such as US-EU disputes and North-South divides. Several factors nonetheless enhance Ottawa's capacities for leverage.

For example, Canada can draw on a reservoir of internationally recognized contributions to global environmental leadership. Ottawa played a key role in the development of the Convention on Long-Range Transboundary Air Pollution (LRTAP) of 1979. Canadian diplomacy led to the 1995 UN agreement on straddling and highly migratory fish stocks, following the turbot war with Spain and Canada's pursuit of international recognition of the right to apply conservation rules on selected areas of the high seas. Canada has been a diligent supporter of the work of conventions such as CITES and those on world heritage (of the UN Educational, Scientific and Cultural Organization [UNESCO]) and the world's wetlands (the Ramsar Convention), and a skilful promoter of new targets for legal development such as forests. The Canadian government provides facilities for the secretariats, in Montreal, of the CBD, NAFTA's Commission on Environmental Cooperation (CEC), and the Multilateral Fund of the Montreal Protocol on the ozone layer. Meetings hosted by Canada, and groupings of states in which Canadian officials played key roles, were critical to the negotiation and progress of the ozone layer, climate change, and biodiversity conventions. Individual Canadians have been important. They include Maurice Strong, who organized and chaired the landmark UN conferences of 1972 and 1992 and has occupied key positions in the UN Environment Program (UNEP), the International Union for the Conservation of Nature (IUCN/World Conservation Union), and the UN; and Jim McNeill, who first in the OECD and then in the Brundtland Commission of the 1980s was instrumental in securing international recognition of the principles of sustainable development. Canadian scientists such as Kenneth Hare, on climate change and nuclear wastes, and Richard Vollenweider, on the eutrophication of lakes and water quality issues, have helped shape both the science and the transnational policy processes in key areas. Despite gaps, Canada also has a domestic environmental regime that is usually more than sufficient to back up its credentials as an international player. Its more general diplomatic capabilities help in the tasks of collaborating with other states, as Canada has done with Malaysia, Costa Rica, Mexico, Japan, and other countries on international forest issues. Canada's location, physical features, and natural resources make it almost by definition a crucial participant in any international arrangements on the Arctic, coastal management, climate change, transboundary pollution problems, protected areas and national parks, and world fisheries and forests issues.

Several developments of the 1990s affected Canadian policies. First, in relation to peacekeeping and development assistance as well as the environment, there was a growing consensus on a need for Canada to be more selective in its attempts at international influence in light of accelerating international demands and domestic fiscal restraint. The extensive network of international environmental institutions makes this a difficult task. DFAIT in 2000 defined the focal points of Canada's international environmental interest as the UN Commission on Sustainable Development, UNEP, the CEC, the Arctic Council, and the Organization of American States.[16] Second, as emphasized in the Liberal government's 1995 foreign policy paper, external policies generally have had to be tailored to meet domestic requirements more clearly, particularly Canada's economic interests. Third, economic globalization has entailed a diminution in Ottawa's capacity, and political will, to engage in across-the-board, proactive multilateralism. Power in the Canadian state, as Peter Phillips puts it, has been moving sideways (to other countries), downwards (to the provinces), upwards (to IGOs), and, finally, 'nowhere—just away'.[17]

Three examples illustrate differing aspects of recent Canadian environmental diplomacy: the CBD and the 2000 Biosafety Protocol; work on international forestry arrangements; and international rules on transboundary pollution.

The push for the CBD in the 1980s came primarily from UNEP. Differing perspectives were represented in Canada's approach, including, within the federal government, the views of Environment Canada, External Affairs, the Canadian Forest Service, and Fisheries and Oceans. The international process resonated with key features of Canadian international environmental policy. It provided a further opportunity, following Canada's leading role in ozone developments in the 1980s, to gain prestige through global leadership. More tangibly, it focused on an instrument that would promote (or, depending on the form it took, could threaten) Canadian interests in relation to agriculture, fisheries, and genetic resources. On critical issues such as technology transfer, global funding mechanisms, and sovereignty over biological resources, it potentially called for the kind of mediating North-South diplomacy that Canada was well able to contribute. Canada's interests were thus grounded in a complex blend of support for environmental multilateralism and an economic stake in outcomes. During the 1980s, for example, Canada, along with the US, France, Britain, West Germany, and Japan, had strenuously resisted developing country strategies through the UN's Food and Agriculture Organization (FAO) to treat hybrid seeds developed from Southern biological resources under 'common heritage' principles, on the grounds of the threat this would pose to intellectual property rights more widely.[18] Concern for the implications of biodiversity regime development for intellectual property rights generally, and resource exports specifically, continued to be a key theme of Canadian approaches to the CBD in 1991–2. At Rio in 1992, Canada worked with other states on several issues, e.g., with the pro-convention forces centred initially on Australia and New Zealand, and with Sweden and Peru on issues surrounding the use of genetic resources, including recognition of their cultural and religious significance. Canada was the first industrialized country to ratify the convention, and produced its follow-up biodiversity strategy in 1995.

Although many of these diverse, and to some extent conflicting, components remained in place in the Canadian policy approach, by the late 1990s the balance among them had shifted. There was a greater readiness to listen to the concerns of the US at the 1995 COP. At Rio the US delegation had been deeply critical of the CBD process. It had strenuously opposed measures that it argued would violate intellectual property rights related to biological resources and restrict the activities of companies in developing countries. Although the Clinton administration signed the CBD in 1993, key provisions remained controversial and ratification was blocked in Congress. From the mid-1990s on, environment and health officials in Ottawa lost ground to others, for example, those in Agriculture and Agri-Food Canada. Further, by the time international negotiations on a Biosafety Protocol began in 1996, the federal government had already formally tilted foreign policy still more towards the promotion of domestic economic interests. Concern for the impacts of multilateral environmental agreements on Canada's export prospects emerged as a crucial criterion. The Biosafety Protocol, then, as opposed to the CBD itself, was viewed in government and the private sector as a more direct threat to Canadian interests in biotechnology and agricultural exports. Specifically, it raised the prospect of importing countries being able under its provisions, through appeal to the precautionary principle and more specifically via the proposed requirement of prior informed consent by the importer, to ban entry of products containing living or genetically modified organisms. From the perspective of agricultural exporters, this would in effect allow importers to use international rules to legitimize protectionist strategies to promote the interests of domestic farming constituencies. Canada joined with other exporting states opposed to this development (the US, Australia, Uruguay, Chile, and Argentina) in the so-called Miami Group.[19] Pressure from the group effectively delayed the conclusion of the pre-negotiation phase of the Protocol during 1999. Canada's key role in this period led, among other things, to a fresh eruption of tensions in bilateral relations with the EU. At the Montreal negotiations in early 2000 the agreement nonetheless went ahead, with many of its key provisions intact, principally as a result of skilful conference diplomacy by Colombia and mediating efforts by a 'compromise group' of states led by Japan, Mexico, Norway, South Korea, and Switzerland. However, as a result of the polarization at Montreal, final agreement could not be reached on all questions. Compromise was possible on some of the key issues through rules requiring exporters to notify importing countries that goods might contain modified organisms. This still left open controversial issues, such as the labelling of products, particularly as Canadian and US trade critics were increasingly viewing EU eco-labelling standards as protectionist mechanisms.

    Canada's lead role during the 1990s in pursuing some form of legally binding instrument on the world's forests represents a further instance of niche diplomacy. The issue combined for Canada the pursuit of interest, promotion of the virtues of multilateralism and international institutions, and North-South bridging diplomacy. However, Canadian approaches were at times in marked contrast to the kinds of biodiversity strategies being urged by the non-governmental environmental community. The process had its origins in developments before the 1992 Rio conference. Canada's economic stake and internationally recognized expertise in forest matters prompted support for a convention to parallel the FCCC and CBD. Forests, however, proved too volatile an issue. Northern and Southern views were frequently in conflict before and during Rio. Threats to tropical forests had become a rallying cry of Western NGOs. For key countries such as Indonesia and Brazil, however, they were vital to economic development, and their exploitation and use were legally protected by the international recognition of sovereign rights contained in UN statements since the early 1970s. Intra-North conflicts erupted on critical issues relating to the place of market forces and state regulation in the use of biological resources. The most that could be achieved at Rio was a statement, emphasized as non-binding, of general principles of sustainable development related to forests, together with related references in Chapter 11 of Agenda 21. It was also evident that the CBD would not become a vehicle for a forests regime, something that Canada and other forest-products exporting states were opposed to.

Canadian forestry and other officials were central players in these events. The momentum carried on beyond Rio, particularly in light of developments in Canada's forest policy and work on the Canadian Biodiversity Strategy. Two major sets of political constraints existed. First, there were already multiple international bodies with forestry mandates. These include the FAO, the International Tropical Timber Organization (ITTO), and the IUCN/World Conservation Union, specifically through its Forest Conservation Program.[20] Proposals for a convention thus had to define requirements that were not already being met in other ways. Second, the main actors in Ottawa, particularly the Canadian Forest Service, Natural Resources Canada, Environment Canada, and DFAIT, recognized that progress towards a convention could not be made without long-term technical co-operation with other leading forest economies. This was in any case viewed as intrinsically worthwhile, whether or not such activities prepared the ground for negotiation of a convention. Collaboration with countries sharing forestry interests similar to those of Canada was thus a part of this overall strategy. Canada became a leading member of a group of 12 countries concerned with issues of conservation and sustainable use in temperate and boreal forests. The group, meeting in what became known as the Montreal Process, produced an initial report to the 1997 World Forestry Congress. The aim has been the development and refinement of a set of internationally agreed criteria on these types of forests, for example, on problems of forest management in relation to global carbon cycles and the functioning of forests as carbon sinks.[21]

Canada also consolidated relations with countries with tropical forest economies. Co-operation with Malaysia in particular led directly to the creation in 1995 of the Intergovernmental Panel on Forests (IPF), a body of the UN Commission on Sustainable Development initially co-chaired by India and the United Kingdom. The IPF was backed by an international task force comprising the main UN and other agencies with forest mandates. It was soon apparent, however, that the necessary consensus for preparatory discussions on options for legally binding instruments was still far away. Canada, meanwhile, continued co-operation with Malaysia, for example, in the international sustainable forest workshop the two countries co-sponsored, together with Japan and Mexico, and with the FAO and ITTO, in Kochi, Japan, in late 1996.[22] The IPF concluded its work in 1997 with recommendations for continued intergovernmental talks.[23] Its successor, the Intergovernmental Forum on Forests (IFF), took shape in the UN's five-year review meetings in 1997 on developments since the Rio conference. Among other things, it was mandated to investigate possible institutional arrangements for world forestry issues, including funding mechanisms, and to report in 2000 to the UN Commission on Sustainable Development. As in earlier discussions, IFF meetings, particularly at Geneva in 1998, again revealed the economic interests and political obstacles in the way of a forestry convention and acknowledged the importance of existing forestry policy arrangements. Even so, Canadian forestry officials continued to hope the process would conclude with a decision to launch international negotiations on some form of legally binding instrument.

Before the completion of the IFF process, Canadian officials opened up a further collaborative mechanism, this time with Costa Rica. The Costa Rica-Canada Initiative (CRCI) became a basis for discussions with other states and key international agencies in support of the institutional discussions of the IFF. The key meeting was held in Ottawa in December 1999. Ralph Goodale, federal Natural Resources Minister, identified three main obstacles to an institutional arrangement for forests: the issues of funding for sustainability initiatives; sovereignty and the right of countries to develop their own natural resources; and the need for continued dialogue on alternative institutional mechanisms. The Canadian view, he stated, was that existing ad hoc arrangements were 'no longer viable'.[24] Canadian officials and forestry experts echoed the need for progress towards a legally binding instrument, arguing among other things that this would also be the most effective means of securing funds from governments, international agencies, and the private sector. The Costa Rican co-chair, Luis Rojas, emphasized the lack of international agreement on processes, institutional arrangements, and funding questions. The final CRCI meeting was nonetheless instrumental in shaping the IFF recommendations of early 2000. This called for a new intergovernmental mechanism that by 2005 would review proposals for an international legal framework on the world's forests. For this purpose it recommended that the UN establish a Forum on Forests, which would hold annual meetings, including meetings at the ministerial level, and would be supported by an international secretariat.

Canada has been a major participant in the transboundary issues handled by the UN Economic Commission for Europe, whose membership comprises not only European states but also Canada and the US. In particular, Canadian officials played key roles in the development and working of the ECE's Convention on Long-Range Transboundary Air Pollution, signed in 1979 and in force from 1983. Subsequent protocols were negotiated on sulphur emissions, nitrogen oxides, and volatile organic compounds (VOCs). A significant feature of LRTAP processes has been the exchange of data among parties as a means of securing compliance and preparing the ground for further legal developments. From the mid-1990s, ECE environmental interest focused increasingly on persistent organic pollutants (POPs). These compounds have been found to have serious human health consequences, especially for people with diets rich in fish and marine mammals, as in

Canada's North. The POPs Protocol of the LRTAP was negotiated in June 1998, along with another on heavy metals, at Aarhus, Denmark. Like the CBD's Biosafety Protocol, it raised issues about the appropriate relations between environmental agreements and international trade regimes.[25]

In the negotiations, Ethel Blondin-Andrew, Secretary of State for Children and Youth, emphasized Canada's special position. Up to 65 per cent of Inuit women had PCB levels in their blood exceeding Canada's health limit by more than five times, and PCBs in the breast milk of Inuit mothers exceeded the average for women in southern Canada by as much as eight times.[26] Canadian officials also pressed for an effective compliance mechanism. In the protocol, which Canada was the first industrialized country to ratify, an international implementation committee was created to carry out periodic reviews of the actions of parties, and a provision was included that this body could act on the basis of evidence of possible non-compliance by a country. For the most part the negotiations, and earlier preparatory work, centred on substances to be included in annexes (production of those in Annex I is eliminated, and restrictions on use are placed on substances in Annex II). A core group of 15 compounds had already been identified. The Aarhus negotiations, however, led to significant exceptions and interpretations. Thus, inclusion of a substance in Annex I did not necessarily mean an immediate halt to production. Heptachlor, for example, was to be banned when the protocol entered into force, but some electrical uses in industry were permitted. PCBs could continue to be used and produced in the transitional economies (Eastern Europe and the former Soviet Union). These countries when ratifying could state when they would implement a production ban before the end of 2005. PCBs (and also DDT) were for this reason included, somewhat ambiguously, in both annexes.[27] In both the POPs and heavy metals protocols, Ottawa was criticized by environmental groups for being too sensitive to industry concerns.

Many of the substances that were the focus of the POPs Protocol were already targets of a separate UNEP process. The international negotiating committee for a proposed global convention met in Montreal, also in June 1998, and continued with sessions in Nairobi in 1999. The convention was finalized in negotiations in Johannesburg in December 2000. Among other things the Montreal meetings examined criteria for selecting POPs. Completion of the LRTAP process was viewed as a regional foundation for this more ambitious project, which was focusing on a group of 12 of the POPs listed in the Aarhus Protocol. However, the North-South dimension made some of the issues already addressed in ECE negotiations still more difficult to resolve. Developing countries pressed the issue of funding mechanisms, and many argued for continued use of DDT.[28] A feature of the UNEP pre-negotiation process was the participation of environmental NGOs, for example, in the working groups at the 1998 Montreal meetings. These groups urged production bans rather than more permissive options of restricted use. As Julia Langer of World Wildlife Fund Canada, argued, 'elimination should be the only approach.'[29]

Trade and the Environment

The 1990s were characterized by a significant rise in the environment-related activities of trade regimes, both regional and global. Many of the architectural questions remain unresolved in continuing debates in the WTO on the relations between trading and environmental rules. The place of multilateral environmental agreements in the global trading system is an issue that divides states and IGOs. UNEP's secretariat, for example, was increasingly critical of WTO trends in the late 1990s, at one point labelling that organization's view of environmental agreements as 'regressive'.[30] The WTO secretariat has consistently emphasized the potential trade-distorting consequences of environmental regulatory practices. As it defined the question in 1998 in relation to food standards: 'How do you ensure that your country's consumers are being supplied with food that is safe to eat—"safe" by the standards you consider appropriate? And at the same time, how can you ensure that strict health and safety regulations are not being used as an excuse for protecting domestic producers?'[31] The WTO has also argued, especially after the collapse of the Seattle talks in 1999, that its approach has been misrepresented or misunderstood by environmental NGOs. Governments, that is, are acknowledged by the WTO to have a right to design and implement their own environmental, plant health, and other regulations; but they violate international trade law when they use related import regulations in a differentiated manner, as the US, for example, was held to have done in the landmark 'shrimp-turtle' ruling in November 1998 following a case initiated by India, Malaysia, Pakistan, and Thailand.

The logics of trade liberalization and environmentalism both comprise rationales that claim a capacity to work more effectively towards at least some of the goals of the other. Trade critics can argue that liberalization is beneficial to the environment because it reinforces incentives to specialization and more efficient uses of natural resources; providing market pricing mechanisms for resources are in place, the environmental impacts of production and use are thus minimized. As the pace of trade liberalization grows, so it strengthens the case for instituting measures of environmental protection and co-operation. Differences in environmental standards, from this perspective, not only lead to less than optimal trade flows, they may increase environmental damage since countries and companies then have incentives to specialize in industries with the weakest environmental regulations.[32] One consequence of these debates has been growing international attention to problems related to countries' inspection regimes and testing laboratories, as in the area of pharmaceutical products. The spread of varying regimes increases the potential for environmental standards, including domestic labelling rules, to be used as non-tariff barriers to trade. Through encouragement by the OECD and other organizations, Canada and other Western states have increasingly explored and used instruments such as mutual recognition agreements, agreed standards for products and processes, and a variety of information-sharing schemes.[33] Continuing uncertainty about the evolution of the WTO's role in setting environmental standards, however, has left many of the larger questions unre-solved. By the end of the 1990s, the US was pressing more insistently for a widened redefinition of the WTO's mandate to incorporate issues on international environmental agendas, while Canada tended to argue for various 'softer' options within the WTO.[34] There has nonetheless been a large area of Canada-US consen-sus on key issues, such as the mutual concern, largely targeting the EU, that eco-labelling practices should not be used as disguised trade-restriction measures.

Many of these questions arise more immediately, as far as Canada is con-cerned, in relation to NAFTA, which entered into force in 1994. Chapter 11 sets out the rules designed to secure non-discriminatory treatment of companies in each country (Canada, the US, and Mexico), that is, governments are obliged to treat companies from other NAFTA countries as equivalent to domestic firms. The parties did not commit themselves to harmonizing regulations, so the continued presence of different rules in different jurisdictions has led unavoidably to dis-putes, as well as to persisting, and often radically opposed, complaints from both trade and environmentalist critics. The agreement also set up the CEC, consisting of the environment ministers of the three national governments, with a mandate that includes the prevention and resolution of 'environment-related trade dis-putes'. The rule on national treatment can be broken by environmental regula-tions, and trade can legally be restricted if products do not meet these, but only in accordance with NAFTA's standard-setting rules. Chapter 9 defines the circum-stances in which countries can enact trade-restricting environmental regulations. The interpretation of these varies. One analyst, Bradley Condon, has defined them in terms of a set of key legal questions. For example: 'Does the standard support the pursuit of a legitimate environmental objective? If a trade restriction is neces-sary, has the least trade-restrictive measure been chosen?'[35]

Canadian and US companies have a long history of criticism of the other country's environmental regulations. Canadian exporters have complained that they were in effect being excluded from US markets, or forced to pay increased costs of market entry, because of federal or state government violations of national treatment principles in such matters as health rules on potato imports, newsprint recycling regulations, minimum-size requirements for lobsters, and asbestos. Ontario's levy on beer cans was an instance of Canadian regulations tar-geted for similar reasons by US companies.[36] By contrast, in the early 1990s debates on NAFTA both US and Canadian environmental groups pointed to likely adverse effects of the agreement, such as environmental damage resulting from a migration of capital to northern areas of Mexico and a continental dilution of environmental rules as jurisdictions competed for investment.[37] Canadian observers have also identified a 'chilling effect' of NAFTA on governments con-templating tighter environmental rules, particularly since the combination of the national treatment rules of Chapter 11 and the standards-setting criteria of Chapter 9 is arguably at odds with the increasingly entrenched place of the pre-cautionary principle in customary international law.[38] Other environmental NGO reservations centre on the secrecy of the formal and informal dispute settlement procedures and the way these strengthen the capacities of companies to protest government measures.

The Canada-US and NAFTA frameworks have produced several key issues where environmental and resource management rules have been alleged to violate national treatment rules. Brief summaries of three illustrate underlying problems.

One of the oldest in Canada-US relations concerns Canadian softwood lumber exports to the US. The issue arose initially out of US criticisms in 1983 of regulatory practices in Canada, particularly related to stumpage. These were identified as subsidies and therefore, in the US view, called for remedies under trade law, specifically the imposition of countervailing duties. The current state of play dates from the agreement of May 1996, which expired in March 2001, under which Canada in effect said it would limit the volume of its exports to the US by way of an annually set tariff rate quota on exports from British Columbia, Alberta, Ontario, and Quebec.[39] The issue remains important for broader trade and environment debates. For environmentalist critics, it appears to establish a secure base for US input into a wide range of Canadian decisions on natural resources policy; for trade critics, it seems to legitimize unacceptable notions of 'managed trade' and indirectly to undermine trade liberalization goals.

The Ethyl/MMT case raised different questions.[40] Bans on leaded fuels led to increasing use of methylcyclopentadienyl manganese tricarbonyl (MMT) as a fuel additive from the late 1970s. The Canadian government in effect banned its use, on human health and pollution grounds, in April 1997. Ottawa took this step in discrete legislation (the Manganese-based Fuel Additives Act) under its constitutional authority to regulate interprovincial and international trade. The action prevented Ethyl, the US producer, from exporting MMT to Canada and selling stockpiles in Canada. The company filed a US$250 million claim against the federal government. It argued that Ottawa's action was discriminatory (because Ethyl was the sole manufacturer) and thus in violation of NAFTA's national treatment provisions, and, appealing to larger issues in international trade law, that it was 'tantamount to expropriation' because of the resulting losses to the company. The US company's case was helped by the relatively weak scientific evidence against MMT. In a 1994 study Health Canada had found no significant evidence of health risks, and a US ban had been overruled by the courts in 1996. In a sense, Ethyl was arguing generally against any form of import restriction, on the grounds that since such measures inevitably help domestic companies and hurt foreign companies, the instrument is inherently discriminatory. The outcome was a reversal for Ottawa. It failed to establish that on procedural grounds the NAFTA tribunal did not have jurisdiction.[41] The import ban was lifted; Ottawa was directed to contribute part of Ethyl's costs and loss of profits (US$13 million) and agreed to provide a written statement explicitly denying there was scientific evidence connecting MMT with risks to human health or pollution problems from cars. Ethyl agreed to drop both its planned Chapter 11 action and a separate constitutional challenge through the Ontario courts.[42]

The reactions of environmental groups were mixed. On the one hand, this was not a simple case of national environmental regulations versus NAFTA. There was no scientific consensus on whether the precautionary principle justified an MMT ban, and the use by Ottawa of its trade powers, as opposed to regulatory authority under environmental law, in a sense muddied the question of whether this was a clear-cut environmental policy issue. On the other hand, the Canadian and US responses to the case seemed to confirm that under NAFTA companies were actors in international law, with a recognized capacity to initiate actions against governments whose environmental standards they disliked. Together with the Myers case, in which an Ohio company claimed compensation for losses resulting from a 1995 ban by Ottawa on PCB exports,[43] the Ethyl/MMT case also indicated to environmentalist critics an alarming lack of transparency in Canada-US procedures.

In a third example, US authorities in 1991 banned ultra-heat-treated (UHT) milk produced by the Lactel company of Quebec from entering Puerto Rico, following changes in that government's milk standards regulations. The Canadian government's initial response was to argue, unsuccessfully, on the basis of equivalency that the Lactel product met Puerto Rico's standards by virtue of their compatibility with the Quebec government's own milk standards. In the subsequent dispute resolution process under the then Canada-US Free Trade Agreement, Ottawa claimed the action by the US violated the national treatment rule because it discriminated against milk produced by Canadian companies. The US defended its action on the grounds that the milk regulations applied to all producers, regardless of whether they were domestic or foreign. The panel found generally in favour of the US position in 1993, maintaining that the Puerto Rico regulations did not restrict trade. However, it accepted that the rules on equivalency of standards needed further exploration, and following an initial study Quebec exports were allowed to resume in 1995.[44]

Law, Statecraft, and Development

International environmental agreements, then, have occupied an expanding space in Canada's continental and multilateral diplomacy. Bilateral relationships with other countries and regions are also affected. Partners are needed for Canada's multilateral environmental diplomacy and its pursuit of convention-shaping goals. Occasional fallout from these processes in terms of damaged bilateral relations has to be repaired. Specific international conventions as well as 'soft' norms and principles have repercussions in more traditional areas of statecraft. Some examples from Canada's bilateral diplomacy are briefly explored below.

Environmental topics have occupied an increasingly important place in Canada's relations with the EU. This is partly because of the rise of issues on multilateral environmental and WTO agendas in which both sides have a stake and partly because of persistent environment-related trade disputes. An agreement on environmental co-operation preceded the Canada-European Community (EC) framework agreement of 1976. This set up a joint co-operation committee mandated to explore sectors of potential in the development of trade and investment links. There are also annual ministerial meetings on the environment. Environment-related issues, for example, sanitary and phytosanitary questions arising from agricultural trade and problems in energy sectors, have been a continuous feature of these exchanges.

Attention to environmental issues was reinforced in the 1990s as Ottawa and Brussels moved to strengthen ties. Two-way annual trade is currently over \$40 billion, up from a late 1970s figure of around \$10 billion.[45] The 1990 Declaration on Canada-EC Relations was followed in 1991 by a joint ministerial statement on environmental co-operation. In the Canada-EU Action Plan of December 1996 both sides agreed to increase efforts to promote the effectiveness of multilateral co-operation on global environmental issues.[46] Multilateral issues impacting on relations (including bilateral links with EU members) included climate change, particularly the 1997 Kyoto negotiations; issues of sustainable forestry management, given Canada's own international initiatives in this sector; and diverse issues related to hazardous wastes and chemicals management, for example, in the context of the Basel Convention on wastes, the Rotterdam Convention of 1998 on prior informed consent in relation to the trade in specified chemicals, and the POPs Protocol and other developments in the LRTAP framework. Canada-EU environmental meetings have also ranged widely over comparative and international questions, including the Arctic environment, responses to environmental problems in the transitional economies of Eastern Europe and the former Soviet Union, the trade significance of the growing European commitment to eco-labelling, and lessons learned from exercises in the greening of government operations.

Environmental issues are viewed as important in part because of the potential these have for threatening economic matters closer to the core of the bilateral relationship. The multilateral level tends to be relatively well insulated, with minimal risks of collateral damage. Even so, on Kyoto issues in 1996–7 and multilateral negotiations on genetically modified organisms in 1999, Canada was caught up in a larger framework of US-EU conflict. Ottawa's tilt towards US positions in the latter context temporarily increased tensions in bilateral relations with Brussels. Two bilateral Canada-EU disputes with environmental aspects (how much depending on the operational definition of the term) had more serious consequences. Canada's conflict with Spain in 1995 over turbot was unusual for the degree of crisis it precipitated in Canada-EU relations. A negotiated resolution was eventually set in the multilateral context of North Atlantic fisheries arrangements, but the short-term repercussions included highly publicized charges from senior EU officials of Canadian violations of international law and a trigger-happy resort to gunboat diplomacy.[47] A long-simmering dispute during the 1990s followed the EU's ban in 1991 on leg-hold traps, a reflection in part of the strength of European environmental and animal rights NGOs. Several years of talks culminated in an agreement with Canada (and also with Russia, the other state concerned) in 1997. There has been a continuous stream of environment-related trade questions. The French government's 1997 ban on asbestos imports was a significant blow to the Quebec industry. Fears of spreading restrictions prompted Ottawa to pursue urgent protective diplomacy in Brussels aimed at deflecting an EU-wide ban. Canadian officials similarly lobbied in the late 1990s against EU plant health regulations that were blocking seed-potato imports from Canada.

Canada's bilateral relations with Japan have been marked by occasional initiatives to promote environmental co-operation, but to a much lesser extent than with the EU. A powerful incentive on Canada's part has been to shift the trade balance away from the historical mix of raw materials exports and finished goods imports. One aim of the Team Canada visit to Japan in September 1999 was thus to promote knowledge of Canada's high-technology industries, including environmental technology.[48] Calls from the early 1980s for more 'comprehensive' relations, particularly from the Japanese side, reflected concerns that long-term bilateral relations would inevitably suffer if they were confined in practice to trade and investment questions and ad hoc responses to trade disputes.

As with the EU, the early 1990s saw renewed efforts to invigorate relations, particularly in light of Prime Minister Brian Mulroney's visit in 1991. The Canada-Japan Forum 2000 Committee, headed on the Canadian side by former Alberta Premier Peter Lougheed, recommended in 1992 various steps towards strengthening relations. A follow-up committee echoed the points in 1995. Environmental co-operation was highlighted as a useful step, particularly in light of the Japanese government's rapidly growing interest in the 1990s in international environmental law and policy.[49] Bilateral talks related to preparations for the Kyoto meetings in 1997 added to the momentum of bilateral environmentalism, as did recurring irritants in environment-related agricultural trade on such issues as potatoes from Canada and apples from Japan. Among other developments, two rounds of low-key environmental discussions were organized in 1996–7, respectively in Japan and Canada, between environment and foreign ministry officials. The seminars, modelled somewhat on the approach taken in Canada-EU meetings, explored bilateral, multilateral, and comparative environmental policy developments. However, this kind of more institutionalized approach failed to take off in the context of relations with Japan and has remained an underexploited instrument. The environmental side of the relationship has continued to develop nonetheless, for example, as a result of the Canadian emphasis on environmental technology during the 1999 Team Canada mission. The potential for collaboration on regional and global forestry issues has also been explored, with Canadian and Japanese officials jointly taking a leading role in the Kochi workshop of 1996.

Environmental questions connected with multilateral legal developments have also played some part in structuring Canada's relations with developing and newly industrializing countries. Given the nature of the UN and its related agencies, securing diplomatic support from key states in the South has become crucial to the success of multilateral environmental initiatives in which Canada has a stake. Canadian co-operation with Costa Rica and Malaysia in the context of a possible forestry agreement was noted earlier. In the framework of the Multilateral Fund of the Montreal Protocol on the ozone layer, Environment Canada has provided training and other assistance for government officials from Brazil, India, Chile, and other countries. The Clean Development Mechanism of the Kyoto Protocol increases the incentives for co-operative projects with developing countries.

Environmental questions are central to Canada's overseas development assistance programs and figure in varying degrees in bilateral relations with states of the South. In part the push has come from, or been reinforced by, growing recognition in the NGO and IGO development communities of the importance of pollution control and the rational use of natural resources in concepts of sustainable human development. A sustainable society has been defined in this context as 'economically viable, socially just and ecologically sound'.[50] The role of the Canadian International Development Agency (CIDA) was officially defined in 1995 as the promotion of 'sustainable development in developing countries', with issues of environmental protection more specifically being listed as one set of six priority areas for the agency.[51]

The place of environmental protection and natural resource projects in CIDA programming varies in different countries and regions.[52] In Africa, these have been a major focus of programs in Zimbabwe, together with projects on HIV/AIDS and the promotion of civil society; by contrast, in Tanzania the emphasis has been more on problems of poverty reduction, women in development, and microfinance. A chronic problem in many countries of the South has been the limited effectiveness of national environmental laws and government agencies. The weakness has major implications for the participation of developing countries in international environmental arrangements such as the climate change regime. Support for institutional development and capacities for environmental law enforcement was a Canadian development assistance priority in relation to Indonesia and the Philippines in the early 1990s. There was a similar focus on aid to strengthen the institutional capacities of the environment department of the Bangladesh government in the late 1990s.

However, development assistance programs have been increasingly subject to budgetary and other constraints, as both effect and cause of complaints that resources have been stretched too thinly across sectors and regions. Declines in overseas development assistance occurred throughout the OECD countries during the 1990s, but by bigger margins in Canada (by 38 per cent between 1991–2 and 1998–9).[53] This was accompanied by a shift in rationales for aid away from Canada's earlier internationalist perspectives towards what Cranford Pratt calls more 'narrowly national' criteria, such as clear benefits for the private sector. The problem with this redefinition, as he points out, is that Canadian responses to global environmental problems are likely to be ineffective if questions of the immediate consequences for Canadians become the basis of international policy.[54]

Canada and the Global Environment

International environmental agreements traditionally impinged minimally on the autonomy of states. In many ways the conventions of the 1970s, for example, constituted a largely technical policy sector separable from the other affairs of governments. The developments of the last 10–15 years have eroded both these notions. The domestic reach and horizontal policy implications of multilateral environmental agreements are extensive, and conventions and convention-making are both constrained by and significant factors in the evolution of international trade arrangements. Environmental diplomacy has thus become a critical part of the overall framework of Canada's environmental union. Environmental policy for Canada, as for other OECD states, is consequently characterized by the emergence of multiple layers and pillars of governance transcending state boundaries, and also by considerable diversity in mechanisms and processes across specific environmental policy sectors. Problems of co-operation among governments at these various levels have been described as 'the central drama of building effective international environmental policies'.[55]

Canada has been a major designer of many of these developments. It has not, though, had a consistently 'environmentalist' foreign policy. This should not be seen as surprising. All states, Canada included, have multiple interests. The diplomatic capabilities of the Canadian state are not available for use for primarily environmental ends. Even without the formal pull exerted by external trade regime developments, the federal government would still have moved during the mid-1990s to make the promotion of economic interests in a competitive continental and world economy the principal architecture for external, and foreign environmental, policies. Yet the process of building and reforming international environmental law and institutions remains crucial to the achievement even of Ottawa's more explicitly interest-based objectives of recent years.

Notes

1 Martha Balis-Larsen et al., 'Canada and US save shared species at risk', *Recovery* 15 (Mar. 2000): 6–7.

2 Andrew Hurrell and Benedict Kingsbury, eds, *The International Politics of the Environment* (Oxford: Clarendon Press, 1992), 2.

3 Miranda A. Schreurs and Elizabeth C. Economy, eds, *The Internationalization of Environmental Protection* (Cambridge: Cambridge University Press, 1997), 6. On the wider significance for Canada of multiple centres of power, see Daniel Wolfish and Gordon Smith, 'Governance and Policy in a Multicentric World', *Canadian Public Policy* 26, Supplement (Aug. 2000): 51–72.

4 *Environment Reporter* 29, 43 (5 Mar. 1999): 2193.

5 J. Fomerand, 'UN Conferences: Media Events or Genuine Diplomacy?', *Global Governance* 2 (1996): 362–4.

6 D.J. Frank et al., 'The Nation-State and the Natural Environment over the Twentieth Century', *American Sociological Review* 65 (2000): 96–116.

7 *International Environment Reporter* 23, 15 (19 July 2000): 556.

8 For a discussion of the 'residual state', see P.G. Cerny, 'Globalization and Other Stories: The Search for a New Paradigm for International Relations', *International Journal* 51 (1996): 596–9.

9 David VanderZwaag, 'The Precautionary Principle in Environmental Law and Policy: Elusive Rhetoric and First Embraces', *Journal of Environmental Law and Practice* 8, 3 (Oct. 1999): 355–9. The Canadian instances he cites are the Oceans Act and the Canadian Environmental Protection Act.

10 See further Edith Brown Weiss, *International Environmental Law: Basic Instruments and References, 1992–99* (New York: Transnational Publishers, 1999); Lynton Caldwell, *International Environmental Policy: From the Twentieth Century to the Twenty-first Century*, 3rd edn, rev. with Paul S. Weiland (Durham, NC: Duke University Press, 1996); W. Burhenne, ed., *International Environmental Law* (London: Kluwer, 1997). Useful sources on current developments in conventions include www.ecolex.org (which includes materials from the IUCN and UNEP environmental law information bases) and www.globelaw.com/frmain.htm.

11 *Global Challenges: Report of the Commissioner of the Environment and Sustainable Development to the House of Commons* (Ottawa: Minister of Public Works and Government Services Canada, 1998), 2–14, 2–16. Canada negotiated the 1923 halibut convention with the US, but initial agreements were negotiated by Britain.

12 *OECD Environmental Data: Compendium 1999* (Paris: OECD, 1999), Table 14.1, 303–13. This lists only agreements signed or ratified by at least one OECD country. It also notes 27 general and 11 miscellaneous agreements.

13 Michael Grubb, with Christiaan Vrolijk and Duncan Brack, *The Kyoto Protocol: A Guide and Assessment* (London: Royal Institute of International Affairs, 1999), 3.

14 Timothy Swanson, 'Why Is There a Biodiversity Convention? The International Interest in Centralized Development Planning', *International Affairs* 75, 2 (Apr. 1999): 307–31.

15 This figure includes non-binding as well as binding instruments. See *Global Challenges*, 2–25, 2–28. Many of these are bilateral environmental agreements between Canada and the US.

16 www.dfait-maeci.gc.ca/sustain/memc-e.asp

17 Peter W.B. Phillips, 'Power and the Federal State in Canada: Is It Being Hollowed Out?', *International Journal* 53, 1 (Winter 1997–8): 60.

18 Philippe Le Prestre and Peter Stoett, 'International Initiatives, Commitments, and Disappointments: Canada, CITES, and the Convention on Biological Diversity', in Karen Beazley and Robert Boardman, eds, *Politics of the Wild: Canada and Endangered Species* (Toronto: Oxford University Press, 2001); Gareth Porter, Janet Welsh Brown, and Pamela S. Chasek, *Global Environmental Politics*, 3rd edn (Boulder, Colo.: Westview Press, 2000), 124–5.

19 Michelle Swenarchuk, 'Canada's heavy-handed trade negotiations', *Intervenor* 24, 3 (July–Sept. 1999): 6; Mark S. Winfield, 'Reflections on the Biosafety Protocol Negotiations in Montreal', at www.cielap.org/infocent/research/MontrealBio.html, pp. 1–2.

20 Richard G. Tarasofsky and David R. Downes, 'Global Cooperation on Forests through International Institutions', in Tarasofsky, ed., *Assessing the International Forest Regime* (Gland: Environmental Law Centre, IUCN, 1999), 97–105.

21 The other countries in the Montreal Process are Argentina, Australia, Chile, China, Japan, Korea, Mexico, New Zealand, Russia, the US, and Uruguay. See further at www.mpci.org and www.ec.gc.ca/agenda21/2000/foresteng.htm#a10d

22 www.un.org/esa/sustdev/iff.htm

23 *Forest Chronicle* 76, 2 (Mar.–Apr. 2000): 223.

24 Ibid., 224; www.nrcan.gc.ca/cfs/crc

25 Kirsten Hillman, 'International Control of Persistent Organic Pollutants: The UN Economic Commission for Europe Convention on Long-Range Transport of Air Pollution, and Beyond', *Review of European Community and International Environmental Law* 8, 2 (1999): 105–22.

26 *Environment Reporter* 29, 10 (3 July 1998): 507–8.

27 Hillman, 'International Control of Persistent Organic Pollutants'. Lindane was added to the group of 15. Other key issues related to import and export controls and wastes (in relation to the Basel Convention).

28 *Environment Reporter* 29, 37, Supplement (22 Jan. 1999): S-31; 29, 39 (5 Feb. 1999): 1930; www.chem.unep.ch/pops

29 *Chemical Regulation Reporter* 22, 15 (10 July 1998): 672.

30 Paper to the WTO's Committee on Trade and Environment (CTE), quoted in *Environment Reporter* 29, 15 (7 Aug. 1998): 748–9. WTO exchanges on related issues with environmental IGOs continued through the CTE in 2000 (*CTE Bulletin* TE/033, 10 July 2000).

31 Cited in Sara Pardo Quintallan, 'Free Trade, Public Health Protection and Consumer Information in the European and WTO Context: Hormone-Treated Beef and Genetically Modified Organisms', *Journal of World Trade* 33, 6 (Dec. 1999): 153.

32 See the policy discussions in Hector Rogelio Torres, 'The Trade and Environment Interaction in the WTO: How Can a "New Round" Contribute?', *Journal of World Trade* 33, 5 (Oct. 1999): 153–5; Matthew A. Cole, 'Examining the Environmental Case against Free Trade', ibid., 183–96.

33 Sherry M. Stephenson, 'Mutual Recognition and Its Role in Trade Facilitation', *Journal of World Trade* 33, 2 (Apr. 1999): 144–5. One problem of information-sharing in the NAFTA context highlighted by state and provincial governments is the added burden this places on them. On the international standards movement and its potential role in relation to the climate change and other multilateral agreements, see *International Environmental Systems Update* 6, 11 (Nov. 1999): 14–15; more generally, see Neil Drobny, 'Environmental Management for the Twenty-First Century', in Tom Tibor and Ira Feldman, eds, *Implementing ISO 14000* (Chicago: Irwin, 1997), 3–14. As Jennifer Clapp and other critics have pointed out, these processes erode still further the boundaries between governmental and private-sector roles in environmental standards-setting. See Clapp, 'The Privatization of Global Environmental Governance: ISO 14000 and the Developing World', *Global Governance* 4, 3 (1998): 295–316.

34 *Environment Reporter* 29, 15 (7 Aug. 1998): 749; 29, 45 (19 Mar. 1999): 2284.

35 Quoted in Alan M. Rugman, John Kirton, and Julie Solway, 'NAFTA, Environmental Regulations, and Canadian Competitiveness', *Journal of World Trade* 31, 4 (Aug. 1997): 136.

36 Ibid., 136–7.

37 Commission for Environmental Co-operation, *Potential NAFTA Environmental Effects: Claims and Arguments, 1991–1994* (Montreal: Commission for Environmental Co-operation, 1996). The CEC later worked on the development of methodologies for more systematic assessments of effects. An initial study was done in relation to intensive cattle feedlot production in the US, corn production in Mexico, and electricity production in all three countries. See Commission for Environmental Co-operation, *Assessing Environmental Effects of the NAFTA: An Analytical Framework (Phase II) and Issue Studies* (Montreal: Commission for Environmental Co-operation, 1999).

38 Remarks by J. Edward Thompson, at the International Bar Association annual conference, Vancouver, cited in *Environment Reporter* 29, 21 (25 Sept. 1998): 1069–70.

39 Gilbert Gagne, 'The Canada-US Softwood Lumber Dispute: An Assessment after Fifteen Years', *Journal of World Trade* 33, 1 (Feb. 1999): 82–3.

40 Juli A. Abouchar and Richard J. King, 'Environmental Laws as Expropriation under NAFTA', *Review of European Community and International Environmental Law* 8, 2

(1999): 210–11; and the summary by Alan C. Swan in *American Journal of International Law* 94, 1 (Jan. 2000): 159–66.

41 For example, Ethyl took action a few days before royal assent to the Manganese-based Fuel Additives Act, so that technically it was not yet a 'measure' that could be objected to.

42 Abouchar and King, 'Environmental Laws as Expropriation', 211.

43 In the Myers case, the US company claimed it lost $US15 million during the federal government's ban on PCB exports between Nov. 1995 and Feb. 1997 (*Environment Reporter* 29, 19 (4 Sept. 1998): 934.

44 Rugman et al., 'NAFTA', 139–42.

45 *Europe towards the New Millennium: The Relevance to Canada* (EU, Conference Board of Canada, DFAIT, 1998).

46 *Europe (Documents)*, No. 2018, 8 Jan. 1997, 3–10.

47 Donald Barry, 'The Canada-EU Turbot War: Internal Politics and Transatlantic Bargaining', *International Journal* 53, 2 (Spring 1998): 277.

48 Ignorance, or skepticism, on the part of Japanese firms was documented in a 1999 survey by the Canadian embassy in Tokyo, reported in *Canada-Japan Trade Council Newsletter* (May-June 1999): 1–2.

49 Ibid. (Jan.-Feb. 1993): 1–5; (July-Aug. 1995).

50 Betty Plewes, Gauri Sreenivasan, and Tim Draimin, 'Sustainable Human Development as a Global Framework', *International Journal* 51, 2 (Spring 1996): 217–18.

51 Tim Draimin and Brian Tomlinson, 'Is There a Future for Canadian Aid in the Twenty-First Century?', in Fen Osler Hampson and Maureen Appel Molot, eds, *Leadership and Dialogue: Canada Among Nations 1998* (Toronto: Oxford University Press, 1998), 150–2.

52 www.acdi-cida.gc.ca

53 Draimin and Tomlinson, 'Is There a Future for Canadian Aid?', 144–5, 153–4. Canadian multilateral aid (through institutions such as the World Bank) fell at a sharper rate than bilateral assistance.

54 Cranford Pratt, 'Competing Rationales for Canadian Development Assistance', *International Journal* 54, 2 (Spring 1999): 313.

55 Konrad von Moltke, 'Trade, Sustainable Development and Commodity Markets', in Agata Fijalkowski and James Cameron, *Trade and the Environment: Bridging the Gap* (The Hague: T.M.C. Asser Instituut/Cameron, May 1998), 142. See P.K. Rao, *The WTO and the Environment* (New York: Palgrave, 2000), part I.

Chapter 11

Globalization, Internationalization, and Liberal Environmentalism: Exploring Non-Domestic Sources of Influence on Canadian Environmental Policy

Steven Bernstein and Benjamin Cashore

The growing economic, social, and political pressures governments face from beyond their borders have meant that policy-making processes are no longer considered to be solely a domestic affair. There is arguably no greater example of these dynamics than the case of Canadian environmental policy, where international institutions, transnational actors, international norms, and market forces have interacted to push domestic environmental policies in directions they otherwise would not have taken.

Just how do these non-domestic factors shape a country's environmental policies? This chapter addresses this question in four analytical steps. First, it puts forward an important distinction between globalization and internationalization to uncover the complex interaction of these non-domestic forces and how they can push policies in ways that the existing scholarly literature has largely failed to recognize. Second, the chapter explains how, in the context of increasingly integrated global markets, an overarching 'liberal environmentalism' norm-complex constrains and directs action on global environmental problems, with implications for what kinds of international agreements are possible and their effects on domestic policies. Third, it reviews three cases of non-domestic/domestic interactions in Canadian environmental policy: forestry, biodiversity (focusing on the 2000 Cartagena Protocol on Biosafety), and, briefly, climate change initiatives (focusing on the Kyoto Protocol to the Framework Convention on Climate Change). These cases provide concrete examples of how the international trends we identify shape domestic policy-making. Finally, the chapter concludes by examining how international forces may be expected to influence future Canadian environmental policy initiatives.

Globalization and Internationalization

For over a decade now, an increasing number of social scientists have explored and debated the effects of increasing global and regional economic integration on domestic public policies.[1] In particular, scholars have debated the degree to which these global pressures constrain policy choices, including Canada's, by forcing countries to adopt similar domestic policies, and whether these pressures push environmental, social, and labour standards upward or downward.[2] Distinguishing between globalization and internationalization advances this debate because it reveals fundamentally different processes at work that constrain domestic policies differently or push them in different directions.[3] Following Doern et al.,[4] we use the term 'internationalization' to refer to the phenomenon whereby policies within domestic jurisdictions face increased scrutiny and participation from actors and/or institutions outside of those jurisdictions. We restrict the definition of 'globalization' to structural economic factors, mainly 'rising levels of trade, [global] finance and foreign direct investment (FDI)',[5] facilitated by reduced transaction costs that enable economic activity to transcend borders more easily.

Globalization is often thought to affect domestic politics, institutions, and policy outputs by putting *downward* pressure on 'wages, working conditions . . . or environmental protection',[6] causing companies to move to countries with lower wages, taxes, and regulations. Certainly the Canadian economy, as one of the world's largest exporters of natural resource products and a recipient of a significant degree of foreign direct investment, can be considered 'globalized'.[7] Yet, in the last 10 years, globalization has not always produced the predicted downward effects. From increased forestry harvesting rules to forest preservation to climate change and biosafety issues, Canada has experienced, in some cases, *upward* pressures on its environmental policies. To be clear, the argument here is not that the resulting environmental policies are adequate to address sufficiently the problems at hand, or that they are immune from a variety of downward pressures from globalization. Rather, our argument is that the effects of non-domestic factors are more complex and interactive than a simple 'race-to-the-bottom' hypothesis suggests.

While globalization clearly affected the way international forces shaped Canadian environmental policy, often the direct source of those pressures came instead from factors we categorize under internationalization. Many pressures affecting Canadian forest management and policy, climate change, and biosafety came not from the market per se, but from international rule-making bodies, international organizations, transnational and domestic environmental non-governmental organizations (ENGOs), and even other governments.

Liberal Environmentalism

While internationalization has acted to mediate and sometimes alter the influence of globalization, Bernstein has found that an international norm-complex, which became entrenched in the 1990s, embraces economic expansion, free trade, and market forces and incentives as a means to address global environmental issues.[8] Norms of liberal environmentalism predicate environmental protection on the promotion and maintenance of a liberal economic order. These norms reflect the view that environmental protection and the preservation of ecosystems, economic growth, and a liberal international economy are compatible, even necessarily linked.

This norm-complex is distinct from the period that stretched from World War II into the 1960s and early 1970s, when environmental concerns first assumed a major place on the international agenda, even up to the 1972 United Nations Conference on the Human Environment in Stockholm. In this period, conservation and environmental protection were seen as largely separate from trade issues (despite some efforts to link them within the OECD and by the Secretariat at the Stockholm conference). Indeed, most states and non-governmental actors understood environmental issues in opposition to economic growth and market forces. It used to be that trade agreements dealt primarily with tariff reductions and were dominated by the participation of trade ministers; environmental agreements addressed solely environmental issues and were dominated by ministers of the environment; and international monetary agreements dealt largely with finance and were dominated by finance ministers.[9]

This sectoralization often resulted in fundamentally conflicting ideas between different sectors about economic development. Thus, at the international trade level following World War II and the Bretton Woods agreements, there was a general trend and agreement to reduce tariffs, which have gradually declined or been eliminated as part of a general pattern of trade liberalization in goods and commodities. International trade agreements, most notably the General Agreement on Tariffs and Trade (GATT) and its successor, the World Trade Organization (WTO), facilitated this process. The Canada-US Free Trade Agreement (FTA) and its successor, the North American Free Trade Agreement (NAFTA), have enhanced this process on the regional level, pushing the continent towards increased economic integration. Critics note that these agreements aim primarily to promote economic growth and trade liberalization, which tends to encourage resource exploitation over environmental preservation.[10] On the other hand, international conferences on the environment focused largely on pollution abatement or conservation and either ignored issues of economic growth and trade, treating them as separate issues, or viewed environment and development goals as being in opposition.[11]

The concept of sustainable development starting in the mid-1980s catalysed a shift in the understandings of state leaders and policy-makers away from this 'sectoralization' and, consequently, changed the framing of international negotiations and institutional activities that touched on both sets of issues. Gradually, trade, finance, and environmental issues became seen as linked, with the consequence that the norms of major trade agreements increasingly permeate the normative framework of environmental protection agreements and negotiations. The old overt conflict between economic development and environmental protection has been reframed within a 'compromise' not only between North and South, but also through the promotion of a particular view of development, one consistent with the rise of liberal economic norms that swept the world following the end of the Cold War. The 1992 Earth Summit in Rio de Janeiro institutionalized this compromise of liberal environmentalism, which, in contrast to the norm-complex at Stockholm, embraced economic development and liberalized trade as a necessary condition to solving ecological problems.

One result is that global civil society started to focus its activities to improve environmental, social, and labour standards on meetings such as the November 1999 WTO Ministerial Conference in Seattle and the OECD-sponsored negotiations on a Multilateral Agreement on Investment (MAI) in the mid- to late 1990s. States as well as corporate and non-governmental actors increasingly recognize that these institutions are fora in which some of the most important rules affecting environmental concerns are being made. The failure of the MAI and the delay of the start of the Millennium round of trade negotiations under the WTO can be attributed at least in part to environmental and labour groups' assertions that these negotiations did not adequately address the environmental, social, and labour consequences of trade and investment. In addition, within the WTO itself, increased pressure to find ways to link these concerns to liberalized trade has become a primary concern.

Market-oriented solutions, such as those consistent with the 'polluter pays principle' (PPP), which aims to internalize the costs of pollution into the price of a product, dominate, while policies that would restrict trade liberalization or distort markets are rejected. As we discuss below, this norm-complex explains why many international policy proposals contrary to this norm-complex have failed, such as efforts to reach a Global Forest Convention, while states have successfully forged agreements where solutions have been found that embrace the market, such as the Convention on Biological Diversity and the Kyoto Protocol.[12]

Recent examples of attempts to promote ecological goals in the context of trade liberalization also include the North American Agreement on Environmental Co-operation (NAAEC), a side agreement to NAFTA.[13] This agreement fits within the constraints of liberal environmentalism as it has oversight powers only, with no binding rules to enforce that might contradict NAFTA trade rules.[14] The creation of the NAAEC reveals the difficulties of implementing liberal environmentalism in practice, as charges of unfair environmental practices become channelled through mechanisms subordinate to the broader liberal trading regime. Partly as a result, environmental groups have looked to the more developed rules and mechanisms regarding trade subsidies as a way to influence environmental policy change.

Canada's traditional support of multilateral co-operation in international affairs also provides an important context to understanding its role in, and responses to, international environmental and trade negotiations. Since World War II, Canadian foreign policy has championed multilateralism as a means to achieve a stable international political and economic environment, a goal reflected in its international environmental and trade policies. Canadian governments also view foreign policy as a means of promoting Canadian values internationally. The compromise of liberal environmentalism has enabled Canada to pursue these goals simultaneously in its foreign policy. However, it has also produced the unintended consequence of focusing attention back on Canada when it fails to live up to the promise of this compromise at home.

The Cases

FORESTRY

The forest sector is exemplary of the ways globalization, internationalization, and liberal environmentalism work to influence domestic forest policy. International negotiations, trade disputes, and eco-labelling initiatives all have influenced domestic policy dynamics in Canada, owing especially to Canada's dependence on foreign markets. Canada's participation in trade agreements also has enabled actors to use international and US trade rules to influence domestic policies. At the same time, the efforts of transnational environmental organizations to use international pressures to influence Canadian domestic forest policy were largely limited to those efforts that embraced, rather than challenged, the liberal environmentalism norm-complex.

The important story in forestry is that globalization, by itself, did not cause much of the policy change in the 1990s, but it allowed non-domestic actors to use market pressures, mainly economic boycotts, to force change. These dynamics are revealed in the Canada-US forest product trade dispute, global forest negotiations, and the move towards eco-labelling in the forest sector.

The Canada-US Softwood Lumber Trade Dispute and Environmentalism
Since 1982, Canada and the United States have been involved in an unrelenting dispute over Canadian exports of softwood lumber. The original claim made by US forest companies was that Canadian provinces subsidize their forest industries by charging below-market prices (stumpage rates) for the rights to harvest provincially owned timber. As stumpage rates increased in the 1980s and 1990s, the US forest company coalition expanded its criticism to other alleged subsidy policies, including raw log export restrictions (which it argued forced down the domestic price). In addition, a highly contested lobby effort in the US Congress criticized Canadian forestry regulations as being environmentally unfriendly. Such criticism has thus far resulted in three different countervail proceedings under US trade law in 1982, 1986, and 1991, with more looming on the horizon.

The US Congress and US adjudication bodies have altered US trade law, partly in response to coalition pressures, so that, although no subsidy was found in 1982, the US reversed itself in 1986 and preliminarily ruled that a subsidy did exist.[15] After Canada abrogated a compromise 1986–91 export tax deal, having argued that stumpage increases had made such a deal irrelevant, the US Commerce Department's International Trade Administration (ITA) ruled again that Canadian provinces were providing a subsidy and the US International Trade Commission again ruled that such a subsidy injured US companies.[16] This time Canada sent the issue to a binational dispute settlement panel under the Canada-

US FTA, which eventually overturned the US finding of subsidy and found that the United States had failed to prove its case.

However, by this time US companies were lobbying heavily in Congress to bring Canada's environmental forestry record squarely into the dispute.[17] They also enlisted the support of Canadian environmental groups for their cause.[18] Canadian provincial and federal governments found themselves defending domestic forestry regulations as much as explicit subsidy allegations. In particular, the US industry argued that Canadian forest companies were not subject to the same environmental restrictions that American companies now faced on US national forest lands.[19] Following these efforts, the US Congress clarified its trade law so that a binational panel finding that the US had not proven its case would be much less likely to occur in the future. As a result, Canada agreed to yet another compromise deal. This time, a voluntary export restraint would limit Canadian softwood lumber exports to the United States to a specific quota. Anything over the quota would be subject to an export tax.[20]

Throughout these developments, a debate raged in Canada over the level of stumpage rates that the four main lumber exporting provinces (British Columbia, Alberta, Quebec, and Ontario) charged their forest companies to harvest provincially owned forest land. The debate was most heated in British Columbia, where softwood lumber exports to the US outnumber exports from all other provinces combined. In the mid-1980s the balance of power began to shift in favour of those who argued that forest companies did not pay a fair price for publicly owned timber, as cash-strapped provincial governments saw higher stumpage fees as a way of solving their budgetary problems.[21] This paved the way for 'structural' increases in British Columbia's provincial stumpage fees in 1987 and 1994.[22]

The 1996 agreement also increased attention to environmental forestry policy, as Canadian environmental groups saw the non-derogation clause of the Softwood Lumber Agreement (SLA) as a tool with which to challenge efforts to streamline BC's Forest Practices Code.[23] As the March 2001 expiration date for the deal approached, this environmental issue was once again coming to the fore.

The softwood lumber dispute reveals that, in the absence of domestic legal tools in Canada enjoyed by environmental groups in the United States, international and domestic environmental groups will cast their net wider, towards trade rules never intended to address environmental issues. In addition, Canadian provinces can use these international pressures to tip the scales domestically to force their own (environmental) policy agendas. They will also do so in a legal context that embraces liberal environmentalism, as it focuses not on increasing alleged protectionist rules, but on eliminating them.

International Institutions and Forestry

Canada's position as a forest 'superpower',[24] owing to its position as the largest exporter of forest products in the world,[25] appeared to afford it a leadership role in international forestry activities and negotiations in the 1990s. However, international activities worked to push the causal arrow somewhat in the opposite direction, with Canadian domestic policy responding to international initiatives as much as directing them. These dynamics are highlighted by the failure to achieve a Global Forest Convention at the 1992 United Nations Conference on Environment and Development (UNCED) or Earth Summit in Rio de Janeiro. Canada was and remains one of the staunchest proponents of a binding international convention, but its efforts continue to appear largely in vain.

In contrast to the successful negotiation of the Biodiversity Convention, the Framework Convention on Climate Change (FCCC), and, although its future is uncertain, the subsequent Kyoto Protocol, the failure of a Global Forest Convention can be explained by its lack of fit within the norm-complex of liberal environmentalism.[26] This poor fit is partly explained by the nature of forest resources themselves, which some perceive as a global commons problem, but which generally fall under the sovereign jurisdiction of individual states (although some forests cross borders). Thus, proposals to address forestry issues have difficulty gaining legitimacy because they can be perceived as violating norms of sovereignty over resources and free trade. Developing countries perceive a threat to the latter norm because they worry that global regulations could in practice operate as disguised barriers to trade that would disproportionately affect developing-country exports. In contrast, climate change, for example, has fared better because although domestic actions are needed, solutions have been developed that operate with the marketplace and free trade, and therefore fit more easily under the legitimating norm-complex of liberal environmentalism. These solutions include international market mechanisms such as tradable permits and other 'flexible' instruments to achieve the goals and targets of the FCCC and Kyoto Protocol. Whether or not these solutions are better for the environment, they have more easily found acceptance owing to their consistency with liberal environmentalism. Solutions that would be perceived as legitimate under liberal environmentalism have remained elusive in the case of a possible forest convention.

The debate at Rio pitted Northern states such as the United States and Canada, which argued for a 'global responsibility' approach, against Southern states such as Malaysia and India, which argued for 'sovereign discretion'. The latter feared that Northern states would dictate how forests within the jurisdiction of Southern states should be managed.[27] Such a direction would have moved these countries more towards the 'command-and-compliance' approach symbolized by Stockholm than towards the new liberal environmental norm-complex institutionalized in other successful agreements at Rio. As a result, negotiations were mired in North-South debates, where the G-77/China bloc of developing countries remained suspicious of Northern intentions on several fronts and refused at the Earth Summit even to consider a binding agreement in which few economic incentives were developed. Developing countries also voiced concerns over inadequate financial and technology transfer commitments from the North, which they argued were required to aid the South in its sustainability obligations.[28]

Instead of a global convention, countries agreed only to a 'non-legally binding authoritative statement of principles for global consensus on the management, conservation and sustainable development of all types of forests', known as the 'forest principles'.[29] Various attempts since 1992 to reinvigorate movement towards a convention have failed.[30]

The lack of international legal teeth behind the forest principles meant that international influences on domestic Canadian forest policy can be traced more to ideas espoused in international negotiations or other policy fora, such as support for biodiversity and the maintenance of ecological processes, which were subsequently taken up in provincial and national forestry initiatives. For example, the 12 per cent land protection commitment of BC's Protected Area Strategy comes from the call of the Brundtland Commission for a tripling of the world's protected areas from the then-current 4 per cent.[31] The 'Statement of Forest Principles' and the 1992 Convention on Biological Diversity also influenced the norms embodied in the biodiversity guidelines of BC's Forest Practices Code. Related concepts such as 'ecosystem management' became the forest management system embraced in BC's Clayoquot Sound, whose slated logging had come under international criticism in 1993.[32] Finally, domestic work under the auspices of the Canadian Council of Forest Ministers (CCFM) led to the establishment of criteria and indicators (C&I) for achieving sustainable forest management in 1995 that fed into the Montreal Process for establishing C&I internationally for temperate and boreal forests. Although debate surrounds the sufficiency of C&I processes for meeting multiple goals of sustainability (ecological, social, and economic),[33] international-domestic interactions clearly affected domestic policies, since the same CCFM process that fed into international processes also led to C&I being written into legislation governing forests in, for example, Ontario and Quebec.

At the national level, international developments also influenced the CCFM's 'National Forest Strategy (1998–2003)'. The report notes that the development of the National Forest Sector Strategy was 'instrumental to Canadian representations at the 1992 United Nations Conference on the Environment and Development' and that this allowed Canada to argue in the international sphere that it was a leader in sustainable forest management.[34] The latest report also focuses Canadian forest policy on the 'forest ecosystem', something absent in its 1987 National Forest Sector Strategy. The 1998 report acknowledges that the Brundtland Commission and the emergence of other international norms caused the CCFM to consider the forest ecosystem as well as social and cultural forest values alongside economic ones.[35]

The Marketplace

Owing to increased international awareness, transnational environmental groups have used the market to create both 'stick' and 'carrot' pressures. On the 'stick' side, ENGOs used Canadian dependence on foreign markets to launch well-publicized boycott campaigns, as Wilson and Poelzer note elsewhere in this volume, first aimed at Clayoquot Sound and later expanded to other regions of British Columbia.[36] These pressures influenced BC policy change by aiding the BC government of the early to mid-1990s to carry out its forest practices and land-use reforms, despite resistance from powerful domestic interests.[37] Environmental groups could claim some success in their efforts to use the marketplace to force policy change.[38] As the softwood lumber dispute reveals, international forces not only affect forest practices through direct domestic policy changes, but may facilitate government and organized interests to initiate and implement their own agendas.

At the same time, environmental groups, led by the World Wide Fund for Nature (WWF), put their efforts towards developing 'carrot' incentives following Rio. They came to the conclusion that rather than expending significant effort to resurrect a failed global forest convention, they could instead directly influence the private sector more quickly through the development of private 'eco-labelling' programs that would recognize those companies practising sustainable forestry. By turning to the market for solutions, this approach fit well with the norm-complex of liberal environmentalism. As a result, the Forest Stewardship Council (FSC) forest certification program was established in 1993, headquartered in Oaxaca, Mexico.[39] Spearheaded by the WWF, the FSC accredits organizations (certifiers) that must perform evaluations to verify that a company's forest operations match 10 established principles and criteria.[40] More specific regional standards are then developed based on these broader principles. The FSC has certified companies in Europe, North America, the former Soviet bloc countries, and developing countries. Owing to Canada's dependence on foreign markets, the FSC has gained considerable attention among forest companies in Canada, especially in British Columbia.

Forest companies and industry associations in Canada began to develop their own 'system-based' sustainable forestry initiatives in response to the FSC's emphasis on environmental performance.[41] Critics argue that these industry processes are less effective because they focus on process rather than performance and because the industry is either directly involved in the case of the Sustainable Forestry Initiative or is the dominant player in the case of the Canadian Standards Association.[42]

Firm-level product differentiation goals may result in the increased use of the FSC and other certification schemes. Recently, Canadian forest giant MacMillan Bloedel (now, after its 1999 takeover, Weyerhaeuser) moved from being a target of Greenpeace boycotts to Greenpeace suitor, promising to halt clear-cutting in old-growth forests and to begin the process of FSC and CSA certification. Transnational environmental groups' end-run around international forest negotiations appeared to produce concrete results in this case. BC's Interfor, another target of transnational groups' boycott efforts, announced that it, too, wished to produce FSC-certified wood.[43] Whether certification will always lead to 'sustainably managed' forests[44] remains unclear. What is clear is that these international efforts have provoked responses by large forest companies in Canada.

While globalization enabled international forces to exert pressure on Canadian forest policy and management practices, the cause of this pressure did not come

from the market itself but from the more recent phenomenon of internationalization, all the while embracing and being constrained by liberal environmentalism.
Indeed, while it is unclear whether ENGO- or industry-initiated programs will
dominate, certification has achieved a great deal of interest exactly because it
embraces the market and fits within the liberal environmentalism norm-complex.

BIOSAFETY

The process that led to the Cartagena Protocol on Biosafety of the Convention on
Biological Diversity, which regulates trade in 'living modified organisms' (LMOs),[45]
illustrates how globalization, internationalization, and liberal environmentalism
intersect to redefine environmental concerns such as trade issues, even when
recent environmental goals appear to be gaining increasing attention vis-à-vis
monetary and trade concerns. Concern over genetically modified organisms
(GMOs) first appeared on the international policy agenda in the years leading up
to the 1992 Rio Earth Summit, as increasing corporate research and development
investments led to significant technological advances in the production of genetically modified crops. Today, 100 million acres of agricultural land in 12 countries,
including Canada and the US, produce genetically modified (GM) crops.[46] The
crops have been genetically manipulated to increase growth rates, to become less
susceptible to pests and disease, and to address human health issues.[47]

Along with these seemingly positive aspects of GMOs, there are concerns over
their effects on the natural environment, particularly over the possibility that even
worse 'super bugs' and 'super weeds'[48] might develop and that GMOs might
forever alter existing natural ecosystems.[49] The problem is that scientific evidence
confirming these ecological fears might not develop until after irreversible harm
occurs. The dominant response internationally to such circumstances has been
the *precautionary principle* debate. While the precautionary principle has been
defined in varied and specific ways,[50] in essence it refers to the position that, in
the face of uncertainty, preventive action is still warranted under conditions associated with a high risk of potentially serious environmental damage. However,
firms, organizations, and countries heavily dependent on trade fear that invoking
pre-emptive policies may harm them unfairly and may encourage thinly disguised
protectionist policies masquerading under the precautionary principle.

In this case, domestic and international environmental groups sought to
expand their hard-fought battles to entrench the precautionary principle as an
acceptable policy within the European Union legal framework to other countries'
domestic policies.[51] This approach illustrates the influence of internationalization,
in which export-dependent agricultural countries such as Canada faced pressure
from non-domestic interests to change their own GMO policies via changes in
international rules.[52] At the same time, the liberal environmentalism norm-
complex severely limited the policy deliberations of international discussions to
those concerning trade rules, closing the door to agreements on rules and procedures governing research, development, and implementation of GMO technology

in isolation. In part, this limited scope is explained by the signing of the Convention on Biological Diversity at Rio, article 19.3 of which, embracing market instruments and liberal economic development, called for the development of a Biosafety Protocol under the CBD framework.[53]

Following Rio, alliances developed over implementation of article 19.3, including the GMO agriculture-exporting 'Miami Group' (consisting of Canada, the United States, Argentina, Australia, Chile, and Uruguay);[54] the European Union, which had already implemented precautionary principle rules for its own internal trade in GMOs; the 'Compromise Group'[55] (Central and Eastern European countries); and the 'Like-Minded Group' (consisting of developing countries, excluding Argentina, Chile, and Uruguay), which sought to limit the introduction of GMOs into their domestic markets.[56]

After a series of informal interactions, a formal meeting was scheduled in Cartagena, Colombia, with the purpose of arriving at agreement. The Cartagena meeting unravelled owing to strong divisions over increased emphasis on the precautionary principle, which, within the liberal environmentalism norm-complex, was treated as subordinate to, and incompatible with, liberal trade as institutionalized through WTO agreements. The main opposition came from Canada, the United States, and other Miami Group countries that refused to allow companies to restrict imports on the basis of the precautionary principle. Doing so, they felt, would in essence be giving up 'gains' they thought they had obtained through WTO processes and rulings that seemed to guarantee market access. The Canadian position was largely governed by concerns within its domestic agricultural sector, as agricultural policy networks dominated foreign policy discussions on the issue. This left Canadian domestic and transnational environmental groups to seek change to Canadian domestic policy through the international route. They expended considerable effort on the Protocol, in the hope that it would bring about a shift in domestic Canadian policy.[57]

Since Cartagena, environmental, social, and labour issues have been increasingly salient on the international rule-making agenda, as evidenced by the failure of the MAI and the failure of the Seattle WTO Ministerial Conference to launch a new round of trade negotiations, in part owing to its inability to deal adequately with these issues. However, despite the apparent opposition to further liberalization these events seem to indicate, the postponing of further trade and investment liberalization in multilateral forums is not likely to undermine liberal environmentalism. Even the organized opposition in Seattle from non-governmental groups focused on demands for increased accountability and attention to environmental, social, and labour standards, not arguments that the WTO be jettisoned. Under these circumstances, the dominance of liberal economic institutions and the norms they embody appear robust under the prevailing liberal environmentalism norm-complex. These concerns nonetheless are indicative of a potential conflict between multilateral environmental agreements and the WTO, a battle that became a major theme in biosafety negotiations.

In this context, a new round of negotiations on LMOs took place in Montreal in January 2000. The Miami Group, led by Canada, was increasingly concerned that the absence of an agreement on LMOs might lead to an unravelling of the existing trading framework and might encourage countries to take more drastic unilateral action.[58]

As a result of these dynamics, negotiators reached an eleventh-hour compromise agreement under which a Protocol would be limited to LMOs and the precautionary principle could be invoked by importing countries as a reason to limit imports. However, the agreement also states that it and other international agreements (i.e., trade agreements such as the WTO) are to be mutually supportive, suggesting either that trade norms are not incompatible with the precautionary principle or that conflicts should not privilege one set of principles (or one international agreement) over the other. In addition, exporting countries are required to explain whether their crops contain genetically modified elements, although the agreement stopped short of differentiating genetically modified from non-genetically modified crops via required labelling.[59] Instead, the Protocol leaves the labelling of LMOs to market pressures, although it also mandates further negotiations on the issue.[60] Regardless, even a mandated labelling solution reflects a reliance on market signals fully consistent with liberal environmentalism norms. The one ambiguity was whether more expanded use of the precautionary principle under this agreement was subordinate to existing treatments at the WTO. The language in the preamble is purposely vague on this front but reflects a dialectic within liberal environmentalism, rather than a challenge to it. The first paragraph explicitly reinforces liberal environmentalism by asserting the 'mutual supportiveness' of trade and environmental agreements.[61] As Gupta notes, the second paragraph 'states categorically that countries negotiating the protocol do not intend to change rights and obligations under other existing agreements', which was demanded by the Miami Group in their efforts to assert the primacy of the WTO.[62] Yet, at the same time, the final principle in the preamble states that 'the previous clause should not be read as subordinating the protocol to other agreements',[63] deliberately creating ambiguity.

It would be a mistake to see advances in the precautionary principle as moving towards greater environmental protection and away from trading norms; quite the opposite occurred, as the agreement entrenched liberal environmentalism by focusing the debate narrowly as a trade issue. The effects of the agreement on Canadian policy and politics were twofold. First, it clearly strengthened the hand of environmental groups whose efforts in Canada to focus increased attention on GMOs had been limited by the agriculture lobby. While Environment Canada had played a limited and relatively minor role in discussions, Environment Minister David Anderson, despite Canada's position as a leader of the Miami Group, was widely cited after the agreement when he said that Canada supports 'the precautionary approach which allows nations to take action even in the absence of scientific certainty' as well as 'the right of every country to restrict the import of LMOs that would harm its biodiversity'.[64]

Second, while the agreement did nothing to stop GMO production or exports, it does put pressure on Canada and other countries to develop specific explanations of the content of their commodities, which may lead to increased domestic attention to the GMO issue. As a result, it may even increase rules on its production. However, given the framing of the issue in the treaty, it only provides limited leverage for those groups that had hoped for wider scrutiny and limitations on the production and development of GMOs.

THE KYOTO PROTOCOL AND CANADA'S RESPONSE TO CLIMATE CHANGE

The chapter by Smith in this volume details the development of the 1997 Kyoto Protocol and the compromise of linking binding emission targets and timetables to market mechanisms, including tradable emission permits, joint implementation, and the Clean Development Mechanism, a compromise legitimated by the liberal environmentalism norm-complex. The story of early Canadian leadership followed by laggard implementation and a 'follow-the-US' foreign climate policy is thus beyond the scope of this chapter. Our brief comments on this case are simply to highlight with a few examples how the climate change story illustrates well the globalization/internationalization interactions identified here, as Canadian domestic policy and politics have clearly been shaped by international negotiations and commitments.

The events leading up to the signing of the Kyoto Protocol epitomize these influences. In the fall of 1997, the looming international negotiations in Kyoto eventually gave Prime Minister Jean Chrétien the ability to break with dominant domestic coal and oil business interests, which strongly opposed an agreement, and eventually to commit Canada to binding greenhouse gas emission reductions. The break came in response to direct pressure from Canada's G-7 partners at the Denver Summit of the Eight in June 1997, subsequent consultations with EU and American leaders, and even direct personal pressure from European leaders, especially German Chancellor Helmut Kohl.[65] Chrétien also drew on domestic environmental group support in agreeing to a set of international rules far beyond what prominent industry associations and lobbies wanted, in part because he wanted to maintain Canada's position and reputation in the international community as a leader on environmental issues.

In this case, the globalized nature of industries responsible for the emission of greenhouse gases contributed to the pressure on Canada to commit to initiate domestic policies beyond what it would have done if climate change were solely a domestic affair. This ironic outcome only makes sense by disentangling globalization and internationalization. Take the case of Alberta, where energy producers prior to Kyoto made the case for deregulation by arguing that to maintain the 'Alberta advantage' (which made its industrial electricity rates much lower than those of many US states, giving it a competitive advantage in regional energy markets) and to benefit from the regionalization of markets under NAFTA, Canada had to follow the OECD trend of deregulation in response to wider pressures of globalization.[66] But the internationalization of energy policy concerns owing to the Kyoto Protocol meant that the competitive environment also had to take into account international commitments being negotiated by Canada's most important trading partner, the United States. Thus, the globalized nature of Alberta's energy sector meant that politically it could not ignore the new commitments that would face its main competitors, namely US states, without opening itself up to possible trade disputes, political pressures, and even long-term competitive pressures owing to being left behind if regulations relating to energy efficiency or incentives for innovation gave US producers a competitive edge in a less carbon-intensive economy. The negotiation of international rules on climate change and the pressures of Canada's broader foreign policy goals and reputation pushed Canada in an opposite direction from what a simple logic of globalization would suggest.

Not only did the negotiations give Canadian ENGOs a degree of policy success they otherwise would not have had, but efforts to implement the Kyoto agreement have altered domestic political struggles and policies as well. For example, while most important players in the energy sector were against the Kyoto Protocol (as were provinces with large coal and oil sectors such as Alberta), once Canada signed the international agreement in Kyoto the industry picture became much more complex. While companies do not fall easily into the camps of proactive and resistant, many companies facing a variety of competitive and organizational pressures (such as the costs/benefits of innovation), as well as consumer, shareholder, moral, and scientific pressures and influences, are in the process of redefining their interests on this issue and positioning themselves to benefit from the possibility of a new competitive environment under the Protocol. New incentives include the possibility of profiting from early action or strategic use of market mechanisms enabled under the Protocol. Policies linked with liberal environmentalism, such as emissions trading, also make it more difficult for industry as a group to resist action, because the fit with domestic liberal economic and sustainable development norms shifts the burden of effort and proof to companies opposed to action to show why they should not have to change. Even formerly resistant provinces such as Alberta are becoming more proactive in their climate change policies under these conditions.

Canadian domestic policy on climate change clearly is moving in ways it would not have in the absence of international pressure from friendly governments, but transnational ENGOs, the evolving Kyoto Protocol, and the wider liberal environmentalism compromise also clearly direct policies along certain paths. In particular, Canadian responses are likely to be possible only to the degree that they are seen as consistent with Canada's competitive and trade goals.

Conclusion

Institutions, rules, and norms interacted with global market pressures in the 1990s to alter fundamentally the directions and choices within Canadian environmental policy. Identifying the related but distinct pressures of globalization, internationalization, and liberal environmentalism permitted us to describe how these forces work and alter Canadian domestic environmental policy. Global economic integration is clearly a large part of the story behind these trends, especially with respect to a country as export-oriented as Canada. However, the lack of support for the hypothesized 'downward' pressure associated with forces of globalization suggests that other forces of internationalization often intersected to shift policies in more complex ways, whether through embracing the market to promote eco-labelling in the forest sector or in promoting global tradable permits in efforts to reduce climate change emissions. Forces of internationalization did not just operate along a market or international rule-making pathway, however. They also operated along a normative pathway (witness Rio's norms on biodiversity, which had an effect in the absence of a Global Forest Convention).

At the same time, these trends were constrained and directed by a liberal environmentalism norm-complex that saw concerns over genetically modified organisms being limited to a *trade* issue, with no consideration to developing global rules on what should, or should not, be permitted in this new technology. So entrenched are most interests within the liberal environmentalism norm-complex that small advances in the use of the precautionary principle were heralded as significant victories for environmentalists. The norm-complex also accounted for the market-oriented directions that forestry and climate change policies embraced. Recognizing these trends not only permits a better understanding of international and domestic environmental policy-making processes, it also permits us to understand what policy doors have been closed and raises the question of whether such doors should be forced back open.

Notes

1 See, e.g., Suzanne Berger and Ronald Dore, eds, *National Diversity and Global Capitalism* (Ithaca, NY: Cornell University Press, 1996); Thomas Risse-Kappen, ed., *Bringing Transnational Relations Back In: Non-State Actors, Domestic Structures and International Institutions* (Cambridge, Mass.: Harvard University Press, 1995).

2 David Vogel, *Trading Up: Consumer and Environmental Regulation in a Global Economy* (Cambridge, Mass.: Harvard University Press, 1995).

3 Steven Bernstein and Benjamin Cashore, 'Globalization, Four Paths of Internationalization and Domestic Policy Change: The Case of Eco-forestry in British Columbia, Canada', *Canadian Journal of Political Science* 33, 1 (2000): 67–99.

4 G. Bruce Doern, Leslie A. Pal, and Brian W. Tomlin, 'The Internationalization of Canadian Public Policy', in Doern, Pal, and Tomlin, *Border Crossings: The Internationalization of Canadian Public Policy* (Toronto: Oxford University Press, 1996), 2.

5 Suzanne Berger, 'Introduction', in Berger and Dore, eds, *National Diversity and Global Capitalism*, 9.

6 Ibid., 12.

7 The forest sector alone makes the largest single contribution to Canada's balance-of-payments surplus, contributing $2.1 billion in 1997 to provincial coffers in the form of

resource rents. See Natural Resources Canada, *The State of Canada's Forests* (Ottawa, Natural Resources Canada, 1997).

8 Steven Bernstein, *The Compromise of Liberal Environmentalism* (New York: Columbia University Press, 2001).

9 Robert O. Keohane and Joseph S. Nye, Jr, 'The Club Model of Multilateral Cooperation and Problems of Democratic Legitimacy', paper presented at the annual meeting of the American Political Science Association, Washington, 31 Aug.-3 Sept. 2000.

10 Paul Stanton Kibel, 'Reconstructing the Marketplace: The International Timber Trade and Forest Protection', *NYU Environmental Law Journal* 5 (1996): 1–63.

11 Bernstein, *The Compromise of Liberal Environmentalism.*

12 Steven Bernstein, 'Logjam in Global Forest Protection: Contesting Liberal Environmentalism', paper presented at the annual convention of the International Studies Association, Minneapolis, 17–21 Mar. 1998. At the time of writing, the future of the Kyoto Protocol was uncertain. Nonetheless, any agreement to replace or modify it is likely to even more strongly embrace market norms and instruments.

13 Pierre Marc Johnson and André Beaulieu, *The Environment and NAFTA: Understanding and Implementing the New Continental Law* (Washington: Island Press, 1996).

14 One possible exception to liberal environmentalism is the Convention on International Trade in Endangered Species. See Kibel, 'Reconstructing the Marketplace'. CITES does provide clear binding rules on the trade in species threatened with extinction. However, it is limited in scope.

15 Gary N. Horlick and Geoffrey D. Oliver, 'Antidumping and Countervailing Duty Law Provisions of the Omnibus Trade and Competitiveness Act of 1988', *Journal of World Trade* 23, 3 (1989): 5–49.

16 Ibid.

17 Ron Wyden, 'Letter to Ambassador Burney', Washington: US Congress, 1992.

18 'Protestors Playing Into Hands of US, Minister Says', *Vancouver Sun*, 20 Oct. 1994, B10; 'Wilderness Committee Stumps for US Industry', *Vancouver Sun*, 18 Oct. 1994, D3.

19 Benjamin Cashore, 'US Pacific Northwest', in Bill Wilson, Kees Van Kooten, Ilan Vertinsky, and Louise Arthur, eds, *Forest Policy: International Case Studies* (Oxon, UK: CABI Publications, 1999), 47–80. These arguments were made in order to maintain their influence in Congress. The ITA and ITC adjudication processes cannot officially take environmental issues into account.

20 Benjamin Cashore, 'Governing Forestry: Environmental Group Influence in British Columbia and the US Pacific Northwest', Ph.D. thesis (University of Toronto, 1997).

21 Benjamin Cashore, 'The Role of the Provincial State in Forest Policy: A Comparative Study of British Columbia and New Brunswick', MA thesis (Carleton University, 1988); James P. Groen, 'British Columbia's International Relations: Consolidating a Coalition-Building Strategy', *BC Studies* 102 (Summer 1994): 25–59.

22 Benjamin Cashore, George Hoberg, Michael Howlett, Jeremy Raynor, and Jeremy Wilson, *In Search of Sustainability: The Politics of Forest Policy in British Columbia in the 1990s* (Vancouver: University of British Columbia Press, 2001), esp. ch. 7.

23 Gordon Hamilton, 'Don't Lower Stumpage, US tells BC', *Vancouver Sun*, 11 Apr. 1997, D1; John Schreiner and Peter Morton, 'Changes to BC Forest Code Fail to Please Environmentalists, US', *Financial Post*, 11 June 1997, 7.

24 Brian Hocking, 'The Woods and the Trees: Catalytic Diplomacy and Canada's Trials as a "Forestry Superpower"', *Environmental Politics* 5, 3 (1996): 448–75.

25 Ministry of Natural Resources, 'Sustaining Forests, Taking Global Action', in *1995–1996 State of Canada's Forests* (Ottawa: Government of Canada, Minister of Natural Resources, 1998).

26 Bernstein, 'Logjam in Global Forest Protection', 17–21. Efforts for a global forest convention can be traced back to the 1980s, when Northern countries and environmentalists focused their attention on tropical deforestation, which helped secure the inclusion of a mandate to conserve tropical forests and their genetic resources in the International Tropical Timber Agreement (ITTA) of 1983, and through its highest decision-making body, the International Tropical Timber Organization (ITTO). Fitting within the norms of liberal environmentalism, the primary mandate of the ITTO remained the regulation of trade in tropical timber. See David Humphreys, 'The Global Politics of Forest Conservation Since the UNCED', *Environmental Politics* 5 (1996): 231–56. After prolonged negotiations on a successor agreement (the ITTA of 1994), consumer countries, including Canada, pledged to manage their own forests sustainably by the year 2000, but outside the context of the ITTO. They reasoned that a pledge within the ITTO would undermine the prospects for a global forest convention, which they wanted to be much broader than the trade-focused ITTA.

27 Gareth Porter and Janet Welsh Brown, *Global Environmental Politics*, 2nd edn (Boulder, Colo.: Westview Press, 1996): 126.

28 Humphreys, 'The Global Politics of Forest Conservation'; Porter and Brown, *Global Environmental Politics*, 115–29; Marc Williams, 'Re-articulating the Third World Coalition: The Role of the Environmental Agenda', *Third World Quarterly* 14 (1993): 7–29.

29 International Development Research Centre, 'The Earth Summit: CD-ROM' (Ottawa: International Development Research Centre on behalf of the United Nations, 1993).

30 In its place, a variety of narrower and/or regional initiatives have taken shape since 1992. New initiatives include the Montreal Process on creating criteria and indicators (C&I) for the conservation and sustainable development of temperate and boreal forests (in which Canada played a major role in formulating and that have influenced provincial forest policies), the Helsinki Process on protecting forests in Europe (which includes a C&I process), negotiations towards a successor to the ITTA, initiatives on labelling and certification schemes (largely led by non-governmental groups and/or industry), and a number of expert and governmental forestry workshops. The only process to focus serious attention on a global convention was the Intergovernmental Panel on Forests (IPF) established in 1995, sponsored by the UN Commission on Sustainable Development (CSD). After two years of discussions that failed to reach consensus on a number of key issues, the Intergovernmental Forum on Forests (IFF) succeeded the IPF. Obstacles concerning trade, sovereignty, and aid continued to plague IFF discussions, suggesting progress towards a forest convention will remain slow. 'Report of the First Session of the CSD Intergovernment Panel on Forests', *Earth Negotiations Bulletin* 13, 3 (11–15 Sept. 1995); 'Summary of IPF-2 Geneva', *Earth Negotiations Bulletin* 13, 45 (24 Aug.-4 Sept. 1998). The IFF process most recently (Oct. 2000) evolved into a permanent UN Forum on Forests (UNFF), a subsidiary body of the UN Economic and Social Council that would carry on work to implement existing agreements and initiatives from the IPF/IFF process. In addition, it would 'consider' within five years the possibility of a mandate for negotiating a binding convention.

31 World Commission on Environment and Development, *Our Common Future* (Oxford: Oxford University Press, 1987).

32 Scientific Panel for Sustainable Forest Practices in Clayoquot Sound, 'Progress Report 2: Review of Current Forest Practice Standards in Clayoquot Sound' (British Columbia, 1994).

33 For a detailed discussion of the conflictual aspects of sustainability criteria and the inadequacy of current C&I processes in Canada to address the diversity of interests and values, or the power imbalances between relevant social groups, see Nilsson Sten and Michael Gluck, 'Sustainability and the Canadian Forest Sector', Interim report IR-00-250 (Laxenburg, Austria: International Institute for Applied Systems Analysis, 2000).

34 Canadian Council of Forest Ministers, 'National Forest Strategy (1998–2003). Sustainable Forests: A Canadian Commitment' (Ottawa: Canadian Council of Forest Ministers, 1998), 3.

35 See ibid. For up-to-date summaries of multilateral negotiations on forests, see International Institute for Sustainable Development, *Earth Negotiations Bulletin* 13, available at: www.iisd.ca

36 Greenpeace Canada, Greenpeace International, and Greenpeace San Francisco, *Broken Promises: The Truth About What's Happening to British Columbia's Forests* (Vancouver, 1997); Canadian Press, 'Greenpeace Steps Up Protests in Europe Against BC Logging', *Vancouver Sun*, 28 Mar. 1998, A4.

37 Personal interview, Michael Harcourt.

38 Bernstein and Cashore, 'Globalization, Four Paths of Internationalization and Domestic Policy Change'.

39 Eric Hansen, 'Certified Forest Products Market Place', in United Nations Timber Committee, ed., *Forest Products: Annual Market Review* (Geneva: United Nations Timber Committee, 1998), 19.

40 Ibid.

41 The Canadian Pulp and Paper Association developed 'Sustainable Forest Management System Standards' under the auspices of the Canadian Standards Association (CSA). The Alberta Forest Products Association developed a similar forest certification process entitled Forest Care, which has already certified Weyerhaeuser operations in Grand Prairie. These systems-based approaches are modelled after the 14001 Environmental Management System of the International Organization for Standardization (ISO). See Fred Gale and Cheri Burda, 'The Pitfalls and Potential of Eco-Certification as a Market Incentive for Sustainable Forest Management', in Chris Tollefson, ed., *The Wealth of Forests: Markets, Regulation and Sustainable Forestry* (Vancouver: University of British Columbia Press, 1997), 414–41.

42 Ibid.; Hansen, 'Certified Forest Products Market Place'; Benjamin Cashore, 'Legitimacy and the Privatization of Environmental Governance: Exploring Forest Certification (Eco-labelling) in the US and Canadian Forest Sectors', unpublished manuscript, Auburn University Forest Policy Center, 2000.

43 Whereas CSA/ISO was trumpeted as a more viable alternative to FSC standards, some individual forest companies such as Weyerhaeuser Canada and Alberta Pacific now say CSA and FSC are both potentially attainable (personal interviews).

44 The Forest Stewardship Council has attempted to sidestep controversies over the term 'sustainably managed' forests, focusing instead on 'well-managed' forests.

45 Discussions first focused on the term 'genetically modified organisms' (GMOs), which included both living organisms and the products produced from them. However, during negotiations, agriculture exporting countries succeeded in limiting the focus to only those organisms that were 'living' and thus had the potential to alter the importing country's natural environment. Ron Sullivan, 'Biosafety protocol compromise', *Earth Island Journal* 15, 2 (2000): 24.

46 John Vidal, 'Global battle rages over GM crops as biotech revolution ploughs on: Out of chaos come international biosafety rules, signed but still to be ratified', *The Guardian* (July 2000): 8.

47 Other apparently beneficial advances include the development of a type of rice that contains vitamin A, designed to combat blindness in millions of children in developing countries around the globe. See John Burgess, 'Talks to Open on Divisive Issue of Gene-Altered Foods', *Washington Post*, 24 Jan. 2000, A8.

48 Paul Jacobs, 'International accord on labeling puts spotlight on genetically modified crops', *Seattle Times*, 1 Feb. 2000, A3.

49 Burgess, 'Talks to Open on Divisive Issue of Gene-Altered Foods'.

50 Aarti Gupta, 'Governing trade in genetically modified organisms: The Cartagena Protocol on Biosafety', *Environment* 42, 4 (2000): 22–33.

51 John Parker, 'Greenpeace holds ship in protest', *Traffic World* 261, 10 (6 Mar. 2000): 39–40; Keith Chadwick, 'European controversy continues over Canadian GM canola seeds', *Chemical Market Reporter* 257, 24 (2000): 10–11.

52 Mark S. Winfield, 'Reflections on the Biosafety Protocol Negotiations in Montreal', unpublished paper, Toronto, 2000.

53 Gupta, 'Governing'; Aaron Crosby and Stas Burgiel, 'The Cartagena Protocol in Biosafety: An Analysis of the Results: An IISD Briefing Note' (Winnipeg: International Institute for Sustainable Development, 2000).

54 The group crystallized as a negotiating bloc only once formal negotiations towards the Cartagena Protocol were under way.

55 Gupta explains that this group consisted of 'for the most part OECD countries that are not key agriculture exporters and are not part of the European Union, including Japan, Mexico, Norway, South Korea, and Switzerland, and later joined by Singapore and New Zealand'.

56 See Gupta, 'Governing'; Crosby and Burgiel, 'The Cartagena Protocol'.

57 See Crosby and Burgiel, 'The Cartegena Protocol'; Winfield, 'Reflections'.

58 Charlie Cray, 'Biosafety truce reached', *Multinational Monitor* 21, 3 (Mar. 2000): 6–7.

59 See ibid.; Ruth Walker, 'Global pact on GMOs approved on Saturday, after a week of talks, 130 nations ratified a trade treaty on engineered food', *Christian Science Monitor*, 31 Jan. 2000, 6.

60 Jim Papanikolaw, 'Biosafety Protocol receives mixed reception from agricultural groups', *Chemical Market Reporter* 257, 6 (2000): 4, 7.

61 See Gupta, 'Governing'.

62 Even prior to the Protocol, high-profile disputes such as that between the EU and the United States and Canada over hormone-modified beef demonstrated the difficulty in reconciling these two principles. In that case, WTO panel and appellate body rulings went against the EU ban on beef because the EU did not conduct a risk assessment. Such an assessment had to bear a 'rational' and 'objective' relationship to the ban under the 1994 WTO Agreement on Sanitary and Phytosanitary Measures, which applied in this case. Significantly, however, the appellate body also ruled that under the SPS agreement, risk assessments need not be based exclusively on laboratory science under controlled conditions, but also on assessments of risks in human societies as they actually exist. Thus, the appellate body ruling overturned the panel on two important grounds: first, it clarified that WTO members could impose higher levels of protection to human health than prevailing international standards as long as such standards were scientifically justified, and, more importantly for this discussion, it opened the door to a broader view of science more consistent with the precautionary principle—opening up the debate on what burden of scientific proof is sufficient to limit trade. See the conclusion in Bernstein, 'The Compromise'. For a succinct summary of the rulings, see Hkån Nordström and Scott Vaughn, WTO Secretariat, *Trade and Environment*, Special Studies #4 (Geneva: World Trade Organization, 1999), Annex 1, paras 140–7.

63 See Gupta, 'Governing'.

64 Wayne Kondro, 'Agreement reached on global biosafety protocol', *The Lancet* 355, 9202 (2000): 477.

65 Interviews with officials and observers involved in Canada's Kyoto preparations.

66 Karen Litfin, 'Advocacy coalitions along the domestic-foreign frontier: Globalization and Canadian climate change policy', *Policy Studies Journal* 28, 1 (2000): 236–52.

Part Two

Cases

Chapter 12

Grounding Environmental Policy: Rural and Remote Communities in Canada

Mary Louise McAllister

Conventionally accepted approaches to public policy are ill-suited to the resolution of complex environmental problems. Traditional policy approaches tend to focus on resolving political disputes over resources, rather than on fostering an effective strategy for long-term sustainability. Moreover, public policy analyses have given short shrift to local environmental policy-making and governance where adverse environmental impacts are most directly felt, particularly in rural and remote areas of Canada. With its resource-based economy, this neglect has serious implications for the country.

Communities in rural regions of the country are subject to the vagaries of fluctuating international markets and external political agendas that are indifferent to the specific needs of rural Canada.[1] It is important to pay attention to these communities if long-term sustainability is to be achieved. In Canada, the resources sector is still the primary engine of the national economy:

> Rural communities provide much employment and economic benefit to all Canadians. Canada's international success and image is based primarily on natural resources. However, rural Canadians are now 'a voice in the wilderness', as they often go unheard. Government must recognize the important contribution from this sector. This recognition should be heard and be celebrated by those of influence, the politicians.—The Mattawa and Area Forestry Committee.[2]

Industrial activities in these resource-intensive regions are important to economic stability. Such activities, however, are accompanied by significant biophysical, socio-economic, and environmental impacts for both rural and urban Canada.

Effective environmental policy-making has been constrained by a number of philosophical and institutional biases. The effects of these constraints are felt most deeply in the hinterland regions of Canada. At the heart of the difficulty is the conventional 'silo' approach to public policy, which L.K. Caldwell noted over 30 years ago: 'Policy analysts and decision-makers have been preoccupied with either narrowly defined problems, or institutional/structural or political issues related to environmental concerns.'[3] Caldwell suggested that comprehensive environmental policy would not be achieved through the pursuit of individual environmental problems taken out of a larger, 'more generalized' context. This argument still holds true today.

In addition to the predictable bureaucratic barriers to effective environmental decision-making, Canada's policy discourse is characterized by federal-provincial jurisdictional disputes, interest-group politics, global competitiveness issues, and, increasingly, the concerns of densely inhabited metropolitan regions. As such, public decision-making does not effectively address the putative goal of environmental policy: long-term sustainability. Advocates of ecosystem or community-based approaches to environmental issues often find that the Canadian policy tool box is ill-equipped to grapple with local concerns that exist on the margins of the national political conscience.

Canada's environmental policy-makers and analysts have shown little appetite for devising strategies that could address local environmental concerns, let alone for delving into the problems of the vast, sparsely populated remote communities of Canada. Yet failure to do so reveals a systemic bias in environmental policy-making with particularly significant implications for the communities most directly affected. As political ecologists and others have noted, the costs and benefits of environmental change are inequitably distributed.[4] The hardest hit are the politically and geographically isolated areas. Moreover, failure to acknowledge effectively those issues related to the unequal allocation of resources is short-sighted from the perspective of the collective interest; regions of Canada are inextricably woven together. The instability of one region has national implications.

A new conceptual approach is required if environmental decision-making is to be effective, particularly with respect to rural regions of Canada. This approach would acknowledge the central role that ecosystem thinking must play in all environmental policy-making if sustainability issues are to be effectively addressed. Catherine Dowling offers the following definition: 'An ecosystem approach can be characterized by six elements including natural environmental planning units, a holistic interdisciplinary approach, cross-scale considerations, inclusive multidisciplinary decision-making, adaptive and flexible management, and an underlying sustainability ethic.'[5] George Francis suggests that this ethic is based on three prerequisites: ecological sustainability, economic vitality, and social equity. He states, 'As an ideal, sustainability meshes well with the desires of most people to achieve decent levels of health and well-being, in pleasant surroundings, with strong community networks, and a diversity of opportunities for work and fulfillment.'[6]

If we accept this definition of sustainability, based as it is on considerations of ecosystem integrity, we require a framework for illustrating and understanding the political factors that affect sustainability. Political ecology provides such a framework. It recognizes the integral role played by politics and the distribution of power in shaping ecosystems. As such, this approach can be used to inform (and critique) Canadian environmental policy as it affects rural regions of Canada. Political ecology may most simply be defined as the study of the role politics plays in shaping the socio-economic and biophysical environment. An examination of some issues related to rural communities (particularly those of northern mining towns) and the political actors involved illustrates the need for a 'nested' approach that can be used to evaluate the environmental implications of complex political forces as well as to craft appropriate policy responses.

Political Ecology: An Analytical Perspective

Political ecologists are primarily concerned with the distribution of environmental costs and benefits according to the relative power of actors operating at different levels (or scales) of decision-making. As Bryant and Bailey note, the poorer, weaker grassroots actors bear the disproportionate costs of environmental problems compared to their wealthy, powerful counterparts (e.g., states, large businesses, and multilateral institutions).[7] Weaker, less influential actors tend to be located in rural and remote parts of the world. In Canada, despite the comparative lack of political influence relative to metropolitan areas, staples-producing regions cannot be easily dismissed for at least three reasons. First, the country still relies on the revenues generated by resource-based activities. The long-term sustainability of Canada as a whole rests in no small measure on the socio-economic and biophysical vitality of rural and remote regions. Second, although grassroots actors have an overall weaker power status, particularly in rural communities, these actors have certain resources that give them some advantages over others. As Bryant and Bailey point out, 'The fact that grassroots organizations are locally organized and run by, and on behalf of, grassroots actors gives them a legitimacy and accountability that is typically lacking in the case of other actors, including many ENGOs.'[8] Finally, the liberal-democratic philosophical basis of the contemporary nation-state requires that the needs of all its regions be given some attention.

In addition to the distribution of costs and benefits, political ecology also considers how and where environmental decisions are taken. If we adopt a sustainability ethic as defined above, the effective management of human interaction with the environment requires a measure of local decision-making and capacity-building in order to respond to the varied needs and requirements of diverse social and ecological boundaries. It is at the local level where everything needs to come together. As George Francis has noted, 'There is no point in having inter-departmental coordinating committees in Ottawa if there is chaos on the ground.'[9] Jim Ellsworth has suggested that effective ecosystem management requires 'boundaries that are small enough to enable stakeholders to conceptualize the ecosystem; identify the interrelationships between social, economic and environmental factors; identify relationships between past decisions and the current state of the ecosystem; and take ownership of ecosystem issues and their solution.'[10] Unfortunately, in recent years, rural communities have experienced offloading without having sufficient resources to achieve the task at hand.

Public decision-making with respect to resources inevitably leads to questions about the distribution of power and control. These resources could include social capital, natural capital, financial capital, commodities, technology, and access to information and decision-making. A modified political ecology approach offers a useful lens through which to consider Canadian environmental policy-making. According to Bryant and Bailey, 'political ecologists start from the premise that environmental change is not a neutral process amenable to technical management. Rather, it has political sources, conditions, and ramifications that impinge on existing socio-economic inequalities and political processes.'[11] The role of actors and their varied types of influence assume a position of prominence at several scales: local, regional, national, and, ultimately, global. Actors seeking to influence agendas at all levels include governments, businesses, environmental non-governmental organizations (ENGOs), and citizens.

Political analyses of the role of actors inevitably revolve around discussions of power. Political ecologists suggest that 'to appreciate the role that power plays in conditioning patterns of human-environmental interaction, it is necessary to adopt a more inclusive understanding of power that encompasses material and non-material considerations as well as the fluidity of power itself.'[12] The environment can be used as a tool with which to exert power and control. As such, both biophysical and socio-economic systems are affected.

In Canada, public policy analyses often ignore the complex human-environmental interrelationships identified by political ecologists. Such analyses tend to use the traditional tools of the trade (institutional or sector analysis) and apply them to 'environmental' issues much as they would transportation, health, or any other narrowly defined sector. Yet, the concept and promotion of sustainability cannot be dealt with on a sector-by-sector basis. It requires a new paradigmatic approach that can deal with complex ecosystems requiring a multi-scaled problem-solving approach. And through such an approach we can begin to understand the challenges facing remote communities.

The Nature of Rural and Remote Communities

What do we mean by 'rural' or 'remote' as distinct from urban places? Definitions vary. Some theorists have defined 'rurality' through spatial determinism, suggesting that the socio-cultural characteristics of a community will reflect the type of living environment or geography of a locality. Others may suggest that economic factors (such as a reliance on primary production) or population density best defines rurality. Still others have argued that rurality can best be understood as 'social representation' subject to various interpretations about its meaning.[13] Phil Ehrensaft provided a useful definition when he identified four factors that distinguish the rural from the urban communities:

> What produces the different outcomes are precisely the simple differences in context identified by widespread intuitive understandings of

what it means to be rural in late twentieth century OECD economies; low versus high population densities and distance from metropolitan labour markets. To this, one could add two other factors; typically higher degrees of economic specialization in sectors which are highly sensitive to prices and phases of the business cycle, and high degrees of oligopolization in the local economy, both of which result in lower flexibility of local institutions and the community as a whole.[14]

This definition is consistent with the challenges faced by the mining regions of Canada, with most of them located in relatively remote or northern areas (with the exception of pits and quarries). These regions are strongly shaped and affected by the external decisions taken by global, national, provincial, and metropolitan actors. Canada's continued reliance on its traditional resource-based, open economy reinforces the inexorable cycle of staples-based production and export-led growth in these regions. In mining and other resource-dependent rural regions, this cycle results in what Jane Jacobs refers to as 'specialized economies like those of supply, clearance and transplant regions' with 'too few homeostatic feedback loops which would allow for self-correction'.[15]

Resource-based towns are limited in their options for diversification. Resource industries themselves are becoming increasingly automated and internationalized and provide fewer guarantees of employment, particularly for those individuals without a university education. Furthermore, northern citizens on average possess a lower level of post-secondary education than those who are educated in the southern urban centres. Many 'low-skilled' jobs in the resource sectors have been replaced by automation. Unemployment rates have been consistently higher in northern parts of the country. Governments, as well as resource industries, have served as the foundations of northern employment and economy. With the accelerated retrenchment of the welfare state in the 1990s, therefore, cuts in the public service hit many northern areas particularly hard. Northern Ontario's employment rate, for example, consistently lags 2–4 percentage points behind the rest of the province.[16]

Residents of remote communities often assert that while the resources sector is still the primary engine of the national economy, this fact is not sufficiently recognized in the redistribution of provincial revenues. Moreover, a frequently stated belief suggests that the 'urban' south lacks an understanding of the role that natural resources play in maintaining the national standard of living. More isolated communities do not possess a great deal of voting power and, therefore, lack political clout with provincial decision-makers when policy decisions are made that affect the well-being of these communities. Ultimately, the situation undermines local sustainability, that is, the ability to achieve 'ecological sustainability, economic vitality, and social equity'.

The Decline of the Welfare State and the Case of Walkerton

In recent years, rural and remote communities faced many new challenges with the impact of downsizing by senior governments and the new responsibilities that accompany offloading. At the same time, health and social costs throughout the industrialized world continue to escalate. These latter trends affect both urban and rural regions, but in the latter case the problems are magnified. Increasingly, for example, we hear news of medical doctors going on strike in more isolated communities as they wrestle with inadequate facilities, staff, and financial resources. Similar problems are encountered with the provision of social services, youth programs, and housing. Moreover, the cost of foods and other goods in these regions is considerably higher. In Kenora, Ontario, for example, it was estimated that food costs an average of 21.4 per cent more than it does in Winnipeg, Manitoba, Kenora's large urban neighbour.[17]

During the 1990s, considerable government rhetoric focused on 'partnerships' and 'less government'. In fact, while many responsibilities have been offloaded to the local jurisdictions, several governments demonstrated some dramatic examples of top-down decision-making. In Ontario, for example, when a new Conservative administration was elected in 1995, the province experienced sweeping legislative changes. During 1996 and 1997, Ontario saw a massive overhaul in the areas of local government, environment, health, and educational and social services. Deep cuts were particularly notable in the area of the environment.

The Ontario government's response to escalating rural concerns came in the form of policies that promoted northern and rural development supported by an unsophisticated growth-based strategy. No recognition was given to the obvious need to support and maintain the environmental basis of the province's wealth, the source of social, natural, and monetary capital. As noted earlier, piecemeal, silo approaches do not come without cost. One example of this occurred in the rural community of Walkerton in southern Ontario. Many rural communities rely on groundwater for their municipal supply, more so than the large Ontario cities located on the Great Lakes. Moreover, urban centres have better developed and funded municipal services that regularly monitor the water quality and supply. In the summer of 2000, seven people died of E. coli poisoning while more than 2,300 became ill in Walkerton. The cause was water contaminated by cow manure during heavy rainfall. On 27 July 2000 the Environmental Commissioner of Ontario, Gordon Miller, submitted a report to the Legislative Assembly critiquing Ontario's environmental laws. He stated that his findings were directly related to the Walkerton tragedy and would be of relevance to the investigation of its causes. The news release from his office stated:

> The contamination of drinking water with E. coli in Walkerton in May is suspected by some experts to be related to contamination of groundwater by runoff from local farms. At the same time . . . Ontario has a 'con-

fused patchwork' of laws and policies on protecting groundwater. The Ministry of the Environment should develop a comprehensive ground-water strategy, Miller says, that would include identifying sources of contamination and their potential effects on health. 'The document I am releasing today is a call for leadership by the Ministry of the Environment. The ministry should introduce legislation that will address the environmental effects of intensive farming and come up with a strat-egy that will protect groundwater. . . . It is essential that the public have confidence in how decisions are being made about managing our groundwater. This is not presently the case.'[18]

The human, social, economic, and environmental costs of the government's failure to maintain effective environmental policies and safeguards far outweigh any possible short-term economic gains achieved by cuts to the Ministry of the Environment and environmentally related programs. While water quality may or may not be a cause for serious concern throughout Ontario, it is logical to assume that overall reductions in inspections, monitoring, and enforcement are going to have the most impact on those regions where there are the fewest human and financial resources available for such tasks. Moreover, these problems are most likely to occur in rural areas where activities such as intensive farming take place.

To be effective, government response to these emerging groundwater problems would need to go beyond the typical policy approach, i.e., examining the impact of intensive farming activities on groundwater and then applying legislation and regulations to manage the environmental impacts of this type of farming. If an ecosystem approach were to be applied, it would be necessary to revamp existing water legislation and regulations. Ecosystem management requires an all-encom-passing surface and groundwater initiative, informed by an understanding of the hydrologic cycle (i.e., the interrelationship between surface water and ground-water) and based on an integrated management approach using watershed-based planning. It has been argued, however, that two problems are associated with this approach, one scientific and the other political:

> In the first instance, it should be noted that given the complexity of the geological environment of aquifers . . . groundwater basins do not always coincide with surface water drainage basins. . . . From a political perspective, it should be noted that watersheds do not coincide with political or economic interactions. Considerable attention will be given to developing inter-jurisdictional agreements that can harmonize both political and environment requirements. Municipalities will need to have more authority to implement effective watershed planning on a local basis in order to reconcile competing land and water use activities.[19]

As the Walkerton issue illustrates, a lack of broader ecosystem planning can lead to environmental impacts that are not readily mitigated. Factors such as global-ization, ideological political shifts towards growth-oriented strategies, and cut-backs to the welfare state all serve as barriers to the adoption of an integrated approach to policy-making. An examination of the impacts of these trends (and counter-trends) can be illustrated through an examination of communities dependent on, or directly affected by, mining-related activities.

Challenges to Mining Communities and the Case of the Adams Mine

Communities often find themselves dealing with the fallout from environmental problems associated with events that happen outside their boundaries, yet they possess limited political authority and resources with which to respond. In the case of mining, these problems can occur at the exploration stages (with the most notable impact affecting relatively isolated Aboriginal communities), during ongoing extractive activities of the mine operation, and, finally, after mine closure when northern mining communities are sometimes left with considerable envi-ronmental impacts and/or few alternative strategies for community development. Two striking examples of this include the abandoned Giant Mine in the Northwest Territories and the Adams Mine at Kirkland Lake, Ontario.

Many mines in Canada have been orphaned, most of them in rural and remote areas, leaving massive environmental liabilities associated with acid rock drainage. The Giant Mine situated near Yellowknife is a case in point. At the mine, 250,000 tonnes of highly toxic arsenic trioxide are stored underground in vaults as a by-product of the mine's many years of processing gold. If the aging and corroding vaults were to break, this arsenic would leach into the surround-ing environment, severely polluting the Mackenzie River watershed and threat-ening the health and integrity of local settlements and communities. It should be recognized that modern mines have extensive closure and reclamation plans that did not exist when many of the abandoned mines were first opened. Nevertheless, many first-hand observers of the Giant Mine are not persuaded that an acceptable policy process is in place to ensure this type of disaster does not happen in the future.[20]

Also of concern with respect to mine closure is the future sustainability of the affected communities. The proposal to use the former Adams Mine in northern Ontario as a waste facility is a useful case through which to examine the kind of environmental risks rural communities often assume on behalf of urban centres if they wish to have economic development. The Adams Mine offers a classic case of centre-periphery dependency viewed through the lens of political ecology. The town of Kirkland Lake always has been economically dependent on global markets. Throughout its history the area has relied on mining and forestry. After the peak of its initial gold boom in 1938, Kirkland Lake experienced its first series of mine closures in 1954. Additional mine closures occurred throughout the 1960s and 1970s. In 1962, a steel corporation from Pittsburgh opened the Adams iron-ore mine, 15 kilometres southeast of Kirkland Lake. The mine, which was later owned by Dofasco, a Canadian company, provided considerable direct and spinoff employment in the area. It closed in 1989, as mining throughout the country experienced a serious downswing in the early 1990s, particularly with the end of the exploration boom. It was in this environment that town leaders looked to other sources of revenue. A controversial proposal emerged suggesting that the closed Adams Mine could be used as a solid waste disposal facility for Metro Toronto. At that time, the mayor of Kirkland Lake, Joe Mavrinac, and others saw this as part of a long-term proposal (which included an industrial park) that would bring half a billion dollars into the community.[21]

The proposed project regained momentum later in the 1990s, as the City of Toronto began to run out of landfill room. The consortium proponents of the project, Rail Cycle North (RCN), noted that the waste would be shipped in closed containers and claimed that the project could be safely managed using the latest technology. They also pointed out that preparation of the pit itself would entail two years of work, cost $50 million, and create many needed jobs for an area with widespread unemployment, including those associated with the railway. The Adams Mine would serve as a landfill site for Toronto's residential waste while the commercial industrial waste would be shipped to Michigan.[22]

Although there was lengthy debate, the majority of the councillors and munic-ipal officials at the nearby communities of Kirkland Lake and Englehart supported the project. Many citizens in the region, however, were vehemently against the proposal. They were concerned about the impact on aquifers if contaminated groundwater leached through fractured rock in the old mine. In 1998, the Environmental Assessment Board approved the proposed project after it deemed that the proponent had addressed its requirements. An environmental group, the Adams Mine Intervention Coalition, appealed the Board's decision to the Ontario Court of Appeal. The appeal was unsuccessful.

The Walkerton groundwater issue heightened local skepticism about govern-ments' collective abilities to prevent serious environmental disasters. Moreover, a number of communities in the region expressed fears about the negative impact the landfill could have on potential tourism, other forms of development, and the region's ability to attract and retain professionals.[23] Up to 1.3 million tonnes of waste per annum would be shipped north on a train. This part of the plan led to concerns associated with the prospect of stench emanating from the trains or even the risk of contamination from possible derailment as the trains passed through communities or stopped at busy crossings.[24]

Two thousand people gathered in Kirkland Lake in protest against the Adams Mine landfill at a rally on 30 July 2000. At that event, MPP David Ramsay claimed, 'This is not just a war over garbage. This is a fight for democracy.' Many local citi-zens in the region joined a number of protest coalitions and asked for a referendum (which was turned down by council). To derail the project, protestors prepared to target Toronto's bid for the 2008 Olympic Summer Games by painting the city as a major polluter: 'How does a small district in Northern Ontario take on one of the world's largest cities?' asked Mr Ramsay. 'You attack its reputation. Becoming Toronto's dump will destroy our reputation. If we must we will destroy theirs.'[25]

The issue went beyond the boundaries of Kirkland Lake to the district of Timiskaming-Cochrane and the Quebec side of Lake Timiskaming. The issues also linked together communities of interests, including elected officials in Ontario and Quebec, Richard Denton, the mayor of Kirkland Lake (who was opposed to the plan), environmental groups, and the Timiskaming First Nation. In addition, one Toronto councillor in particular, Jack Layton, actively lent his support to the protestors and was backed up by some other councillors and citizens of Toronto who were sympathetic to the cause. Networks of protestors included the Adams Mine Intervention Coalition, the Temiskaming Federation of Agriculture, and the Temiskaming Environmental Action Committee. First Nations bands with land claims covering the area of the Adams Mine asked the federal government to conduct an environmental assessment. The federal government does not have jurisdiction in the region but it does have responsibility for First Nations concerns. The federal agency announced that it would make a decision about whether to initiate the assessment during the fall of 2000.

Despite much opposition to the plan, Toronto City Council approved it with a vote of 36–20.[26] Another final vote was scheduled to take place a few months later, in the autumn. One *Globe and Mail* editorial argued that the decision is a 'recognition that those who live in rural areas or small towns benefit from the commercial and industrial engine of Toronto, which is both a market and a major provincial taxpayer, and that urban dwellers do not suddenly acquire horns because they try to benefit from an asset of under populated regions—open space not in use or in demand.'[27] What this argument failed to acknowledge is that Toronto's economic power as an 'industrial engine' allows this metropolitan area to influence the long-term futures of these northern communities without absorbing any of the possible environmental costs (socio-economic or biophysical) of its actions. As Val Plumwood has noted in another context:

> There is clearly a serious problem for the ecological rationality of any system that allows those who have most access to political voice and decision-making to be also those most relatively remote from the ecological degradation it fosters, and those who tend to be least remote from ecological degradation and who bear the worst ecological consequences to have the least access to voice and decision power.[28]

Rural communities, however, cannot be readily dismissed, particularly when they are able to organize a broad coalition of support. This proved to be the situation during the final vote on the Adams Mine proposal in October in Toronto when 'one of the most divisive municipal debates in recent memory took place.'[29] The protracted debate extended over a period of four days and was accompanied by procedural delaying tactics by some councillors as well as angry protests from citizens. On 11 October 2000, Toronto City Council voted by a margin of 32–24 to send the trash to the Adams Mine. The Council passed 50 amendments to the proposal. One of the most important amendments was that the RCN consortium, not the City of Toronto, would be financially responsible for any unforeseen legal changes during the 20 years of the contract, including regulatory changes that might raise the costs of operations. The city did not want to absorb potential costs for unlimited unforeseen liability. As a result of these changes, the deal fell through and Toronto decided to send the waste in trucks to Michigan (raising a new set of issues with potentially affected communities).[30] When reviewing this issue, some may declare the failed deal a victory for the coalition of groups and citizens that opposed the Adams Mine proposal. Others may argue that the final result was simply a matter of economics and that the business plan had never made sense when there were other lower-priced alternatives.[31]

This case reveals an interesting set of dynamics at work. Kirkland Lake, as with so many other resource-based communities, depends on external financing as well as global demand and markets for its viability. After a number of mine closures and with the overall depressed state of the northern economy during the past 20 years, community leaders have been looking for alternatives. Lacking an ability to attract a diversity of economic opportunities because of their remote location, northerners found themselves torn between wanting the economic opportunities associated with receiving Toronto's waste, and not wanting the associated potential environmental risk. The decision of the elected city councils was not viewed by many of their constituents as legitimate. Northern citizens, operating outside of their elected councils, have proven themselves capable of mobilizing to effect change if they are able to draw on a broad and diverse support base. The impact of their efforts stimulated a lengthy debate in Toronto City Council that in turn led to a careful examination of the proposed deal and the subsequent amendments. All of this raises interesting political questions about the role of elected councillors in a representative democracy and the demands of citizens to participate actively in decisions that vitally affect them. Who gets to decide and how? After the decision, northern municipal leaders were once again charged with the task of exploring new avenues to invigorate the region's economy.

A Sustainable Mining Community

How well a community survives and sustains itself will depend on a number of factors: its relative influence on political agendas (which is often determined by size and location), the diversity of its economic base, government policy decisions at all levels, and the health, energy, adaptability, and active engagement of its citizenry. Also, centre-periphery relations will vary from community to community. It is important not to underestimate the diversity of rural and remote towns and their own ability to effect change. This is particularly the case with the larger, more diversified northern cities with good airport facilities, which can now serve as commuting centres for many resource-based fly-in operations.[32] The bigger towns, such as Sudbury, Ontario, and Prince George, British Columbia, act as economic hubs for the northern region. These northern urban cities are located at the centre of communications and transportation links by air and road, and serve as supply centres for a variety of resource-based activities. In these locations, municipalities are often able to establish many high-tech businesses based on natural resources.

Sudbury, a mining town long dominated by Inco and Falconbridge, has been diversifying into initiatives based on advanced technologies. For example, the Northern Centre for Advanced Technology was established 'to help resource industries in Northern Ontario design, produce and manufacture tools and instruments they can market around the world.'[33] The Sudbury Regional Development Corporation and Laurentian University have also collaborated on developing a centre for resource-based research and consulting services. By the end of the twentieth century, Sudbury was becoming known globally as a source of innovation in mining equipment, robotics, and technology. As one observer of Sudbury noted in 1994:

> Sudbury no longer exists in any single time or place. It has one foot in the past and one in the present, one foot in the Canadian Shield and one in Toronto, one foot in the hinterland and one in the heartland. . . . Traditional local economies might falter, local psyches might be infiltrated and homogenized by larger ones, but the natural and built landscapes will always serve as a constant grounded reminder of where you are and why you are there, and thus provide the strength to move forward with confidence.[34]

Sudbury also has experienced significant improvement in terms of its biophysical environment. In the last 30 years of the twentieth century, Sudbury moved from having a reputation as a 'moonscape', caused by sulphur-dioxide emissions, to a globally recognized 'green' role model for other mining communities. Extensive land, air, and watershed initiatives were stimulated by the work of local groups such as the Sudbury Environmental Enhancement Program and the Vegetative Enhancement Technical Advisory Committee, as well as by the mining companies, provincial ministries, the university, and other associations and groups.[35]

It is difficult, therefore, to make blanket predictions about the impacts of the retrenchment of the welfare state and changes in the economy and technology on northern communities relative to their southern counterparts. Much will depend on the size, location, health, diversity, and spirit of a community. Nevertheless, mining and other resource-based communities are increasingly subject to the vagaries of the global marketplace as they lose the buffers provided by a postwar nation-building strategy that actively promoted resource development. As noted in the cases above, resource-based communities are now paying the largest costs associated with the cumulative socio-economic and biophysical impacts of primary industrial activities. As discussed below, the actions of multilateral institutions, multinational corporations, domestic public- and private-sector organizations, and grassroots players all respond and contribute to a complex set of dynamics that ultimately determine the sustainability of mining and other rural communities.

Actors in Environmental Decision-Making: Global to Local

The activities of global institutions very much shape the overall economic and environmental context for resource-dependent communities. The World Bank and other international financial institutions, structured as they are on liberal principles of free trade, have contributed to a global trading regime that hastens the pace of unsustainable resource extraction and development. The desire to acquire much-needed revenues sees local communities competing to attract global industries engaged in large-scale extractive activities. These development enterprises do not come without environmental cost.

Various international actors and organizations have recognized the problems associated with these developments. As a result, mining corporations are being pressured to address issues of community sustainability, which have become a matter of international and public discussion at a number of conferences and meetings throughout the world. While experiences vary, the general tone of the discussions has included an increasing recognition by corporations and governments that communities are legitimate players in determining the evolving future of mining activities. Further, a general recognition is emerging that affected local communities should expect compensation from negative impacts and a share of the benefits from mineral development. Global awareness of community concerns led to the establishment of the International Council on Metals and the Environment (ICME) in 1991 to promote good environmental and health policies in the metals industry. It has official standing and interacts actively with United Nations agencies such as the UN Environment Program (UNEP) and participates in the work of the Organization for Economic Co-operation and Development (OECD).[36] Members include major mining companies from around the world. One of the first initiatives of the ICME was to adopt its Environmental Charter. Under the Charter, companies pledge to meet applicable environmental laws and regulations and to advance environmental protection while minimizing risk where regulations are inadequate. Their Community Responsibility Principles include respect for local cultures, meaningful consultation with communities as stakeholders, mitigating the adverse effects of mining activities in these communities while promoting social, economic, and institutional development, and respecting the laws and goals of the governments where the development is taking place.[37]

On an individual basis, mineral companies have not traditionally addressed social or economic concerns of a community. In the past 20 years, efforts by multinational (publicly visible) companies to address biophysical impacts have significantly improved, although many challenges, associated with such problems as tailings spills and contamination of local water supplies, remain. Problems that can be addressed by technological solutions (rather than those associated with social or cultural concerns) are something with which the engineering and scientifically trained mining profession can most readily identify. Nevertheless, large multinational companies are now being pressured to address the social health of communities and have been taking initiative in this area. As yet, however, these companies have not developed well-integrated strategies for dealing with these concerns.

Domestic governments play a vital role in shaping the future of mining communities. In Canada, where over 150 communities depend in part or completely on mining, goals similar to those of the ICME have been articulated in government documents and public consultation exercises.[38] In the late 1990s, the federal department of Natural Resources Canada engaged in a multi-stakeholder consultation process of developing indicators for sustainable development to help managers and policymakers assess the environmental sustainability of mineral operations and the factors affecting those operations. Community sustainability was one of the valued goals of the exercise. In recent years, government appears to have taken a role as a provider of information to and about rural Canada; as well, it is becoming an advocate and facilitator of local initiatives.[39] In Canada, this approach is readily identified through government documents and vision statements as well as in the use of public round tables and public consultation. A number of initiatives were targeted towards the promotion of local sustainable communities. Natural Resources Canada, for example, has been actively engaged in developing such projects as the Green Municipal Enabling Fund and the Green Municipal Investment Fund (which promote 'eco-efficiency' in communities), the Sustainable Communities Initiative (aimed at facilitating high-speed community interconnections through communications technologies), and Community Capacity-Building (directed towards rural, remote, and Aboriginal communities for decision-making).[40]

While such programs appear to be useful ventures, how effective will they be in meeting the needs of rural communities, particularly in the quest to help them to chart their own course for the future? The past century saw the erosion of civic and social networks based on local territories with the development of the welfare state and its associated centralizing political and economic forces. In addition, private-sector economic actors increasingly became distanced, physically and socially, from the local communities affected by their decisions (e.g., executives of resource companies moved to urban centres rather than staying in the company town). Recently, government initiatives to amalgamate local governments and other public services, along with new developments in transportation and communications, have all served to undermine traditional community boundaries. Moreover, citizens living in the rural or more remote areas of Canada will often assert that provincial decisions are taken with insufficient attention devoted to the needs of their communities.

As the Adams Mine case indicates, residents of remote and rural regions are not prepared to accept decisions that deeply affect their own communities without adequate public consultation. In particular, resistance takes place when the results are heavily influenced by politicians and officials in capital cities whose immediate concerns and perspectives are most often shaped by issues peculiar to their own large metropolitan areas. The past few decades have seen a number of citizens in northern communities setting up political action groups, participating on consensus-based round tables, and working out co-management arrangements. While these initiatives do not point to a sea change in governing relationships, they do suggest a shift in some of the dynamics affecting centre-periphery relationships. Val Plumwood has written that:

> the political and communicative empowerment of those least remote from ecological harms must form an important part of strategies for eco-logical rationality. There are many specific contextual forms this empow-erment might take, such as access for community action groups to resources like public funding, but its general conditions surely require institutions which encourage speech and action from below and deep forms of democracy where communicative and redistributive equality flourish across a range of social spheres.[41]

A number of factors contribute to some signs of emerging political action in rural and remote communities. These include the growth of citizen and group activism and a general public skepticism about the effectiveness of the state in its ability to maintain a healthy and stable economy, society, or environment. Increased activism of rural, northern, or remote communities, however, does not necessarily mean sustainable decision-making. A number of groups are more con-cerned with attracting investment than with maintaining environmental sustain-ability. One group of prospectors and developers in northern Ontario initiated a very successful campaign in the early 1990s called Save Our North to draw atten-tion to the economic concerns of northerners who saw a dramatic decrease in mineral exploration in the region. Such initiatives may bring some much-needed attention to the issues facing northern mining communities, but to what extent should local governments and other local actors determine environmental policy? Some would argue that these local communities are not well positioned to give sufficient weight to long-term sustainability when they are concerned about more immediate needs for development, employment, and revenues, particularly in depressed regions with few opportunities for diversification.

One line of thought, 'subsidiarity', suggests that decision-making should be pushed down to the level of government that can most effectively deal with the issue. But this does not mean absolute decentralization. As John Bryden notes in his discussion of sustainable rural communities, 'The issue here is not so much that central policies need to be abandoned, but rather that in the formulation and implementation of policy, all levels have a legitimate, and different, role to play.'[42] The environmental health of rural and remote communities requires a nested approach: one that recognizes the interdependent relationships between the biophysical and socio-economic forces, the relationship between political power and ecological impacts, and the different scales at which environmental decisions take place.

Federal and provincial governments and other actors have a role to play in ensuring that long-term sustainability is not traded off for short-term economic opportunities and that other, more sustainable options be identified. Traditional public policy approaches with a liberal democratic framework, however, will not suffice because they do not address inherent issues related to the sustainability of desired biophysical and socio-economic systems. John Dryzek proposes an alternative approach, what he refers to as ecological democracy:

> Ecological democracy blurs the boundary between human social systems and natural systems. . . . Ecological problems and issues transcend established governmental jurisdictions, such that democratic exercises may need to be constituted in order to fit the size and scope of particular issues. When established authority in governmental jurisdictions is recalcitrant then such fora may need to be constituted as oppositional democratic spheres. [43]

These oppositional spheres are diverse and may come in the forms of non-governmental organizations operating at the international, regional, or local levels, or in networks organized around watershed and bioregional needs and requirements. As Dryzek suggests, however, 'the kinds of values that can survive authentic democratic debate are those oriented to the interests of the community as a whole, rather than selfish interests within the community (or outside it).'[44] These interests include sensitivity to local ecological contexts. It is debatable whether or not it is necessary to come up with a new term or type of democracy to achieve Dryzek's goal. Perhaps what is required is a redefinition or a reconceptualization of the public interest, one that recognizes the importance of long-term sustainability, as has been defined here, coupled with a policy environment that can respond to the complex requirements of an ecosystem approach to decision-making.

Traditional national policy responses need to be replaced with approaches that can identify and deal proactively with the forces that cause environmental degradation, recognizing the important role that local actors and communities must play to achieve long-term biophysical and socio-economic sustainability. Similar to the canaries in the mine, rural and remote communities are the first to suffer the effects of environmental degradation while being least able to do anything about the situation. A proactive approach would also recognize the complex interplay of forces and actors at different scales. John Bryden suggests that, given these conditions, 'Local knowledge and learning are therefore crucial, as is flexibility of systems of support to meet diverse conditions.'[45] Furthermore, he asserts that communities can be supported with knowledge from other places and issues that affect their own circumstances. They will need to be able to build networks and alliances with other local actors as well as with regional, national, and international players. The state itself will need to be able to provide flexible responses to address the needs of the communities.

Conclusion

Conventional approaches to environmental policy-making will not be sufficient if the goal is long-term sustainability. Environmental policy-making and analysis generally tend to focus on specific problems, particular political institutions, environmental issues, or various sets of actors. This is often done without situating the issue within the broader context of the complex biophysical and socio-economic factors that interact in a variety of ways and on different scales from the global to the local. Moreover, policy-making traditionally has been about finding the politically acceptable solution, rather than one that includes a sustainability ethic. External forces particularly affect rural and remote regions where primary industrial activities such as mining are located. More sophisticated approaches to environmental policy are needed to address effectively the challenges facing rural Canada.

Political ecology offers a useful framework for considering these challenges. This approach emphasizes the need to develop strategies that recognize the complex sources of environmental problems, factors that are not readily dealt with by limited policy responses. Political ecology also acknowledges that the poorer and weaker actors tend to bear a disproportionate cost of environmental problems, the ramifications of which go beyond the affected communities. This has certainly held true in Canada's rural and remote regions, particularly in the North. The decline of the welfare state has served to intensify the problems facing these regions in terms of social, health, biophysical, and economic issues. The water contamination issue in the rural community of Walkerton, Ontario, illustrates the need for environmental policy to be based on integrated strategies that include a variety of decision-makers from all levels of government and related communities of interest. Such an approach benefits everyone, not just those regions most hurt by the lack of integrated strategies.

Mining communities offer an excellent case for a political ecology analysis. To achieve long-term sustainability, all mining communities rely on the favourable disposition of various factors and actors. Favourable factors may include a good geographic location, a rich resource base, supportive historical patterns of development, strong community networks, diverse economies, and competitive advantage. Actors include international organizations that can pressure international corporations to adopt a community sustainability ethic, governments capable of devising effective strategies oriented towards long-term viability of communities, and, finally, strong local grassroots networks working towards economic, social, and ecological diversity while positioning their communities for the inevitable day that the mines close. Effective policy can be devised only through a comprehensive understanding of the interconnected role these factors play in the sustainability of communities.

The Adams Mine at Kirkland Lake, Ontario, serves to illustrate the relative level of control many northern citizens have over the external forces affecting their environment. The economic challenges and problems northerners face are significant. Moreover, if they do choose economic development, they are often asked to bear a disproportionate amount of the environmental costs. Local actors, however, do have political resources at their disposal. Local activist groups, whether they are advocating for mining or the environment, are increasingly making their voices heard through the media. Networks of grassroots organizations can have a significant impact on the agenda of the state. Moreover, northern communities are diversifying with the introduction of new information technologies. While some communities are in a state of inevitable decline, others, such as Sudbury, are taking advantage of their mining history and technological expertise to develop value-added economic enterprises. At the same time, different actors have mobilized to improve the regional environment both biophysically and socially. At the global and national levels, corporations and associations are becoming increasingly aware that to do business and to develop a mine without considering the host community can result in poor economic performance and a higher level of risk for the company. Especially with the benefit of the Internet, ENGOs and other actors play an important oppositional role in the international arena.

Canada has a history of political stability, a wealthy resource-based economy, government programs to redistribute some of that wealth, and a measure of tolerance for public expression. As such, rural regions in Canada have an advantage over their counterparts in other parts of the world, even though they are disadvantaged internally vis-à-vis the more populated areas of the country. Rural communities located in countries with politically unstable regimes, limited (to non-existent) social safety nets, huge disparities between rich and poor, and high levels of illiteracy have far fewer means to shape their own environment. It has been noted, however, that 'some of the historical advantages of being born in a rich country such as Canada, even if one lives in a very remote place, are smaller than they were 20 or 30 years ago, and likely to become even smaller in the future.'[46] It is time, therefore, for policy-makers and analysts to devise a nested approach to decision-making, locally to globally, that is receptive to community needs as well as adaptable to changing conditions in natural and social systems. This is a daunting task given existing ideological, political, and economic barriers to the achievement of such a goal. Nevertheless, a policy framework of this kind is needed to effectively recognize and respond to the complex forces and interrelationships that support desired ecosystems and sustainable communities.

Notes

The author would like to thank both George Francis for providing his insights into sustainability and communities and Debora VanNijnatten for her perceptive comments. Any errors or misinterpretations are the author's own.

1 The term 'rural' is used broadly in this chapter to refer to non-urban regions, including remote and northern areas of Canada.

2 Canada, House of Commons, *Think Rural: Report of the Standing Committee on Natural Resources*, Andy Mitchell, Chairman, March 1997, 2.

3 Lynton Keith Caldwell, *Environment: A Challenge to Modern Society* (Garden City, NY: Natural History Press, 1970), 21.

4 Raymond L. Bryant and Sinéad Bailey, *Third World Political Ecology* (London: Routledge, 1997), 28.

5 Institute for Research on Environment and Economy, *Ecosystem Management: Meeting the Challenges of Community Initiatives, Proceedings of a Workshop* (Cornwall, Ont.: University of Ottawa, 10 May 1995), 13.

6 Francis, personal communication.

7 Bryant and Bailey, *Third World Political Ecology*, 34.

8 Ibid., 184.

9 Francis, personal communication.

10 Jim Ellsworth, 'Ecosystem Management: New Forms of Governance: Serving and Assisting Citizen-based, Sustainable Ecosystem Initiatives', in Institution for Research on Environment and Economy, *Ecosystem Management*, 55.

11 Bryant and Bailey, *Third World Political Ecology*, 28.

12 Ibid., 39.

13 Mark Shucksmith, 'Conceptualizing Post-industrial Rurality', in John Bryden, ed., *Towards Sustainable Rural Communities* (University School of Rural Planning and Development, University of Guelph, 1994), 125–31.

14 Philip Ehrensaft, 'Restructuring Rural Institutions', ibid., 154.

15 Jane Jacobs, *Cities and the Wealth of Nations: Principles of Economic Life* (New York: Vintage, 1985), 224.

16 'Unemployment rates paint a bleak picture', *Northern Ontario Business* (Mar. 1997).

17 Allison Bray, 'Welfare Slashes Deep', *Winnipeg Free Press*, 18 Dec. 1995, A1.

18 Environmental Commissioner of Ontario, 'News Release: Urgent Need to Protect Groundwater, Environmental Commission Says', Toronto, 27 July 2000.

19 William O. Karvinen and Mary Louise McAllister, *Rising to the Surface: Emerging Groundwater Policy Trends in Canada* (Kingston: Centre for Resource Studies, Queen's University, 1994), 124–5.

20 Joint news release of Mine Watch Canada and Yukon Conservation Society, 'Taxpayers to Pay for Massive Cleanup at Northern Mines', 2 Sept. 1999.

21 Joe Mavrinac, 'Kirkland Lake', in Matt Bray and Ashley Thomson, eds, *At the End of the Shift: Mines and Single-Industry Towns in Northern Ontario* (Toronto: Dundurn Press, 1992), 149–54.

22 'Toronto Joint Committee Believes That Adams Mine Project Will Work: Recommends It', *Temiskaming Speaker*, 26 July 2000.

23 'TMA Hears Concerns Importing Waste Will Damage Other Opportunities in the District', *Temiskaming Speaker*, 12 Apr. 2000.

24 'Taking aim at the Trash Train', *Globe and Mail*, 14 Aug. 2000, A2.

25 'Heat turned up in fight against Adams Mine landfill project', *Temiskaming Speaker*, 2 Aug. 2000.

26 'Toronto to Send its Garbage North', *Globe and Mail*, 3 Aug. 2000, A1.

27 'The Politics of Trash', *Globe and Mail*, 14 Aug. 2000, A14.

28 Val Plumwood, 'Inequality, Ecojustice, and Ecological Rationality', in John S. Dryzek and David Schlosberg, eds, *Debating the Earth: The Environmental Politics Reader* (New York: Oxford University Press, 1998), 573.

29 'Toronto's garbage is going north', *The Record*, 12 Oct. 2000, A3.

30 'City kills Adams Mine deal', *Globe and Mail*, 21 Oct. 2000, A1.

31 John Barber, 'Recycled numbers still add up to a rubbish deal', *Globe and Mail*, 21 Oct. 2000, A30.

32 Whitehorse Mining Initiative, *Searching for Gold: The Whitehorse Mining Initiative, A Multi-stakeholder Approach to Renew Canada's Minerals and Metals Sector* (Whitehorse, Yukon, 14 Oct. 1994), 150.

33 Michael Whitehouse, 'NORCAT exploring new opportunities for the resource sector', *Northern Ontario Business* (Feb. 1997).

34 Michael Whitehouse, 'Sudbury's sense of place will always be grounded in the Canadian Shield', *Globe and Mail*, 9 Feb. 1994, A20.

35 David Lees, 'Green Rebirth', *Canadian Geographic* (May-June 2000): 61–70.

36 International Council on Mining and Environment, Introduction, 1999: http://206.191.21.210/icme

37 International Council on Metals and the Environment, *Environmental Charter*, 29 Jan. 1999: http://206.191.21.210/icme/Envchar.htm

38 Whitehorse Mining Initiative, *Vision Statement* (Whitehorse, Yukon, Oct. 1994).

39 Ibid., 163.

40 Natural Resources Canada, 'The Path Forward to Sustainable Development Strategy 2000: A Discussion Paper', July 2000, 37–41.

41 Plumwood, 'Inequality, Ecojustice, and Ecological Rationality', 573.

42 John Bryden, 'Towards Sustainable Rural Communities: From Theory to Action', in Bryden, ed., *Towards Sustainable Rural Communities*, 225.

43 John S. Dryzek, *The Politics of the Earth* (New York: Oxford University Press, 1997), 201.

44 Ibid., 200.

45 Bryden, 'Towards Sustainable Rural Communities', 226.

46 Richard Long, 'The Role of the State in a Rural Development "Partnership"', in Bryden, ed., *Towards Sustainable Rural Communities*, 163.

Chapter 13

Canadian Smog Policy in a Continental Context: Looking South for Stringency

Debora L. VanNijnatten and W. Henry Lambright

Gone are the days when Canadians tuned into their morning television or radio broadcasts merely to catch the daily weather report and decide whether an umbrella might need to be packed along with lunch. Instead, the late 1980s brought us daily ultraviolet radiation reports to remind us of the depletion of the ozone layer and the attendant heightened risks of skin cancer. We now also watch for 'smog alert' days when children, the elderly, and those with respiratory ailments are encouraged to remain indoors and healthy adults are told to refrain from exercising outdoors. For those of us who live in the populous northeastern portions of the continent or in heavily populated areas along the west coast, smog has become a part of our daily lives during the summer months. We can see it lie heavily across the horizon and we are increasingly aware of its effects on our health.

Not surprisingly, smog also has become a salient political issue in Canada. The most significant obstacle to taking effective action in this area, however, is that air pollution is a regional problem that transcends conventional political boundaries and requires co-operation among many levels of government. Both within Canada and in North America more broadly, various transboundary institutions and processes designed to encourage collaboration between jurisdictions in the management and reduction of air pollution have been established. These mechanisms have enabled policy-makers to make considerable progress in terms of furthering our understanding of air pollutant interactions and mapping the pathways that pollutants tend to travel across the continent. This knowledge also has enabled policy-makers to turn their attention to the next step necessary for achieving reductions in air pollutants: harmonizing air quality standards across different jurisdictions so that significant emission reductions will result. Policy harmonization is a considerably more difficult task, however.

In Canada, independent action on the part of the provinces, and thus the persistence of varying policy regimes at the subnational level, remains a stumbling block to co-ordinated national action on air pollution. Attempts at collaborative intergovernmental (federal-provincial) policy-making through the Canadian Council of Ministers of the Environment, whose agreements are non-binding on provinces, have not secured policy actions that would result in serious emission reductions. However, continental pressures emanating from both the national and subnational levels in the US, on a backdrop of critical comment from the trilateral NAFTA Commission on Environmental Co-operation, have had more success in spurring action, especially on the part of Canada's largest smog-producer, Ontario. Contrary to the concerns of those who believe that 'downward harmonization' of Canadian policy and standards will result from increased continentalization, continental pressures and processes have provided the impetus for increased stringency in Canadian air quality policy.

Smog: What Is It?

'Smog' is a term used to describe a smoky, foggy mixture of air pollutants that can be seen as a brownish haze on the horizon. Although the science of and interactions among air pollutants are extremely complex, the primary ingredients of smog are ground-level ozone and fine airborne particles. Ground-level, or tropospheric, ozone (not to be confused with the stratospheric ozone layer, some 15–50 kilometres above the earth's surface, that protects us from cancer-causing ultraviolet radiation) is a colourless and highly irritating gas that forms just above the earth's surface. It is a secondary pollutant produced when two air pollutants, nitrogen oxides (NO_x) and volatile organic compounds (VOCs), react with each other in the presence of strong sunlight.[1]

Both NO_x and VOCs result from a variety of sources. NO_x result primarily from the burning of fossil fuels (coal, oil, and gas) in electricity generation, industry, and automobiles. Coal-burning produces the highest levels of NO_x. VOCs include a diverse class of compounds, also the results of fuel combustion and of the evaporation of liquid fuels and solvents. Refineries, chemical manufacturers, and drycleaning and painting operations are sources of VOCs. High ozone levels are caused by the presence of NO_x and VOCs, hot temperatures, direct sunlight, and the stagnation of air over several days. Smog incidences thus depend on weather conditions and the most frequent episodes in Canada occur in the period from May to September.

Ground-level ozone is harmful to human health. In fact, the 1996 federal NO_x/VOC Science Assessment concluded that there is no safe level of human exposure to ground-level ozone.[2] The health effects of ozone primarily involve respiratory ailments and inhibition or interference of the immune system's ability to defend the body. That ozone could lead to irreversible changes in the lungs of children, whose immune systems and lungs are still developing, is of particular concern here.[3] Ozone also damages vegetation and has been linked to declines in crop and forest productivity.[4]

Airborne particles, or particulate matter, consist of minute solids or liquids in air that vary in size and chemical composition. Particulate matter (PM) gives smog its colour and affects visibility. Studies and government policy have focused on two groups of particulates: PM10 (less than 10 microns across, about 1/8 the width of human hair) and PM2.5 (less than 2.5 microns across, also known as fine particles).[5] Particles can be both primary (emitted directly to the air) and secondary (formed through chemical reactions involving other air pollutants such as sulphur dioxide, SO_2). The main sources of particulates include thermal power plants, vehicle emissions, incineration, and industrial activities such as mining and quarrying. Other contaminants such as heavy metals and persistent organic pollutants may be absorbed into particulates, thereby increasing their toxicity. Particles, especially fine particles, also pose a serious health risk, as they can become deeply lodged in the lungs and the respiratory system has no means of expelling them.[6] There does not appear to be any seasonal pattern to particulate concentrations.

Smog is generally perceived as a primarily urban and central Canadian/west coast issue, although smog can affect areas as far as 800 kilometres away from pollution sources. The smoggiest region in the country is along the Windsor-Quebec City corridor, where national air quality objectives are exceeded on as many as 25 per cent of summer days.[7] This corridor, containing almost half the Canadian population, also receives up to half of its airborne pollution from the US, especially the Detroit, Ohio Valley, and Cleveland areas. Perhaps not surprisingly, then, Windsor, Ontario, directly across the river from Detroit, is Canada's smoggiest city, while Long Point, Ontario, a rural area on the north shore of Lake Erie, experiences the highest and most frequent ozone episodes in Canada.[8] The Lower Fraser Valley in British Columbia also experiences ground-level ozone concentrations that exceed national guidelines, although less frequently. In this area, smog precursors are generated mainly from local automobile emissions trapped by the surrounding mountains. The southern Atlantic region, especially the Saint John, New Brunswick, area, receives most of its smog from the northeastern US states, although smog incidences here are less intense and less frequent.

The Rise of Smog as a Political Issue in Canada

The appearance of smog on the political agenda in Canada can be associated with a number of developments over the last decade or so. First, the high number of instances of ozone levels exceeding tolerable limits in the mid- to late 1980s alerted the public to the extent of the smog problem. Over the period 1983–8, ground-level ozone often exceeded the national guideline, or 'Objective', of 82 parts per billion (ppb) on an hourly average. A historically bad smog season arising out of the hot, stagnant weather conditions during the summer of 1988, when the ozone Objective was exceeded on close to 50 days, brought the issue to a head and attracted media headlines.[9] Environment Canada's own research showed that, although levels of air pollutants such as carbon monoxide, sulphur dioxide, and airborne particles declined over the period 1979–93, ground-level ozone increased.[10] Then, in 1992, Toronto's air quality was rated as being worse than that of Chicago, Boston, or Atlanta.[11] Moreover, the ozone problem has continued; for example, in 1996 the Toronto area experienced 40 smog alert days during the spring and summer months.[12] In 1998 the first smog-alert of the season was issued on 15 May, the earliest since 1988.

Second, a series of Health Canada and Environment Canada studies making causal linkages between ground-level ozone and health effects appeared in the 1990s.[13] In the mid-1990s, Environment Canada had carried out an extensive multi-stakeholder review of the current state of knowledge on ground-level ozone in conjunction with its NO_x/VOC Scientific Assessment. The Assessment drew together all aspects of scientific knowledge, including human health analyses, in support of resolving the ground-level ozone problem. One of its major conclusions was that 'there is no discernible human health threshold for ground-level ozone',[14] which, at the very least, indicated that current standards were inadequate. The studies that generated the most controversy, however, were those attempting to put 'numbers' to the air quality problem. One Health Canada study suggested that 6 per cent of all respiratory admissions to hospitals in Canada were smog-related, that air pollution could be linked to 5,000 premature deaths each year in 11 major Canadian cities, and that all of this accounted for $1 billion in health-care costs every year. Moreover, a study conducted about the same time for the Canadian Council of Ministers of the Environment (CCME) estimated that, in the years 1997–2020, cleaner air resulting from lower-emission vehicles and fuels could provide health and ecological benefits of approximately a billion dollars a year.[15]

The oil industry has objected strongly to such reports, calling them 'advocacy rather than science'.[16] Politicians and public interest groups, on the other hand, have been quick to highlight the health concerns associated with air pollution. When unveiling BC's new and highly controversial automobile emissions standards in 1996, Environment Minister Moe Shihota noted that 'If you can't breathe, nothing else matters.'[17] The Ontario Medical Association and the OntAIRio Campaign, a non-partisan campaign created by the Sierra Club, the Toronto Environmental Alliance, and the David Suzuki Foundation, have called for an 85 per cent reduction in NO_x and a 75 per cent reduction in SO_2 because smog constitutes a 'health crisis'.[18] A poll conducted in January 2000 by the Angus Reid Group found that 54 per cent of Ontarians believe that air pollution is already negatively affecting their health and 79 per cent believe that it will eventually affect their health, while 59 per cent said that someone in their family was already suffering ill effects from poor air quality.[19] The link between air pollution and ill health appears to have been made in the minds of the public.

Third, debates in the late 1990s about the appropriate direction of national air pollution policies in the United States have galvanized environmental groups on both sides of the border, garnered considerable media attention, especially in central Canada, and engaged both federal and provincial governments. The main point of contention in the US air quality policy arena is that the country's 1990 Clean Air Act exempted many older, mainly coal-burning, power plants from meeting stringent air emission limits. At the time, policy-makers were assured by industry that these older plants would be shut down; this did not prove to be the case. According to the US Public Interest Research Group, the excess pollution generated by these older plants, which emit up to 10 times the amount of a new plant, accounted for 51 per cent of all SO_2 and 18 per cent of all NO_x emissions in

1997.[20] Moreover, these older plants are concentrated in the midwestern states of Ohio, Pennsylvania, and Indiana, where emissions are then carried on prevailing winds to the northeastern states as well as to Ontario and Quebec. The northeastern states have thus pushed for changes to national air quality legislation so that midwestern emissions must be reduced. Central and eastern Canadian provinces have an obvious interest in the outcomes associated with such efforts.

The Policy and Regulatory Framework in Canada

Air pollution, like most environmental issues in Canada, is subject to the vagaries of shared jurisdiction. No doubt there are many who would agree with Pollution Probe's assessment that 'Confused government jurisdiction over air quality is . . . a major problem, and has greatly inhibited efforts to address issues such as Canada's smog problem.'[21] Indeed, both provincial and federal governments hold key jurisdictional levers in the area of air quality. The federal government, through its jurisdiction over international and interprovincial affairs and taxation and spending powers, as well as its general power to make laws for the 'Peace, Order and Good Government' of Canada, can work to reduce smog that crosses provincial and national borders. In addition, it can regulate federal sources of air emissions directly, as well as fuel content and emission standards for new vehicles.[22] The federal government also can regulate to protect human health. The provinces, however, possess many important powers in terms of regulating air quality; they are responsible for most aspects of roads and highways, urban planning and transportation, fuel taxes, licensing and inspection of vehicles, and emissions from industrial facilities and other sources. Given this patchwork of jurisdiction and the transboundary nature of air pollution, effective co-operation between the two levels of government in this area is essential.

The provinces establish air quality standards for levels of smog-related pollutants within their boundaries. The federal government does set non-binding, science-based guidelines for ambient levels (in the surrounding atmosphere) of 'criteria' air pollutants (ozone, SO_2, NO_x, VOCs, CO), known as National Air Quality Objectives (NAQOs). However, provincial governments have the option of adopting these objectives as guidelines or as legally enforceable standards. As noted above, the national Objective for ground-level ozone is 82 ppb, although this standard is under revision. There are no national Objectives for PM10 and PM2.5 at present, although standards do exist in BC and Ontario. Air pollution is measured at approximately 140 national pollution surveillance sites across Canada operated by the national, provincial, and municipal governments. The provinces tend to fashion their policies in a manner consistent with the national Objectives, although they possess a plethora of additional regulations and programs, some of which are described in Chapter 8 of this volume and which differ from province to province.

Successive federal ministers have referred to the need for federal leadership in establishing national environmental standards relating to air pollutants. The key legislation at the federal level in terms of smog reduction is the recently revised Canadian Environmental Protection Act (CEPA). CEPA gives the federal Minister of the Environment a number of powers that can be exercised on behalf of the environment, including the ability to declare a substance toxic, as explained by Valiante in Chapter 1.[23] Ozone itself has not yet been declared toxic, although a select number of VOCs, precursors to smog, have been declared toxic. Particulate matter has been assessed as toxic under the CEPA process and the federal government has indicated that it will regulate both particles and their precursor air pollutants.[24] Overall, however, the federal government appears not to have employed the regulatory tools provided by CEPA to the extent that it might have in terms of regulating air quality improvements.[25]

The other major federal legislation addressing smog is the Motor Vehicle Safety Act (MVSA) under which emission standards for new vehicles are established. In 1996 the federal government legislated new mandatory emission controls under the authority of the MVSA that set more stringent limits on tailpipe emissions of CO, NO$_x$, hydrocarbons, and diesel particulates. Previously, the federal government had a Memorandum of Understanding with vehicle manufacturers under which the manufacturers volunteered to implement stricter US federal emission controls for cars sold in Canada.[26]

Domestic Dynamics: The Failure of Intergovernmentalism

Intergovernmentalism in Canada does not have a particularly good track record with regard to achieving high levels of environmental protection in Canada generally, nor has it proven effective in terms of air quality policy. Yet intergovernmentalism, whereby federal and provincial officials work together via institutions and processes established outside of formal legal channels (e.g., legislatures), increasingly has been employed in the field of environmental protection. Governments argue that co-operation through the CCME offers the promise of higher levels of environmental protection nationally. Critics counter that the CCME, despite its capable secretariat and the plethora of task groups and committees working on various issues, has no authority to enforce agreements negotiated by participating ministers.[27] Certainly, both environmental policy observers and the federal Commissioner of the Environment and Sustainable Development have expressed concerns that CCME agreements tend not to be stringent enough and rarely possess the mechanisms necessary for effective implementation and accountability.[28] These concerns also apply to CCME activities in the area of smog.

The CCME first undertook to address the problem of ground-level ozone, and bring about some co-ordination in provincial approaches, in the late 1980s. The result was the three-phase 1990 NO$_x$/VOC Management Plan, developed in consultation with industry and environmental interests and containing 59 separate initiatives to resolve the problem of ground-level ozone by 2005. During Phase 1 of the Plan (1990–4), a national prevention program was to be established, interim targets for NO_x and VOC reductions were to be negotiated, and studies on which to base final reduction targets were to be conducted. During Phase 2 (1994–7), caps on NO_x and VOCs would be established and additional remedial measures for ozone problems were to be identified. Final adjustments to the caps and remedial measures were to be made during Phase 3 (1997–2000).[29] Then, the implementation tasks were to be shared among the agreement partners.

In the early to mid-1990s, the CCME endorsed several guidelines under the 1990 Plan to reduce emissions of NO_x and VOCs from specific stationary sources. It also endorsed the recommendations of its own Task Group on Cleaner Vehicles and Fuels that governments develop more stringent national fuel and emission standards as well as vehicle inspection and maintenance programs. The CCME then went on to develop codes of practice that provinces could follow in setting up their own programs. Both the guidelines and the codes of practice were non-binding. Another working group also discussed options for national standards for sulphur content in fuel; in addition to being implicated in the formation of airborne particles, sulphur also interferes with the advanced, low-polluting emissions systems in new vehicles (see discussion below).[30] This group was unable to agree on a direction and put forward a number of policy options instead.

In 1993, the CCME and their counterparts in the Council of Energy Ministers, together comprising a Joint Ministers Meeting (JMM), signed the Comprehensive Air Quality Management Framework for Canada. This was a mechanism to further co-ordinate government actions on air quality issues of regional, national, and international scope. Under the agreement, a co-ordinating committee was established, the National Air Issues Co-ordinating Committee (NAICC), comprised of federal and provincial assistant deputy ministers from environment and energy departments. The NAICC has various task groups to address specific issues, such as hazardous air pollutants, acidifying emissions, and, of particular interest here, smog. A Stakeholders Advisory Group comprised of industry and non-governmental organization representatives provides input on air issues generally.

In the mid-1990s, as some of the activities identified under Phase 1 of the 1990 Plan were implemented, a task group of the NAICC worked on drafting a detailed plan of action for Phase 2 for consideration by the JMM. However, there was no consensus within the ministerial body on what further national actions should be taken and, after some delay, the federal government decided to proceed alone, delivering a Phase 2 Federal Smog Management Plan in 1997. This Phase 2 Plan publicized the results of the 1996 NO_x/VOC Scientific Assessment, outlined 'next steps' to be taken by federal departments and, in a departure from the 1990 CCME Plan, addressed particulate matter as well as ground-level ozone.[31]

Shortly after the Phase 2 Plan release, the Commissioner of the Environment and Sustainable Development undertook an evaluation of the 1990 NO_x/VOC Management Plan as the major national smog policy. The resulting report noted that, whereas the Plan provided 'sound strategic direction' for addressing

Canada's smog problem, federal and provincial governments never reached agreement on the details of a framework for implementing it.

> Environment Ministers originally agreed to negotiate federal-provincial partnership agreements within one year, outlining who would do what by when. When no such agreements were prepared, the Plan was destined to fail. An appropriate accountability regime was never put in place to clarify the roles, responsibilities and expected performance of each level of government.[32]

Although governments agreed on an ultimate goal (consistent attainment of 82 ppb ozone across the country) and a general approach for achieving this, they failed to set out interim reduction targets, prevention, remedial and study programs, means for monitoring, and consequences for non-performance. The Commissioner expressed particular concern about the informal, ad hoc nature of the monitoring network in Canada, which was vulnerable to diminishing commitments by the various federal, provincial, and municipal governments. As a result, argued the Commissioner's report, the federal government and, by extension, the provinces are not able to show the degree to which activities under the 1990 Plan have contributed to reductions in smog.[33] Finally, the report noted that the emissions reduction activities envisioned under the three-phase Plan were not enough to address the severity of the ground-level ozone problem in Canada in any case.

Some observers are hopeful that new Canada-wide standards for ozone and particulate matter, negotiated under the Canada-Wide Accord on Environmental Harmonization, will be more successful in bringing about emission reductions. Both ground-level ozone and particulate matter were identified as priorities for the development of such standards, and the standard-setting process for these pollutants has been ongoing since 1998. The major criticism of the standards developed under the Canada-Wide Accord is that they are not legally enforceable, just as other CCME agreements are not enforceable. The Accord itself is replete with phrases such as 'if a consensus is not achieved in any given area, governments are free to act with their existing authorities' and 'all governments retain their legislative authorities.'[34] Governments may be more accountable for meeting standards under the Accord, as each government is to undertake clearly defined responsibility for environmental performance and will report publicly on its results. The Accord also contains provisions for setting clear objectives, sharing information, evaluating agreements themselves, reporting regularly to the public, and rectifying non-performance.[35] The implementation of standards under the Accord is not mandatory, however, and any province can withdraw from a Standards Agreement on three months' notice. Moreover, as Harrison notes in Chapter 7, provinces are given considerable flexibility to develop control strategies to achieve Canada-wide standards, and these strategies can be regulatory or voluntary.

In the case of ozone and particulate matter, the draft standards agreed to by CCME members in late 1999 were much criticized. The new standard for ozone by 2015 was to be 65 ppb, averaged over an eight-hour period. The previous suggested guideline was 82 ppb over a one-hour period, twice as stringent as the standards in most provinces, but environmentalists argued that this standard would allow for higher one-hour readings on a given day.[36] The new standard for PM2.5 by 2010 was to be 30 micrograms per cubic metre (mpcm), which was more stringent than the 1999 Ontario standard of 120 mpcm. Annual reporting would commence in 2011, although comprehensive five-year reports would be compiled as of 2005. There were, however, no specific reduction commitments for point or mobile emission sources by federal or provincial governments, as the emphasis was on ambient standards.

While average urban concentrations of NO_x decreased between 1989 and 1996 in Canada, VOC levels have shown little change and trends in both pollutants vary significantly from one location to another.[37] Moreover, population growth, increased emissions from greater use of vehicles, and higher consumption of energy threaten to drive up ozone levels. Finally, recent science conducted on both ozone and particulate matter indicates that concentrations much lower than the current national standards cause adverse health effects.[38] It is clear, then, that significant reductions in ozone-causing pollutants must still be achieved. It is also clear that intergovernmental efforts and agreements formulated under the auspices of the CCME over the 1990s generated guidelines for provincial action, but did not bring about vigorous provincial policy action to generate serious reductions in emissions of smog-precursors.

Continental Pressures at Multiple Levels

Canadians constantly are told by their politicians that air pollutants from the US transported on prevailing winds into Canada cause up to half of the ground-level ozone in southwestern Ontario and up to 75 per cent of the ozone in the southern Atlantic region.[39] Certainly, then, co-operation between the two countries to reduce this flow of pollutants is necessary; while Canadian governments and industry can make reductions in smog-causing pollutants to reduce ozone levels, the problem also requires action on the other side of the border. This fact may partly account for past inaction on the part of provincial policy-makers, especially in Ontario. Yet recent Canada-US interactions on the issue of transboundary smog, at both subnational and national levels, have forced Canadian provincial and national governments to define further their policy stances and, especially in the case of Ontario, to take more decisive measures to reduce smog-causing emissions. Emissions reporting and work by the NAFTA Commission on Environmental Co-operation (CEC) on the long-range transport of air pollutants have also aided in keeping air quality on the agenda of Canadian governments.

SUBNATIONAL ACTIVITIES

There are bound to be some tensions between Canada and the US in environmental negotiations because of differences in their policy approaches. First, while Canada has chosen to adopt non-regulatory approaches to achieve reductions in smog-causing emissions, such as the CCME's NO_x/VOC Management Plan and Ontario's Smog Accord, the Americans are more cautious about such mechanisms and more prone to employ regulatory tools. Second, environmental spending by Canadian federal and provincial governments has fallen behind spending by US federal and state governments, a fact that has not gone unnoted by the American environmental policy community. Third, and perhaps most importantly, the power of the provinces and the increasing 'intergovernmentalization' of environmental policy-making in Canada, whereby the federal government can encourage national action but cannot force the provinces to comply, are not features of the American context. As Hoberg notes in Chapter 9, the US states are subordinated to the national level in the field of environmental protection and the federal Environmental Protection Agency (EPA) sets and enforces national pollution standards on the states. The EPA may delegate the implementation of standards to the states, but these activities are subject to active federal oversight.

This is not to say that there are no policy differences among the US states. The northeastern states and California tend to have the most stringent programs in place, especially in terms of vehicle emissions. This policy pattern is likely the result of a number of factors, including the severity of pollution problems in these regions, federally mandated reduction requirements, and, in the case of the Northeast, co-operative policy initiatives within the region. As indicated above, there is considerable tension between the 'upwind' midwestern states and 'downwind' northeastern states. Research by such bodies as the Northeastern States for Coordinated Air Use Management (NESCAUM) has shown that wind flow does move pollution from the nation's Midwest to the Northeast and that the industrial Midwest is a major source of NO_x, a key component of smog.[40] As a result, northeastern states have found it difficult to comply with federal EPA ambient air quality standards because, although they have undertaken emissions reduction actions themselves, these actions are countered by the transboundary pollution that comes their way. Organizations like NESCAUM and the Ozone Transport Commission have enabled northeastern states to make common cause with each other and lobby federal officials for accelerated action on emissions reduction in the Midwest. More recently, northeastern states have petitioned the EPA under provisions of the 1990 Clean Air Act to force emissions reductions in the Midwest.[41]

Ontario, Canada's largest smog producer, occupies an uneasy position between these state factions. On the one hand, the province has close economic, political, and environmental (in terms of water pollution) ties with the Great Lakes states (Illinois, Indiana, Michigan, Minnesota, New York, Ohio, Pennsylvania, and Wisconsin), which count among their numbers the coal-burning midwestern states. On the other hand, the province also suffers from midwestern pollution and has common cause with the states of the Northeast and Middle Atlantic regions (Connecticut, Delaware, District of Columbia, Maine, Maryland, Massachusetts, New Hampshire, New Jersey, New York, Rhode Island, Vermont, and sometimes Virginia) in reducing the source of that pollution. However, when one compares air pollution policies in the Great Lakes states, the northeastern states, and the high-smog provinces (British Columbia, Ontario, Quebec, and New Brunswick), the central Canadian provinces appear to resemble their Great Lakes neighbours more than their stringent northeastern counterparts, especially with regard to vehicle emission reduction programs. British Columbia is an outlier among the provinces as it resembles more the northeastern states and California.

The policy similarities and differences in the states and provinces have been highlighted in the ongoing debate about proposed new air quality standards in the US. In July 1997, the EPA issued new air quality standards for ozone (80 ppb over an eight-hour period) and particulate matter, specifically PM2.5 (15mpcm). The agency's current PM10 standard was to remain the same, at 50 mpcm. The new, more stringent standards were justified on health grounds[42] and strongly supported by the downwind northeastern states and Canadian provinces. They were vigorously opposed, however, by the midwestern states and their industries, and these opponents decided to mount a legal challenge to the new standards. In response to a suit brought forward by these interests, the Court of Appeals for the District of Columbia held that the EPA, in issuing the new standards, had exceeded its constitutional authority and that its proposal was 'an unconstitutional delegation of legislative power'.[43] The Court explained that 'what the EPA lacks is any determinate criterion for drawing lines' to determine where the standards should be. The EPA then turned to the US Supreme Court for a review of the Appeal Court's decision.

Ontario's interventions in the US debate have appeared contradictory. During 1997, Ontario's Minister of Environment travelled to a number of US states in an effort to build support for co-operative action on transboundary air pollution. Ontario and Quebec also attempted to solicit support from the Great Lakes states at the 1997 annual meeting of Great Lakes governors and premiers to aid provincial efforts aimed at combatting transboundary pollution.[44] The next year, however, Ontario Premier Mike Harris did not attend the annual meeting, which had been viewed as an opportunity for the province to air its views on smog entering Ontario from the United States. Shortly thereafter, the Great Lakes governors rejected requests from Quebec and Canada to support more stringent air quality standards.[45] During 1998, however, the EPA proposed a new standard for NO_x emissions produced by coal-fired plants. The new standard, which would apply to 22 eastern states and cover the aging coal-fired plants in the Midwest, aimed to cut NO_x emissions by 28 per cent starting in 2003. Yet both Ontario and the government of Canada failed to file full submissions with the EPA during its consultation period on the new standards.[46]

Also in 1998, NESCAUM expressed concern that deregulation in the electricity industry in both countries would significantly increase power production at low-cost, coal-burning (and high-polluting) utility plants.[47] Ontario has been in the process of downsizing its nuclear capacity and introducing full wholesale and retail competition into the province's electricity market by 2000. As nuclear generating plants have been closed, the shortfall in generating capacity has been made up both by boosting the capacity of existing coal-fired generating plants and by purchasing power from coal-fired utilities in the US. The result: a 47 per cent increase in air emissions during the first six months of 1998.[48] Moreover, environmentalists in Canada were concerned that the Ontario government would sell its coal-fired generating plants without first ensuring that the plants be retrofitted to use cleaner-burning natural gas.

In 1999, the Ontario government stated its intention to intervene in the EPA's appeal case in support of the new, more stringent ozone and particulate standards. Ontario's Premier Harris was reminded, however, via a letter from the Attorney General for the state of New York, that Ontario's NO_x emission rates were three times higher than the rates allowable under the new EPA regulations.[49] In fact, the Attorney General went so far as to note that the Ontario government's failure to reduce NO_x emissions might result in the overturn of the EPA regulations on trade competitive grounds. This did not happen, however, and it was the decision of the US Court of Appeal that was overturned. The EPA's ozone and particulate standards, more stringent than anything enacted by governments in Canada,[50] were upheld.

BILATERAL AND TRILATERAL INTERVENTIONS

There are good reasons to conclude that recent policy changes in Canada, especially in Ontario, can be linked to bilateral and trilateral interventions. The 1991 Canada-US Air Quality Agreement provides for the study and control of air pollutants that cross the Canada-US border. It was originally geared towards reducing the air pollutants that contribute to acid rain—SO_2 and NO_x—and both nations have been successful in reducing SO_2 emissions by more than 40 per cent. There has been less progress in reducing NO_x emissions, however. As of 1997, efforts began to extend the Agreement and develop a 'Smog Annex' to address transboundary smog. Formal bilateral discussions took place throughout 2000 on a backdrop of the court challenge to the EPA's proposed ozone regulations and accompanied by considerable media attention on both sides of the border. Throughout 1999, prior to formal negotiations, both Canadian and American environmental groups criticized lax Canadian environmental policies in a range of areas and it was frequently pointed out that the US was taking more stringent actions to deal with smog-causing air pollutants. The implication, as with the acid rain negotiations of the 1980s, was that Canada should 'clean up its own backyard' before asking the Americans to take further action. Federal Environment Minister David Anderson, in the run-up to bilateral negotiations, was quick to employ this line of argument, noting that Canada must demonstrate it is serious about smog reduction at home before seeking guarantees from the Americans to cut their emissions.[51]

In the context of these negotiations, the focus increasingly turned to Ontario, Canada's largest smog producer. Ontario's 1997 Drive Clean Program, the first air quality initiative of the Progressive Conservative Harris government, had received mixed reviews. Some groups praised the government for moving forward and introducing a vehicle emissions inspection program. Others criticized the loopholes in the program, such as the exemption for recreational vehicles, trucks, buses, and cars built before 1980, and the 'leeway' factor that allows cars to emit certain levels of pollutants and still be declared clean.[52] Still others noted that the Drive Clean Program would likely penalize lower-income Ontarians and would be inefficient in terms of actually reducing the most life-threatening pollutants.[53]

In the same month that Drive Clean was introduced, the NAFTA Commission on Environmental Co-operation made public its first comparative study of pollutant releases and transfers in the US states and Canadian provinces. The study, based on 1994 data, ranked Ontario as the third-largest source of pollution in North America after Texas and Tennessee. Quebec ranked twelfth, while Alberta ranked seventeenth. Ontario's Environment Minister responded that the CEC's data did not reflect current conditions.[54] He did promise to unveil more stringent air emission standards, however. A first step, in late 1997, was to put into effect an 'interim' PM10 standard of 50 mpcm over a 24-hour period.[55]

At the same time, the CEC released a report on the long-range transport of air pollutants in North America.[56] The report stated that long-range persistent air pollutants posed significant threats to human health and the environment and that pollution prevention, achieved through trilateral co-operation between Canada, the US, and Mexico, was the best strategy for reducing deleterious emissions. The CEC had also studied transboundary pollution transport within the northeastern US and eastern Canada, and expressed concern about the trend towards the closing of monitoring stations as governments cut environmental budgets. At this point, Ontario had undertaken deeper cuts to its environmental budget and personnel than any other state or province.

With the January 1998 release of its Smog Accord, however, Ontario appeared impervious to these broader, continental pressures. The Accord had been the result of a year and a half of consultations with industry, environmentalists, and scientists, and it was hoped that the Accord would represent a consensus of all stakeholders. However, environmental groups withdrew from the process when it was decided that the Accord would rely on voluntary efforts by industry, rather than government regulations, to reduce NO_x and VOC emissions by 45 per cent by 2015. The program was also to receive no additional funding or staff to monitor progress.[57] Pollution Probe, a participant in the consultations, found itself unable to endorse the Accord 'due to the serious lack of substantive commitments to emissions reductions'.[58] The Ontario Medical Association criticized the government for promoting voluntary programs and for failing to impose mandatory standards that might more quickly address health effects. The Canadian Institute for Environmental Law and Policy noted that the plan contained no specific implementation commitments to require reductions from industrial or mobile sources by federal or provincial governments.[59] In response, Ontario's Environment Minister declared: 'We think it's only fair to give industry a first crack at doing it this way before going the regulatory route.'[60] The minister did promise, however, that the government would enact mandatory provisions if the targets were not met by industry.

In May, Ontario's Environmental Commissioner, in her second annual report, also criticized the voluntary approach adopted by the government in the Smog Accord. She noted that the plan 'provided no details of how almost half the smog reductions needed by its target year of 2015 can be achieved'.[61] The Commissioner also criticized the government's reliance on voluntary measures to meet air quality targets, its lack of support for municipal transit systems, the under-enforcement of regulations because of substantial budget cuts, and its failure to force industry to adopt new emissions reduction technology.

Later in 1998, the Ontario Ministers of Environment, Energy, and Economic Development were publicly accused of working behind the scenes to weaken the federal government's new sulphur content regulations while publicly advocating stringent standards.[62] Indeed, the Environment Minister had declared himself 'embarrassed' about the level of sulphur content in his province's fuels, the highest in North America. For the purposes of comparison, Ontario averaged 530 parts per million (ppm) sulphur content in gasoline in 1997 while the American average was 347 ppm.[63] However, a memo obtained under Access to Information indicated that Ontario officials had lobbied hard against the new stringent federal regulations. In late 1998, despite considerable protest from gasoline refineries in Ontario (and, apparently, Ontario officials),[64] the federal government announced new regulations under CEPA to reduce the sulphur content of gasoline by 90 per cent by 2005. The new sulphur content standard of 30 ppm will eventually match California's, the most stringent jurisdiction in North America. Vehicle manufacturers, who have spent an estimated $13 billion on new emissions technology, lauded the reduction goals in the regulations but lamented the implementation time frame. They had wanted the low-sulphur regulations to take effect immediately in order to protect their emissions systems.[65]

However, 1998 ended with Ontario's announcement that new legislation would provide the government with additional powers to enforce environmental laws more effectively and a Smog Patrol Program would enable ministry officials to work with enforcement agencies to target trucks and buses with visible exhaust emissions.

Meanwhile, Canadian officials and environmentalists worried that Ontario's weak air pollution policies might scuttle the Canada-US negotiations on a smog treaty. The federal Environment Minister pointed to Ontario as the key to successful negotiations, saying that 'if we don't have Ontario doing as much as the Americans, the Americans are unlikely to listen to the Canadian government.'[66] A spokesperson for the OntAIRio Campaign asserted: 'The key to Canada negotiating a reduction in smog coming to us from the United States is in our being prepared to impose the same technological cleanup on our coal-fired plants that the Americans are putting on theirs. . . . The government of Ontario has refused to make that cleanup happen.'[67] It was estimated that, if the EPA's new requirements on NO$_x$ emissions from coal-fired plants came into force, the level of emissions in the US would be two to four times lower than in Ontario.[68] Ontario Hydro's emission rates in 1997 alone were 300 per cent higher than would be allowable under the new US standards.[69] After a sustained campaign by environmental groups in the province, the Ontario government promised that the five coal-burning plants owned by Ontario Power Generation Corp., which generate as much air pollution as five million cars,[70] would not be sold without commitments that they would be retrofitted to burn cleaner-burning fuels.[71]

In September 1999 the CEC made public another pollutant release and transfer report showing that Ontario had moved up (or down, depending on one's perspective) in the state-province rankings. The province was now the second-largest polluter in North America, after Texas. The Ontario government was quick to dismiss the report, arguing that it was based on a 'flawed methodology'.[72]

Then, in the midst of extensive media coverage of the first Canada-US meeting to discuss the Smog Annex, and contrary to its initial approach in the Smog Accord, Ontario reached into its regulatory tool box. The Environment Minister announced that the government would mandate a modest but immediate 5 per cent reduction in NO$_x$ by electric utilities.[73] This target was compared with the 1998 EPA standards for NO$_x$ reductions in the national media and found wanting. However, the Ontario government announced shortly thereafter that the province would match whatever standards were instituted by the US Environmental Protection Agency to reduce smog-causing emissions if these were tougher than the province's own standards. Moreover, an emissions trading system for NO$_x$ was to be established, with an overall mandatory cap on emissions that would gradually decrease. Under the system, companies would be allowed to buy 'pollution credits' to offset emissions above the new ceilings, provided that the credits were bought from companies that have cut their emissions. The province would also require expanded annual reporting on emissions of all criteria pollutants, an activity that used to be voluntary.

The first meeting between Canada and the US in February 2000 was described by the two governments as 'co-operative and productive'.[74] Discussions centred mainly on technical and organizational issues central to the negotiations, such as the timing and scope of the negotiations as well as the elements to be included in the actual Annex. Negotiators also set out a work plan for future meetings in the summer and fall. It was agreed that the Annex would be a 'reciprocal arrangement' with commitments for emissions reductions by both countries in those regions identified as upwind sources contributing to transboundary flows.[75] Separate reduction targets and timetables for achieving them would be negotiated for each region at these later meetings, with a formal agreement to be signed by the end of the year, preferably before the US presidential election. The overall goal was to be a 45 to 50 per cent reduction in emission levels.

After this first round of Canada-US talks and directly prior to the second round, the federal government unveiled an 'updated' Clean Air Strategy. Federal officials announced new restrictions on SO_2 and NO_x, promised to declare particulate matter toxic under CEPA (which would force the government to regulate within two years), and stated the government's intention to seek tighter time frames to reduce emissions in negotiations with the provinces.[76] The federal and provincial governments did indeed meet that same month under the auspices of the CCME to discuss smog once more. After difficult negotiations, governments agreed to implement differential reduction targets by 2010, with Ontario reducing its emissions output by 45 per cent (as per its Smog Accord, although the target date is five years earlier), Quebec by more than 20 per cent, and Alberta and BC by 10 per cent.[77] The overall goal is to reduce smog by 20 per cent and to achieve a new national ozone Objective of 65 ppb. Although these standards are more stringent, this agreement suffers from the same limitations as the CCME's 1990 Plan; the provinces are responsible for implementation and there are no real penalties for non-compliance. Yet, the federal Environment Minister argued that this agreement was different, as the provinces were now 'serious' about meeting the commitments. Specifically, federal officials claimed that the agreement was made possible because Ontario withdrew its objections to the accelerated time frame.[78] Certainly, one significant difference in the context of this round of intergovernmentalism was that the regulatory landscape had shifted somewhat in Ontario. An Ontario spokesperson stated that the province had moved on the issue because of its concerns about health effects and because 'we think it will be helpful in terms of our negotiations with the Americans.'[79]

The June and August Canada-US negotiations yielded further progress on key elements of the Smog Annex, although the most substantial discussions relating to emission reductions were addressed in September and October. Both governments were committed to completing talks before the presidential election in November, as it was feared that a new Bush administration would be less favourably disposed towards bilateral environmental agreements. After four rounds of intense negotiations, as well as extensive informal consultations, a final draft of the Ozone Annex to the 1991 Air Quality Agreement was released on 13 October 2000. In both countries, defined pollution 'regions' (central and southern Ontario and southern Quebec in Canada; 18 eastern states and the District of Columbia in the US) were to make NO_x and VOC emission reductions. The US agreed to reduce NO_x emissions by 35 per cent by 2007, which would represent a 70 per cent reduction in American emissions from power plants and other major industrial sources. For its part, Canada agreed to place a cap on NO_x emissions from Ontario power plants of 39 kilotonnes (representing a 50 per cent reduction) and five kilotonnes in Quebec.[80] Moreover, Canada agreed to harmonize with those of the US its emission reduction regulations for cars, vans, light trucks, diesel engines, fuel standards, and small engines for off-road equipment. Finally, annual reporting and joint analysis of transboundary transport were also features of the Annex.

The federal Minister of the Environment declared himself 'very pleased' with the newly minted agreement, although Ontario's Environment Minister, Dan Newman, declared that the federal government had 'sold out' to the Americans by not requiring deeper reductions of their southern neighbours.[81] In response, Anderson noted that Ontario had been the main obstacle to getting an even tougher package: 'Nobody has done more to make this deal difficult than the province of Ontario, and no individual has done more than Dan Newman. For him to claim this is a sellout by the feds is an extraordinary attempt to revise history.'[82]

Conclusion

As of 2001, it is evident that Ontario has reluctantly retreated from its obvious preference for voluntarism as a policy approach to reducing air emissions and has tentatively reached into its regulatory tool box. This does not appear to be the result of pressure generated through intergovernmentalism or from the Canadian federal government, which for the most part has appeared content, or has felt forced, to work within federal-provincial collaborative institutions. The track record of the various intergovernmental agreements over the 1990s does not indicate real success in producing stringent provincial, or indeed national, policies to address air quality problems.

On the other hand, pressures emanating from south of the border with US federal officials and northeastern state representatives appear to have been more effective in prodding Canada, especially Ontario, to take action to reduce smog-causing emissions. It should also be noted, however, that portrayals of Ontario as a potential 'treaty-breaker' have been effectively emphasized by Canadian officials. In addition, Canadian environmental groups have just as effectively (and consistently) highlighted the weaknesses in federal and especially Ontario air quality policies in comparison with American policies. Moreover, the CEC pollutant release reports have served to focus public attention on Ontario as a jurisdiction whose environmental record is less than enviable. The Commission's work on long-range air pollutant transport also has aided in keeping the issue on the political agenda.

It is significant in this case of air quality policy that the various 'levels' of continental pressures—subnational via the northeastern US states, bilateral Canada-US, and trilateral CEC—worked in the same direction, putting pressure on Canada, especially Ontario, to act. Pressure from the midwestern states to delay action was overcome by this troika as well. The interesting question here is what is likely to transpire in cases where there is tension between the levels of continental pressures, especially between bilateral Canada-US negotiations and state-province (perhaps even regional groupings of states and provinces) environmental relations, such that these pressures are operating in very different directions.

   This case also adds to the existing literature that demonstrates the relevance of studying continental influences on Canadian domestic environmental policy. Far from serving to weaken standards, viewed as inevitable by many in both the social and environmental policy communities, continental pressures have generated 'upward' pressures on Canadian smog policy. Without these broader pressures, Canadian policy-making very likely would have languished in failed intergovernmentalism and voluntarism or, at the very least, policy progress would have evolved much more slowly.[83] It is perhaps not surprising, as Wilson points out in Chapter 3, that many Canadian environmental groups are beginning to look to American and North American institutions and processes as a way of encouraging, even forcing, policy change by Canadian governments.

Notes

1 It should be noted here that some research indicates that NO_x play an ambiguous role in the formation of ozone: in some cases increased levels of NO_x may actually decrease ozone levels. 'Breathless (What's wrong with the air in Toronto?)', *Toronto Life* 31, 2 (Febr. 1997): 50–9.

2 Atmospheric Environment Service, Environment Canada, *Canadian 1996 NO_x/VOC Science Assessment: Summary for Policy Makers* (Toronto: Multi-Stakeholder NO_x/VOC Science Program, Oct. 1997), 2.

3 Canadian Pulp and Paper Association, *Compendium of Air Issues and Air Issues Management Initiatives Involving the Federal Government of Canada*, Aug. 1997, 1–2.

4 http://www.ec.gc.ca/smog/facts.htm. Accessed 25 Sept. 1999.

5 Ibid.

6 Ibid.

7 Ibid.

8 Ibid.

9 Environment Canada, 'Indicator: Average levels of air pollutants in Canadian cities', *Urban Air Quality: National Environmental Indicator Series*, SOE Bulletin No. 96–1 (Spring 1996).

10 Ibid.

11 M. Mittelstaedt, 'Toronto's Air Quality Worst of Six Cities', *Globe and Mail*, 28 Mar. 1992, A5.

12 'Implications of New Federal Emission Regulations', *Canada AM*, CTV, 4 Mar. 1997.

13 R.T. Burnett et al., 'Association between Ozone and Hospitalization for Respiratory Diseases in 16 Canadian cities', *Environmental Research* 72 (1997): 24–31; Burnett et al., 'The Role of Particulate Size and Chemistry in the Association between Summertime Ambient Air Pollution and Hospitalization for Cardiorespiratory Diseases', *Environmental Health Perspectives* 105, 6 (June 1997): 614–20; Burnett et al., ' Effects of the Urban Ambient Air Pollution Mix on Daily Mortality Rates in 11 Canadian Cities', *Canadian Journal of Public Health* 89, 3 (May-June 1988): 152–6.

14 Atmospheric Environment Service, *Canadian 1996 NO_x/VOC Science Assessment*, 2.

15 Commissioner of the Environment and Sustainable Development, 'Smog: Our Health at Risk', in *1997 Annual Report*, ch. 4, 8.

http://www.oag-bvg.gc.ca/domino/reports.nsf/html/c004ce.html

16 'Ontario pumps out dirtiest gasoline: Report blames ageing refineries, cheap crude for over-the-top sulphur levels', *Ottawa Citizen*, 2 Mar. 1998, A1.

17 'Auto industry upset with tough new BC smog rules', Canadian Press, 8 Dec. 1995.

18 Sierra Club of Canada, 'The OntAIRio Campaign: Ontarians will vote for clear air!', news release: http://www.sierraclub.ca/national/media/poll-feb10-99.html. Accessed 16 Feb. 2000.

19 Ibid.

20 'US pollution loopholes hurting Ontario: Report by US Public Interest Research Group', Canadian Press, 13 July 1998.

21 J. Morrow and E. Schwartzel for Pollution Probe, 'Regarding Air Quality Issues and the CEPA Review', presented to the House of Commons Committee on Environment and Sustainable Development, Sept. 1994, 2.

22 Ibid., 1.

23 Commissioner of the Environment and Sustainable Development, 'Smog: Our Health at Risk'.

24 Ibid.

25 Morrow and Schwartzel for Pollution Probe, 'Regarding Air Quality Issues', 2. It should be noted, however, that the federal government was given new authority to control vehicle and other engine emissions in the amendments to CEPA in 1999, which may provide an impetus for new regulations.

26 Ibid., 4.

27 For a detailed discussion of the CCME and its workings, see Chapter 7 in this volume by Harrison.

28 See K. Harrison, *Passing the Buck: Federalism and Canadian Environmental Policy* (Vancouver: University of British Columbia Press, 1996); Harrison, 'The Regulator's Dilemma: Regulation of Pulp Mill Effluents in the Canadian Federal State', *Canadian Journal of Political Science* 29, 3 (1996): 469–96; D. VanNijnatten, 'Intergovernmental Relations and Environmental Policy-Making: A Cross-National Perspective', in P. Fafard and K. Harrison, eds, *Managing the Environmental Union* (Kingston: Institute of Intergovernmental Relations and Saskatchewan Institute for Public Policy, 2000); Auditor General of Canada, 'Involving Others in Governing, Accountability at Risk', in *1999 Annual Report*, ch. 23; Commissioner of the Environment and Sustainable Development, 'Streamlining Environmental Protection Through Federal-Provincial Agreements: Are They Working?', in *1999 Annual Report*.

29 Commissioner of the Environment and Sustainable Development, 'Smog: Our Health at Risk'.

30 *Environmental Policy & Law* 9, 1 (Apr. 1998): 681.

31 Environment Canada, Natural Resources Canada, Transport Canada, *Phase 2 Federal Smog Management Plan* (Ottawa: Government of Canada, Nov. 1997).

32 Commissioner of the Environment and Sustainable Development, 'Smog: Our Health at Risk', 4.

33 Ibid., 26.

34 CCME, *CCME Harmonization Initiative*. http://www.ccme.ca/ccme/harmonization/plain/html. Accessed 24 Apr. 1998.

35 Commissioner of the Environment and Sustainable Development, 'Streamlining Environmental Protection Through Federal-Provincial Agreements: Are They Working?'.

36 D. Williamson, 'Air quality standards ambiguous', *Windsor Star*, 4 Dec. 1999, A1, A5.

37 Commissioner of the Environment and Sustainable Development, 'Smog: Our Health at Risk', 11.

38 For example, a Health Canada review of 22 mortality studies showed that ground-level ozone has statistically significant health effects at 15 ppb, well below the national objective of 82 ppb. *Environmental Policy & Law* 10, 1 (Apr. 1999): 829.

39 However, it is also argued that 'Ontario's own geography—its huge expanse of hydro-carbon-producing forests, its agricultural land cheek by jowl with industrial cities, its southern third surrounded by three vast, biologically active bodies of water—plays a relatively unstudied role in its air chemistry and air quality.' In 'Breathless (What's wrong with the air in Toronto?)'.

40 P. Miller et al., 'The Long-Range Transport of Ozone and Its Precursors in the Eastern United States', Boston: Northeastern States for Coordinated Air Use Management, 1997.

41 L. Parker and J. Blodgett, 'Air Quality: EPA's Ozone Rule, OTAG, and Section 126 Petitions—A Hazy Situation?', Washington: Congressional Research Service, Environmental and Natural Resources Division, 98–236, 15 June 1999.

42 USEPA, Office of Air and Radiation, Office of Air Quality Planning and Standards, 'EPA's Revised Ozone Standard', http://www.epa.gov/ttn/oarpg/naaqsfin/o3fact.html. Accessed 8 Feb. 2000.

43 *American Trucking Association, Inc. v. USEPA*, 97–1440 and 97–1441 (D.C. Cir. 14 May 1999), Summary of Decision.

44 M. Winfield and G. Jenish, *Ontario's Environment and the Common Sense Revolution: A Four Year Report* (Toronto: Canadian Institute for Environmental Law and Policy, Sept. 1999), A31.

45 Ibid., A36.

46 Ibid., A34.

47 Ibid.

48 'Hydro blamed for pollution from U.S. Utility's electricity purchase skirts law, environmentalists say', *Toronto Star*, 10 Sept. 1998, A12.

49 Canada News Wire: http://www.newswire.ca/releases/May1999/17/c4744.html. Accessed 16 Feb. 2000.

50 The CCME's new Canada-wide standards for ozone are more stringent, but they are non-binding.

51 'Smog cleanup begins at home: Feds urge Ontario to set an example', *Windsor Star*, 11 June 2000, A1, A2.

52 E. Reguly, 'Drive Clean clouded by loopholes', *Globe and Mail*, 11 Mar. 1999, B2.

53 P. Coninx, 'Motorists' money will go up in smoke', *Globe and Mail*, 16 Sept. 1997, A17; R. Howard, 'Vehicle emissions testing dismissed as costly', *Globe and Mail*, 1 Sept. 1998, A4.

54 *Environmental Policy & Law* 8, 6 (Sept. 1997): 594.

55 Ibid., 8, 9 (Dec. 1997): 627.

56 Commission for Environmental Co-operation, *Continental Pollutant Pathways: An Agenda for Cooperation to Address Long-Range Transport of Air Pollution in North American* (Montreal, 1997).

57 Brennan, 'Smog plan toothless, critics say', *Windsor Star*, 21 Jan. 1998, A1.

58 http://www.pollutionprobe.org/air/smogplan.html. Accessed 20 June 2000.

59 CIELAP, 'Why the Proposed Canada-Wide Standards Fail to Protect Health and Environment: Analysis from the Canadian Institute for Environmental Law and Policy', Toronto, June 2000: http://www.cielap.org/infocent/research/cws.html

60 R. Brennan, 'Smog plan toothless, critics say'.

61 *Environmental Policy & Law* 9, 2 (May 1998): 685.

62 M. Mittelstaedt, 'Sterling's flip-flop elicits anger', *Globe and Mail*, 7 Nov. 1998, A11.

63 'Canada moving before US on cleaner fuels', *Environmental Policy & Law* 9, 8 (Nov. 1998): 753.

64 'Oilpatch could face $1.7 billion hit: Environment minister's proposal to cut sulphur levels in gasoline would mean major upgrading charged to refineries', *Financial Post*, 4 Mar. 1997, 3.

65 'Ontario pumps out dirtiest gasoline: Report blames aging refineries, cheap crude for over-the-top sulphur levels', *Ottawa Citizen*, 2 Mar. 1998, A1.

66 'Smog cleanup begins at home'.

67 I. Sturino, 'Ontario smog may hinder cleanup talks', *Globe and Mail*, 11 Feb. 2000, A23.

68 'Smog cleanup begins at home'.

69 M. Mittlestaedt, 'U.S. pollution rules may cost Ontario Hydro millions', *Globe and Mail*, 29 Sept. 1998, A6.

70 Ontario Clean Air Alliance, 'Ontario's Dirty Secrets: 5 coal plants add up to a big smog problem', news release: http://www.cleanair.web.net/whatsew/dirtysee.html. Accessed 16 Feb. 2000.

71 R. Mackie, 'Environmentalists victorious in fate of coal-burning plants', *Globe and Mail*, 18 May 2000, A8.

72 *Environmental Policy & Law* 10, 6 (Sept. 1999): 887.

73 M. Mittelstaedt, 'Ontario moves to cut smog, acid rain', *Globe and Mail*, 25 Jan. 2000, A8.

74 'Canada-U.S. Ozone Negotiations: Joint U.S.-Canada Statement', news release, Ottawa, 16 Feb. 2000: http://www.dfait-maeci.gc.ca/geo/usa/ozone_neg-e.asp. Accessed 24 July 2000.

75 Environment Canada, 'Fact Sheet: Ozone Annex under the 1991 Canada-U.S. Air Quality Agreement': http://www.ec.gc.ca/press/00615_f_e.htm. Accessed 24 July 2000.

76 M. MacKinnon, 'Smog-fighting strategy to be unveiled', *Globe and Mail*, 19 May 2000, A1.

77 A. Duffy, 'Provinces pledge to cut smog by 2010', *Edmonton Journal*, 7 June 2000, A6.

78 R. Seguin, 'Ministers agree to air-quality target', *Globe and Mail*, 7 June 2000, A7.

79 Ibid.

80 Minister of the Environment, 'U.S.-Canada Ozone Annex Negotiations, Negotiators Joint Statement', news release, Washington, 13 Oct. 2000.

81 Mark MacKinnon and Richard Mackie, 'Canada, U.S. agree to cut smog', *Globe and Mail*, 14 Oct. 2000, A7.

82 Ibid.

83 The obvious exception here is British Columbia, which has struck out on its own in terms of policy development in this area. One important intervening factor in BC's case is that its air quality problem is not transboundary to the extent it is in central Canada and it does not have to, or cannot, wait for foreign action.

Chapter 14

Sound Science and Moral Suasion, Not Regulation: Facing Difficult Decisions on Agricultural Non-Point-Source Pollution

Éric Montpetit

Canadian farming, still largely a way of life in the immediate postwar period, has increasingly become a modern industry like any other. Between 1981 and 1996, the total number of farms decreased from 320,000 to 260,000. During the same period, however, the proportion of large farms, those with revenues of $500,000 and more, rose from 6 per cent to 10 per cent. As a result, the average annual growth rate in agriculture over the past 10 years has been positive, at 3.5 per cent.[1] In short, agricultural production in Canada is increasingly concentrated and intensive.

Such intensity and concentration engender environmental stress. Modern farming produces significant quantities of wastes and relies on toxic chemicals as well as potentially damaging biotechnologies. The geographical distance between areas of livestock production and areas of intensive cultivation exacerbates this stress.[2] Where intensive animal farming occurs, the quality of waste frequently outweighs the need for crop fertilization. In contrast, zones of intensive cultivation are often relatively free of livestock farming, thereby requiring a greater reliance on chemical fertilizers. Cultivation intensity also necessitates the use of pesticides and herbicides that present some environmental risks.

The environmental stress caused by agriculture often translates into soil degradation, air pollution, and water pollution. Tillage and chemical fertilization (as opposed to manure fertilization) can render soil vulnerable to erosion, while the use of heavy machinery causes soil compaction. Intensive animal production is often associated with problems of odours, while both livestock farming and field crops are said to contribute to the problem of carbon monoxide releases into the atmosphere.[3] Fertilizers, biological or not, as well as pest-control chemicals often leak into streams and rivers as well as groundwater. Once in the water, nutrients stimulate biological activity and create serious distortion of ecosystems. Chemicals threaten fish and aquatic plants, and water polluted with agricultural waste and chemicals may pose human health risks.[4] And, unlike soil compaction and even odours, technology appears insufficient to address problems of water quality in agricultural zones.

Public authorities increasingly recognize agricultural pollution as a public policy problem.[5] Despite years of investment in industrial and municipal pollution control, water quality in several areas remains rather poor. This poor water quality, environmental officials often suggest, is attributable to non-point-source pollution, especially agricultural pollution. Even agricultural officials recognize the importance of environmental protection in agricultural areas. In 1989, in *Growing Together*, a major federal farm policy document, Agriculture Canada listed 'sustainability' as one of the four pillars of Canadian agricultural policy. In 1995, the federal and provincial ministers of agriculture promised to co-ordinate their efforts 'to effectively deal with the challenges and seize the opportunities presented by increasing public interest in environmental sustainability'.[6] Two years later, the federal department, now known as Agriculture and Agri-Food Canada, published a strategy for an 'environmentally sustainable agriculture'.[7]

Despite the seriousness of agricultural pollution and despite officials' awareness of this problem, the Canadian federal government has shied away from adopting stringent regulatory agri-environmental standards, preferring instead to employ science-based moral suasion, a voluntary approach. In response to the idea that moral suasion is well-suited to non-point-source pollution, this chapter argues that policy feedback and regulatory aversion have predisposed federal officials to this type of policy instrument. Further, bureaucratic capacity, weak in the environmental sector and strong in agriculture, has combined with federalism to encourage federal policy-makers to exclude command-and-control regulations from their policy instrument arsenal and to rely solely on science-based moral suasion.

The Canadian Approach to Agricultural Pollution

Committed to agricultural sustainability in a manner similar to Canada, the European Union has regulated soil fertilization to protect water quality. The EU Nitrate Directive requires member states to take measures to limit the application of nitrate to 170kg per hectare.[8] In the United States, large livestock operations, commonly called Concentrated Animal Feeding Operations (CAFOs), are regulated under section 502 of the US Clean Water Act and are subject to National Pollutant Discharge Elimination System permit requirements, which prohibit any direct discharge of agricultural waste into the environment. If these requirements only pertain to point-source agricultural pollution, so-called 'section 319 programs' indirectly regulate land fertilization. Through '319' programs, the US Environmental Protection Agency exercises a leadership role in the development of pollution control management plans to address non-point source agricultural pollution.[9] Also, since 1985 the US Department of Agriculture has administered rather generous conservation programs.[10]

Canadian policies for agricultural pollution do not compare favourably with those in Europe and the US. The Canadian federal government, despite its environmental commitment, has chosen to refrain from adopting command-and-control regulations or conditional grant programs. The Canadian Environmental Protection Act (CEPA), revamped in 1999, contains no provision that would allow for the regulation of agricultural practices. Sections 116 to 119 of the Act do address nutrients, but they restrict the regulatory power of Environment Canada to cleaning products. The rationale invoked for exempting agricultural fertilizers was that they are already regulated under the Fertilizers Act.[11] Yet, while the Fertilizers Act deals with the marketing of fertilizers and the setting of labelling and toxicity standards, it does not address their use by farmers.[12] This Act certainly fails to regulate the land application of unprocessed agricultural wastes.

CEPA does offer support for the National Program of Action for the Protection of the Marine Environment from Land-Based Activities (NPA), the objective of which is to identify priorities in terms of pollution abatement on land as well as recommend improved planning and management processes where appropriate. However, the program gives agricultural pollution a low priority, with higher priority being placed on municipal and industrial sources of pollution.[13]

One should not conclude from this, however, that the federal government does nothing about agricultural pollution. In fact, the NPA reaffirms the importance of initiatives such as the St Lawrence Action Plan VISION 2000, a program whose current emphasis is non-point-source agricultural pollution. Yet the approach privileged under the St Lawrence Action Plan and other Ecosystem Initiatives sponsored by the federal government contrasts with those of Europe and the US, as the Canadian approach does not rest on command-and-control regulations or on the provision of grants in exchange for the adoption of agricultural practices with a low environmental impact. Instead, the federal government prefers to rely on moral suasion backed by sound scientific knowledge.[14] For example, Part Three of the new CEPA, which pertains to information-gathering, makes it a central task of Environment Canada to 'operate and maintain an environmental monitoring system, conduct research and studies and publish information'. Knowledge produced in this manner should serve to set 'non-regulatory science-based targets or recommended practice'.[15] Canadian policy-makers appear to assume that, once equipped with scientific knowledge, environmental officials and other environmentally concerned citizens will be effective at persuading polluters to change their practices. In several areas of concern, regulatory sanctions and financial incentives are perceived as costly and less efficient.

This is certainly the case with respect to agricultural pollution. The Agri-Environmental Indicator Project is arguably the most important agri-environmental initiative of the federal government. Far from a regulatory initiative, the project's objective is to produce scientific information on the environmental impact of agricultural practices. This scientific information, it is assumed, will demonstrate 'the progress being made by the agriculture sector' and support 'the development of strategies and actions targeted at areas and resources that remain at environmental risk'.[16] Significantly, the state agency responsible for the Agri-Environmental Indicator Project is not Environment Canada but Agriculture and Agri-Food Canada. Accustomed to providing services to farmers, Agriculture and Agri-Food Canada prefers to educate farmers about the environmental impact of their practices rather than to enforce environmental regulations.

The Nature of Agricultural Pollution or Policy Feedback?

It has been suggested by some observers that command-and-control regulatory policy instruments, arguably adequate to deal with point-source pollution, are limited in their efficiency when it comes to agricultural non-point-source pollution. Command-and-control regulations, it is argued, are successful when monitoring is efficient enough to catch violators and when sanctions are applied. This is not problematic for point-source pollution, which is released into the environment in large quantities at the end of the pipes or chimneys of a limited number of industrial plants and municipalities. In contrast, each farm releases a small quantity of pollutants into the environment at a time. Yet, the large number of farms releasing small amounts of pollutants over long periods of time results in significant impacts on the environment. Monitoring can be very costly for regulators precisely because agricultural pollution is so hard to pinpoint and originates from such a large number of farms. Moreover, when agriculture-related pollutants, such as nutrients, heavy metals, or bacteria, are found in watercourses, it is nearly impossible to establish liability.[17] For these reasons, governments have been advised to move away from command-and-control regulations and to rely to a greater extent on moral suasion and self-regulation to tackle such pollution problems. Once properly informed, so the reasoning goes, farmers will realize the benefits of adopting practices that minimize environmental disruptions.[18]

Soil erosion was a major concern in Ontario and western Canada in the 1980s. It also was identified as a major source of water pollution and was seen as posing a threat to the long-term viability of agriculture.[19] As a result, the federal government, often in collaboration with provincial governments, launched a series of programs,[20] the objective of which was to gather knowledge on practices to minimize soil erosion and then to convince farmers to adopt these practices. These programs turned out to be very successful and a large proportion of Ontario and western Canadian farmers adopted new seeding technologies in order to leave crop residues on their fields and prevent soil erosion. Buoyed by this experience, federal officials had every reason to believe that moral suasion, backed by scientific knowledge, was a particularly effective policy instrument for dealing with agricultural pollution. In opting for moral suasion, the Canadian government, such officials would argue, simply made an optimal policy instrument choice.

Yet, in the case of soil erosion, it was in the interest of farmers to adopt soil protection practices. The loss of topsoil was threatening yields and needed to be compensated with expensive fertilizers. Farmers quickly discovered that it was profitable to adopt so-called 'no-till technologies'. The same, however, cannot be said of all 'environmentally friendly' agricultural practices. For example, building sealed manure storage facilities increases production costs without increasing productivity. Establishing buffer zones between watercourses and agricultural land reduces areas of production. Moreover, biological means of controlling pests are not as efficient as chemicals. In short, it is far from clear that moral suasion can be as functional with all aspects of agricultural pollution as it was with soil erosion.

Even those who agree that the nature of agricultural pollution requires innovative environmental approaches have suggested that moral suasion is not enough. They argue that agricultural pollution would be best addressed when instruments of various types, including command-and-control regulations, are employed in tandem.[21] Ribaudo writes that 'farmer interest in education, technical, and financial assistance is enhanced when the threat of regulations is in the background.'[22] This idea is not entirely new, nor is it particular to the agricultural policy arena. Several environmental studies have concluded that moral suasion, command-and-control regulations, and financial incentives are each unlikely to be efficient when used alone. Writing about environmental policy in general, Lotspeich argues that 'the relevant choice is not between two approaches, but rather one of the correct mix of market and CAC [command-and-control] instruments.'[23] In short, functionality in the agricultural context offers a poor explanation for the Canadian emphasis on moral suasion and the exclusion of command-and-control regulations.

The success of soil protection programs surely had a feedback effect,[24] as it reinforced the belief held by federal officials that moral suasion was the appropriate policy instrument to deal with agricultural pollution. This is a different perspective, however, from one that argues that policy-makers have opted for moral suasion because it is the optimal alternative in agriculture. As a matter of fact, as noted above, European and American policy-makers chose radically different regulatory policy instruments to address problems very similar to those in Canada, indicating that singular past policy experiences matter.

Regulatory Aversion

Policy feedback from soil protection programs partly explains the preference of Canadian government officials for science-based moral suasion. It does not, however, explain why they have refrained from mixing moral suasion with command-and-control regulations. This section argues that Canadian federal policy-makers have developed an aversion for command-and-control regulations and, moreover, that this aversion has recently been institutionalized. It is thus difficult in Canada to elaborate new regulations, environmental or otherwise.

The North American Free Trade Agreement and the World Trade Organization have brought about increased competition in several business sectors, including agriculture.[25] As a result, business concerns about production costs have grown and regulatory costs have become a favourite target. Business groups, including farm groups, argue with increasing frequency that government regulations constitute an unjustified burden. In the current context of capital mobility, they suggest, Canada must deregulate to avoid capital flight.

While it may be premature to suggest that Canada participates in a global race to the bottom,[26] this deregulatory discourse has led policy-makers to launch a review of existing regulations and submit the adoption of new regulations to a rigid, rational decision-making process. Since 1992 the federal decision-making process has consisted of six steps: a demonstration that the level of risk requires regulations; public consultations; a cost-benefit analysis; minimization of the impact on business competitiveness; minimization of the costs for Canadians; and a demonstration that enforcement capacity is adequate.[27] Lemaire argues that this process amounts to a 'regulation for regulations'.[28] While the objective of this screening process for regulations was to curb what was perceived to be an excessive tendency to regulate, the result appears to be the institutionalization of a bias against command-and-control regulations. Conscious of the effort required to obtain approval for command-and-control regulations, government agencies are thus more likely to favour less demanding instruments. Moral suasion is one such instrument, as it is not subjected to such a strict approval process.

The rational decision-making process for the approval of command-and-control regulations, combined with the policy feedback from soil-protection programs, then, offers a powerful explanation for the general preference of federal officials in Canada for science-based moral suasion. This sharply contrasts with the European Union, often considered a regulatory state itself.[29] Still, we need to understand why the preference for moral suasion has been incorporated into actual policies.

Federal Bureaucratic Capacities

Generally speaking, business interests are concentrated while environmental interests are diffuse. This renders environmental groups more likely to be the victims of the free-rider problem: mobilization is difficult because no one can be excluded from enjoying any benefits accruing from its activities.[30] As a result, environmental groups are unlikely to have sufficient resources to press for the adoption of high environmental standards. This problem is particularly acute in agriculture, where an awareness of the environmental impact of practices is relatively recent. With limited resources, environmental groups have experienced difficulties in taking on this issue and, simultaneously, maintaining their activities on traditional environmental problems such as nuclear waste and industrial pollution. As a result, their efforts have been concentrated on a narrow range of agri-environmental issues, essentially pesticide registration and usage.

The transformation of agriculture, specifically its increased concentration and intensification, has, in some places, encouraged the organization of concerned citizens. These groups, however, often frame the issue of agricultural pollution as a 'not-in-my-backyard' (NIMBY) problem, as they are organized locally and devote significant efforts to opposing the siting of new farm operations. Appearing as if they are primarily concerned with the value of the countryside properties of their members, these groups have not enjoyed much credibility in demanding higher environmental standards for agriculture.[31] In short, the emergence of new groups has not compensated for the weakness of the more traditional environmental groups on agricultural pollution.

The comparative environmental policy literature, however, suggests that the weakness of environmental groups can be partly compensated for by strong environmental government bureaucracies.[32] It may be assumed that Environment Canada officials are among those state actors in Ottawa most likely to oppose the general bias against command-and-control regulations. After all, the traditional role of the environmental official has been to enforce regulations. If it is indeed the case that Environment Canada officials are inclined to oppose a bias towards command-and-control regulations, they appear to be in a rather weak position to do so. Study after study has concluded that Environment Canada is a weak bureaucracy. For example, Doern and Conway conclude that the ministry:

> ultimately failed to convince the political centre and other departments that environmental issues were real and threatening their own continuance—that they were not just public opinion and the views of environmentalists. The DOE [Department of the Environment] started the 1990s buoyed by the Green Plan but still facing a phalanx of ministers and policy mandarins who felt that the environment/economy was a trade-off. It had not made a convincing case in the Ottawa system that the environment had moved from an amenity concern to a vital issue.[33]

In Chapter 6 of this volume, Doern examines some of the difficulties Environment Canada faces as a result of changing political priorities and complex relations with other departments. Even if Environment Canada is committed to stringent command-and-control regulations on behalf of diffuse interests, it can rarely translate this commitment into policy.

Moreover, Environment Canada faces opposition within the agricultural policy field. Agriculture is one of the few economic sectors with its own ministry and, as mentioned above, the mandate of this ministry is to provide services to farmers. Farmers expect Agriculture and Agri-Food Canada to help them become competitive internationally and the ministry can count on relatively important resources to do just that. Naturally, with increasing knowledge about the environmental impact of agriculture, Agriculture and Agri-Food Canada has also developed somewhat of an interest in the environment. On the one hand, environmental problems such as soil erosion constitute threats to the long-term viability of agriculture. On the other hand, environmentalism can endanger the competitiveness of agriculture, as environmental regulations add to production costs. Agriculture and Agri-Food Canada, therefore, has become a powerful advocate for a softer approach to agricultural pollution. Equipped with a rationale constructed on the basis of the success of soil erosion programs in the 1980s, the ministry's involvement in environmental issues is tentative.[34] Assuming that Environment Canada is committed to high agri-environmental regulatory standards, it faces a strong bureaucratic opponent in Agriculture and Agri-Food Canada.

A similar tension exists between the US Department of Agriculture and the US Environmental Protection Agency (EPA). However, as Hoberg points out in Chapter 9, this latter agency is much more influential in Washington than Environment Canada is in Ottawa. As the American regulations mentioned above attest, the EPA still has the capacity to compensate for the potential weakness of environmental groups concerned with agricultural pollution. In Canada, Environment Canada is deprived of a similar capacity. In addition, Agriculture and Agri-Food Canada safeguards farmers against increases in environmental regulatory costs. Playing a leadership role in agri-environmental policy,[35] Agriculture and Agri-Food Canada ensures that pollution problems are addressed in ways that serve farmers best. One might say, insofar as the environment is concerned, that the federal ministry is in a position of conflict of interest, and this has meant privileging science-based moral suasion over command-and-control regulations.

Federalism

Officials from both the environment and agriculture ministries participate in the formulation of public policy. The negotiations that take place among them affect policy choices and agricultural officials, supported by farm groups, have a higher capacity than environmental officials to have their policy preferences formulated into policies. Yet the last word on these policies does not belong to bureaucrats, but to politicians, and the preferences of politicians are not as affected as those of bureaucrats by factors such as policy feedback or processes of regulatory approval. It is thus somewhat of a puzzle why politicians appear to have accepted science-based moral suasion and excluded the possibility of command-and-control regulation as a possible policy instrument to tackle agricultural pollution. It is argued here that the dynamics of federalism allow federal politicians to avoid making difficult decisions about agricultural pollution.

As is mentioned throughout this volume, Canadian provinces have important environmental responsibilities due to their jurisdiction over natural resources. Yet the federal government has jurisdiction over oceans, navigation, commerce, and criminal law, as well as taxing, spending, and residual powers, and thus it can play an important environmental role. In fact, as Valiente explains in Chapter 1, court decisions regarding the environmental division of powers have been largely favourable to the federal government and have yet to establish clear limits on federal competence. As Harrison argues in Chapter 7, if the federal government has often been content to leave environmental responsibilities with the provinces, it is not because the constitutional division of powers prohibits federal interventions.[36] And this is even more the case with respect to agricultural pollution. Section 95 of the Constitution Act establishes a concurrent jurisdiction in agriculture, subject to federal pre-eminence. Clearly, federal politicians are not constitutionally prevented from approving stringent command-and-control agri-environmental regulations.

While they are not prevented from doing so, however, the adoption of command-and-control regulations has the potential to become politically risky. It is farmers who would bear the main costs associated with stringent command-and-control agri-environmental regulations, as opposed to the costs of gathering scientific information and educating farmers, which would be distributed among taxpayers. Farmers also are well organized to campaign against politicians, whereas the potential beneficiaries of command-and-control agri-environmental regulations are dispersed. Vacationers, residents of the countryside, and everyone who has access to a watercourse are likely to appreciate a cleaner environment. But coming from different walks of life, these citizens are unlikely to organize themselves on behalf of politicians advocating stringent agri-environmental regulatory standards. As mentioned above, some countryside residents might organize themselves to oppose the siting of farm operations, but they are unlikely to seek or obtain regulations of a more general nature.

While science-based moral suasion diffuses some benefits, it concentrates others. In fact, farmers might learn not only about the environmental impact of their practices, but also about alternative practices that may increase profitability. Again, the profitable soil-protection practices mentioned above were the result of science-based moral suasion. As for those alternative practices that are costly, moral suasion leaves farmers free to ignore them. In short, science-based moral suasion involves low political risk and perhaps even some political gains, while command-and-control agri-environmental regulations are considerably more risky and carry little potential for political gains.

Public opinion can nevertheless turn against politicians if they are perceived as environmentally irresponsible. The Walkerton tragedy in Ontario offers one such example. The federal constitution, however, allows federal politicians to avoid blame if moral suasion turns out to be insufficient to protect the rural environment. Federal politicians can play with the 'fuzziness' of the division of powers to claim that the responsibility to regulate rests with the provinces. In fact, provinces have long insisted that their exclusive jurisdiction over natural resources be recognized, and the federal government certainly will not dispute this jurisdiction when environmental problems arise. In other words, federal politicians can easily pass the buck on environmental problems.[37]

Regulatory decentralization then poses a problem as provinces, to a greater extent than the federal government, are exposed to regulatory competition. In hog production, for example, where environmental problems are endemic, provinces intensively compete for markets and investments. To obtain these markets and investments, they may be tempted to maintain environmental standards lower than those of their neighbouring provinces. Montpetit and Coleman argue that Quebec has adopted agri-environmental standards much higher than those of Ontario, suggesting that a race to the bottom between the two provinces is not occurring.[38] Quebec's Auditor General has revealed, however, that the province displays a high level of toleration for the violations of its agri-environmental standards.[39] In short, Quebec politicians, in appearance more inclined to protect the environment, are not immune to pressures for lower regulatory costs.

Conclusion

Agricultural concentration and intensity carry environmental risks. Governments, including the federal government, have committed themselves to the development of policies to manage risks associated with modern agricultural practices. However, in sharp contrast to Europe and the United States, Canada has opted for a voluntary approach: science-based moral suasion. The federal government appears to have abandoned the alternative of command-and-control regulations.

Some would argue that the nature of agricultural pollution is well-suited to the use of moral suasion because its non-point-source character renders regulatory monitoring excessively costly. This opinion is convincingly contested in the environmental policy literature, however. Moral suasion and command-and-control regulations would be more efficient when used together rather than alone. Thus, the nature of agricultural pollution provides a poor explanation for the policy choice to exclude command-and-control regulations from the federal agri-environmental policy approach.

Instead, the preference for moral suasion is best explained by a policy feedback from the soil protection programs of the 1980s. The success of these programs has served to convince federal officials that science-based moral suasion was the correct approach to address problems of agricultural pollution. An avoidance of command-and-control regulations, on the other hand, was motivated by an institutionalized aversion to this type of policy instrument, as the approval of federal regulations is tightly controlled by a rational decision-making process.

Assuming that officials from Environment Canada remain more committed to command-and-control regulations, the bureaucratic capacity of the ministry does not allow them to overturn the more general preference for science-based moral suasion. The strength of Agriculture and Agri-Food Canada ensures the dominance of this ministry in agri-environmental policy formulation. And while command-and-control regulations are generally politically costly, federalism offers a discount on the political costs that could be associated with endorsing science-based moral suasion. This conclusion raises concerns about the capacity of the Canadian federal state to manage properly the environmental risks associated with the intensification and concentration of farming.

Notes

1 Agriculture and Agri-Food Canada, *A Portrait of the Canadian Agri-Food System* (Ottawa: Agriculture and Agri-Food Canada, 1999).

2 Owen J. Furuseth, 'Restructuring of Hog Farming in North Carolina: Explosion and Implosion', *Professional Geographer* 49, 4 (1997): 391–403.

3 Food and Agriculture Organization of the United Nations, *Sustainability Issues in Agricultural and Rural Development Policies: Vol. 1* (Rome: FAO, 1995).

4 Ken Kilpatrick, 'Concern Grows about Pollution from Megafarms', *Globe and Mail*, 30 May 2000. http://www.globeandmail.com/

5 Agriculture Canada, *Ontario Farm Groundwater Quality Survey* (Ottawa: Agriculture Canada, 1993); David Berryman and Isabelle Giroux, *La contamination des cours d'eau par les pesticides dans les régions de culture intensive de maïs au Québec: Campagne d'échantillonnage de 1992 et 1993* (Québec: Ministère de l'Environnement et de la Faune, 1994).

6 Federal and Provincial Ministers of Agriculture, *National Environment Strategy for Agriculture and Agri-Food* (Ottawa: Agriculture and Agri-Food Canada, 1995), 1.

7 Agriculture and Agri-Food Canada, *Agriculture in Harmony with Nature: Strategy for Environmentally Sustainable Agriculture and Agri-Food Development in Canada* (Ottawa: Agriculture and Agri-Food Canada, 1997).

8 Éric Montpetit, 'Europeanization and Domestic Politics: Europe and the Development of a French Environmental Policy for the Agricultural Sector', *Journal of European Public Policy* 7, 4 (2000): 576–92.

9 Carolyn M. Johns, 'Non-Point Source Water Pollution Management in Canada and the US: A Comparative Analysis of Institutional Arrangements and Policy Instruments', paper presented at the annual meeting of the Canadian Political Science Association, Sherbrooke, 1999.

10 Walter N. Thurman, *Assessing the Environmental Impact of Farm Policies* (Washington: AEI Press, 1995).

11 Environment Canada, *A Guide to the New Canadian Environmental Protection Act* (Ottawa: Minister of Public Works and Government Services, 2000), 13.

12 The Pesticides Act is similar.

13 Federal/Provincial/Territorial Advisory Committee on Canada's National Program of Action for the Protection of the Marine Environment from Land-based Activities, *Canada's National Program of Action for the Protection of the Marine Environment from Land-based Activities (NPA)* (Ottawa: Minister of Public Works and Government Services Canada, 2000), 7.

14 The goal of the St Lawrence Action Plan Vision 2000, phase three, is 'to educate the key players in agriculture about environmental problems'.

15 Environment Canada, *A Guide*, 5.

16 Agriculture and Agri-Food Canada, *Environmental Sustainability of Agriculture: Report of the Agri-Environmental Indicator Project* (Ottawa: Minister of Public Works and Government Services Canada, 2000).

17 Alfons Weersink et al., 'Economic Instruments and Environmental Policy in Agriculture', *Canadian Public Policy* 24, 3 (1998): 311–14; Johns, 'Non-Point Source Water Pollution Management'.

18 OECD, *Sustainable Agriculture: Concept, Issues and Policies in OECD Countries* (Paris: OECD, 1995); Joyti K. Parikh, ed., *Sustainable Development in Agriculture* (Dordrecht: Martinus Nijhoff, 1988).

19 Standing Committee on Agriculture, Fisheries and Forestry, *Soil at Risk* (Ottawa: Senate of Canada, 1984).

20 The Soil and Water Environmental Enhancement Program (SWEEP) and the National Soil Conservation Program.

21 Weersink et al., 'Economic Instruments', 321; Richard N.L. Andrew, 'Environmental Regulation and Business Self-Regulation', *Policy Science* 31 (1998): 177–97.

22 Marc O. Ribaudo, 'Lessons Learned about the Performance of USDA Agricultural Nonpoint Source Pollution Programs', *Journal of Soil and Water Conservation* 53, 1 (1998): 9.

23 Richard Lotspeich, 'Comparative Environmental Policy: Market-Type Instruments in Industrialized Capitalist Countries', *Policy Studies Journal* 26, 1 (1998): 85–104. See also Marie-Louise Bemelmans-Videc and Evert Vedung, 'Conclusions: Policy Instrument Types, Packages, Choices, and Evaluation', in Bemelmans-Videc, Ray C. Rist, and Vedung, eds, *Carrots, Sticks & Sermons: Policy Instruments & Their Evaluation* (New Brunswick, NJ: Transaction Publishers, 1998), 263.

24 Paul Pierson, 'When Effect Becomes Cause: Policy Feedback and Political Change', *World Politics* 45 (1998): 595–628.

25 Grace Skogstad, 'Agricultural Policy', in G. Bruce Doern, Leslie A. Pal, and Brian W. Tomlin, *Border Crossings: The Internationalization of Canadian Public Policy* (Toronto: Oxford University Press, 1996).

26 See F.W. Scharpf, *Governing Europe: Effective and Democratic?* (New York: Oxford University Press, 1999), ch. 3.

27 Secrétariat du Conseil du Trésor, *Gérer la réglementation au Canada: Réforme de la réglementation et processus réglementaires* (Ottawa: Ministre des Approvisionnements at Services, 1996).

28 Donald Lemaire, 'The Stick: Regulation as a Tool of Government', in Bemelmans-Videc, Rist, and Vedung, eds, *Carrots, Sticks & Sermons*, 66–7.

29 Giandomenico Majone, *La Communauté européenne: un État régulateur* (Paris: Montchrestien, 1996).

30 Mancur Olson Jr, *The Logic of Collective Action: Public Goods and the Theory of Groups* (Cambridge, Mass.: Harvard University Press, 1971).

31 Laura B. DeLind, 'The State, Hog Hotels, and the Right to Farm', *Agriculture and Human Values: Journal of the Agriculture, Food, and Human Values Society* 12 (1995): 34–44.

32 David Vogel, 'Representing Diffuse Interests in Environmental Policymaking', in R. Kent Weaver and Bert A. Rockman, eds, *Do Institutions Matter? Government Capabilities in the United States and Abroad* (Washington: Brookings Institution, 1993), 270.

33 G. Bruce Doern and Thomas Conway, *The Greening of Canada: Federal Institutions and Decisions* (Toronto: University of Toronto Press, 1994), 82.

34 In deciding to ban alachlor, a herbicide, Hoberg argues that Agriculture Canada went against the interests of farmers to preserve the legitimacy of its regulatory responsibilities. George Hoberg Jr, 'Risk, Science and Politics: Alachlor Regulation in Canada and the United States', *Canadian Journal of Political Science* 23, 2 (1990): 257–77.

35 As mentioned above, Agriculture and Agri-Food Canada is responsible for what appears to be the main agri-environmental initiative of the federal government: the Agri-Environmental Indicator Project.

36 Kathryn Harrison, *Passing the Buck: Federalism and Canadian Environmental Policy* (Vancouver: University of British Columbia Press, 1996), ch. 3.

37 Ibid.

38 Éric Montpetit and William D. Coleman, 'Policy Communities and Policy Divergence in Canada: Agro-Environmental Policy Development in Quebec and Ontario', *Canadian Journal of Political Science* 32, 4 (1999): 691–714.

39 Louis-Gilles Francoeur, 'Un porc sur cinq est produit au noir au Québec', *Le Devoir*, 19 June 2000, A2.

Chapter 15

Dollar Discourse: The Devaluation of Canada's Natural Capital in Canadian Climate Change Policy

Heather A. Smith

Climate change is a problem so complex that solving it 'will truly put human institutions and ingenuity to the test.'[1] The definition of the problem, even the assumption that there is a problem, is contested. In Canada, proposed solutions are actively debated by a varied set of stakeholders, including numerous departments of the federal government, provincial governments, industry of all types ranging from the insurance industry and the energy industry to the forestry industry, environmental non-governmental organizations, and the Canadian public. Climate change is a hot issue, literally and figuratively.

While recognizing the complexity of the issue and the numerous stakeholders involved, the aim of this chapter is to provide the reader with a snapshot of Canada's international behaviour. The focus is on Canada's behaviour since the negotiation of the 1992 Framework Convention on Climate Change (FCCC), with an emphasis on Canada's position at the third Conference of Parties (COP) meeting in 1997 at Kyoto, Japan. I argue that, while Canada has been an active participant in the international climate change negotiations, our policy post-1992 has been driven by concerns for potential negative economic impacts arising from reductions in greenhouse gas emissions. As a result, Canada has sought means to reduce emissions at the lowest economic cost to domestic stakeholders.

Adopting a foreign policy perspective and focusing on the events in the late 1990s has its limitations, for example, the difficulty of capturing the essence of the evolution of our climate change policy. Canada was a leader in the early stages of this issue, but as the issue evolved, so, too, did Canada's position. We moved away from rhetorical leadership to the position of a faithful member in a coalition committed to ensuring 'the most cost-effective implementation possible'[2] of the Kyoto Protocol. The forces that shape our policy now are unlikely to change dramatically in the near future and, thus, one should not expect Canada to break from this coalition.

A second limitation of the foreign policy point of view is that the domestic part of the equation is not given full treatment. This is not to suggest that domestic influences are ignored. As will be seen, in order to understand Canada's international behaviour at least three sets of explanatory variables must be considered: the influence of science, variables external to Canada such as the position of the United States and the ideology of globalization, and domestic determinants such as the provinces and industry. The categorization of these variables simplifies a very complicated reality, but this approach provides us with some insights into the interplay of forces that shape Canadian climate change policy.

Canada and Climate Change

The emergence of climate change on the international political agenda dates back to 1988 when a series of ministerial and non-ministerial meetings preceded the beginning of the negotiations on the Framework Convention on Climate Change (FCCC). Negotiations on the FCCC began in January 1991. As I have argued elsewhere,[3] the difficult FCCC negotiations were characterized by divisions between the United States and the European Union, the developed and developing states, and among developing states themselves. During this time, Canada played the role of mediator, attempting to bridge the gap between the Bush administration and the European Union (EU). These divisions continue to this day and are considered below in the discussion of the Kyoto negotiations.

Ultimately, the FCCC included a loosely worded commitment by countries with the 'aim of returning individually or jointly to their 1990 levels the anthropogenic emissions of carbon dioxide and other greenhouse gases not covered by the Montreal Protocol'.[4] The FCCC also recognized the common but differentiated responsibilities of states and did not demand commitments from developing states.

In 1992, Canada signed and ratified the FCCC. However, the commitment to stabilization came with the expectation of implementation. Meeting the 1992 commitment proved difficult for Canada for a variety of reasons, including an apparent lack of political will, the desire to maintain parity in position with the United States, and resistance from influential domestic forces.

The FCCC came into force in March 1994 and the first Conference of Parties was held in Berlin in March 1995. At this meeting, commitments and progress to date were reviewed. Progress was deemed inadequate, as it was clear that several states, including Canada and the United States, would not meet the 1992 commitment. As a result, states agreed to the Berlin Mandate, which committed them to the development of a legally binding protocol by the third Conference of Parties in Kyoto, Japan.

International diplomacy leading up to the third Conference of Parties (COP3) meeting in December 1997 continued to be marked by division. The European Union consistently squared off against the American-led JUSSCANNZ (Japan, United States, Canada, Australia, and New Zealand and sometimes including Norway, Iceland, and Switzerland) coalition, particularly over issues of targets and timetables. However, in 1995 the Intergovernmental Panel on Climate Change (IPCC), an intergovernmental body of scientific experts, published its Second Assessment Report, which reported that 'there is now a discernible human influence on global climate.'[5] The US administration, now under Bill Clinton, accepted the scientific evidence and, prior to Kyoto, publicly announced that it would pursue emissions reductions, thus signalling a willingness to move away from the previous US blocking position. Members of the JUSSCANNZ coalition quickly fell in step.

After tense and drawn out negotiations, the Kyoto Protocol was adopted by consensus by the meeting's delegates. It was agreed that Annex I states (typically, developed states) would reduce emissions by an average of 5.2 per cent below 1990 levels by 2008–12. This reduction would be achieved through the adoption of state-specific national limits. Therefore, the US agreed to a 7 per cent reduction and Canada to a 6 per cent reduction, while states such as Australia and Iceland were allowed to increase emissions by 8 per cent and 10 per cent, respectively.

This does not mean that the Americans, Canadians, and JUSSCANNZ coalition members were acting altruistically. Rather, JUSSCANNZ demanded that, in exchange for more stringent reduction commitments, the Kyoto Protocol must include several 'flexibility mechanisms'. Among the three such mechanisms adopted in the Protocol, the first was the establishment of an international emissions trading regime. Joint implementation, the second mechanism, 'allows any Annex I Party to transfer to, or acquire from any other such Party emission reductions units resulting from projects aimed at reducing greenhouse gas emissions at source, or enhancing anthropogenic removal by sinks.'[6] The Protocol also introduced a third flexibility mechanism, the Clean Development Mechanism (CDM), which 'allows certified emission reductions resulting from sustainable development projects in developing countries to be funded by Annex I parties.'[7] The US, as well as Canada and Australia, had demanded the inclusion of carbon sinks, primarily in the form of forests. Finally, the JUSSCANNZ coalition clashed with developing states over the need for the latter to adopt voluntary commitments. In the end, no commitments were required of developing states.

The Kyoto Protocol is a testimony to diligent negotiation, but whether or not it even comes into force is altogether another issue. Entry into force requires ratification by 'enough industrial countries to represent at least 55 per cent of industrial country emissions'.[8] The difficulty is this: the US Senate, prior to Kyoto, passed the Byrd-Hagel resolution that 'the Senate would refuse to ratify any treaty that did not contain commitments to limit greenhouse gas emissions for developing countries.'[9] The Senate action is driven by a concern for US competitiveness, as it is assumed that if the US adopts policies to reduce emissions the country's gross national product will suffer as a result of capital flight to states that do not have similarly strict regulations. From this perspective, Kyoto is seen as a recipe for creating an unfair trade advantage for less developed states. The likelihood of American ratification of the Protocol in the near future is thus limited and much depended on the outcome of the 2000 presidential election. The ultimate success of Republican George W. Bush, the son of the former President, in a hotly contested vote count has meant that this likelihood is diminished considerably.

Since the Kyoto meeting, states have met at COP4 in Buenos Aires and COP5 in Bonn. The work of these meetings has been to flesh out and more carefully define the provisions of the Protocol. The division between the US-led coalition, now called the Umbrella Group, and the EU continues. The EU has called for caps on the use of the flexibility mechanisms, whereas the Umbrella Group, driven by the fear of negative economic impacts associated with domestic reduction activities, has rejected the call for caps. The unflinching support for flexibility mechanisms by Canada, the US, and other Umbrella Group members has been viewed by other parties as a means by which the advocates can 'buy themselves out of their obligations'.[10] The Umbrella Group's stance also has been described as 'climate fraud',[11] because the use of flexibility mechanisms is seen as a way of avoiding reductions at home.

The Canadian government is committed to addressing the issue of climate change in multilateral fora. We want to be at the table. At Kyoto, functioning as a member of the American-led coalition, Canada has supported calls for voluntary commitments by developing states, pushed for flexibility mechanisms, and advocated the inclusion of carbon sinks. Since Kyoto, Canada has been party to the rejection of caps on the flexibility mechanisms and has strongly encouraged the participation of the private sector in the development and implementation of the flexibility mechanisms.

Explaining Canada's International Behaviour: The Science

The question posed here is 'how might we explain Canada's international behaviour?' In response to this question, the balance of this chapter addresses the three sets of variables identified in the introduction. The analysis begins with an assessment of the role of science, after which external and domestic variables are considered in subsequent sections.

Canadian climate change policy is informed by a general acceptance of the broad scientific consensus on climate change. It is an accepted fact that there is a natural greenhouse effect. It is also accepted that both the concentration and emission of greenhouse gases, such as carbon dioxide (CO_2) and methane, have increased and, as a result, some warming of the earth's surface has occurred. The latter phenomenon is known as the 'enhanced greenhouse effect'.

More importantly, the federal government accepts that there is a link between anthropogenic activities and climate change, and policy-makers have accepted the findings of the IPCC that human activities have a discernible impact on climate. In the words of Environment Minister David Anderson, 'there can be no doubt that human activity has had a profound effect on the impact of the global ecosphere, and that we are stretching the earth's carrying capacity.'[12] Anderson has also stated: 'The trends in global temperature are unmistakable. The 1990s saw the warmest surface temperatures since accurate measurement began around 1860, and climatologists estimate that they are warmer than any time in the past 1200 years.'[13]

The acceptance of climate change as a human-induced problem is important because, if one chose to argue that the science is inaccurate, then the definition of the problem, indeed the very assumption that there is a problem, is under challenge. One's definition of the problem as legitimate or illegitimate directly translates into policy prescriptions; if there is 'no problem', then all of the actions taken to date to address climate change would be seen as irrelevant, hasty, or ill-conceived. There are those who make this argument in the Canadian context. The Fraser Institute, for example, while accepting that some warming has occurred and that human use of fossil fuels has caused an increase in atmospheric CO_2 levels, questions whether or not CO_2 causes warming. According to the Institute, scientific evidence suggests 'that humans are not dramatically affecting climate, and that the minor changes that are occurring are benign or may even be beneficial'.[14] If one followed the logic of the Fraser Institute, this might justify continued unabated emissions, which is problematic.

In any case, concern for the projected impacts of climate change does seem to inform Canadian behaviour. According to a 1991 study, some of the potential environmental impacts specifically related to Canada[15] include northern crop and forest ecosystem shifts, the increased potential for drought causing economic loss in the agriculture sector, and possible impacts on freshwater fisheries. More recently, the Canada Country Study, an enormous undertaking that considered the social, biological, and economic impacts of climate change, noted that climate change could extend the summer outdoor recreation season while shortening the winter recreation season. Projected changes could 'generally enhance thermal regimes for commercial agriculture'.[16] In terms of human health, projected indirect impacts include the return of malaria to southern Canada and the area in which populations are susceptible to dengue and yellow fever may extend northward into Canada.[17]

The federal government appears to accept such impact assessments. In the view of David Anderson, 'the effects of this human induced temperature increase threaten the entire ecosystem. Polar ice caps and glaciers are already rapidly melting, increasing global sea levels.'[18] Recent budgetary commitments of $60 million to fund the Canadian Foundation for Climate and Atmospheric Sciences for the advancement of climate science also indicate a government commitment to strengthening Canada's capacity to address the issue of climate change.[19]

While the scientific argument that climate change is caused by human activity has been accepted by the Canadian government, it appears that the government is not willing to accept scientific calls for significant reductions in greenhouse gas emissions. As early as 1990, scientists called for dramatic reductions. The Scientific Declaration of the 1990 Second World Climate Conference, for example, stated that 'in order to stabilize carbon dioxide emissions by the middle of the 21st century at about 50 per cent of the pre-industrial concentrations, a continuous world-wide reduction of net carbon dioxide emissions by 1 or 2 [per cent] per year starting now would be required.'[20] Anderson has stated that 'science tells us that if we, as humans, are to prevent dangerous interference with the world's climate system, more will need to be done.'[21] Yet one must assume that the government does not accept that we have reached dangerous levels of interference, because the Canadian commitment to address climate change in no way reflects the emission requirements advocated by the international scientific community.

Science is important to our understanding of Canadian behaviour because, at the very least, the knowledge that the scientific community shares with politicians has helped to define the nature of this issue area. The federal government has accepted this definition and has acted in the recognition that climate change has the potential to affect all Canadians. Policy decisions, however, are ultimately the product of political choices. 'Although science may provide a major input into environmental decision-making, it does not itself determine the decision.'[22] That the federal government has not acted to reduce emissions dramatically is suggestive of the influence of competing visions on the implications of climate change. Rather than constructing the issue as environmentally dangerous, danger is being defined in economic terms.

Explaining Canada's Behaviour: The International Dimension

A general acceptance of the science explains why Canada is active in international climate change negotiations, but this does not explain Canada's coalition membership, its predilection for market mechanisms, or its advocacy on behalf of voluntary commitments for developing states. International variables, working in conjunction with domestic determinants, offer insight into this policy position. First, the position of the United States on the climate change issue is integral to Canadian policy development. Second, the structure of the international political economy and, in particular, the liberal economic emphasis on economic growth and competitiveness, elsewhere called the ideology of globalization, is fundamental to understanding Canadian behaviour.

As Macdonald and Smith argue, the position of the United States on this issue is of vital importance and has significantly influenced the Canadian position.[23] A recent intergovernmental document describing the international context of the climate change issue supports this claim: 'Careful consideration of the approaches and likely actions of our major trading partners is essential to ensure that our domestic industries are not negatively impacted, and in fact benefit from new opportunities within a carbon-constrained world.'[24] Concerns for competitiveness vis-à-vis the United States explain to a great extent Canada's commitment to the JUSSCANNZ coalition.

The influence of the United States not only conditions Canada's coalition membership, it could also determine whether or not Canada ratifies the Kyoto Protocol. Kyoto could come into force without the US, but as Christopher Flavin notes, 'due to concerns over competitiveness as well as fairness, neither the Europeans nor the Japanese wish to move forward without an agreement that includes the world's largest greenhouse gas emitter.'[25] Canada is not likely to ratify the Protocol without US participation because of Canadian concerns about competitiveness.

Canada's advocacy on behalf of voluntary commitments for developing states is also situated in the globalization discourse and is related to concerns about competitiveness. At the heart of the North-South division are issues relating to:

> the attribution of responsibility or the burden-sharing arrangement adopted by Parties in reducing emissions. . . . This has traditionally been the most divisive of all issues within the Convention, pitting developing countries (who advocate a formula based on historical contributions to atmospheric CO_2 or per capita emissions) against developed countries concerned with carbon leakage, international competitiveness and general economic well being.[26]

Canada and other members of the JUSSCANNZ coalition are committed to finding the most cost-effective means of reducing greenhouse gas emissions. The concerns for competitiveness rest on the fact that, to meet the 6 per cent reduction agreed to at Kyoto, the overall emissions reductions for Canada alone amount to approximately 25 per cent below the 'business-as-usual' projected levels of 2010.[27] For an energy-intensive country such as Canada, this is a staggering requirement. Projections for economic impacts are discussed further in the next section.

Concerns for domestic economic impacts, coupled with the perceived inequity of the international commitments for emission reductions, explain both Canada's advocacy of voluntary commitments and its demands for the inclusion of flexibility mechanisms in the Kyoto Protocol. Critical for Canada, both at Kyoto and in subsequent Conference of Parties meetings, has been 'getting the right deal'. The right deal, in the words of the Environment Minister, is one that 'ensure[s] a level playing field with our trading partners and competitors' and 'help[s] maximize economic and trade opportunities for Canadian businesses'.[28] The right deal has to include mechanisms that provide opportunities for offsetting the need to reduce emissions domestically. The flexibility mechanisms provide those opportunities and, in spite of intentions to reduce emissions at home, Canada's rejection of caps on the percentage of allowable reductions through flexibility mechanisms suggests that these mechanisms would provide for most of the reductions.

Explaining Canada's International Behaviour: The Domestic Determinants

It is difficult to dissociate international from national variables because they are intertwined. That said, three significant domestic factors affecting the development and implementation of Canadian climate change policy can be identified, including the economic discourse informing Canadian foreign policy, the provinces, and industry.

The domestic processes, it should be noted, are much richer and more detailed than is outlined here. The stakeholders are numerous, and besides industry itself include federal government departments such as the Department of Foreign

Affairs and International Trade (DFAIT), Natural Resources Canada, the Department of Finance, and Industry Canada. Furthermore, environmental non-governmental organizations such as the Pembina Institute and Friends of the Earth Canada play important watchdog roles. Finally, the Canadian public could play a vital role in the resolution of this issue. However, a detailed treatment of all these stakeholders is beyond the scope of this chapter.

Canadian climate change policy is consistent with the foreign policy priorities identified by the federal government in its 1995 statement, *Canada in the World*. One of the key priorities identified at that time was the 'promotion of prosperity and employment'.[29] In practice, this has translated into an orientation towards economically efficient and effective foreign policy. It should come as no surprise, then, that Canadian climate change policy is designed and presented in a manner consistent with this orientation. While a concern for the environment is present, economic growth and international competitiveness are the prime motivators.

The concern for potential negative economic impacts and the desire to find low-cost options are influenced by predictions of economic impacts. Canada has been able to achieve some reductions, thus lowering the projected gap between commitments and emissions, but there is a long way to go to meet the Kyoto commitment.[30] The Canada Country Study offers us a fair assessment of the debate surrounding costs. The study recognizes that many incalculable costs are related to unanticipated impacts, the costs of adaptation, and costs of catastrophic events. The 'best-guess cost estimate' provided in the study suggests that 'the impact of climate change on Canada could be $8–$16 billion annually, based on a 1995 Canadian GDP of $776 billion.'[31] While very carefully phrased, these potential economic costs clash with expectations of continued economic growth.

Yet, the emphasis on economic growth and competitiveness is not simply a reflection of a government philosophy that reinforces and legitimates the ideology of globalization; it is also a reflection of the influence of the provinces. The provinces have, and will continue to have, an enormous role in the development and particularly the implementation of climate change policy. The power of the provinces derives from their constitutional jurisdiction over natural resources and the recognition that the federal government, while it can negotiate international accords with limited provincial input, is constrained in its ability to implement international conventions that affect provincial jurisdiction.[32] Recognizing the fundamental importance of the provinces in the implementation of climate change strategies, the federal government and provincial governments came together after the United Nations Conference on Environment and Development to form the Joint Ministers of Energy and Environment (JMM). This has become the 'principal intergovernmental decision-making forum on climate change'.[33] The JMM is supported by the National Air Issues Steering Committee and National Air Issues Co-ordinating Committee on Climate Change (NAICC-CC).[34] It is through these bodies that the 1995 National Action Program was developed.

The National Action Program outlined a variety of strategies for addressing climate change in the Canadian context. The emphasis was on voluntary, cost-effective strategies. Consistent with the theme noted above, the National Action Program emphasized actions that 'are cost-effective, enhance opportunities at home and maintain or improve Canada's competitiveness abroad.'[35] Thus, the Program supported voluntary initiatives, such as Canada's Climate Change Voluntary Challenge and Registry Program for industry, and advocated for mechanisms such as joint implementation as a means of offsetting domestic emissions requirements.

Prior to Kyoto, the federal, provincial, and territorial energy and environment ministers agreed to Canada's positions for Kyoto. Ministers 'agreed that it is reasonable to seek to reduce aggregate greenhouse gas emissions in Canada back to 1990 levels by approximately 2010.'[36] That the federal government broke with this agreement prior to Kyoto is suggestive of the importance placed by the federal government on its international credibility in this area. It is also suggestive of the power of the dynamics in the negotiations themselves. What is important here is that there is a confluence between the JMM statement and the general positions of the federal government. For example, the same press release stated that 'Limiting our emissions must be done in ways that carefully consider our international competitiveness, trade balance and regional economies.'[37] The ministers also emphasized 'the importance of flexibility elements in the agreement, the advance of science and technology, and the appropriate involvement of developing countries'.[38] The importance of being consistent with trading partners was also highlighted. Finally, and reflecting the provincial concerns about the distribution of economic impacts, Ty Lund, the Alberta Minister of Environment at that time, was quoted as saying: 'Together, we will address our international commitments in such a way that no region or sector is asked to bear an unreasonable share of the burden.'[39]

The parallels between the federal position internationally and the federal-provincial statements are striking, and suggest a recognition of the need to include the provinces as full partners in the national process. While the federal government did break from the agreed reductions commitment, this must be seen as related to demands for the inclusion of flexibility mechanisms in the Kyoto Protocol. The provinces were enraged with the federal unilateralism but were soon placated with the agreement at a December 1997 First Ministers' meeting to engage in a process of reviewing the full implications of the Kyoto Protocol prior to Canadian ratification. This process began in 1998 and is ongoing.

The influence of the provinces must not be underestimated. Their demands for full participation in the Kyoto implementation process have been met and they will play a vital role in the future direction of this policy issue. Their power comes from their constitutional prerogative and their desire for flexibility mechanisms. Canada's demand for developing countries' participation is informed by provincially specific concerns about competitiveness and economic growth.

Finally, we turn to industry, particularly the oil, gas, and coal industries that have been included in the development of government policy. Industry is divided on the issue of climate change. The Coal Association of Canada, prior to Kyoto, rejected a stabilization commitment as 'impossibility compounded'.[40] Even when addressed in light of a stabilization commitment and not reductions such as those agreed to in Kyoto, the Coal Association predicted that 'the loss of one coal mining job will lead to the loss of 7 or 8 associated jobs.'[41] Concerns for negative impacts on employment, investment, and the economy arising out of the Kyoto agreement are echoed by Imperial Oil president Bob Peterson, who has stated that 'meeting the Kyoto targets means that as Canadians we have effectively agreed to limit the size of our economy.'[42]

While the concerns noted above have struck a chord with policy-makers, some companies, such as Suncor and TransAlta, have been actively engaged in the process and are strong proponents of emissions trading, joint implementation, and the CDM. Suncor has increased investments in alternative and renewable energy projects and has committed to stabilizing its net emissions to 1990 levels.[43] For its part, TransAlta Utilities has stated that 'using the Protocol's flexibility mechanisms and a combination of grandfathering and new technology, TransAlta can achieve zero net emissions of greenhouse gas from our Canadian operations by 2024.'[44] The key for TransAlta is the existence of international offsets; otherwise the predictions for emission reductions change dramatically.

The influence of industry can be seen in the federal government's insistence on the inclusion of flexibility mechanisms in the Kyoto Protocol and its advocacy on behalf of participation by the private sector in any actions taken. Industries such as TransAlta and Suncor have framed climate change as an opportunity for economic gain rather than loss. However, the key lies in the provisions of the Protocol. The flexibility mechanisms must be attractive to industry, because otherwise one could expect the federal government to incur the full wrath of oil and gas interests.

The primary domestic determinants of Canadian climate change policy, then, are the government's emphasis on economic competitiveness and growth, provincial governments, and industry. While the dynamics at the domestic level are undoubtedly more complex than is depicted here, this portrait suggests a convergence of interests, at least at the level of discourse.

Conclusion

The argument that Canada is committed to addressing the issue of climate change in a multilateral, cost-effective manner is reasonably straightforward. What is less straightforward is what lies behind this argument. One might argue that Canada's behaviour is realistic and rational, given the implications of climate change, i.e., 'we must protect Canadian industry and Canadian jobs.' The approach thus far has been to avoid putting Canada's economic well-being in jeopardy, while trying to find the best means of addressing the global issue of climate change. For Canadian policy-makers, the environmental impacts are a long way off, if indeed they do occur, but the potential economic impacts are of immediate concern. This argument has its merits, though it is not the position taken here.

Without a doubt, many committed individuals within the Canadian government have dedicated long hours, in an era of limited resources, to tackling this issue. Yet, the reality is that 'the environment' is a marginalized policy area. The government recognizes the potential environmental implications of the issue and has committed some resources to the advancement of science and public education, and it also has supported the efforts of Canada's negotiators. This is to be applauded. But climate change is a global issue, with global implications. The Manitoba flood and central Canadian ice storms of recent years show us that we are not immune to the forces of nature. Governments around the world, including the Canadian government, seem to be playing a 'wait-and-see' game with the environment; they prefer to wait and see if predicted environmental impacts become reality and they appear content to focus on short-term economic concerns. In the meantime, Canadian industry will seek offsets and Canadian citizens will continue to live a 'business-as-usual' lifestyle. If the impacts do become a reality, decisive action will need to be taken to protect Canada and its citizens. One must wonder whether or not it will then be too late.

Notes

1 Christopher Flavin, 'Last Tango in Buenos Aires', *World Watch* (Nov./Dec. 1988): 17.

2 Federal/Provincial/Territorial Ministers of Energy and Environment, *National Implementation Strategy on Climate Change*, International Context, Feb. 2000, 24.

3 Heather A. Smith, 'Canadian Federalism and International Environmental Policy Making: The Case of Climate Change', *Working Paper 5* (Kingston: Queen's University Institute of Intergovernmental Relations, 1998).

4 United Nations, General Assembly, Framework Convention on Climate Change, (A/AC.237/18 (Part II)/Add.1, 15 May 1992), 8.

5 World Meterological Organization. 'Statement on the Occasion of the Second Conference of Parties of the UN Framework Convention on Climate Change' by G.O.P. Obassi, Secretary-General of the WMO, 1: http://www.wmo.ch/web/Press/sgspeech.html

6 Federal/Provincial/Territorial Ministers of Energy and Environment, *National Implementation Strategy on Climate Change*, 16.

7 Ibid.

8 Flavin, 'Last Tango', 16.

9 Hermann E. Ott, 'The Kyoto Protocol to the UN Framework Convention on Climate Change—Finished and Unfinished Business', Wuppertal Institute, Feb. 1998, 2: http://www.wuppertalinst.org/WI/Projects_e/Kyoto/Kyoto_Protokoll.html

10 Herman E. Ott, 'Emissions Trading in the Kyoto Protocol—Finished and Unfinished Business', */linkages/journal/* 3, 4 (26 Oct. 1998): 1.

11 'China Rejects Poor Countries Joining Climate Fight', *Planet Ark*: http://www.planetark.org/dailynews...m?newsid = 2441&newsdate = 04-Nov-1998

12 Environment Canada, 'The Environmental Challenge in the 21st Century', Speaking Notes for the Hon. David Anderson, Minister of Environment, at the Globe 2000 Opening Plenary, Vancouver, 22 Mar. 2000, 3.

13 Ibid.

14 Laura Jones, 'The Top Three Problems with Signing a Treaty to Reduce Greenhouse Gas Emissions', Vancouver: Fraser Institute, 1: http://www.fraserinstitute.ca/publ...rum/1997/november/cover_story.html

15 Canadian Climate Change Board, 'Climate Change and Climate Impacts: The Scientific Perspective', *Climate Change Digest* (Ottawa: Minister of Supply and Services Canada, 1991), 18–20.

16 Environment Canada, *The Canada Country Study: National Summary for Policy Makers*, 14: http://www.ec.gc.ca/climate/ccs/policysummary_e.htm

17 Ibid., 24.

18 Environment Canada, 'The Environmental Challenge in the 21st Century', 3.

19 Government of Canada, 'Budget 2000: Enhancing Climate and Atmospheric Research', 1: http://www.ec.gc.ca/budget/cc3_e.htm

20 Statement of the Scientific and Technical Sessions, *Environmental Policy and Law* 20, 6 (1990): 222.

21 Environment Canada, Speaking Notes for the Hon. David Anderson, Minister of the Environment, to the Ministerial Forum on the Kyoto Mechanisms, 8 Oct. 1999, 2.

22 Lynton Keith Caldwell, *Between Two Worlds: Science, the Environmental Movement, and Policy Choice* (Cambridge: Cambridge University Press, 1992), 13.

23 See Douglas Macdonald and Heather Smith, 'Promises Made, Promises Broken: Questioning Canada's Commitments to Climate Change', *International Journal* 55, 1 (Winter 1999–2000): 107–24.

24 Federal/Provincial/Territorial Ministers of Energy and Environment, *National Implementation Strategy on Climate Change*, 7.

25 Flavin, 'Last Tango', 16.

26 Federal/Provincial/Territorial Ministers of Energy and Environment, *National Implementation Strategy on Climate Change*, 27.

27 Environment Canada, Speaking Notes for the Hon. David Anderson, Minister of the Environment, to the Alliance for Responsible Environmental Alternatives, 1999 National Climate Change Conference, 7 Oct. 1999, 1.

28 Environment Canada, Speaking Notes for the Hon. David Anderson, at the 3rd Annual Voluntary Challenge and Registry Awards, 2 Mar. 2000, 2.

29 Government of Canada, *Canada in the World* (Ottawa: Supply and Services Canada, 1995), 10.

30 The 1995 National Action Program on Climate Change 'projected that greenhouse gas emissions would be 13% higher in the year 2000 than in 1999. Progress is being made in lowering the projected "gap" to 8% by 2000.' See Environment Canada, *Canada's Second National Report on Climate Change: Actions to Meet Commitments Under the Framework Convention on Climate Change*, 1997, xiii.

31 Environment Canada, *The Canada Country Study: National Summary for Policy Makers*, 7.

32 For a detailed discussion of provincial jurisdiction over the environment, see Chapter 1 by Valiante. For a detailed discussion of the dynamics of federal-provincial relations, see Chapter 7 by Harrison.

33 National Climate Change Secretariat, 'Key Players', 1: http://www.nccp.ca/html/play.htm

34 For a discussion of the role of these organizations in the formation of smog policy, see Chapter 13.

35 Environment Canada, *Canada's National Action Program on Climate Change* (Ottawa: Minister of Supply and Services, 1995), 10.

36 Natural Resources Canada, News Release: 'Canada's Energy and Environment Ministers Agree to Work Together to Reduce Greenhouse Gas Emissions', news release, 12 Nov. 1997, 1: http://www.nrcan.gc.ca/css/imb/hqlib/jmme97.htm

37 Ibid.

38 Ibid.

39 Ibid.

40 Canadian Coal Association, 'Issues Relating to International Negotiations on Climate Change: Implications of Current Proposals', a brief presented to Energy Ministers' Conference, St John's, 1997, 5.

41 Canadian Coal Association, speech by Donald O. Downing, president of the Coal Association of Canada, 'International Climate Change Negotiations: The Implications for Canada's Coal Industry', 1997, 6.

42 Canadian Press, 'Defiant in the Face of Environmental Protestors Hurling Pennies, Imperial Oil President Bob Peterson Insists the Kyoto Agreement on Global Warming is Bad Science and Flawed Public Policy', 21 Apr. 2000.

43 Pr Newswire Association, 'Suncor Commits $100 Million to Alternative and Renewable Energy', 27 Jan. 2000.

44 TransAlta Utilities, *Beyond Kyoto: TransAlta's Blueprint for Sustainable Thermal Power Generation*, n.d., 1.

Chapter 16

Canada's Threatened Wildlife: Civil Society, Intergovernmental Relations, and the Art of the Possible

Robert Boardman

Wildlife species issues often appear quaint, far from the real battles over pollution or the sustainable use of natural resources. The 1916 Canada-US agreement for the protection of migratory birds has been described as 'a child of sentiment', on the grounds it originated not in economic conflict but rather in ethical discourse.[1] Yet the politics of species at risk in Canada is not only central to broader environmental agendas, it is grounded in a diversity of interests. Species survival requires the protection of habitats and it is thus part of the politics of land use. And although this is an area traditionally characterized by the programs of private conservation organizations, effective and long-term wildlife protection also requires the active participation of governments. This makes species survival a tough interjurisdictional issue, and also brings it into the terrain of ideological conflict over the role of the twenty-first-century state.

This chapter examines the evolution and political dynamics of Canada's arrangements for the protection of species at risk. It looks first at the problems of threats to wildlife, and then focuses on three closely interconnected policy arenas: the activities of non-governmental environmental organizations; processes linking Canada with North American, Arctic, and global developments; and national regime-building efforts and the politics of redefining relations among Canada's governments on questions of species at risk. Each is an important basis of wildlife politics in itself, and each is also a context for understanding the federal government's two attempts to create endangered species legislation, namely in proposals for a Canadian Endangered Species Protection Act (CESPA), which died on the order paper before the 1997 election, and for a Species at Risk Act (SARA), which suffered the same fate before the election of November 2000.

Species as Issues

The politics of species at risk in Canada has been shaped by varying mixtures of complacency, misconception, and vigorous support for and opposition to the goals of protection. There are still remnants of the images of the 'superabundance' of wildlife that characterized attitudes in the nineteenth and early twentieth centuries, despite growing evidence even then of declines in bison and other populations.[2] The place that wild species have had in identity politics and literatures, and in perceptions of national parks as Canadian icons, has reinforced the view that problems of spaces and species are not 'issues' of a conventional political kind. This both helps and hinders nature conservation groups. Some underlying problems tend to be hidden. Cities, even if they could be made environmentally clean through the control of pollution, still leave large ecological footprints that destroy or transform habitats. Apart from the politics of isolated urban green spaces, however, these costs tend not to be noticed or to generate the political activity associated with the more tangible phenomena of air and water pollution.

Issues of wild species protection are closely connected with the politics of protected areas. Wild plants and animals need habitats. As Jane Smart has noted in relation to global plant conservation, this is 'not rocket science'.[3] However, there are differing policy implications, depending on the relative emphasis placed on species or on ecological systems. A focus on areas normally includes consideration of wildlife questions. Particular species, such as large herbivores or grizzly bears, may be identified as keystones or indicators of the ecological health of areas. Policy approaches centring on species are complementary, but tend to have a differing slant. The species become the focal point, and protection of habitat the means. Further, effective wildlife protection cannot be achieved by looking only at legally protected areas such as national parks or biosphere reserves. Species do not confine themselves to designated areas, though the presence of these influences population dynamics and behaviour. Many wildlife species have ranges that include the properties of private landowners. Protected areas require both buffers and other zones marking them off from other forms of land use, and also corridors connecting them. Otherwise we risk merely 'protecting disconnected vignettes of nature in isolated national parks'.[4] Protection of ecological integrity has been a critical goal of national parks since the 1960s, but these have multiple mandates. Wildlife habitat in parks is affected by stressors such as roads, buildings, and other infrastructure. Annual visitors to Canada's national parks vary from very low, for example 0.01 per square kilometre in Ellesmere, to chronic and extreme levels in Point Pelee (28,600) and Prince Edward Island (30,232).[5]

Related issues have surfaced in debates on Ottawa's approaches to endangered species legislation since the mid-1990s. Critics from environmental organizations attacked these for paying too little attention to the habitat protection needs of species. Others, however, argued that public opinion was being misled by a confusing use of scientific terms. A species may be threatened in Canada, for example, but have stable populations in other parts of its range in the US, or it may occur in other countries. Research sponsored by the Fraser Institute maintains that the inflation of lists of threatened and endangered species by the addition of large numbers of subspecies or local populations, or of species that are at risk in Canada but not elsewhere, gives a distorted view of the magnitude of the problem.[6]

Driving the scientific arguments for protection have been two broad, interconnected rationales. Instrumental arguments set species in 'use' or sustainability contexts. Wildlife species from this perspective are beneficial or hazardous to us, and should be managed accordingly. Agriculture and forestry benefit from the existence of wild gene pools. Pharmacological research has increasingly investigated and used compounds derived from wild plants in the development of cancer and other therapies. Much of the argument for protection of species at risk, however, is grounded in notions of their intrinsic worth. Piping plovers and burrowing owls do not have constituencies of supporters because they are seen to be useful. There are practical implications of these debates in terms of government organization and the design of legislation. Wildlife issues fall variously under agencies of governments dealing with natural resources or heritage protection. There are divergent views, too, about whether the designation of species as threatened or endangered should include those in commercial use, for example, in fisheries. Ecosystems, moreover, have their own complex dynamics that include changes in species balances over time. They do not have 'a "starting point" in the past that could offer straightforward criteria for evaluating present conditions.'[7] In the recent geological past, British Columbia was covered by ice except for parts of the north of Vancouver Island and the western Queen Charlotte islands. Most of the province's endemic plant species are located in these areas.[8] Such considerations do not mean that protecting natural areas and species should be abandoned as hopelessly arbitrary, but they force complex choices on planners.

Various terms are used to describe categories of species at risk.[9] The Committee on the Status of Endangered Wildlife in Canada (COSEWIC) meets annually to review the status of selected species in these categories. Following the May 2000 meeting in Ottawa, the updated listing contained 353 species. New listings in the 'endangered' category included a population of the tailed frog in the interior of British Columbia and a spike-rush found in wetlands habitats in Nova Scotia.[10]

Human activities impacting on habitats constitute the most significant source of threats to wildlife. These vary from incremental changes in particular localities to 'the wholesale conversion of natural systems for agriculture, ranching, and urban development'.[11] Specific threat factors include chemicals and metals from industrial, agricultural, mining, or other activities. Polychlorinated biphenyls (PCBs) have been found in killer whales off Vancouver Island, mercury in loons in parts of Quebec, and DDT in some Point Pelee species. Overhunting was a significant threat to some species a century ago, for example, the sea otter of the west coast. The introduction of a species often has multiple ecological consequences. Global climate change has been identified as an increasingly important twenty-first-century factor in relation to Canadian species of amphibians, butterflies, freshwater fish, and coral, and more generally through its probable effects on vegetation.

Species Politics: Groups and Publics

Environmental groups with interests in species at risk are diverse. Two aspects are significant in terms of the politics of protection. First, many organizations operate autonomously as conservation actors with their own programs and projects.

Particularly in view of government cutbacks since the mid-1980s, these, and part-nership arrangements with government agencies, have become an increasingly important component of national frameworks of species protection and recovery. Second, although many groups remain staunchly 'non-political', some also aim to influence the legislative planning and wildlife programs of governments.

Both aspects intersect with public attitudes on species at risk. Groups rely on voluntarism. Much data collection for monitoring the status of particular species has traditionally been reliant on volunteers, as in the Ontario Christmas Bird Count from the early 1900s.[12] Public attitudes towards species issues have been influenced at different times by groups and the media and by developments in government programs. The end of the 1970s, for example, saw a significant rise in public attention to issues of threatened wildlife and in support for the projects of the World Wildlife Fund (WWF) and the Canadian Wildlife Federation (CWF).[13] During the 1960s the CBC's *The Nature of Things* focused on natural resources and the capacity of science and technology to solve problems, but in the 1980s and 1990s the emphasis shifted more to the fragility of natural ecosystems and threats to wildlife species.[14] A series of studies sponsored since the 1980s by the Canadian Wildlife Service (CWS) of Environment Canada has found continued levels of strong support for wilderness values. Related economic activities were valued at over $5 billion in 1991 and over $11 billion in 1996.[15] Polls conducted for the CWS prior to Ottawa's introduction of endangered species legislation in 1996 indicated that more than 83 per cent of Canadians attached high or moder-ate value to the protection of species at risk;[16] a Decima poll of October 1999 found that 74 per cent of respondents would support significant measures to protect threatened wildlife. However, other polls in the late 1990s also suggested that Canadians ranked health care, unemployment, and national unity signifi-cantly ahead of environmental protection.[17] And for many Canadians, wildlife and nature have been oversold. One writer has criticized the novels and poetry of the 1980s for failing to satisfy the hankering of urban youth in Toronto for real stories—about 'anything but bloody loons'.[18]

Attitudes can constrain species recovery and management programs. Volunteers are more difficult to find for projects on reptiles than on birds or love of nature may prompt the picking of threatened orchids. A landscape that includes lakes being killed by acid rain may still have aesthetic appeal that lulls the concern of those admiring it. The culling of deer populations in parks tends to be resisted by the public.[19] Bear and wolf programs require broad supportive attitudes; there is a stretch of interconnected wolf habitat covering areas of the northeastern United States, Quebec, and New Brunswick. Effective wolf recovery programs depend on at least tacit support from local communities and the satisfying of concerns about physical risks to persons, as well as acceptance of the likely consequences in terms of declines in populations of moose, deer, and caribou.[20]

The conservation activities of groups have in many cases broadened into sus-tained networks of co-operation with other organizations. Although collaborative efforts are common, relations among groups are not consistently harmonious. Hunting issues create cleavages. Ducks Unlimited has extensive wetlands conservation programs but is criticized on these grounds by some other groups. Several characteristic conservation roles can be identified.

First, non-governmental organizations (NGOs) are a source of data for species recovery programs. Systematic data collection on threatened plants began in 1973 following the establishment by the Canadian Botanical Association of a Rare and Endangered Plants Committee. Data on species are typically gathered by nature trusts prior to negotiating management or easement arrangements with landowners. Data-gathering by conservation groups is also a critical feature of endangered species recovery projects. Surveys by the Vancouver Island Marmot Recovery Foundation have indicated that as a result of threats from forestry, estimated numbers of marmots declined from 350 to 71 in the period 1990–8.[21]

Second, many organizations are directly involved in programs of habitat protection. In the mid-1990s, protected lands were owned or managed by groups such as the Nature Conservancy of Canada (32,000 km²), Wildlife Habitat Canada (15,000 km²), and the Federation of Ontario Naturalists (530 km²).[22] Nature trusts and other organizations have become increasingly significant in developing conservation relations with private landowners. In Nova Scotia, about three-quarters of land is privately owned, making agreements with landowners essential for long-term species protection goals. Landowners can make easement and other agreements with organizations such as the Nova Scotia Nature Trust. These specify restrictions on the use of the land or provide for its management by outside bodies, which then apply to future owners.[23]

Third, organizations fund species recovery and habitat protection projects by local groups. WWF-Canada has major conservation programs on endangered spaces, endangered species, wildlife toxicology, and Latin America. Wildlife Habitat Canada was set up in 1984 by federal and provincial government environmental and wildlife agencies and conservation groups, and operates as a private organization. Among other activities in the late 1990s, it funded projects on wetlands conservation (through the framework of the North American Waterfowl Management Plan), including marsh restoration in Prince Edward Island; the monitoring of burrowing owls in Alberta; and fisheries habitat (in collaboration with the federal Department of Fisheries and Oceans).[24] In 1985 it undertook the first design and sale of stamps, which hunters had to buy when applying for migratory bird permits and which were made available also for sale to the public.

Fourth, environmental groups with species interests co-operate with government agencies. Species protection in Canada has historically been characterized by such interactions, as in the growing collaboration between University of Toronto scientists and Ontario government agencies in the 1930s.[25] WWF-Canada, the Canadian Nature Federation (CNF), and the CWF traditionally have been members of COSEWIC alongside the wildlife agencies of the federal, provincial, and territorial governments. Protected area networks are associated with NGO-government connections through organizations such as the Canadian Biosphere Reserves Association (CBRA), the Canadian Parks and Wilderness Society (CPAWS), and the Canadian Council on Ecological Areas (CCEA), which among other activities promotes scientific work on the classifying and documenting of North America's ecological regions.[26]

Through projects and in the discourses of conferences, newsletters, and Web sites, group conservation activities often are interwoven with debate on government policies and programs. Attempts to influence governments, directly or indirectly through education, are an integral part of the tasks of many groups. Compared with their US counterparts, though, Canadian organizations historically have been limited in terms of funding, memberships, and access to legislatures, the courts, executives, and environmental bureaucracies.[27]

The requirements for species and habitat protection implicate a wide range of jurisdictions. Yet like all politics, conservation politics is local politics. Much group activity has focused on problems of particular species and sites, or on specific economic projects and government policies. The CNF has had an active interest over several decades in plover habitat in the Maritimes. In the late 1990s, groups in Alberta intensified earlier criticisms of the provincial government's plans for protected areas, specifically on the grounds that the habitat of grizzly bears, wolverines, and other species of the Foothills were being overlooked because of the area's rich natural gas and timber resources.[28] Arguments about the habitat needs of species have been central to a number of zoning and planning issues in southern Ontario, for example over the Red Hill valley in Hamilton and the Oak Ridges moraine north of Toronto. The trans-jurisdictional logic of species and habitat protection takes some groups into Canada-US issues. The CPAWS and other groups have proposed the creation of a large protected region linking the Algonquin Park region of Ontario with the Adirondacks in New York. Appeals to the global or national ecological importance of sites are significant in some cases, as in the successful campaign by conservation groups in 1999 that led Amoco to drop consideration of a pipeline through a significant aspen ecosystem in Rumsey, Alberta.

Conservation groups have developed similar critiques of the federal government's endangered species legislation proposals, for a Canadian Endangered Species Protection Act (CESPA) in 1996-7, and a Species at Risk Act (SARA) in 2000. Effective habitat protection and recognition of the central role of scientific bodies in the determination of the threat status of wildlife species were identified as key requirements of legislation. Ottawa's frameworks were widely criticized for failing to recognize core ecological principles. Thus, while CESPA contained provisions against the taking of species, conservation groups maintained that this overly literal interpretation of 'protection' was of little value without a commitment to sustained measures to protect habitat.[29] The argument was developed forcefully in a letter on SARA planning signed by 631 scientists and sent to Prime Minister Chrétien in February 1999: 'without nationwide, comprehensive habitat conservation—an essential part of species protection—the endangered species bill will be meaningless.'[30] As David Coon of the Conservation Council of New Brunswick put it in relation to SARA in the spring of 2000, 'It's not the killing of endangered species by companies or people that's the important issue here, it's the habitat.'[31] Critics who acknowledged Ottawa's limited room for legislative manoeuvre objected to its failure in the 2000 bill to provide even for strong protection of species at risk on lands clearly under federal jurisdiction or to extend protective measures by way of Ottawa's powers in relation to fisheries and migratory or transboundary species.

The position of COSEWIC was for these reasons a central issue in debates on the two federal bills. For many environmental groups, ecological legitimacy demanded two things: that COSEWIC should be able to make open scientific decisions, untarnished by political, economic, or other considerations; and that the designation of a species in one of the COSEWIC categories of risk would then automatically set in motion agreed measures of protection. Alternative models (diluting the voice of environmental organizations or scientific experts in the COSEWIC structure, giving ministers or cabinets final listing power, or vesting governments with significant discretionary powers in relation to species recovery programs) have been strenuously resisted by groups.

The federal government's preparations on endangered species legislation provided multiple opportunities for groups to inject such arguments into the policy process. These included the 14 public consultation workshops held across Canada in 1995 on national endangered species protection requirements, the hearings on CESPA in 1996 of the House of Commons Standing Committee on the Environment, and the intensive consultations launched after the 1997 federal election by Environment Canada in its efforts to craft a restructured bill. A key feature of group politics was the setting up of the Canadian Endangered Species Coalition (CESC) in 1994 by six leading conservation organizations, as Wilson points out in Chapter 3.[32] In the 1995 consultations, representatives of environmental groups stressed the need for strong federal legislation, complementary measures by the provinces, independent scientific decision-making in designations of species, and incentives for landowners to protect habitat.[33] Presentations to the Commons environment committee led to several amendments, for example, on the independence of individual COSEWIC members and on a requirement for the Environment Minister to order emergency protection of a species within 60 days of its designation as endangered or threatened.[34]

It has been clear since 1995 that federal endangered species protection is not a minor issue of interest only to birders and conservation groups. Diverse industrial, agricultural, forestry, and resource sectors have been affected and have a stake in any protection or recovery measures regulating land use.[35] A central issue is the economic costs of protecting species, particularly the question of financial compensation for landowners, whether families or large companies, who might be subjected to species-protection projects as a result of government decisions. A representative of the New Brunswick Federation of Woodlot Owners said in 2000 in response to SARA: 'Today you are operating your woodlot and tomorrow you are told you must reduce or stop cutting. That's money out of a family's yearly income.'[36] Some critics, particularly those fearful of a spread to Canada of endangered species legislation of the US kind, broadened the attack on federal plans into a defence of property rights.[37]

However, to characterize debates as a polarization between economic interests and species-protection claims is simplistic. The spectrum of arguments from representatives of industrial, resource, agricultural, and other sectors has made for significant overlap and has provided the possibility of cross-fertilization with environmentalist viewpoints. Economic self-interest has persuaded some companies of the utility of having at least minimally intrusive endangered species legislation in place at both federal and provincial levels. The importance of exports to the Canadian forest products and mining sectors has highlighted their vulnerability to European NGO campaigns restricting access to overseas markets, a power already demonstrated in the 1980s and 1990s in relation to seal hunting and animal trapping.[38]

The failure of CESPA on the order paper in 1997 led to exchanges among a variety of groups in the Species at Risk Working Group (SARWG). This was set up following workshops of farmers and environmentalists later that year initiated by the National Agriculture Environment Committee.[39] The aim was to explore, in an informal setting, possible frameworks for species-at-risk protection that would be broadly acceptable to multiple stakeholders. There was agreement on the need for incentives to landowners to engage in species protection, for compensation where protective measures required land-use restrictions, for effective habitat protection, and in general for what was later called the 'spongy stick' strategy of accommodation, negotiation, and partnership among diverse groups. Proposals circulated in 1998 called for co-operative partnerships, recognition of the rights of landowners and resource users, species listings by an independent scientific body, government funding for research, recovery programs and compensation, and changes to tax laws to create positive incentives to landowners to protect species on their properties.[40]

Transnational Connections

Species at risk in Canada are affected in several ways by transnational factors. First, many species and their habitats straddle the boundaries of the Canadian state. Many plants at risk have parts of their ranges in the US and reach their northern limits in southern Canada. All bird species on the COSEWIC threatened and endangered lists occur also in the US, as do about 70 per cent of animals and plants. Some species, such as the leatherback turtle, travel among several countries. Around three-quarters of Canadian bird species are migratory. In addition to those with bilateral routes, many species migrate among Canada, the US, and Mexico, including over 280 birds, 17 fish, eight whales, and four sea turtles.[41]

Among the more famous long-distance travellers are the monarch butterfly, the eastern population of which migrates between sites in Canada and Mexico and is threatened by agricultural chemicals and loss of critical milkweed habitat on its routes; and the semipalmated sandpiper, which migrates from nesting sites in northern Canada to winter in South America by way of the Minas Basin in Nova Scotia. Whooping cranes in Wood Buffalo National Park are vulnerable to factors such as extreme weather conditions and habitat threats and oil spills en route to and in their wintering grounds in Texas. The protection of species at risk in Canada thus requires international agreements, and this requirement has repercussions on Canadian developments.

Second, some of these species face problems as a result of the illegal and lucrative international trade in wildlife. Trade in black bear parts, particularly since the late 1980s, reflects traditional practices in some Asian cultures, such as medical use of the gall bladder for treatment of fevers and skin lesions and consumption of paw meat as a health food.[42] The illegal trade in peregrine falcons prompted a major investigation by Canadian and US enforcement agencies in the early 1980s. Another operation in 1999–2000 focused on the import and sale in Ontario of internationally protected tropical birds. Operation Duckfoot, a two-year undercover operation in the late 1990s into the illegal big-game trade in Alberta, led to a series of prosecutions under the province's wildlife legislation.[43] In testimony to the House of Commons Heritage Committee in 2000 on Ottawa's new parks bill, the Public Service Alliance of Canada called for the arming of wardens in parks.[44]

Third, many environmental NGOs define their identities partly as Canadian and partly as continental or global. Some leading organizations have transborder origins. The CNF started out in the 1930s as an extension of the US-based Audubon Society. WWF-Canada was formed in 1967 as the national chapter of the international WWF network, which was set up a few years earlier in part as a funding mechanism for the Switzerland-based International Union for the Conservation of Nature (IUCN). Since the late 1970s the Canadian Committee for IUCN has linked conservation groups with significant international interests. The global dimensions of wildlife protection issues are important for many. There was growing interest in the 1980s and 1990s in the international ivory trade, whaling, game-ranching, and other issues focused on in the biannual Conferences of the Parties of the Convention on International Trade in Endangered Species (CITES). Environmental groups have been highly critical of the equivocal positions of the official Canadian delegations on the issues of Japanese and Norwegian whaling. Canadian organizations and their NGO counterparts in other countries have become increasingly important in international governance arrangements on wildlife species, for example in the gathering and publicizing of data on countries' compliance with international agreements.[45]

Fourth, the federal government is actively engaged in a large number of international agreements on species.[46] Definitions of wildlife issues and objectives thus extend beyond Canada's borders. International agreements also form a key element in Ottawa's delicate balancing act among the provinces on species-at-risk issues, since the Canadian constitution defines international relations and trade as federal responsibilities. This expanding network of international arrangements in turn affects Canadian programs and wildlife politics. Canada's ratification of the Convention on Biological Diversity (CBD), a product of the 1992 Rio Summit, arguably carried with it an obligation to follow through with a federal endangered species law (though another, short-lived, interpretation was that the terms of the CBD could be satisfied through the creation of a 'national' framework that might not entail additional federal legislation). International calls for action are often publicized by groups. Some are taken up by Ottawa as part of its rationale for strengthening the national regime and the federal government's role in this. These have included the World Conservation Strategy of 1980 (and its revised form in 1991), the World Charter for Nature (1982), and the report of the Brundtland Commission (1987). The international 'presence' in Canada's conservation community also influences conservation politics more indirectly, as in the push that the Montreal meetings of the IUCN World Conservation Congress in 1996 gave to endangered species debates.

Canada is part of two large regions of shared species and multiple jurisdictions. Participation in continental arrangements originated in the 1916 Canada-US Migratory Birds convention. The agreement, and the implementing of the Migratory Birds Convention Act, survived early criticisms from British Columbia and Nova Scotia and a constitutional challenge by Prince Edward Island.[47] It became the basis for a growing network of Canada-US protection measures and migratory bird sanctuaries, particularly through the North American Waterfowl Management Plan. A protocol signed in 1995 reaffirmed the importance of protecting habitat in both countries, and a framework agreement of 1997 on co-operation among governments (state and provincial as well as federal) provided for the development of lists of target species.[48] Since 1980 the Canadian Wildlife Service has given increasing attention to Mexico in light of the routes of many migratory species.[49]

Canada is also a partner in multi-state arrangements for species in the Arctic. Ottawa has signed over 30 international agreements dealing with various aspects of environmental protection in the region.[50] Co-operation with other Arctic countries grew on an ad hoc basis in the 1950s and 1960s, culminating in the international polar bear agreement of 1973. For species protection programs, Canada currently co-operates with other Arctic nations in the Program for the Conservation of Arctic Flora and Fauna (CAFF), the first meeting of which was held in Ottawa in 1992. Particular areas of concentration have included conservation work on murres and eiders, problems in the expansion of protected area networks in the Arctic, and rare vascular plants.[51] Even so, for many species the Arctic is not an adequate ecological framework; 279 of the 360 bird species that breed in the Arctic migrate to spend winters in non-Arctic countries.[52]

In addition to North American and Arctic arrangements on species protection, Canada has also traditionally been a leader in global activities aimed at species and ecosystem protection. Particularly important are the networks of protected areas based on international agreements for protecting wetlands (the Ramsar Convention) and for establishing biosphere reserves. In 1999, Canada had 36 and six sites respectively designated under these agreements, with a total protected area of over 130,510 km².[53] There are also six World Heritage natural sites in Canada. These areas typically overlap with other designations. For example, existing national parks are the basis for the Waterton biosphere reserve in Alberta, and the Niagara Escarpment biosphere reserve is based on a combination of a national park, private land, provincial lands, and a marine conservation area.[54]

Canada ratified CITES in 1975. Its appendices, the main focus of meetings of the parties, define various degrees of restrictions on international trade in species and their parts. While global issues related to developing countries tend to predominate, Canada is involved because of its listed species (including the leatherback turtle and burrowing owl), debates in the non-governmental conservation community about its stand on international questions such as whaling, and the growth of the illegal wildlife trade. This trade has produced allegations that Canada is used for international 'laundering' operations. Difficult enforcement problems arise in Canada as in other countries over 'look-alike' items, for example, gall bladders from different bear species. This was a key factor leading to the Canadian (and US) listing of the American black bear on Appendix II of CITES at the 1992 Conference of the Parties.[55] However, Canada, along with the US and Mexico, did not join the Bonn Convention of 1979 on the protection of migratory species. This is partly because it is argued to duplicate existing North American arrangements, partly because of criticism of the inclusion of various fish species.

Governments and the National Framework

Much of the controversy surrounding endangered species issues from the mid-1990s revolved around Ottawa's legislative plans. However, the federal role is only one part of the protracted evolution of a national framework for species protection. It was not until 1996 that a more comprehensive agreement was reached, which, among other things, incorporated consensus on the federal government's place in the overall regime.

The provinces' constitutional authority in areas of natural resources has made them in many ways the primary actors on wildlife issues generally and, though less consistently, on endangered species questions specifically. Ontario had waterfowl hunting regulations in place in the early 1870s. The existence of a patchwork of differing provincial regulations presented initial problems for the implementation of the 1916 Canada-US Migratory Birds Convention. Measures by provincial governments to protect threatened spaces gathered momentum from the early 1990s, for example, in the major extension of protected-area planning in north-central British Columbia in late 2000. These developments were responses to several factors, including pressures from local conservation organizations, rising public interest, and federal-provincial agreement in 1990 on the outlines of a national wildlife policy. Even so, legislative provisions varied. Nova Scotia's endangered species law of 1998 comprised important conservation features, such as acknowledgement of the role of COSEWIC, and compensation for landowners. By the end of the decade a number of provinces had enacted endangered species legislation (see VanNijnatten, Chapter 8). Planning for provincial legislation and programs on endangered species and protected areas often has involved broad-ranging consultative processes, as in Alberta in 2000 following the inclusion of protected-area provisions in that province's Natural Heritage Act introduced the previous year.[56] The place of protected areas in Ontario's Lands for Life program in the late 1990s was likewise controversial. Conservation groups, including CPAWS, WWF-Canada, and the Federation of Ontario Naturalists, successfully campaigned for expanded protected areas.

Provincial developments also were shaped in part by concerns about the growth and future expansion of Ottawa's role. Several governments, receptive to representations from agricultural, resource, mining, and other sectors and alert to possible threats to their capacities to run provincial economies, criticized CESPA in 1996 as a significant intrusion into provincial jurisdiction. Among specific concerns was the issue of migratory species or those with a large transborder range, which comprise a large proportion of Canada's species at risk. Provincial critics pointed out that if Ottawa secured a crucial role here (as an extension of its constitutional authority in international matters), it could potentially open the way to a federal 'takeover' of many species. More generally, the provinces objected to CESPA because, as William Amos writes, 'they felt they were being asked to accept a regime which solidified the notions of federal leadership and provincial junior partnership.'[57] The Alberta government was an early critic of SARA in 1999–2000, questioning both its constitutionality and its compatibility with the 1996 National Accord.[58] To be credible, though, such criticisms also implied a need for more effective provincial measures, and so in a sense helped indirectly to promote endangered species protection by legitimizing alternative conceptions of the national framework.

There have been long-standing criticisms by Aboriginal organizations of the principles and practices of endangered species protection measures, for example in relation to Canada's implementation of CITES. For First Nations critics, the national parks system is weak to the extent that it has failed to protect critical wildlife habitat, especially of species with ranges across park boundaries.[59] The planning of federal endangered species legislation in the 1990s and the growth of provincial measures coincided with important developments in relation to Aboriginal land claims and issues of traditional hunting, fishing, and forestry rights. Relations among actors have reflected persisting ambiguities about the constitutional status of Aboriginal organizations and their roles in environmental and resource governance. At stake are crucial questions about the scope of the regulatory authority of the federal government in relation to wildlife species.

Aboriginal organizations tended to respond to federal legislative plans in the 1990s by demanding a voice in conservation mechanisms and by seeking recognition of their management authority in relation to species. In the 1995 consultations, the Grand Council of the Cree of Quebec called for Aboriginal representation on scientific committees responsible for determining the status of wildlife species and emphasized the importance of their existing powers in relation to moose, Brant geese, and other populations.[60] Federal and provincial policy statements on wildlife since 1990 have repeatedly acknowledged the importance of integrating traditional ecological knowledge into wildlife planning. It was almost a decade, however, before a decision was made to include a person with Aboriginal ecological knowledge in the membership of COSEWIC.[61]

Conflicting interpretations of Ottawa's place in the environmental union have shaped species-at-risk politics. Ottawa's historical presence in the area has been largely a product of its constitutional authority in relation to federal lands and to Canada's international relations and trade. Other aspects, including criminal law and its position as the national government, have figured in approaches to federal endangered species policy. The Canada Wildlife Act of 1973 was a first major attempt to secure legislative recognition of the federal government's role. This provided a basis for action on species near extinction, for public education, and for initiatives such as the creation of marine protected areas. However, it failed to specify mechanisms for protecting species on federal lands or for assuring longer-term preventive or recovery strategies.[62] Crucial aspects of Ottawa's traditional species-at-risk powers arose from implementing legislation in relation to two international agreements: the Migratory Birds Convention Act, for the Canada-US Migratory Birds Convention; and the Wild Animal and Plant Protection and Regulation of International and Interprovincial Trade Act, the implementing legislation for CITES.[63] As broader debates on the structures of federalism intensified in the 1980s and 1990s, Environment Canada increasingly emphasized Canada's international responsibilities as a legitimizing basis for federal programs.

Federal government programs on species at risk, as opposed to issues of wildlife management more generally, date from 1950. CWS staff began work that year on trumpeter swans, an endangered migratory species, at Valhalla Lake, Alberta.[64] Projects followed on the whooping crane and peregrine falcon, particularly as evidence mounted of threats to birds from pesticides and, in the case of falcons, from the illegal wildlife trade. Such projects routinely involved co-operation with provincial wildlife agencies. It was apparent at least from the early 1970s, however, that the absence of an agreed national framework would continue to restrict Ottawa's role and its capacity to respond to the proliferating issues on global biodiversity agendas.[65]

The path to an effective national framework has nonetheless been painfully slow and, at the time of writing in early 2001, is still far from complete. The continued absence of federal endangered species legislation puts Canada significantly out of step with other Western countries, including those such as the US and

Australia that also have complex problems of multiple jurisdictions.[66] Politically and constitutionally, the only way for Ottawa to secure a national role for itself has been to build on a foundation of agreements with the provinces. Federal species-at-risk authority has thus depended in part on there being effective provincial laws and programs. Increasingly during the 1990s federal ministers and officials characterized Ottawa's endangered species role as 'complementary' to the efforts of the provinces and territories.

The 1970s and 1980s saw steady growth in federal activities. The Wildlife Act of 1973 was followed by work on CITES enforcement questions from 1975. There was a marked expansion of endangered species work in the CWS after 1985. The protected-area networks grew. A policy on marine areas was announced in 1986. Co-operation with the provinces also intensified. COSEWIC was founded in 1977, the Committee on the Recovery of Nationally Endangered Wildlife (RENEW) in 1988. By 1990, the federal and provincial governments had agreed on the National Wildlife Policy. Specific federal endangered species legislation, however, was not yet on the agenda. The 1990 Green Plan referred to the newly minted national wildlife policy, adding vaguely, and in deference to provincial sensitivities, that federal lands would be 'managed appropriately to meet protection and recovery needs'. Ottawa also declared its aim of producing recovery programs for all species at risk within federal jurisdiction by 1993.[67]

Several factors changed this dynamic in the early 1990s. Pressure from scientists and conservation organizations for endangered species legislation mounted. Sympathetic MPs took up the cause in association with groups, as in the private member's bill on endangered species and habitats introduced by a British Columbia MP, Robert Wenman, in 1991. A crucial development was Canada's adherence to the CBD in 1992 and subsequent work on the Canadian Biodiversity Strategy.[68] Following commitments by the Liberals in the 1993 election campaign, CESPA was eventually introduced in October 1996. Attracting almost universal condemnation from environmental groups, the provinces, Aboriginal organizations, industry and resource associations, and private landowners, the bill died on the order paper in 1997.[69] This was despite what Environment Canada saw as the key to the success of the bill, the agreement on a national framework for species at risk negotiated with the provincial governments and announced shortly before the introduction of CESPA. The Liberal government made it clear after the 1997 election that a revised bill would be drawn up. Intensive rounds of consultations were held with provincial governments, environmental organizations, and other stakeholders over the next two years.[70]

By the end of the decade, the climate of political debate surrounding species at risk was significantly different from that of the mid-1990s. Some environmental critics argued that no federal legislation was better than a rehashed version of CESPA. Some provinces and private-sector interests remained opposed to almost any form of a possible federal bill. The mounting pace of provincial legislation and programs, particularly in Ontario, British Columbia, Alberta, and Nova

Scotia, also highlighted the costs of the continued absence of a federal species-at-risk law. Public attention to the issue was reinforced in the late 1990s by renewed controversy over the ecological deterioration of Banff and other national parks.[71] Serious problems, including threats to wildlife species and a lack of adequate scientific expertise in parks management, were documented in the report of the Panel on Ecological Integrity in Canada's National Parks at the end of 1999. The federal government introduced a parks bill in March 2000 designed to provide stricter regulation of commercial developments within and near parks. There was also more institutionalized co-operation among federal departments on species and habitat issues in the late 1990s. In 1998, Environment Canada joined with Agriculture and Agri-Food Canada, Natural Resources, Fisheries and Oceans, and the Canadian Museum of Nature in the Federal Biosystematics Partnership, which was later represented on COSEWIC.

SARA, introduced in April 2000, shared some of the aims and approaches of CESPA, but with some key differences. Like its predecessor, it was set firmly in the context of the evolving post-1996 framework of federal-provincial endangered species co-operation, and its form reflected divisions of principle and approach among federal cabinet ministers. It still lacked the degree of habitat protection demanded by scientists and conservation groups, even in relation to lands and species clearly under federal jurisdiction. It also failed to make COSEWIC unequivocally the final voice on species designations and the initiation of recovery programs. Rather, the Committee was to be the source of recommendations on endangered species listings submitted by the Environment Minister to the federal cabinet. SARA was tougher than CESPA in proposing sanctions under Ottawa's criminal law powers for violators. The general principles of negotiation with landowners, and funding for compensation as well as for species research and recovery, met with qualified approval from a variety of environmental and industry groups.[72]

Steps to consolidate a national framework intensified from 1995 in parallel with the protracted CESPA-SARA process. These were a prerequisite not only for co-ordinated national policies and programs on species at risk, but also for Ottawa's own legislative prospects. Some elements—particularly COSEWIC, the annual federal-provincial/territorial wildlife conference, and meetings of the Wildlife Ministers Council of Canada (WMCC)—were already present as institutional expressions of co-operative, and occasionally combative, relations among governments. Efforts to formalize relations from the late 1970s had led initially to agreement in 1982 on a set of guidelines for wildlife policy and then to the National Wildlife Policy of 1990. Although this did not explicitly anticipate federal endangered species legislation, it in many ways set the agenda for the developments of the 1990s. It was 'a national policy, providing a framework for federal, provincial, territorial, and non-governmental policies and programs that affect wildlife'. The governments committed themselves to the completion and maintenance of a comprehensive and ecologically representative system of protected areas. Encouragement would also be given to species and habitat protection on private lands through consideration of such measures as tax credits to landowners, differential property taxes, and management agreements between landowners and conservation organizations.[73]

COSEWIC was set up in 1977 following the federal-provincial/territorial wildlife conference held in Fredericton, and made the first of its annual species designations in 1978. The membership consisted of representatives from provincial and territorial wildlife agencies, the CWS and other federal agencies, conservation organizations (CNF, CWF, and WWF-Canada), as well as the scientific experts chairing its species subcommittees. Without federal endangered species legislation, however, it had an uncertain status. It was Canada's scientific authority for designating threatened and endangered species, but it was a body whose decisions, as COSEWIC itself repeatedly emphasized to supporters and opponents alike, formally had no legal consequences.

The Committee became a contentious issue in the late 1990s. Environmental groups lobbied to strengthen its independence. Some wanted to make it more of an arm's-length creature of the federal government, as opposed to a body accommodating the views of provincial and territorial governments. Provincial and industry critics sought to dilute the powers of groups and scientific experts and to maximize governmental discretion on listings, emergency responses, and recovery programs. In March 1999, federal and provincial ministers (now meeting as the Canadian Endangered Species Conservation Council [CESCC], established as part of the 1996 deal) formulated new terms of reference for COSEWIC. These emphasized its 'independence, openness, transparency, and scientific integrity.' The basic structure was retained, of decision-making by COSEWIC based on advice from its eight subcommittees (renamed species specialist groups). Members, formally approved by CESCC, were to consist of one wildlife expert from each province and territory; representatives from federal agencies (CWS, DFO, Parks Canada, and the Canadian Museum of Nature representing the Federal Biosystematics Partnership); chairs of the subgroups; and at least three NGO members. Though the expectation was that the traditional non-governmental members (CNF, CWF, and WWF-Canada) would remain, the revised procedures called for CESCC to solicit nominations from the non-governmental conservation community.[74] As noted earlier, a decision was made the following year to include a member with traditional Aboriginal knowledge.

RENEW was founded in 1988 by Canada's wildlife agencies, with a broad federal, provincial, territorial, and non-governmental membership, to devise and oversee recovery plans for species at risk designated by COSEWIC. It steadily expanded its operations during the 1990s, particularly in light of the increased resources being devoted by the CWS to endangered species questions. By 1996–7 RENEW spending on species recovery programs totalled $3.7 million.[75]

CESPA and SARA thus fitted into these evolving federal-provincial contexts. Both were characterized by a lingering, and probably irresolvable, ambiguity about Ottawa's place in national frameworks. The negotiation by provincial wildlife agencies and the CWS of a dual agreement, on a national accord and a national framework for the protection of species at risk, endorsed by the wildlife ministers in Charlottetown in October 1996, was a prerequisite for federal legislation. CESPA was tabled in the Commons later that month. The 1996 agreement enshrined the principle of co-operation among Canada's governments. These were to pursue species and habitat protection through 'complementary federal and provincial/territorial legislation, regulations, policies, and programs'. The CESCC was created as the vehicle to achieve this, and COSEWIC was formally recognized as the scientific advisory body for these purposes.[76] SARA could thus be described in December 1999 by the federal Environment Minister, David Anderson, as an element in a three-part strategy on species at risk. The other two parts were partnerships with the provinces and territories by means of the 1996 National Accord and the promotion of stewardship by private landowners, First Nations, and others.[77] In other formulations, though, Environment Canada placed relatively more emphasis on Ottawa's retention of some aspects of the national leadership role: 'Where combined federal and provincial efforts and private stewardship efforts are not sufficient to protect species and identified critical habitat, the Government of Canada would deploy measures to ensure protection.'[78] Even so, this broader intergovernmental context stiffened Environment Canada's resistance to the kinds of changes to SARA still being sought during the spring and summer of 2000 by environmentalist critics. David Anderson insisted in mid-September that anything more than minor adjustments would likely derail the bill. The early election call shortly afterwards made this a moot point.

The Politics of Species at Risk

As Oscar Wilde said of parents in *The Importance of Being Earnest*, to lose one 'may be regarded as a misfortune; to lose both looks like carelessness.' During the 1990s the federal government crafted two endangered species bills, CESPA and SARA, each of which attracted, and in many of their detailed provisions reflected, sustained criticisms from environmental groups, the provinces, and other key players. Both were lost, their fates sealed by the election calls respectively in 1997 and 2000. Neither, moreover, offered the prospect of an effective and comprehensive framework of species protection and recovery. As critics from leading conservation organizations were quick to point out, provisions for habitat protection were weak, and the process for designating species at risk was to culminate in a political rather than a scientific decision. A third effort that began as SARA was reintroduced in February 2001.

Ecological considerations, particularly the ranges and habitat needs of species, nonetheless continue to underline the requirement for sound federal species-at-risk legislation. These factors also confirm the critical role of transborder and other international arrangements. The need for a federal statute was less clear to many governments and other actors at the start of the 1990s, at the time of the Green Plan and the national wildlife policy. By the close of the decade, however, a series of developments, i.e., commitments in the CBD in 1992, the quickening pace and uneven coverage of provincial measures, the federal-provincial agreements of 1996 that brought wildlife issues into line with other features of the harmonization politics of the mid-1990s, and Ottawa's participation in international forums such as the CITES conferences of the parties, had made its continued absence much more problematic.

Yet the gap clearly does not mean that no national arrangements for species at risk are in place. Canada's governments collaborate on endangered species questions through a variety of evolving institutional mechanisms. Non-governmental organizations are central to conservation and recovery efforts by gathering data, managing ecologically sensitive lands, and educating publics. Whether all of this, with or without specific federal endangered species legislation, will be sufficient to arrest the trend of mounting threats to Canada's wild species of fauna and flora remains to be seen. But the grounds for optimism remain shaky. The underlying causes of these threats will likely persist and even intensify. The wildlife artist Robert Bateman has written that he sees each year 'how the number and variety of birds on Canada's landscape has diminished, from songbirds in Ontario to seabirds in British Columbia.'[79] The seriousness of the aggregate threat will depend to a large extent on the adequacy of long-term measures by governments and conservation organizations to stem specific threats to the ecological integrity of national parks and the viability of Canada's other protected areas, to manage disruptions to habitats outside these areas in ways that minimize impacts on wildlife populations, and to control the sources and effects of climate change.

Notes

1 Kurkpatrick Dorsey, *The Dawn of Conservation Diplomacy: United States-Canadian Wildlife Protection Treaties in the Progressive Era* (Seattle: University of Washington Press, 1998), 165.

2 Janet Foster, *Working for Wildlife: The Beginning of Preservation in Canada*, 2nd edn (Toronto: University of Toronto Press, 1998), 63–5.

3 Jane Smart, 'Plants in Peril', *Oryx* 33, 4 (1999): 279. In general, see Monte Hummel, ed., *Protecting Canada's Endangered Spaces: An Owner's Manual* (Toronto: Key Porter, 1995). On the complementary role of ex situ conservation, see *The State of Canada's Environment* (Ottawa: Government of Canada, 1996), 14–27.

4 J. Sanderson and L.D. Harris, eds, *Landscape Ecology: A Top-Down Approach* (Boca Raton, Fla: Lewis, 2000), 13. See also Andrew F. Bennett, *Linkages in the Landscape: The Role of Corridors and Connectivity in Wildlife Conservation* (Gland: IUCN, 1999). On the limitations of protected areas, see John B. Theberge, 'Ecology, Conservation, and Protected Areas in Canada', in Philip Dearden and Rick Collins, eds, *Parks and Protected Areas in Canada: Planning and Management* (Toronto: Oxford University Press, 1993), 142–3.

5 *State of the Parks: 1997 Report* (Ottawa: Public Works and Government Services Canada, 1998), 25.

6 Laura Jones, with Liv Fredricksen, *Crying Wolf? Public Policy on Endangered Species in Canada* (Vancouver: Fraser Institute, 1999), 7–8.

7 Yrjo Haila, 'The North as/and the Other: Ecology, Domination, Solidarity', in F. Fisher and M.A. Hajer, eds, *Living with Nature: Environmental Politics as Cultural Discourse* (Oxford: Oxford University Press, 1999), 54–5.

8 Gerald B. Straley et al., *The Rare Vascular Plants of British Columbia*, Syllogeus Series No. 59 (Ottawa: National Museums of Canada, 1985), 5.

9 The categories are 'extinct' (a species no longer exists); 'extirpated' (a species no longer in Canada, but occurring elsewhere); 'endangered' (one 'facing imminent extirpation or extinction'); 'threatened' (a species facing endangerment unless actions are taken to check limiting factors); and 'vulnerable' (of 'special concern', for example because of human activities). The designation 'rare' was discontinued in 1990. Confusions over the terms 'endangered' and 'threatened', used loosely in conservation debates to refer to a diverse range of wildlife issues, led to increasing policy use of the collective term 'species at risk' in the late 1990s. Lists of 'species' in these various categories conventionally include subspecies or geographically restricted populations.

10 Environment Canada, news release, 8 May 2000.

11 Ted Mosquin, Peter G. Whiting, and Don E. McAllister, *Canada's Biodiversity: The Variety of Life, Its Status, Economic Benefits, Conservation Costs and Unmet Needs* (Ottawa: Canadian Museum of Nature, 1995), 66.

12 See, for example, the calls for volunteers on a variety of projects listed in *Wildlife Watchers: Report on Monitoring* 4 (Mar. 1998): 1–3.

13 J. Alexander Burnett, 'A Passion for Wildlife: A History of the Canadian Wildlife Service, 1947–1997', *The Canadian Field Naturalist* 113, 1 (1999): 148–9; John A. Livingston, *The Fallacy of Wildlife Conservation* (Toronto: McClelland & Stewart, 1981).

14 Glenda Wall, 'Science, Nature, and "The Nature of Things": An Instance of Canadian Environmental Discourse, 1960–1994', *Canadian Journal of Sociology* 24, 1 (1999): 61–5.

15 *The Importance of Wildlife to Canadians: Highlights of the 1991 Survey* (Ottawa: Canadian Wildlife Service, 1993), 3–4; *The Importance of Nature to Canadians* (Ottawa: Canadian Wildlife Service, 2000).

16 Burnett, 'A Passion for Wildlife', 152.

17 Loren Vanderlinden and John Eyles, 'Public Perspectives on Biodiversity: Models and a Case Study', in Stephen Bocking, ed., *Biodiversity in Canada: Ecology, Ideas, and Action* (Peterborough, Ont.: Broadview Press, 2000), 265–6.

18 Russell Smith, 'CanLit Takes It to the Street' (review), *Globe and Mail*, 23 May 1998, D10.

19 A 'Bambi effect' may influence the attitudes of older Canadians who saw the Disney feature in the 1940s and 1950s. See Vanderlinden and Eyles, 'Public Perspectives on Biodiversity', 260. A related issue arose in 2000 in connection with growing beaver populations in parts of Manitoba.

20 S. Larivière et al., 'Status and Conservation of the Gray Wolf (*Canis lupus*) in Wildlife Reserves of Quebec', *Biological Conservation* 94, 2 (2000): 150.

21 Gloria Galloway, 'Captive Breeding Program considered for Marmots', *National Post*, 1 May 1999, A1.

22 Mosquin et al., *Canada's Biodiversity*, App. 8, 182.

23 Nova Scotia Nature Trust, *Land Conservation: Options for Landowners* (Halifax: NSNT, 1998), 8–11.

24 Wildlife Habitat Canada, *Annual Report 1997*, 3–5.

25 Stephen Bocking, *Ecologists and Environmental Politics: A History of Contemporary Ecology* (New Haven: Yale University Press, 1997), 154–5.

26 *Eco* 12 (Nov. 1998): 1–2.

27 John E. Carroll, *Environmental Diplomacy: An Examination and a Prospective of Canadian-United States Transboundary Environmental Relations* (Ann Arbor: University of Michigan Press, 1983), 18–20.

28 Jill Mahoney, 'Protected Areas Needed for Foothills Wildlife, Timber, Groups Say', *Globe and Mail*, 13 Oct. 1999, A5.

29 William A. Amos, 'Federal Endangered Species Legislation in Canada: Explaining the Lack of a Policy Outcome', MA thesis (University of British Columbia, 1999), 60–75.

30 Anne McIlroy, 'Scientists Start Playing Hardball to Protect Animals', *Globe and Mail*, 25 Feb. 1999, A16.

31 Michael Tutton and Lisa Hrabluk, 'Bill doesn't go far enough, say environmentalists', *New Brunswick Telegraph Journal*, 12 Apr. 2000, A8.

32 Amos, 'Federal Endangered Species Legislation', 61–2.

33 *Report on Public Consultation: A National Approach to Endangered Species Conservation in Canada* (Ottawa: CWS, 1995), 3–5.

34 House of Commons, Committee on Environment and Sustainable Development, 4th Report, Issue No. 5 (Meetings 44–78), 1997, 5:63.

35 There were presentations from over 20 industrial, resource, and other groups to the Commons environment committee on CESPA. They included the Mining Association of Canada, Canadian Pulp and Paper Association, Canadian Federation of Agriculture, Canadian Cattlemen's Association, United Fishermen and Allied Workers Union, and the Industrial, Wood, and Allied Workers of Canada.

36 Peter deMarsh, quoted in Tutton and Hrabluk, 'Bill doesn't go far enough'.

37 Robert J. Smith and M. Danielle Smith, 'Endangered Species Protection: Lessons Canada Should Learn from the United States Endangered Species Act', *Property Rights Journal* 1, 1 (1997): 18–23.

38 Gordon Peeling and Tony Rotherham, 'Everyone's Business', *Globe and Mail*, 10 Apr. 2000.

39 The group included representatives of the Canadian Pulp and Paper Association, Mining Association of Canada, National Agriculture Environment Committee, Sierra Club of Canada, CNF, and CWF.

40 Rita Morbia and Elizabeth May, 'Unlikely Allies Join to Protect Canada's Species at Risk', *Global Biodiversity* 8, 3 (1998): 21; Elizabeth May, 'A Challenge for Canadians', *Recovery: An Endangered Species Newsletter* 15 (Mar. 2000): 2.

41 Canadian Wildlife Service, *Wild Travelers: Migratory Wildlife Shared by Canada, the United States and Mexico* (Ottawa: CWS, 1998), 7.

42 L.J. Gregorich, *Poaching and the Illegal Trade in Wildlife and Wildlife Parts in Canada* (Ottawa: CWF, 1992), 45–6.

43 Government of Alberta, news release, No. 00–032, 12 Apr. 2000.

44 Leanne Yohemas-Hayes, 'National Park Wardens Want Guns for Protection', *Globe and Mail*, 19 May 2000, A7.

45 M.J. Bowman, 'International Treaties and the Global Protection of Birds: Pt. II', *Journal of Environmental Law* 11, 2 (1999): 298.

46 In general, see P. van Heijnsbergen, *International Legal Protection of Wild Fauna and Flora* (Amsterdam: IOS Press, 1997), ch. 6 (species) and ch. 9 (habitats and protected areas).

47 Dorsey, *The Dawn of Conservation Diplomacy*, 232–3; Foster, *Working for Wildlife*, ch. 6 and App., 225–36. New Brunswick, though, temporarily withdrew from wildlife protection on the grounds that this now fell under Ottawa's jurisdiction.

48 Robert Milko, *Migratory Birds Environmental Assessment Guideline* (Ottawa: CWS, 1998), 5–6; Martha Balis-Larsen et al., 'Canada and US Save Shared Species at Risk', *Recovery: An Endangered Species Newsletter* 15 (Mar. 2000): 6–7.

49 Canadian Wildlife Service, *CWS Latin American Program: The First Thirteen Years, 1980–93* (Ottawa: CWS, 1994), 1–2. Canadian attention to these questions was reinforced by Canada's joining the Organization of American States in 1989 and Ottawa's subsequent ratification of the hemisphere convention of 1940. Latin America has also become a major focus of WWF-Canada.

50 'Making International Environmental Agreements Work: The Canadian Arctic Experience', in *Report of the Commissioner of the Environment and Sustainable Development to the House of Commons, 1999* (Ottawa: Public Works and Government Services Canada, 1999), ch. 6, 10–13. John England has been among critics of underfunding of Arctic research generally. See England, 'An Urgent Appeal to the Government of Canada to Proclaim Our Northern Identity', *Arctic* 53, 2 (2000): 204–12.

51 CAFF, *Strategic Plan for the Conservation of Arctic Biological Diversity* (Akureyri: CAFF Secretariat, 1998). Since 1996 CAFF has been integrated into the Arctic Council.

52 CAFF, *Strategic Plan*, 4.

53 *OECD Environmental Data: Compendium 1999* (Paris: OECD, 1999), 152–3. By comparison, the US figures are respectively 17 and 47, with a total area of 11,780 km^2. See also Hal Eidsvik, 'Canada, Conservation and Protected Areas: The International Context', in Dearden and Collins, eds, *Parks and Protected Areas in Canada*, 273–90.

54 Leif Helmer, 'Working Together to Protect and Promote the Thousand Islands: An Assessment of Regional Capacity to Support a Biosphere Reserve', MES thesis (Dalhousie University, 2000), 27.

55 Michael 't Sas-Rolfes, 'Assessing CITES: Four Case Studies', in Jon Hutton and Barnabas Dickson, eds, *Endangered Species, Threatened Convention: The Past, Present and Future of CITES* (London: Earthscan, 2000), 83. On CITES-related issues generally, see Philippe Le Prestre and Peter Stoett, 'International Initiatives, Commitments, and Disappointments: Canada, CITES, and the Convention on Biological Diversity', in Karen Beazley and Robert Boardman, eds, *Politics of the Wild: Canada and Endangered Species* (Toronto: Oxford University Press, 2001), ch. 9.

56 Government of Alberta, news release, No. 00–034, 20 Apr. 2000.

57 Amos, 'Federal Endangered Species Legislation', 116.

58 Ed Struzik, 'Alberta May Fight Endangered Species Legislation', *National Post*, 12 Apr. 2000, A11.

59 Lawrence Berg, Terry Fenge, and Philip Dearden, 'The Role of Aboriginal Peoples in National Park Design, Planning, and Management in Canada', in Dearden and Collins, eds, *Parks and Protected Areas in Canada*, 233. On protected areas in the North and their relationship with Aboriginal societies and values, see D. Scott Slocombe, 'Hinterlands, Wilderness, and Protected Areas in Northern Canada', in R. Gerald Wright, ed., *National Parks and Protected Areas: Their Role in Environmental Protection* (Oxford: Blackwell Science, 1996), 369–88.

60 *Report on Public Consultation*, 86.

61 More generally, see Deena Clayton, 'The Benefits of Traditional Knowledge', *Recovery: An Endangered Species Newsletter* 14 (Oct. 1999): 2; Russel Lawrence Barsh, 'Taking Indigenous Science Seriously', in Bocking, ed., *Biodiversity in Canada*, 153–74.

62 Charles Haines, 'Threatened Wildlife in Canada: Assessing the Need for a Federal Endangered Species Act', MES thesis (Dalhousie University, 1995), 81–3.

63 *Compliance and Enforcement Policy for Wildlife Legislation* (Ottawa: Environment Canada, 1999), 5. Other statutes with provisions related to species or protected areas include the National Parks Act, Oceans Act, Canadian Environmental Assessment Act, and Canadian Environmental Protection Act.

64 Burnett, 'A Passion for Wildlife', 139.

65 Ibid., 146.

66 Robert Boardman, 'Risk Politics in Western States: Canadian Species in Comparative Perspective', in Beazley and Boardman, eds, *Politics of the Wild*, ch. 8.

67 Environment Canada, *Canada's Green Plan* (Ottawa: Government of Canada, 1990), 84–5.

68 Environment Canada, *Conserving Wildlife Diversity: Implementing the Canadian Biodiversity Strategy* (Ottawa: Environment Canada, 1998). Conservation groups argued strongly against the view that CBD obligations could be met without new federal legislation. See further CWS, *Endangered Species Legislation in Canada: A Discussion Paper* (Ottawa: Environment Canada, 1994), 3–5.

69 William Amos, Kathryn Harrison, and George Hoberg, 'In Search of a Minimum Winning Coalition: The Politics of Species-at-Risk Legislation in Canada', in Beazley and Boardman, eds, *Politics of the Wild*, ch. 7.

70 Christine Stewart, 'Working Together on Species at Risk', *Recovery: An Endangered Species Newsletter* 13 (June 1999).

71 On problems in Parks Canada resulting from government reorganization and deficit-cutting, see Rick Searle, *Phantom Parks: The Struggle to Save Canada's National Parks* (Toronto: Key Porter, 2000), ch. 5.

72 Hugh Winsor, 'Industry, Green Lobby gang up on Species Bill', *Globe and Mail*, 13 Mar. 2000, A4.

73 Wildlife Ministers Council of Canada, *A Wildlife Policy for Canada* (Ottawa: CWS, 1990), 5, 19; and the report by Paul Griss at 53rd Federal-Provincial/Territorial Wildlife Conference, St John's, 20–3 June 1989 (Ottawa: CWS, 1989), 136–7.

74 www.cosewic.gc.ca/COSEWIC/TOR-COSEWIC_March99.cfm. Useful earlier evaluations include Francis R. Cook and Dalton Muir, 'The Committee on the Status of Endangered Wildlife in Canada: History and Progress', *Canadian Field-Naturalist* 98, 1 (1984): 63–70; Jacques Prescott and B. Theresa Aniskowicz, 'Helping Endangered Species: COSEWIC and RENEW', *Canadian Biodiversity* 2, 1 (1992): 23–30.

75 Burnett, 'A Passion for Wildlife', 150–1.

76 www.cws-scf.ec.gc.ca/sara/strategy/accord_e.htm. An over-literal reading of this phrasing might be that, depending on the adequacy of other measures, federal endangered species legislation is unnecessary; however, this interpretation would be contrary to the spirit of the accord.

77 David Anderson, 'Canada's Plan for Protecting Species at Risk: An Update', *Recovery: An Endangered Species Newsletter* 15 (Mar. 2000): 4.

78 Environment Canada, *2000–2001 Estimates. Part III: Report on Plans and Priorities*. Available at www.ec.gc.ca/rpp/index.htm

79 Robert Bateman, 'Stop the Politics of Neglect', *Globe and Mail*, 23 Oct. 2000, A13.

Chapter 17

Some Aspects of the 'New Biotechnology' and its Regulation in Canada

William Leiss and Michael Tyshenko

Genetically modified organisms, or GMOs, are being developed steadily, with continued growth of the biotechnology sector predicted well into the next century. This chapter looks at the degree of 'fit' between biotechnology processes and products, on the one hand, and the older federal legislation, last amended over a decade ago, under which it is reviewed and regulated. This chapter deals solely with genetic engineering, or the changing and moving of traits between different species of plants and animals; other biotechnology techniques, such as cloning, new reproductive technologies, and stem cell research, do not move new traits between species and are not discussed here. Assessing the risks associated with genetic engineering, new biotechnology, and emerging technologies has presented a new challenge to government departments, which now must evaluate ever-increasing numbers of genetically modified products seeking approval for production and distribution to consumers.

What Is Genetic Engineering?

The biology underlying the creation of genetically engineered organisms is complex and will be described here only briefly. Since plants are the target of the majority of genetic manipulations, the following overview focuses on plant genetics, but this technical description applies to other organisms that are genetically modified as well. As all plants grow and develop, their embryonic cells become specialized into leaf, stem, or root cells. Each tissue has specific functions that the mature plant needs to survive; these different cell types make different kinds and amounts of proteins. Many of the plant structures and enzymes are made of proteins, and most of the processes that occur are influenced by enzymes, which are also proteins.

The proteins present in different cells and tissues have been studied extensively for some species. Each cell has several thousand different proteins, but most of the proteins are very rare; less than a few hundred proteins in total may be moderately abundant, and only a few may be very abundant. Proteins are also differentially expressed, with some being found in all cells and at all times during growth and development, while others are present only in a particular tissue or at a specific time. The most common way for a cell to control protein production is to control which genes are 'turned on', a process that works as follows. The building blocks of proteins are different amino acids, and the order of amino acids and the length of the chain are unique for each kind of protein. Each unique amino acid sequence is specified by the gene code on a chromosome in the cell's nucleus. Therefore, a gene is a functional piece of deoxyribonucleic acid (DNA) that contains the code necessary for making a specific protein. Genes are present in different places along the length of the chromosomes. In addition, every cell contains all of the DNA and genes on chromosomes, which code for the proteins made in all of the tissues and organs that an individual plant will need. However, only those genes whose proteins are needed in a particular cell will be used by that cell. These are the active genes. The other genes just sit there on the chromosomes, inactive in that cell but active somewhere else in the plant.

Whether a gene is active or not depends on complex interactions between the DNA and other molecules in the cell. Specifically, a typical gene can be divided into two main parts. The first part is a stretch of DNA responsible for interacting with the cell or the environment, and is called the promoter. The second part actually contains the code for the order of amino acids in the protein, and is called the coding sequence. When the gene is active or turned on, the promoter is interacting with other molecules in a way that allows the coding sequence to direct the synthesis of a specific protein through a series of complex steps.

Genetic engineering can be defined as the process of manipulating the pattern of proteins in an organism by altering its existing genes. Either new genes are added or existing genes are changed so that they are made at different times or in different amounts. Because the genetic code is similar in all species, genes taken from one species can function in another: 'For example with genetic engineering researchers have added genes to potatoes from bacteria, viruses, chickens, and moths.'[1] Also, promoters or the 'on switch' from one coding sequence can be removed and placed in front of another coding sequence to change when or where the protein is to be made.

Recombinant DNA (rDNA) techniques are methods of molecular biology that allow researchers to identify specific genes and allow for their manipulation. Typically, genes with favourable characteristics from a wide range of organisms may be introduced into recipient organisms, such as a food crop. These new characteristics can be introduced using a number of techniques, including: by injection into the nucleus of the cell with a tiny needle; by electrical shock of the cells, which briefly depolarizes the membrane allowing for DNA uptake; by attaching the DNA to small metal particles and using a 'gene gun' to shoot the particles into the cells; or by using viruses and bacteria engineered to infect cells with the transgenic DNA. In all methods, the newly engineered DNA must find its way into the nucleus and become incorporated into the plant's own genetic material. Once incorporated into the host at the DNA level, the introduced gene functions like all other genes of the host. This process of transplanting desired traits from one organism to another is called 'transformation' or more commonly 'gene splicing'. The resulting products from recombinant manipulations are termed 'transgenics' or 'genetically modified organisms' (GMOs).[2]

Since Canadian legislation was amended in 1988 to include products of biotechnology, the science knowledge base for molecular biology manipulation and knowledge of organisms at the genetic level has been increasing at remarkable speed. Complete genetic code with all encoded gene sequences has been determined for several bacteria, yeast strains, the fruit fly, and nematodes. Genome projects for higher model biological systems, including other yeast strains, the mouse, and humans, are nearing completion. The 'sequencing' phase of the Human Genome Project was completed in July 2000, well ahead of its original schedule.[3] New types of molecular biology, such as bio-informatics and molecular database mining, are emerging to deal with the enormous amount of genome data.[4] Innovation in genomics science continues at a dizzying pace as newer methods and scientific breakthroughs continue to push back the older boundaries of biology. The result of new techniques of gene manipulation, together with the compilation of genome databases, has expanded the identified number of genetically useful traits available to scientists for gene transfers.

Before genetic modification through applications of molecular biology was available, plant scientists relied entirely on conventional cross-breeding, which restricts the scope of genetic manipulations to those traits found within the same species or in closely related species. This limited the number of traits and also usually introduced less desirable genes closely linked to the trait of interest. The drawback of conventional cross-hybridization is that it involves recombination of thousands of genes on whole chromosomes, while recombinant DNA techniques transfer or modify one or a few well-characterized genes. Researchers now prefer recombinant DNA techniques since new target genes can be directly inserted into a non-related organism without the difficulties of conventional cross-hybridization. The power of genetic modification techniques, in terms of specificity and potentially useful traits, has increased as new methods of gene transfer have been developed. Recombinant DNA techniques are used to achieve the same goals that biotechnology developers have sought through conventional crossing methods of genetic modification; however, rDNA techniques have the power to move novel traits between two completely different organisms.

The Regulatory Structure for Biotechnology

Canada amended many of its regulatory acts to include a very broad definition of biotechnology, focusing on the safety of the end products. In Canada and the United States, regulators ruled on the first genetically modified products during the early 1990s and approved the commercial use of bacterial chymosin, an enzyme for use in making cheese products. Yeast and fungi were also some of the early genetically modified organisms approved. The US Food and Drug Administration (FDA) approved the first genetically modified crop plant, called the 'Flavr Savr' tomato, developed by Calgene Inc., affirming that it was as safe as other commercial tomatoes, and this product set the precedent for all other genet-ically modified products to follow.[5]

In 1988, Canadian federal legislation was amended in several instances to include a very broad definition of biotechnology: 'Biotechnology means the appli-cation of science and engineering to the use of living organisms or parts or prod-ucts of living organisms in their natural or modified forms.' This broad definition was used as a catch-all to embrace all of the emerging new biotechnology that was producing genetically modified plants and animals. Under regulations made pursuant to this definition, genetically modified products of agriculture were mainly regulated by three of the amended Acts, the Seeds Act, the Fertilizers Act, and the Feeds Act (feeds intended for livestock). The amendments to the Fertilizers Regulations concerning genetic engineering apply to all novel supple-ments, which are substances that improve the physical condition of the soil or improve plant growth or crop yields. Under the Seeds Act, genetically modified plants are those that have what is called a 'novel trait' (the result of moving or altering a gene). A trait is novel when the transferred bit makes a difference of 2 per cent or more in the organism to which it has been transferred.[6] Once a novel trait has been identified, it must be approved and field-tested before sale in Canada. An assessment is done using molecular, biochemical, and other data to determine whether the nutritional and other characteristics of food products made from plants with novel traits may be expected to be identical to those derived from similar plants that did not have those novel traits; if they are, the two groups of products are said to be 'substantially equivalent'.[7]

Plants with novel traits have been assessed and released into the environment since 1988 under confined conditions in Canada following guidelines promulgated by Agriculture and Agri-Food Canada (AAFC). Once the health and environmen-tal safety questions with respect to an unconfined release are addressed, author-ization is granted for a release of a particular plant with a novel trait. Thereafter (with few exceptions), the plant can be grown in any quantity or in any location without notifying Agriculture and Agri-Food Canada. Animal products of the new biotechnology are regulated under the Health of Animals Act as a class of prod-ucts known as 'veterinary biologics'.

A single genetically modified plant or animal product may have many cross-cutting aspects, spanning plant regulation, animal regulation, environmental safety, and health safety. Canadian regulation of biotechnology attempts to ensure that a regulatory framework is in place to protect human and animal health and the environment and also to promote innovation, encourage biotechnology venture capital investment, and support technology transfer from university research to the marketplace. The various federal Acts, as shown in Table 17.1, are designed to regulate the end products of biotechnology applications (plants and animals with novel traits), and not the scientific and technological processes themselves (the processes of molecular biology that make gene transfer within and across species possible) in the new biotechnology.

Some Problems with Canadian Biotechnology Regulations

One of the problems with Canadian regulation concerning recombinant biotechnology is that the government's current definition of biotechnology is now 10 years old and there has been an ever-increasing discrepancy between the pace of biotechnology innovation and the underlying concept on the part of government that the new biotechnology is 'business-as-usual'. The reality is that the scope and pace of biotechnology have changed dramatically. Scientific innovation has resulted in a large number of new laboratory techniques, and the result is an increased number of applications stemming from biotechnology. However, innovation in the genetic manipulations of plants and animals is still in its infancy, with only the first wave of single-gene modifications having reached the consumer and the environment.

Figure 17.1 shows the numbers of submissions of genetically modified plants, each of which must be evaluated and approved before field trials are allowed. In

Table 17.1: Classification and Government Regulation of Canadian Biotechnology Products

Products Regulated	Federal Department(s)	Act	Regulations
Feeds, including novel feeds	Agriculture and Agri-Food Canada	Feeds Act	Feeds Regulations
Supplements, including novel supplements (both microbial and chemical)	Agriculture and Agri-Food Canada	Fertilizers Act	Fertilizers Regulations
Veterinary biologics	Agriculture and Agri-Food Canada	Health of Animals Act	Health of Animals Regulations
Plants, including plants with novel traits, including forest trees	Canadian Food Inspection Agency	Seeds Act	Seeds Regulations
Products for uses not covered under other federal legislation	Environment Canada Health Canada	Canadian Environmental Protection Act	New Substances Notification Regulations
Baculovirus, pesticides, and biocides	Health Canada	Pest Control Products Act	Pest Control Products Regulations
Transgenic fishes	Department of Fisheries and Oceans (proposed)	Fisheries Act	Regulations on Transgenic Fishes (proposed)
Drugs, cosmetics, medical devices, and novel foods	Health Canada	Food and Drugs Act	Food and Drugs Regulations; Medical Devices Regulations

Source: Adapted from: http://www.cfia-acia.agr.ca/english/reg/rege.shtml

1988 (when the Seeds Act was amended to include the new GMO products derived from genetic engineering), only 10 genetically engineered plants and 14 field trials needed to be assessed; a decade later there were 148 submissions and 812 field trials to be assessed. The scope and exponential increase in the number of genetic manipulations could not have been predicted in 1988 ûnder the then modified legislation to include a broad definition of biotechnology that would apply to plants with novel traits. The number of plants being genetically altered has dramatically increased and now includes alfalfa, broccoli, barley, mustard, canola, corn, grapevine, potato, soybean, sugar beet, and wheat.

The applications of genetic manipulations have also developed well beyond what was known when the legislation was amended in 1988. In the late 1980s, plants were undergoing genetic modifications to improve characteristics such as tolerance to chemical herbicides, increased resistance to pests, and increased resistance to disease. The resulting food products were also modified to reduce processing costs, increase shelf life, and yield better flavour and enhanced nutritional properties. Now, the number and type of genetic applications have been broadened to include: novel herbicide tolerance, viral resistance, fungal resistance, pharmaceuticals (drug production), chemical production, orphan drug production, and production of various modified oils, and future genetic manipulations boast of plants that will contain attenuated viruses to act as vehicles for vaccine delivery.[8] The pace of science, which has accelerated in recent years, is in the process of turning plants into drug and chemical bio-reactors and miniature oil refineries. But the Seeds Act, for example, was not designed to regulate pharmaceuticals, drugs, and vaccine production. To be assessed properly, the types of genetic alterations now occurring

Figure 17.1: Number of Submissions and Field Trials of Genetically Engineered Plant Material under the Seeds Act, 1988–1998

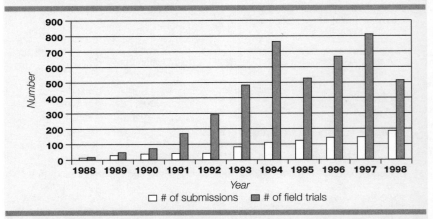

Source: Canadian Food Inspection Agency, Plant Health and Production Division, Plant Biotechnology Office. http://www.cfia-acia.agr.ca/english/plaveg/pbo/triesse.shtml

require extensive scientific expertise encompassing molecular biology, ecology, evolution, pharmacology, medicine, virology, plant and animal physiology, biochemistry, organic chemistry, molecular modelling, and genetics.

In addition, the growth of the biotechnology industry has resulted in a dramatic increase in the number of genetic manipulations of plants and animals. Figure 17.2 shows the results of a patent database search for all applications that contain keywords 'plant and recombinant' or 'animal and recombinant'. Companies apply for patents seeking to protect their rights while they develop new technology or develop new genetically modified organisms. The patent applications are written to be as broad as possible, and Figure 17.2 shows the number of applications that 'potentially' may use genetic engineering in plants and animals. The most current numbers from the patent database show about 4,500 applications for plant transformations alone that could eventually seek Canadian regulatory approval (although it is unlikely that all the patent applications will be developed to completion and make it into the Canadian marketplace).

The general trend at present, as seen in Figures 17.1 and 17.2, shows that about 10 per cent of all patent submissions eventually are developed as novel plants or genetically modified animals and seek submission for approval or field-testing. Granting approval for plants with novel traits also involves having the field-trial data collected, and these data, too, must be assessed before final approval is granted. Field trial numbers also have continued to increase, since single submissions sometimes require multiple field trials. To date, only 35 decision documents for plants with novel traits have been completed by the Canadian

Figure 17.2: Patent Database Full-Text Boolean Search Using Key Words: 'plant and recombinant' and 'animal and recombinant'

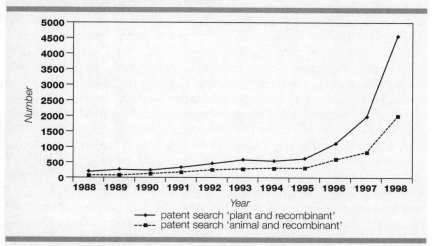

Source: US patent full-text database: http://164.195.100.11/netahtml/search-bool.html

Food Inspection Agency (CFIA).[9]

We conclude this section with a brief note on some structures in other countries. Germany has stringent laws regarding genetic manipulation, amended to be less stringent in 1990 (the 'Gene Law' reduced approval times for new projects and facilities while a central federal office, Zentrale Kommission fuer Biologische Sicherheit, still controls all licensing of genetic experimentation). In the United States, the FDA oversees GMOs; the European Union (EU) has a regulatory structure set out in the Deliberate Release Directive (90/220). Since 1992, 18 genetically modified (GM) products, including crops, vaccines, and flowers, have been approved for commercial use in the EU; however, no new applications have been acted upon since 1998, when a moratorium was put into place. Several Eastern European countries are drafting specific legislation to co-ordinate with EU rules for trade in GMO products; Bulgaria was the first Eastern European country to enact specific GMO legislation.[10]

Understanding the Risks of the New Biotechnology: Plant GMOs

Risks associated with plant biotechnology applications fall into two major categories, human health risks (such as allergens) and environmental risks. Environmental risks include out-crossing of genetically modified plants with wild relatives, acceleration of insect resistance, and effects on non-target species. What follows is a brief summary of the risks identified to date, starting with environmental risks.[11]

Through plant biotechnology, new, desirable characteristics are engineered into major crops, such as 'herbicide tolerance' for canola (making the canola plant immune to the effects of a herbicide that will kill surrounding weeds) and 'insect tolerance' for corn (where the cells in the corn plant express toxins lethal to insects, such as the corn borer, that attack the plant). Since these characteristics will then be found in all of the plant's cells, including the pollen it produces, various risks arise that are associated with 'gene transfer' or 'gene flow', which refers to the possibility that the new characteristics will be dispersed in the environment and cause unintended harmful effects to other plants and insects. Where plants are concerned, this is called 'out-crossing', that is, fertilization of either other domestic or wild species with the modified pollen. Where insects are concerned, risks involve both the possibility that increased resistance to particular toxic agents will develop in the target insects and that other insects not so targeted will accidentally be exposed to the toxins. Such gene transfer is regarded as inevitable, and both the environmental assessments of the novel characteristics and crop management practices in the field are designed to minimize the risks associated with gene flow within 'acceptable' limits.

Unintended gene transfer from GM plants to wild plant species is likely where the plant is the 'outbreeding' type (cross-fertilization occurs among distantly related parent plants) and there are numerous wild 'relatives' in the nearby environment. This is true of canola. If the engineered characteristic is herbicide tolerance, then the transfer of that characteristic to those wild relatives is undesirable for a number of reasons, such as reduction of biodiversity and lowered effectiveness of the herbicide for weed control. Unintended transfers also can occur just because both modified and non-modified types of the same crops are being grown in the same general environment, and where it is important for a variety of reasons for the two types to be kept separate—for example, because farmers growing non-GM types of canola may be part of a supply chain in which products will be advertised to consumers as being 'GM-free', or simply because it interrupts the farmer's established crop management and rotation strategies.[12] Finally, it would be possible for two GM varieties engineered for tolerance to two different herbicides to cross, making the progeny plants tolerant to both (a process known as 'gene stacking'), rendering crop management by farmers more difficult and raising the possibility that this new characteristic could spread further in the environment.

Management of these types of risks involves primarily the use of minimum isolation distances between modified and non-modified crops, albeit with the realization that, as mentioned above, some unintended gene transfer is inevitable. This will be a more serious consideration if and when plants are engineered widely for production of vaccines or pharmaceutical products, in which case strict isolation requirements will have to be strongly enforced.

'Insect tolerance' is achieved by engineering a new function into the plant genome, whereby all of the plant's cells can express a substance that is toxic to the insects that cause damage to the plant (e.g., the corn borer or the Colorado potato beetle). So far all such engineered crops use the same device for this purpose, namely, the bacterium *Bacillus thuringiensis* (Bt), which is also sprayed on crops as a conventional insecticide; since Bt is a naturally occurring organism, these insecticidal sprays containing Bt are used by producers growing 'organic' crops. Widespread use of insecticides of all types always brings with it the risk of pest resistance, and the genetic engineering of insecticides into plants is no exception. The recommended procedure for reducing this risk is the use of 'refugia', that is, alternating GM and non-GM varieties of the same crops in sections, creating refuges for the insect pests and inhibiting the development of resistance. However, it is expected that Bt resistance in pest insects and weeds will certainly occur.[13]

The need for refuges illustrates a major, ongoing issue in the risk controversies over GM crops. Just as with the case of gene flow discussed above, measures against insect resistance are dependent on management practices at the farm level. In other words, regulatory approval of the GM crop varieties, including an assessment of their environmental risks and the options for controlling those risks, is granted on the assumption that appropriate management practices will be followed by those who are using the engineered crop varieties. This procedure effectively transfers responsibility for risk management from the regulator to the user, who may or may not have the ability to discharge that responsibility.[14]

In addition to insect resistance, the engineering of new toxins into plants raises the possibility of unintended effects on non-target organisms. Possible adverse effects of engineered *Bt* on monarch butterflies have dominated both scientific and media exchanges on this point for some time now. The risk arises from the possibility that pollen from corn crops engineered to express *Bt* toxins can contaminate neighbouring stands of milkweed, on which monarch butterflies feed. Controversy derived from an initial laboratory study reported in 1999, the results of which were disputed by other scientists, spread all over the world; the ongoing disputes had not yet died down when a second study, published in an academic journal in August 2000 but immediately picked up by the media (where dissenting opinions of other scientists also were reported), raised the profile of this issue once again.[15]

A special controversy has persisted about the use of so-called 'antibiotic resistance marker genes' in GM crops. These marker genes have been used as a laboratory tool to help technicians identify when the desired genetic modifications (such as insect tolerance) have been successfully carried out: 'Plants that contain a gene for resistance to an antibiotic will grow on material that contains that antibiotic, whereas if the genes have not been successfully inserted the plants will not grow. Because the "marker gene" is linked to the other gene, those plants that have grown on the antibiotic will also contain the gene for resistance to the insect pest.'[16] Even though the defenders of this practice maintain that the antibiotic-resistance genes will not 'flow' out of the plants and into the environment, there has been a good deal of criticism of it nonetheless, especially since the matter of accelerating antibiotic resistance in general (which is entirely unrelated to this usage in plant genetics) is a matter of great concern. In its 1998 expert report on GM foods issues, the Royal Society stated:

> it is no longer acceptable to have antibiotic resistance genes present in a new GM crop under development for potential use in foodstuffs. In particular, researchers in both academia and industry should not produce GM plants containing genes that confer resistance to those antibiotics that are used to treat infections in animals or humans.

This position has been adopted by agencies of the UK government.[17]

In the domain of human health risks, a matter that concerns many citizens (to the surprise of scientists) is the possibility that the engineered DNA in GM crops will become inserted in their own genetic material through the consumption and digestion of food products. This is perhaps an understandable error, for no one takes responsibility for explaining genetic engineering and technology clearly to the public, which is apparently just supposed to take the bland assertions of 'safety' from government regulators at face value. Within the regulatory system, the most serious health concern has focused on allergenicity risk, that is, the possibility that allergens could become accidentally inserted into food crops and thereafter show up in widely consumed food products. This in fact occurred in one of the first genetic food-modification attempts. Pioneer Hi-Bred International Inc., a biotechnology company in Iowa, produced a soybean containing a gene from the Brazil nut in hopes of increasing the protein content of soybeans. Scientists at the University of Nebraska found that the new gene, which had increased the soybean's nutritional value, also caused a severe immune reaction in people with nut allergies; Pioneer Hi-Bred immediately discontinued the production of its genetically modified soybeans before they reached stores.[18] However, the production of genetically modified organisms by using genes not known to cause allergy, as well as gene products that have no protein sequence similarity to known allergens, has turned out to be much more difficult to assess, mainly due to the lack of methods to test for protein allergenicity. Astwood et al. attempted to model a method for testing GMO-expressing foreign proteins and allergen stability during digestion, but the fact remains that methods for testing and assessing allergenicity are still being worked out, even for well-known food allergens. Currently, health risks for new proteins being expressed in GMOs, including their synergistic potential and use in secondary or tertiary products, cannot be accurately determined.[19]

Finally, we must at least mention the issue of labelling GM food products. Many have suggested that labelling genetically modified items being sold in stores is a responsible and ethical way to inform the consumer and so allow her or him to make a personal choice. But such labelling of items produced by biotechnology is problematic for a number of reasons.[20] For example, many individuals might not understand what genetic engineering is, and thus the labelling would convey very little usable information. Moreover, the enforcement and monitoring of labelling claims, including claims of products being 'GM-free', could prove to be a daunting task.

Understanding the Risks of the New Biotechnology: Xenotransplantation

Xenotransplantation involves the transfer of tissue from one animal to another of a different species. During the 1920s and 1930s, several doctors tried to transplant organs from goats, lambs, monkeys, and pigs into various patients; these xenografts all soon failed, for reasons that were not understood at the time, until the immunologic basis of rejection of foreign tissues was discovered during the mid-1940s. In 1954, Joseph Murray and his colleagues at Brigham Hospital in Boston performed the first truly successful kidney transplant; immunologic tissue rejection was avoided by transplanting a kidney between identical twin brothers whose organs were indistinguishable to each other's immune systems. Subsequently, doctors were able to transplant kidneys from unrelated donors by administering immunosuppressive drugs such as cyclosporin that blocked the recipient's immune response to foreign proteins. Medical practitioners now can transplant a host of organs, including heart, lung, liver, and pancreas between human hosts, using such drugs to prevent immune rejection. However, of the thousands of patients in North America who are very good candidates for organ transplantation, less than half receive a donated organ due to persistent shortages of donors. Using tissue and organs from animals is thought to be a promising way of overcoming such shortages.[21]

During the 1960s and 1970s, while successful human-to-human organ transplants were being developed, medical researchers continued to investigate exactly why organs transplanted between widely different species failed so rapidly. A major cause, they learned, was that human blood contains antibody molecules that bind to the foreign tissues. Antibodies are normally directed against infectious microbes but also respond to foreign components of transplanted organs. The attachment of these antibodies then activates special complement proteins in the blood, triggering the destruction of the graft. The hyperacute rejection of foreign tissue, which begins within minutes after the xenotransplant surgery, destroys the small blood capillaries in the transplanted organ, causing massive internal bleeding and tissue death.

Although this immune reaction presents an imposing barrier to xenotransplantation, recent experiments suggest that scientists may yet overcome it using molecular biology techniques. In 1992, researchers created a genetically modified pig; by the addition of a human gene, all of the pig's blood vessels expressed human proteins on their inner walls. It is believed that the presence of these human proteins will actively prevent human complement proteins and antibodies from doing damage following tissue transplantation. The transgenic pig organs have capillaries that will not be damaged since they are masked with human proteins and will not trigger the human immune system. Although untested so far in a human host, organs from these transgenic pigs have functioned for as long as two months in monkeys.[22]

Xenotransplantation raises many ethical and public health concerns as well as new types of risks, most notably the risk of animal infections crossing the 'species barrier' into the persons receiving tissue transplants and then to the public at large. Most concerns about cross-species disease transfer focus on viruses, especially those with long latency. Examples of animal viruses crossing to humans include HIV, which appears to have originated with the simian immunodeficiency virus (SIV) in Africa. In 1997 an avian virus that had previously infected only chickens and ducks crossed to humans; hundreds of thousands of chickens were slaughtered to contain the outbreak.[23] Such a virus may lead to either 'zoonosis' or 'xenozoonosis', the latter being an infectious agent introduced to humans by transplanted tissue. Viruses arising by zoonotic infection, such as influenza, are already known to be transmissible from pigs to humans, but these are unlikely to be a major problem in xenotransplantation, since donor animals would be maintained in carefully controlled, disease-free environments. Xenozoonotic viruses, on the other hand, are potentially more dangerous, since they may not be identifiable with current tests, and by definition their pathogenic behaviour is unknown. Such viruses may cause acute or chronic infectious diseases or could be oncogenic, causing cancers such as leukemia.

To understand the risk of using pig xenotransplants, for example, it is necessary to understand which diseases may be transmissible between the pig donor and human host. Recently, researchers have discovered that the porcine endogenous retrovirus (PERV) can infect human cells.[24] Both PERV-A and PERV-B have been shown to be able to infect different pig and human cell lines; these retroviruses bear some similarity to the gibbon-ape-leukemia virus, which itself originated from a mouse retrovirus that is oncogenic. There are also many other endogenous viral sequences lurking in the pig genetic material, the significance of which is even more difficult to quantify. There is some potential for these pig retroviruses to mutate in human hosts or recombine with human retroviruses and produce completely new pathogens. The result might be quite dangerous, for unlike the viruses that bring on the short-lived swine flu, certain retroviruses are potentially cancer-causing and could produce lifelong infection.[25]

The patent applications of three US companies to produce chimeric pig-human organs raise several interesting questions concerning associated health risks, as well as moral and ethical concerns and the adequacy of Canadian regulation. The transgenic pigs and their future offspring expressing the human gene product were imported from Britain into Canada for experimental organ transplants into humans, but Health Canada never inspected them. The imported pigs were processed by Agriculture and Agri-Food Canada just as if they were hogs used for ham or bacon (and thus were the responsibility of the Canadian Food Inspection Agency), despite the fact that the pigs obviously would never be used for food. Some government officials questioned why the pigs were allowed to enter Canada at that time, when policies and regulations for undertaking xenotransplantation were just beginning to be formulated. Meanwhile, although a pig-human organ transplant was already scheduled to occur in the near future, at the end of 2000 Canadian governments still had not conducted any public consultation on this issue or fully assessed the risks associated with viral transmission between humans and pigs. It would seem sensible to regulate this animal GMO under the Health of Animals Act as a veterinary biologic, since pig organs for xenografts are genetically modified to possess a novel trait. Instead, under Health Canada procedures, and apparently ignoring the novel trait, the genetically modified pigs are considered to be 'medical devices'.[26] This confusion about the status of animal tissues for xenotransplantation reveals the patchwork nature of the current legislative framework for the new biotechnology.

Regulation of Biotechnology Risk: Product or Process?

As noted above, the current regulatory regime for biotechnology products in Canada uses a network of existing legislation and departmental mandates to assess health and environmental risks and to align its evaluation methods with those of its international trading partners. The primary federal departments and agencies involved are Health Canada, Environment Canada, and the Canadian

Food Inspection Agency, operating under eight different Acts of Parliament. The rationale for this approach is explained as follows:

> Biotechnology uses living organisms, or parts of living organisms, to make new products or provide new methods of production. This broad description covers all organisms, their parts and products, whether developed traditionally or through the newer molecular techniques such as genetic engineering. . . . departments and agencies now regulating products developed using traditional techniques and processes are responsible for regulating products developed using biotechnology techniques and processes.

This approach is also used, entirely or in large part, by many of Canada's trading partners.[27]

The scientific rationale for the approach was enunciated in a report published in 1987 by an expert panel appointed by the US National Academy of Sciences, and it was reaffirmed by a similar group in 2000.[28] The rationale takes the form of three statements:

1 'There is no evidence that unique hazards exist either in the use of rDNA techniques or in the movement of genes between unrelated organisms.'
2 'The risks associated with the introduction of rDNA-engineered organisms are the same in kind as those associated with the introduction of unmodified organisms and organisms modified by other methods.'
3 'Assessment of the risks of introducing rDNA-engineered organisms into the environment should be based on the nature of the organism and the environment into which it is introduced, not on the method by which it was produced.'

As mentioned earlier, humans have been doing genetic modification in domesticated plants and animals through selective breeding for millennia; and in the twentieth century, before the advent of molecular biology, other modern techniques (such as radiation) have been used as a way of selecting for desired traits. All this may properly be called indirect genetic manipulation, because genetic structures carried within cells could not be accessed as such and the manipulation occurred at the level of the whole plant or animal, in earlier times, or at the cellular level more recently. On the other hand, genetic manipulation using molecular biology accesses genes directly, which was possible only after the discovery of the structure of DNA; the applications resulting from this new direction are only about 20 years old. We could refer to these as the 'pre-molecular' and 'molecular' phases of plant genetics.[29]

In Canada, the lead federal regulators for plant biotechnology applications, Agriculture and Agri-Food Canada and now the Canadian Food Inspection

Agency, have argued that there is a strong element of continuity from 'traditional practices' (i.e., selective breeding) to the 'new biotechnology' (i.e., modern genetic engineering).[30] During hearings on biotechnology regulation held by the House of Commons Standing Committee on Environment and Sustainable Development in mid-1996, a senior AAFC official provided a general perspective along these lines, where the single phrase 'new or traditional biotechnology' was said to cover a process of continuous evolution that has proceeded through four stages: (1) plant cultivation and animal husbandry; (2) selective breeding of plants and animals; (3) gene transfer within the same species; (4) gene transfer among different species.[31]

This perspective reinforces the rationale for the current regulatory approach: 'Under the regulatory framework, Agriculture and Agri-Food Canada assesses the traits of the final products rather than the actual processes of biotechnology, with the belief that genetically engineered organisms are not fundamentally different from traditionally bred organisms.'[32] But a different note is struck by the following passage from the same document:

> Through new biotechnology techniques, scientists can modify the characteristics of organisms for our benefit in a more controlled way than with traditional practices. . . . These techniques allow the transfer of genes to be carried out in a very controlled way, so that only one or a few desirable traits are transferred at a time. Furthermore, these technologies can be used to introduce desirable traits from outside the species, something that is not possible with traditional breeding methods.

The first quotation says that 'genetically engineered organisms are not fundamentally different from traditionally bred organisms', whereas the second says that the new technology does something 'that is not possible with traditional breeding methods.' The first suggests that no new authority is needed; the second at least puts the question we have raised on the table for discussion, and we shall return to it in our concluding section.

Another prominent feature of the regulatory stance taken by Canadian federal departments is what may be called a highly restrictive perspective on risk.[33] For the regulators, as expressed in their slogan of 'science-based risk assessment', risk is restricted only to those hazards that may be characterized with precision by scientific practice, such as the ones described above (herbicide and insect tolerance). It is indeed very important for the public to be protected against such risks through the existence of regulatory oversight. However, it has also been known for some time now that among the public, which is not generally expert in the science of molecular biology, or in other sciences, there is a quite different perspective on risk, one that is much broader in scope than that of the regulators and that is permeated by values different from those that govern scientific practice. This differing value structure is revealed in the comprehensive public attitude surveys on biotechnology done in Europe.[34] The main conclusions are: (1) perceived usefulness of the biotechnology product is a precondition of citizen support; (2) people seem prepared to accept some risk as long as there is a perception of usefulness *and* no moral or ethical concern; and (3) most importantly, moral doubt (that is, a sense that something is 'wrong') can act as a veto on people's willingness to accept specific biotechnology applications. In other words, the regulator's concept of 'safety' (acceptable risk) is not the final or overriding consideration; rather, a looser but also deeply held sense of 'right and wrong' is the decisive criterion for public acceptance.

This is where the 'process' *versus* 'product' distinction becomes relevant. As shown earlier, biotechnology regulators maintain that, since there are no *unique* risks associated with genetic modification, there is no need for a unique form of regulatory oversight for GM applications of any kind. In other words, the regulators say that it would make no sense to regulate the process of biotechnology (that is, directly moving genes themselves among different organisms), as opposed to the various products (for example, herbicide-tolerant canola or insect-resistant corn plants), because the relevant risks are in the end products, not in the process that created them. Moreover, these risks are similar to most of those with which we are already familiar as a result of conducting regulatory oversight of food products made from 'conventional' (non-GM) crops—risk factors such as toxicity (for example, from pesticide residues), bacteria and other pathogens, allergenicity, digestibility, nutritional deficiencies, and so on. Again, this list contains important risks against which the public needs to be protected through competent and diligent regulatory supervision. But it is not a complete list of the risks that concern the public.

The intense and still growing public controversies over biotechnology are, in our opinion, a strong indication that many among the public do indeed wish the process of so-called 'new' biotechnology itself (the engineering of new organisms through molecular biology) to be the subject of specific regulatory oversight. This is what is implicit in the now-famous term 'Frankenfood' and its cousins (when Japanese scientists first cloned a pig in the summer of 2000, it was immediately designated 'Frankenpig'), namely, a perceived concern about what ultimately may be the type of creations that emerge from the science of modern molecular biology, and whether or not those creations will be consistent with our moral sense of right and wrong or instead give rise to a new and troubling dimension of 'moral risks'.[35] What the public senses, albeit unclearly, that is different about the 'new biotechnology' (as opposed to the farmers' conventional and age-old practices of selective breeding) is its *inherently unlimited* character, the fact that every new stage of understanding leads to an enhanced capacity to manipulate more thoroughly the genomes of all plants and animals, including humans. Some manipulations that can be imagined are so repugnant to our moral sensibility that they must be forbidden. Are we supposed to wait until we are confronted with those actually existing products, along with their makers' assurances that they are 'safe', and only then express our repugnance?

On the contrary, what we must have is an anticipatory public oversight that looks broadly at the general features of all the genetic manipulations that are proceeding along the way from laboratory science to new product development, and that applies not only scientific criteria but also a range of ethical judgements to those intended manipulations. This requires the creation of a unique, specialized regulatory body at a national level, working in parallel (but entirely independent of) the existing departmental regulatory agencies charged with assuring product safety. Such a proposed agency was described in the 1998 Royal Society statement on genetically modified plants for food use as an 'over-arching body' or 'super-regulator' that would have responsibility for the 'wider issues' surrounding genetic modification. This idea is further elaborated below.

Conclusion

Looming in the future are applications of biotechnology far more complex than the ones we have seen so far: genetically engineered food crops involving multiple transgenic insertions, eugenics using genetic screening (modification of inherited human traits), and gene therapy (elimination of undesirable inherited human traits and single-gene diseases). Science will make possible, should we wish to have them, the construction of human-animal chimeras for organ harvesting or of quasi-human living entities.[36] Some of these futuristic biotechnology applications may never come to pass (although it would be unwise to take this for granted), but of some things we can be certain—that scientific research on such things as genetic markers for human disease, aging, and intelligence will continue; that the methods of moving genetic materials between species will be explored and refined; and that the potential commercial applications of any such research that promises attractive medical benefits will be well-funded by the biotechnology industry.

Our society and others missed a golden opportunity to 'do the right thing' when the need for the regulation of the new biotechnology appeared during the 1980s, namely, to apply an appropriate risk-management approach to this task, one that had learned from the mistakes of previous epochs. When the first versions of a new approach to health and environmental risk management appeared on the scene, in the 1970s, they had to be applied retrospectively to major industries, such as chemicals and nuclear power, which had grown up and prospered in the absence of society's having proper regulatory structures in place. Much was learned in the battles to impose a new structure on those industries; for example, the differences between 'expert' and 'public' assessments of risk and the need to encompass both (the nuclear industry never did learn to appreciate this important point). But like other nations, Canada failed to seize the opportunity, when the new biotechnology came along, to apply these lessons.

This failing had two aspects, both of which are explored well in Katherine Barrett's recent doctoral thesis. First, governments everywhere, ever anxious to prove themselves as good economic managers by 'picking winners' among new technologies, became aggressive promoters of the new biotechnology. Their promotional orientation inevitably dictated how they would approach their responsibilities for assessing and regulating this new industrial sector. Their desire to find an approach that would encourage a fledgling sector to develop quickly is illustrated well in the fact that their regulatory rationale, based on the process/product distinction, only appeared after the first generation of product development in industrial laboratories was well under way. Moreover, the chosen regulatory framework was constructed in a virtually secret dialogue between industry and government officials; the public was invited in and introduced to the subject only after the fact, after governments were already committed to its basic structure.[37] These self-imposed limitations on regulatory responsibility also inhibited Canadian federal departments from freely engaging the public in discussions on a wider range of issues. No communications program from these departments to date, dealing with products of the new biotechnology, has included a balanced account of risks and benefits, and controversial issues often elicit a response from 'official spokespersons' that is either confrontational or merely inarticulate.[38]

Second, the core concept in that basic structure was an excessively narrow construction of the concept of risk. Only risks characterized by the science of plant biology itself would be admitted into the calculus, and all of them were confined by definition to product-based risks. The structure of regulatory discourse about the new biotechnology had decided, before the public was ever invited into the debate, to rule out a priori any considerations having to do with the process of using molecular biology to create new organisms. The discussion would be about product safety and nothing else. This apparently clever strategy allowed industry to get its first-generation products into the marketplace with a minimum of fuss, but it overlooked the fact that, these days, there is no guarantee that the public will passively accept a 'definition of the situation' that institutions seek to impose arbitrarily on public discourse. [39]

There is a certain lack of public confidence in the new biotechnology that, in our opinion, will not easily be repaired. In our view, a new public institutional structure is required, one that acts truly independently of industrial interests and that is charged with taking the widest possible purview of all the relevant aspects, especially moral and ethical aspects, of the potential social consequences of applications of the new biotechnology.[40]

In the new biotechnology (the 'molecular' phase of biotechnology), there is a marked qualitative increase in the human capacity to manipulate genomes of all organisms, plant and animal, including the transfer of genetic material across greatly different species. It seems to us that there is a sufficiently important qualitative difference between these two pre-molecular and molecular phases of genetic manipulation to justify the introduction of a generic oversight mechanism for the latter. In other words, we need a designated 'gene regulator' to oversee the processes of molecular biology with respect to the suitability of specific genetic manipulations intended to be introduced into the environment,[41] that is, an agency that would be a regulatory authority separate from, and superior to, the multi-departmental apparatus for the assessment of product safety previously described.

It is at least possible to see in the present achievements and future promises of molecular biology the prospect of a qualitative change in human technology, which also opens up for human societies qualitatively different issues of ethics and sensibility, because there is almost no limit to the genetic manipulations that can take place when science can operate directly on DNA. In this sense the process at stake here—the creation of transgenic entities through the direct manipulation of DNA using molecular biology—may be sufficiently unique, and may have ethical implications for human societies sufficiently profound in nature, that it ought to be the subject of a unique form of oversight.[42]

Finally, whether or not there is any warrant for a new level of oversight based on considerations of health and environmental safety, there is another reason entirely to consider such a course of action: as a response to what we earlier referred to as the poorly articulated public concerns about the present and future of genetic manipulation. In other words, given what is thought and imagined about this technology and its ultimate operational capacities, it is advisable to provide another level of regulatory oversight for no other reason than as a means of additional reassurance to the public.[43] This need not be seen as pandering to the lowest common denominator of understanding or as 'giving in' to the current critics of GM technologies, especially those who do not share the basic tenets and values of the modern scientific community.[44] It also need not be envisioned as a heavy regulatory burden, duplicating unnecessarily what already exists, but rather—to use the words of the Royal Society report referred to earlier—as a body with 'an ongoing role to monitor the wider issues associated with the develop-ment of GM plants'.[45] Obviously, the mandate and operational authority of such a body would require clear description and clear differentiation from the product-based safety reviews that now exist. But in the end, as a practical matter, it may be more efficient to provide this additional layer of public reassurance than to fight an endless rearguard action against the dark shadows conjured up in imag-ination by fears of what a newly potent science of genetics might bring.

Notes

1 US National Research Council, *Genetically Modified Pest-Protected Plants: Science and Regulation* (Washington: National Academy Press, 2000), 22.

2 M. Crouch, 'How the terminator terminates: An explanation for the non-scientist of a remarkable patent for killing second generation seeds of crop plants'. Washington: Edmonds Institute, 1998. http://www.bio.indiana.edu/people/terminator.html

3 C. O'Brian, 'Entire E. coli genome sequenced—at last', *Nature* 385 (Feb. 1997): 472; see also http://www.ornl.gov/hgmis/project/about.html

4 M. Boguski, 'Bioinformatics', *Current Opinions in Genetics and Development* 4 (1994): 383–8.

5 US Food and Drug Administration, 'Direct food substance affirmed as generally recognized as safe; chymosin enzyme preparation derived from Escherichia coli K-12', *Federal Register*, 23 Mar. 1990, vol. 57, 10932–6; US Food and Drug Administration, 'Direct food substances affirmed as generally recognized as safe; chymosin enzyme preparation derived from genetically modified Kluyveromyces marxianus (Hansen) Van Der Walt variety lactis (Dombrowski) Johannsen et Van Der Walt', *Federal Register*, 25 Feb. 1992, vol. 57, 6476–9; US Food and Drug Administration, 'Direct food substances affirmed as generally recognized as safe; chymosin enzyme preparation derived from Aspergillus niger Van Tieghem variety awamori (Nakazawa) Al-Musaliam', *Federal Register*, 7 May 1993, vol. 58, 27197–203; E.L. Flamm, 'How FDA approved chymosin: a case history', *Bio/Technology* 9 (1991): 349–51; L.S. Kahl, 'Summary of consultation with Calgene, Inc., concerning Flavr Savr tomatoes', FDA, 17 May 1994.

6 http://www.ec.gc.ca/cceb1/eng/97biochem.html, reporting substances that are products of micro-organisms under the new substances notification regulations. Section 2.3.4, Proteins subject to the 'Two Percent Rule'.

7 For detailed information on the evaluations of GMO plants, see the Web site of Professor Douglas Powell, Department of Plant Science, University of Guelph: http://www.plant.uoguelph.ca/safefood

8 D. Weiner and R. Kennedy, 'Genetic Vaccines', *Scientific American* (July 1999).

9 http://www.cfia-acia.agr.ca/english/plaveg/pbo/pntvcne.shtml, Status of Regulated Plants with Novel Traits (PNTs) in Canada: Environmental Release, Novel Livestock Feed Use, Variety Registration and Novel Food Use.

10 J. Hodgson, 'Bulgaria gets Eastern Europe's first gene release body', *Nature Biotechnology* 14 (Oct. 1996): 1212. In general, see the 'Special Issue: Precautionary Regulation—GM Crops in the European Union', *Journal of Risk Research* 3, 3 (July 2000).

11 Some useful short summaries of the environmental risks of plant GMOs are: B.J. Miflin, 'Crop Biotechnology: Where Now?', *Plant Physiology* 123 (May 2000): 17–27; Sir Robert May, 'Genetically Modified Foods: Facts, Worries, Policies and Public Confidence', Feb. 1999: http://www.dti.gov.uk./ost/ostbusiness/gen.html; the Royal Society, 'Statement: Genetically modified plants for food use', Sept. 1998: www.royalsoc.ac.uk. A very complete discussion of the range of risk factors will be found in US National Research Council, *Genetically Modified Pest-Protected Plants: Science and Regulation* (Washington: National Academy Press, 2000), ch. 2. A readable account of the risks and benefits of genetically modified food crops is Alan McHughen, *Pandora's Picnic Basket: The Potential and Hazards of Genetically Modified Foods* (New York: Oxford University Press, 2000).

12 Heather Scoffield, 'Canola farmer fights seed invasion', *Globe and Mail*, 14 Aug. 2000, B1, B4.

13 Bette Hilemen, 'Views differ sharply over benefits, risks of agricultural biotechnology', *Chemical & Engineering News* (21 Aug. 1995): 8–17; The Gene Exchange, 'Research confirms risks of transgenic crops'. Washington, 1996.

14 The same is true, of course, of the use of conventional pesticides.

15 The first study, by J. Losey et al., 'Transgenic pollen harms monarch larvae', appeared as a note in *Nature* 399 (20 May 1999): 214; a summary of other scientists' comments and research findings on the issue is available at: http://www.fooddialogue.com/monarch/index.html. The second study, by L. Hansen Jesse and J. Obrycki, 'Field deposition of Bt transgenic corn pollen: lethal effects on the monarch butterfly', *Oecologia*, Springer-Verlag, 19 Aug. 2000, can be read on-line at: http://athene.em.springer.de/cgi/view-hd.pl?/search97cgi/s97_cgi?action=view&Vdk VgwKey=%2Fjour%2Fjour%2F00442%2Fcontents%2F00%2F00502%2Fpaper%2Fs00 4420000502ch100%2Ehtml&queryZIP=#LINK_HL0. See also the article by Heather Scoffield in *Globe and Mail*, 25 Aug. 2000, A2.

16 The Royal Society, 'Genetically modified plants for food use', 8.

17 Ibid.

18 J. Nordlee, S. Taylor, J. Townsend, L. Thomas, and R. Bush, 'Identification of a Brazil-nut allergen in transgenic soybeans', *New England Journal of Medicine* 334 (1996): 688–92.

19 J. Astwood, J. Leach, and R. Fuchs, 'Stability of food allergens to digestion *in vitro*', *Nature Biotechnology* 14 (Oct. 1996): 1269–73.

20 There is a good discussion of this issue in McHughen, *Pandora's Picnic Basket*, ch. 12.

21 J. Stoye, 'No clear answers on safety of pigs as tissue donor source', *The Lancet* (29 Aug. 1998): 666–7; L. Chapman, T. Folks, D. Salomon, A. Patterson, T. Eggerman, and P. Noguchi, 'Xenotransplantation and xenogenic infections', *New England Journal of Medicine* (30 Nov. 1995): 1498–1501.

22 F. Bach and H. Fineberg, 'Call for moratorium on xenotransplants', *Nature* 391 (1998).

23 P. Collignon, 'Controversies in Healthcare. Xenotransplantation: do the risks outweigh the benefits?', *Medical Journal of Australia* 168 (May 1998): 516–19.

24 Japanese scientists claimed the first successful cloning of a pig, which makes xeno-transplantation much more feasible: *Science* 18 (Aug. 2000): 1118–19. At the same time, other scientists reported that PERV can infect humans. See I. Polejaeva et al., 'Cloned pigs produced by nuclear transfer from adult somatic cells', *Nature* 407 (Aug. 2000): 505–9; L. Van der laan et al., 'Infection by porcine endogenous retrovirus after islet xenotransplantation in SCID mice', *Nature* 407 (Aug. 2000): 501–4.

25 C. Patience, Y. Takeuchi, and R. Weiss, 'Infection of human cells by an endogenous retrovirus of pigs', *Nature Medicine* 3, 3 (1997): 282–6. So far, in a small number of short-term clinical trials using pig liver tissue, usually as external dialysis filters for patients waiting for human liver donors, the patients have not tested positive for the presence of a pig retrovirus: *Science* 279 (1998).

26 http://www.hc-sc.gc.ca/hpb-dgps/therapeut/zfiles/english/btox/notices/noticetohos-pitals_e.html, on the clinical use of viable animal cells, tissues, or organs to treat patients. Accessed 29 Mar. 1999.

27 A useful summary can be found in the 'Factsheet: The Federal Regulatory System', included in the information site on the National Biotechnology Strategy: http://www.ic.gc.ca/cmb/welcomeic.nsf/558

28 US National Academy of Sciences, *Introduction of Recombinant DNA-Engineered Organisms into the Environment: Key Issues* (Washington: National Academy Press, 1987); US National Research Council, *Genetically Modified Pest-Protected Plants: Science and Regulation* (Washington: National Academy Press, 2000). The quotations in the text are from p. 44 of the latter report.

29 Cf. the distinction made by David Dennis, who writes on his Web site: 'Biotechnology is defined as the transfer of genes using the techniques of molecular biology to gener-ate transgenic plants. It does not refer to methods used by modern plant breeders.' http://www.performanceplants.com/FAQ.htm

30 Contrast the definition given by David Dennis (above, note 29) with the following state-ment from material (dated Aug. 1997) posted on the CFIA Web site: 'Biotechnology involves using biological processes to produce substances beneficial to agriculture, the environment, industry, and medicine. In fact, we have used biotechnology to make everyday products for thousands of years.' http://www.cfia-acia.agr.ca/english/ppc/biotech/whatbio.htm

31 Standing Committee, transcript of hearing, meeting no. 19 (16 May 1996), testimony of Dr Brian Morrissey, AAFC. The current wording on the traditional versus new biotech-nology distinction is on the CFIA Web site at: http://www.cfia-acia.agr.ca/english/ppc/biotech/geninfo.htm (last updated Aug. 1997).

32 AAFC, *Biotechnology in Agriculture: General Information* (Ottawa, 1995).

33 For a valuable discussion of this point, Katherine J. Barrett, 'Canadian Agricultural Biotechnology: Risk Assessment and the Precautionary Principle', Ph.D. thesis (University of British Columbia, 1999).

34 'Eurobarometer', *Nature* (26 June 1997).

35 See the section entitled 'Cloning: Down the road towards moral risks', in William Leiss, Inaugural Lecture for the Research Chair in Risk Communication and Public Policy, University of Calgary (Mar. 1999: text and illustrations files): http://www.ucalgary.ca/ ~ wleiss/news/inaugural_lecture.htm

36 A frightful application of biotechnology, which we do not have time to deal with here, is the bioengineering of virulent bacteria and viruses for warfare, in the form of 'biological weapons' such as micro-organisms and viruses that have been genetically modified to make them more deadly. One is described as a recombinant Ebola-smallpox chimera called 'Ebolapox', in which the infection possesses the characteristic severe internal hemorrhaging of the Ebola virus but also the contagiousness of smallpox. At present about 18 countries are reportedly known to have, or are suspected of having, a capacity to develop such biological weapons. Ricki Lewis, 'Bioweapons research proliferates', *The Scientist* (27 Apr. 1998); Richard Preston, 'Annals of warfare, the bioweaponeers', *The New Yorker* (9 Mar. 1998): 52–65.

37 Perhaps the most powerful constraint on the Canadian regulators was their perceived need to conform (for trade harmonization reasons) to the US model, which first made the choice on how to approach the regulation of the new biotechnology. So far as excluding the public is concerned, it is likely that this was not at all an explicit decision; rather, it is the 'normal' procedure for governments to make policy choices first and then to design a public consultation process that leaves out the most basic issues from consideration.

38 Asked to respond to a newspaper story about the invasion of GM canola plants into neighbouring fields, a spokesperson for CFIA stated: 'That is a question that has been raised. That is my response.' Heather Scoffield, 'Canola farmer fights seed invasion', *Globe and Mail*, 14 Aug. 2000, B4.

39 Monsanto Inc. was awarded a US patent entitled: Control of Plant Gene Expression, 3 Mar. 1998 (M. Oliver, J. Quisenberry, N. Trolinder, G. Lee, and D. Keim, US Patent Number 5,723,765). The patent's main invention is to genetically engineer crops that produce seeds that are reproductively sterile in the second generation. This would make it impossible for farmers to save and replant seeds, making them dependent on the seed suppliers. Over 1.4 billion people, mostly living in less developed countries, depend on farm-saved seeds. The public backlash associated with Monsanto's terminator gene patent and its potential impact has been nothing less than incredible. Genetic engineering of plants to produce sterile seeds has been renounced as a 'morally offensive application of agricultural biotechnology'. Intense hostility worldwide towards this developing technology has been a public relations disaster for Monsanto. See http://www.rafi.org/web/allnews-one.shtml?dfl = allnews.db&tfl = allnews-one-frag.ptml&operation = display&ro1 = recNo&rf1 = 112&rt1 = 112&usebrs = true

40 Some of the broader issues involving the international context are briefly noted in a report issued by the national academies of seven countries and regions: *Transgenic Plants and World Agriculture* (Washington: National Academy Press, 2000).

41 This section draws on the concluding section in William Leiss, 'The Trouble with Science: Public Controversy over GM Foods' (Jan. 1999): http://www.ucalgary.ca/ ~ wleiss/news/trouble_with_science.htm

42 The great majority of current genetic manipulations in plant biology are confined to plant genes.

43 Regular news about new stages of completion in the Human Genome Project will produce, among other things, an enormous increase in public concerns about genetic manipulation.

44 One of the most active groups in Internet discussions on GM foods is the Natural Law Party.

45 The purview of such a body should extend to the full range of expected manipulations (plant, animal, human).

Appendix: Select Bibliographies for Environmental Issues

· Urban Environment

· Arctic/Northern Environment

· Energy and Fuels
    Oil and Gas
    Hydroelectricity
    Nuclear Power
    Alternative Fuels

· Waste Management
    Solid Waste
    Hazardous Waste

· Fisheries Management
    Atlantic Fisheries
    Pacific Fisheries

· Great Lakes Water Quality

Urban Environment

Alternatives Journal 22, 2 (Apr.-May 1996). Issue devoted to 'Green Communities'. View list of articles at: http://www.fes.uwaterloo.ca/alternatives/

Alternatives Journal 24, 1 (Winter 1998). Issue devoted to 'Cars vs Transit'.

Alternatives Journal 26, 3 (Summer 2000). Issue devoted to 'The End of Sprawl: Ways to redesign cities for better living'.

British Columbia Roundtable on the Environment and the Economy. 'State of sustainability: urban sustainability and containment'. Victoria, 1994.

Canada Mortgage and Housing Corporation, International Relations Division and Federation of Canadian Municipalities. *Ecological City: Canada's Overview*. Ottawa: CMHC, 1995.

Canadian Urban Institute and the Urban Environment Centre. 'A Municipal Primer on the United Nations Conference on Environment and Development: A Report'. Winnipeg and Ottawa: Canadian Council of Ministers of the Environment and Federation of Canadian Municipalities, 1994.

Canadian Urban Transit Association. 'The Environmental Benefits of Urban Transit: A Report'. Toronto: Transit/Environment Task Force, 1990.

Dearden, P., and B. Mitchell. *Environmental Change and Challenge: A Canadian Perspective*. Toronto: Oxford University Press, 1998. Ch. 13: 'Urban Environmental Management'.

Draper, D. *Our Environment: A Canadian Perspective*. Toronto: ITP Nelson, 1998. Ch. 13: 'Lifestyle Choices and Sustainable Communities'.

Federation of Canadian Municipalities and Canadian Urban Research on the Environment. *Canadian Municipal Environmental Directory*. Ottawa, 1995.

Hetherington, T., C. Rutter, and S. Farina. *The Green Links: Educator's Guide to the Urban Environment*. New Westminster, BC: Douglas College, May 1997.

Maclaren, V. *Developing Indicators of Urban Sustainability: A Focus on the Canadian Experience*. Toronto: ICURR Publications, 1996.

Lambright, W.H. 'Urban Reactions to the Global Warming Issue: Agenda Setting in Toronto and Chicago', *Climate Change* 34 (1996): 463–78.

Land Owner Resource Centre. *Maintaining Healthy Urban Cities*. Toronto and Hull, Que.: Ministry of Natural Resources and Human Resources Development Canada, 1998.

Lemon, J. 'Urban planning in twentieth century North America: From success to irrelevancy?', *University of Toronto Quarterly* 62, 4 (Summer 1993): 441–55.

Mitlin, D., and D. Satterthwaite. *Cities and Sustainable Development: Background Paper Prepared for Global Forum '94*. London: International Institute for Environment and Development, Human Settlements Program, 1994.

Ouellet, P. *Environmental Policy Review of 15 Canadian Municipal Plans*. Toronto: ICURR Publications, 1993.

Perks, W., J. Bilkhu, and D. Thimpson. *The Integration of Environmental Assessment and Municipal Planning*. Toronto: ICURR Publications, 1996.

Platt, R.H., R.A. Rowntree, and P.C. Muick. eds, *The Ecological City: Preserving and Restoring Urban Biodiversity*. Amherst: University of Massachusetts Press, 1994.

Rees, W.E., and M. Roseland. 'Sustainable Communities: Planning for the 21st Century', *Plan Canada* 31, 3 (1991): 15–26.

Roseland, M. 'Linking Affordable Housing and Environmental Protection: The Community Land Trust as a Sustainable Urban Development Institution', *Canadian Journal of Urban Research* (Dec. 1992): 162–81.

Stren, R., ed. *Sustainable Cities: Urbanization and the Environment in International Perspective*. Scarborough, Ont.: HarperCollins Canada, 1991.

Tomalty, R. *Ecosystem Planning for Canadian Urban Regions*. Toronto: ICURR Publications, 1994.

_____ and D. Pell. 'Sustainable Development in Canadian Cities: Current Initiatives'. Ottawa: Canada Mortgage and Housing Corporation, Centre for Future Studies in Housing and Living Environments, 1996.

_____ and S. Hendler. 'Green Planning: Striving towards Sustainable Development in Ontario's Municipalities', *Plan Canada* 31, 3 (1991): 27–32.

Internet Sources
Federation of Canadian Municipalities Ten-Point Action Plan for Sustainable Communities
http://www.fcm.ca/newfcm/Java/frame.htm

Intergovernmental Committee on Urban and Regional Research
http://www.icurr.org

National Air Pollution Surveillance Network (monitors and assesses the quality of the ambient air in Canadian urban centres)
http://www.etcentre.org/naps

Canadian Journal of Urban Research
http://www.uwinnipeg.ca/ ~ ius/cjur.htm

Canadian Urban Institute
http://www.canurb.com

Internet Sources—City of Toronto
'City of Toronto: Smog'
http://www.city.toronto.on.ca/health/smogalert.htm

Frameworks for Applying Sustainability in the City of Toronto
http://www.utoronto.ca/envstudy/INI498/salsbergf.htm

The Official Site of the City of Toronto
www.city.toronto.on.ca

Toronto Environmental Alliance
http://www.torontoenvironment.org/

Toronto in Transition
http://www.metrotor.on.ca/transition/

University of Toronto Study: 'Moving Ahead: Encouraging Environmentally Sustainable Transportation in the City of Toronto'
http://www.utoronto.ca/envstudy/INI498/dadflten.htm

Arctic/Northern Environment

Alternatives Journal 22, 4 (Oct.-Nov. 1996). Issue devoted to 'Diamond Mining and Northern Sustainability'.

Arctic Bulletin.

Axworthy, L. 'Circumpolar cooperation key to Canada's new northern vision', *Canadian Speeches* 13, 5 (Nov.-Dec. 1999): 62–7.

Canada, Indian and Northern Affairs. *The Arctic Environmental Strategy: Five Years of Progress.* Ottawa, 1996.

Canadian Environmental Assessment Agency. *NWT Diamonds Project: Report of the Environment Assessment Panel.* Ottawa, 1996.

Condon, R.G. 'Arctic bibliography: a guide to current Arctic and sub-Arctic periodicals', *Arctic Anthropology* 27, 2 (1990): 113–22.

Henry, G.H., A.S. Dyke, and J.H. England. 'Canada's crisis in arctic science: the urgent need for an arctic science and technology policy', *Arctic* 51, 2 (1998): 183–97.

International Work Group for Indigenous Affairs. *Arctic Environment: Indigenous Perspectives.* Copenhagen: IWGIA document no. 69, 1991.

Johnston, M.E., G.D. Twynam, and W. Haider, eds. *Shaping Tomorrow's North: The Role of Tourism and Recreation.* Thunder Bay: Lakehead University, 1998.

McKinley, R. 'Northern clean-up continues, but toxic risk still present', *Windspeaker* 16, 6 (Oct. 1998): 12–13.

Northern Perspectives, published by the Canadian Arctic Resources Committee. Full text available at: http://www.carc.org/pubs/np.htm. See, for example, issues devoted to:

'Persistent Organic Pollutants: Are We Close to a Solution?': 26, 1 (Fall-Winter 2000).

'Impact and Benefit Agreements: Tools for Sustainable Development?': 25, 4 (Fall-Winter 2000).

'Arctic Contaminants: An Unfinished Agenda': 25, 3 (Fall-Winter 1998–9).

'Diamond Mining and the Demise of Environmental Assessment in the North': 24, 1–4 (Fall-Winter 1996).

'Environmental Clean-up and Sustainable Development in the Circumpolar Arctic': 21, 4 (Winter 1993–4).

Northwest Territories, Resources, Wildlife and Economic Development. *Pressures on the Arctic Ecosystem from Human Activities.* Yellowknife, 1998.

Page, Robert. *Northern Development: The Canadian Dilemma.* Toronto: McClelland & Stewart, 1986.

Rothwell, D.R. 'Australian and Canadian initiatives in polar marine environmental protection: a comparative review', *Polar Record* 34, 191 (1998): 305–16.

Tennberg, M. *Arctic Environmental Cooperation: A Study in Governmentality.* Aldershot: Ashgate, 2000.

Tynan, C., and D. DeMaster. 'Observations and predictions of Arctic climatic change: potential effects on marine mammals', *Arctic* 50, 4 (Dec. 1997): 308–22.

VanOostdam, J. 'Human health implications of environmental contaminants in Arctic Canada: A review', *Science of the Total Environment* 230, 1–3 (1 June 1999): 1–82.

Welch, H.E. 'Marine Conservation in the Canadian Arctic: A Regional Overview', *Northern Perspectives* 25, 1 (1995): 5–17.

Woo, M.-K., and D.J. Gregor, eds. *Arctic Environment: Past, Present and Future.* Hamilton, Ont.: Department of Geography, McMaster University, 1992.

Young, O.R. *Creating Regimes: Arctic Accords and International Governance.* Ithaca, NY: Cornell University Press, 1998.

Internet Sources
Canadian Arctic Resources Committee
http://www.carc.org/

Environment Canada, The Arctic Ecosystem
http://www.mb.ec.gc.ca/nature/ecosystems/da00s04.en.html

Environment Canada, The Green Lane (Media Advisory)
http://www.ec.gc.ca/press/arctoz_m_e.htm

Government of the Northwest Territories—Land and Environment
http://www.gov.nt.ca/agendas/land/index.html

Health Canada, Northern and Arctic Environment 1996–7
http://www.hc-sc.gc.ca/msb/fnihp/artic_e96.htm

The International Arctic Environment Data Directory
http://www.grida.no/add/add-data.htm

Nunavut Planning Commission
http://npc.nunavut.ca/eng/index.html

University of Waterloo on the Arctic environment
http://www.arts.uwaterloo.ca/ANTHRO/rwpark/ArcticArchStuff/Environment.html

Yukon Department of Renewable Resources
http://www.renres.gov.yk.ca/

Energy and Fuels

OIL AND GAS

Alberta Energy and Utilities Board. *Alberta Oil and Gas Industry: Annual Statistics for 1998*. Calgary, 1999.

Alberta Environmental Centre. *Cattle and the Oil and Gas Industry in Alberta: A Literature Review with Recommendations for Environmental Management*. Calgary: Alberta Cattle Commission, 1996.

Alberta Health, Health Surveillance Branch and Clean Air Strategic Alliance. *Assessment of Respiratory Disorders in Relation to Solution Gas Flaring Activities in Alberta: Report*. Edmonton, 1998.

Ballem, J. *The Oil and Gas Lease in Canada*. Toronto: University of Toronto Press, 1999.

Canada, Energy, Mines and Resources. *2020 Vision: Canada's Long-Term Energy Outlook*. Ottawa: Energy and Fiscal Analysis Division of Energy, Mines and Resources Canada, 1990.

_____. Natural Resources Canada. *Canadian Natural Gas in the United States, Reliable and Environmentally Responsible*. Ottawa, 1994.

_____. *Energy Efficiency Trends in Canada*. Ottawa, 1996.

_____. Statistics Canada. Manufacturing, Construction and Energy Division, Energy Section. *Oil and Gas Extraction 1998*. Ottawa, 1999.

Feldman, D.L. 'Revisiting the energy crisis: How far have we come?', *Environment* 37, 4 (1995): 16–20, 42–4.

Francis, W. 'Burning questions about gas flares', *Environment Views and Network News* 1, 1 (1997): 18–19.

Freeman, S.D. 'Put energy conservation front and center', *Policy Options* 17, 3 (1996): 11–13.

Gaoshe, L. *The Impact of the Vancouver Island Natural Gas Pipeline Construction on Water Quality*. Victoria: BC Environmental Policy Review and Disaster Preparedness Planning, 1993.

Gibson, G., E. Higgs, and S.E. Hrudey. 'Sour Gas, Bitter Relations', *Alternatives Journal* 24, 2 (1998): 26–31.

Harker, P. 'Energy and Minerals in Canada', in B. Mitchell, ed., *Resource and Environmental Management in Canada: Addressing Conflict and Uncertainty*. Toronto: Oxford University Press, 1995, 286–309.

Hill, R., P. O'Keefe, and C. Snape. *The Future of Energy Use*. London: Earthscan Publications, 1995.

Lax, A. *Political Risk in the International Oil and Gas Industry*. Scarborough, Ont.: Prentice-Hall Canada, 2000.

Nikiforuk, A. 'It makes them sick: Alberta farmers claim their livelihoods, livestock and health have been compromised by increasing oil and gas developments', *Canadian Business* 72, 2 (Fall 1999): 46–51.

Story, K. 'Managing the Impacts of Hibernia: A Mid-Term Report', in Mitchell, ed., 310–34.

Vitello, C. 'Trouble in the Oil Patch: Sabotage Renews Interest in Potential Sour-Gas Flaring Hazards', *Hazardous Materials Management Magazine* 11, 2 (Apr.-May 1999): 10–14.

Internet Sources
Canadian Gas Association

http://www.cga.ca/

Canadian Petroleum Products Institute
http://www.icpp.ca/cppi.html

Natural Resources Canada, Oil Division
http://www.nrcan.gc.ca/es/erb/od/

Natural Resources Canada, Natural Gas Division
http://www.nrcan.gc.ca/es/erb/ngd/

Pembina Institute for Appropriate Development
http://www.pembina.org/

HYDROELECTRICITY

Allaby, J. 'Electrical Enterprise: Small is Beautiful When it Comes to Hydro Power', *Canadian Geographic* 110 (Oct.-Nov. 1990): 48–52.

BC Hydro. *Environmental, Social and Economic: BC Hydro 1999 triple bottom line report.* Vancouver: BC Hydro, 1999.

Berkes, F. 'The Intrinsic Difficulty of Predicting Impacts: Lessons from the James Bay Hydro Project', *Environmental Impact Assessment Review* 8, 3 (1988): 201–20.

Bruce, M. 'Water and Waterscapes: Some Conflicting Interests', *Environments* 24, 1 (1996): 97–104.

Canada. *Guidelines for the Environmental Impact Statement for the Proposed Great Whale River Hydroelectric Project: Background Information.* Ottawa: Great Whale Public Review Support Office, 1992.

_____. *Hydroelectric Potential Development of the Lower Churchill River in Labrador: A Large Element in Reducing Canada's Greenhouse Gas Emissions.* Ottawa: Canadian Intergovernmental Conference Secretariat, 1997.

Chamberland, A., C. Belanger, and L. Gagnon. 'Atmospheric emissions: Hydro-electricity versus other options', *Ecodecision* 19 (Winter 1996): 56–60.

Clugston, M. 'Power Struggle: Plans for a $12 b hydro project straddling the Labrador-Quebec border heal old wounds and re-open others', *Canadian Geographic* 118, 7 (Nov.-Dec. 1998): 58–76.

Day, J.C., K. Boudreau, and N. Hackett. 'Emerging Institutions for Bilateral Management of the Columbia River Basin', *American Review of Canadian Studies* 26, 2 (Summer 1996): 217–32.

Freeman, N. *The Politics of Power: Ontario Hydro and its Government, 1906–1995.* Toronto: University of Toronto Press, 1996.

Froschauer, K. *Provincial Hydro Expansions: Required to Serve Industrial Development in Canada and Continental Integration (Ontario, Quebec, Labrador, Manitoba, British Columbia).* Ottawa: Carleton University, 1993.

Hydro-Québec. *Environmental Performance Report, 1999.* Available at: http://www.hydro-quebec.com/publications/enviro_perf_rep_1999/index.html

Manore, J.L. *Cross-Currents: Hydroelectricity and the Engineering of Northern Ontario.* Waterloo, Ont.: Wilfrid Laurier University Press, 1999.

Mathew, R. *Comparative Study of Hydroelectric Projects in Canada and India.* Available at: http://www.pages.hotbot.com/photo/roymathew/canada.html

McCutcheon, S. *Electric Rivers: The Story of the James Bay Project.* Montreal: Black Rose Books, 1991.

Internet Sources

Canadian Hydropower Association
http://www.canhydropower.org

Canadian Hydro Developers Inc.
http://www.canhydro.com

BC Hydro
http://eww.bchydro.bc.ca/

Hydro-Québec
http://www.hydro.qc.ca/

Manitoba Hydro
http://www.hydro.mb.ca/

Newfoundland & Labrador Hydro
http://www.nlh.nf.ca/

NUCLEAR POWER

Canada, Atomic Energy Control Board. *Radioactive Emission Data from Canadian Nuclear Generating Stations, 1986 to 1995*. Hull, Que., July 1997.

_____. *Canadian National Report for the Convention on Nuclear Safety*. Ottawa: Government of Canada, 1998.

_____. *Policy on Protection of the Environment: Proposed Regulatory Policy*. Ottawa,1998.

Canada, Department of Finance. *1999–2000 Estimates, Part III, Report on Plans and Priorities: Atomic Energy Control Board*. Ottawa: Public Works and Government Services Canada, Canadian Government Publishing, 1999.

Canadian Environmental Assessment Agency. *Report of the Nuclear Fuel Waste Management and Disposal Concept*. Hull, Que., Feb. 1998.

Carbon, M. *Nuclear Power: Villain or Victim? Our Most Misunderstood Source of Energy*. Madison, Wis.: Pebble Beach Publishers, 1997.

Durham Nuclear Awareness, 'Pickering Nuclear Station Unsafe . . . Maintenance Backlog Out of Control', media release, 6 May 1997. Available at:
http://www.ccnr.org/dna_release.html

'Final chapter in Chernobyl saga', *Toronto Star*, 13 Dec. 2000, A20.

Gonzalez, A. 'Chernobyl—ten years after: Global experts clarify the facts about the 1986 accident and its effects', *IAEA Bulletin*. Available at:
http://www.iaea.or.at/worldatom/inforesource/bulletin/bull383/gonzalez.html

Gordon, S. 'The greening of the atom: Atomic Energy of Canada wants to shift the long-running battle over nuclear energy to its critics' environmental turf', *Financial Post Magazine* (Nov. 1998): 14–20.

Greber, M.A., E.R. Frech, and J.A.R. Hiller. *The Disposal of Canada's Nuclear Fuel Waste: Public Involvement and Social Aspects*. Chalk River, Ont., AECL–10712, COG–93–2, 1994.

Hine, D., et al. 'Public opposition to a proposed Nuclear Waste Repository in Canada: An investigation of cultural and economic effects', *Risk Analysis* 17, 3 (1997): 293–302.

Lee, W. 'Fallout: Privatizing bigger public services would have hidden cost we rarely expect. Just look at Ontario Hydro's nuclear plants', *The Megazine* 30, 1 (July-Aug. 1996): 30–4.

Lermer, G. 'The Dismal Economics of Candu', *Policy Options* 17, 3 (1996): 16–20.

Martin, D.H. 'The CANDU Syndrome: Canada's Bid to Export Nuclear Reactors to Turkey'. Ottawa: Campaign for Nuclear Safety, Sept. 1997. Available at: http://www.ccnr.org/turkey_syndrome_2.html

Mehta, M. 'Re-Licensing of Nuclear Facilities in Canada: The "Risk Society" in Action', *Electronic Journal of Sociology* (1997). Available at: http://www.sociology.org/content/vol003.001/mehta.html

Nuclear Inforing. 'Nuclear Power: Energy for Today and Tomorrow'. Available at: http://pw1.netcom.com/ ~ res95/energy/nuclear.html

Ontario. Legislative Assembly. Select Committee on Ontario Hydro Nuclear Affairs. *Report of the Select Committee on Ontario Hydro Nuclear Affairs*. Toronto, 1997.

Plummer, D. 'Nuclear waste: Coming soon to a hole near you?', *Canadian Dimension* 30, 5 (1996): 52–4.

Stothart, P. 'Nuclear electricity: The best option given the alternatives', *Policy Options* 17, 3 (1996): 14–16.

Internet Sources

Canadian Coalition for Nuclear Responsibility
http://www.ccnr.org/

Canadian Nuclear Safety Commission
http://www.aecb-ccea.gc.ca

Canadian Nuclear Association
http://www.cna.ca

Canadian Nuclear Society
http://www.cns-snc.ca

Energy Probe
http://www.energyprobe.org/energyprobe/index.cfm

Natural Resources Canada, Nuclear Energy Division
http://nuclear.nrcan.gc.ca

Nuclear Information and Resource Service
http://www.nirs.org/

Nuclear-Related WWW Sites
http://www.nci.org/nci-hot.htm

ALTERNATIVE FUELS

AhYou, K., and G. Leng. *Renewable Energy in Canada's Remote Communities*. Ottawa: Natural Resources Canada, 1999.

Baird, V. 'Here comes the sun, and the wind and the rain', *New Internationalist* 284 (Oct. 1996): 20–3.

Bartels, D. 'A rare good thing: the Hopi solar project and barriers to the use of renewable energy technologies', *Alternatives Journal* 21, 4 (Oct.-Nov. 1995): 36–40.

Burke, D. 'Ground-source heating: The wave of the future?', *Canmore Leader*, 18 Mar. 1997, A14.

Canadian Wind Energy Association National Conference. *National Conference of the Canadian Wind Energy Association: Proceedings, 1995*. Calgary, 1995.

Clode, D.-G. 'Sunlight power for the 21st century?', *Ecodecision* 21 (Summer 1996): 8–9.

Cochrane, L. *Assessment of the Potential Use of Biomass Resources as a Sustainable Energy Source in Saskatchewan*. Saskatoon: Saskatchewan Energy Conservation and Development Authority, 1994.

Gill, L. *The Environmental Benefits and Economics of Hydrogen as a Vehicle Fuel in Canada*. Canadian Energy Research Institute, Study No. 82, 1998.

Gipe, P. 'Wind energy comes of age: windpower has become a commercial generating technology capable of meeting a considerable part of our electrical energy needs', *Ecodecision* 19 (Winter 1996): 52–5.

Ledger, B. 'Garbage in, power out: collecting landfill gas has a double environmental benefit', *Canadian Consulting Engineer* 39, 3 (1998): 34–40.

Natural Resources Canada. *1998–99 Year-End Report of Activities Under the Renewable Energy Deployment Strategy, REDI*. Ottawa: Government of Canada, 1999.

_____. 'Anderson announces funding for Ballard fuel cell technology'. Available at: http://www.nrcan.gc.ca/css/imb/hqlib/9619.htm

_____. *Renewable Energy Deployment Initiative (REDI): Encouraging Heating and Cooling Using Renewable Sources*. Ottawa: Government of Canada, 1998.

_____. *Renewable Energy Strategy: Creating a New Momentum*. 1996. Available at: http://nrn1.nrcan.gc.ca/es/new/denis2.htm

_____, Energy Demand Branch. *Efficiency and Alternative Energy Programs in Canada*. Ottawa: Government of Canada, 1995.

_____, Renewable and Electrical Energy Division. *Renewable Energy Strategy: Creating a New Momentum*. Ottawa: Government of Canada, 1996.

Pembina Institute. *Lost Opportunities: Canada and Renewable Energy*. 1999. Available at: http://www.pembina.org/pubs/cre.htm

Schwartzman, D. 'Solar Communism', *Science and Society* 60, 3 (Fall 1996): 307–31.

Tulley, A. 'The age of wind power dawns in Alberta', *Canadian Geographic* 114, 2 (1994): 12.

Internet Sources

Blue Energy Tidal Power
http://www.bluenergy.com

Canadian Renewable Fuels Association
http://www.greenfuels.org

Canadian Sustainable Energy
http://www.newenergy.org

Canadian Wind Energy Association
http://www.canwea.ca

Energy and Environment: Links and Resources
http://www.zebu.uoregon.edu/energy.html

Natural Resources Canada, Renewable and Electrical Energy Division
http://www.nrcan.gc.ca/es/erb/reed

Waste Management

SOLID WASTE

Chang, E., D. Macdonald, and J. Wolfson. 'Who killed CIPSI?', *Alternatives Journal* 24, 2 (1998): 21–5.

Crittenden, G. 'The Blue Box Conspiracy'. First appeared in *The Next City*. Available at: http://www.solidwastemag.com/library/related/blue.htm

Fenton, R. 'Pulling in the same direction: Private waste stewardship and municipal waste management planning', *Alternatives Journal* 19, 2 (1993): 25–30.

Jackson, J. *Resources—Not Garbage: Municipal Solid Waste in Ontario*. Toronto: Canadian Institute for Environmental Law and Policy, Mar. 1999. Available at: http://www.cielap.org/infocent/research/swaste.html

Journal of Solid Waste Technology and Management.

La Plante, B., and M. Lukert. 'Impact on Newsprint Recycling Policies on Canadian Waste Production and Forests', *Canadian Public Policy* 20, 4 (Dec. 1994): 400–14.

Maclaren, V. 'Waste Management: Moving Beyond the Crisis', in B. Mitchell, ed., *Resource and Environmental Management in Canada: Addressing Conflict and Uncertainty*. Toronto: Oxford University Press, 1995, 29–54.

Menzies, D. 'Waste Blues'. First appeared in *The Financial Post Magazine* (Sept. 1997). Available at: http://www.solidwastemag.com/library/Wasteb1.htm

Munroe, G. *User-Pay Systems for Solid Waste Management in Canadian Municipalities*. Toronto: ICURR Publications, Sept. 1999.

Nova Scotia, Department of the Environment. *Solid Waste Resource Management in Nova Scotia: 1996–97 Status Report*. Halifax, 1997.

Resource Integration Systems Ltd. *Case Studies of Leading-edge Solid Waste Diversion Projects*. Ottawa: Environment Canada, Hazardous Waste Branch, Waste Treatment Division, 1996.

Sinclair, A.J. 'Assuming Responsibility for Packaging and Packaging Waste', *Electronic Green Journal* 12 (2000). Available at: http://egj.lib.uidaho.edu/egj12/sinclair1/index.html

Solid Waste Management and Recycling.

Thorpe, Beverly. 'Industry's Environmental Responsibility beyond the Point of Sale: True Waste Reduction Through Extended Producer Responsibility: A Challenge for Quebec'. Brief Submitted to the BAPE (Bureau d'Audiences Publiques sur l'Environnement) Commission of Enquiry on Solid Waste Management. Montreal: Greenpeace Quebec, Aug. 1997.

Ungar, S. 'Recycling and the Dampening of Concern: Comparing the Roles of Large and Small Actors in Shaping the Environmental Discourse', *Canadian Review of Sociology and Anthropology* 35, 2 (May 1998): 253–76.

Internet Sources

Nova Scotia, Department of the Environment, Waste-Resource Management Publications
http://www.gov.ns.ca/envi/wasteman/Pubs.htm

Ontario, Ministry of the Environment
http://www.ene.gov.on.ca/waste.htm

Recycling Council of Ontario
http://www.rco.on.ca/

Solid Waste and Recycling: Canada's magazine on collection, hauling, processing and disposal
http://www.solidwastemag.com/

Solid Waste Association of North America
http://www.swana.org

HAZARDOUS WASTE

Canadian Institute for Environmental Law and Policy. *Ontario: Open for Toxics.* Toronto, June 2000. Available at:
http://www.cielap.org/infocent/research/index.html#waste.

Davis, C. *The Politics of Hazardous Waste.* Scarborough, Ont.: Prentice-Hall Canada, 1993.

Hazardous Materials Management Magazine. Available at: http://www.hazmatmag.com/

McFarlane, D. 'Beyond NIMBY: Hazardous Waste Siting in Canada and the United States', *Journal of Politics* 58, 1 (Feb. 1996): 258–61.

O'Neill, K. 'Out of the Backyard: The Problems of Hazardous Waste Management at a Global Level', *Journal of Environment and Development* 7, 2 (1998): 138–63.

Smith, D. 'The Kraken Wakes: Corporate Social Responsibility and the Political Dynamics of the Hazardous Waste Issue', *Industrial Crisis Quarterly* 5, 3 (1991): 189–207.

Rabe, B. *Beyond NIMBY: Hazardous Waste Siting in Canada and the United States.* Washington: Brookings Institution Press, 1994.

Winfield, M. *Hazardous Waste and Toxic Substances.* Toronto: Canadian Institute for Environmental Law and Policy, n.d. Available at:
http://www.cielap.org/infocent/research/hazwaste.html

Internet Sources

Environment Canada, Hazardous Waste

http://www.ns.ec.gc.ca/pollution/hazardouswaste.html

Fisheries Management

ATLANTIC FISHERIES

Akiba, O. 'Policy issues and challenges in Canadian management of the Atlantic fisheries', *Environmental Conservation* 24, 2 (1997): 159–67.

Applebaum, B. 'Straddling stocks—international law and the Northwest Atlantic Problem', *Canadian Bulletin of Fisheries and Aquatic Sciences* 226 (1993): 193–210.

Arnason, R. 'Minimum information management in fisheries', *Canadian Journal of Economics* 23, 3 (1990): 630–53.

Barry, D. 'The Canada-European Union turbot war: internal politics and transatlantic bargaining', *International Journal* 53, 2 (Spring 1998): 253–84.

Blades, K. *Net Destruction: The Death of Atlantic Canada's Fishery*. Halifax: Nimbus Publishing, 1995.

Canada, Fisheries and Oceans Canada. *Integrated Fisheries Management Plan*. Ottawa, 1997. Available at:
http://www.gfc.dfo.ca/fish_mgmt/mgmt_plan/crab_19–e.html

_____. *Government Response to the Report of the Standing Committee on Fisheries and Oceans: The East Coast Report*. Ottawa, 1998.

Charles, A. 'Living with uncertainty in fisheries: Analytical methods, management priorities and Canadian groundfishery experience', *Fisheries Research Amsterdam* 37, 1–3 (Aug. 1998): 37–50.

Conservation Council of New Brunswick. 'Respecting Nature and Community: Beyond Crisis in the Fisheries', *Ecological Fisheries Project Bulletin* 3 (1995). Available at: http://www.web.apc.org/-nben/ecofish.htm

Coward, H., R. Ommer, and T. Pitcher, eds. *Just Fish: Ethics and Canadian Marine Fisheries*. St John's: ISER Books, 2000.

Crawford, S., B. Morito, B. Shuter, C. Minns, and C. Olver. 'Toward a definition of conservation principles for fisheries management', *Canadian Journal of Fisheries and Aquatic Sciences* 54, 11 (Nov. 1997): 2720–5.

Crowley, R., B. McEachern, and R. Jasperse. 'A review of federal assistance to the Canadian fishing industry, 1945–1990', *Canadian Bulletin of Fisheries and Aquatic Sciences* 226 (1990): 339–67.

Eggen, M. 'The sinking feeling', *Alternatives Journal* 23, 1 (1997): 7.

Food and Agriculture Organization, United Nations. Code of Conduct for Responsible Fisheries. Available at:
http://www.fao.org/waicent/faoinfo/fishing/agreem/codecond/codecon.htm

Gardner, M. 'Input controls vs. rights-based management: The political economy of fisheries management in Atlantic Canada', *Aquatic Living Resources* 8, 3 (1995): 267–77.

Gauldie, R. 'Fisheries management science: A plea for conceptual change', *Canadian Journal of Fisheries and Aquatic Sciences* 52, 9 (1995): 2059–61.

Gough, J. 'A historical sketch of fisheries management in Canada', *Canadian Bulletin of Fisheries and Aquatic Sciences* 226 (1993): 5–53.

Harding, C. 'A review of the major marine environmental concerns off the Canadian east coast in the 1980s'. Halifax: Department of Fisheries and Oceans, 1992.

Harris, L. 'The East Coast Fisheries', in B. Mitchell, ed., *Resource and Environmental Management in Canada*. Toronto: Oxford University Press, 1995, 13–150.

House of Commons Standing Committee on Fisheries and Oceans. *The East Coast Report: An Interim Report*. Ottawa, 1998.

Hutchings, J.A., and R.A. Myers. 'What can be learned about the collapse of a renewable resource? Atlantic Cod, *gadus morhua*, of Newfoundland and Labrador', *Canadian Journal of Fisheries and Aquatic Sciences* 51, 9 (1994): 2126–46.

_____, C. Walters, and R.L. Haedrich. 'Is scientific inquiry incompatible with government information control?', *Canadian Journal of Fisheries and Aquatic Sciences* 54, 5 (1997): 1198–1210.

Mathews, D.R. *Controlling Common Property: Regulating Canada's East Coast Fishery.* Toronto: University of Toronto Press, 1993.

Neis, B. 'Fishers' ecological knowledge and stock assessment in Newfoundland', *Newfoundland Studies* 3, 2 (1992): 155–78.

_____ and L. Felt, eds. *Finding Our Sea Legs: Linking Fishery People and Their Knowledge with Science and Management.* St John's: ISER Books, 2000.

Northern Cod Review Panel. *Independent Review of the State of the Northern Cod Stock: Final Report* (the Harris Report). Ottawa: Department of Fisheries and Oceans, 1990.

Parfit, M. 'Diminishing returns: Exploiting the ocean's bounty', *National Geographic* 188, 5 (1995): 2–37.

Parsons, L. *Management of Marine Fisheries in Canada.* Ottawa: National Research Council Canada, Department of Fisheries and Oceans, 1993.

_____ and W. Lear. *Perspectives on Canadian Marine Fisheries Management.* Ottawa: NRC Research Press, 1994.

Richards, L., and J. Maguire. 'Recent international agreements and the precautionary approach: New directions for fisheries management science', *Canadian Journal of Fisheries and Aquatic Sciences* 55, 6 (June 1998): 1545–52.

Rivard, D., and J. Maguire. 'Reference points for fisheries management: The eastern Canadian experience', *Canadian Special Publication of Fisheries and Aquatic Sciences* 120 (1993): 59–65.

Schram, G.G., and N. Polunin. 'The high seas "commons": Imperative regulation of half our planet's surface', *Environment Conservation* 22, 1 (1995): 3.

Internet Sources

Fisheries and Oceans Canada, Fisheries Management

http://www.gfc.dfo.ca/fish_mgmt/ressource_mgmt/index-e.html

Fisheries and Oceans Canada

http://www.maritimes.dfo.ca/

Fisheries Resources Conservation Council

http://www.ncr.dfo.ca/frcc/index.htm

National Service Standards: Fisheries Management Sector

http://www.ncr.dfo.ca/communic/fish_man/nss/fishman.htm

PACIFIC FISHERIES

Anderson, R., M. Harrison, and D. Anderson. 'U.S., Canada Spent 6 Years on Fishing Agreement', *Seattle Times*, 6 June 1999.

'Canada, U.S. Sign Salmon Pact', *Toronto Star*, 1 July 1999.

DeCloet, D. 'The apartheid fishery is scuttled: the provincial court rules Ottawa's Aboriginal Fishing Strategy illegal', *British Columbia Report* 9, 23 (9 Feb. 1998): 11.

Fraser River Action Plan. *Fact Sheet 2: Pollution in the Fraser.* Available at: http://yvrwww1.pwc.bc.doe.ca/ec/frap/fr-fs2.html

Glavin, T. 'Dead reckoning: confronting the crisis in Pacific fisheries', *Canadian Geographic* 116, 5 (Sept.-Oct. 1996): 76-7.

_____. 'Sea of change: As West Coast fisheries collapse, human activity is blamed', *Canadian Geographic* 119, 4 (May-June 1999): 38-48.

Grafton, R., and H. Nelson. 'Fishers' individual salmon harvesting rights: An option for Canada's Pacific fisheries', *Canadian Journal of Fisheries and Aquatic Sciences* 54, 2 (1997): 474-82.

Griffin. S. 'Something fishy's going on: an insider's look at the salmon fishing industry in BC', *Briarpatch* 28, 5 (June 1999): 9-12.

House of Commons Standing Committee on Fisheries and Oceans. *The West Coast Report: An Interim Report.* Ottawa, 1998.

Kenny, E. 'East, west disputes oceans apart', *Victoria Times Colonist*, 11 July 1995, A5.

Kenworthy, T., and S. Pearlstein. 'U.S., Canada Reach a Landmark Pact on Pacific Salmon Fishing', *Washington Post*, 4 June 1999.

Leaman, B. 'Reference points for fisheries management: The western Canadian experience', *Canadian Special Publication of Fisheries and Aquatic Sciences* 120 (1993): 15-30.

McDaniels, T., M. Healey, and R. Paisley. 'Cooperative fisheries management involving First Nations in British Columbia: An adaptive approach to strategy design', *Canadian Journal of Fisheries and Aquatic Sciences* 51, 9 (1994): 2115-25.

Munro, G., T. McDorman, and R. McKelvey. 'Transboundary fishery resources and the Canada-United States Pacific Salmon Treaty', *Canadian-American Public Policy* 33 (Fall 1998): 1-48.

'Pacific Fisheries for Tomorrow', *Pacific Tidings* 7, 3 (1995): 5-6.

Paisley, R.K. *Regional Marine Issues Overview Paper—West Coast.* Ottawa: Canadian Arctic Resources Committee/Canadian Nature Federation, 1994.

Pinkerton, E. 'Local fisheries co-management: A review of international experience and their implications for salmon management in British Columbia', *Canadian Journal of Fisheries and Aquatic Sciences* 51, 10 (1994): 2363-78.

'Saving the Wild Chinook', *Pacific Tidings* 8, 2 (1995): 3-4.

Springer, A.L. 'The Pacific Salmon Controversy: Law, Diplomacy, Equity, and Fish', *American Review of Canadian Studies* 27 (1997): 385-409.

Stewart, C., and R. Rogers. 'Prisoners of their histories: Canada-US conflicts in the Pacific salmon fishery', *American Review of Canadian Studies* 27 (1997): 253-69.

Stoffer, P. 'The United States Hooked a Big One with the Liberals' Fishing Deal', *Ottawa Citizen*, 15 June 1999.

Taylor, E. 'Fishing for control: former enemies join forces as BC coastal communities seek to manage their own fisheries', *Alternatives* 24, 2 (Spring 1998): 7-8.

Terry, T. 'Anderson faults Canadian rigidity on salmon treaty: The federal fisheries minister says the lack of an agreement benefits Americans, not us', *Vancouver Sun*, 24 Apr. 1999, A4.

Internet Sources

Fisheries and Oceans Canada
http://www.maritimes.dfo.ca/

Fisheries and Oceans Canada (Pacific Region): Fisheries management
http://www.pac.dfo-mpo.gc.ca/ops/fm/fishmgmt.htm

Great Lakes Water Quality

'An overview of Canadian law and policy governing Great Lakes water quality management', *Case Western Reserve Journal of International Law* 18 (Winter 1986): 109–53.

Barlow, M. 'Our water's not for sale', *Canadian Perspectives* (Winter 1999): 6.

Caldwell, L. 'Disharmony in the Great Lakes basin: institutional jurisdictions frustrate the ecosystem approach', *Alternatives Journal* 20, 3 (July–Aug. 1994): 26–33.

Canada, Department of Foreign Affairs and International Trade. 'Amendments to International Boundary Waters Treaty to Protect Great Lakes from Bulk Water Removals', news release No. 250, 22 Nov. 1999. Available at: http://198.103.104.118

Canada and United States. *Great Lakes Water Quality Agreement of 1978: Agreement, with Annexes and Terms of Reference, between the United States of America and Canada, signed at Ottawa, November 22, 1978.* Windsor, Ont. and Washington: International Joint Commission, 1978. Available at: http://www.ijc.org/ijcweb-e.html

Focus (Bulletin of the International Joint Commission). Available at: http://www.ijc.org

Fuller, K., H. Shear, and J. Wittig. *The Great Lakes: An Environmental Atlas and Resource Book.* Chicago: Great Lakes National Program Office, US Environmental Protection Agency/Government of Canada, 1995.

Gilbertson, M. 'Are causes knowable? Some consequences of successional versus toxicological interpretations of the Great Lakes Water Quality Agreement', *Canadian Journal of Fisheries and Aquatic Sciences* 54, 2 (Fall 1997): 483–95.

Hartig, J. 'Great Lakes remedial action plans: fostering adaptive ecosystem-based management processes', *American Review of Canadian Studies* 27, 3 (Fall 1997): 437–58.

_____, M.A. Zarull, T.M. Heidtke, and H. Shah. 'Implementing ecosystem-based management: Lessons from the Great Lakes', *Journal of Environmental Planning and Management* 41, 1 (1998): 45–75.

Hartig, P.D., J.H. Hartig, D.R. Lesh, D.G. Lowrie, and G.H. Wever. 'Practical application of sustainable development in decision-making processes in the Great Lakes Basin', *International Journal of Sustainable Development and World Ecology* 3 (1996): 31–46.

Inscho, F., and M. Durfee. 'The Troubled Renewal of the Canada-Ontario Agreement Respecting Great Lakes Water Quality', *Publius* 25, 1 (Winter 1995): 51–69.

International Joint Commission. *The IJC and the 21st Century.* Ottawa, 1997.

_____. *Beacons of Light* = *'des lumières dans la nuit': Successful Strategies toward Restoration in Areas of Concern under the Great Lakes Water Quality Agreement: Special Report.* Ottawa, 1998.

_____. *Water Use Reference.* 1999. Material on IJC reports and public hearings available at: http://www.ijc.org/

_____. *Ninth Biennial Report on Great Lakes Water Quality.* Ottawa, 1998.

_____. *Protection of the Waters of the Great Lakes: Final Report to the Governments of Canada and the United States.* Ottawa, 22 Feb. 2000.

Kreutzwiser, R.D. 'Water Resources Management: Canadian Perspectives and the Great Lakes Water Levels Issue', in B. Mitchell, ed., *Resource and Environmental Management in Canada: Addressing Conflict and Uncertainty.* Toronto: Oxford University Press, 1995, 259–85.

Muldoon, P., and J. Jackson. 'Keeping the zero in zero discharge: phasing out persistent toxic substances in the Great Lakes Basin', *Alternatives Journal* 20, 4 (Sept.–Oct. 1994): 14–20.

National Research Council of the United States and the Royal Society of Canada. *The Great Lakes Water Quality Agreement: An Evolving Instrument for Ecosystem Management.* Washington: National Academy Press, 1985

Rabe, B. 'The Politics of Ecosystem Management in the Great Lakes Basin', *American Review of Canadian Studies* 27, 3 (Autumn 1997): 411–36.

Schwartz, A.M. 'Canada-U.S. Environmental Relations: A Look at the 1990s', *American Review of Canadian Studies* 24, 4 (Winter 1994): 489–508.

_____. 'The Canada-U.S. Environmental Relationship at the Turn of the Century', *American Review of Canadian Studies* 30, 2 (Summer 2000): 207–26.

Scoffield, H. 'Canada-U.S. commission urges Great Lakes water-export ban', *Globe and Mail*, 19 Aug. 1999, A2.

Internet Sources

Environment Canada, Great Lakes
http://www.cciw.ca/glimr/intro-e.html

International Joint Commission
http://www.ijc.org

Great Lakes Commission
http://www.glc.org/

Great Lakes Fishery Commission
http://www.glfc.org

Great Lakes Research Consortium
http://www.esf.edu/glrc/

Great Lakes United
http://www.glu.org/

Contributors

Steven Bernstein is an Assistant Professor of International Relations at the University of Toronto. His book *The Compromise of Liberal Environmentalism* (2001) examines the evolution of international environmental norms. His other publications and ongoing research examine the internationalization of public policy, transnational environmental politics, institutionalization and change in world politics, and theory and evidence in social science research.

Robert Boardman is a Professor of Political Science at Dalhousie University. He is a specialist in international environmental institutions and the post-socialist world order. He is co-editor, with Karen Beazley, of *Politics of the Wild: Canada and Endangered Species* (2001) and author of *The Political Economy of Nature: Environmental Debates and the Social Sciences* (2001).

Benjamin Cashore is an Assistant Professor of Forest Policy and Economics at Auburn University. His research interests include globalization and the forest sector, the political economy of US-Canada forest products trade, and forest industry sustainability initiatives. Recent publications have appeared or are forthcoming in *Policy Sciences*, the *Canadian Journal of Political Science*, *Canadian Public Administration*, and *Canadian-American Public Policy*. He is a co-author of *In Search of Sustainability: The Politics of Forest Policy in British Columbia in the 1990s* (2000).

G. Bruce Doern is a Professor in the Carleton Research Unit on Innovation, Science and Environment in the School of Public Administration, Carleton University and holds a joint Research Chair in Public Policy in the Politics Department, University of Exeter. His most recent books include *Risky Business: Canada's Changing Science-Based Regulatory Regime* (2000, edited with Ted Reed), and *Changing the Rules: Canada's Regulatory Regimes and Institutions* (1999, with Margaret Hill, Michael Prince, and Richard Schultz).

Kathryn Harrison is an Associate Professor of Political Science at the University of British Columbia. She is the author of *Passing the Buck: Federalism and Canadian Environmental Policy*, co-author of *Risk, Science, and Politics: Regulating Toxic Substances in Canada and the United States*, and co-editor of *Managing the Environmental Union*. Her current research concerns alternative environmental policy instruments, including voluntary agreements, ecolabels, and information dissemination.

George Hoberg is an Associate Professor of Political Science and Forest Resource Management at the University of British Columbia. He is a specialist on Canadian and American environmental and forest policy and on the impact of North

American integration on Canada. He is a co-author of *In Search of Sustainability: The Politics of Forest Policy in British Columbia in the 1990s* (2000) and editor of *Scope for Choice: Canada in a New North America* (2001).

Michael Howlett is a Professor of Political Science at Simon Fraser University who specializes in public policy analysis, Canadian political economy, and Canadian resource and environmental policy. He is co-author of *In Search of Sustainability: The Politics of Forest Policy in British Columbia in the 1990s* (2000), *Canadian Natural Resource and Environmental Policy: Political Economy and Public Policy* (1997), *Studying Public Policy: Policy Cycles and Subsystems* (1995), and *The Political Economy of Canada* (1992, 1999).

W. Henry Lambright is a Professor of Political Science and Public Administration, and Director of the Center for Environmental Policy and Administration at The Maxwell School of Citizenship and Public Affairs, Syracuse University. He is the author of *Powering Apollo: James E. Webb of NASA* (1995) and *Technology and U.S. Competitiveness: An Institutional Focus* (1992). Recent articles have appeared in *Prometheus, Policy Studies Journal, Canadian-American Public Policy,* and *Public Administration Review.*

William Leiss, FRSC, is a Professor in the School of Policy Studies, Queen's University, and Research Chair in Risk Communication and Public Policy in the Faculty of Management, University of Calgary. He is the author of *The Domination of Nature* (1972), *The Limits to Satisfaction* (1976), *Under Technology's Thumb* (1990), and *Risk Issue Management: A New Approach to Risk Controversies* (2001), and is co-author of *Risk and Responsibility* (1994) and *Mad Cows and Mother's Milk* (1997). He is currently (1999–2001) President of the Royal Society of Canada.

Douglas Macdonald is a Lecturer in the Environmental Studies Program, Innis College, University of Toronto. Earlier in his career he worked as an environmental policy consultant and served from 1982 to 1988 as Executive Director of the Canadian Institute for Environmental Law and Policy. He is the author of a number of applied and academic environmental policy reports and articles, as well as *The Politics of Pollution* (1991).

Mary Louise McAllister is an Associate Professor in the Department of Environmental and Resources Studies at the University of Waterloo. Her research interests include urban and rural community sustainability, land-use issues and conflict resolution, and Brazil/Canada studies. She is co-author of *A Stake in the Future: Redefining the Canadian Mineral Industry* (1997) and recent articles have appeared in *Mineral and Energy,* the *Journal of Environmental Planning and Management,* and the *Bulletin of the Canadian Institute of Mining and Metallurgy.*

Éric Montpetit is an Assistant Professor of Comparative Public Policy at École nationale d'administration publique. He belongs to the Collectif de recherche sur la gouvernance and he has published numerous articles on agricultural and environmental policy in such journals as *World Politics*, the *Journal of European Public Policy*, and the *Canadian Journal of Political Science*.

Gregory Poelzer is Co-ordinator of the Northern Studies Program and an Associate Professor of Political Science at the University of Northern British Columbia. His recent articles have appeared or are forthcoming in *Post-Soviet Geography and Economy*, *Prospering Together: The Economic Impacts of Aboriginal Title Settlement in BC* (edited by Rosyln Kunin), and *Regions in Russia* (edited by Pater J. Stavrakis et al.).

Heather Smith is an Assistant Professor of International Studies at the University of Northern British Columbia. She is a specialist in Canadian foreign policy, particularly on the issue of climate change. Recent publications have appeared in *Environment and Security* and *International Journal*.

Michael Tyshenko is a Ph.D. student in the Department of Biology, Queen's University. He possesses a strong background in both molecular biology and science policy (and has both an M.Sc. and an MPA). His current doctoral research deals with cryopreservation and genetic engineering of fruit flies and tissue culture cell lines using antifreeze genes.

Marcia Valiante is an Associate Professor of Law in the Faculty of Law, University of Windsor, who specializes in environmental law. Recent publications have appeared in the *Journal of Environmental Law and Practice* and in two edited collections, *Environmental Law and Policy* (1998) and *Global Governance: Drawing Insights from the Environmental Experience* (1997).

Debora L. VanNijnatten is an Assistant Professor of Political Science at Wilfrid Laurier University. Her research has focused on multi-stakeholder consultation, science/policy linkages, voluntary initiatives, and Canadian-American policy. Recent publications have appeared or are forthcoming in *Policy Studies Journal*, *Canadian-American Public Policy, Managing the Environmental Union* (edited by Patrick Fafard and Kathryn Harrison), and *Risk Issue Management: A New Approach to Risk Controversies* (by William Leiss).

Jeremy Wilson is a Professor of Political Science at the University of Victoria, where he teaches courses in Canadian politics, public policy, and global environmental issues. He is the author of *Talk and Log: Wilderness Politics in British Columbia, 1965–96* (1998) and a co-author of *In Search of Sustainability: The Politics of Forest Policy in British Columbia in the 1990s* (2000).

Index